The New McCall's Cookbook

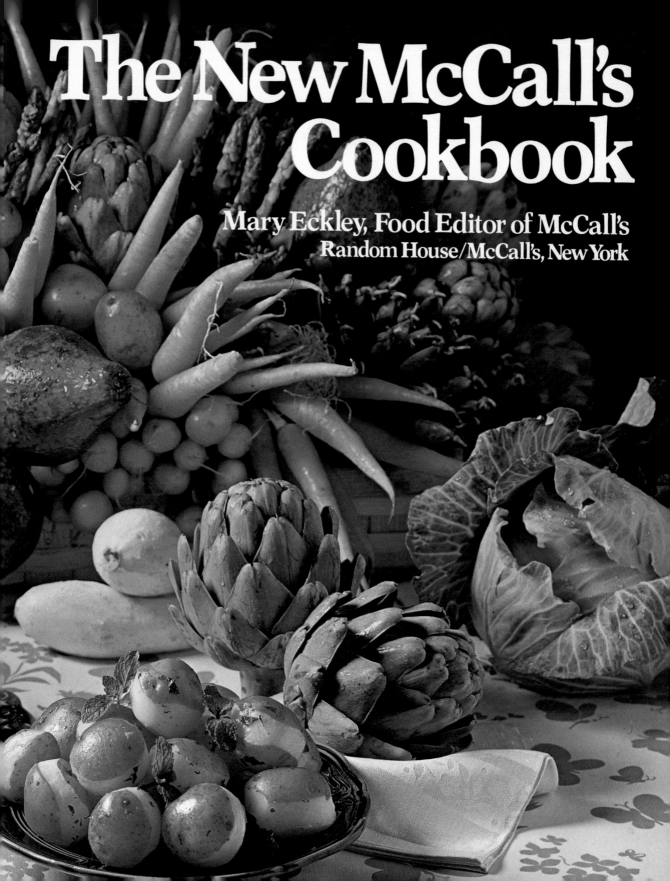

The New McCall's Cookbook

Mary Eckley, Food Editor of McCall's

Random House/McCall's, New York

Copyright © 1963, 1964, 1965, 1966, 1967, 1968, 1969,
1970, 1971, 1972, 1973 by The McCall Publishing
Company
All rights reserved under International and Pan-
American Copyright Conventions. Published in the
United States by Random House, Inc., New York, and
simultaneously in Canada by Random House of
Canada Limited, Toronto.
Library of Congress Cataloging in Publication Data
Eckley, Mary, comp.

   The new McCall's cook book.

   1. Cookery. I. McCall's magazine. II. Title.
TX715.E182   641.5   73-4828

ISBN 0-394-48518-1 (red)
ISBN 0-394-48785-0 (green)
ISBN 0-394-48783-4 (yellow)
ISBN 0-394-48784-2 (blue)
Text composition by University Graphics, Inc.,
Shrewsbury, New Jersey. Color separations by Offset
Separations, Inc., 437 Madison Avenue, New York.
Printed and bound by Von Hoffmann Press, Inc.,
St. Louis, Missouri.

Manufactured in the United States of America
First Edition
98765432

Contents

1 Introduction to Cooking
Page 9

McCall's Cooking School • How to Tackle a Recipe • How to Measure Correctly • Common Food Weights and Measures • About Oven Temperatures • Basic Top-of-the-Range Cooking Terminology • Other Cooking Terminology • Cutting Terminology • Basic Cooking Utensils • The Right Way to Carve

2 Appetizers
Page 43

Hors d'oeuvres and Canapés • First Courses

3 Beverages
Page 67

Coffee • Tea • Fruit Drinks and Punches • Milk and Ice-Cream Drinks • Alcoholic Drinks • Serving Wine

4 Quick Breads
Page 83

Sweet Quick Breads • Muffins • Biscuits • Coffeecakes • Cornbread • Quick Breads with Bakery Breads • Pancakes and Waffles

5 Yeast Breads
Page 99

Tips for Bread Bakers • Kneaded Breads • Sweet Yeast Breads • Sweet Rolls • Batter Breads

6 Cakes and Frostings
Page 117

Notes on Cakes • One-Bowl or "Quick" Cakes • "Butter" or Conventional Cakes • Sponge and Angel Cakes • Poundcake • With Cake Mixes • Frostings • How to Frost a Layer Cake • Glazes • Fillings

7 Cookies
Page 145

Hints for Cookie Bakers • Drop Cookies • Rolled Cookies • Refrigerator Cookies • Molded Cookies • Bar Cookies

8 Desserts and Dessert Sauces
Page 163

Cheesecakes • Cream Puffs, Crullers, Fritters • Custards and Puddings • Fruit Desserts • Gelatine Desserts • Ice Cream Desserts • Homemade Ice Creams and Frozen Desserts • Sherbets • Soufflés • Shortcakes and Kuchens • Some Special Desserts • Dessert Sauces

9 Eggs and Cheese   Page 221

All about Eggs • Know the Eggs You Buy • How to Cook Eggs • Scrambled Eggs • Omelets • Special Egg Dishes • Cheese • Cheese with Fruit

10 Fish   Page 237

Purchasing • Storage • Broiling Fish • The Beauty of Baking • In Praise of Poaching • A-Sizzle on the Grill

11 Shellfish   Page 249

Availability • Clams • Crabmeat • Lobster • Oysters • Scallops • Shrimp

12 International Cooking   Page 263

Chinese • English • French • German • Greek • Irish • Italian • Japanese • Mexican • Spanish • Scandinavian

13 Jams, Jellies and Preserves   Page 327

Preserved Perfection • Directions for Sterilizing Glasses and Jars • Test for Jellying Point • Jellies, Jams and Conserves • A Harvest of Pickles and Relishes • Quick and Easy Relishes

14 Meats   Page 345

What to Look For • Storage of Meat • Basic Meat Cookery • Beef • Roast Beef • Broiling and Pan-Broiling • Braising • Simmering • Ground Beef • Frankfurters • Pork • Ham • Lamb • Veal • Variety Meats • Game

15 Pies and Small Pastries   Page 409

Tips for Pie Bakers • Pastry and Pie Shells • Fruit Pies • Very Special Pies • Cream Pies, Chiffon Pies • Deep-Dish Pies, Dumplings, and Tarts

16 Poultry   Page 435

Buying and Storage • Test Your Terminology • Chicken • Cornish Hen • Goose • Duckling • Capon • Turkey • Stuffing

17 Rice, Grains and Pasta

Page 457

Rice • Grains and Cereals • Pasta (Macaroni, Spaghetti and Noodles)

18 Salads and Salad Dressings

Page 467

Green Salads • Know Your Salad Greens • Mixing Salad Greens • Care of Salad Greens • Main-Dish Salads • Vegetable Salads • Fruit Salads • Gelatine Salads • Creamy Dressings • Salad Dressings

19 Sauces and Gravies

Page 495

Sauces for Meat, Fish, Poultry and Vegetables • Gravy

20 Soups

Page 505

Consommés • Cream Soups • Hearty Soups • Cold Soups • With Canned Soups

21 Vegetables

Page 523

Vegetable Preparation and Cooking Chart • Vegetables and Potatoes

22 Holiday Delights

Page 557

Candies • Cookies • Fruitcakes • Holiday Specialties

23 Menus for Entertaining

Page 571

Brunch Menus • Luncheon • Buffet Menus • Cocktail Menus • Dinner Menus • Holiday Menus

24 Nutrition and Meal Planning, Low-Calorie Cooking

Page 577

Basic Nutrition Plan • Eating for Health and Beauty • A Week of Menus with Recipes • Basic Diet Pattern • Low-Calorie Recipes

Index

Page 593

Introduction to Cooking

Herb Butter:
1 cup butter or regular margarine, softened
2 tablespoons chopped parsley
1-1/2 teaspoons dried tarragon leaves
1 clove garlic, crushed
3/4 teaspoon salt
1/8 teaspoon pepper

6 boned whole chicken breasts (each 3/4 lb)
3/4 cup unsifted all-purpose flour
3 eggs, well beaten
1-1/2 cups packaged dry bread crumbs
Salad oil or shortening
    for deep-frying

Chicken Kiev

1. To make Herb Butter: In a small bowl, with rubber scraper, thoroughly mix butter, parsley, tarragon, garlic, salt, and pepper. On a sheet of foil, shape into 6-inch square. Freeze until firm—about

2. 40 minutes. Meanwhile, wash chicken; dry well on paper towels. Using a small sharp knife, carefully remove skin. Cut each breast in half. To flatten chicken, place each half, smooth side down, on

3. sheet of waxed paper; cover with second sheet. Using a mallet or side of saucer, pound chicken to about 1/4-inch thickness, being careful not to break the meat. Cut frozen butter into 12 pats.

4. Place a pat of the herb butter in center of each piece of chicken. Bring the long sides of the chicken over butter; fold ends over, making sure that no butter is showing; fasten each piece with

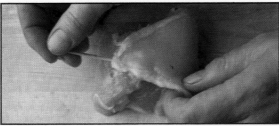

5. toothpicks. This is very important to keep the herb butter inside during frying. Roll each chicken piece in the flour on a sheet of waxed paper. Dip each in beaten eggs and roll in crumbs,

6. coating evenly. Then shape each piece, with palms of hands, into triangles (see Picture 7, below). Refrigerate, covered, until chilled for about 1 hour. In a Dutch oven or large, heavy

7. saucepan, slowly heat salad oil or shortening (3 inches deep) to 360F on deep-frying thermometer. Add the chicken pieces, 3 at a time. Fry, turning with tongs, until browned—5

8. minutes. Drain. (Do not pierce coating.) Keep warm in 200F oven 15 minutes (no more) in a large pan lined with paper towels. Makes 8 servings.

1/2 cup unseasoned warm
   mashed potato or packaged
   instant mashed potato
1-1/2 cups warm water
   (105 to 115 F)
2 pkg active dry yeast
1/2 cup sugar
1 tablespoon salt

2 eggs
1/2 cup butter or regular
   margarine, softened
6-1/2 cups unsifted all-purpose
   flour

Melted butter, or 1 egg, beaten
   with 2 tablespoons water
Poppy or sesame seed

Refrigerator Potato Rolls

1. Prepare mashed potato as package label directs for 1/2 cup, omitting salt and butter. Pour warm water into a large bowl. (First rinse bowl in hot water.) If possible, check temperature of hot water with thermometer. The temperature should be no less than 105F and no more than

2. 115F. Water that is too hot will kill yeast; water that is too cold will slow down yeast action and rolls will not be as light. Sprinkle the yeast over water; add sugar and salt, stirring with wooden spoon until completely dissolved. Let stand a few minutes; the mixture will start to bubble slightly.

3. Add 2 eggs, the soft butter, warm mashed potato and 3 cups flour. With portable electric mixer at high speed, beat just until smooth. Add 2 cups flour, beating with wooden spoon until flour is incorporated in dough. Add remaining 1-1/2 cups flour, mixing with hands, until the dough is

4. smooth and stiff enough to leave side of bowl. (This takes place of kneading to develop the gluten in the flour.) Brush top of dough with 1 tablespoon melted butter; cover with waxed paper and dish towel. Let rise in refrigerator 2 hours, or until double in bulk. Remove from refrigerator.

5. Punch down with fist. Cover and refrigerate. Dough can be refrigerated from one to three days, punching it down once a day. About 2 hours before serving, remove dough from refrigerator; shape. For crescents (picture 7): Remove one third of dough from refrigerator. On lightly floured

6. pastry cloth, divide dough in half. With rolling pin covered with lightly floured stockinette, roll each half into a 10-inch circle. Brush with 1 tablespoon melted butter. Cut into 6 wedges. Starting at wide end, roll up each wedge toward the point. Place on a greased cookie sheet, 2 inches

7. apart, point side down. Curl ends inward slightly. For figure eights and snails (picture 8): Remove one third of dough from refrigerator. On lightly floured surface, with palms, roll into a 12-inch rope. Divide into 12; roll each into a 12-inch strip. On greased cookie sheet, pinch ends

8. together and twist once into an 8. Snails: Press one end of a strip to greased cookie sheet; wind strip around itself; tuck other end underneath. Fan-tans (picture 9): Roll one third of dough into 15-by-8-inch rectangle. Spread with butter. With sharp knife, cut dough lengthwise into 5 (1-1/2-inch)

9. strips. Stack strips; cut into 12. Place cut side up in greased, 2-1/2-inch muffin-pan cups. To bake: Cover with towel; let rise in warm place (85F) until double in bulk—1 hour. Preheat oven to 400F. Brush with butter or with egg and seeds. Bake 12 minutes, or until golden. Serve warm. Makes 36.

3 lb boneless chuck or round, cut into
   1- to 1-1/2- inch cubes
1/3 cup all-purpose flour
2-1/2 teaspoons salt
1/4 teaspoon pepper
1/4 cup butter or margarine
1 bay leaf
1-1/2 teaspoons dried thyme leaves
1/2 cup chopped celery tops
1 small onion, stuck with 4 whole cloves
2 parsley sprigs
1 lb peeled small yellow onions (about 8)

1 lb medium carrots pared and halved crosswise
1-1/2 lb small new potatoes, pared or scrubbed
   with skins on (about 10)
2 medium white turnips, pared and quartered,
   or 4 small, pared and halved
1-1/2 cups celery, cut into 1-inch pieces

Parsley Dumplings:
2 cups packaged biscuit mix
2 tablespoons chopped parsley
1 egg
1/2 cup milk

Beef Stew with Parsley Dumplings

1. On waxed paper, roll beef cubes in flour mixed with salt and pepper, coating evenly on all sides. Reserve remaining flour mixture for later. In hot butter in 6-quart Dutch oven, brown beef well on all sides, turning with tongs. Do not overcrowd. As

2. beef is browned, remove, and set aside. Continue browning rest. Takes 30 minutes in all to give rich flavor and brown color. Return beef to Dutch oven; add bay leaf, thyme, celery, onion with cloves, parsley sprigs. Toss to coat with drippings. Add

3. 4 cups water; bring to boiling; reduce heat, and simmer, covered, 2 hours. Add onions, carrots, potatoes; simmer, covered, 20 minutes; add turnips and celery; simmer 10 minutes. During this 10 minutes, make Dumplings: In medium

4. bowl, combine biscuit mix and parsley; stir in egg and milk, mixing with fork just until blended. Drop batter by 10 rounded tablespoonfuls onto gently boiling stew (on meat or vegetables, not in liquid—this makes dumplings soggy), 2 to 3

5. inches apart, allowing for expansion. Cook, uncovered, over low heat 10 minutes. Cover tightly; cook 10 minutes longer. Using slotted spoon, remove dumplings to heated baking dish; keep warm in oven. In small bowl, combine 3 tablespoons

6. reserved flour mixture (see Step 1) with 1/4 cup water, stirring until smooth. Stir gently into stew; simmer 5 minutes, or until the mixture is thickened. Replace dumplings on top of stew to serve. Reheat, covered, until hot. Makes 8 servings.

2 tablespoons butter or margarine
1 cup finely chopped onion
1-1/2 lb ground chuck or lamb
1 clove garlic, crushed
1/2 teaspoon dried oregano leaves
1 teaspoon dried basil leaves
1/2 teaspoon cinnamon
1 teaspoon salt
Dash pepper
2 cans (8-oz size) tomato sauce

Cream Sauce:
2 tablespoons butter
   or margarine
2 tablespoons flour
1/2 teaspoon salt
Dash pepper
2 cups milk
2 eggs

1/2 cup grated Parmesan cheese
1/2 cup grated Cheddar cheese
2 tablespoons dry bread crumbs

2 eggplants (1-lb, 4-oz size), washed and dried
Salt
1/2 cup butter or margarine, melted

Moussaka

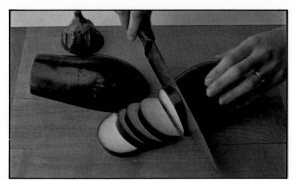

1. Meat Sauce: In hot butter in 3-1/2-quart Dutch oven, sauté onion, chuck, garlic, stirring until brown—10 minutes. Add herbs, spices, tomato sauce; bring to boiling, stirring. Reduce heat; simmer, uncovered, 1/2 hour. Halve unpared eggplant

2. lengthwise; slice crosswise, 1/2 inch thick. Place in bottom of broiler pan; sprinkle lightly with salt; brush lightly with melted butter. Broil, 4 inches from heat, 4 minutes per side, or until golden. Make Cream Sauce: In medium saucepan, melt

3. butter. Remove from heat; stir in flour, salt, and pepper. Add milk gradually. Bring to boiling, stirring until mixture is thickened. Remove from heat. In small bowl, beat eggs with wire whisk. Beat in some hot cream-sauce mixture; return mixture to

4. saucepan; mix well; set aside. Preheat oven to 350 F. To assemble casserole: In bottom of a shallow 2-quart baking dish (12 by 7-1/2 by 2 inches, pictured), layer half of eggplant, overlapping slightly; sprinkle with 2 tablespoons each grated

5. Parmesan and Cheddar cheeses. Stir bread crumbs into meat sauce; spoon evenly over eggplant in casserole; then sprinkle with 2 tablespoons each Parmesan and Cheddar cheeses. Layer rest of eggplant slices, overlapping, as before. Pour cream

6. sauce over all. Sprinkle top with remaining cheese. Bake 35 to 40 minutes, or until golden-brown and top is set. If desired, brown top a little more under broiler—1 minute. Cool slightly to serve. Cut in squares. Makes 12 servings.

10- to 12-lb fully cooked bone-in ham
1 cup sliced onion
2 bay leaves
1/4 cup brown sugar, packed
4 sprigs parsley
6 whole cloves
3 whole black peppercorns
1 pint beer

Glaze:
1/2 cup brown sugar, packed
1/4 cup honey
Whole cloves

Curried Fruit:
1/4 cup butter, melted
1/2 cup light-brown sugar, packed
1 tablespoon curry powder
1 can (1 lb, 14 oz) peach halves, drained
1 can (13-1/4 oz) pineapple chunks, drained

Summer Baked Ham

1. Preheat oven to 325F. Place ham, fat side up, in shallow roasting pan. Place onion and bay leaves on ham; sprinkle with sugar, parsley, cloves, and peppercorns. Insert meat thermometer in center of thickest part, away from bone. Pour

2. beer into pan around ham. Cover pan tightly with foil. Bake, basting every 30 minutes with beer in pan, using a baster, about 3 hours, or until meat thermometer registers 130F. (Remove the ham from the oven; take off foil; baste.) Make

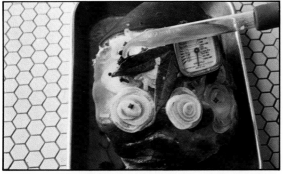

3. Glaze: When ham is done, remove it from roasting pan, and pour off all fat and drippings. Reserve 2 tablespoons of drippings (not fat); combine with brown sugar and honey. Return ham to roasting pan. Increase oven temperature to

4. 400F. With sharp knife, carefully remove any skin. To score: Make diagonal cuts in fat (be careful not to cut into meat), 1/4 inch deep and 1-1/4 inches apart, using ruler, to form a diamond pattern. Stud the center of each diamond

5. shape with a whole clove. To glaze the ham: Brush the surface with half of the honey glaze; return ham to oven, and bake 30 minutes longer, basting every 10 minutes with more of the glaze. To make Curried Fruit: Mix butter, sugar, and

6. curry. In 1-1/2-quart casserole, toss fruit with sugar mixture. Bake, uncovered, 30 minutes in same oven. Serve along with ham. See How to Carve a Whole Ham in the Introduction to Cooking. Makes 20 servings.

Sauce:
1/3 cup olive or salad oil
1-1/2 cups finely chopped onion
1 clove garlic, crushed
1 can (2 lb, 3 oz) Italian tomatoes, undrained
1 can (6 oz) tomato paste
2 tablespoons chopped parsley
1 tablespoon salt
1 tablespoon sugar
1 teaspoon dried oregano leaves
1 teaspoon dried basil leaves
1/4 teaspoon pepper

Manicotti:
6 eggs, at room temperature
1-1/2 cups unsifted all-purpose flour
1/4 teaspoon salt

Filling:
2 lb ricotta cheese
1 pkg (8 oz) mozzarella cheese, diced
1/3 cup grated Parmesan cheese
2 eggs
1 teaspoon salt
1/4 teaspoon pepper
1 tablespoon chopped parsley
1/4 cup grated Parmesan cheese

Baked Manicotti with Cheese Filling

1. Make Sauce: In hot oil in 5-quart Dutch oven, sauté onion and garlic 5 minutes. Mix in rest of sauce ingredients and 1-1/2 cups water, mashing tomatoes with fork. Bring to boiling; reduce heat. Simmer, covered, stirring occasionally, 1 hour.

2. Make Manicotti: In medium bowl, combine 6 eggs, flour, 1/4 teaspoon salt, and 1-1/2 cups water; with electric mixer, beat just until smooth. Let stand 1/2 hour or longer. Slowly heat 8-inch skillet. Pour in 3 tablespoons batter, rotating

3. skillet quickly to spread batter evenly over bottom. Cook over medium heat until top is dry but bottom is not brown. Turn out on a wire rack to cool. Continue until all batter is used. As manicotti cool, stack them with waxed paper between them.

4. Preheat oven to 350F. Make Filling: In large bowl, combine ricotta, mozzarella, 1/3 cup Parmesan, eggs, salt, pepper, and parsley; beat with wooden spoon to blend well. Spread about 1/4 cup filling down the center of each manicotti, and roll

5. up. Spoon 1-1/2 cups sauce into each of two 12-by-8-by-2-inch baking dishes. Place eight rolled manicotti, seam side down, in single layer; top with five more. Cover with 1 cup sauce, sprinkle with Parmesan. Bake, uncovered, 1/2 hour, or un-

6. til bubbly. To freeze: Line baking dish with foil; assemble as directed. Fold foil over to seal, and freeze in dish. When frozen, remove dish. To serve: Unwrap; place in dish; thaw 1 hour. Bake, covered, 1 hour in 350F oven. Each dish serves 6.

Hollandaise Sauce:
3 egg yolks
2 tablespoons cold water
1/2 cup (1 stick) butter or regular margarine
2 tablespoons lemon juice
1/8 teaspoon salt
Dash cayenne

Béarnaise Sauce:
1/4 cup tarragon vinegar
1/4 cup dry white wine
2 tablespoons finely chopped
   fresh tarragon or 2 teaspoons
   dried tarragon leaves
1 tablespoon chopped
   shallot or onion

1/8 teaspoon coarsely ground black pepper
1 tablespoon chopped parsley
3 egg yolks
1/2 cup (1 stick) butter or regular margarine
1 tablespoon chopped fresh tarragon or parsley

The Difficult Sauces

1. Make Hollandaise: In top of double boiler, with wire whisk, beat egg yolks with water just until blended. Cook over hot, not boiling, water, stirring constantly with whisk, until mixture begins to thicken—about 1 minute. Add butter, 1 tablespoon

2. at a time (cut stick of butter into 8 pieces), beating continuously after each addition until butter is melted and mixture smooth before adding next piece of butter—takes about 5 minutes in all. Hot water in double-boiler base should not touch

3. bottom of pan above; water should not be allowed to boil. (If it should start to bubble, add a little cold water at once to cool it.) Sauce curdles easily over high heat. Remove double-boiler top from hot water before adding lemon. Using a wire

4. whisk, slowly beat in lemon juice, then salt and cayenne, beating just until sauce becomes thick as mayonnaise. To keep warm: Add cold water to hot water in bottom of double boiler to make lukewarm; replace sauce, covered, over water, not heat.

5. Make Béarnaise: In small saucepan, combine vinegar, wine, tarragon, shallots, pepper, and parsley; bring to boiling, stirring. Reduce heat, and simmer, uncovered, to reduce to 1/4 cup—about 8 minutes. Strain into a measuring cup, pressing

6. herbs to extract juice. Let cool. Cook egg yolks, as in Step 1, using 2 tablespoons tarragon liquid for water. Continue with Steps 2, 3, and 4, using 2 tablespoons tarragon liquid for lemon. Add chopped herb. Serve warm or cold. Makes 1 cup.

1 piecrust mix or pastry for 2-crust pie
1 cup sugar
2 tablespoons flour
1 teaspoon cinnamon
1/8 teaspoon nutmeg

1/4 teaspoon salt
7 cups thinly sliced, pared tart
  cooking apples (2-1/2 lb)
2 tablespoons lemon juice
2 tablespoons butter or regular margarine

Perfect Apple Pie

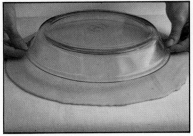

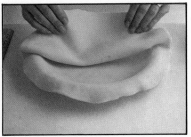

1. Make pastry as package directs. Handling gently, shape pastry into ball. Divide in half; form each half into a round; then flatten each with palm of hand. On lightly floured pastry cloth, roll out

2. half of pastry into a 12-inch circle, using a ball-bearing rolling pin. Roll with light strokes from center to edge, lifting rolling pin as you reach edge. Place a 9-inch pie plate on pastry circle; pastry

3. should be 1 inch wider all around. Fold pastry in half; carefully transfer to plate, making sure fold is in center of plate. Unfold pastry, fit carefully into pie plate, pressing gently with

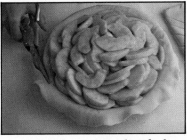

4. fingers, so pastry fits snugly all around. Do not stretch; refrigerate. Preheat oven to 425F. In small bowl, mix sugar, flour, cinnamon, nutmeg, and salt. In large bowl, toss the apples with

5. lemon juice. Add sugar mixture to sliced apples; toss lightly to combine. Roll out remaining pastry into 12-inch circle (see Step 2). Fold over in quarters; cut slits for steam vents. Turn apple

6. mixture into pastry-lined plate, mounding up in center to support top crust. Dot apples with butter cut in small pieces. Using scissors, trim overhanging pastry to measure 1/2 inch from rim of plate.

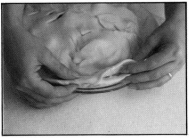

7. Place folded pastry so that point is at center of filling, and unfold. Using scissors, trim overhanging pastry (for top crust), to measure 1 inch from edge, all around. Moisten the edge of bot-

8. tom pastry with a little water. Fold top pastry under edge of bottom pastry. With fingers, press edge together to seal, so juices won't run out. Press upright to form a standing rim. Crimp edge:

9. Place thumb on edge of pastry at an angle. Pinch dough between index finger and thumb. Repeat at same angle all around. Bake 45 to 50 minutes, till apples are tender, crust golden. Serves 8.

Cake:
1 cup unsifted unsweetened cocoa
2 cups boiling water
2-3/4 cups sifted all-purpose flour
2 teaspoons baking soda
1/2 teaspoon salt
1/2 teaspoon baking powder
1 cup butter or regular margarine, softened
2-1/2 cups granulated sugar
4 eggs
1-1/2 teaspoons vanilla extract

Frosting:
1 pkg (6 oz) semisweet chocolate pieces
1/2 cup light cream
1 cup butter or regular margarine
2-1/2 cups unsifted confectioners' sugar

Filling:
1 cup heavy cream, chilled
1/4 cup unsifted confectioners' sugar
1 teaspoon vanilla extract

Perfect Chocolate Cake

1. In medium bowl, combine cocoa with boiling water, mixing with wire whisk until smooth. Cool completely. Sift flour with soda, salt, and baking powder. Preheat oven to 350F. Grease well and lightly flour three 9-by-1-1/2-inch layer-cake pans.

2. In large bowl of electric mixer, at high speed, beat butter, sugar, eggs, and vanilla, scraping bowl occasionally, until light—about 5 minutes. At low speed, beat in flour mixture (in fourths), alternately with cocoa mixture (in thirds), beginning

3. and ending with flour mixture. Do not overbeat. Divide evenly into pans; smooth top. Bake 25 to 30 minutes, or until surface springs back when gently pressed with fingertip. Cool in pans 10 minutes. Carefully loosen sides with spatula; remove

4. from pans; cool on racks. Frosting: In medium saucepan, combine chocolate pieces, cream, butter; stir over medium heat until smooth. Remove from heat. With whisk, blend in 2-1/2 cups confectioners' sugar. In bowl set over ice, beat until it

5. holds shape. Filling: Whip cream with sugar and vanilla; refrigerate. To assemble cake: On plate, place a layer, top side down; spread with half of cream. Place second layer, top side down; spread with rest of cream. Place third layer, top side

6. up. To frost: With spatula, frost sides first, covering whipped cream; use rest of frosting on top, swirling decoratively. Refrigerate at least 1 hour before serving. To cut, use a thin-edged sharp knife; slice with a sawing motion. Serves 10 to 12.

Cake:
8 egg whites
3 cups sifted all-purpose flour
1 teaspoon baking powder
Salt
2 cups granulated sugar
1 tablespoon grated orange peel
2 tablespoons grated lemon peel
8 egg yolks

2 cups butter or regular margarine
2 tablespoons lemon juice

Glaze:
1 tablespoon butter
1 pkg (1 lb) confectioners' sugar
1/3 cup lemon juice
1 teaspoon grated lemon peel

First, separate eggs, turning yolks into one large bowl and whites into another. Let egg whites warm to room temperature —about 1 hour. Preheat oven to 350F.

Poundcake

1. With a little shortening, lightly grease bottom and side of a 10-inch tube pan. Sprinkle with a little flour. Rotate to coat inside of pan evenly; shake out excess flour.

2. Sift flour on waxed paper. Gently spoon into 1-cup measure; level off. Measure 3 cups flour in all. Turn back into sifter, along with baking powder and 1/4 tea-

3. spoon salt. Sift onto waxed paper; set aside. With mixer at high speed, beat egg whites with 1/4 teaspoon salt till foamy throughout. Beat in 1 cup sugar,

4. 1/4 cup at a time, beating well after each addition. Beat until soft peaks form when beater is slowly raised. On foil or waxed paper, grate orange and lemon

5. peels on fine grater; measure. In large bowl, at high speed, with same beater (don't wash), beat butter with one cup sugar until light and fluffy—5 minutes. Beat

6. in yolks until light and fluffy. At high speed, beat in peels, lemon juice, and 2 tablespoons water until smooth. Divide flour mixture into thirds; at low speed,

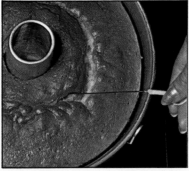

7. blend in, 1/3 at a time, just until combined—takes about 1 minute. At low speed, blend in egg whites, half at a time, just until blended, scraping bowl and

8. guiding batter into the beater. (Be sure not to overmix.) Turn batter into prepared pan, cleaning bowl with rubber scraper. Bake, in middle of oven, 60 minutes, or

9. until cake tester inserted in center comes out clean. Cool on rack 15 minutes. Gently loosen sides with spatula; turn out; cool. Blend glaze ingredients; drizzle over cake.

8 egg whites
6 egg yolks
4 tablespoons butter or regular
  margarine, softened
2 tablespoons granulated sugar
1/2 cup all-purpose flour

3/4 cup Dutch-process
  unsweetened cocoa
1 cup granulated sugar
1/4 teaspoon salt
2 cups milk
1 teaspoon vanilla extract

1/4 teaspoon cream of tartar
1 cup heavy cream, chilled
1/4 cup confectioners' sugar

Preheat oven to 350F. Place oven
rack on lowest rung in oven.

Chocolate Soufflé

1. Separate eggs: Crack shell, keeping yolk in one half, white in other. Turn yolk from one half into the other, letting white run into a small bowl, yolk into another. Pour each white into large bowl; let stand to warm 1 hour. With

2. 1 tablespoon butter, grease 2-quart soufflé dish. Fold 26-inch piece waxed paper lengthwise in thirds. Grease with 1 tablespoon butter. Form 2-inch collar around the dish; tie. Sprinkle dish, paper with 2 tablespoons sugar. In

3. medium-size, heavy saucepan with wire whisk, mix flour, cocoa, 3/4 cup sugar, the salt. Gradually blend in milk. Cook, stirring, over medium heat, until mixture comes to boil (large bubbles break on surface). Beat

4. yolks with a wire whisk. Beat in some of cocoa mixture. Gradually stir yolk mixture into rest of mixture in saucepan. Add 2 tablespoons butter and the vanilla, stirring until they are combined. Set aside to cool slightly. Add

5. cream of tartar to egg whites. With electric mixer at high speed, beat just until soft peaks form when beater is slowly raised; scrape side of bowl several times with rubber scraper so that egg whites are beaten throughout.

6. Add 1/4 cup granulated sugar, 2 tablespoons at a time, beating well after each addition. Beat just until stiff peaks form when beater is raised. Whites will be shiny and satiny. Turn a third of cocoa mixture over top of egg whites.

7. Using a wire whisk or rubber scraper, gently fold mixture into whites, using under-and-over motion, just until combined. Fold in rest of cocoa mixture a half at a time. Caution: Overfolding reduces the volume. Using a rubber

8. scraper, gently turn soufflé mixture, without stirring, into prepared dish set in a large baking pan; clean out bowl with scraper. Smooth top with a metal spatula. Place pan and dish in oven on bottom rack. Pour hot

9. water into pan to measure 1 inch. Bake 1-1/4 hours. With rotary beater, beat cream with confectioners' sugar until stiff. Chill. To serve, remove collar. Break the top of the soufflé with fork. Serve with cream to 8.

The New McCall's Cookbook, as you have seen, begins with a selection of cooking schools that are so popular in *McCall's* Magazine. You can apply the cooking techniques illustrated here to many of the recipes in the rest of the book.

The sections that follow include all the best-loved recipes that have appeared over the years in *McCall's* Magazine. They are recipes that you've requested again and again—from our cooking contests, from our famous treasuries, from around the world.

We've tested and retested these in our kitchens, even more than the usual number of times, to give you a collection of great recipes that really work.

The book starts from the beginning with the beginner. It explains how to tackle a recipe and how to measure, defines cooking terms, and in the *McCall's* fashion, takes you step by step through the various procedures. In the Nutrition and Meal Planning chapter are simple rules for planning nutritionally balanced meals, with a week of menus.

For those of you who are more experienced, there's an interesting section on international cooking; menus for entertaining; ideas for the working woman who needs to cook quickly and well.

Preparing meals every day is still the homemaker's greatest chore. But we think cooking can and should be something beyond a chore, beyond necessity. It can be one of the truly creative arts, and a deeply satisfying, personal one, since it is done for the pleasure and well-being of those we love.

Mary Eckley
Food Editor, *McCall's*

Illustrations by Larry Coultrip
Mary Norton, assistant on the manuscript
Photographs by George Ratkai
Design by Lidia Ferrara

How to Tackle a Recipe

1. Read the recipe all the way through before you turn a hand. Every word!

2. Check your supplies to see if you have all the ingredients called for.

3. See if you have the right equipment to work with. Nothing is more frustrating than to be in the middle of a recipe and find you haven't the right pan or pot.

4. If you aren't familiar with an ingredient listed, look it up, so you'll recognize it the next time.

5. At this point, get out all ingredients and all equipment.

6. Do as much preparation prior to combining ingredients as you possibly can—following recipe directions exactly, of course.

7. Last but not least, follow the recipe to the letter. It is only the experienced cook who can take liberties with or make changes in a recipe. All recipes published today are thoroughly tested, and the directions given should be followed meticulously. You'll be a happier cook if you . . .

• Make it a habit to trim, peel, scrape foods over waxed paper or paper towels to save work.

• Keep a damp cloth close at hand. Cooking is more fun and more successful when your hands and kitchen are tidy.

• Wash pots, pans, utensils as you work.

• Wipe off your range each time you use it.

• Preheat your oven for all baking—unless recipes say not to.

• Wipe off tops of salad-oil, catsup, chili-sauce, mustard bottles or jars every time you use them.

• Do not cut or increase recipes unless you are skilled enough to recognize the difference in pan sizes and/or cooking time necessitated by the change.

How to Measure Correctly

1. Use only standard measuring cups and spoons. Any recipe you follow has been tested with standard equipment.

2. Make all measurements level.

3. In measuring dry ingredients or fats, use the standardized metal cups that come in nests and hold 1/4, 1/3, 1/2, and 1 cup.

4. In measuring dry ingredients (flour, confectioners' sugar, etc.), heap the cup or spoon to overflowing; then level off excess with a straight-edge knife or spatula.

5. When recipe calls for sifted flour, sift before you measure. Never pack the flour down by banging the cup on the table.

6. In measuring fats, bring to room temperature if stored in refrigerator; then press firmly into spoon or cup, and level off with straight-edge knife or spatula. One stick of butter or margarine measures 1/2 cup, or 8 tablespoons. Many wrappers have a printed measuring guide. Tape one to your kitchen ruler for handy reference.

7. When measuring liquids, use the standard glass liquid measuring cup, with lip, marked off in quarters and thirds. Always place cup on a flat surface, and measure at eye level.

8. Brown sugar should always be packed firmly into the measuring cup or spoon, then leveled off with a knife or spatula. If lumpy, roll with rolling pin before measuring.

9. When measuring molasses, syrup or honey, pour liquid into cup or spoon. Do not dip measuring utensil into the heavy liquid. Scrape out thoroughly, with a rubber scraper, all liquid that clings to inside.

10. If confectioners' sugar looks lumpy, it is advisable to roll it with a rolling pin before measuring. If recipe calls for sifted confectioners' sugar, press through sieve to sift.

Memorize the following common weights and measures to save time and assure accuracy. Make sure all measurements are level.

Common Food Weights and Measures

Dash: less than 1/8 teaspoon
1 tablespoon: 3 teaspoons
4 tablespoons: 1/4 cup
5-1/3 tablespoons: 1/3 cup
8 tablespoons: 1/2 cup
10-2/3 tablespoons: 2/3 cup
12 tablespoons: 3/4 cup
16 tablespoons: 1 cup
1 fluid ounce: 2 tablespoons
1 cup: 1/2 pint (liquid)
2 cups: 1 pint
2 pints (4 cups): 1 quart
4 quarts: 1 gallon
8 quarts: 1 peck (dry)
4 pecks: 1 bushel
16 ounces: 1 pound

About Oven Temperatures

We cannot overemphasize the need for correct oven temperature. Nor can we stress too strongly the need to follow the temperature indicated in the recipe. Many a good roast or cake has been ruined because the oven temperature was not correct.

Once a year, at least, have your oven checked by the utility company that serves your area. Read the manufacturer's booklet about your range, study it—because the people who make the range know best how you should treat it for maximum service. It's a good idea to use an oven thermometer as well to make certain that oven temperature is correct.

Temperature (Degrees F)	Term
250 to 275	Very slow
300 to 325	Slow
350 to 375	Moderate
400 to 425	Hot
450 to 475	Very hot
500 to 525	Extremely hot

Basic Top-of-the-Range Cooking Terminology

Bring to the boiling point, or bring to a boil, means the step before cooking. You'll know that water or any liquid is reaching that point when bubbles appear at the bottom, rise to the top, and break. When all liquid is in motion, it has come to a boil.
Boil means to cook at the boiling point. When this point is reached, adjust heat to maintain it.
Boil rapidly means the point at which liquid goes into rapid motion; the surface breaks into small, lumpy waves. A rapid boil won't cook food faster; but for some uses, it is better: to start cereals (keeps particles separated) and to evaporate soup, jam or other liquids.
Full, rolling boil means the point at which the liquid rises in the pan, then tumbles into waves that can't be stirred down. It usually occurs in heavy sugar mixtures, like candy or frosting, in jelly making when jelly is almost done or when liquid pectin is added.
Simmer means to cook just below the boiling point; adjust the heat to maintain this stage. In simmering, the food cooks so slowly the surface moves slightly; no bubbles show.
Steam means to cook by steam in a closed container. Dumplings and puddings are examples. You can cook by steam under pressure in less time than usual, with a pressure cooker.
Blanch means to remove skins from fruits, vege-

tables or nuts by letting them stand in boiling water until skins peel off easily. Occasionally, it is necessary to drain off the first water and add more boiling water.

Poach means to cook eggs, fish, vegetables in liquid at or below simmering, or to cook eggs over water in a special pan.

Steep means to let a food stand in hot liquid, below boiling, to extract flavor, color, or both.

Parboil means to cook food in a boiling liquid until partially done. This is usually a preliminary step to further cooking. Beans and ham, for instance, are parboiled, later baked.

Scald means to heat liquids like milk almost to boiling; tiny bubbles will appear at edge. Or when freezing or canning vegetables, heat by steam or in boiling water.

Other Cooking Terminology

Bake: To cook by dry heat, usually in the oven. When applied to meats and vegetables, this is called roasting.

Barbecue: To roast meats very slowly on a spit or rack over heat, basting with a seasoned sauce.

Baste: To moisten foods (usually roasting meats) while cooking, with meat drippings, melted fat, or sauces, to prevent drying and to add flavor.

Beat: To work a mixture smooth with a regular, hard, rhythmic movement.

Blend: To mix thoroughly two or more ingredients.

Braise: To brown meat or vegetables in a small amount of hot fat and cook slowly, tightly covered. In some recipes, you add other liquids after the initial browning.

Broil: To cook directly under a flame or heating unit or over an open fire or grill.

Brush: To spread food with butter or margarine or egg, using a small brush.

Candy: To cook fruit in a heavy sugar syrup until transparent, then drain and dry. (Orange peel, for example.) Also, to cook vegetables with sugar or syrup to give a coating or glaze when cooked.

Caramelize: To melt sugar slowly over very low heat until sugar is liquid, brown and caramel flavored.

Coat: To roll foods in flour, nuts, sugar, crumbs, etc., until all sides are evenly covered; or to dip first into slightly beaten egg or milk, then to cover with whatever coating is called for in recipe.

Coddle: To cook slowly and gently in water just below the boiling point. Eggs are frequently coddled.

Combine: To mix all ingredients.

Cook: To prepare food by applying heat in any form.

Cream: To beat shortening until smooth, creamy and light, with wooden spoon or beater. Usually applied to shortening when combined with sugar; *e.g.,* in making cakes.

Crisp: To make firm and brittle in very cold water or in refrigerator (lettuce, other greens, for example).

Cut: (1) To break up food into pieces, with a knife or scissors. (2) To combine shortening with dry ingredients by working together with two knives used scissor fashion, or with pastry blender. Usually applied to pastry making.

Devil: To coat with a hot seasoning, such as mustard or a hot sauce. Eggs are "deviled" when the yolk is mixed with hot seasonings.

Dissolve: To make a liquid and a dry substance go into solution.

Dot: To scatter small amounts of butter, nuts, chocolate and so forth over the surface of a food.

Dredge: To coat food with some dry ingredient, such as seasoned flour or sugar.

Dust: To sprinkle a food or coat lightly with flour or sugar.

Flambé: To cover a food with brandy or cognac, etc.; then light, and serve flaming; *e.g.,* plum pudding.

Fold: To combine two ingredients—more often than not, beaten egg whites and batter—very gently with a wire whisk or rubber scraper, using an under-and-over motion, until thoroughly mixed.

Fry: (1) To cook in a small amount of fat on top of stove; also called "sauté" and "pan-fry." (2) To cook a food in a deep layer of hot fat, called "deep-frying." The aim is to produce foods with a crisp golden-brown crust and a thoroughly cooked interior without letting them absorb too much fat. The kind, quantity and temperature of the fat are important in accomplishing this result.

Garnish: To decorate any foods. Nuts, olives, parsley and so forth are called garnishes when used to give a finish to a dish.

Glacé: To coat with a thin sugar syrup cooked to the crack stage.

Glaze: To cover with aspic; to coat with a thin sugar syrup; to cover with melted fruit jelly. Cold meats, fish, fruit, etc., are often glazed.

Grill: See "Broil."

Knead: To work and press dough hard with the heels of your hands so the dough becomes stretched and elastic.

Marinate: To let food stand in acid such as lemon juice, tomato juice, wine, or in an oil-acid mixture like French dressing. Acts as a tenderizer, steps up flavor.

Melt: To heat solid food, like sugar or fat, until it becomes liquid.

Mix: To stir, usually with a spoon, until ingredients are thoroughly combined.

Pan-broil: To cook, uncovered, on a hot surface, usually a skillet. The fat is poured off as it accumulates.

Pan-fry: To cook or fry on top of range in a hot, uncovered skillet with little or no fat. Steaks, chops, potatoes are frequently cooked this way.

Pare: To cut away coverings of vegetables and fruits.

Peel: To strip or slip off outer coverings of some vegetables or fruit.

Plank: To bake or broil meat, fish, or vegetables on a wooden or metal plank.

Pot-roast: To brown meat in a small amount of fat, then finish cooking in a small amount of liquid.

Preheat: To heat oven to stated temperature before using.

Purée: To press fruits or vegetables through a sieve or food mill or blend in an electric blender until food is pulpy. Sauces, soups, baby foods, vegetables are often puréed.

Reduce: To boil a liquid until you have a small, concentrated amount.

Roast: To cook meat or vegetables in an oven by dry heat. See "Bake."

Sauté: To fry foods until golden and tender, in a small amount of fat on top of range. See "Fry."

Scallop: To arrange foods in layers in a casserole, with a sauce or liquid, and then bake. Usually has a topping of bread crumbs.

Score: To cut narrow gashes, part way through fat, in meats before cooking; *e.g.,* in steaks to prevent curling, or to cut diamond-shaped gashes part way through fat in ham just before glazing.

Scramble: To stir or mix foods gently while cooking, as eggs.

Sear: To brown surface of meat over high heat, either on top of range or in oven.

Shirr: To break eggs into a dish with cream or crumbs; then bake.

Sift: To put dry ingredients through a fine sieve.

Skewer: To thread foods, such as meat, fish, poultry, vegetables, on a wooden or metal skewer so they hold their shape during cooking.

Sterilize: To heat in boiling water or steam for at least 20 minutes, until living organisms are destroyed.

Stew: To cook foods, in enough liquid to cover, very slowly—always below the boiling point.

Stir: To mix, usually with a spoon or fork, until ingredients are worked together.

Toast: To brown and dry the surface of foods with heat, such as bread and nuts.

Toss: To tumble ingredients lightly with a lifting motion.

Whip: To rapidly beat eggs, heavy cream, etc., in order to incorporate air and expand volume.

Cutting Terminology

Chop means to cut food into smaller pieces, usually with large knife and cutting board. One hand holds knife tip on board; the other moves blade up and down, cutting through the food.

Mince means to cut food in pieces, but finer than chopped. Mincing takes the same steps: Use cutting board and sharp knife, chopping knife and wooden bowl, or scissors—just do it longer.

Grind means to put food through chopper. Choppers have two or three blades. Use a blade with smaller holes to grind foods fine; one with larger holes for coarse chopping or grinding.

Flake means to break or pull apart a food, like chicken or fish, that divides naturally. All you do is follow these divisions, pulling at them gently with one or two forks. Or flake with your fingers.

Cube means to cut a solid into little cubes from about 1/2 inch to 1 inch.

Dice means to cube but to make the cubes smaller —less than 1/2 inch. Use a cutting board and a very sharp knife, or a special cubing gadget.

Grate means to tear off coarse-to-fine particles of food with a hand grater or mechanical device.

Sliver means to cut or split into long, thin strips, with a knife on a cutting board.

Shred means to cut or tear in long, narrow pieces. The fineness varies—recipes often say that foods should be "finely" or "coarsely" shredded. Use a hand or mechanical shredder; or cut crisp vegetables, like cabbage, to shreds with a sharp knife.

Julienne means to cut potatoes or vegetables into matchlike sticks.

Basic Cooking Utensils

The utensils and tools you use for cooking are your best kitchen friends. They determine to a great extent your cooking success or failure. Consider these points when buying utensils:

1. Buy things of good quality—you'll be using these utensils for a long time.

2. Consider your needs, and buy to suit them. If you are not heavy coffee drinkers, for instance, buy a smaller-size coffee maker.

3. Buy matched sets of utensils or tools if what you want is included in the set—if not, buy various kinds to suit your needs.

4. Select utensils of standard sizes. These will generally have their size and/or capacity stamped on the bottom or indicated on a label.

5. Some things such as paring knives and spoons are used in different parts of the kitchen at the same time—save time and steps by having duplicates of these. We call it storage at the point of first use.

6. Buy enough basic cooking utensils (see below) to start with, and add to these as you need them and as your cooking skills increase.

Pans for Top-of-Range Use:
1 coffee maker, size to suit family
1 double boiler—1-1/2 quarts
1 Dutch oven—4 to 6 quarts
1 small frying pan—7″ to 8″ top diameter

1 large frying pan with fitted cover—9″ to 10″ diameter
1 griddle
3 saucepans with covers—1 quart, 2 quarts, and 3 quarts
1 teakettle—2-1/2 quarts

Pans for Oven Use:
1 shallow baking dish—1-1/2 quarts
2 layer-cake pans— 8″ or 9″ x 1-1/2″ deep
1 square cake pan—8″ x 8″ x 2″ or 9″ x 9″ x 2″
2 casseroles—1-1/2 quarts, 3 quarts
2 cookie sheets—15-1/2″ x 12″
6 custard cups—5 or 6 ounce
2 loaf pans—9″ x 5″ x 3″
1 muffin pan with 6 to 12 individual cups
1 oblong pan—13″ x 9-1/2″ x 2″
1 pie plate—9″ diameter
1 shallow roasting pan with rack
1 tube pan—10″ x 4″

Preparation and Measuring Tools:
1 biscuit cutter
1 bottle opener and corkscrew
1 bread or cutting board
1 can opener
1 colander
1 flour sifter
1 French cook's knife
1 fruit reamer

1 set assorted graters
1 jar opener
1 pair kitchen shears
1 ladle
1 long-handled, slotted metal spoon
1 long-handled, 2-tined kitchen fork
1 nest mixing bowls—4 sizes
1 minute timer
1 narrow spatula—3/4″ wide
1 pair tongs
1 pancake turner
1 paring knife
1 pastry blender
1 pastry brush
1 potato masher
1 rolling pin
1 rotary beater
2 rubber scrapers—one narrow, one wide
1 slicing knife (8–9″ blade)
1 set standard dry measuring cups
3 standard liquid measuring cups—1 cup, 2 cups
  and 4 cups
1 set standard measuring spoons
1 medium-large strainer
1 small strainer
1 vegetable brush
1 vegetable peeler
1 wire rack
1 wooden spoon
Nice to Have:
apple corer
baster
bread knife with serrated or scalloped edge
butter-ball paddles
cake tester
assorted cutters for cookies, doughnuts, biscuits
food grinder or chopper
French wire whisk
funnel

garlic press
grapefruit knife
ice-cream spade
jelly-roll pan—15-1/2″ x 10-1/2″ x 1″
knife sharpener
melon-ball cutter
molds—large and individual for puddings and
  salads
mortar and pestle for crushing garlic, herbs and
  seeds
nutmeg grater
pastry cloth and rolling-pin cover
pepper mill
poultry pins
slicer for eggs, tomatoes
soufflé dish
strawberry huller
thermometers—roast meat, deep-fry, candy
For Storage:
bins for fruits and vegetables
bread box
canister set
cookie jar
covered cake plate
juice jug
refrigerator dishes with covers
waxed paper, aluminum foil, plastic sandwich
  wrap and bags
For Cleanup:
dishcloths and/or sponges
dish drainer
dish-draining rack
dishpan
dish towels
garbage can
paper towels
pot holders
wastebasket

The Right Way to Carve

The equipment you need to carve any type of meat or bird is a long carving knife or slicer, a short auxiliary knife, and a two-pronged fork. The knives should be sharp enough to slice easily.

Because a roast continues to cook after it leaves the heat, remove it from the oven just before it is done, and let it stand 15 to 20 minutes. The juices settle; it will carve more easily and be tastier. Be sure that hot meat goes to the table on a hot platter and cold meat on a cold platter.

How to Carve Roast Turkey

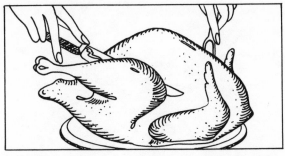

1. Turkey is placed with legs to carver's right. Plunge fork into bird just below breast, to give firm support, being careful not to puncture breast. With carving knife, slice thigh and leg from body.

2. Pull thigh and leg away—joint should give easily. If necessary, cut through joint at socket, using a sharp, small auxiliary knife. Lift to small platter, to carve later.

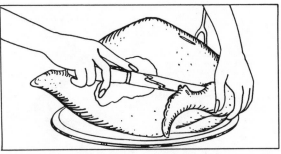

3. Grasp wing in left hand; pull from body as far as possible. Work knife through joint; twist wing from body. Place on small platter.

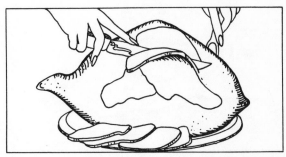

4. Carve thin slices (parallel to breastbone) the full sweep of the breast, from top to bottom. Slice enough breast meat for first servings.

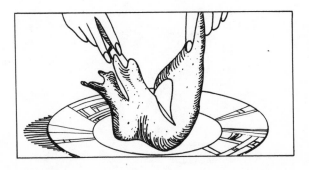

5. Holding leg in left hand, separate it from thigh, with small knife.

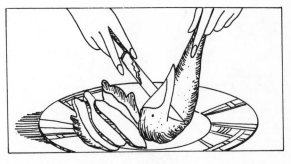

6. Holding thigh with fork, cut long, thin slices, with auxiliary knife.
Then, holding leg in hand, carve thick slices. Include white and dark meat in each serving. Carve other side of turkey for second servings.

How to Carve Leg of Lamb

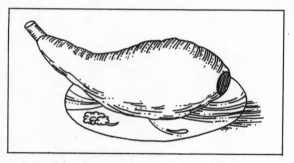

1. Leg of lamb is placed so that the thick, meaty section is on the side nearest the carver. (If a left leg, shank will be at carver's left; if right, at his right.)

2. Insert fork firmly in the large end of leg; cut 2 or 3 lengthwise slices from the thin side of the leg (the side away from the carver).

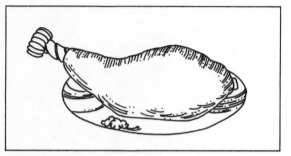

3. Turn lamb so it rests on the surface just cut; the thick, meaty section will be in an upright position.

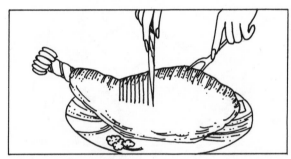

4. Insert fork firmly into the thick, meaty section. Starting at the shank end, cut slices (1/4 inch thick) down to large leg bone, cutting as many slices as needed.

5. With fork still in place, run knife along leg bone to release all the slices.

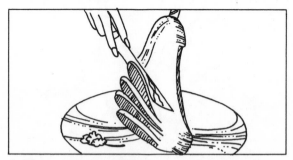

6. Then cut more slices from underside.

How to Carve a Whole Ham

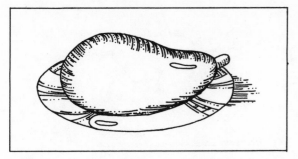

1. Ham is placed so that the bone end (shank) is at carver's right, fat side up. Insert fork into the heavy end of ham (butt).

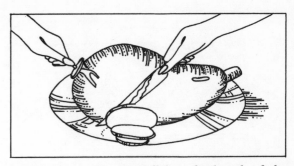

2. Cut 2 or 3 slices, parallel to the length of the ham, from the thin side. (Thin side of ham will face carver if the ham is a left one; it will face away from carver if ham is a right one.)

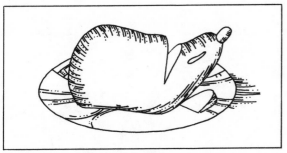

3. Using fork and hand, turn ham so it rests on cut surface. Cut a small wedge-shape piece from the shank end of ham; remove piece to side of platter.

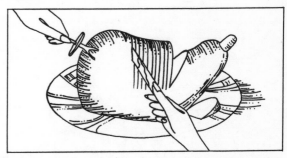

4. With fork steadying ham, start slicing at the wedge-shape cut, cutting thin horizontal slices down to leg bone. (Use long, sawing motions to cut.)

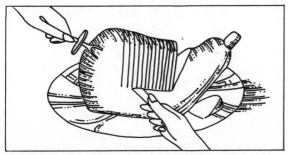

5. Insert knife at the wedge-shape cut at shank end. Run knife parallel to leg bone to release slices.

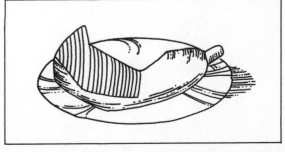

6. For more servings, turn ham back to its original position, fat side up. Cut additional slices at right angles to the bone.

How to Carve a Standing Rib Roast

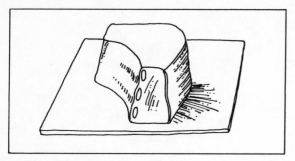

1. Place the roast on a platter or on a wooden board, cut side up, with the rib side of the roast at the carver's left.

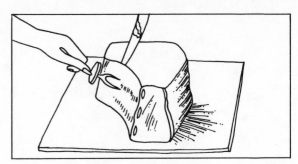

2. Plunge the fork between the two rop ribs, to get a firm grip on the roast. (A fork that is equipped with a hand guard is a good protection.) Beginning at the outside edge of the roast, draw the carving knife (its blade should be 8 or 9 inches long) across the roast to the rib side.

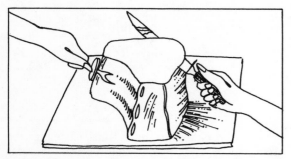

3. Release this first slice by cutting vertically along the full length of the rib bone with the point of the carving knife.

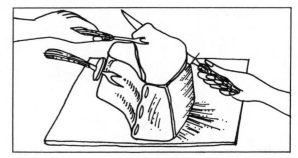

4. The first slice is usually fairly thick. Remaining slices, however, may vary from 1/8 to 1/4 inch thick, depending on personal preference. Lift off each slice as it is cut, with the aid of an auxiliary fork, to a serving platter or to an individual dinner plate.

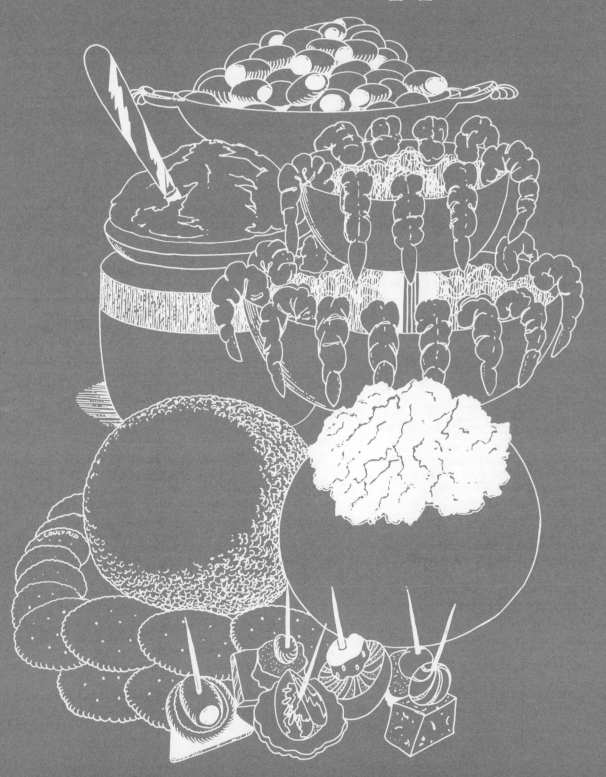

Hors d'oeuvres and Canapés

As the name suggests, appetizers are intended to whet, and not satisfy, the appetite.

In keeping with the trend toward lighter eating, hostesses are serving fewer hors d'oeuvres. But at a cocktail party, the hors d'oeuvres take the place of a light supper and must be more plentiful.

A few rules: If hors d'oeuvres cannot be eaten in the fingers, provide small plates with forks.

It is preferable to have fewer, very delicious ones, being careful not to duplicate flavors. Hot ones should be really hot. Heat a few at a time and serve at once, or for a larger party, keep them hot in a chafing dish.

Almost all the recipes that follow can be made several hours ahead, ready just for serving or last minute heating.

Marinated Artichokes

2 pkg (9-oz size) frozen artichoke hearts
1/2 cup tarragon vinegar
1/4 cup olive oil
4 teaspoons sugar
2 teaspoons finely cut fresh tarragon or 1 teaspoon dried tarragon leaves

1. Cook artichoke hearts as the label directs. Drain, and turn into medium bowl.
2. In small bowl, combine vinegar, oil, sugar, and tarragon; stir until sugar dissolves. Pour over artichoke hearts.
3. Refrigerate, covered, overnight or several days. Carefully turn artichoke hearts occasionally.
4. To serve: Arrange in shallow serving dish, and garnish with sprigs of fresh tarragon, if desired. Pass hors-d'oeuvre picks.
Makes 12 hors-d'oeuvre servings.

Stuffed Grape Leaves

Filling:
2 tablespoons butter or margarine
2 tablespoons chopped onion
2 cups fluffy cooked rice
2 tablespoons olive or salad oil
1 teaspoon salt
1/8 teaspoon pepper
2 tablespoons chopped parsley

1 jar (16 oz) vine leaves, drained and separated
2 tablespoons lemon juice
1 cup tomato juice

1. Make filling: In hot butter in small skillet, sauté onion until golden. Add the rice, oil, salt, pepper, and parsley; mix well.
2. Lay vine leaves, shiny side down, on flat surface. Place 1 teaspoon rice mixture on each.
3. Fold sides of each leaf over filling; then roll up, starting from narrow end. Place stuffed leaves, seam side down, close together, in bottom of medium skillet.
4. Pour lemon and tomato juices over them. Set a heavy plate or pie plate on top, to keep rolls in place during cooking.
5. Bring to boiling; reduce heat, and simmer, covered, 20 minutes. Remove from heat. Cool to room temperature. Refrigerate rolls until they are cold.
6. To serve: Lift out of liquid with slotted utensil. If desired, brush with olive oil, to make leaves shiny.
Makes 48.

Guacamole Dip with Crisp Vegetables

1 medium tomato, peeled
2 ripe avocados (about 1-1/2 lb in all)
1/4 cup finely chopped onion
2 tablespoons finely chopped canned chile
   peppers
1-1/2 tablespoons white vinegar
1 teaspoon salt
Chilled cauliflowerets
Crisp celery sticks
Green onions
Radishes
Cucumber sticks

1. In medium bowl, crush tomato with potato masher.
2. Halve avocados lengthwise; remove pits and peel. Slice avocados into crushed tomato; then mash until well blended.
3. Add onion, chile pepper, vinegar, and salt; mix well.
4. Place guacamole in bowl. Surround with vegetables.
Makes about 2 cups.

Pickled Mushrooms

1 tablespoon salt
1 lb fresh button mushrooms
1/2 cup chopped onion
1 clove garlic, finely chopped
1/4 cup chopped parsley
2 bay leaves
1/8 teaspoon pepper
1/2 teaspoon dried thyme leaves
2 cups white wine
2 cups white vinegar
1/2 cup olive or salad oil
2 tablespoons lemon juice

1. Add salt to 6 cups cold water. Wash mushrooms in this; drain.
2. Combine remaining ingredients in large saucepan. Add mushrooms; bring to boiling point.
3. Then reduce heat, and simmer, covered, 8 to 10 minutes, or until mushrooms are tender. Cool.
4. Refrigerate, covered, at least 1 hour, or until ready to use.
Makes 6 servings.

Eggplant Appetizer

1 large eggplant
1/2 cup plus 2 tablespoons olive or salad oil
2-1/2 cups sliced onion
1 cup diced celery
2 cans (8-oz size) tomato sauce
1/4 cup red-wine vinegar
2 tablespoons sugar
2 tablespoons drained capers
1/2 teaspoon salt
Dash pepper
12 pitted black olives, cut in slivers
Toast rounds

1. Wash eggplant; cut into 1/2-inch cubes.
2. In 1/2 cup hot oil in large skillet, sauté eggplant until tender and golden-brown. Remove eggplant, and set aside.
3. In 2 tablespoons hot oil in same skillet, sauté onion and celery until tender—about 5 minutes.
4. Return eggplant to skillet. Stir in tomato sauce; bring to boiling. Lower heat, and simmer, covered, 15 minutes.
5. Add vinegar, sugar, capers, salt, pepper, and olives. Simmer, covered and stirring occasionally, 20 minutes longer.
6. Refrigerate, covered, overnight.
7. To serve: Turn into serving bowl. Surround with toast rounds.
Makes 6 to 8 appetizer servings.

Mousse of Chicken Livers

1/2 cup sweet butter
1 large onion, sliced (1 cup)
1-1/4 lb chicken livers
1 hard-cooked egg
1-1/2 tablespoons cognac
1/2 teaspoon salt
Dash pepper
Chopped green onion

1. In 2 tablespoons hot butter in skillet, sauté sliced onion until tender—about 10 minutes. Remove from skillet.
2. Heat remaining butter in same skillet. Add chicken livers, and sauté over medium heat 3 to 5 minutes, or until golden-brown. Liver should be pink inside.
3. Put half the sautéed onion, chicken livers, egg, and cognac in blender; blend at low speed just until smooth. Turn into bowl. Repeat with rest of onion, livers, egg, and cognac. Stir in salt and pepper. Turn into crock or small bowl.
4. Refrigerate, covered, until well chilled—overnight. Garnish with green onion. Serve with toast or crackers.
Makes 3 cups.

Spring Dip

1/4 cup heavy cream
2 cups creamed cottage cheese
1/4 cup grated raw carrot
1/4 cup thinly sliced green onions
1/4 cup finely chopped green pepper
6 radishes, sliced very thin
Dash freshly ground black pepper
Dash dill weed

1. Stir cream into cottage cheese. Add remaining ingredients, and mix well.
2. Refrigerate. Serve with raw vegetables.
Makes about 3 cups.

Pineapple-Cheese Ball

2 pkg (8-oz size) cream cheese, softened
1 can (8-1/2 oz) crushed pineapple, drained
2 cups chopped pecans
1/4 cup finely chopped green pepper
2 tablespoons finely chopped onion
1 tablespoon seasoned salt
Canned pineapple slices
Maraschino cherries
Parsley sprigs
Assorted crackers

1. In medium bowl, with fork, beat cream cheese until smooth. Gradually stir in crushed pineapple, 1 cup pecans, the green pepper, onion, and salt.
2. Shape into a ball. Roll in remaining nuts. Wrap in plastic film or foil.
3. Refrigerate until well chilled—overnight.
4. To serve: Place cheese ball on serving board. If desired, garnish with pineapple slices, cherries, and parsley. Surround with crackers. Let guests help themselves.
Makes about 40 appetizer servings.
Note: Any leftover cheese mixture can be reshaped and refrigerated, for use another day.

Cocktail Olives

2 cups olive, salad, or peanut oil
1/2 cup white vinegar
1 lemon-peel spiral
3 dried hot red chiles
8 whole black peppercorns
1 tablespoon salt
1-1/2 teaspoons dried thyme leaves
2 bay leaves
1/2 teaspoon dried tarragon leaves
1 teaspoon dried marjoram leaves
2 cans (2-oz size) anchovy fillets
2 jars (4-oz size) pitted large green olives, drained
1 jar (4 oz) pimientos, drained
1 can (5-3/4 oz) pitted large ripe olives, drained
3 cloves garlic
1 sprig parsley
3 tablespoons capers

1. In large jar (about 2-quart size), combine oil, vinegar, lemon peel, chiles, black peppercorns, salt, thyme, bay leaves, tarragon, marjoram; stir to combine.
2. Drain anchovies; add oil from anchovies to above mixture. Cut anchovies in half crosswise; use to fill cavities in green olives.
3. Cut pimientos in strips; use to fill cavities in black olives.
4. Crush 1 clove garlic; sliver other 2 cloves garlic; add garlic and olives to jar, along with parsley and capers.
5. Let stand, covered, at room temperature at least 3 days before serving.
Makes about 2 quarts.
Note: If storing for longer time, refrigerate, and let warm to room temperature before serving.

Cocktail Macadamias

1 jar (7 oz) Macadamia nuts
2 tablespoons butter or margarine, melted
1/2 teaspoon seasoned salt
1/4 teaspoon liquid hot-pepper seasoning
1/4 teaspoon paprika
1/4 teaspoon garlic salt

1. Preheat oven to 375F.
2. In shallow baking pan, toss nuts with butter, seasoned salt, hot-pepper seasoning, and paprika.
3. Bake 10 minutes.
4. Drain nuts on paper towels. Sprinkle with garlic salt. Serve slightly warm.
Makes 1-1/4 cups.

Savory Edam Cheese

1 whole Edam cheese (about 1-3/4 lb)
1 cup beer or ale
1/4 cup butter or regular margarine, softened
1 teaspoon caraway seed
1 teaspoon dry mustard
1/2 teaspoon celery salt

1. Let cheese stand at room temperature until it is soft—about 1 hour.
2. Remove a slice, about an inch thick, from top. With spoon, scoop out cheese from slice and from cheese, keep red shell intact. Discard top. Refrigerate shell.
3. Grate scooped-out cheese on fine grater into medium bowl. Let stand until very soft.
4. Add beer, butter, caraway seed, mustard, and celery salt; mix until well blended. Fill cheese shell with mixture, mounding high.
5. To store: Wrap cheese in plastic film, then in foil. Store in refrigerator several weeks.
6. To serve: Let stand at room temperature until soft enough to spread.
Makes 3 cups.

Caviar-Cream-Cheese Ball

2 pkg (8-oz size) cream cheese
1 jar (4 oz) red caviar, slightly drained
Party pumpernickel slices

1. Let cream cheese stand at room temperature, to soften—about 1 hour. Then, on serving tray, shape into a mound about 5 inches in diameter; flatten top. Refrigerate, covered.
2. To serve: Spoon caviar over top of cream cheese, letting a little drizzle over side. Surround with pumpernickel. If desired, decorate with holly.
Makes 30 servings.

Holiday Cheese Ball

4 pkg (3-oz size) cream cheese, softened
6 oz blue cheese, softened
6 oz processed Cheddar-cheese spread
2 tablespoons grated onion
1 teaspoon Worcestershire sauce
1/8 teaspoon monosodium glutamate
1 cup ground pecans
1/2 cup finely chopped parsley
Assorted crackers

1. In medium bowl, combine cheeses, onion, Worcestershire, and monosodium glutamate. Beat until well blended.
2. Stir in 1/2 cup pecans and 1/4 cup parsley. Shape into a ball. Wrap in waxed paper or plastic film, then in foil.
3. Refrigerate overnight.
4. About 1 hour before serving, roll cheese ball in remaining pecans and parsley. Place on serving plate, and surround with crackers.
Makes about 30 appetizer servings.

Blue-Cheese Spread

1/2 lb natural blue cheese, sieved
2 pkg (3-oz size) cream cheese
1/4 teaspoon Worcestershire sauce
1/4 teaspoon paprika
Dash salt
Dash cayenne
3 tablespoons port

1. Let cheeses warm to room temperature.
2. Combine with remaining ingredients in large electric-mixer bowl. Beat, at high speed, until thoroughly combined and smooth.
To store: Fill small crocks; seal tops with melted paraffin. Keep refrigerated.
Makes 1-3/4 cups.

Cheddar-Beer Spread

1/2 lb mild Cheddar cheese, grated
1/2 clove garlic, crushed
Dash cayenne
1 tablespoon Worcestershire sauce
1/2 teaspoon dry mustard
1/2 cup beer

1. Combine cheese, garlic, cayenne, Worcestershire, mustard, and beer in medium bowl.
2. Mix until very smooth.
3. To store: Fill crock, and seal top with melted paraffin. Keep refrigerated several weeks. Then serve as a cocktail spread. Remove from refrigerator 1/2 hour before serving.
Makes 1-1/2 cups.

Cheese-Pâté Pineapple

2 pkg (3 oz size) cream cheese
2/3 cup prepared brown mustard
2-1/2 lb natural sharp Cheddar cheese, grated
1 jar (2 oz) small pimiento-stuffed olives, drained
1 fresh green pineapple frond

1. In a large bowl, combine cream cheese and mustard; with electric mixer at medium speed, beat until well blended. At low speed, gradually beat in grated cheese until well combined.
2. Turn mixture onto wooden board. With hands, knead until smooth and pliable. Refrigerate, covered, until chilled and able to be molded—about 45 minutes.
3. With hands, roll mixture into a cylinder. Stand cylinder on cookie sheet. Mold into pineapple shape, about 5-1/2 inches high, 15 inches around at widest part, 10-1/2 inches at narrowest part.
4. Cut olives crosswise into 1/4 inch thick slices. Carefully place olive slices on cheese in straight horizontal rows, arranging them so vertical rows run on diagonal. Using wooden pick, make diagonal lines, 1/8 inch deep, between rows of olive slices. Cover with plastic film.
5. Refrigerate still on cookie sheet until serving time (overnight, if desired).
6. To serve: With broad spatula, carefully remove cheese-pineapple from cookie sheet to serving platter, standing it upright on broadest end. Place pineapple frond on top. Surround with small crackers, for spreading. Let stand at room temperature about 30 minutes before serving.
Makes enough to spread 180 crackers.

Swiss-Cheese Fritters

Salad oil or shortening for deep-fat frying
1-1/2 cups (6 oz) grated natural Swiss or Gruyère cheese
3 tablespoons flour
1/2 teaspoon salt
1/4 teaspoon pepper
1/4 teaspoon dry mustard
4 egg whites
1/2 cup packaged dry bread crumbs

1. In deep skillet or deep-fat fryer, slowly heat salad oil or shortening (at least 2 inches) to 375F on deep-frying thermometer.
2. Combine cheese, flour, salt, pepper, and mustard on sheet of waxed paper.
3. In medium bowl, beat egg whites until stiff peaks form when beater is slowly raised. Gently fold cheese mixture into egg whites until well combined.
4. Shape by tablespoonfuls into 1-inch balls; roll in bread crumbs.
5. Deep-fry a few at a time, turning once, 1-1/2 minutes, or until golden-brown on both sides. Drain on paper towels.
6. Serve hot, on wooden picks, as an hors d'oeuvre. Or pass in a basket.
Makes 22 fritters.

Cheddar in Sherry

2 tablespoons soft butter or margarine
1 teaspoon dry mustard
Few grains cayenne
1/2 lb Cheddar cheese
5 tablespoons sherry

1. Cream butter with mustard and cayenne.
2. Grate cheese very finely. Mix with sherry.
3. Add butter mixture, and blend thoroughly. Makes 1-1/4 cups.

Cheese-Bacon Puffs

2 eggs
1 cup finely grated Cheddar cheese
2 teaspoons grated onion or onion juice
1/2 teaspoon dry mustard
6 slices white bread
24 (1-inch) bacon squares

1. Preheat oven to 375F.
2. In small bowl, beat eggs with fork. Add grated cheese, onion, and the dry mustard; stir until they are well blended.
3. Trim crust from bread; cut each slice into quarters, to make 24 squares in all. Arrange in shallow baking pan. Spoon heaping teaspoonful cheese mixture on center of each bread square. Top each with a piece of bacon.
4. Bake 15 minutes, or until bread is toasted and topping is slightly puffed.
Makes 2 dozen puffs.

Swiss Cheese Fondue

1 clove garlic, split in half
1 lb. natural Swiss cheese, grated
Dash salt
Dash pepper
1-1/2 to 2 cups dry white wine
2 tablespoons cornstarch
2 tablespoons light rum or kirsch
1 loaf French or Italian bread, cut into 1-inch cubes

1. For making fondue, use a rather deep baking dish with a glazed interior, a flameproof-glass saucepan, or a crockery utensil. Never use a metal pan.
2. Rub bottom and side of baking dish with garlic. Put cheese, salt, and pepper into dish; add enough wine almost to cover.
3. Cook over medium heat, stirring constantly, just until cheese melts—no longer. Cheese and wine will not be blended yet.
4. Now make a smooth paste of cornstarch, rum, and about 2 tablespoons water. Using wire whip, stir cornstarch mixture into melted cheese and wine.
5. Cook over medium heat, stirring, 2 to 3 minutes, or until fondue is as creamy and thick as medium white sauce.
6. To serve: Set fondue over a chafing-dish flame or candle warmer. Each bread cube should be speared with a fork and dipped into warm fondue. Makes about 3 cups.

Swiss-Cheese-and-Tomato Fondue

1 clove garlic, split
1 lb natural Swiss cheese, grated
1-1/4 cups dry white wine
1 can (8 oz) tomato sauce
Dash salt
Dash pepper
2 tablespoons cornstarch
1 long loaf French or Italian bread

1. For fondue, use a fondue pot, deep baking dish with glazed interior, flameproof-glass saucepan, or crockery utensil. Never use a metal pan.
2. Rub bottom and side of fondue pot with cut sides of garlic. Place cheese, 1 cup wine, the tomato sauce, salt, and pepper in pot.
3. Cook over medium heat, stirring constantly, just until cheese melts. Remove from heat. (Do not cook longer, even though cheese and wine are not blended.)
4. In small bowl, make a smooth paste of cornstarch and remaining wine. With a wire whisk, mix the cornstarch mixture into the cheese mixture.
5. Return to medium heat; cook, stirring constantly, 2 to 3 minutes, or until fondue is creamy and as thick as medium white sauce.
6. To serve: Set fondue over low flame or candle warmer. Cut bread in 1-inch cubes, for dipping into fondue.
Makes 12 servings.

Hot Cheese Pastries

Filling:
2 pkg (8-oz size) cream cheese, softened
1/2 lb Greek cheese (feta), crumbled
1 egg
3 tablespoons butter or margarine, melted

1 pkg (1 lb) prepared phyllo-pastry or strudel-pastry leaves
1 cup butter or margarine, melted

1. Make filling: In small bowl of electric mixer, combine cream cheese, Greek cheese, egg, and 3 tablespoons butter; beat at medium speed until well blended and smooth.
2. Preheat oven to 350F.
3. Place 2 leaves of phyllo pastry on board; brush with melted butter. Cut lengthwise into strips about 2 inches wide.
4. Place 1 teaspoon filling at end of a strip. Fold over one corner to opposite side, to make a triangle. Continue folding, keeping triangle shape, to other end of strip. Arrange the filled triangle on an ungreased cookie sheet. Repeat with the remaining strips.
5. Repeat with other pastry leaves.
6. Bake 20 minutes, or until deep golden-brown. Serve hot.
Makes about 7 dozen.
Note: If desired, make and bake ahead. Cool; then refrigerate, covered, overnight. To serve: Arrange on cookie sheet; bake in 350F oven about 10 minutes, or until heated.

Chile con Queso with Raw Vegetables

1/4 cup butter or margarine
1/2 cup finely chopped onion
1 can (1 lb) tomatoes, undrained
1-1/2 to 2 cans (4-oz size) green chiles (see Note),
    drained and chopped
1/2 teaspoon salt
1 lb Monterey Jack cheese, cubed
1/2 cup heavy cream

1. In hot butter, in medium skillet, sauté onion until tender. Add tomatoes, chiles and salt, mashing tomatoes with fork. Simmer, stirring occasionally, 15 minutes.
2. Add cheese cubes, stirring until cheese is melted. Stir in cream. Cook, stirring constantly, 2 minutes.
3. Remove from heat, and let stand 15 minutes. Serve warm, in a casserole over a candle warmer, as a dip with carrot sticks, celery hearts, cucumber sticks and large corn chips.
Makes 10 to 12 servings.
Note: Use larger amount of green chiles, if you like this really hot.

Greek Cheese Pie

9-inch unbaked pie shell
3/4 lb feta cheese, cut into small pieces
1 cup light cream
3 eggs
1/2 teaspoon dried thyme leaves
1 teaspoon cornstarch
Dash pepper
1 small clove garlic, crushed
9 large pitted ripe olives
7 large pitted green olives
1 pimiento, cut into strips

1. Preheat oven to 425F. Prick crust well with fork; place in freezer 10 minutes.
2. Bake pie shell 10 minutes; cool.
3. Blend cheese in electric blender with cream and eggs until smooth. Add thyme, cornstarch, and pepper; blend. Stir in garlic. Turn into pie shell.
4. Bake pie 10 minutes. Arrange olives over top; bake 25 minutes longer, or until filling is set. Decorate with pimiento strips. Serve warm.
Makes 8 servings.
Note: This pie may be made early in the day and reheated for serving.

Quiche Lorraine

Pie Shell:
1/2 pkg (10- or 11-oz size) piecrust mix
1 tablespoon soft butter

Swiss-Cheese Filling:
1/2 lb sliced bacon
1-1/2 cups grated natural Swiss cheese (6 oz)
3 eggs
1-1/2 cups light cream
3/4 teaspoon salt
Dash nutmeg
Dash cayenne
Dash black pepper

1. Make piecrust mix as the label directs, sprinkling some of water over all of the pastry mix, tossing it lightly with a fork after each addition, and pushing dampened portion of the mixture to the side.
2. Shape the pastry into a ball. Then wrap it in waxed paper, and refrigerate until you are ready to make pie shell.
3. On lightly floured surface, roll the pastry to an 11-inch circle; roll with light strokes, from the center out to the edge, alternating the directions.
4. If the rolled circle of piecrust is too irregular in shape, trim off any bulges around edge, to use as patches. Then gently press the patches in place on the pastry, and smooth them with the rolling pin.

5. Fold pastry in half, and lift to a 9-inch pie plate, with fold in center.

6. Now unfold the pastry, and fit it very carefully into the pie plate.

7. Fold the edge under; make rim. Crimp rim decoratively.

8. Spread bottom of the pie shell with butter. Refrigerate until using.

9. Preheat the oven to 375F.

10. Fry bacon until it's crisp; drain on paper towels. Crumble into bits, and sprinkle over bottom of the pie shell.

11. Sprinkle grated cheese over bacon.

12. In medium bowl, with rotary beater, beat eggs with cream, salt, nutmeg, cayenne, and black pepper until mixture is well combined, but not frothy.

13. Place pie shell on middle shelf in oven. Pour egg mixture into pie shell.

14. Bake 35 to 40 minutes, or until the top is golden and center is firm when it is gently pressed with a fingertip.

15. Let cool on a wire rack for 10 minutes before serving.

Makes 12 hors d'oeuvre servings.

Parmesan-Cheese Leaves

1 cup unsifted all-purpose flour
1/2 cup butter or regular margarine, cut into
   small pieces
1 cup grated Parmesan cheese
1/4 teaspoon salt
Dash pepper
Dash cayenne
1 egg, slightly beaten

1. In medium bowl, combine flour and butter. With pastry blender or 2 knives, used scissors fashion, cut butter into flour until butter particles are the size of small peas.

2. With fork, stir in cheese, salt, pepper, and cayenne.

3. Sprinkle evenly with 2 tablespoons cold water. Toss with fork.

4. Form into a ball with hands; then flatten slightly.

5. Between sheets of waxed paper, on a slightly damp surface, roll out to 1/4-inch thickness.

6. Using leaf-shape or scalloped cookie cutters (about 2-1/2 inches), cut out pastry. Place in plastic freezer container, with waxed paper between layers. Cover; freeze.

7. When ready to use: Preheat oven to 400F. Place frozen pastries, about 1 inch apart, on ungreased cookie sheets.

8. Brush tops lightly with egg.

9. Sprinkle with a little paprika, if desired. Bake, still frozen, 10 minutes, or until golden. Serve warm. Nice with consommé.

Makes about 2 dozen.

Williamsburg Cheese Straws

1 cup sifted* all-purpose flour
1/2 teaspoon salt
1/4 teaspoon dry mustard
1/8 teaspoon cayenne
1/3 cup butter or margarine
1 cup grated sharp Cheddar cheese
1-1/2 tablespoons ice water
1 teaspoon celery seed
* Sift before measuring.

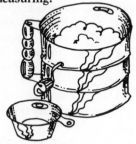

1. Into medium bowl, sift flour with salt, mustard, and cayenne. With pastry blender, cut in butter and half the cheese until mixture resembles coarse crumbs.
2. Add water; stir lightly to blend. Shape into a ball.
3. Preheat oven to 350F.
4. On lightly floured surface, roll out pastry 1/8 inch thick. Sprinkle with remaining cheese. Fold dough in half; roll out 1/8 inch thick again. With pastry wheel or knife, cut into strips 3 inches long and about 1/2 inch wide. Sprinkle with celery seed. Place on ungreased cookie sheets.
5. Bake about 12 minutes, or until pale brown. Serve warm.
Makes about 5 dozen.
Note: These may be frozen; reheat at 300F at serving time.

Pissaladière

2 pkg pie-crust mix*
10 large ripe tomatoes (about 5 lb)
2 tablespoons olive or salad oil
1/4 cup butter or margarine
3 Spanish onions (2 lb), thinly sliced
1/2 cup grated Parmesan cheese
1 teaspoon dried rosemary leaves
2 cans (2-oz size) anchovy fillets
15 ripe olives, halved
Olive oil
* Pastry for 2 crusts in each package.

1. Prepare pie crust, both packages at same time, as label directs.
2. On lightly floured pastry cloth, or waxed paper, roll out pastry, 1/4-inch thick to form a rectangle, about 17 by 12 inches. Fit into a 15-by-10-by-1-inch jelly-roll pan; trim edges. Refrigerate.
4. To remove skin from tomatoes: Hold tomato on fork over flame just until skin "pops" or dip in boiling water until skin loosens. Seed and cut tomatoes in very small pieces. In hot olive oil, in large skillet, cook the tomatoes over high heat, until the water evaporates and the tomatoes form a paste—about 15 minutes.
5. Preheat oven to 375F.
6. In hot butter, in skillet, sauté the onions until they are soft and slightly golden.
7. Sprinkle the bottom of the pastry with the grated cheese. Layer the onions evenly over cheese; sprinkle with rosemary. Then make a layer of the tomato mixture over all.
8. Arrange anchovies in rows on top, 5 lengthwise and 4 crosswise to make a lattice effect. In center of each square, place an olive half. Brush each olive with a little olive oil.
9. Bake 35 minutes, or until crust is golden and baked through.

10. Let cool slightly. Then brush with a little olive oil. Cut into 30 squares with an olive in the center of each.
Makes 30 servings.

Swedish Meatballs

4 eggs, slightly beaten
2 cups milk
1 cup packaged dry bread crumbs
4 tablespoons butter or margarine
1 cup finely chopped onions
2 lb ground chuck
1/2 lb ground pork
Salt
Dill weed
1/4 teaspoon allspice
1/4 teaspoon nutmeg
1/4 teaspoon ground cardamom
1/3 cup flour
1/4 teaspoon pepper
2 cans (10-1/2-oz size) condensed beef broth, undiluted
1 cup light cream

1. In a large bowl, combine the eggs, milk, and dry bread crumbs.
2. In 2 tablespoons hot butter in large skillet, sauté chopped onion until soft—about 5 minutes. Lift out with slotted spoon. Add to bread-crumb mixture, along with ground meats, 3 teaspoons salt, 1/2 teaspoon dill weed, the allspice, nutmeg, and cardamom. With a wooden spoon or your hands, mix well to combine.
3. Refrigerate, covered, for 1 hour.
4. Shape meat mixture into 60 meatballs.
5. Preheat the oven to 325F.
6. In remaining hot butter, sauté meatballs, about one-third at a time, until browned all over. Remove as browned to two 2-quart casseroles.
7. Remove the skillet from heat. Pour off all but 1/4 cup drippings; stir in flour, 1/2 teaspoon salt, and the pepper. Gradually stir in beef broth. Bring to boil, stirring constantly. Add cream and 1 teaspoon dill weed. Pour over meatballs in casseroles.
8. Bake, covered, 30 minutes. Garnish top of meatballs with fresh dill sprigs, if desired.
Makes 20 servings.

Beef-Tartare Canapés

3/4 lb ground beef round
1 egg
3 tablespoons finely chopped onion
3 tablespoons finely chopped watercress
3 anchovy fillets, finely chopped
3 tablespoons drained capers
1/4 teaspoon salt
Dash pepper
1 loaf (10 oz) Italian bread, about 14 inches long
Butter or margarine

1. In medium bowl, combine beef, egg, onion, watercress, anchovies, capers, salt, and pepper; mix lightly with fork until well combined. Refrigerate, covered.
2. Cut a 1/2-inch-thick slice from each end of bread; set aside. Remove soft bread center from entire loaf, using a long-bladed serrated knife and leaving 1/2-inch-thick shell. Pack beef mixture into loaf, filling from each end. Replace ends; secure with wooden picks.
3. Wrap loaf in foil, and refrigerate until chilled—about 1 hour.
4. To serve: Place loaf on board, and cut into slices about 1/2 inch thick. Spread bread lightly with butter.
Makes 26 slices.

Steak Tartare

2 lb ground beef round
1/2 cup finely chopped onion
1/2 cup capers, drained
8 anchovy fillets, finely chopped
4 egg yolks
1 teaspoon salt
1/8 teaspoon pepper
1/4 cup finely chopped watercress
Unsalted saltine crackers or small rounds of
  rye bread

1. In large bowl and using 2 forks, lightly toss all ingredients, except the crackers, until they are well combined.
2. Mound on a serving platter.
3. Refrigerate, covered, until ready to serve—2 to 3 hours.
4. Surround with the crackers or rye bread.
Makes 20 servings.
To make more decorative: Turn meat mixture into a fancy mold. To serve: Unmold, and garnish with anchovy strips and capers.

Savory Steak Slices

1-1/2 lb flank steak
1/3 cup soy sauce
1/3 cup rum
2 tablespoons salad oil
Watercress sprigs
1/4 cup sliced radishes
Party rye bread slices, lightly buttered

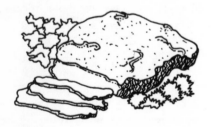

1. Trim excess fat from steak. Wipe steak with damp paper towels.
2. Combine soy sauce and rum in large, shallow dish. Place flank steak in mixture. Refrigerate, covered, turning occasionally, 24 hours.
3. Remove steak from rum mixture. Brush steak lightly with oil. Place in broiler pan without rack.
4. Broil steak, 6 inches from heat, 1 minute on each side. Then turn, and broil 5 minutes longer. Turn again; broil 5 minutes more, or until medium rare.
5. Let cool, occasionally brushing steak with pan juices. Refrigerate, lightly covered, until serving.
6. To serve: Cut steak into thin slices, on the diagonal. Arrange on serving board or platter. Garnish with watercress sprigs and sliced radishes. Place basket of bread slices nearby.
Makes about 40 hors d'oeuvre servings.

Rumaki

16 chicken livers
1 cup soy sauce
1/2 cup cream sherry
16 slices bacon, halved crosswise

1. Wash chicken livers; dry well on paper towels.
2. Cut each liver in half, removing any stringy portion. Turn livers into a large bowl.
3. Combine soy sauce and sherry; mix well. Pour over chicken livers; toss lightly to mix well.
4. Wrap each halved chicken liver with half a bacon slice; secure with wooden pick. Arrange on broiler rack in broiler pan. Brush each side with soy mixture.
5. Broil, 3 inches from heat, 2 or 3 minutes on each side, turning once or twice, until bacon is crisp and livers are cooked through.
Makes 32.

Party Pâté

3 lb chicken livers
6 tablespoons butter or margarine
1/3 cup chopped onion
1 tablespoon dried savory leaves
1 tablespoon dried tarragon leaves
6 tablespoons cognac
1/2 cup light cream
5 eggs
1-1/2 tablespoons salt
1/4 teaspoon pepper
2 bay leaves
8 slices bacon

Glaze:
1 tablespoon unflavored gelatine
1 cup dry white wine
1/2 teaspoon dried tarragon leaves
1/2 teaspoon chopped parsley

Decoration:
10 ripe olives
1 green olive
1 jar (4 oz) roasted pimientos

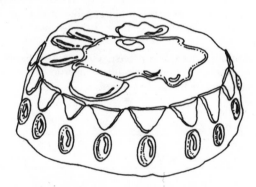

1. Day before: Trim any white part from chicken livers; wash livers and dry on paper towels.
2. In hot butter in skillet, sauté onion and dried herbs until onion is golden. Add chicken livers; sauté, stirring, about 5 minutes. Cut up livers.
3. In bowl, combine livers, cognac, cream, eggs, salt, and pepper; mix well. Put mixture through blender, about one third at a time, to make a smooth purée.
4. Preheat oven to 400F. Line a 1-3/4-quart round casserole with bacon slices. Arrange bay leaves in bottom of casserole.
5. Pour liver mixture into casserole; place in pan of very hot water (water should measure 1 inch). Bake 1 hour.
6. Remove casserole from hot water; let cool completely on wire rack. Refrigerate, covered, overnight. Next day, unmold: Loosen edge with spatula; turn out on a tray. Remove bacon; smooth surface with spatula. Refrigerate.
7. Prepare Glaze: Sprinkle gelatine over 1/4 cup water in small saucepan; let stand 5 minutes to soften. Add wine, tarragon, and parsley; stir over low heat until mixture is hot and gelatine is dissolved; strain if desired.
8. Set pan in ice water; let stand, stirring, until thickened—15 minutes.
9. Meanwhile, arrange slices of the olives and pimiento around edge and on top of pâté, to form design of your choice. Spoon with half of glaze, covering completely. Refrigerate pâté to set glaze—30 minutes. Reheat remaining glaze; cool and spoon over chilled pâté. Refrigerate until serving time to set glaze. Garnish with parsley, if desired. Serve with pumpernickel or toast rounds.
Makes 40 servings.

Smoked-Salmon Canapés

1 pkg (3 oz) cream cheese, softened
2 teaspoons finely cut fresh dill
8 slices party pumpernickel
6 oz smoked salmon, thinly sliced
4 teaspoons capers

1. In small bowl, blend cream cheese and dill. Spread on pumpernickel slices. Cut each slice into three triangles.
2. Cut salmon into 24 strips, each 3 inches by 1/2 inch. Roll up each strip loosely, and stand one roll on each triangle of bread. Top salmon with capers. Arrange on serving plate, and garnish with dill sprigs, if desired.
Makes 24.

Liver Pâté en Gelée

1-1/2 teaspoons unflavored gelatine
1 cup canned condensed beef broth
4 canned whole mushrooms
1 can (4-3/4 oz) liver pâté
1 tablespoon butter or regular margarine
1 teaspoon brandy
Thin slices toast

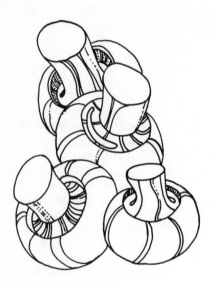

1. In small saucepan, sprinkle gelatine over 1/4 cup undiluted broth; let stand 5 minutes, to soften. Heat over low heat, stirring constantly, until gelatine dissolves. Remove from heat. Add remaining broth.
2. Place 1-1/2-cup decorative mold in pan of ice and water. Spoon about 2 tablespoons gelatine mixture into mold. Let stand a few minutes, until almost set.
3. Cut mushrooms in half. Arrange, in a pattern, on set gelatine in mold. Add enough more gelatine mixture to cover mushrooms.
4. In small bowl, combine liver pâté, butter, brandy. With electric mixer or fork, beat until combined.
5. Turn mixture into empty liver-pâté can, making top even; invert onto waxed paper. With can opener, remove end of can. Lift can, and carefully push pâté, through can, onto center of set gelatine in mold, being careful to keep its shape.
6. Spoon remaining chilled gelatine mixture around and over pâté. Refrigerate, covered, 3 hours, or until firm.
7. To unmold: Run sharp knife around edge of mold. Invert over serving plate. Place a hot, damp dishcloth over mold; shake gently to release. Lift off mold.
8. Remove crusts from toast; cut toast diagonally in quarters. Arrange triangles around mold. Or serve mold with crackers, if you wish.
Makes 8 servings.

Herring in Dill Sauce

1 cup prepared mustard
1 cup olive oil
1/4 cup vinegar
3 tablespoons lemon juice
1/2 cup chopped fresh dill
1 teaspoon pepper
1-1/2 teaspoons salt
1-1/2 teaspoons whole allspice
2 tablespoons sugar
8 salt-herring fillets
Fresh dill sprigs

1. Combine mustard and oil in small bowl; beat, with rotary beater, until as thick as mayonnaise.
2. Gradually beat in vinegar and lemon juice, then dill, pepper, salt, allspice, and sugar.
3. Rinse herring; drain well on paper towels. Place in large glass bowl; cover with sauce.
4. Refrigerate, covered, at least 3 days.
5. To serve: Cut into 1-inch pieces; serve with wooden picks. Garnish with dill sprigs.
Makes 10 to 12 servings.

Herring in Sour Cream

2 cans (6-oz size) matjes-herring fillets, or 3
    matjes-herring fillets
1 medium onion
24 whole black peppercorns
2 bay leaves
3/4 cup dairy sour cream
1/4 cup sauterne

1. Rinse fillets in cold water; drain; dry on paper towels. Cut crosswise into 1-inch pieces. Then slice onion into thin rings.
2. In medium bowl, layer onion rings, black peppercorns, bay leaves, herring pieces.
3. Combine sour cream, wine. Pour over herring mixture, mixing gently to combine.
4. Refrigerate, covered, 8 hours, or overnight.
Makes 2 cups; 6 appetizer servings.
Note: Herring in Sour Cream may be stored, covered, in refrigerator 3 days.

Swedish Cold Salmon with Mustard Sauce

5- to 6-lb fresh salmon
1/4 cup sugar
1/4 cup salt
1 tablespoon white pepper
1 large bunch fresh dill, snipped
Mustard Sauce, below
Party rye or pumpernickel bread

1. Two days before: With sharp knife, carefully remove skin from salmon. Cut salmon in half along bone; remove bone.
2. Combine sugar, salt, and pepper; mix well. Use about one third of sugar mixture to sprinkle both sides of salmon, lightly rubbing into surface.
3. On tray, covered with waxed paper, place one salmon half. Cover with half of snipped dill. Place other half of salmon, cut side sprinkled with rest of dill, on top.
4. Place a bread board on top of fish; weigh down with very heavy skillet or iron. Refrigerate two days.
5. During refrigeration, sprinkle two more times with sugar mixture, turning fish and basting with juices in tray.
6. When ready to serve, lightly dry salmon with paper towels. If desired, garnish with fresh dill and thin lemon slices. Slice thinly. Serve with Mustard Sauce and dark bread.
Makes 20 servings.

Mustard Sauce

1/2 cup prepared brown mustard
1/2 cup sugar
1/2 cup salad oil
1/2 cup chopped fresh dill
1/4 cup white-wine vinegar

In small bowl, combine mustard, sugar, and salad oil; mix well with wooden spoon. Add dill and wine vinegar; beat well. Refrigerate, covered, until well chilled—several hours.
Makes 1-1/2 cups.
Note: If stronger mustard flavor is desired, add dry mustard to taste.

Clams Oregano

2 dozen clams in shells, well scrubbed
3/4 cup butter or margarine, melted
1 cup packaged dry bread crumbs
2 cloves garlic, crushed
2 tablespoons chopped parsley
2 tablespoons grated Parmesan cheese
4 teaspoons lemon juice
1 teaspoon dried oregano leaves
1/8 teaspoon liquid hot-pepper seasoning
Rock salt
Lemon wedges
Parsley sprigs

1. In large kettle, bring 1/2 inch water to boiling. Add clams; simmer, covered, until clams open—6 to 10 minutes.
2. Meanwhile, combine butter with bread crumbs, garlic, chopped parsley, Parmesan, lemon juice, oregano, and hot-pepper seasoning.
3. Remove clams from kettle; discard top shells. Remove clams from bottom shells; chop coarsely; add to crumb mixture. Spoon into bottom shells.
4. Place a layer of rock salt, 1/2 inch deep, in a large roasting pan or two shallow casseroles; sprinkle with water to dampen.
5. Arrange filled clam shells on salt. Run under broiler just until golden-brown—about 5 minutes. Garnish with lemon wedges and parsley sprigs. Serve at once.
Makes 8 servings.

First Courses

Today's entertaining is more relaxed and informal; often, it's buffet. A first course, if served at all, may be a part of the cocktail hour. Or to facilitate service, a first course served cold may already be on the table when guests sit down.

Many of the first courses that follow make interesting luncheon or supper dishes; such as Pâté Tart and the Asparagus-and-Swiss-Cheese Tart. For other first course suggestions, see the chapters on soups, shellfish and salads.

Caviar: The Taste of Luxury

The best quality of fresh caviar is made with a minimum of salt. The word "Malossol" on a jar is not, as some may think, the name of a variety of fresh caviar; literally, it means "little salt" in Russian, or mildly salted.

What makes caviar so expensive is that it is extremely perishable and must be refrigerated with utmost care on its journey from Iran or Russia, home of the sturgeon. If the temperature goes below 28 degrees, it will freeze and be ruined; above 32 degrees, it spoils.

Beluga, a gray caviar, largest grained, is the costliest food in the world.

Osetra, a smaller caviar, is lower in price.

Sevruga, prized by experts, is the smallest.

Pressed Caviar, lowest priced and popular with many connoisseurs, is made of small eggs of Beluga that drop out during grading and are pressed into a mass, thick as marmalade.

Red Caviar, made from salmon roe, is not a "true" caviar, like sturgeon caviar; but it is appetizing, delicious, and modestly priced. Caviar of whatever variety should be served well chilled, in a well-chilled crystal or china dish in a bed of finely chopped ice. A tablespoonful, or two generous teaspoonfuls, of caviar would make one good average serving.

Purists eat it without any embellishments—just dark bread and sweet butter. Other caviar lovers may add trimmings, like a sprinkling of hard-cooked eggs, the yolks and whites chopped separately; sour cream; chopped onion; warm toast, crisp crackers. Traditionally, chilled dry champagne or ice-cold vodka is served with any caviar.

Avocado Halves, California Style

2 tablespoons chili sauce
2 tablespoons catsup
1 tablespoon vinegar
1 tablespoon sugar
1 teaspoon Worcestershire sauce
6 dashes Tabasco
5 tablespoons lemon juice
3 large ripe avocados, chilled

1. Make sauce: Combine chili sauce, catsup, vinegar, sugar, Worcestershire, Tabasco, and 2 tablespoons lemon juice. Mix well.
2. Refrigerate several hours, to chill well.
3. At serving time, peel avocados; cut in half; remove pits. Brush cut sides with 3 tablespoons lemon juice. Fill cavities with sauce (see Note). Serve as first course.
Makes 6 servings.
Note: Or use your favorite bottled salad dressing.

Eggs en Gelée

6 eggs
2 env unflavored gelatine
2 cans (12-1/2-oz size) chicken consommé
1/2 cup sauterne
1 tablespoon tarragon vinegar
3/4 teaspoon salt
Boiling water
12 fresh tarragon leaves
4 tablespoons liver pâté
1 teaspoon heavy cream

1. Gently lower eggs into boiling water in medium saucepan. Take pan off heat; cover; let stand 3 to 5 minutes. Cool eggs under cold water, to prevent further cooking.
2. Sprinkle gelatine over 1 cup consommé in small saucepan, to soften. Stir over low heat, to dissolve gelatine. Stir in rest of consommé, the sauterne, vinegar, and salt. Set aside.
3. Pour boiling water over tarragon leaves; drain; then plunge leaves into ice water.
4. Beat pâté with heavy cream until smooth. Place in pastry bag with small star tip.
5. Place 6 (6-oz) oval molds or custard cups in pan of ice and water. Spoon 1 tablespoon gelatine mixture into each mold. Let stand about 5 minutes, or until gelatine is just set. Then arrange 2 drained tarragon leaves on gelatine in each mold. Pipe liver paté in little stars or in a ring around the leaves. Cover with another tablespoon of gelatine mixture, being careful to keep decoration intact. Let stand until the gelatine is firm.
6. Meanwhile, carefully peel eggs. Place an egg in center of each mold on firm gelatine layer. Pour enough gelatine mixture around the eggs just to cover them.
7. Refrigerate molds, along with any remaining gelatine mixture, until firm.
8. To unmold: Dip molds in hot water; invert onto individual serving plates, and shake gently to release. Garnish with parsley, if desired, and remaining gelatine, chopped.
Makes 6 servings.
Note: The yolks of these eggs should be soft in the center, so be careful not to overcook.

Anchovy Antipasto Salad

2 cans (2-oz size) anchovy fillets, drained
1/4 cup diced pickled beets
2 tablespoons finely chopped green pepper
1 tablespoon finely chopped onion
1 tablespoon drained capers
2 tablespoons olive or salad oil
4 teaspoons red-wine vinegar
1/2 teaspoon sugar
1/2 teaspoon dried oregano leaves
Dash pepper
Crisp chicory leaves
Hard-cooked-egg wedges
Whole pickled beets
Drained capers

1. In bowl, combine anchovies, diced beets, green pepper, onion, 1 tablespoon capers.
2. In jar with tight-fitting lid, combine oil, vinegar, sugar, oregano, pepper; shake vigorously. Pour over anchovy mixture, and toss.
3. Refrigerate, covered, at least 2 hours.
4. To serve: Spoon on chicory on serving plate. Garnish with egg, beets, capers. Pass chunks of Italian bread.
Makes 4 servings.

Shrimp Cocktail

1-1/2 lb Boiled Shrimp, page 259

Sauce:
1/2 cup chili sauce
1 tablespoon prepared horseradish
1 tablespoon lemon juice
2 teaspoons Worcestershire sauce
1/4 teaspoon salt
Dash cayenne

Shredded lettuce
6 lemon wedges

1. Prepare Boiled Shrimp. Refrigerate.
2. Make Sauce: In small bowl, combine all ingredients except lettuce and lemon; mix well. Refrigerate, covered, at least 3 hours.
3. To serve: Arrange shredded lettuce in 6 sherbet dishes. Divide shrimp among dishes; then spoon some sauce over each. Garnish with lemon wedges.
Makes 6 servings.

Blini

1-1/2 cups milk
1 tablespoon sugar
1 teaspoon salt
1 pkg active dry yeast
1/2 cup warm water (105 to 115F)
2 cups sifted all-purpose flour
4 eggs, separated
1/2 cup butter or margarine
1/2 cup heavy cream
2 cups dairy sour cream
1 lb black or red caviar

1. In small saucepan, heat milk just until bubbles form around edge of pan; remove from heat. Stir in sugar and salt. Let cool to lukewarm.
2. Sprinkle yeast over warm water in large bowl, stirring until dissolved.
3. Gradually add flour and lukewarm milk mixture, mixing until smooth.
4. Beat egg yolks well; stir into batter. Cover with towel; let rise in warm place, free from drafts, until tripled in bulk—about 3 hours.
5. Melt butter in small saucepan. Let milk residue settle to bottom; use clear butter for blini.
6. Beat egg whites until very stiff. Whip heavy cream.

7. Fold egg whites, then cream, then 3 tablespoons clear melted butter into batter. Let stand 30 minutes.

8. Slowly heat large skillet or griddle. Grease with about 1 teaspoon melted butter. Use 1 tablespoon batter for each blini. Cook until bubbles form and surface becomes slightly dry; turn, and cook until golden-brown on underside. Repeat, adding more butter as needed. Keep cooked blini warm in uncovered shallow pan in a warm (300F) oven.

9. Serve warm, with remaining melted butter, sour cream, and caviar.

Makes 5 dozen.

Eggs Mayonnaise

1-1/4 cups mayonnaise or cooked salad dressing
1/3 cup chili sauce
1 teaspoon grated onion
1 tablespoon chopped parsley
Dash cayenne
2 tablespoons vinegar
1 teaspoon Worcestershire sauce
1 teaspoon prepared horseradish
3 cups shredded lettuce
8 hard-cooked eggs, chilled and halved

1. In medium bowl, with rotary beater, beat mayonnaise, chili sauce, onion, parsley, cayenne, vinegar, Worcestershire, and horseradish until well blended.

2. Refrigerate mixture, covered, until serving.

3. To serve: Arrange lettuce on 8 salad plates. Place 2 egg halves on each. Spoon about 3 tablespoons mayonnaise mixture over each serving.

Makes 8 servings.

Melon with Prosciutto

1/4 lb sliced prosciutto (Italian ham) or baked
   Virginia ham
1 (2-1/2-lb) honeydew melon, well-chilled
1 lemon
1 lime

1. Cut prosciutto into 1-inch strips.

2. Cut melon in half; scoop out seeds and fibers. Cut half into six wedges; remove rind.

3. Roll each melon wedge in strip of ham. Serve garnished with lemon and lime wedges.

Makes 6 servings (2 wedges per person).

Grilled Grapefruit with Kirsch

4 grapefruit, halved
1 cup sugar
1 cup kirsch

1. Cut out centers and remove seeds from each grapefruit half. Cut around each section with grapefruit knife, to loosen.

2. Sprinkle each half with 2 tablespoons sugar, then with 2 tablespoons kirsch.

3. Broil, 4 inches from heat, about 5 minutes, or until bubbly and brown. Garnish with maraschino cherries and mint sprigs, if desired.

Makes 8 servings.

Cold Ratatouille

1 medium green pepper
1-1/2 medium zucchini (1/2 lb)
1/4 lb medium mushrooms
1/2 medium eggplant (1/2 lb)
6 tablespoons salad or olive oil
1/2 cup thinly sliced onion
1 clove garlic, crushed
2 medium tomatoes (3/4 lb), peeled and cut
   into wedges
1 teaspoon salt
1/8 teaspoon pepper
2 tablespoons chopped parsley

1. Wash pepper; halve. Remove ribs and seeds. Cut lengthwise into 1/4-inch-thick slices.
2. Scrub zucchini. Cut on diagonal into 1/4-inch-thick slices. Wash mushrooms; slice lengthwise, right through stems, 1/4 inch thick.
3. Wash eggplant; do not peel. Cut lengthwise into quarters; then cut crosswise into 1/4-inch slices.
4. In 2 tablespoons hot oil in medium skillet, sauté green pepper, mushrooms, onion, and garlic 5 minutes, or until onion is transparent. With slotted spoon, remove to medium bowl.
5. Add 2 tablespoons oil to skillet. In hot oil, sauté zucchini, turning frequently, until tender—about 10 minutes. With slotted utensil, remove from skillet to same bowl.
6. Add remaining oil to skillet. In hot oil, sauté eggplant, turning occasionally, until tender—5 minutes.
7. Return vegetables to same skillet. Layer half of tomato wedges on top. Sprinkle with salt, pepper, and 1/2 tablespoon parsley. Stir gently to mix.
8. Layer remaining tomato on top. Sprinkle with 1/2 tablespoon parsley.
9. Simmer mixture, covered, over low heat 10 minutes.
10. Remove cover; cook 5 minutes longer, basting occasionally with pan juices, or until liquid has evaporated.
11. Turn into large, shallow serving dish. Refrigerate, covered, until very well chilled—several hours.
12. Sprinkle with remaining parsley.
Makes 8 servings.

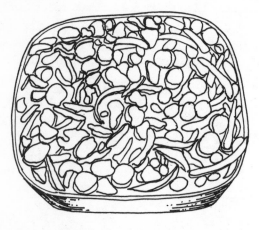

Lobster Cocktail

Cocktail Sauce:
3/4 cup chili sauce
1 to 2 tablespoons prepared horseradish
2 teaspoons lemon juice
1/4 teaspoon salt
Dash cayenne
1/2 teaspoon Worcestershire sauce

2 teaspoons salt
3 (5-oz size) frozen rock-lobster tails, unthawed
Shredded lettuce
6 lemon wedges

1. Make Cocktail Sauce: In small bowl, combine all ingredients through Worcestershire sauce; mix well.
2. Refrigerate sauce, covered, several hours, or overnight.
3. Meanwhile, in large saucepan, bring 2 quarts water and 2 teaspoons salt to boiling. Add lobster tails; return to boiling.
4. Reduce heat; simmer, covered, 8 minutes.
5. Drain lobster tails; let cool. Cut away undershell from each tail. Remove meat in one piece; cut into chunks.

6. Refrigerate until well chilled.

7. To serve: Arrange some shredded lettuce in each of 6 sherbet dishes.

8. Divide lobster into dishes. Spoon sauce over it. Garnish with lemon.

Makes 6 servings.

Scallops Provençal

1 lb bay or sea scallops
2 tablespoons lemon juice
1/2 lb fresh mushrooms
2 lb fresh tomatoes, or 1 can (1 lb) whole tomatoes, drained
5 tablespoons olive or salad oil
4 shallots, sliced
4 parsley sprigs, chopped
1 small clove garlic, crushed
1/2 teaspoon salt
Dash white pepper
1/2 teaspoon dried thyme leaves
1/2 teaspoon dried oregano leaves

1. In medium bowl, toss scallops with lemon juice.
2. Wipe mushrooms; slice lengthwise, right through stem, about 1/8 inch thick. Toss with scallops.
3. If using fresh tomatoes, scald in boiling water; peel; remove seeds; chop pulp coarsely.
4. In 2 tablespoons hot oil in 8-inch skillet with tight-fitting cover, sauté half of shallot and parsley with the garlic just until golden. Add tomato, salt, pepper, thyme, and oregano. Cook, covered, over low heat, 20 minutes, stirring occasionally to break up tomatoes. Uncover, and cook for 5 more minutes.
5. In 3 tablespoons hot oil in large skillet, sauté remaining shallot and parsley, stirring, about 5 minutes. Add scallops and mushrooms; cook, uncovered, over high heat 10 minutes, shaking pan and stirring frequently.
6. Stir in tomato mixture; cook 2 minutes longer. Serve at once.

Makes 6 first-course servings. Or serve to 4 with rice, as a main course.

Pâté Tart

9-inch unbaked pie shell
3 cans (4-3/4-oz size) liver pâté
1/4 cup minced onion
2 cloves garlic, crushed
Nutmeg
2 eggs
1 cup heavy cream
1/2 teaspoon salt
Dash cayenne
1 cup finely grated natural Swiss cheese (1/4 lb)
1/3 cup grated Parmesan cheese

1. Prepare pie shell; refrigerate until ready to use.
2. Preheat oven to 375F.
3. In medium bowl, combine pâté, onion, garlic, and 1/4 teaspoon nutmeg; mix well. Spread evenly over bottom of pie shell.
4. In medium bowl, with rotary beater, beat eggs with cream, salt, dash nutmeg, and the cayenne until well combined but not frothy. Stir in cheeses.
5. Pour into prepared pie shell; bake 40 to 45 minutes, or until top is golden and firm when gently pressed with fingertip.
6. Let cool in pan on wire rack about 1 hour. Serve warm, cut into wedges.

Makes 6 to 8 first-course servings; 12 hors d'oeuvre servings.

Asparagus-and-Swiss-Cheese Tart

1 pkg (11 oz) piecrust mix
1 pkg (10 oz) frozen cut asparagus
1-1/2 cups heavy cream
2 eggs
1/4 teaspoon nutmeg
1 teaspoon salt
2-1/4 cups coarsely grated natural Swiss cheese

1. Preheat oven to 450F.
2. Prepare piecrust as the label directs. On floured pastry cloth, with a stockinette-covered rolling pin, roll pastry to form 13-inch circle. Use to line an 11-inch pie plate. Flute edge.
2. Prick bottom and side of pastry all over with fork. Bake 10 minutes; prick again if necessary. Let cool. Reduce oven temperature to 375F.
3. Pour 1/2 cup boiling water over asparagus in medium saucepan; return to boiling. Boil, covered, 5 minutes, or until tender. Drain. Dry on paper towels to remove excess moisture.
4. Place in blender with cream, eggs, nutmeg, and salt; blend at high speed 1 minute, or until smooth. Stir in 1-1/2 cups grated cheese to mix well.
5. Turn into pastry shell. Bake 20 minutes. Remove from oven. Sprinkle remaining 3/4 cup grated cheese over top, forming a lattice pattern. Return to oven about 3 minutes, or until cheese melts slightly. Serve warm.
Makes 6 servings.

Coquilles Saint Jacques

1 teaspoon lemon juice
1/2 teaspoon salt
2 lb sea scallops, washed and drained
4 tablespoons butter or margarine
1/4 cup finely chopped onion
1/4 lb mushrooms, sliced; or 1 can (3 oz) sliced
    mushrooms, drained
1/3 cup flour
Dash pepper
1 cup light cream
1/2 cup milk
1 cup grated Gruyère cheese
1/2 cup dry white wine
1 tablespoon lemon juice
1 tablespoon chopped parsley
1/2 cup packaged dry bread crumbs
2 tablespoons butter or margarine, melted

1. In medium saucepan, combine 1 cup water, 1 teaspoon lemon juice, and the salt; bring to boiling. Add scallops; simmer, covered, 6 minutes, or till tender. Drain on paper towels.
2. In 4 tablespoons hot butter in medium saucepan, sauté onion and mushrooms until tender—about 5 minutes. Remove from heat; stir in flour and pepper until well blended. Gradually stir in cream and milk.
3. Bring to boiling, stirring. Reduce heat, and simmer, stirring frequently, until quite thick—4 to 5 minutes. Add cheese, and stir until melted. Remove from heat.
4. Carefully stir in wine, lemon juice, and parsley. Then add scallops. Turn into 8 scallop shells or a 1-1/2-quart casserole.
5. Mix bread crumbs and melted butter; sprinkle over scallops. Place shells on cookie sheet.
6. Broil, 4 inches from heat, until golden-brown— 2 to 3 minutes.
Makes 8 servings.

Beverages

It's always beverage time, always beverage weather, whether it's morning, noon, night or the hours in between; summer or winter; surrounded by the family, entertaining friends or relaxing alone. Be as festive, as ceremonial or as casual as you please in serving beverages.

Coffee

What's the key to a really satisfying cup of coffee, one that's full-bodied and just plain good? The secret of perfect coffee (no matter which method you use: drip, vacuum, percolator, espresso) is as simple as this: Fresh coffee, exactly measured; fresh water; a thoroughly clean coffee maker; immediate service. Directly after the coffee is brewed, throw away the grounds. Once the vacuum can or paper bag of coffee is opened, store in refrigerator and use it up within a week. If coffee has gone stale, don't use it. The right size coffee maker is important: If you're a two-cup family, use a small coffee maker, and save the large one for company.

The best way to measure coffee is to use a standard measuring scoop or its equivalent.

Use two level tablespoonfuls of coffee to three quarters of a standard liquid measuring cup (not a coffee cup) of water. Concerning grinds: A drip grind is good, unless the coffee maker specifies differently. Brew it just under the boiling point, but never let coffee boil.

Measure instant coffee as label directs.

"American," "French," "Italian," describe the kind of roast. Italian coffee is roasted longest. American is roasted shortest and is lighter in color and flavor.

Some of the coffeehouse coffees popular today are: Cappuccino—a beverage composed of equal parts of steaming strong coffee and steaming milk, poured into a cup, sugared, topped with whipped cream and sprinkled with cinnamon or nutmeg. Good!

Viennese coffee—strong black coffee always topped with whipped cream; sometimes spiced.

Caffè Espresso—made in a special type of coffee-pot, pressurized with steam. There are small, simple espresso makers for home use.

Turkish coffee—a sweet, heavy brew of pulverized coffee.

Irish coffee—a strong black coffee with Irish whisky added, topped with whipped cream.

Coffee Made in a Percolator

6 cups fresh cold water
1 cup percolator or drip-grind coffee

1. Fill bottom section of an 8-cup percolator with water.
2. Measure the coffee into basket, placed on stem. Insert stem in pot.
3. Over medium heat, percolate coffee 10 minutes, timing from point when liquid first shows color.
4. Immediately remove basket with coffee grounds; replace cover.
5. If coffee is not served at once, keep hot over very low heat; do not let it boil.
Makes 8 servings.

Coffee Made in a Vacuum-Type Coffee Maker

6 cups fresh cold water
1 cup silex or drip-grind coffee

1. Fill lower bowl of an 8-cup vacuum-type coffee maker with water.

2. Attach upper bowl securely to lower bowl, adjusting filter. Measure coffee into upper bowl; cover.

3. Over medium heat, bring water to boiling (most of water will rise to upper bowl). Stir several times; let stand over heat about 2 minutes.

4. Remove from heat; let coffee return to lower bowl. Immediately detach upper bowl with coffee grounds. Cover coffee.

5. If coffee is not served at once, keep hot over very low heat; do not let it boil.

Makes 8 servings.

Coffee Made in a Drip Coffeepot

1 cup drip-grind coffee
6 cups boiling water

1. Assemble an 8-cup drip coffeepot: Put coffee section in place. (If using filter paper, insert before putting in coffee.) Measure coffee into coffee section. Place water section on top of coffee section.

2. Pour boiling water into water section. Cover; let stand until all water has dripped through coffee.

3. Detach water and coffee sections; discard grounds; replace cover.

4. If coffee is not served at once, keep hot over very low heat; do not let it boil.

Makes 8 servings.

Coffee for a Crowd

2 gallons plus 1/2 cup fresh cold water
Cheesecloth*
1 lb regular-grind coffee
3 eggs, slightly beaten
3 eggshells, crushed
* Cheesecloth should be 1 yard wide and 2 yards long; fold it to make double thickness 1 yard square.

1. In large kettle, bring 2 gallons water to full, rolling boil.

2. Meanwhile, soak cheesecloth (or sugar sack large enough so coffee will only half fill it); rinse well.

3. In medium bowl, combine coffee, eggs, shells, and 1/2 cup cold water; mix well. (Eggs and shells will clarify coffee.)

4. Put coffee mixture into sack; tie with strong cord long enough to fasten to handle of kettle.

5. When water has boiled, reduce heat to just below boiling point. Tie sack to kettle handle; submerge.

6. Over low heat, brew coffee 10 minutes, pushing sack up and down in water several times.

7. Remove sack, letting all liquid drain into kettle. Keep coffee hot.

Makes enough for 40 (5-1/2-oz) servings.

Caffè Espresso

Use dark-roast Italian coffee, fine grind, with fresh cold water in a special caffè-espresso pot. Follow manufacturer's directions. Serve hot in demitasse cups, with a twist of lemon peel in each, if desired.

Tea

On the average, each American drinks 180 cups and glasses of tea each year. Quite surprising, when you consider what the earliest American settlers did with tea.

In general, teas fall into three classifications. All three types come from the same tea bush; it's what happens after the leaves are picked that makes them different.

Black Tea undergoes a special processing treatment—oxidation—that turns the leaves black and produces a brew with a rich, hearty flavor. Over 97 percent of the tea consumed in America is the black type.

Oolong Tea is semi-oxidized. Its leaves are partly brown, partly green. It brews light in color.

Green Tea is not oxidized, so the leaves stay green in color. It too is light in color when brewed.

To Brew a Cup of Tea

Bring fresh, cold water to a full rolling boil. The teapot itself should be heated with boiling water. Allow one teaspoonful of tea (or one tea bag) per person. Add the briskly boiling water, and let the tea steep 3 to 5 minutes. To make tea in a cup, simply place a tea bag in the cup and pour on boiling water. With instant tea, measure one level teaspoonful into a cup; add the briskly boiling water.

Because China tea is so delicate, it is served without milk. This is also true of the teas flavored with spices. With other teas, you may or may not add milk, as you prefer. Many people like their tea with a slice of lemon, sometimes stuck with cloves. Whatever you do, it's most important that freshly made tea be served while it is piping hot.

Hot Tea for 25

1 quart boiling water
2/3 cup loose tea

1. To make concentrate: Pour 1 quart boiling water over 2/3 measuring cup of loose tea.
2. Cover; let stand 5 minutes.
3. Stir and strain into quart pitcher or teapot. (Use within 4 hours; store at room temperature.)

4. To serve: Have ready a large pot of very hot water. Pour 2 tablespoons concentrate into teacup. Fill cup with hot water. By varying amount of concentrate, you can vary tea strength.
Makes about 25 cups.
For Iced Tea: Pour about 2-1/2 tablespoons concentrate into a glass; add ice and cold water.
Makes 20 glasses.

Iced Tea

8 to 10 tea bags, tags removed
1 quart cold water
Crushed ice or ice cubes
Sugar
Lemon

1. Combine tea bags and water in a glass pitcher; refrigerate, covered, at least 6 hours or overnight, no longer.
2. Remove tea bags, squeezing against side of container.
3. To serve, pour into ice-filled glasses. Add sugar and lemon to taste.
Makes 6 servings.

Fruit Drinks and Punches

Icy-cold beverages like these on a steaming-hot day are the very essence of refreshment, as our steaming-hot beverages on icy-cold days are great chill removers.

There are many interesting variations and combinations using canned and fresh fruits, fruit juices and nectars. Iced drinks look best in high glasses. Exception, punch. Whether hot or cold, punch is most properly served from a punch bowl into small cups with handles.

Fancy ice cubes give a lovely party touch, and they are very easy. Before freezing them, add a little green or red food color. Or add curls of lemon or orange peel; whole maraschino cherries with their stems; thin slices of orange, lemon, lime. It's best to use freshly boiled or distilled water if you want clear cubes.

Cup of Cheer

1 cup sugar
12 whole cloves
2 (2-inch pieces) cinnamon sticks
6 cups grapefruit juice
3 cups orange juice
1 quart cider

1. In saucepan, combine sugar, 1/2 cup water, the cloves, and cinnamon; bring to boiling. Reduce heat, and simmer 20 minutes. Strain.
2. In large bowl, combine fruit juices and cider; mix well. Stir in sugar syrup.
3. Reheat, and serve hot. This punch is also very good chilled. It may be made up to 2 weeks ahead, and reheated over and over, as needed. If desired, garnish with orange slices and cinnamon sticks.
Makes 26 punch-cup servings.

Hot Mulled Cider

1 gallon cider
1/2 cup light-brown sugar, firmly packed
(optional)
8 to 10 (3-inch) cinnamon sticks, broken into
  pieces
10 to 15 whole allspice
20 to 25 whole cloves

1. In 6-quart kettle, bring all ingredients to boiling;
simmer, uncovered, about 30 minutes. Strain
through a double layer of cheesecloth.
2. Refrigerate the cider until needed. Reheat for
serving. Place a cinnamon-stick stirrer in each
mug, if desired.
Makes 12 to 15 servings.

Fresh Lemonade

3 lemons
3/4 cup sugar
Ice cubes
Maraschino cherries with stems, drained

1. With a sharp knife, very thinly slice lemons
crosswise. Discard end slices and seeds.
2. Put lemon slices into a large bowl or sturdy
pitcher. Add the sugar.
3. With a wooden spoon or potato masher, pound
until the sugar is dissolved and slices are broken.
4. Add 1 tray of ice cubes and 2 cups cold water.
Stir until very cold.
5. To serve: Pour lemonade, along with lemon
slices, into glasses. Garnish each glass with a
cherry.
Makes 5 cups, or 4 tall glasses.

Fresh-Orange Spritzer

2 cans (6-oz size) frozen orange-juice concentrate
1 bottle (1 pt, 12 oz) club soda, chilled
3 tablespoons lemon juice
Ice cubes

1. In large pitcher, combine orange-juice concentrate and 1 cup cold water; stir until orange juice is
thawed.
2. Add soda, lemon juice, and 2 cups cubes.
Makes 8 (6-oz) servings.

Golden Refresher

1 cup sugar
1 teaspoon whole cloves
Dash salt
1 piece (2-inch) cinnamon stick
3/4 cup lemon juice
2 cups orange juice
1 pint orange sherbet
3 bottles (10-oz size) carbonated lemon drink
  or ginger ale, well chilled
Maraschino cherries with stems
Mint sprigs

1. In medium saucepan, combine sugar, 2 cups
water, the cloves, and salt. Bring to boiling, stirring to dissolve sugar; reduce heat, and simmer 10
minutes. Add cinnamon stick; cool.
2. Combine lemon and orange juices with cooled
syrup; mix well; refrigerate until very cold—
several hours.
3. To serve: In each of four tall glasses, pour 1 cup
juice; drop in 1 large spoonful of sherbet; fill glass
with carbonated drink. Stir; garnish with cherry
and mint sprig.
Makes 4 servings.

Pineapple-Orange Blush

2-1/2 cups orange juice
1 can (1 pint, 2 oz) pineapple juice
1/2 cup lemon juice
1/2 cup maraschino-cherry juice (see Note)
1 bottle (12 oz) ginger ale, chilled
1 pkg (16 oz) frozen whole strawberries, thawed

1. In large punch bowl, combine orange, pineapple, lemon, and cherry juices; mix well. Refrigerate several hours or overnight, or until well chilled.
2. To serve, add ginger ale and strawberries; mix well. Serve over ice, if desired.
Makes 2 quarts; 8 servings.
Note: From a bottle of maraschino cherries.

Milk and Ice-Cream Drinks

These are enjoyed by anybody old enough to send a tall spoon down into a tall glass to raise a dollop of something ice cold and creamy. In fact, almost all these drinks are easy enough for the small fry to make themselves.

Old-Fashioned Hot Chocolate

2 squares unsweetened chocolate
3 tablespoons sugar
Dash salt
3 cups milk
Whipped cream (optional)

1. In saucepan, over very low heat, melt chocolate in 1 cup water, stirring constantly until blended.
2. Stir in sugar and salt; bring to boiling, stirring. Reduce heat, and simmer 3 minutes.
3. Gradually add milk; heat thoroughly.
4. Just before serving, beat with rotary beater. Serve at once, topped with whipped cream, if desired.
Makes 1 quart, 4 to 6 servings.
For Mocha Chocolate: Substitute 1 cup strong coffee for 1 cup water.
For Orange Chocolate: Mix 1 tablespoon grated orange rind with sugar.
For Mint Chocolate: Add 1/4 teaspoon peppermint extract just before serving.

Spiced Chocolate Drink

1 pkg (6 oz) semisweet chocolate pieces
1/4 cup sugar
Dash salt
2 cups milk
1 cup light cream
1/4 teaspoon cinnamon
1/8 teaspoon nutmeg
1 teaspoon vanilla extract

1. In heavy 3-quart saucepan, bring 1 cup water to boiling. Add chocolate pieces, sugar, and salt; stir constantly over medium heat just until chocolate is melted and mixture is smooth.
2. Add milk, cream, cinnamon, and nutmeg. Bring just to boiling, stirring. Remove from heat. Add vanilla.
3. Just before serving, beat with rotary beater until foamy. Serve warm, or refrigerate to serve cold.
Makes 6 servings.

Spiced Cocoa

1-1/2 cups sweetened cocoa
1/2 teaspoon cinnamon
1/4 teaspoon nutmeg
2 tablespoons sugar
2 cups boiling water
3 cups milk
8 marshmallows

1. Combine cocoa, cinnamon, nutmeg, and sugar in large saucepan. Gradually stir in water, then milk.
2. Heat carefully, stirring often; be careful not to scorch.
3. Serve the cocoa hot, topped with marshmallows.
Makes 8 servings.

Orange Eggnog

1 cup cold milk
1 egg
1 cup cold orange juice
Dash nutmeg

Combine all ingredients in medium bowl or blender. Beat with rotary beater or blend until frothy. Serve at once.
Makes 2 servings.

Spicy Eggnog

1/2 cup sugar
Dash allspice
1/4 teaspoon cinnamon
1/8 teaspoon nutmeg
3 eggs, separated
2 cups milk, chilled
1 cup light cream, chilled
Nutmeg

1. Combine sugar, allspice, cinnamon, and 1/8 teaspoon nutmeg.
2. In large bowl of electric mixer, at high speed, beat egg whites until soft peaks form.
3. Gradually beat in half of sugar mixture until stiff peaks form.
4. In small bowl, beat egg yolks until lemon-colored. Gradually beat in remaining sugar mixture until thick and smooth.
5. Thoroughly fold into whites. Stir in milk and cream; mix well.
6. Serve well chilled, each serving sprinkled with nutmeg.
Makes 12 servings.

Frosted Strawberry Float

1/2 pint box fresh strawberries
1/4 cup sugar
3 cups milk, chilled
1/2 pint strawberry ice cream

1. Gently wash berries in cold water. Drain, and hull.
2. Crush, with a potato masher, in medium bowl. Stir in sugar.
3. Gradually add milk, beating with rotary beater. Spoon in ice cream; stir until it starts to melt. Serve in tall glasses.
Makes 4 servings.

Ice-Cream Milk Shakes

Peanut-Butter: In electric blender,* blend at high speed, for 1 minute, 1 cup milk and 2 tablespoons creamy peanut butter. Add 2 No. 16 (or medium) scoops vanilla ice cream; blend 1 minute longer. Makes 2 cups.

* All milk shakes can be made using a rotary beater or a portable electric mixer and 1-quart measure or medium bowl.

Strawberry: Substitute 2 tablespoons strawberry jam for peanut butter, adding a drop or two of red food color.

Raspberry: Substitute 2 tablespoons raspberry jam for peanut butter, adding a drop or two of red food color.

Pineapple: Substitute 3 tablespoons drained, canned crushed pineapple for peanut butter.

Banana: Substitute 1/2 medium-size ripe banana, cut in small pieces, for peanut butter.

Maple Milk Shake

2 cups milk
1/2 cup maple syrup
1 pint soft vanilla ice cream

1. In large bowl, with rotary beater, beat all ingredients until well combined.
2. Serve at once in glasses.
Makes 4 servings.

Mocha Frosted

2 cups strong coffee,* chilled
3/4 cup chocolate milk
1-1/2 cups soft coffee ice cream
*Use 2 tablespoons instant coffee, dissolved in 2 cups boiling water.

1. Combine coffee, milk, and 1 cup ice cream in medium bowl; beat with rotary beater just until smooth.
2. Pour into 3 or 4 tall glasses. Top with rest of ice cream.
Makes 3 or 4 servings.

Strawberry Milk Shake

1 pkg (16 oz) frozen sliced strawberries, slightly thawed
3 cups milk

1. Turn half of strawberries into blender container; add 1-1/2 cups milk. Cover; blend until smooth; pour into pitcher.
2. Blend rest of strawberries and milk; add to pitcher. Serve well chilled.
Makes 6 servings.

Soda Suggestions

Orange-Sherbet Freeze: Put 2 scoops orange sherbet in a large glass. Spoon on 2 teaspoons orange marmalade. Fill to top with ginger ale; stir well, with a long spoon. Top with 2 tablespoons drained canned mandarin-orange sections.

Root-Beer Float: Put 2 scoops ice cream (any flavor) in a large glass. Fill to top with root beer; stir well, with a long spoon.

Chocolate-Mint Soda: In a large glass, combine 2/3 cup milk, 1 tablespoon canned chocolate syrup, few drops peppermint extract; stir well, with a long spoon. Add 2 scoops vanilla ice cream. Fill to top with ginger ale; stir well. Top with 2 tablespoons whipped cream. Streak with 1 teaspoon chocolate syrup.

Double Strawberry Soda: Put 2 scoops strawberry ice cream in a large glass. Spoon 1 tablespoon strawberry jam over ice cream. Fill to top with ginger ale; stir well, with a long spoon.

Pineapple-Lemon Soda: Put 2 scoops lemon sherbet and 1/4 cup drained pineapple chunks in a large glass. Fill to top with ginger ale; stir well, with a long spoon.

Makes 1 serving.

Alcoholic Drinks

The brimming punch bowl, iced or steaming, says "Welcome." Our cheerful drinks are modern versions of old stand-bys, along with many more recently in vogue.

Christmas Punch

1 can (6 oz) frozen lemon-juice concentrate, undiluted
1 can (6 oz) frozen orange-juice concentrate, undiluted
1 cup sugar
1/4 cup angostura bitters
3 egg whites
1 bottle (3/4 quart) daiquiri cocktail, chilled
1 bottle (1 pint, 12 oz) club soda, chilled
1 tray ice cubes
1 bottle (4/5 quart) champagne, chilled

1. In pitcher or bowl, combine frozen concentrates, sugar, and bitters. When juices are thawed, stir until they are well blended and sugar is dissolved.
2. Refrigerate fruit-juice mixture until it is well chilled—several hours or overnight.
3. Just before serving, beat egg whites until stiff.
4. In punch bowl, combine fruit-juice mixture, daiquiri cocktail, and club soda. With wire whisk or rotary beater, gently beat in egg whites. Add ice cubes.
5. Pour champagne into punch at table.
Makes about 24 (4-oz) servings.

Pink-Champagne Punch Bowl

Strawberry Ice Ring:
2 quarts distilled or boiled water
1 dozen large strawberries, washed

8 bottles (4/5-quart size) pink champagne, well
   chilled

1. Make Strawberry Ice Ring: Pour distilled water, to measure about 1 inch, into a 2-quart ring mold. Arrange unhulled berries in bottom. Freeze until firm. Gradually pour in distilled water to fill mold. Freeze until firm—several hours.
2. When ice ring is frozen, unmold: Place mold in warm water just until ice begins to loosen. Turn out ice ring onto waxed paper. Return to freezer at once, until ready to use.
3. At serving time, half fill punch bowl with champagne. Float ice ring in bowl. Add more champagne, to fill bowl three fourths full. Add more champagne as needed.
Makes 24 servings; 48 (4-oz) glasses.
Note: If possible, refrigerate punch bowl or fill with ice water, to chill.

Cranberry-Bourbon Punch

1 quart bottled cranberry juice
1 can (1 pt, 2 oz) pineapple juice
1 cup orange juice
1/2 cup lemon juice
1 cup bourbon
2 bottles (1-pt, 12-oz size) ginger ale, chilled

1. In punch bowl, combine fruit juices and bourbon. Refrigerate until well chilled.
2. Just before serving, pour in ginger ale.
Makes 20 to 25 punch-cup servings.
Note: Make punch ahead, and use some to fill and freeze in an ice-cube tray. Float cubes in punch bowl.

Daiquiri Punch

Ice Block, below
Frosted Punch Bowl, below
1 bottle (16 oz) daiquiri mix*
6 tablespoons superfine sugar
2-1/2 cups light rum
1/2 cup curaçao or cointreau
2 dozen ice cubes
1 bottle (1 pint, 12 oz) club soda, chilled
* Without liquor.

1. Day ahead, prepare Ice Block and Frosted Punch Bowl.
2. In pitcher or bowl, combine daiquiri mix and sugar, and stir until sugar is dissolved. Add rum and curacao.
3. Refrigerate, stirring occasionally, until well chilled—about 3 hours.
4. To serve: Place Fern Ice Block in Frosted Punch Bowl. Place half of daiquiri mixture and 1 dozen ice cubes in electric blender; blend, at high speed, 15 to 20 seconds. Pour into punch bowl. Repeat with remaining mixture and ice. Stir in club soda.
Makes about 20 (4-oz) servings.
Note: You may use 2 (6-oz) cans frozen daiquiri mix. If blender is not available, crush ice cubes very fine. Place with daiquiri mixture in jar with tight-fitting lid. Shake vigorously 1 minute.

Ice Block

Day before using, make Ice Block: Fill a bowl with 2 quarts water, and let stand at room temperature 1 hour. Stir occasionally to release air bubbles. Mound 2 trayfuls of ice cubes in a 2-quart, fancy round mold; fill with the water. Freeze until firm. To unmold: Dip mold in warm water until ice loosens; turn out on waxed paper. Return to freezer if not using at once.

Frosted Punch Bowl

Beat 1 egg white with 1 tablespoon water. Use to brush a band about 1-1/2 inches wide on outside of punch bowl, at top. Sprinkle sheet of waxed paper with granulated sugar. Roll edge of bowl in sugar, to frost it. Let stand at room temperature about 20 minutes; then roll in sugar again. Set aside to dry—3 to 4 hours or overnight.

Champagne Punch

1 large bunch seedless green grapes (about 1-1/2 lb)
2 cups sauterne
1 cup cognac
2 tablespoons sugar
2 bottles (7-oz size) club soda, chilled
6 strawberries, hulls on, washed (optional)
1 bottle (4/5 quart) champagne, chilled

1. Day ahead: Wash grapes; place on small tray. Place in freezer.
2. Several hours before serving: In pitcher or bowl, combine sauterne, cognac, and sugar; stir until sugar is dissolved. Refrigerate.
3. To serve: Pour sauterne mixture into punch bowl. Stir in soda. Add frozen grapes and the strawberries.
4. Pour champagne into punch just before serving. Makes about 16 (4-oz) servings.

Ella Brennan's Milk Punch

1-1/2 cups bourbon or brandy
1-1/2 pints half-and-half (see Note)
1 teaspoon vanilla extract
2-1/2 tablespoons confectioners' sugar
1/2 cup heavy cream
Nutmeg

1. Combine bourbon, half-and-half, and vanilla. Stir in sugar until dissolved. Cover; refrigerate several hours, or until very well chilled.
2. Just before serving, whip cream until stiff. Pour bourbon mixture into punch bowl or glass serving bowl. Set bowl in a bowl of crushed ice, if desired.
3. Spoon whipped cream on punch. Sprinkle with freshly grated nutmeg.
Makes 8 or 9 punch-cup servings.
Note: Half-and-half is half milk and half cream.

Planter's-Punch Bowl

3 cups chilled orange juice
1-1/2 cups chilled lemon juice
1 cup chilled fresh lime juice
3 cups chilled pineapple juice
1 cup light rum
1 cup rye whisky
1/2 cup confectioners' sugar
Ice Ring, below

1. Combine juices, rum, rye, and confectioners' sugar in a punch bowl; blend well.
2. Float Ice Ring on punch.
Makes about 20 (4-oz) punch-cup servings.

Ice Ring

4 candied red cherries, halved
16 pieces angelica, 1 inch long
8 lemon or lime slices, 1/4 inch thick

1. Choose a ring mold that will fit your punch bowl; place it in freezer until well chilled. Rinse inside of mold with cold water; return to freezer until thin coating of ice forms.
2. Arrange cherries, rounded side down and evenly spaced, in bottom of mold. Place two pieces of angelica on each cherry, extending at side, to resemble leaves.
3. Slowly add about 1/4 cup cold water, or just enough to cover the cherries slightly (too much water would dislodge fruit). Freeze until firm.
4. Arrange lemon slices directly over cherries; add just enough cold water to cover slightly. Freeze until firm.
5. Fill mold to top with cold water; freeze until firm.
6. When ready to use, run cold water over mold, to loosen; unmold. Float ring on punch in bowl.

Old English Eggnog

6 egg yolks
1 cup granulated sugar
2 quarts light cream
1 pint cognac
1 cup light rum
6 egg whites
1/2 cup confectioners' sugar

1. In large bowl, beat egg yolks until thick. Gradually add granulated sugar, beating until light.
2. Add cream; beat until very well combined. Slowly stir in cognac and rum. Refrigerate, covered, until well chilled.
3. About 1 hour before serving, beat the egg whites until they are foamy. Gradually add the confectioners' sugar, beating well after each addition. Continue beating until soft peaks form when the beater is slowly raised.
4. Gently fold into egg-yolk mixture.
5. Refrigerate, covered, until serving time.
Makes about 28 (4-oz) servings.

Peach-Brandy Eggnog

6 egg yolks
1 cup confectioners' sugar
1-2/3 cups peach brandy (4/5 pint)
1 cup cold milk
1 pint heavy cream, whipped
Freshly ground nutmeg

1. In large bowl, with electric mixer at medium speed, beat egg yolks until light. Gradually beat in sugar.
2. Slowly pour in brandy while beating constantly. Let rest about 10 minutes. Gradually beat in milk.
3. Refrigerate, covered, until very well chilled— 3 hours or longer.
4. To serve: Pour brandy mixture into chilled punch bowl. Gently fold in whipped cream just to blend. Grate or sprinkle nutmeg over top.
Makes 10 to 12 punch-cup servings.

Rum Swizzles

6 cups grapefruit juice
3 cups orange juice
1 quart cider
12 whole cloves
2 (2-inch) pieces cinnamon stick
2 cups grenadine
1 to 2 cups amber rum
3 or 4 drops angostura bitters
8 drops red food color

1. In 6-quart saucepan, combine grapefruit juice, orange juice, cider, cloves, and cinnamon stick. Bring to boiling; reduce heat, and simmer, covered, 30 minutes. Strain to remove spices.
2. Return mixture to large saucepan. Stir in grenadine, rum, bitters, and food color; mix well.
3. To serve hot, bring to boiling, covered. If desired, garnish each serving with a cinnamon stick and orange slice.
4. To serve cold, serve in chilled punch bowl over ice cubes. If desired, float orange slices stuck with cloves on top.
Makes about 4 quarts.
Note: Very good, without rum, as a nonalcoholic punch, too.

Whisky-Sour Punch

1 can (6 oz) frozen orange-juice concentrate, undiluted
1 can (6 oz) frozen lemon-juice concentrate, undiluted
1 tablespoon angostura bitters
2 tablespoons sugar
1 jar (8 oz) maraschino cherries
1 bottle (3/4 quart) whisky-sour cocktail, chilled
1 bottle (1 pint, 12 oz) club soda, chilled
Ice Block, page 78
1 large navel orange, thinly sliced
1 lemon, thinly sliced

1. In pitcher or bowl, combine frozen fruit-juice concentrates, bitters, sugar, and syrup drained from maraschino cherries. When juices are thawed, stir until well blended. Refrigerate, with cherries, until well chilled—several hours or overnight.
2. To serve: In punch bowl, combine fruit-juice mixture, whisky-sour cocktail, and club soda; mix well.
3. Float Ice Block in punch. Place cherries, orange and lemon slices around ice.
Makes about 18 (4-oz) servings.

Wassail Bowl

4 small oranges
Whole cloves
3 bottles (12-oz size) ale
3 cups dark rum
2/3 cup sugar
1/8 teaspoon ginger

1. Preheat oven to 350F.
2. Stud unpeeled oranges with cloves 1/2 inch apart. Place in shallow pan; bake, uncovered, 30 minutes.
3. In large saucepan, combine ale, rum, sugar, and ginger; bring just to boiling, stirring until sugar is dissolved.
4. Place hot oranges in punch bowl; pour hot ale mixture over them. Serve hot, in punch cups.
Makes 15 punch-cup servings.

Syllabub

3 cups cream sherry or Madeira
2 cups sugar
1/3 cup lemon juice
1 tablespoon grated lemon peel
2 cups heavy cream

1. In small punch bowl, combine sherry, sugar, lemon juice, and peel; stir until sugar is dissolved.
2. Refrigerate, covered, several hours or overnight.
3. Just before serving, beat cream until soft peaks form. Spoon over sherry mixture. Fold together just until combined.
Makes about 16 (4-oz) servings.

Piñas Coladas

1/2 cup cream of coconut (see Note)
1 cup unsweetened pineapple juice, chilled
2/3 cup light rum
2 cups crushed ice

1. Refrigerate 6 cocktail glasses, to chill well—about 1 hour.
2. In electric blender, combine cream of coconut, pineapple juice, rum, and ice; cover, and blend at high speed 1/2 minute.
3. Pour into chilled glasses. If desired, serve with a pineapple spear.
Makes 1 quart; 8 servings.
Note: Cream of coconut may be purchased as coconut-milk cream.

Sangría

1-1/2 cups Spanish red wine
1 to 2 tablespoons sugar
1/2 orange, sliced
2 tablespoons Cointreau
2 tablespoons brandy
1 bottle (6 oz) club soda, chilled
12 ice cubes

1. In pitcher, combine wine and sugar. Stir until sugar is dissolved. Add orange slices, Cointreau, and brandy.
2. To serve: Add soda and ice; mix well.
Makes about 2-1/2 cups.

Rosé-Wine Spritzer

1 bottle (4/5 quart) rosé wine, chilled
1 bottle (12 oz) club soda, chilled
Ice cubes

1. Pour wine and soda into large pitcher; stir just to combine. Add ice cubes.
2. Serve in chilled wineglasses.
Makes 8 (6-oz) servings.

Serving Wine

Americans have learned very rapidly about wines. You remember the stories of G.I.'s stationed in Europe who started by drinking a whole bottle of port wine or dark sherry before their food and, when their stomachs rebelled, quickly learned how much better it was for their livers and their enjoyment if they took first a dry aperitif (dry sherry, dry vermouth, or perhaps a glass of white wine), then a dry wine with their food, then afterward a brandy or sweet after-dinner drink.

Today, Americans are drinking wine regularly, and this is the only way to learn about it.

A red wine is suitable with anything except something with a very delicate flavor, such as Dover sole, just as a white wine may be drunk with anything, providing your palate has taught you that you would need a full-bodied white burgundy (and not a delicate Chablis) to complement a pungent beef stew or even a roast of beef.

The fragrance of a red wine is improved if you remove the cork an hour or so before you drink it, and "room temperature" is best, whereas a white wine or rosé should be lightly chilled, but not enough so that you lose part of the fragrance or the taste. Don't forget, it is the fragrance and the taste that account for the cost of the wine.

Wine must be stored in a cool, dark place, with the bottle on its side so that the cork is wet.

Allow one bottle of table wine for every two persons for a regular meal. For a festive occasion, if you add a different wine for dessert, one bottle for four might be enough.

Forget the rules and let your own palate teach you the pleasures of serving wine.

Quick Breads

"Quick bread" is a term used to describe bread leavened by baking powder or baking soda, instead of yeast. Sweet breads, biscuits, muffins and pan- cakes are all quick breads—quick to make because no rising period is required.

Sweet Quick Breads

It's hard to buy these sweet breads, so if you want to serve them, you'll have to make them. Use them when you entertain, particularly at afternoon teas or luncheons when a fruit salad is the main course. Natural-food lovers might serve them as dessert.

These breads make very welcome holiday gifts. Whole loaves may be wrapped in a moistureproof, vaporproof wrap, and stored in the refrigerator for short periods or in the freezer.

McCall's Best Nut Bread

2-1/2 cups sifted* all-purpose flour
3 teaspoons baking powder
1/2 teaspoon salt
1 egg, beaten
1 teaspoon vanilla extract
3/4 cup sugar
1/4 cup butter or margarine, melted, or salad oil
1-1/4 cups milk
1 cup finely chopped walnuts or pecans
* Sift before measuring.

1. Preheat oven to 350F. Grease a 9-by-5-by-3-inch loaf pan.
2. Sift flour with baking powder and salt.
3. In large bowl, combine egg, vanilla, sugar, and butter. Using wooden spoon or portable electric mixer, beat until well blended. Add milk, blending well.
4. Add flour mixture, beating until smooth. Stir in nuts.
5. Pour batter into prepared pan; bake 60 to 65 minutes, or until cake tester inserted in center comes out clean.
6. Let cool in pan 10 minutes. Remove from pan; cool completely on wire rack. To serve, cut into thin slices.
Makes 1 loaf.

Date-Nut Bread

4 cups pitted dates
2 cups coarsely chopped walnuts
2 cups boiling water
2-3/4 cups unsifted all-purpose flour
1-1/2 teaspoons baking soda
1 teaspoon salt
1/2 cup butter or regular margarine, softened
1-1/4 cups light-brown sugar, firmly packed
2 eggs
1 teaspoon vanilla extract

1. With scissors, cut dates into thirds into large bowl. Add nuts and boiling water. Let cool to room temperature—about 45 minutes.
2. Meanwhile, grease 2 (8-1/2-by-4-1/2-by-2-1/2-inch) loaf pans. Sift flour with baking soda and salt. Set aside.
3. Preheat oven to 350F.
4. In large bowl, with electric mixer at high speed, beat butter with sugar, eggs, and vanilla until smooth.
5. Add cooled date mixture; mix well. Add flour mixture; beat with wooden spoon until well com- bined. Turn into prepared pans.

6. Bake 1 hour and 10 minutes, or until cake tester inserted in center comes out clean. Cool in pans 10 minutes; remove to wire rack, and let cool completely.
Makes 2 loaves.

Holiday Banana Bread

1-3/4 cups sifted* all-purpose flour
2/3 cup sugar
3 teaspoons baking powder
1/2 teaspoon salt
1/4 teaspoon baking soda
1/3 cup regular margarine
1 cup mashed very ripe banana (2 or 3)
2 eggs
1/2 cup chopped walnuts
1/4 cup chopped candied citron
1/4 cup chopped candied orange peel
1/4 cup chopped candied cherries
1/4 cup chopped candied pineapple
1/4 cup dark raisins
* Sift before measuring.

1. Preheat oven to 350F. Grease well a 9-by-5-by-3-inch loaf pan.
2. Into large bowl, sift flour with sugar, baking powder, salt, and soda. With pastry blender, cut in margarine until mixture resembles coarse crumbs.
3. Add banana and eggs; with electric mixer at low speed, beat 2 minutes.
4. Add nuts, candied fruit, and raisins; beat until well blended. Turn into prepared pan.
5. Bake 1 hour and 10 minutes, or until cake tester inserted in center comes out clean.
6. Let cool in pan on wire rack 10 minutes. Remove from pan; let cool completely on rack. Wrap with plastic film, then in foil, and store overnight before serving.
Makes 1 loaf.

Lemon Tea Bread

2 cups unsifted all-purpose flour
1-1/2 teaspoons baking powder
1/4 teaspoon salt
1/2 cup butter or regular margarine
1 cup sugar
2 eggs
1/3 cup milk
1/2 cup chopped walnuts
2 teaspoons grated lemon peel

Syrup:
1/4 cup lemon juice
1/3 cup sugar

1. Lightly grease 9-by-5-by-3-inch loaf pan. Preheat oven to 350F.
2. Sift flour with baking powder and salt; set aside.
3. In large bowl of electric mixer, at medium speed, beat butter with 1 cup sugar until light and fluffy. Add eggs, one at a time, beating well after each addition; beat until very light and fluffy.
4. At low speed, beat in flour mixture alternately with milk, beginning and ending with flour mixture; beat just until combined.
5. Stir in nuts and lemon peel. Turn batter into prepared pan. Bake 55 to 60 minutes, or until cake tester inserted in center comes out clean.
6. Make Syrup: In small saucepan, combine lemon juice and sugar; cook, stirring, 1 minute, or until syrupy. Pour evenly over bread as soon as it is removed from oven.
7. Let cool in pan 10 minutes. Remove to wire rack; let cool completely.
Makes 1 loaf.

Pineapple-Apricot-Nut Loaf

2-3/4 cups sifted* all-purpose flour
3 teaspoons baking powder
1/4 teaspoon baking soda
1/4 teaspoon salt
3/4 cup sugar
1/3 cup butter, melted
1 egg
1/3 cup milk
1 cup canned crushed pineapple, undrained
1/3 cup chopped dried apricots
1/4 cup light raisins
1 tablespoon chopped candied green cherries
   or citron
1 cup chopped walnuts
* Sift before measuring.

1. Preheat oven to 350F. Grease and flour 9-by-5-by-3-inch loaf pan. Sift flour with baking powder, soda, and salt; set aside.
2. In large bowl, combine sugar, melted butter, and egg; using wooden spoon, beat until ingredients are well blended.
3. Add milk, pineapple, apricots, raisins, and cherries; blend well.
4. Add flour mixture; beat just until combined. Stir in nuts. Turn into prepared pan.
5. Bake 1-1/4 hours, or until cake tester inserted in center comes out clean.
6. Let cool in the pan 10 minutes. Remove from pan; let cool completely on wire rack.
Makes 1 loaf.

Savory Cheese Bread

2 cups sifted* all-purpose flour
2 teaspoons baking powder
1 tablespoon sugar
1/2 teaspoon salt
1/4 cup butter or regular margarine, cut into 4
   parts
1 cup grated sharp natural Cheddar cheese (1/4 lb)
1 tablespoon grated onion
1-1/2 teaspoons dried dillweed
3/4 cup milk
1 egg, slightly beaten
* Sift before measuring.

1. Preheat oven to 350F. Lightly grease a 9-by-5-by-3-inch loaf pan.
2. Sift flour with baking powder, sugar, and salt into a large bowl.
3. With 2 knives or pastry blender, cut in butter until mixture resembles coarse crumbs. Stir in cheese, onion, and dill, to mix well.
4. Combine milk and beaten egg; pour into flour mixture all at once. Stir quickly with a fork just to moisten flour mixture.
5. Turn into prepared pan. Bake 40 to 45 minutes, or until cake tester inserted in center comes out clean.
6. Let cool in pan 10 minutes. Turn out on wire rack to cool completely, or serve slightly warm.
Makes 1 loaf.

Prune Bread

1-1/2 cups (8 oz) dried prunes
2 cups unsifted all-purpose flour
3/4 cup sugar
1 teaspoon baking soda
1/2 teaspoon salt
1 egg
2 tablespoons melted shortening or salad oil

1. In medium saucepan, combine prunes with 1-1/2 cups water; bring to boiling. Reduce heat, and simmer, covered, 10 minutes.
2. Preheat oven to 350F. Grease bottom of an 8-1/2-by-4-1/2-by-2-5/8-inch loaf pan. Sift flour with sugar, baking soda, and salt; set aside.
3. Drain prunes, reserving liquid. Pit prunes, and chop. Add to reserved liquid, and measure. Add water if needed to make 2 cups.

4. In large bowl, combine egg and shortening; with electric mixer at medium speed, beat well. Add prune mixture; beat until well blended.
5. Add flour mixture; beat at low speed just until smooth. Turn into prepared pan.
6. Bake 50 to 60 minutes, or until cake tester inserted in center comes out clean.
7. Let cool in pan on wire rack 10 minutes. Remove from pan; cool completely on rack. Then wrap in plastic film or foil, and refrigerate overnight before slicing.
Makes 1 loaf.

Pumpkin Loaves

2 cups unsifted all-purpose flour
1/2 teaspoon salt
1/2 teaspoon baking powder
1 teaspoon baking soda
1 teaspoon ground cloves
1 teaspoon ground cinnamon
1 teaspoon ground nutmeg
2 cups sugar
3/4 cup butter or regular margarine, softened
2 eggs
1 can (1 lb) pumpkin

1. Lightly grease two 9-by-5-by-3-inch loaf pans. Preheat oven to 325F.
2. Sift flour with salt, baking powder, soda, and spices; set aside.
3. In large bowl of electric mixer, at medium speed, beat sugar with butter just until blended. Add eggs, one at a time, beating well after each addition; continue beating until very light and fluffy. Beat in pumpkin. At low speed, beat in flour mixture until combined.
4. Turn batter into prepared pans, dividing evenly. Bake 1 hour and 15 minutes, or until cake tester inserted in center comes out clean.
5. Let cool in pans 10 minutes. Turn out onto wire racks to cool completely.
Makes 2 loaves.

Muffins

Surprise your family with homemade Buttermilk Bran Muffins for Sunday breakfast. Or serve the Cheese Muffins with a salad at lunch. They're absurdly easy to make. What is known as the "muffin method"—that is, adding all the liquid ingredients to all the dry—is often used for other quick breads and for simple cakes, as well.

Muffins keep well, so if you don't eat all you've made for a meal, wrap the remainder in saran or foil, and refrigerate or freeze them, to serve at another meal. But be sure to heat them before serving.

Buttermilk Bran Muffins

1 cup sifted* all-purpose flour
2 teaspoons baking powder
1/2 teaspoon baking soda
3/4 teaspoon salt
3 cups whole-bran cereal
1/2 cup seedless raisins
1/3 cup shortening
1/2 cup sugar
1 egg
1 cup buttermilk
* Sift before measuring.

1. Preheat oven to 400F. Grease bottoms of 12 (3-inch) muffin-pan cups, or line each with paper liner.
2. Sift flour with baking powder, soda, and salt into medium bowl. Add bran and raisins; mix well.
3. In large bowl, using wooden spoon, cream shortening with sugar until light and fluffy. Beat in egg.
4. Using fork, add flour mixture alternately with buttermilk, stirring only until dry ingredients are moistened. Do not beat. Batter will be lumpy.
5. Quickly dip batter into muffin-pan cups, filling not quite two thirds full. Bake 20 to 25 minutes, or until golden.
6. Loosen edge of each muffin with spatula; turn out. Serve hot.
Makes 12.

Blueberry Cake Muffins

2 cups sifted* all-purpose flour
1-1/2 teaspoons baking powder
1/4 teaspoon salt
1/2 cup butter or regular margarine, softened
1 cup granulated sugar
2 eggs, unbeaten
1 teaspoon vanilla extract
1/2 cup milk
1 cup fresh or thawed frozen and drained
    blueberries
Confectioners' sugar
* Sift before measuring.

1. Preheat oven to 375F. With paper liners, line 18 muffin-pan cups (2-1/2 by 1-1/4 inches), or grease them well.
2. Sift flour with baking powder and salt. Set aside.
3. In large bowl, with electric mixer at high speed, beat butter with granulated sugar, eggs, vanilla until light and fluffy—about 4 minutes—occasionally scraping side of bowl and beaters with rubber scraper.
4. At low speed, beat in flour mixture (in fourths) alternately with milk (in thirds), beginning and ending with flour mixture. Beat just until smooth.
5. With rubber scraper, gently fold in blueberries just until combined.
6. Scoop about 1/4 cup batter into each prepared muffin cup, to fill each about two thirds full.
7. Bake 20 to 25 minutes, or until golden-brown and cake tester inserted in center comes out clean.
8. Remove muffins to wire rack; let cool slightly.
9. Serve warm or cold, sprinkled with confectioners' sugar.
Makes 18 muffins.

Brown-Sugar Muffins

Topping:
1/4 cup light-brown sugar, packed
1/4 cup sifted all-purpose flour
2 tablespoons butter or margarine
2 teaspoons ground cinnamon

Batter:
1-1/3 cups sifted* all-purpose flour
1-1/2 teaspoons baking powder
1/2 teaspoon salt
1/4 cup butter or regular margarine, softened
1/2 cup light-brown sugar, packed
1 egg
1/2 cup milk
* Sift before measuring.

1. Preheat oven to 375F. Lightly grease bottoms of 12 (2-1/2-inch) muffin-pan cups.
2. Make Topping: In small bowl, combine topping ingredients; mix until crumbly.
3. Make Batter: Sift flour with baking powder and salt.
4. In large bowl of electric mixer, at medium speed, beat butter until fluffy. Beat in brown sugar, then egg until very light and fluffy. At low speed, blend in milk, then flour mixture, just until combined. Divide evenly into muffin cups.
5. Sprinkle topping over each muffin. Bake 15 to 18 minutes, or until cake tester inserted in center comes out clean.
6. Cool slightly in pan on wire rack. Gently remove from pan. Serve warm.
Makes 12.

Cheese Muffins

2 cups sifted* all-purpose flour
1/4 cup sugar
3 teaspoons baking powder
1/2 teaspoon salt
1/8 teaspoon cayenne
1/2 cup grated sharp Cheddar cheese
1 cup milk
1/4 cup salad oil or melted shortening
1 egg, slightly beaten
* Sift before measuring.

1. Preheat oven to 425F. Grease bottoms of 14 (2-1/2-inch) muffin-pan cups.
2. Sift flour with sugar, baking powder, salt, and cayenne into large bowl. Stir in cheese.
3. Measure milk in 2-cup measure. Add oil and egg; beat with fork to mix well.
4. Make a well in center of flour mixture. Pour in milk mixture all at once; stir quickly, with fork, just until dry ingredients are moistened. Do not beat. Batter will be lumpy.
5. Using 1/4-cup measuring cup (not quite full), quickly dip batter into muffin cups, filling each slightly more than half full. (Dip only once for each muffin cup.)
6. Bake 15 to 20 minutes, or until golden and cake tester inserted in center comes out clean.
7. Loosen edge of each muffin with spatula; turn out. Serve hot.
Makes 14 muffins.

Date-Nut Muffins

2 cups sifted* all-purpose flour
1/4 cup sugar
3 teaspoons baking powder
1 teaspoon salt
1 cup finely chopped dates
1/4 cup finely chopped walnuts
1 cup milk
1/4 cup salad oil or melted shortening
1 egg
* Sift before measuring.

1. Preheat oven to 400F. Grease bottoms of 12 (3-inch) muffin-pan cups, or line each with paper liner.
2. Sift flour with sugar, baking powder, and salt into medium bowl. Add dates and nuts.
3. Measure milk in 2-cup measure. Add oil and egg; beat with fork to mix well.
4. Make a well in center of dry ingredients. Pour in milk mixture all at once; stir quickly, with fork, just until dry ingredients are moistened. Do not beat. Batter will be lumpy.
5. Quickly dip batter into muffin-pan cups, filling not quite two thirds full. Bake 20 to 25 minutes, or until golden.
6. Loosen edge of each muffin with spatula; turn out. Serve hot.
Makes 12.

Biscuits

McCall's step-by-step method for biscuits gives you the kind of perfection you hope you'll get and seldom do. Biscuits should be served as soon as they are baked, piping hot, so butter can melt into them deliciously. Our drop biscuits are great for beginners—they're quicker and easier to make; there's no kneading and no rolling out. Try the cheese biscuits too.

Baking-Powder Biscuits

2 cups sifted* all-purpose flour
3 teaspoons baking powder
1 teaspoon salt
1/3 cup shortening
About 3/4 cup milk
* Sift before measuring.

1. Preheat oven to 450F. Sift flour with baking powder and salt into medium bowl.
2. Cut shortening into flour mixture, with a pastry blender or 2 knives (used scissors-fashion), until mixture resembles coarse cornmeal.
3. Make a well in the center. Pour in 2/3 cup milk all at once. Stir quickly round the bowl with a fork. If mixture seems dry, add a little more milk, to form dough just moist enough (but not wet) to leave side of bowl and form ball.
4. Turn out dough onto a lightly floured surface, to knead. Gently pick up dough from side away away from you; fold over toward you; press out lightly with palm of hand. Give the dough a quarter turn. Repeat ten times.
5. Gently roll out dough, from center, to 3/4-inch thickness.

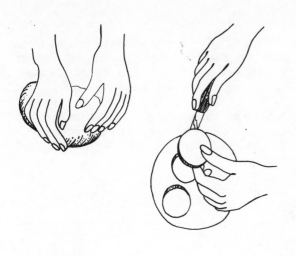

6. With floured 2-1/2-inch biscuit cutter, cut straight down into dough, being careful not to twist cutter.

7. Place on ungreased cookie sheet; bake 12 to 15 minutes.

Makes 8 (2-1/2-inch) biscuits.

Note: To prepare ahead: Make biscuits through first part of Step 7; refrigerate up to 3 hours. Let warm 15 minutes to room temperature, while preheating oven; bake as directed. Serve at once.

Drop Biscuits: Make Baking-Powder Biscuits, increasing milk to 1 cup. Do not knead or roll out. Drop dough, by tablespoonfuls, onto lightly greased cookie sheet; bake at 450F for 10 minutes, or until golden-brown. Makes 20.

Cheese Biscuits: Adding 3/4 cup grated sharp Cheddar cheese to sifted dry ingredients, make Baking-Powder Biscuits.

Coffeecakes

The ones we've included here are easier to make than our equally delicious yeast coffeecakes. They're nice enough to serve to guests at brunch or with afternoon coffee. The guests probably won't believe you made them; but that's part of the fun, isn't it?

Streusel-Layered Coffeecake

Streusel Mixture:
1/2 cup light-brown sugar, firmly packed
2 tablespoons soft butter or margarine
2 tablespoons all-purpose flour
1 teaspoon cinnamon
1/2 cup coarsely chopped walnuts (optional)

Batter:
1-1/2 cups sifted* all-purpose flour
2-1/2 teaspoons baking powder
1/2 teaspoon salt
1 egg
3/4 cup granulated sugar
1/3 cup butter or margarine, melted
1/2 cup milk
1 teaspoon vanilla extract
* Sift before measuring.

1. Preheat oven to 375F. Grease an 8-by-8-by-2-inch baking pan or a 9-by-1-1/2-inch layer-cake pan.

2. Make Streusel Mixture: In small bowl, combine brown sugar, 2 tablespoons soft butter, 2 tablespoons flour, the cinnamon, and nuts; mix with fork until crumbly. Set aside.

3. Make Batter: Sift flour with baking powder and salt. Set aside.

4. In medium bowl, with rotary beater, beat egg until frothy. Beat in sugar and butter until well combined. Add milk and vanilla. With wooden spoon, stir in flour mixture until well combined.

5. Turn half of batter into prepared pan. Sprinkle evenly with half of streusel mixture. Repeat with remaining batter and streusel mixture.

6. Bake 25 to 30 minutes, or until cake tester inserted in center comes out clean. Cool slightly in pan on wire rack. Serve warm.

Makes 9 servings.

Blueberry Sally Lunn

2 cups sifted* all-purpose flour
3 teaspoons baking powder
1/2 teaspoon salt
1/2 cup soft butter
1/2 cup granulated sugar
2 eggs
3/4 cup milk
1 cup blueberries, washed and drained
2 tablespoons light-brown sugar
1/2 teaspoon cinnamon
* Sift before measuring.

1. Preheat oven to 375F. Grease an 8-by-8-by-2-inch pan. Sift flour, baking powder, salt. In large bowl of electric mixer, combine butter, granulated sugar, eggs; beat at high speed until fluffy.
2. At low speed, add dry ingredients alternately with milk. Fold in blueberries. Turn into prepared pan; sprinkle with brown sugar and cinnamon.
3. Bake about 35 minutes. Serve warm.
Serves 9.

Sour-Cream Crumbcake

2 cups sifted* all-purpose flour
1 teaspoon baking powder
1/2 teaspoon baking soda
1/4 teaspoon salt
1/2 cup soft butter or margarine
1 cup sugar
3 eggs
1 teaspoon vanilla extract
3/4 cup dairy sour cream

Crumb Topping:
1/2 cup sugar
1/4 cup sifted all-purpose flour
2 tablespoons soft butter or margarine
1 teaspoon cinnamon
Confectioners' sugar
* Sift before measuring.

1. Preheat oven to 350F. Grease well and flour a 9-inch tube pan.
2. Sift flour with baking powder, baking soda, and salt; set aside.
3. In large bowl of electric mixer, at high speed, beat butter, sugar, eggs, and vanilla until light and fluffy—about 5 minutes—occasionally scraping bowl with rubber scraper.
4. At low speed, beat in flour mixture (in fourths) alternately with sour cream (in thirds), beginning and ending with flour mixture. Beat just until smooth—about 1 minute.
5. Turn batter into prepared tube pan.
6. Bake 50 minutes, or until cake tester inserted in center comes out clean.
7. Meanwhile, make Topping: In small bowl, combine all topping ingredients; toss lightly, with fork, until mixture is crumbly.
8. Remove cake from oven; sprinkle crumb topping evenly over top. Return to oven 10 minutes.
9. Let cool, in pan, on wire rack 10 minutes. Remove from pan; sprinkle crumb-topped surface with confectioners' sugar. Serve warm.
Makes 10 servings.

Cornbread

Certain meals seem to demand cornbread, and when they do, stir up a batter of McCALL's own, or a lovely variation thereof, and serve piping hot! The cornbread mixes are very good too.

Cornbread

1 cup sifted* all-purpose flour
2 tablespoons sugar
3 teaspoons baking powder
1/2 teaspoon salt
1 cup yellow cornmeal
1 egg, beaten
1/4 cup salad oil or shortening, melted
1 cup milk
* Sift before measuring.

1. Preheat oven to 425F. Grease an 8-by-8-by-2-inch baking pan.
2. Sift flour with sugar, baking powder, and salt. Add cornmeal, mixing well; set aside.
3. In medium bowl, combine egg, salad oil, and milk, mixing well. Add flour mixture, stirring only until flour mixture is moistened.
4. Spoon batter into prepared pan; bake 20 to 25 minutes, or until golden-brown. To serve, cut into squares. Serve hot, with butter.
Makes 9 servings.

Corn Muffins

1. Preheat oven to 425F. Grease bottoms of 12 (2-1/2-inch) muffin-pan cups, or line each with paper liner.
2. Prepare batter for Cornbread, above: Sift flour with sugar, baking powder, and salt into large bowl. Add cornmeal; mix well.
3. In medium bowl, combine egg, salad oil, and milk; beat with fork to mix well.
4. Make a well in center of flour mixture. Pour in milk mixture all at once; stir quickly, with fork, just until dry ingredients are moistened. Do not beat. Batter will be lumpy.
5. Quickly dip batter into muffin-pan cups, filling not quite two thirds full. Bake 15 to 20 minutes, or until golden.
6. Loosen edge of each muffin with spatula; turn out. Serve hot.
Makes 12.

Double Cornbread

1 cup sifted* all-purpose flour
1 cup yellow cornmeal
4 teaspoons baking powder
1 teaspoon salt
1/4 cup sugar
2 eggs, slightly beaten
1 cup milk
3 tablespoons butter or regular margarine, melted
1 can (8-3/4 oz) cream-style corn (1 cup)
* Sift before measuring.

1. Preheat oven to 425F. Grease a 9-by-9-by-1-3/4-inch baking pan.
2. Sift flour with cornmeal, baking powder, salt, and sugar; set aside.
3. In medium bowl, combine eggs, milk, butter, and corn. Add flour mixture, stirring only until flour mixture is moistened.
4. Spoon batter into prepared pan; bake 25 to 30 minutes, or until cake tester inserted in center comes out clean and top is golden-brown. To serve, cut into squares. Serve hot.
Makes 9 servings.

Southern Spoon Bread

1 cup yellow or white cornmeal
1 teaspoon salt
2 cups boiling water
2 tablespoons butter or margarine
1 cup milk
3 egg whites
3 egg yolks, slightly beaten
1 teaspoon baking powder

1. Preheat oven to 375F. Grease a 2-quart casserole or a 12-by-8-by-2-inch baking dish.
2. In medium saucepan, gradually stir cornmeal and salt into boiling water. Cook, over medium heat, stirring constantly, until consistency of thick mush. Remove from heat.
3. Add butter and milk; beat until smooth. Let cool to room temperature.
4. Meanwhile, beat egg whites until stiff peaks form when beater is raised; set aside.
5. Using same beaters, beat egg yolks until thick and lemon-colored.
6. Stir egg yolks and baking powder into cooled cornmeal mixture, mixing well. Then gently fold in egg whites until well combined.
7. Turn into prepared casserole; bake 40 to 50 minutes, or until golden-brown and puffy.
8. To serve, spoon from casserole (or, if baked in oblong dish, cut into squares), and serve hot, with butter.
Makes 8 servings.

Corn Sticks

1-1/4 cups yellow cornmeal
2/3 cup unsifted all-purpose flour
1/4 cup sugar
1 tablespoon baking powder
1/2 teaspoon salt
1 egg
1 cup milk
1/4 cup salad oil

1. Preheat oven to 425F. Grease 2 corn-stick pans.
2. In medium bowl, stir cornmeal with flour, sugar, baking powder, and salt. Add egg, milk, and oil. With wire whisk or rotary beater, beat just until smooth—about 1 minute. Turn into prepared corn-stick pans.
3. Bake 12 to 15 minutes, or until golden-brown. Turn out of pans. Serve hot.
Makes 14.

Popovers

Butter or margarine
4 eggs
1-1/4 cups milk
1/4 cup butter or regular margarine, melted
1-1/4 cups sifted* all-purpose flour
1/2 teaspoon salt
* Sift before measuring.

1. Preheat oven to 400F. Grease well, with butter, 8 custard cups.
2. Beat eggs well with rotary beater; then beat in milk and melted butter.
3. Sift flour with salt; beat into egg mixture until smooth.
4. Pour into prepared custard cups, placed, not too close together, on a large cookie sheet. Bake 50 minutes. Serve hot.
Makes 8.

Quick Breads with Bakery Breads

There are ever so many great ways of using the bread you buy at your grocer's. The variety of things you can do to make it more interesting is limited only by your imagination—and ours!

Hot, Crisp Herb Bread

1 loaf French bread
1/2 cup soft butter or margarine
1/2 teaspoon paprika
1/2 teaspoon dried rosemary leaves
1/4 teaspoon dried thyme leaves
1/4 teaspoon dried marjoram leaves
1/8 teaspoon seasoned salt

1. Preheat oven to 400F.
2. At 1-inch intervals, make diagonal cuts in bread; don't cut through bottom.
3. In small bowl, combine remaining ingredients until well blended. Spread mixture between bread slices.
4. Wrap bread completely in foil; bake 15 to 20 minutes, or until herb butter is melted and bread is hot.
Makes 8 servings.

Garlic Bread

1 loaf French bread
1/2 cup soft butter or margarine
1 clove garlic, crushed
3 tablespoons grated Parmesan cheese
1 teaspoon dried marjoram leaves
1/4 teaspoon pepper
Dash cayenne

1. Preheat oven to 350F.
2. At 1-inch intervals, make diagonal cuts in loaf; don't cut through bottom.
3. In small bowl, combine remaining ingredients until well blended. Spread mixture between bread slices.
4. Place bread on ungreased cookie sheet; sprinkle top with few drops water.
5. Bake about 10 minutes, or until butter is melted and bread is hot. Serve immediately.
Makes about 12 servings.

Strawberry-Jam Crescents

1/3 cup strawberry jam
2 tablespoons chopped walnuts
1 pkg (8 oz) refrigerator crescent rolls
1/2 cup confectioners' sugar
1 tablespoon butter or margarine
1 tablespoon milk

1. Combine jam and walnuts well.
2. Preheat oven to 375F.
3. Unroll crescent-roll dough. Cut along perforations to make 8 pieces.
4. Spread each with jam-walnut mixture, dividing evenly. Roll up as the label directs.
5. Place, 2 inches apart, on a lightly greased cookie sheet; bake 10 to 15 minutes, or until golden.
6. Meanwhile, in small bowl, mix sugar, butter, and milk until smooth.
7. Remove crescents to wire rack. Spread tops with icing. Serve warm.
Makes 8 crescents.

Crispy Herb Rolls

1 loaf unsliced white bread
1 cup soft butter or margarine
1/2 teaspoon paprika
2 teaspoons snipped fresh thyme or rosemary
    leaves*
* Or use 1 teaspoon dried thyme or rosemary
leaves

1. Preheat oven to 375F.
2. With serrated bread knife, completely trim crust from bread.
3. Cut loaf in half, lengthwise. Make a cut down center of each half, being careful not to cut all the way through.
4. Then make 3 cuts crosswise, being careful not to cut all the way through. Place on wire rack in shallow pan.
5. With wooden spoon, cream butter with paprika and thyme until well blended. Spread evenly over sides and top of bread.
6. Bake 15 minutes, or until crisp and golden. To serve, cut apart with scissors or knife.
Makes 16 small servings.

Salt Crescent Rolls

2 pkg (8-oz size) refrigerated crescent dinner rolls
1 egg, slightly beaten
2 teaspoons coarse salt

1. Preheat oven to 375F.
2. Shape crescents, and place on cookie sheet, as the label directs.
3. Brush crescents with egg; sprinkle with salt.
4. Bake 12 minutes, or until golden-brown. Serve warm.
Makes 16 crescents.
Sesame or Poppy-seed Crescents: In Step 3, omit salt; sprinkle with sesame or poppy seeds. Bake as directed.

Pancakes and Waffles
Buttermilk Pancakes

3 eggs
1 cup sifted* all-purpose flour
3 teaspoons baking powder
1/2 teaspoon salt
2 teaspoons granulated sugar
1 teaspoon light-brown sugar
1/2 cup buttermilk
2 tablespoons butter or margarine, melted
* Sift before measuring.

1. In large bowl of electric mixer, at high speed, beat eggs until light and fluffy—about 2 minutes.
2. Into eggs, sift flour with baking powder, salt, and granulated sugar. Add brown sugar; beat until smooth.
3. Stir in buttermilk and butter just until combined; do not overbeat.
4. Meanwhile, slowly heat griddle or heavy skillet. To test temperature, drop a little cold water onto hot griddle; water should roll off in drops.
5. Use 1/4 cup batter for each pancake; cook until bubbles form on surface and edges become dry.

Turn; cook 2 minutes longer, or until nicely browned on underside.

6. Serve hot with butter and maple syrup.
Makes 8 (4-inch) pancakes.

Blueberry Buttermilk Pancakes

1. To Buttermilk Pancakes Batter, gently add 1 pkg (12 oz) thawed frozen blueberries, drained; or 1-1/4 cups fresh blueberries. Stir just until combined. Be careful not to break berries as you stir.

2. Cook and serve pancakes as directed above.
Makes 12 (4-inch) pancakes.

French Toast

4 slices white bread, 3/4 inch thick*
3 eggs
3/4 cup milk
1 tablespoon granulated sugar
1/4 teaspoon salt
2 tablespoons butter or margarine
Confectioners' sugar or cinnamon-sugar
* Or use 2 thin slices, put together.

1. Arrange bread in single layer in 9-inch-square baking dish.

2. In small bowl, with rotary beater, beat eggs, milk, granulated sugar, and salt until blended. Pour over bread; turn slices to coat evenly.

3. Refrigerate, covered, overnight, or at least 4 hours.

4. In hot butter in skillet, sauté bread until golden —about 4 minutes on each side. Sprinkle with confectioners' sugar or cinnamon-sugar, and serve with bacon and syrup. Or serve with frozen sliced strawberries.
Makes 4 servings.

Griddlecakes

1 cup sifted* all-purpose flour
2 teaspoons baking powder
1/2 teaspoon salt
2 tablespoons sugar
1 egg
1 cup milk
3 tablespoons butter or margarine, melted
* Sift before measuring.

1. Sift flour with baking powder, salt, and sugar into medium bowl.

2. With rotary beater, beat egg. Add milk and butter; beat until well mixed.

3. Pour into dry ingredients; beat only until combined—batter will be lumpy.

4. Meanwhile, slowly heat griddle or heavy skillet. To test temperature, drop a little cold water onto hot griddle; water should roll off in drops.

5. Use about 1/4 cup batter for each griddlecake; cook until bubbles form on surface and edges become dry. Turn; cook 2 minutes longer, or until nicely browned on underside. Serve with whipped butter, below.
Makes 8 (4-inch) griddlecakes.

Whipped Butter

1/4 lb sweet or salt butter

1. Let butter stand, at room temperature, in small bowl of electric mixer 30 minutes.
2. Beat at low speed until smooth; then beat at high speed until light and fluffy (about 10 minutes in all).
3. Mound high in small bowl. Serve at room temperature.
Makes about 1 cup.

H.R.M.'s Favorite Waffles

4 eggs
2 cups sifted* all-purpose flour
1 teaspoon salt
1 teaspoon baking soda
1 teaspoon baking powder
2 cups buttermilk; or 1 cup dairy sour cream,
**   mixed with 1 cup milk**
1 cup melted butter
* Sift before measuring.

1. Preheat waffle iron.
2. Beat eggs until light.
3. Sift together flour, salt, soda, and baking powder.
4. Add flour mixture and buttermilk alternately to beaten eggs, beginning and ending with flour mixture. Add melted butter; blend thoroughly.
5. For each waffle, pour batter into center of lower half of waffle iron until it spreads to 1 inch from edge—about 1/2 cup.
6. Lower cover on batter; cook as manufacturer directs, or until waffle iron stops steaming. Do not raise cover during baking.
7. Carefully loosen edge of waffle with fork; remove. Serve hot, with butter and Strawberry Syrup, below.
Makes 8 waffles.

Strawberry Syrup

1 pkg (12 oz) thawed frozen sliced strawberries
2 teaspoons cornstarch
1 teaspoon lemon juice

1. Drain strawberries, reserving liquid. In medium saucepan, combine 1 tablespoon strawberry liquid and the 2 teaspoons cornstarch; stir until smooth.
2. Add remaining liquid, the berries, and lemon juice; bring to boiling, stirring. Sauce will be slightly thickened and translucent. Serve warm.
Makes about 1-1/2 cups.

Yeast Breads

The fragrance of bread baking in the kitchen is so heavenly we think it should be bottled and sprayed about! There is something about baking bread that's deeply satisfying, and nothing makes a family feel more pampered.

Tips for Bread Bakers

Flour: Our bread recipes were tested using all-purpose flour. In each recipe, we specify whether it is to be sifted or unsifted before measuring.

Yeast: Yeast is available in two forms—active dry and compressed. The active dry yeast keeps well for several months, but should be used before the expiration day on the package. Keep it, in its package, on a cool shelf. Dissolve active dry yeast in warm water (105 to 115F). Water that is too hot will kill yeast. Water that is too cold will slow down yeast action considerably.

Compressed yeast is more perishable. It will keep 1 to 2 weeks under refrigeration. Dissolve compressed yeast by crumbling it into lukewarm water (95F).

Yeast is a living plant that needs warmth to grow, so the water or milk in which you dissolve it must be warm; so must the bowl in which the dough is mixed.

In growing, yeast forms the gas that makes the bread light. Unlike baking powder, its action is continuous; so the flour mixture needs a framework capable of holding the gas over a period of time. This framework is provided by the gluten in the flour.

Stirring or beating or kneading flour and liquid develops the gluten, and the gluten traps the leavening gas, so the bread rises.

Kneaded Breads: When all the ingredients have been combined, most recipes suggest kneading the dough. This is simply mixing and blending by hand a dough that is too stiff to mix with a spoon. Doughs that are kneaded contain more flour than those that are not, and the gluten framework is strong enough to hold the gas in tiny pockets, so the resulting bread is fine and evenly textured, with a smoothly rounded top.

Kneading: Turn out dough onto lightly floured board or pastry cloth. With floured hands, pick up dough. Fold dough over toward you, then push it down and away from you, with heel of hand. Give dough a quarter turn; repeat kneading, developing a rocking rhythm. Continue kneading and turning 10 minutes, until dough is smooth and elastic and blisters appear on surface.

Rising: The room in which dough rises must be warm. The ideal temperature is 85F. Cover the dough with a towel, and keep it away from drafts. If your room is chilly, place the dough in an unlighted oven, with a large pan of hot water on the rack below the bowl, to hasten rising.

Crust: If bread is baked in a loaf pan, there will be a break between the sides and the top crust, and both sides of the bread will have a uniform, well-shaped appearance.

For a tender, soft crust, brush it with shortening after you take it from the oven, and cover it with a towel. For a crisp crust, omit the shortening, and let the bread cool without covering it. For a highly glazed crust, varnish the loaf, before baking, with an egg yolk beaten into a tablespoonful of water; use a pastry brush to apply it.

To Shape Loaf

1. On lightly floured pastry cloth, stretch or roll dough until it is about 27 inches long (3 times as long as pan in which it will be baked).

2. Fold dough into thirds, pressing or rolling, to break any air pockets, until dough is a 7-inch square.

3. Fold dough into thirds, from opposite direction, pressing with fingers to break any air pockets.

4. Seal edge and ends of loaf by pinching together. Roll under palm of hand to smooth shape of loaf.

5. Place, seam side down, in lightly greased 9-by-5-by-3-inch pan.

6. Brush top of shaped loaf with melted butter. Cover with towel; let rise in warm place (85F), free from drafts, until double in bulk—about 1 hour. When a finger poked into dough leaves an indentation, rising is sufficient. Sides of dough should reach top of pan.

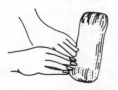

McCall's Basic White Bread

2 cups milk
3 tablespoons sugar
1 tablespoon salt
1/4 cup butter or regular margarine
1/4 cup warm water (105 to 115F)
2 pkg active dry yeast
6-1/2 to 7 cups sifted* all-purpose flour
2 tablespoons melted butter or margarine
* Sift before measuring.

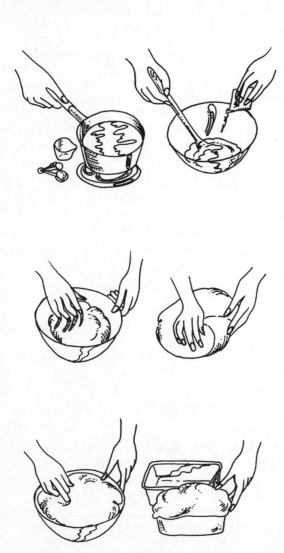

1. In small saucepan, heat milk just until bubbles form around edge of pan. Remove from heat. Add sugar, salt, and 1/4 cup butter, stirring until butter is melted. Let cool to lukewarm (a drop sprinkled on wrist will not feel warm).

2. If possible, check temperature of warm water with thermometer. Sprinkle yeast over water in large bowl, stirring until dissolved. Stir in milk mixture.

3. Add half the flour; beat, with wooden spoon, until smooth—about 2 minutes. Gradually add remaining flour, mixing it in with hand until dough is stiff enough to leave side of bowl.

4. Turn out dough onto lightly floured board. Cover with the bowl; let rest 10 minutes. Knead by folding dough toward you, then pushing down and away from you, with heel of hand. Give dough a quarter turn; repeat kneading, developing a rocking rhythm. Continue kneading and turning 10 minutes, or until dough is smooth and elastic and blisters appear on surface.

5. Place in lightly greased large bowl; turn dough to bring up greased side. Cover with towel; let rise in warm place (85F), free from drafts, about 1 hour, or until double in bulk. When two fingers poked into dough leave indentations, rising is sufficient. Punch down dough with fist; turn out onto lightly floured pastry cloth. Divide in half; shape each half into smooth ball. Cover with towel; let rest 10 minutes. Shape each portion into loaf, and place in pan, according to the shaping directions, page 101.

6. Brush top of each loaf with 1 tablespoon melted butter. Cover with towel; let rise in warm place (85F), free from drafts, until double in bulk, or until sides of dough reach tops of pans—about 1 hour.

7. Meanwhile, preheat oven to 400F.

8. Bake loaves 40 to 50 minutes—tops should be well browned and sound hollow when rapped with knuckle. Remove from pans immediately; cool well on wire rack, away from drafts.

Note: If a lighter-color crust is desired, cover top of loaves with brown paper or aluminum foil after bread has baked 25 minutes.

Makes 2 loaves.

Caraway Rye Bread

2 cups warm water (105 to 115F)
2 pkg active dry yeast
1 tablespoon salt
1/4 cup light molasses
2 tablespoons butter or regular margarine,
  softened
1 to 2 tablespoons caraway seed, to taste
3-1/2 cups sifted* rye flour
3 to 3-1/2 cups sifted* all-purpose flour
Cornmeal
1 egg white, slightly beaten
Caraway seed or coarse salt
* Sift before measuring.

1. If possible, check temperature of warm water with thermometer. Sprinkle yeast over water in large bowl, stirring until dissolved.
2. Add salt, molasses, butter, caraway seed, rye flour, and 1-1/2 cups all-purpose flour; beat, with wooden spoon, till smooth—2 minutes.
3. Gradually add rest of all-purpose flour; mix in with hand until dough leaves side of bowl.
4. Turn dough onto lightly floured board. Dough will be stiff. Knead until smooth—about 10 minutes.
5. Place in lightly greased large bowl; turn to bring up greased side. Cover with towel; let rise in warm place (85F), free from drafts, until double in bulk —about 1 hour.
6. Grease large cookie sheet; sprinkle with cornmeal.
7. Punch down dough. Turn out onto lightly floured pastry cloth. Divide in half.
8. To make round loaves: Shape each half into a smooth ball; tuck edges under. Place, 5 inches apart, on prepared cookie sheet.
9. To make oval loaves: Shape each half into a ball. Roll each into a 10-inch loaf, tapering ends. Place, 3 inches apart, on cookie sheet.
10. Cover with towel; let rise in warm place (85F), free from drafts, until double in bulk—about 40 minutes.
11. Meanwhile, preheat oven to 375F.
12. Bake bread 50 minutes, or until loaf sounds hollow when rapped with knuckle. Remove to wire rack. Brush tops of loaves with egg white; sprinkle with caraway seed; cool.
Makes 2 loaves.

Old-Fashioned Potato Bread

Packaged instant mashed potato
2 pkg (1/4-oz size) active dry yeast
2 cups warm water (105 to 115F)
1/4 cup sugar
1 tablespoon salt
1/2 cup butter or regular margarine, softened
7-1/2 to 7-3/4 cups unsifted all-purpose flour
2 tablespoons butter or margarine, melted

1. Make instant mashed potato for 2 servings as package label directs, using liquid but omitting butter and seasonings. Measure 1 cup.
2. In large bowl, sprinkle yeast over warm water; stir until dissolved. Stir in sugar and salt until dissolved.
3. Add 1 cup mashed potato, 1/2 cup softened butter, and 3-1/2 cups flour. With electric mixer at medium speed, beat until smooth—about 2 minutes.

4. Gradually add 4 cups more flour, mixing with hands until dough is smooth and stiff enough to leave side of bowl; mix in remaining 1/4 cup flour if needed.

5. Turn out dough onto lightly floured board. Knead until dough is smooth and elastic and small blisters appear on surface—about 10 minutes.

6. Place in lightly greased large bowl; turn dough, to bring up greased side. Cover with towel; let rise in warm place (85F), free from drafts, until double in bulk—about 1 hour.

7. Turn out dough onto lightly floured pastry cloth or board. Divide in half. Roll out one half into a 16-by-8-inch rectangle; roll up, starting at one end. Press ends even; pinch to seal; tuck under loaf.

8. Place, seam side down, in greased 9-by-5-by-3-inch loaf pan. Brush surface lightly with some of the melted butter. Repeat with other half of dough.

9. Let loaves rise in warm place (85F), free from drafts, until sides come to top of pan and tops are rounded. Set oven rack at lowest level. Preheat oven to 400F.

10. Bake 30 to 40 minutes, or until crust is deep golden-brown and loaves sound hollow when tapped. If crust becomes too brown, cover with a piece of brown paper.

11. Turn out of pans onto wire racks; brush tops with remaining melted butter. Let cool completely. Makes 2 loaves.

Whole-Wheat Bread

2 cups milk
1/2 cup light-brown sugar, packed
1 tablespoon salt
1/4 cup butter or regular margarine
1 cup warm water (105 to 115F)
2 pkg active dry yeast
7 cups unsifted whole-wheat flour
1-1/4 cups unsifted all-purpose flour
3 tablespoons butter or margarine, melted

1. In small saucepan, heat milk until bubbles form around edge of pan; remove from heat. Add sugar, salt, and 1/4 cup butter; stir until butter melts; cool to lukewarm.

2. If possible, check temperature of water with thermometer. Sprinkle yeast over water in large bowl, stirring until dissolved. Stir in milk mixture.

3. Add 4 cups whole-wheat flour; beat vigorously with wooden spoon until smooth. Gradually add remaining whole-wheat flour and the all-purpose flour, mixing in last of it with hand until dough is stiff enough to leave side of bowl.

4. Turn out dough onto lightly floured pastry cloth or board. Knead until dough is smooth and elastic—about 10 minutes.

5. Place in lightly greased large bowl; turn dough to bring up greased side. Cover with towel; let rise in warm place (85F), free from drafts, until double in bulk—about 1 hour.

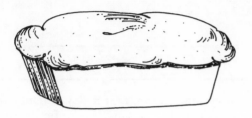

6. Turn out dough onto lightly floured pastry cloth or board. Divide in half. Let rest, covered, 10 minutes. Roll out one half into a 16-by-8-inch rectangle; roll up, starting at one end. Press ends even; pinch to seal; tuck under loaf.

7. Place, seam side down, in greased 9-by-5-by-3-inch loaf pan. Brush surface lightly with some of the melted butter. Repeat with other half of dough.

8. Let loaves rise in warm place, free from drafts, until sides come to top of pans and tops are rounded—about 1 hour.

9. Place oven rack in middle of oven. Preheat oven to 400F.

10. Bake 35 to 40 minutes, or until crust is deep golden-brown and loaves sound hollow when tapped. (If crust seems too brown after 35 minutes of baking, cover with foil or brown paper.)

11. Turn out of pans onto wire racks; brush tops with remaining melted butter. Serve slightly warm, or let cool completely.

Makes 2 loaves.

Swedish Limpa Bread

2-1/2 cups warm water (105 to 115F)
2 pkg active dry yeast
1 tablespoon salt
1/4 cup light or dark molasses
1/2 cup light-brown sugar, packed
1/4 cup soft butter or regular margarine
2 tablespoons grated orange peel
1 teaspoon anise seed
4 cups unsifted rye flour
4-1/2 cups unsifted all-purpose flour
Cornmeal
2 tablespoons butter or regular margarine, melted

1. If possible, check temperature of water with thermometer. Sprinkle yeast over water in large bowl, stirring until dissolved.

2. Add salt, molasses, brown sugar, 1/4 cup butter, the orange peel, anise seed, and rye flour. With wooden spoon, beat vigorously until smooth.

3. Gradually add all-purpose flour; mix in with hand until dough leaves side of bowl. Dough will be stiff.

4. Turn out dough onto lightly floured pastry cloth or board. (Use all-purpose flour for pastry cloth or board.) Knead until smooth and elastic—about 10 minutes.

5. Place in lightly greased large bowl; turn dough to bring up greased side. Cover with towel; let rise in warm place (85F), free from drafts, until double in bulk—about 1-1/2 hours.

6. Grease a large cookie sheet; sprinkle sheet lightly with cornmeal.

7. Punch down dough. Turn out onto lightly floured pastry cloth or board. Divide in half.

8. Shape each half into a smooth ball, 6 inches in diameter; tuck edges under. Place on opposite ends of cookie sheet. (To make oval loaf, shape into a loaf 8 inches long, tapering ends.) With sharp knife, cut 3 diagonal slashes on top of loaf—about 1/4 inch deep.

9. Cover with towel; let rise in warm place, free from drafts, until double in bulk—1 to 1-1/2 hours.

10. Preheat oven to 375F. Bake on middle shelf of oven 30 to 35 minutes; cover with foil or brown paper the last 10 minutes. Remove to rack; brush with melted butter. Serve slightly warm, or let cool completely.

Makes 2 loaves.

Swiss Braided Loaves

1-1/2 cups milk
3 tablespoons sugar
1 tablespoon salt
1/4 cup butter or regular margarine
1/2 cup warm water (105 to 115F)
2 pkg active dry yeast
2 eggs
7 cups unsifted all-purpose flour
2 tablespoons butter or margarine, melted
1 egg yolk
1 tablespoon sesame or poppy seed

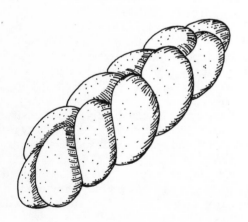

1. In small saucepan, heat milk just until bubbles form around edge of pan. Remove from heat. Add sugar, salt, and 1/4 cup butter, stirring until butter is melted. Cool to lukewarm.

2. If possible, check temperature of warm water with thermometer. Sprinkle yeast over water in large bowl, stirring until dissolved. Stir in milk mixture.

3. Add eggs and half of flour; beat with wooden spoon until smooth—about 2 minutes. Gradually add remaining flour, mixing in flour with hand until dough is stiff enough to leave side of bowl.

4. Turn out dough onto lightly floured pastry cloth or board. Knead until smooth and elastic—about 10 minutes.

5. Place in lightly greased large bowl; turn dough over to bring up greased side. Cover with towel; let rise in warm place (85F), free from drafts, about 1 hour, or until double in bulk.

6. Turn out dough onto lightly floured pastry cloth or board. Divide in half; divide each half into 3 equal parts. Using palms of hands, roll each part into a 14-inch-long strip. Braid 3 strips; pinch ends together. Repeat with remaining strips. Place each braid on greased large cookie sheet. Brush each with 1 tablespoon melted butter. Cover with dish towel.

7. Let rise in warm place, free from drafts, until double in bulk—about 50 to 60 minutes.

8. Place oven rack in middle of oven. Preheat oven to 400F.

9. Brush surface of each loaf with egg yolk mixed with 2 tablespoons water. Sprinkle with sesame or poppy seed.

10. Bake 35 to 40 minutes, or until a rich golden-brown. (If crust seems too brown after 25 minutes of baking, cover with foil or brown paper.) Remove to wire rack to cool. Serve warm or cold.

Makes 2 braids.

Sweet Yeast Breads

Spiral Cinnamon Raisin Bread

1-1/2 cups milk
1/4 cup sugar
2 teaspoons salt
1/2 cup butter or regular margarine
1-1/2 cups raisins
1/2 cup warm water (105 to 115F)
2 pkg active dry yeast
3 eggs
7-1/2 cups unsifted all-purpose flour
1/2 cup sugar
2 teaspoons cinnamon
1/4 cup butter or regular margarine, melted

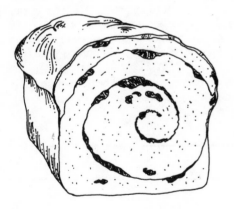

1. In small saucepan, heat milk until bubbles form around edge of pan; remove from heat. Add 1/4 cup sugar, the salt, 1/2 cup butter, and the raisins; stir until butter melts; cool to lukewarm.
2. If possible, check temperature of water with thermometer. Sprinkle yeast over water in large bowl, stirring until dissolved. Stir in milk mixture.
3. Add eggs and 4 cups flour; beat vigorously with wooden spoon until smooth—about 2 minutes.
4. Gradually add remaining flour; mix in last of it with hand until dough is stiff enough to leave side of bowl.
5. Turn out dough onto lightly floured pastry cloth or board. Knead until smooth and elastic—about 10 minutes.
6. Place in lightly greased large bowl; turn dough over to bring up greased side. Cover with towel; let rise in warm place (85F), free from drafts, until double in bulk—about 1-1/2 hours.
7. In small bowl, mix 1/2 cup sugar and the cinnamon.
8. Turn dough out onto lightly floured pastry cloth or board. Divide in half. Roll out one half into 16-by-8-inch rectangle. Sprinkle with 3 tablespoons cinnamon-sugar, reserving rest. Starting at narrow end, roll up jelly-roll fashion. Pinch edges and ends together to seal. Tuck ends under to give a smooth shape.
9. Place, seam side down, in greased 9-by-5-by-3-inch loaf pan. Brush surface lightly with 1 tablespoon melted butter. Cover with towel. Repeat with other half of dough.
10. Let rise in warm place, free from drafts, until sides come to top of pan and tops are rounded—about 1 hour.
11. Place oven rack in middle of oven. Preheat oven to 375F.
12. Brush each loaf with remaining melted butter, and sprinkle with cinnamon-sugar. Bake 35 to 40 minutes—tops should be well browned. (If crust seems too brown after 25 minutes of baking, cover with foil or brown paper.) Baked loaf should sound hollow when tapped with knuckle.
13. Remove from pan immediately; cool slightly on wire rack, away from drafts. Serve warm.
Makes 2 loaves.

Babka

1 cup milk
1/4 cup warm water (105 to 115F)
2 pkg active dry yeast
1/2 cup sugar
1 teaspoon salt
1/2 cup butter or regular margarine, softened
4 eggs
1 egg yolk
4-1/2 cups unsifted all-purpose flour
1/2 cup seedless raisins

Topping:
1 egg white
2 tablespoons flour
2 tablespoons sugar
1/4 teaspoon cinnamon
2 tablespoons butter or margarine

1. In small saucepan, heat milk until bubbles form around edge. Remove from heat; cool to lukewarm.
2. If possible, check temperature of warm water with thermometer. In large bowl, sprinkle yeast over water, stirring until dissolved. Add lukewarm milk, 1/2 cup sugar, the salt, 1/2 cup butter, the eggs, egg yolk, and 3 cups flour. With electric mixer at medium speed, beat until smooth and blended. With wooden spoon, stir in 1-1/2 cups flour; beat vigorously 2 minutes, or until dough leaves side of bowl. Mix in raisins.
3. Cover with towel; let rise in warm place (85F), free from drafts, until double in bulk—about 1 hour.
4. Grease and flour 9-inch springform pan. Turn dough into prepared pan. Cover with towel; let rise in warm place (85F), free from drafts, until dough is 1/2 inch from top of pan—about 1 hour.
5. Meanwhile, preheat oven to 350F.
6. Make Topping: Beat egg white with 1 tablespoon water; use to brush top of babka. Mix flour, sugar, cinnamon, and butter; sprinkle on babka.
7. Bake 60 minutes, or until cake tester inserted in center comes out clean. Cool in pan on wire rack 15 minutes.
8. To serve: Remove side and bottom of springform pan. Cut in wedges. Serve warm, if desired.
Makes 16 servings.

Sweet Rolls

Sweet-Roll Dough

3/4 cup milk
1/2 cup sugar
2 teaspoons salt
1/2 cup butter or regular margarine
1/2 cup warm water (105 to 115F)
2 pkg active dry yeast
2 eggs, beaten
4-1/4 cups unsifted all-purpose flour
Soft butter or margarine

1. Heat the milk just until bubbles form. Add sugar, salt, and 1/2 cup butter; stir to dissolve. Cool to lukewarm.
2. If possible, check temperature of warm water with thermometer. Pour into large, warm bowl. Sprinkle the yeast over water, and stir to dissolve.
3. With a wooden spoon, stir in milk mixture, beaten eggs, and 2 cups flour; beat until smooth—about 2 minutes.
4. Gradually add rest of the flour, beating until dough is stiff, smooth, and cleans side of bowl. Turn into large, greased bowl. Brush with soft butter.
5. Cover the bowl with foil; refrigerate for 2 hours. Dough will rise to top. (May be refrigerated up to 3 days.)

6. To use: Cut off amount needed; refrigerate the remainder. Shape and bake as directed, below. Makes 2 dozen rolls.

Crescents

1/3 cup light-brown sugar, firmly packed
1/3 cup finely chopped walnuts
3/4 teaspoon cinnamon
1/3 Sweet-Roll Dough, page 108
2 tablespoons butter or margarine, melted
1 egg yolk
Bottled cinnamon sugar

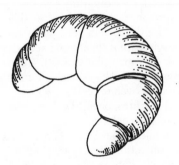

1. Lightly grease a large cookie sheet.
2. In small bowl, toss the brown sugar, chopped walnuts, and cinnamon, mixing them well.
3. On lightly floured surface, pat dough into a round; let rest 5 minutes.
4. Roll out dough to a 12-inch circle; brush with butter. Sprinkle with brown-sugar mixture to within 1/2 inch of edge. Cut into 8 equal pie-shape wedges. (See diagram.)
5. Starting from wide end, roll up each wedge toward point. Place, with center point down, 2 inches apart, on prepared cookie sheet. Curve ends to form crescents.
6. Cover loosely with sheet of waxed paper. Set in warm place (85F), free from drafts, until double in bulk—about 45 minutes. Meanwhile, preheat oven to 350F.
7. With fork, beat egg yolk with 1 tablespoon water. Use to brush tops of rolls. Sprinkle lightly with cinnamon sugar.
8. Bake 15 minutes, or until golden-brown.
9. Let cool slightly on wire rack.
Makes 8.

Blueberry Surprises

1/3 Sweet-Roll Dough, page 108
1/3 cup blueberry preserves
1 tablespoon butter or margarine, melted
Streusel Topping (see Bow Ties)
Confectioners' sugar

1. Lightly grease 8 muffin-pan cups.
2. Divide dough evenly into 8 pieces. On lightly floured surface, roll each piece of dough into a 3-1/2-inch round.
3. In center of each round, place a heaping teaspoonful of blueberry preserves. (See diagram.)
4. Moisten edge with water; bring sides together over filling; pinch with fingers to seal.
5. Place in prepared muffin cups, pinched side down. Brush with butter; then sprinkle with Streusel Topping.
6. Let rise in warm place (85F), free from drafts, until double in bulk—30 to 40 minutes. Meanwhile, preheat oven to 350F.
7. Bake 15 minutes, or until golden-brown.
8. Remove to wire rack; let cool slightly. Sprinkle with confectioners' sugar. Serve while still warm.
Makes 8.

Bear Claws

1/3 Sweet-Roll Dough, page 108
3 tablespoons butter or margarine, melted
Bottled cinnamon sugar
1/4 cup chopped walnuts
1/3 cup chopped raisins
1 teaspoon grated lemon peel

Sugar Glaze:
1/2 cup sifted confectioners' sugar
1/4 teaspoon vanilla extract
2 teaspoons milk

1. Lightly grease a large cookie sheet.
2. On lightly floured surface, shape dough into a round; let rest 5 minutes.
3. Roll dough to an 18-by-9-inch rectangle. Brush with half of butter; then sprinkle generously with cinnamon sugar, leaving a 1/4-inch edge all around.
4. Combine walnuts, raisins, and lemon peel. Sprinkle evenly over sugared surface.
5. From longer side, fold 1/3 of the dough over. Then bring opposite side over this, to make a 3-layer strip, 18 by 3 inches. Pinch together to seal.
6. With sharp knife, cut strip crosswise into 6 sections. On folded side of each, make 3 (1-inch) cuts, evenly spaced. (See diagram.)
7. Arrange on prepared cookie sheet. Separate "claws" slightly. Brush tops with rest of butter. Cover loosely with a sheet of waxed paper.
8. Let rise in warm place (85F), free from drafts, until double in bulk—about 45 minutes. Meanwhile, preheat oven to 350F.
9. Bake 15 minutes, or until golden-brown. Let cool slightly on wire rack.
10. Meanwhile, make Sugar Glaze: In small bowl, combine confectioners' sugar, vanilla extract, and milk; mix well. Pour over warm rolls, to glaze thinly.
Makes 6.

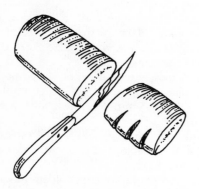

Horns

1/3 Sweet-Roll Dough, page 108
2 tablespoons butter or margarine, melted
Raspberry or strawberry preserves
Creamy peanut butter (optional)
1 egg yolk
1/4 cup toasted, sliced almonds or chopped
   peanuts

1. Lightly grease a large cookie sheet.
2. On lightly floured surface, shape dough into a round; let rest 5 minutes.
3. Roll out dough to a 12-inch circle. Brush with melted butter; then spread with the preserves or with a combination of peanut butter and preserves to within 1/2 inch of the edge.
4. With sharp knife, cut into 8 equal pie-shape wedges. Beginning at narrow end, roll up each wedge to within 1-1/2 inches from edge. (See diagram.)
5. Make 3 or 4 (1-inch) cuts at wide end of each one. Bring up strips over filling. Pinch edges, to seal.

6. Place horns on cookie sheet; cover loosely with sheet of waxed paper.

7. Let rise in warm place (85F), free from drafts, until double in bulk—about 45 minutes. Meanwhile, preheat oven to 350F.

8. With fork, beat egg yolk slightly with 1 tablespoon water. Use to brush tops of rolls. Sprinkle with almonds or peanuts.

9. Bake 15 minutes, or until golden-brown. Let cool on wire rack.

Makes 8.

Pinwheels

1/3 Sweet-Roll Dough, page 108
Apricot or cherry preserves, or prune butter
1 egg yolk

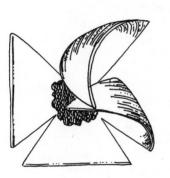

1. Lightly grease a large cookie sheet.

2. On lightly floured surface, shape dough into a round; let rest 5 minutes.

3. Pinch off a small piece of dough for centers. Roll rest of dough into a rectangle, 15 by 10 inches. With sharp knife or pastry wheel, cut into 6 (5-inch) squares. (See diagram.)

4. Arrange squares, 1-1/2 inches apart, on prepared cookie sheet. From each corner of each square, make cut at 45-degree angle, 2-1/2 inches long.

5. In center of each square, place 1 tablespoon preserves.

6. To make pinwheels: Bring every other point of dough to center of square; then press in the center, to fasten.

7. Roll out small piece of dough 1/8 inch thick. Cut 6 rounds, using a 1-1/4-inch round cutter. Moisten bottom of rounds slightly with water; place in center of each pinwheel, to cover points. Cover loosely with a sheet of waxed paper.

8. Let rise in warm place (85F), free from drafts, until double in bulk—about 45 minutes. Meanwhile, preheat oven to 350F.

9. With fork, beat egg yolk slightly with 1 tablespoon water. Use to brush tops of rolls.

10. Bake 15 minutes, or until golden-brown. Let cool on wire rack.

Makes 6.

Bow Ties

Streusel Topping:
2 tablespoons soft butter or margarine
2 tablespoons light-brown sugar
1/2 teaspoon cinnamon
1/3 cup unsifted all-purpose flour

1/3 Sweet-Roll Dough, page 108
1/4 cup butter or margarine, melted
Bottled cinnamon sugar
Confectioners' sugar

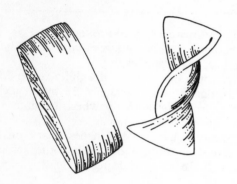

1. Make Streusel Topping: Combine butter with sugar, cinnamon, and flour; mix well. Set aside until ready to use.
2. Lightly grease a large cookie sheet.
3. On lightly floured pastry cloth, roll dough to a rectangle 20 by 10 inches. Spread surface with half of melted butter; then sprinkle generously with cinnamon sugar.
4. Fold over dough in half, from long side, to form a rectangle 20 by 5 inches.
5. Cut crosswise into 2-1/2-inch strips, making 8 (5-by-2-1/2-inch) strips. (See diagram.)
6. Place strips on prepared cookie sheet, making a twist in center of each, to give a bow effect.
7. Brush tops with rest of melted butter. Sprinkle with Streusel Topping; cover loosely with a sheet of waxed paper.
8. Let rise in warm place (85F), free from drafts, until double in bulk—about 45 minutes. Meanwhile, preheat oven to 350F.
9. Bake 15 minutes, or until golden-brown. Remove to wire rack; let cool slightly. Sprinkle with confectioners' sugar. Serve while still warm.
Makes 8.

Stollen

3/4 cup milk
1/2 cup granulated sugar
1/2 teaspoon salt
1 pkg active dry yeast
1/4 cup warm water (105 to 115F)
5 cups unsifted all-purpose flour
1 cup dark raisins
1 tablespoon grated lemon peel
1 jar (4 oz) candied red cherries, coarsely chopped
1 jar (8 oz) diced mixed candied peel
1/2 cup finely chopped blanched almonds
1 cup butter or regular margarine, softened
1/2 teaspoon nutmeg or mace
2 eggs
1/4 cup butter or margarine, melted
Confectioners' sugar

1. In small saucepan, heat milk just until bubbles form around edge of pan; remove from heat. Add granulated sugar and salt, stirring until dissolved. Let cool to lukewarm (a drop on wrist won't feel warm).
2. In large bowl that has been rinsed in hot water, sprinkle yeast over warm water (if possible, check temperature of warm water with thermometer); stir until dissolved.
3. Stir in milk mixture and 2 cups flour; beat with wooden spoon until smooth—at least 2 minutes.
4. Cover bowl with towel; let rise in warm place (85F), free from drafts, until double in bulk—1-1/2 hours. Grease 2 cookie sheets.
5. To risen dough in bowl, add the raisins, lemon peel, candied fruit, almonds, softened butter, nutmeg, eggs, and remaining flour. Mix with wooden spoon until blended. Turn out onto lightly floured surface; knead until fruit and nuts are well distributed—about 5 minutes.

6. Divide dough in half; shape each half into a ball. Roll or pat one ball into an oval 10 inches long and 6 inches across at widest part. Brush with 1 tablespoon melted butter.

7. Fold dough in half lengthwise. Place on prepared cookie sheet. Press folded edge lightly, to crease; then curve into crescent shape. Repeat with other ball of dough.

8. Cover stollen with towels; Let rise in warm place (85F) until double in bulk—1-1/2 to 2 hours.

9. Preheat oven to 375F.

10. Bake 25 to 30 minutes, or until nicely browned. Brush tops of stollen with remaining melted butter.

11. Remove to wire racks; cool.

12. To store: Wrap in plastic film, then in foil. Store in refrigerator or freezer several weeks.

13. To serve: Let warm to room temperature. Just before serving, sprinkle with confectioners' sugar. Makes 2 stollen.

Jelly Doughnuts

1/2 cup milk
1/3 cup sugar
1 teaspoon salt
1/3 cup butter or regular margarine
2 pkg active dry yeast
1/2 cup warm water (105 to 115F)
3 egg yolks
3-3/4 cups sifted* all-purpose flour
Raspberry or strawberry jam or jelly
Egg white
Salad oil for deep-frying
Sugar
* Sift before measuring.

1. Heat milk in small saucepan until bubbles form around edge of pan; remove from heat. Add 1/3 cup sugar, the salt, and butter; stir until butter is melted. Let cool to lukewarm.

2. In large bowl, sprinkle yeast over warm water (if possible, check temperature of water with thermometer). Stir until dissolved.

3. Add milk mixture, egg yolks, and 2 cups flour. With electric mixer at medium speed, beat until smooth—about 2 minutes.

4. With wooden spoon, beat in remaining flour; beat until smooth.

5. Cover with foil; let rise in warm place (85F), free from drafts, until double in bulk—about 1 hour.

6. Punch down dough. Turn out onto lightly floured surface; turn over, to coat with flour. Knead 10 times, or until dough is smooth. Divide in half.

7. Roll out half of dough to 1/4-inch thickness. Cut into 12 (3-inch) rounds. Place 1 teaspoon jam in center of half of rounds; brush edge with egg white. Top with remaining rounds, and press together firmly to seal. Arrange on floured cookie sheet. Repeat with rest of dough.

8. Cover with towel; let rise until double in bulk— about 45 minutes.

9. Meanwhile, in deep-fat fryer or heavy skillet, slowly heat salad oil (2 inches deep) to 350F on deep-frying thermometer.

10. Gently drop doughnuts, 3 or 4 at a time, into hot oil. Fry, turning as they rise to surface, turning once again, until golden-brown—about 4 minutes in all. (Break one open to test for doneness; fry others longer if necessary.)

11. Remove with slotted utensil. Drain on paper towels. While still warm, dust with sugar.

Makes 12.

Batter Breads

The easiest and quickest yeast breads to make are batter breads. In these the batters are beaten vigorously instead of being kneaded. For this reason they have a more open, lacy texture, and the top and break will be more uneven. In color, aroma, flavor and all-around goodness, they are comparable to kneaded breads. However, they do not keep as well and are best when freshly baked.

Honey Whole Wheat Casserole Bread

1 cup milk
3/4 cup shortening
1/2 cup honey
2 teaspoons salt
2 pkg active dry yeast
3/4 cup warm water (105 to 115F)
3 eggs, slightly beaten
4-1/2 cups unsifted all-purpose flour
1-1/2 cups whole-wheat flour
1 teaspoon soft butter or margarine

1. In small saucepan, heat milk until bubbles form around edge of pan; remove from heat. Stir in shortening, honey, and salt until shortening is melted. Cool to lukewarm.

2. Sprinkle yeast over warm water in large bowl; stir until yeast is dissolved. Stir in milk mixture and eggs.

3. Combine all-purpose and whole-wheat flours. Add two thirds flour mixture to yeast mixture; with electric mixer at low speed, beat until blended. Then beat at medium speed until smooth—about 2 minutes. With wooden spoon, gradually beat in remaining flour mixture. Then beat, stretching dough 20 to 30 times.

4. Cover with waxed paper and a towel. Let rise in warm place (85F), free from drafts, until double in bulk—about 1 hour.

5. Lightly grease a 2-1/2- or 3-quart casserole or heatproof bowl. Punch down dough, and beat with spoon until smooth—about 30 seconds. Turn into casserole. Cover, and let rise until double in bulk—20 to 30 minutes.

6. Preheat oven to 375F.

7. With a sharp knife, cut a 4-inch cross about 1/2 inch deep in top of dough.

8. Bake 45 to 50 minutes, or until bread is nicely browned and sounds hollow when rapped with knuckle.

9. Remove from casserole to wire rack. Rub butter over top of bread. Serve slightly warm. Cut in wedges.

Makes 1 round loaf.

Virginia Sally Lunn

1 cup milk
2 tablespoons sugar
1 teaspoon salt
1/3 cup butter or regular margarine
1/2 cup warm water (105 to 115F)
1 pkg active dry yeast
3 eggs
4 cups sifted* all-purpose flour
* Sift before measuring.

1. In small saucepan, heat milk until bubbles form around edge of pan; remove from heat.
2. Add sugar, salt, and butter, stirring until butter is melted; let cool to lukewarm.
3. If possible, check temperature of warm water with thermometer. Sprinkle yeast over water in large bowl of electric mixer; stir to dissolve.
4. Add milk mixture, eggs, and all of flour; at medium speed, beat till smooth—2 minutes.
5. Cover with waxed paper and towel; let rise in warm place (85F), free from drafts, until double in bulk and bubbly—about 1 hour.
6. Grease two 9-by-5-by-3-inch loaf pans.
7. With wooden spoon, beat batter vigorously 1/2 minute. Pour batter evenly into prepared pans. Cover with towel; let rise in warm place (85F), free from drafts, to within 1 inch of tops of pans—about 45 minutes.
8. Meanwhile, preheat oven to 350F.
9. Bake loaves 35 to 40 minutes, or until golden-brown. Remove from pans to wire rack. Serve hot, slicing with a serrated knife.
Makes 2 loaves.

Anadama Batter Bread

3/4 cup boiling water
1/2 cup yellow cornmeal
3 tablespoons shortening
1/4 cup light molasses
2 teaspoons salt
1/4 cup warm water (105 to 115F)
1 pkg active dry yeast
1 egg
2-3/4 cups sifted* all-purpose flour
1/4 teaspoon salt
1 teaspoon yellow cornmeal
1 teaspoon soft butter or regular margarine
* Sift before measuring.

1. Lightly grease a 9-by-5-by-3-inch loaf pan.
2. In large bowl, pour boiling water over cornmeal. Stir in shortening, molasses, and salt; let cool to lukewarm.
3. If possible, check temperature of warm water with thermometer. Sprinkle yeast over warm water in large bowl of electric mixer, stirring until dissolved. Stir into cornmeal mixture.
4. Add egg and half the flour; beat 2 minutes at medium speed, frequently scraping down side of bowl and beaters with rubber scraper. Add rest of flour; beat 1 minute longer.
5. Spread batter evenly in prepared pan, using a buttered spatula to smooth top. Cover with towel; let rise in warm place (85F), free from drafts, until double in bulk—about 1-1/2 hours. Then sprinkle top with salt and cornmeal.
6. Meanwhile, preheat oven to 375F.
7. Bake loaf 50 to 55 minutes, or until it sounds hollow when rapped with knuckle. Remove from pan to wire rack. Brush top with butter; cool completely.
Makes 1 loaf.

Brioche

1/2 cup warm water (105 to 115F)
1 pkg active dry yeast
1/4 cup sugar
1 teaspoon salt
1 teaspoon grated lemon peel
1 cup soft butter or regular margarine
6 eggs
4-1/2 cups sifted* all-purpose flour
1 egg yolk
* Sift before measuring.

1. If possible, check temperature of warm water with thermometer. Sprinkle yeast over water in large bowl of electric mixer; stir until dissolved.

2. Add sugar, salt, lemon peel, butter, 6 eggs, and 3 cups flour; at medium speed, beat 4 minutes. Add remaining flour; at low speed, beat until smooth—about 2 minutes.

3. Cover bowl with waxed paper and damp towel; let rise in warm place (85F), free from drafts, until double in bulk—about 1 hour. Refrigerate, covered, overnight.

4. Next day, grease 24 (3-inch) muffin-pan cups.

5. Stir down dough with wooden spoon. Dough will be soft. Turn out onto lightly floured board; divide in half. Return half to bowl; refrigerate until ready to use.

6. Working quickly, shape three fourths of dough on board into a 12-inch roll. With floured knife, cut into 12 pieces. Shape each into ball; place in prepared muffin cup.

7. Divide other fourth of dough into 12 parts; shape into balls. With finger, press indentation in center of each large ball; fill with small ball.

8. Cover with towel; let rise in warm place (85F), free from drafts, until double in bulk—about 1 hour.

9. Meanwhile, shape refrigerated half of dough, and let rise, as directed.

10. Preheat oven to 400F.

11. Combine egg yolk with 1 tablespoon water; brush on Brioche. Bake 15 to 20 minutes, or until golden-brown. Serve hot or cold.

Makes 24.

Cakes & Frostings

Cake baking is still very much an art—a very demanding and precise one.

For best results, first read the recipe all the way through. Follow the recipe exactly. Don't make substitutions or changes. Since accurate measurements are essential, use standard measuring cups, spoons and cake pans.

Notes on Cakes

1. All our cake recipes were tested using sifted all-purpose or cake flour, unless stated otherwise. This means that the flour must be sifted before measuring.

2. Our cake recipes were tested using double-acting baking powder.

3. When a recipe calls for shortening, use one of the soft emulsifier types, such as Snowdrift, Crisco, Spry, or Fluffo.

4. Do not substitute shortening in recipes that specifically call for butter or margarine.

5. Our cake recipes were tested using large eggs.

6. Make sure all ingredients are at room temperature.

7. For best results, use only pans that are the size recommended in the recipe. To measure pans: For diameter, width, or length, measure across the top of pan with ruler, from one inside edge to the other. For depth, measure inside of side wall.

8. To ensure even and delicate browning of cakes, use metal cake pans with a bright, shiny finish. If using oven-glass cake dishes, decrease oven temperature 25 degrees, to prevent overbrowning.

9. If baking a single cake, place on rack in center of oven. If baking two layers, place both on same rack in center of oven, being careful pans do not touch sides of oven or each other. If baking three layers, adjust oven racks to divide oven into thirds; do not place one pan directly over another.

10. Do not open oven door to test cake until minimum baking time has elapsed.

TEST FOR DONENESS

1. Cake will have shrunk slightly from side of pan.
2. Surface will spring back when gently pressed with fingertip.
3. A wire cake tester or wooden pick inserted near center will come out clean.

TO REMOVE CAKES FROM PANS

Layer Cakes: Carefully run a knife or metal spatula around edge of cake, to loosen from pan; invert on wire rack; remove pan. Then place another wire rack on top of cake; invert again, so cake cools right side up.

Tube Cakes: Using an up-and-down motion, run a knife or metal spatula carefully around edge of cake and around tube, to loosen cake from pan. If tube pan does not have a lift-out bottom, hit pan sharply on table; then invert pan, and turn out cake.

TO CUT CAKES

Angel-Food, Chiffon, and Sponge Cakes: Use a knife with a serrated edge. Cut cake gently, back and forth, with a sawing motion.

Frosted Layer Cakes: Use a knife with a thin, sharp edge. Rinse knife in hot water after making each cut.

TO FREEZE CAKES

Kinds to Freeze: All types of unfrosted cake may be frozen.

Frosted Cakes: Cakes frosted with butter or fudge frostings may be frozen successfully. Do not freeze cakes with whipped-cream or fluffy frostings. Freeze cakes, unwrapped, until frosting is firm; then wrap in freezer wrap; label, and freeze. If possible, place wrapped cake in a box when freezing, to prevent crushing.

Unfrosted Cakes: Wrap completely cooled cakes in freezer wrap; label, and freeze. When freezing layer cakes, wrap each layer separately. If possible, place wrapped cake in a box when freezing, to prevent crushing.

Length of Storage: Unfrosted cakes may be stored in freezer 2 to 3 months. Frosted cake may be stored only 1 to 2 months.

TO THAW CAKES

Unfrosted Layers: Let stand, still wrapped, at room temperature about 1 hour. Let larger cakes stand, still wrapped, about 2 hours.

Frosted Cakes: Remove freezer wrap. Let stand at room temperature until thawed—about 2 hours.

TO STORE CAKES

Cover loosely with moistureproof wrap; or place under a "cake saver" or large, inverted bowl, or in a tightly covered cake tin. Store cakes with whipped-cream or cream fillings in refrigerator.

One-Bowl or "Quick" Cakes

One-bowl cakes are those in which the ingredients are mixed in one bowl according to a strict formula. They are a good choice for the apprentice cake baker as they are the easiest type to make other than a cake mix. They are at their best when freshly baked; they do not keep as well as the other types of cakes.

McCall's Best Gold Cake

2-1/2 cups sifted* cake flour
1-1/2 cups sugar
1 teaspoon salt
3 teaspoons baking powder
1/2 cup shortening
1-1/4 cups milk
5 egg yolks (1/2 cup)
1 teaspoon vanilla extract, or 2 teaspoons grated lemon peel, or 1 tablespoon grated orange peel
* Sift before measuring.

1. Preheat oven to 350F. Grease well and flour three 8-by-1-1/2-inch layer-cake pans, or two 9-by-1-1/2-inch layer-cake pans, or a 13-by-9-by-2-inch baking pan.
2. Into large bowl of electric mixer, sift flour with sugar, salt, and baking powder.
3. Add shortening and 3/4 cup milk. At medium speed, beat 2 minutes, occasionally scraping side of bowl and guiding mixture into beaters with rubber scraper.
4. Add egg yolks, vanilla, and remaining milk; beat 2 minutes longer.
5. Pour batter into prepared pans; bake layers 30 to 35 minutes; oblong 35 to 40 minutes; or until surface springs back when gently pressed with fingertip.
6. Cool in pans 10 minutes. Remove from pans; cool thoroughly on wire racks. Fill and frost as desired.

Applesauce-Date Cake

2 cups unsifted all-purpose flour
2 teaspoons baking soda
1 teaspoon cinnamon
1/2 teaspoon allspice
1/2 teaspoon nutmeg
1/4 teaspoon cloves
1/4 teaspoon salt
2 eggs
1 cup light-brown sugar, firmly packed
1/2 cup butter or regular margarine, softened
2 cups hot applesauce
1 cup chopped dates
3/4 cup coarsely chopped walnuts
1/2 recipe for Cream Cheese Frosting, page 141

1. Preheat oven to 350F. Grease well and flour a 9-by-9-by-2-inch baking pan.
2. Into large bowl of electric mixer, sift flour with baking soda, cinnamon, allspice, nutmeg, cloves, and salt. Then add the eggs, brown sugar, soft butter, and 1 cup hot applesauce; at low speed, beat just until the ingredients are combined.
3. At medium speed, beat 2 minutes longer, occasionally scraping the side of the bowl and guiding mixture into the beater with a rubber scraper.
4. Add remaining applesauce, dates, and walnuts; beat 1 minute. Pour batter into prepared pan.
5. Bake 50 minutes, or until cake tester inserted in center comes out clean. Let cool in pan 10 minutes. Remove from pan, and let cool on wire rack.
6. Frost top of cooled cake with Cream-Cheese Frosting. Cut into 9 squares.
Makes 9 servings.

Favorite One-Egg Cake

2 cups sifted* cake flour
1 cup sugar
2-1/2 teaspoons baking powder
1 teaspoon salt
1/3 cup shortening
1 cup milk
1 egg
1 teaspoon vanilla extract
* Sift before measuring.

1. Preheat oven to 350F. Grease well and flour two 8-by-1-1/2-inch layer-cake pans, or a 9-by-9-by-1-3/4-inch baking pan.
2. Into large bowl of electric mixer, sift flour with sugar, baking powder, and salt.
3. Add shortening and milk. At medium speed, beat 2 minutes, occasionally scraping side of bowl and guiding mixture into beaters with rubber scraper.
4. Add egg and vanilla; beat 2 minutes longer.
5. Pour batter into prepared pans; bake layers 25 to 30 minutes; square 30 to 35 minutes; or until surface springs back when gently pressed with fingertip.
6. Cool in pans 10 minutes. Remove from pans; cool thoroughly on wire racks. Fill and frost as desired.

Silvery White Cake

4 egg whites
2-1/4 cups sifted* cake flour
1-1/2 cups sugar
3-1/2 teaspoons baking powder
1 teaspoon salt
1/2 cup shortening
1 cup milk
1-1/2 teaspoons vanilla extract, or 1 teaspoon
   vanilla extract plus 1/4 teaspoon almond extract
* Sift before measuring.

1. In small bowl, let egg whites warm to room temperature—about 1 hour.
2. Meanwhile, preheat oven to 350F. Grease well and flour two 8-by-1-1/2-inch layer-cake pans, or two 9-by-1-1/2-inch layer-cake pans, or a 13-by-9-by-2-inch baking pan; or line bottoms of pans with waxed paper and grease.
3. Into large bowl of electric mixer, sift flour with sugar, baking powder, and salt.
4. Add shortening, 3/4 cup milk, and vanilla. At low speed, beat only until ingredients are combined.
5. At medium speed, beat 2 minutes, occasionally scraping side of bowl and guiding mixture into beaters with rubber scraper.
6. Add unbeaten egg whites and rest of milk; beat 2 minutes longer.
7. Pour batter into prepared pans; bake layers 30 to 35 minutes; oblong 35 to 40 minutes; or until surface springs back when gently pressed with fingertip.
8. Cool in pans 10 minutes. Remove from pans; cool thoroughly on wire racks. Fill and frost as desired.

Sour-Cream Fudge Cake

2 squares unsweetened chocolate
2 cups sifted* cake flour
1-1/2 cups sugar
1 teaspoon baking soda
1 teaspoon salt
1/2 cup shortening
1 cup dairy sour cream
2 eggs
1 teaspoon vanilla extract
* Sift before measuring.

1. Preheat oven to 350F. Grease well and flour two 8-by-1-1/2-inch layer-cake pans, or a 13-by-9-by-2-inch baking pan.
2. Melt chocolate over hot, not boiling, water; let cool.
3. Into large bowl of electric mixer, sift flour with sugar, soda, and salt.
4. Add shortening and sour cream. At medium speed, beat 2 minutes, occasionally scraping side of bowl and guiding mixture into beaters with rubber scraper.
5. Add eggs, vanilla, chocolate, and 1/4 cup hot water; beat 2 minutes longer.
6. Pour batter into prepared pans; bake layers 30 to 35 minutes; oblong 35 to 40 minutes; or until surface springs back when gently pressed with fingertip.
7. Cool in pans 10 minutes. Remove from pans; cool thoroughly on wire racks. Fill and frost as desired.

Scotch Chocolate Cake Squares

2 cups sifted* all-purpose flour
2 cups granulated sugar
1/2 teaspoon salt
1/2 cup regular margarine
1/2 cup shortening
1/4 cup unsweetened cocoa
2 eggs, slightly beaten
1/2 cup buttermilk
1 teaspoon baking soda
1 teaspoon cinnamon
1 teaspoon vanilla extract

Icing:
1/2 cup regular margarine
1/4 cup unsweetened cocoa
6 tablespoons milk
1 pkg (1 lb) confectioners' sugar
1 teaspoon vanilla extract
2 cups flaked coconut
1 cup chopped pecans
* Sift before measuring.

1. Preheat oven to 350F. Into large bowl, sift flour with granulated sugar and salt; set aside. Grease a 13-by-9-by-2-inch baking pan.
2. In small saucepan, combine 1/2 cup margarine, the shortening, 1/4 cup cocoa, and 1 cup water; bring to boiling. Pour over flour mixture.
3. Add eggs, buttermilk, soda, cinnamon, and 1 teaspoon vanilla; with portable electric mixer, beat just until smooth. Immediately pour into prepared pan.
4. Bake 40 to 45 minutes, or until surface springs back when gently pressed with fingertip.
5. Meanwhile, make Icing: In medium saucepan, combine margarine, cocoa, and milk; bring just to boiling. Remove from heat.
6. Add sugar and vanilla; with spoon, beat until smooth. Stir in coconut and nuts. Spread over hot cake as soon as it is removed from oven. Cool in pan on wire rack. Cut into squares.
Makes 15 servings.

Gold Petits-Fours Cake

1-1/4 cups sifted* cake flour
3/4 cup sugar
1-3/4 teaspoons baking powder
1/2 teaspoon salt
1/4 cup shortening
2/3 cup milk
1 teaspoon vanilla extract, or 1 teaspoon grated
    lemon peel, or 2 teaspoons grated orange peel
3 egg yolks
* Sift before measuring.

1. Preheat oven to 350F. Grease well and flour an 11-by-7-by-1-1/2-inch baking pan.
2. Into large bowl of electric mixer, sift flour with sugar, baking powder, and salt.
3. Add shortening, milk, and vanilla.
4. At low speed, beat 30 seconds, scraping side of bowl with rubber scraper. At medium speed, beat 2 minutes.
5. Add egg yolks; continue beating 1 minute longer, or until batter is smooth.
6. Pour batter into prepared pan; bake 20 to 25 minutes, or until surface springs back when gently pressed with fingertip.
7. Cool in pan 10 minutes. Remove; cool completely on wire rack.
Use to make Pink and White Petits Fours, page 134.

Pineapple Upside-Down Cake

2 cans (8-1/4-oz size) sliced pineapple (8 slices)
1/4 cup butter or regular margarine
2/3 cup light-brown sugar, firmly packed
8 maraschino cherries, drained
1/4 cup pecan halves or broken walnuts
1 cup sifted* all-purpose flour
3/4 cup granulated sugar
1-1/2 teaspoons baking powder
1/2 teaspoon salt
1/4 cup shortening
1/2 cup milk
1 egg
Whipped cream
* Sift before measuring.

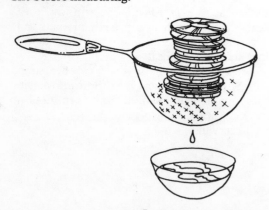

1. Preheat oven to 350F. Drain pineapple, reserving 2 tablespoons of the syrup.
2. Melt butter in a 10-inch heavy skillet, over low heat. (See Note.) Add brown sugar, stirring until sugar is melted. Remove from heat.
3. Arrange drained pineapple on sugar mixture in skillet. Fill centers of pineapple slices with cherries and spaces between slices with pecans. Set skillet aside.
4. Into medium bowl, sift flour with granulated sugar, baking powder, and salt. Add shortening and milk. With electric mixer at medium speed, beat 2 minutes.
5. Add egg and reserved pineapple syrup; beat 2 minutes longer. Pour cake batter over pineapple in skillet, spreading evenly.
6. Bake 40 to 45 minutes, or until cake springs back when gently pressed with fingertip.
7. Let stand on wire rack just 5 minutes. With small spatula, loosen cake from edge of skillet. Cover with serving plate; invert; shake gently; then lift off pan.
8. Serve the cake warm. Top individual servings with whipped cream. Or top with small spoonfuls of vanilla ice cream, if desired.
Makes 8 servings.
Note: If skillet does not have an iron or heat-proof handle, wrap handle in aluminum foil.

Apricot Upside-Down Cake: Make and bake as above, substituting 1 can (1 lb, 1 oz) unpeeled apricot halves, drained well on paper towels, for sliced pineapple and syrup from apricots for pineapple syrup. Arrange apricots, cut side up, on brown-sugar mixture, and surround with cherries and nuts.

Easy Upside-Down Cake with Cake Mix: Make either of fruit toppings in skillet, as directed above. Then prepare a package of 2-layer yellow-cake mix as label directs. Measure 2-1/2 cups batter, and pour over fruit. Turn remaining batter into greased and floured 8-inch layer-cake pan, and bake along with upside-down cake. If desired, freeze plain layer for dessert another day.

"Butter" or Conventional Cakes

"Butter" cakes, since they have a high fat content, are made by the "creaming" or conventional method of mixing. Directions for this method are given in the cake recipes that follow.

McCall's Best Devil's-Food Cake

3 squares unsweetened chocolate
2-1/4 cups sifted* cake flour
2 teaspoons baking soda
1/2 teaspoon salt
1/2 cup butter or regular margarine, softened
2-1/2 cups light-brown sugar, firmly packed
3 eggs
2 teaspoons vanilla extract
1/2 cup sour milk** or buttermilk
1 cup boiling water
Quick Fudge Frosting, page 140
* Sift before measuring.
** To sour milk: Place 1-1/2 teaspoons lemon juice or vinegar in measuring cup. Add milk to measure 1/2 cup. Let stand a few minutes before using.

1. Melt chocolate over hot, not boiling, water. Let cool.
2. Preheat oven to 350F. Grease well and flour two 9-by-1-1/2-inch layer-cake pans; or three 8-by-1 1/2-inch layer-cake pans.
3. Sift flour with soda and salt; set aside.
4. In large bowl of electric mixer, at high speed, beat butter, sugar, eggs, and vanilla until light and fluffy—about 5 minutes—occasionally scraping side of bowl with rubber scraper.
5. At low speed, beat in chocolate.
6. Beat in flour mixture (in fourths), alternately with milk (in thirds), beginning and ending with flour mixture. Beat just until smooth—about 1 minute.
7. Beat in water just until mixture is smooth. Batter will be thin.
8. Pour batter into prepared pans; bake 30 to 35 minutes, or until surface springs back when gently pressed with fingertip.
9. Cool in pans 10 minutes. Remove from pans; cool thoroughly on wire racks. Fill and frost with Quick Fudge Frosting, or as desired.

McCall's Best Chocolate Loaf Cake

1 cup boiling water
2 squares unsweetened chocolate, cut-up
2 cups sifted* all-purpose flour
1/4 teaspoon salt
1 teaspoon baking soda
1/2 cup butter or regular margarine, softened
1 teaspoon vanilla extract
1-3/4 cups light-brown sugar, firmly packed
2 eggs
1/2 cup dairy sour cream
Confectioners' sugar
* Sift before measuring.

1. In small bowl, pour boiling water over chocolate; let cool.
2. Meanwhile, preheat oven to 325F. Grease well and flour a 9-by-5-by-3-inch loaf pan.
3. Sift flour with salt and soda; set aside.
4. In large bowl of electric mixer, at high speed, beat butter, vanilla, sugar, and eggs until light and fluffy—about 5 minutes—occasionally scraping side of bowl with rubber scraper.
5. At low speed, beat in flour mixture (in fourths), alternately with sour cream (in thirds), beginning and ending with flour mixture.
6. Beat in chocolate mixture just until combined.
7. Pour batter into prepared pan. Bake 60 to 70 minutes, or until cake tester inserted in center comes out clean.
8. Cool in pan 15 minutes. Remove from pan; cool thoroughly on wire rack. Serve sprinkled with confectioners' sugar, or frost as desired.

Clove Cake with Caramel Frosting

3 cups sifted* all-purpose flour
1 tablespoon ground cloves
1 tablespoon ground cinnamon
1 teaspoon baking powder
1/2 teaspoon baking soda
1/8 teaspoon salt
1 cup seedless raisins
1 cup shortening, butter, or regular margarine, softened
2-1/4 cups sugar
5 eggs
1 cup buttermilk or sour milk**
Easy Caramel Frosting, page 140
* Sift before measuring.
** To sour milk: Put 1 tablespoon lemon juice or vinegar into measuring cup. Add milk to make 1 cup.

1. Preheat oven to 350F. Lightly grease 10-by-4-inch tube pan.
2. Sift 2-3/4 cups flour with the cloves, cinnamon, baking powder, soda, and salt; set aside. Toss raisins with remaining flour.
3. In large bowl of electric mixer, at medium speed, beat shortening until creamy. Gradually add sugar, beating until mixture is light and fluffy—about 5 minutes.
4. In small bowl, beat eggs until very light and fluffy. Blend into sugar mixture at medium speed, using rubber scraper to clean side of bowl.
5. At low speed, alternately blend flour mixture (in thirds), and milk (in halves), into sugar-egg mixture, beginning and ending with flour mixture. Beat only until blended. Stir in floured raisins.
6. Pour batter into tube pan; bake 60 to 65 minutes, or until cake tester inserted in the center of the cake comes out clean.
7. Cool in pan on wire rack 20 minutes. Gently loosen with a spatula; turn out of pan onto rack. Cool completely—about 1 hour.
8. Frost with Caramel Frosting.
Makes 16 servings.

Marble Loaf Cake

1-1/2 squares unsweetened chocolate
2-1/2 cups sifted* cake flour
3/4 teaspoon salt
3 teaspoons baking powder
1/2 cup butter or regular margarine, softened
1-1/2 cups sugar
3 eggs
3/4 teaspoon vanilla extract
3/4 cup milk
* Sift before measuring.

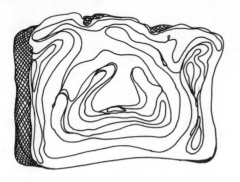

1. Melt chocolate over hot, not boiling, water. Let cool.
2. Preheat oven to 350F. Grease and flour a 9-by-5-by-3-inch loaf pan.
3. Sift flour with salt and baking powder; set aside.
4. In large bowl of electric mixer, at medium speed, beat butter and sugar until light.
5. Add eggs and vanilla, beating until very light and fluffy.
6. At low speed, beat in flour mixture (in fourths), alternately with milk (in thirds), beginning and ending with flour mixture.
7. In medium bowl, combine about one third batter with chocolate, mixing well.
8. Spoon plain and chocolate batters, alternately, into prepared pan. With spatula or knife, cut through batter, forming a Z.
9. Bake 65 minutes, or until cake tester inserted in center comes out clean.
10. Cool in pan 15 minutes. Remove from pan; cool thoroughly on wire rack. To serve, cut in thin slices.

McCall's Best Spicecake

2-1/2 cups sifted* cake flour
1 teaspoon baking powder
1 teaspoon baking soda
1 teaspoon salt
1 teaspoon cinnamon
1/2 teaspoon ground cloves
1/8 teaspoon pepper
1/2 cup butter or regular margarine, softened
1/2 cup light-brown sugar, firmly packed
1 cup granulated sugar
2 eggs
1 teaspoon vanilla extract
1-1/4 cups buttermilk
* Sift before measuring.

1. Preheat oven to 350F. Grease well and flour two 8-by-1-1/2-inch layer-cake pans, or a 13-by-9-by-2-inch baking pan.
2. Sift flour with baking powder, soda, salt, cinnamon, cloves, and pepper.
3. In large bowl of electric mixer, at high speed, beat butter, sugars, eggs, and vanilla until light and fluffy—about 5 minutes—occasionally scraping side of bowl with rubber scraper.
4. At low speed, beat in flour mixture (in fourths), alternately with buttermilk (in thirds), beginning and ending with flour mixture. Beat just until smooth—about 1 minute.
5. Pour batter into prepared pans; bake layers 30 to 35 minutes; bake oblong 40 to 45 minutes; or until surface springs back when gently pressed with fingertip.
6. Cool in pans 10 minutes. Remove from pans; cool thoroughly on wire racks. Fill and frost as desired.

Macaroon Cake

6 eggs
1 cup shortening
1/2 cup regular margarine
3 cups sugar
1/2 teaspoon almond extract
1/2 teaspoon coconut extract
3 cups sifted* cake flour
1 cup milk
2 cans (3-1/2-oz size) flaked coconut
   or 2 cups grated fresh coconut
* Sift before measuring.

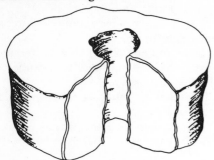

1. Separate eggs, placing whites in a large bowl, yolks in another large bowl. Let whites warm to room temperature—about 1 hour.
2. Preheat oven to 300F. Grease a 10-inch tube pan.
3. With electric mixer at high speed, beat egg yolks with shortening and margarine until well blended. Gradually add sugar, beating until light and fluffy. Add extracts; beat until blended.
4. At low speed, beat in flour (in fourths), alternately with milk (in thirds), beginning and ending with flour.
5. Add coconut; beat until well blended.
6. Beat egg whites just until stiff peaks form. With wire whisk or rubber scraper, gently fold whites into batter until well combined. Turn into prepared pan.
7. Bake 2 hours, or until a cake tester inserted near center comes out clean.
8. Cool in pan on wire rack 15 minutes. Remove from pan; cool thoroughly on wire rack.
Makes 12 to 16 servings.

Walnut-Raisin Cake

1 cup seedless raisins
1 cup walnuts
1 teaspoon baking soda
1 cup boiling water
1-1/2 cups sifted* all-purpose flour
1 teaspoon cinnamon
1/4 teaspoon salt
1/2 cup butter or regular margarine
1 cup sugar
1 egg
2 egg yolks
1 teaspoon lemon juice
1 teaspoon vanilla extract
Easy Caramel Frosting, page 140
Walnut halves
* Sift before measuring.

1. Preheat oven to 325F. Grease lightly, with butter, a 9-by-5-by-3-inch loaf-pan.
2. Coarsely chop raisins and 1 cup walnuts; place in medium bowl. Add baking soda; then stir in boiling water. Set aside.
3. Sift flour with cinnamon and salt. Set aside.
4. In large bowl, with electric mixer at medium speed, beat butter until creamy. Add sugar, a little at a time, beating until light and fluffy. Stop beater once or twice; scrape down side of bowl with rubber spatula.
5. Add egg and egg yolks, one at a time, beating after each addition and scraping down side of bowl with rubber spatula. Beat until light and fluffy. Add lemon juice and vanilla.
6. With wooden spoon, beat in flour mixture, in fourths, alternately with raisin mixture, in thirds, beginning and ending with flour mixture. Pour batter into prepared pan.
7. Bake 1 hour and 15 minutes, or until top springs back when lightly pressed with fingertip and cake has pulled away from pan at edge.

8. Cool in pan on wire rack 5 minutes. With small spatula, loosen around edge. Turn out on wire rack; turn top up; let cool completely.

9. Frost top with Butterscotch Frosting, letting some run down side. Decorate with walnut halves. Or sprinkle cake with confectioners' sugar, if you prefer. To serve, slice in 1/2-inch-thick slices.
Makes 15 servings.

Chocolate Fudge Cake

4 squares (1-oz size) unsweetened chocolate
1/2 cup hot water
1-3/4 cups granulated sugar
Cake flour
1 teaspoon baking soda
1 teaspoon salt
1/2 cup butter or regular margarine, softened
3 eggs
2/3 cup milk
1 teaspoon vanilla extract
Chocolate Butter-Cream Frosting, page 141

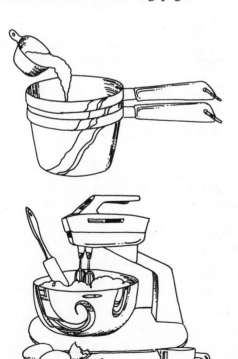

1. Cut 2 waxed-paper circles to fit bottoms of 2 (9-by-1-1/2-inch) round layer-cake pans. Lightly grease bottoms and sides of pans; place waxed paper in pans.

2. In top of double boiler, combine chocolate and hot water. Place over hot, not boiling, water, stirring constantly, until chocolate is melted—mixture will be thick.

3. Add 1/2 cup sugar; cook, stirring, until sugar is dissolved—about 2 minutes. Remove from hot water; let cool while preparing batter.

4. Preheat oven to 350F. Sift flour onto sheet of waxed paper. Measure 2 cups. Sift measured flour with soda and salt. Set aside.

5. In large bowl of electric mixer, at medium speed, beat butter until light. Gradually add rest of sugar; beat until very light and fluffy—at least 5 minutes. Stop beater several times, and scrape down side of bowl with rubber spatula.

6. Add eggs, one at a time, beating well after each addition and scraping down side of bowl.

7. At low speed, add flour mixture (in fourths), alternately with milk (in thirds), beginning and ending with flour mixture. Beat after each addition just until blended.

8. Add chocolate mixture and vanilla; beat at low speed just until well blended—do not overbeat. Turn into pans, dividing evenly.

9. Bake 25 to 30 minutes, or until top of cake springs back when gently pressed in center with fingertip.

10. Let cool in pans on wire rack 10 minutes. With small spatula, loosen edges. Place cake rack over one layer; invert; remove pan. Peel off waxed paper. Repeat with second layer. Let cool completely.

11. Just before frosting cake, make Chocolate Butter-Cream Frosting.
Makes 8 to 10 servings.

Tomato-Soup Spice Cake with Cream-Cheese Frosting

4 cups unsifted all-purpose flour
1-1/2 teaspoons baking soda
2 teaspoons cinnamon
1 teaspoon ground cloves
1/2 teaspoon nutmeg
1 cup butter or regular margarine, softened
1 lb light-brown sugar
2 eggs
1 can (10-1/2 oz) condensed tomato soup, undiluted
2 cups chopped walnuts
1 cup dark raisins
Cream-Cheese Frosting, page 141

1. Preheat oven to 350F. Grease a 13-by-9-by-2-inch baking pan.
2. Sift flour with soda, cinnamon, cloves, and nutmeg. Set aside.
3. In large bowl, with electric mixer at high speed, cream 1 cup butter until light. Gradually beat in brown sugar until light. Add eggs, and beat until fluffy.
4. Combine soup with enough water to measure 2 cups; mix well.
5. At low speed, add flour mixture (in fourths), to sugar mixture, alternately with soup mixture (in thirds), beginning and ending with flour mixture. Beat just until combined.
6. Fold in nuts and raisins. Turn into prepared pan.
7. Bake 55 to 60 minutes, or until cake tester inserted in center comes out clean.
8. Cool in pan on wire rack 30 minutes. Turn out of pan; let cool completely on rack.
9. Frost top with Cream-Cheese Frosting. Cut into squares.
Makes 15 to 18 servings.

Oatmeal Praline Cake

1-1/2 cups boiling water
1 cup raw quick-cooking rolled oats
1-1/2 cups unsifted all-purpose flour
1 teaspoon baking soda
1 teaspoon cinnamon
1 teaspoon nutmeg
1/2 cup butter or regular margarine
1 cup granulated sugar
1 cup light-brown sugar, firmly packed
2 eggs
1 teaspoon vanilla extract

Topping:
3 tablespoons butter or regular margarine
3/4 cup light-brown sugar, firmly packed
3/4 cup shredded coconut
1/2 cup coarsely chopped walnuts
1 egg
3 tablespoons milk

1. Pour boiling water over rolled oats in small bowl; stir with a fork, to mix well. Let stand 40 minutes, to cool.
2. Preheat oven to 350F. Grease and flour a 9-by-9-by-2-inch baking pan.
3. Sift together flour, soda, cinnamon, and nutmeg. Set aside.
4. In large bowl, with electric mixer at medium speed, beat 1/2 cup butter until creamy. Add granulated sugar and 1 cup brown sugar, a little at a time, beating until light and fluffy.
5. Add 2 eggs, one at a time, beating after each addition; then beat until light and fluffy. Beat in vanilla.
6. Add rolled-oat mixture, mixing until well combined.
7. At low speed, beat in flour mixture, until completely mixed.
8. Turn batter into prepared pan. Bake 50 minutes, or until top springs back when gently pressed with fingertip.
9. Meanwhile, make Topping: In small bowl, combine all topping ingredients. Spread over hot cake.

10. Return cake to oven. Bake 10 minutes longer, or until topping is golden.
11. Cool in pan on wire rack. Cut into squares. Makes 12 servings.

Sponge and Angel Cakes

True sponge and angel cakes contain no fat or baking powder. They owe their lightness and leavening to stiffly beaten egg whites.

Chiffon cakes are modified spongecakes. The proportion of eggs is lower; baking powder is used for leavening; oil is added for richness.

Jelly rolls are made from a spongecake batter baked in a jelly-roll pan. They must be rolled up while still warm and pliable.

McCall's Best Angel-Food Cake

1-3/4 cups egg whites (12 to 14)
1-1/4 cups sifted* cake flour
1-3/4 cups sugar
1/2 teaspoon salt
1-1/2 teaspoons cream of tartar
1 teaspoon vanilla extract
1/2 teaspoon almond extract
* Sift before measuring.

1. In large bowl, let egg whites warm to room temperature—about 1 hour.
2. Meanwhile, preheat oven to 375F.
3. Sift flour with 3/4 cup sugar; resift 3 times; set aside.
4. With portable electric mixer, at high speed, beat egg whites with salt and cream of tartar until soft peaks form when beater is slowly raised.
5. Gradually beat in remaining sugar, 1/4 cup at a time, beating well after each addition. Continue beating until stiff peaks form when beater is slowly raised.
6. With rubber scraper or wire whisk, gently fold extracts into egg whites until combined.
7. Sift flour mixture, one fourth at a time, over egg whites. With wire whisk or rubber scraper, using an under-and-over motion, gently fold in each addition with 15 strokes, rotating bowl a quarter of a turn after each addition.
8. Then fold an additional 10 strokes; flour mixture should be blended into egg whites.
9. With rubber scraper, gently push batter into ungreased 10-inch tube pan. With spatula or knife, cut through batter twice.
10. With rubber scraper, gently spread batter in pan until it is smooth on top and touches side of pan.
11. Bake, on lower oven rack, 35 to 40 minutes, or until cake springs back when gently pressed with fingertip.
12. Invert pan over neck of bottle; let cake cool completely—about 2 hours.
13. With spatula, carefully loosen cake from pan; remove. Serve plain, or frost as desired.
Makes 16 servings.

Mocha Chiffon Cake

1 cup egg whites (7 or 8)
2 teaspoons instant coffee
1/2 cup sifted* unsweetened cocoa
3/4 cup boiling water
1-3/4 cups sifted* cake flour
1-3/4 cups sugar
1-1/2 teaspoons baking soda
1 teaspoon salt
1/2 cup salad oil
7 egg yolks
2 teaspoons vanilla extract
1/2 teaspoon cream of tartar
* Sift before measuring.

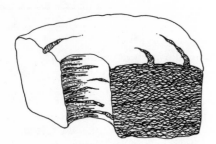

1. In large bowl of electric mixer, let egg whites warm to room temperature—about 1 hour. Meanwhile, preheat oven to 325F.
2. Combine coffee and cocoa in small bowl. Add boiling water, stirring until smooth. Let cool.
3. Sift flour with sugar, soda, and salt into large bowl. Make well in center.
4. Pour in salad oil, egg yolks, vanilla, and cooled coffee mixture. With spoon or portable electric mixer, beat just until smooth.
5. Sprinkle cream of tartar over egg whites; with mixer at high speed, beat until very stiff peaks form when beater is slowly raised. Do not underbeat.
6. Pour batter over egg whites; with rubber scraper or wire whisk, using an under-and-over motion, gently fold into egg whites just until blended.
7. Turn into ungreased 10-inch tube pan; bake 60 minutes, or until cake springs back when gently pressed with fingertip.
8. Invert pan over neck of bottle; let cake cool completely—about 1-1/2 hours.
9. With spatula, carefully loosen cake from pan; remove. Serve plain, or frost as desired.
Makes 10 to 12 servings.

Coconut Chiffon Loaf Cake

1/2 cup egg whites (3 or 4)
1 cup sifted* cake flour
2/3 cup sugar
1-1/4 teaspoons baking powder
1/2 teaspoon salt
1/4 cup salad oil
3 egg yolks
2 teaspoons coconut extract
1/2 teaspoon vanilla extract
1/4 teaspoon cream of tartar
1/2 cup flaked coconut
* Sift before measuring.

1. Let egg whites warm to room temperature in large bowl of electric mixer—about 1 hour. Meanwhile, preheat oven to 325F.
2. Sift flour with sugar, baking powder, and salt into another large bowl. Make well in center.
3. Add, in order, oil, egg yolks, 1/3 cup water, coconut and vanilla extracts; beat, with spoon, until smooth.
4. In large bowl of electric mixer, at high speed, beat egg whites with cream of tartar until stiff peaks form when beater is slowly raised.
5. With wire whisk or rubber scraper, using an under-and-over motion, gently fold egg-yolk mixture, along with coconut, into egg whites just until blended.
6. Pour into ungreased 9-by-5-by-3-inch loaf pan; bake 50 minutes, or until cake springs back when gently pressed with fingertip.
7. Invert cake by hanging pan between 2 other pans; let cool completely—about 1 hour.

8. With sharp knife, cut edges of cake from sides of pan; hit pan sharply on table; turn out cake.
9. To serve: Slice cake into 3/4-inch slices.
Makes 10 to 12 servings.

McCall's Best Daffodil Cake

White Batter:
1-3/4 cups egg whites (12 to 14)
1-1/4 cups sifted* cake flour
1-3/4 cups sugar
1/2 teaspoon salt
1-1/2 teaspoons cream of tartar
1-1/2 teaspoons vanilla extract

Yellow Batter:
5 egg yolks
2 tablespoons cake flour
2 tablespoons sugar
1 tablespoon grated orange peel
* Sift before measuring.

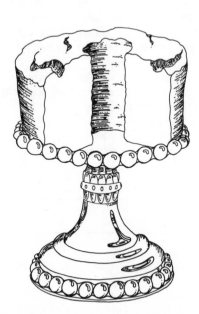

1. In large bowl, let egg whites warm to room temperature—about 1 hour.
2. Meanwhile, preheat oven to 375F.
3. Make White Batter: Sift flour with 3/4 cup sugar; resift 3 times. Set aside.
4. With portable electric mixer, at high speed, beat egg whites with salt and cream of tartar until soft peaks form when beater is slowly raised.
5. Gradually beat in remaining sugar, 1/4 cup at a time, beating well after each addition. Continue beating until stiff peaks form when beater is slowly raised.
6. With rubber scraper or wire whisk, gently fold vanilla into egg whites until well combined.
7. Sift flour mixture, one fourth at a time, over egg whites. With wire whisk or rubber scraper, using an under-and-over motion, gently fold in each addition with 15 strokes, rotating bowl a quarter of a turn after each addition.
8. Then fold an additional 10 strokes; flour mixture should be completely blended into egg whites. Put one third batter into medium bowl.
9. Make Yellow Batter: In small bowl, combine egg yolks with cake flour and sugar. With portable electric mixer, at high speed, beat until thick and lemon-colored. Stir in orange peel.
10. With rubber scraper or wire whisk, using an under-and-over motion, gently fold egg-yolk mixture into one third batter, with 15 strokes.
11. For marbled effect, spoon batters alternately into an ungreased 10-inch tube pan, ending with white batter on top. With spatula or knife, cut through batter twice.
12. With rubber scraper, gently spread batter in pan until it is smooth on top and touches side of pan.
13. Bake, on lower oven rack, 35 to 40 minutes, or until cake springs back when gently pressed with fingertip.
14. Invert pan over neck of bottle; let cake cool completely—about 2 hours.
15. With spatula, carefully loosen cake from pan; remove. Serve plain, or frost as desired.
Makes 16 servings.

Fresh-Orange Spongecake

6 egg whites
1-3/4 cups sifted* all-purpose flour
1/2 teaspoon salt
1-1/2 cups sugar
6 egg yolks
6 tablespoons fresh orange juice
1 tablespoon grated orange peel
* Sift before measuring.

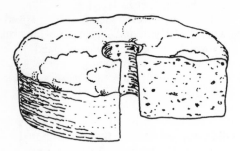

1. In large bowl of electric mixer, let egg whites warm to room temperature—about 1 hour.
2. Meanwhile, preheat oven to 350F.
3. Sift flour with salt; set aside.
4. With electric mixer, at medium speed, beat egg whites until foamy. Gradually beat in 1/2 cup sugar, beating after each addition.
5. Continue beating until soft peaks form when beater is slowly raised. Set aside.
6. In small bowl of electric mixer, at high speed and with the same beaters, beat egg yolks until thick and lemon-colored.
7. Gradually beat in remaining sugar; continue beating until mixture is smooth and well blended.
8. At low speed, blend in flour mixture, guiding mixture into beaters with rubber scraper.
9. Add orange juice and orange peel, beating just until combined—about 1 minute.
10. With wire whisk or rubber scraper, using an under-and-over motion, gently fold egg-yolk mixture into egg whites just until blended.
11. Pour batter into an ungreased 10-inch tube pan; bake 35 to 40 minutes, or until cake springs back when gently pressed with fingertip.
12. Invert pan over neck of bottle; let cake cool completely—about 1 hour.
13. With spatula, carefully loosen cake from pan; remove. Serve plain or sprinkled with confectioners' sugar, or frost as desired.
Makes 12 servings.

Fresh Lemon Spongecake: Substitute 1/4 cup fresh lemon juice for orange juice, and lemon peel for orange peel, in recipe above.

Hot-Milk Spongecake

1/2 cup milk
1 cup sifted* all-purpose flour
1 teaspoon baking powder
1/4 teaspoon salt
3 eggs (2/3 cup)
1 cup sugar
1 teaspoon vanilla extract
* Sift before measuring.

1. In small saucepan, heat milk until bubbles form around edge of pan. Remove from heat; set aside.
2. Preheat oven to 350F.
3. Sift flour with baking powder and salt; set aside.
4. In small bowl of electric mixer, at high speed, beat eggs until thick and lemon-colored. Gradually add sugar, beating until mixture is smooth and well blended—about 5 minutes.
5. At low speed, blend in flour mixture just until smooth.

6. Add warm milk and vanilla, beating just until combined.

7. Pour batter immediately into an ungreased 9-by-9-by-1-3/4-inch baking pan or two greased and floured 8-by-1-1/2-inch layer-cake pans; bake 25 to 30 minutes, or until cake springs back when gently pressed with fingertip.

8. Invert square cake by hanging between 2 other pans; let cool completely. Remove from pan. Let layer cakes cool in pans 10 minutes. Remove from pans; cool thoroughly on wire racks. Serve plain, or frost as desired.

Note: If a larger cake is desired, double amounts of ingredients above. Use large bowl of electric mixer. Bake in an ungreased 10-inch tube pan 35 to 40 minutes. Invert pan over neck of bottle; let cake cool completely.

Jelly-Roll Cake

4 eggs
3/4 cup sifted* cake flour
1 teaspoon baking powder
1/2 teaspoon salt
3/4 cup granulated sugar
Confectioners' sugar
1 cup raspberry preserves
* Sift before measuring.

1. In small bowl of electric mixer, let eggs warm to room temperature—about 1 hour.

2. Preheat oven to 400F. Lightly grease bottom of 15-1/2-by-10-1/2-by-1-inch jelly-roll pan; then line bottom of pan with waxed paper.

3. Sift flour with baking powder and salt; set aside.

4. At high speed, beat eggs until very thick and lemon-colored. Beat in granulated sugar, 2 tablespoons at a time; continue beating 5 minutes longer, or until very thick.

5. With rubber scraper, gently fold in flour mixture just until combined.

6. Turn into prepared pan, spreading evenly. Bake 9 minutes, or just until surface springs back when gently pressed with fingertip.

7. Meanwhile, on a clean tea towel, sift confectioners' sugar, forming a 15-by-10-inch rectangle.

8. Invert cake on sugar; gently peel off waxed paper.

9. Starting with narrow end, roll up cake (towel and all); place, seam side down, on wire rack to cool—20 minutes.

10. Gently unroll cake; remove towel. Spread with raspberry preserves; roll up again.

11. Place, seam side down, on serving plate; let stand, covered, at least 1 hour before serving.

12. To serve, sift confectioners' sugar over top; slice on diagonal. Serve with a bowl of chilled sweetened whipped cream, if desired.

Makes 8 to 10 servings.

Poundcake

Poundcake, delicious and moist, traces its name to its ingredients. The old-time poundcake recipe called for a pound of each of the basic ingredients —sugar, butter, flour and eggs. Our modern versions are adaptations of the original recipe—just as good, less difficult to make.

Walnut Poundcake Loaf

5 eggs
1-1/2 cups sifted* all-purpose flour
1/2 teaspoon baking powder
1 cup butter or regular margarine
1/2 teaspoon vanilla extract
1 cup sugar
3/4 cup finely chopped walnuts
* Sift before measuring.

1. Preheat oven to 325F. Grease well and flour 9-by-5-by-3-inch loaf pan.
2. Separate eggs, putting whites in large bowl.
3. Sift flour with baking powder; set aside.
4. In large bowl of electric mixer, at medium speed, cream butter and vanilla until light. Gradually add 1/2 cup sugar, beating until very light and fluffy.
5. Then add egg yolks, one at a time, beating well after each addition.
6. At low speed, beat in flour mixture only until combined. Stir in walnuts.
7. Beat egg whites, with rotary beater or portable electric mixer, just until soft peaks form when beater is slowly raised.
8. Add remaining sugar, 2 tablespoons at a time, beating until stiff peaks form when beater is slowly raised.
9. With wire whisk or rubber scraper, using an under-and-over motion, gently fold egg whites into batter just until combined.
10. Pour batter into prepared pan; bake 1 hour and 10 minutes, or until cake tester inserted in center comes out clean.
11. Cool in pan, on wire rack, 15 minutes. Then turn out on rack, cool completely. To serve, slice thinly.
Makes one loaf.

Pink and White Petits Fours

2 pkg (1-lb, 1-oz size) poundcake mix*
4 eggs
Apricot Glaze, page 143
Fondant Frosting, page 141
Pink and green cake-decorating tubes
* Or make Gold Petits-Fours Cake, page 122

1. Preheat oven to 350F. Lightly grease and flour a 15-1/2-by-10-1/2-by-1-inch jelly-roll pan.
2. Prepare both packages of poundcake mix as package label directs, using 4 eggs and liquid called for.
3. Turn into prepared pan. Bake 30 to 35 minutes, or until top springs back when pressed with fingertip.

4. Cool 10 minutes in pan. Turn out on wire rack; let cool completely.

5. Meanwhile, make Apricot Glaze and Fondant Frosting.

6. Using a 2-inch heart-shape cookie cutter, cut out hearts from cooled cake. (You'll have 32 or 33.)

7. To glaze cakes: Place on fork, one at a time. Hold over bowl of glaze, and spoon glaze over cake, completely covering top and side.

8. Place cakes, uncoated side down and 2 inches apart, on wire racks placed on cookie sheets. Let stand until glaze is set—at least 1 hour.

9. To frost: Place glazed cakes on fork, one at a time. Spoon frosting over cake, to run over top and down side evenly. Frost half of cakes white and half pink.

10. Let cakes dry completely on wire racks—about 1 hour. Repeat frosting if necessary. Let dry.

11. To decorate: Make little posies and leaves with decorating tubes, or drizzle any remaining frosting over tops. Refrigerate several hours. Let stand at room temperature 1 hour before serving.
Makes 32 or 33.

Chocolate Poundcake

3 cups sifted* all-purpose flour
1/2 cup unsweetened cocoa
1/2 teaspoon baking powder
1/4 teaspoon salt
1 cup butter or regular margarine, softened
1/2 cup soft shortening
3 cups sugar
5 eggs
1-1/4 cups milk
2 tablespoons grated unsweetened chocolate
1 tablespoon vanilla extract
* Sift before measuring.

1. Sift flour with cocoa, baking powder, and salt; set aside.

2. Lightly grease and flour a 10-inch tube pan. Preheat oven to 350F.

3. In large bowl of electric mixer, at medium speed, beat butter, shortening, sugar until light and fluffy—about 5 minutes.

4. Add eggs, one at a time, beating well after each addition.

5. With mixer at low speed, beat in flour mixture, in 4 additions, alternately with milk, in 3 additions, beginning and ending with flour mixture. Add grated chocolate and vanilla.

6. Turn batter into prepared pan. Bake 1 hour and 15 to 20 minutes, or until cake tester inserted in center comes out clean.

7. Let cool in pan on wire rack 10 minutes. Turn out of pan; let cool completely on rack. If desired, serve with whipped cream and shaved chocolate.
Makes one 10-inch cake.

With Cake Mixes

Modern cake mixes are very good and very easy to use.

Here we present some favorite ways to use cake mixes.

White-and-Gold Angel Cake

1 pkg (14-1/2 oz) angel-food-cake mix
1 tablespoon grated lemon peel
1 teaspoon lemon juice
Yellow food color
Confectioners' sugar

1. Preheat oven to 375F.
2. Prepare cake mix as package label directs. Divide batter in half.
3. Into half of batter, fold lemon peel and juice and 10 drops food color just until combined.
4. Spoon white and yellow batters alternately into ungreased 10-inch tube pan. Cut through batter twice with spatula or rubber scraper. Smooth top of batter with rubber scraper, pressing batter gently against side of pan.
5. Bake and cool as the label directs. Sprinkle top with confectioners' sugar before serving.
Makes 12 servings.

Chocolate-Mousse Dessert Cake

1 pkg angel-food-cake mix
1 square unsweetened chocolate, grated

Cocoa-Cream Filling and Frosting:
3 cups heavy cream
1-1/2 cups sifted confectioners' sugar
3/4 cup unsweetened cocoa
1 teaspoon unflavored gelatine
2 teaspoons vanilla extract
1/4 teaspoon salt

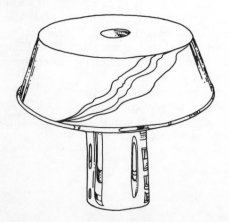

1. Preheat oven and prepare cake mix as package label directs, adding grated chocolate to the flour mixture.
2. Turn batter into ungreased 10-inch tube pan; bake 30 to 40 minutes, or until surface springs back when gently pressed with fingertip.
3. Invert pan over neck of bottle. Let cake hang to cool completely.
4. Meanwhile, make Cocoa-Cream Filling and Frosting: Refrigerate cream, confectioners' sugar, and cocoa (in large bowl) until very cold.
5. Sprinkle gelatine over 2 tablespoons cold water; let stand 5 minutes to soften. Heat, stirring, over hot water until dissolved. Let cool.
6. Add vanilla and salt to chilled cream. Beat with portable electric mixer until stiff enough to hold its shape.

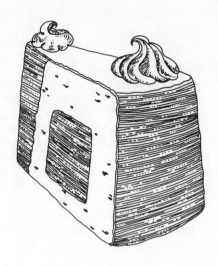

7. Remove 3 cups cocoa cream; into this, stir the cooled gelatine. Use for filling cake.

8. To prepare cake for filling: Remove cake from pan; place upside down on cake plate. Cut 1-inch slice, crosswise, from top of cake; set aside. With knife, outline a cavity in cake, leaving 1-inch-thick walls.

9. With a spoon, carefully remove cake from this area, leaving a 1-inch-thick base. Reserve 1-1/4 cups crumbled cake.

10. Fill cavity in cake with gelatine mixture. Replace top of cake.

11. Mix 1/2 cup cocoa cream with reserved cake pieces. Use to fill center hole of cake.

12. Frost top and side of cake with remaining cocoa cream. Refrigerate until well chilled—several hours or overnight. Just before serving, decorate top with rosettes of whipped cream and grated chocolate, if desired.

Makes 10 to 12 servings.

Neapolitan Cake

1 pkg (1 lb, 2-1/2 oz) yellow-cake mix
1 square unsweetened chocolate
Red food color
Seven-Minute Frosting, page 142 (See Note)
1/8 teaspoon red food color

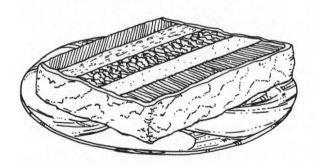

1. Preheat oven to 350F. Grease and flour 2 (9-by-1-1/2-inch) layer-cake pans.

2. Prepare cake mix as package label directs. Measure 1-1/3 cups batter into small bowl; stir in chocolate until well blended. Measure another 1-1/3 cups batter into small bowl; stir in several drops red food color.

3. Turn the plain, chocolate, and pink batters into prepared pans, dividing evenly. To marble, swirl batters together with a spatula, first using a folding motion, then making a Z through batter.

4. Bake 25 to 30 minutes, or until cake tester inserted in center comes out clean. Cool in pans on wire rack 10 minutes. Remove from pans; cool thoroughly on rack.

5. Make Seven-Minute Frosting, as directed; add food color. Use to fill and frost top and side of cake.

Makes 8 to 10 servings.

Note: Or use 1 package (6-1/2 oz) fluffy-white-frosting mix as the label directs.

Frostings

How to Frost a Layer Cake

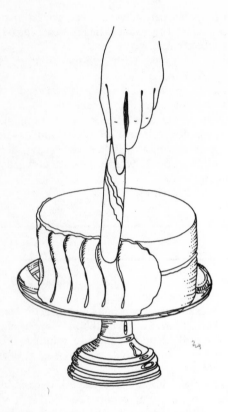

1. Be sure both cake and frosting are cool.
2. Brush off all loose crumbs with a pastry brush; trim off any ragged edges with kitchen scissors.
3. Select a cake plate or tray that will set off the cake to the best advantage. It should be flat and at least 2 to 3 inches larger in diameter than the cake.
4. Cut 4 strips of waxed paper, each 10 by 3 inches. Place strips, overlapping, around edge of cake plate. Invert a cake layer in the center of the cake plate. If there is a difference in thickness of the layers, use the thicker or thickest for the bottom.
5. Using a flexible metal spatula, spread top of bottom layer smoothly with frosting or filling, almost to the outer edge.
6. Place the next layer, right side up, on first layer. Repeat with other layers. If layers have a tendency to slide, anchor them with wooden picks or wooden skewers until the filling has set, before frosting side and top of cake.
7. Spread side of cake with a thin coating of frosting, to set crumbs. Then spread frosting from top edge down over the side, making sure cake is completely covered. If frosting is fluffy or creamy type, swirl as you spread.
8. Pile the remaining frosting on top, and spread it lightly to the edge, swirling it as you spread.
9. If you wish to sprinkle the top and side with grated chocolate, coconut, or finely chopped nuts, this should be done while the frosting is still moist.
10. When cake frosting is set, carefully pull out waxed-paper strips.

Coffee Butter Frosting

1/3 cup butter or regular margarine, softened
3-1/2 cups sifted confectioners' sugar
1 tablespoon instant coffee
3 tablespoons hot milk
1 teaspoon vanilla or rum extract, or brandy flavoring

1. In medium bowl, combine butter, sugar, coffee, and 2 tablespoons hot milk and the vanilla.
2. With portable electric mixer at medium speed, or wooden spoon, beat mixture until smooth and fluffy.
3. If frosting seems too thick to spread, gradually beat in a little more hot milk.
Makes enough to fill and frost an 8-inch or 9-inch two-layer cake.

Chocolate Whipped-Cream Filling and Frosting

2 cups heavy cream
1 cup sifted confectioners' sugar
1/2 cup sifted unsweetened cocoa
1/8 teaspoon salt

1. Combine all ingredients in medium bowl. Refrigerate, covered, 30 minutes.
2. With portable electric mixer at high speed, or rotary beater, beat mixture until stiff. Refrigerate until ready to use.

Makes enough to fill and frost an angel-food or chiffon cake split crosswise into 3 layers; or to spoon over individual slices of an angel-food or chiffon cake.

Mocha Whipped-Cream Filling and Frosting: Combine 2 tablespoons instant coffee with rest of ingredients.

Chocolate Sour-Cream Frosting

1 pkg (6 oz) semisweet-chocolate pieces
1/2 cup dairy sour cream
Dash salt

1. Melt chocolate pieces in top of double boiler, over hot water. Remove top of double boiler from hot water.
2. Add sour cream and salt. With portable electric mixer at medium speed, or rotary beater, beat frosting until creamy and of spreading consistency.

Makes enough to frost top and side of an 8-inch or 9-inch two-layer cake; or top of a 13-by-9-by-2-inch cake; or top and side of a 10-inch tube cake.

Note: To make enough frosting to fill and frost an 8-inch or 9-inch two-layer cake, use 1-1/2 pkg (6-oz size) semisweet-chocolate pieces and 3/4 cup dairy sour cream.

Cocoa Cream Frosting

1/3 cup light cream or evaporated milk, undiluted
1/4 cup butter or regular margarine, softened
1/4 teaspoon salt
1/2 cup sifted unsweetened cocoa
1 teaspoon vanilla extract, or 1/2 teaspoon rum
    extract
3 cups sifted confectioners' sugar

1. In small saucepan, heat cream until bubbles form around edge of pan. Let cool slightly.
2. In medium bowl, combine butter, salt, cocoa, vanilla, 1/4 cup hot cream, and 1-1/2 cups sugar.
3. With portable electric mixer at medium speed, or wooden spoon, beat mixture until smooth.
4. Gradually add remaining sugar, beating until smooth and fluffy. If frosting seems too thick to spread, gradually beat in a little more hot cream.

Makes enough to fill and frost an 8-inch or 9-inch two-layer cake.

Note: If frosting is too thin, set in bowl of ice water. Beat until thick enough to spread.

Quick Fudge Frosting

2 squares unsweetened chocolate
1/4 cup butter or regular margarine, softened
3 cups sifted confectioners' sugar
1/8 teaspoon salt
1/4 cup hot light cream or evaporated milk,
    undiluted
1 teaspoon vanilla extract, or 1/2 teaspoon rum
    extract

1. Melt chocolate over hot water. Remove from heat; let cool.
2. In medium bowl, combine butter, sugar, salt, and 3 tablespoons hot cream. With wooden spoon, or portable electric mixer at medium speed, beat until mixture is smooth.
3. Add chocolate; continue beating until frosting is thick enough to spread. Add vanilla.
4. If frosting seems too thick, gradually beat in a little more hot cream.
Makes enough to fill and frost an 8-inch or 9-inch two-layer cake.

Peanut-Butter Frosting

2 tablespoons butter or regular margarine,
    softened
1/2 cup creamy or chunk-style peanut butter
3 cups sifted confectioners' sugar
1 teaspoon vanilla extract
1/4 to 1/3 cup milk or light cream

1. In small bowl, combine butter, peanut butter, sugar, vanilla, and 1/4 cup milk.
2. With portable electric mixer at medium speed, or wooden spoon, beat frosting until creamy and of spreading consistency. If frosting seems too thick to spread, gradually beat in a little more milk.
Makes enough to fill and frost an 8-inch or 9-inch two-layer cake.

Easy Caramel Frosting

1/2 cup butter or regular margarine
1 cup light-brown sugar, firmly packed
1/3 cup light cream or evaporated milk, undiluted
2 cups unsifted confectioners' sugar
1 teaspoon vanilla extract, or 1/2 teaspoon maple
    extract

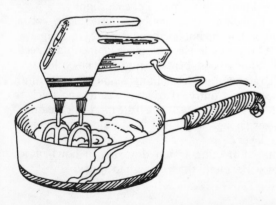

1. Melt butter in small saucepan, over low heat. Remove from heat.
2. Add brown sugar, stirring until smooth. Over low heat, bring to boiling, stirring; boil, stirring, 1 minute. Remove from heat.
3. Add cream; over low heat, return just to boiling. Remove from heat; let cool to 110F on candy thermometer, or until bottom of saucepan feels lukewarm.
4. With portable electric mixer at medium speed, or wooden spoon, beat in 2 cups confectioners' sugar until frosting is thick. If frosting seems too thin to spread, gradually beat in a little more confectioners' sugar. Add vanilla.
5. Set in bowl of ice water; beat until frosting is thick enough to spread and barely holds its shape.
Makes enough to frost top and side of an 8-inch or 9-inch two-layer cake; or top of a 13-by-9-by-2-inch cake.

Cream-Cheese Frosting

1 pkg (8 oz) cream cheese, softened
1 tablespoon butter or regular margarine
1 teaspoon vanilla extract
1 lb confectioners' sugar

1. In medium bowl, with electric mixer, at medium speed, beat cheese with butter and vanilla until creamy.
2. Add confectioners' sugar; beat until light and fluffy. Spread thickly over top of cake; make swirls with knife.
Makes 2-1/2 cups.

Chocolate Butter-Cream Frosting

4 squares (1-oz size) unsweetened chocolate
1/2 cup butter or regular margarine
1 egg
2-2/3 cups confectioners' sugar
1 teaspoon vanilla extract
1/8 teaspoon salt

1. Fill large bowl half full of ice cubes; add 1/2 cup cold water.
2. In top of double boiler, combine chocolate and butter. Place over hot, not boiling, water, stirring occasionally, until chocolate is melted. Remove from hot water.
3. Quickly stir in egg. Add sugar, 1/3 cup water, the vanilla, and salt; stir until well blended.
4. Place pan in prepared ice water. With portable electric mixer at high speed, beat until of spreading consistency—about 5 minutes.
Makes enough to fill and frost a 9-inch layer cake.

Fondant Frosting

2-3/4 cups granulated sugar
Dash salt
1/4 teaspoon cream of tartar
3 to 3-1/2 cups sifted confectioners' sugar
1/2 teaspoon almond extract
Red food color

1. In medium saucepan, combine granulated sugar, salt, and cream of tartar with 1-1/2 cups water. Over low heat, cook, stirring, until sugar is dissolved.
2. Over medium heat, cook, without stirring, to 226F on candy thermometer.
3. Transfer to top of double boiler; let cool to lukewarm (110F on candy thermometer).
4. With wooden spoon, gradually beat in just enough confectioners' sugar to make frosting thick enough to coat spoon but thin enough to pour. Add almond extract. Remove half of frosting (about 1-1/2 cups) to small bowl. Add a few drops red food color, to tint a delicate pink.
5. Keep white frosting over hot, not boiling, water, to keep thin enough to pour. If frosting is too thin, add a little more confectioners' sugar; if too thick, thin with a little warm water. After using white frosting, heat pink frosting, and use in same way.
Makes 3 cups.

Orange Frosting

2 tablespoons butter or regular margarine, softened
2 egg yolks
1 tablespoon grated orange peel
4 cups sifted confectioners' sugar
2 to 3 tablespoons orange juice

1. In small bowl of electric mixer, combine butter, egg yolks, orange peel, sugar, and 2 tablespoons orange juice.
2. With mixer at medium speed, beat until frosting is smooth and easy to spread. If frosting seems too thick to spread, gradually beat in a little more orange juice.
Makes enough to frost top and side of a 10-inch tube cake.

Orange Glaze: Prepare half recipe, adding enough orange juice so glaze can be poured over top of a 10-inch tube cake and run unevenly down sides.

Seven-Minute Frosting

2 egg whites (1/4 cup)
1-1/2 cups granulated sugar
1 tablespoon light corn syrup, or 1/4 teaspoon cream of tartar
1 teaspoon vanilla extract

1. In top of double boiler, combine egg whites, sugar, corn syrup, and 1/3 cup water.
2. With portable electric mixer or rotary beater, beat about 1 minute to combine ingredients.
3. Cook over rapidly boiling water (water in bottom should not touch top of double boiler), beating constantly, about 7 minutes, or until stiff peaks form when beater is slowly raised.
4. Remove from boiling water. Add vanilla; continue beating until frosting is thick enough to spread —about 2 minutes.
Makes enough to fill and frost an 8-inch or 9-inch two-layer cake; or to frost a 13-by-9-by-2-inch cake.

Coffee Spice: Beat in 2 teaspoons instant coffee, 1 teaspoon cinnamon, and 1/2 teaspoon nutmeg along with vanilla.

Seafoam Frosting: Substitute 1-1/2 cups light-brown sugar, firmly packed, for 1-1/2 cups of the granulated sugar.

Pink Peppermint: Omit vanilla. Add 1/2 teaspoon peppermint extract and few drops red food color. Fold in 1/4 cup finely crushed peppermint candy.

Coconut: Reduce vanilla to 1/2 teaspoon, and add 1/2 teaspoon coconut flavoring. Sprinkle top and side of cake with 1 can (3-1/2 oz) flaked coconut.

Four-Minute Frosting: Make Seven-Minute Frosting, halving each ingredient and beating over boiling water only 4 minutes. Makes enough to frost 12 cupcakes; or top of an 8-inch or 9-inch square cake.

Apricot Glaze

1-1/2 cups apricot preserves
1/2 cup sugar

1. In medium saucepan, combine preserves, sugar, and 1/2 cup water; bring to boiling, over medium heat. Boil, stirring, 5 minutes.
2. Remove from heat. Press through sieve into a bowl.
Makes 1-1/2 cups.

Chocolate Glaze

2 tablespoons butter or margarine
1 square unsweetened chocolate
1 cup sifted confectioners' sugar
2 tablespoons boiling water

1. Melt butter and chocolate over hot water. Remove from heat; let cool.
2. In small bowl, combine chocolate mixture with remaining ingredients.
3. With rotary beater, beat just until mixture is smooth and well combined. (Glaze seems thin, but will thicken on standing.)
Makes about 1/2 cup.

Lemon Glaze

1 tablespoon butter or regular margarine
1 pkg (1 lb) confectioners' sugar
1/3 cup lemon juice
1 teaspoon grated lemon peel

In medium bowl, with wooden spoon, beat butter, sugar, lemon juice and peel until smooth. Then drizzle over cake, letting it run down sides.
Makes 3/4 cup.

Broiled Coconut Topping

1/4 cup soft butter or regular margarine
1/4 cup light cream or evaporated milk, undiluted
1/2 cup light-brown sugar, firmly packed
1 cup flaked or shredded coconut

1. In small bowl, combine all ingredients; mix well.
2. Spread evenly over top of hot 8-inch or 9-inch square cake.
3. Run under broiler, 4 inches from heat, 2 to 3 minutes, or until topping is bubbly and golden. Cool cake in pan on wire rack; serve slightly warm.

Lemon Filling

4 egg yolks
1/2 cup sugar
1/4 cup lemon juice
2 teaspoons grated lemon peel
1 tablespoon heavy cream

1. In top of double boiler, with rotary beater, beat egg yolks with sugar until smooth.
2. Stir in lemon juice and peel; cook over boiling water, stirring, 5 to 8 minutes, or until mixture thickens.
3. Remove from heat. Stir in cream; cool.
Makes 1 cup, or filling for an 8-inch two-layer cake.

Fresh-Orange Filling

3/4 cup sugar
2-1/2 tablespoons cornstarch
1/8 teaspoon salt
1/2 cup orange juice
2 tablespoons grated orange peel
2 tablespoons lemon juice
2 tablespoons butter or regular margarine

1. In small saucepan, combine sugar with cornstarch and salt.
2. Gradually stir in orange juice and 1/2 cup water; over medium heat, bring to boiling, stirring. Boil 1 minute. Remove from heat.
3. Stir in remaining ingredients. Cool well.
Makes 1-1/2 cups.

Chocolate-Custard Filling

1 pkg (6 oz) semisweet-chocolate pieces
1/2 cup soft butter or regular margarine
2/3 cup sifted confectioners' sugar
2 egg yolks
1 teaspoon vanilla extract
2 egg whites

1. Melt chocolate in top of double boiler, over hot water. Remove from heat; let cool.
2. In small bowl of electric mixer, at medium speed, beat butter until light. Add sugar gradually, beating until very light and fluffy.
3. Add egg yolks, one at a time, beating after each addition.
4. Gradually beat in chocolate. Add vanilla.
5. With rotary beater, beat egg whites just until stiff peaks form. With rubber scraper, using an under-and-over motion, fold egg whites into chocolate mixture just until blended.
Makes 2 cups.

Vanilla-Cream Filling

1/2 cup sugar
1/4 cup cornstarch
1/4 teaspoon salt
2 cups milk
4 egg yolks, slightly beaten
1 teaspoon vanilla extract

1. In medium saucepan, combine sugar with cornstarch and salt.
2. Gradually add milk; over medium heat, bring to boiling, stirring. Remove from heat.
3. Add half of hot mixture to egg yolks; mix well. Gradually return to saucepan, stirring.
4. Over medium heat, bring to boiling, stirring. Remove from heat. Add vanilla. Cool completely before using to fill cake.
Makes 2 cups.
Coconut-Cream Filling: Add 1/2 cup flaked coconut and 1/2 teaspoon almond extract along with vanilla.
Chocolate-Cream Filling: Increase sugar to 3/4 cup. Combine 1/4 cup sifted unsweetened cocoa with sugar, cornstarch, and salt.
Makes 2 cups.

Cookies

Cookies are popular the world around. As a matter of fact, they have a very national character. We in this country use many of the recipes brought to us by settlers, early and late. Our repertoire of cookies is, therefore, as rich and varied as our background.

There are dropped cookies, rolled cookies, refrigerator (icebox) cookies and molded cookies, bar cookies—all easy to make, and all keep well in a jar or a covered tin.

Making Cookies

1. Our cookie recipes were tested using sifted all-purpose flour, unless stated otherwise. This means that flour must be sifted before measuring.
2. The back of any large baking pan may be substituted for a cookie sheet. Use greased or ungreased, as recipe directs.
3. If you are baking one sheet of cookies at a time, place oven rack in center of oven. If you are baking two sheets, place racks to divide oven into thirds.

If tops of cookies do not brown properly, move to a higher rack the last few minutes of baking.
4. Bright, shiny baking sheets ensure delicately browned cookies. They should be at least an inch shorter and narrower than the oven, to allow for circulation of heat.
5. Check cookies when minimum baking time is up. To cool, remove with wide spatula to wire racks. Do not overlap.

Storing Cookies

Line bottom of container with waxed paper; place a sheet of waxed paper between each two layers of cookies. Store different types of cookie in separate containers.
Soft Cookies: Store in container with tight-fitting lid. Slices of apple or orange in container help keep

cookies moist. Change fruit often.
Crisp Cookies: Store in container with loose-fitting lid. If cookies lose their crispness, heat at 300F about 5 minutes before serving.
Bar Cookies: Store in pan, tightly covered, in refrigerator.

Freezing Cookies

Drop- or Rolled-Cookie Dough: Pack in freezer containers; label, and freeze. To use, thaw dough in refrigerator until it is easy to handle. Prepare and bake as recipe directs.
Refrigerator-Cookie Dough: Form dough into a roll. Wrap in foil or plastic film; seal; label, and freeze. To use, cut frozen dough into slices, and bake as

recipe directs.
Baked Cookies: All types of cookie may be frozen. Wrap cooled cookies in foil or plastic film; seal; label, and freeze. Fragile cookies should be packed in freezer containers; label, and freeze. To thaw: Let stand, unwrapped, at room temperature 15 minutes.

Mailing Cookies

Select only cookies that will hold up in the mail. Bar and drop cookies are good for mailing.
Wrap each cookie separately in waxed paper or saran. Or put in pairs, and wrap each pair.
Line heavy-cardboard box with foil or waxed paper. Pack cookies in box. Stuff corners and any

spaces with crushed waxed paper, cotton or marshmallows so cookies are secure; place crushed waxed paper on top of cookies. Cover; secure with tape. Wrap in heavy brown paper; tie securely. Clearly print address and return address. Attach "Fragile" sticker.

Drop Cookies

Drop cookies are the easiest kind to make, as they are made from a soft dough and dropped from the spoon directly onto the baking sheet. Actually, "dropped" is a little misleading—the mixture must be stiff enough to be pushed from the spoon.

Dropped cookies can be soft, with a cakelike texture, crisp or even brittle. Their shape is irregular because they spread while baking. Here we give a wide variety of recipes for these delicious cookies.

Benne-Seed Cookies

1/2 cup sesame or benne seeds
1 cup unsifted all-purpose flour
1/4 teaspoon baking powder
1/8 teaspoon salt
3/4 cup butter or regular margarine, softened
1 cup light-brown sugar, firmly packed
1 egg
1 teaspoon vanilla extract

1. Put sesame seeds in heavy skillet. Place over medium heat, stirring constantly, until seeds are golden-brown. Set aside.
2. Sift flour with baking powder and salt; set aside.
3. In large bowl, combine butter, brown sugar, egg, and vanilla. With electric mixer at medium speed, beat until smooth.
4. Using wooden spoon, beat in flour mixture and toasted sesame seeds until well blended.
5. Refrigerate, covered, 2 hours.
6. Preheat oven to 375F. Drop dough by slightly rounded teaspoonfuls, 2 inches apart, onto ungreased cookie sheet. Flatten each cookie with a small spatula.
7. Bake 10 to 12 minutes, or just until lightly browned around edge. Let cookies stand about 1 minute. Then remove to wire rack; let cool completely.
Makes 5 dozen.

Molasses-Raisin Drop Cookies

1/2 cup boiling water
1/4 cup shortening
1/2 cup light molasses
1/2 cup sugar
1 egg, unbeaten
2-1/2 cups unsifted all-purpose flour
1 teaspoon salt
1 teaspoon baking powder
1/2 teaspoon baking soda
1 teaspoon ginger
1 teaspoon cinnamon
1 cup seedless raisins

1. Preheat oven to 375F. Grease well several cookie sheets.
2. Pour boiling water over shortening in mixing bowl; stir until melted. Stir in molasses and sugar, then the unbeaten egg; mix well.
3. Sift flour with salt, baking powder, baking soda, ginger, and cinnamon. Add to molasses mixture; stir to mix well. Stir in raisins.
4. Drop dough by rounded tablespoon on prepared cookie sheets, about 1 inch apart. Bake on top shelf of oven, 8 to 10 minutes. Let cool on wire rack. Store in cookie tin with a piece of apple.
Makes 2 dozen.

Glazed Ginger Cookies

2-1/2 cups sifted all-purpose flour
1/2 teaspoon salt
1 teaspoon baking powder
1/4 teaspoon baking soda
1 teaspoon cinnamon
1/2 teaspoon cloves
1 teaspoon ginger
1/2 cup shortening
1/2 cup light-brown sugar, firmly packed
1 egg
1/2 cup light molasses
1 tablespoon vinegar
1/2 cup seedless raisins (optional)

Glaze:
2 cups sifted confectioners' sugar
2 to 3 tablespoons milk

1. Sift flour with salt, baking powder, soda, cinnamon, cloves, and ginger; set aside.
2. In large bowl, with wooden spoon, or portable electric mixer at medium speed, beat shortening, sugar, and egg until light and fluffy.
3. Stir in molasses, vinegar, and 1/2 cup water. Mixture will look curdled.
4. Gradually stir in flour mixture until smooth. Stir in raisins. Refrigerate 30 minutes.
5. Meanwhile, preheat oven to 375F. Lightly grease cookie sheets.
6. Drop by slightly rounded teaspoonfuls, 2 inches apart, onto cookie sheets.
7. Bake 10 to 12 minutes, or until set. Remove to wire rack; cool partially.
8. Make Glaze: In medium bowl, combine sugar and milk; stir unitl smooth.
9. Spread top of cookies with glaze while still slightly warm. Decorate, if desired, with additional raisins.
Makes about 4 dozen.

Orange-Oatmeal Cookies

1 cup unsifted all-purpose flour
1/2 teaspoon baking soda
1/2 teaspoon salt
1/2 cup shortening
1 cup light-brown sugar, firmly packed
1 egg
1 tablespoon grated orange peel
2 tablespoons orange juice
1 cup raw quick-cooking oats
1/2 cup seedless raisins
1/2 cup coarsely chopped walnuts

1. Preheat oven to 350F. Lightly grease cookie sheets. Sift flour with baking soda and salt; set aside.
2. In large bowl, with electric mixer at medium speed, beat shortening, brown sugar, and egg until fluffy.
3. At low speed, beat in orange peel and orange juice. Then beat in flour mixture just until combined. Stir in oats, raisins, and nuts.
4. Drop by tablespoon, 2 inches apart, onto prepared cookie sheets.
5. Bake 15 to 18 minutes, or until golden. Remove to wire rack; cool.
Makes about 2-1/2 dozen.

Easy No-Roll Sugar Cookies

1 cup butter or regular margarine, softened
1 cup sugar
1 egg
2 cups sifted all-purpose flour
1/2 teaspoon salt
1/2 teaspoon baking soda
1/2 teaspoon cream of tartar
1 teaspoon vanilla extract

1. Preheat oven to 400F.
2. In large bowl of electric mixer, at medium speed, cream butter with sugar and egg until very light and fluffy.
3. Sift flour with salt, baking soda, and cream of tartar right into bowl. Beat at low speed until well combined; beat in vanilla.
4. Drop by rounded teaspoon onto ungreased cookie sheet. Dip bottom of glass in sugar and press cookies to flatten slightly.
5. Bake 8 to 10 minutes, until golden. Cool on wire rack.
Makes 4 dozen.

Rolled Cookies

For rolling cookies it's best to use a pastry cloth on the pastry board and a stockinette cover on the rolling pin. Flour should be rubbed into both and the excess brushed off. Rolled cookies are made from dough stiff enough to roll thin. Thorough chilling of the dough is necessary; otherwise it will be too soft to roll without adding more flour, which will make less tender cookies. The dough should be rolled a little at a time, leaving the rest to chill in the refrigerator.

Brown-Sugar Shortbread Cookies

1 cup butter or regular margarine, softened
1/2 cup light-brown sugar, firmly packed
2-1/2 cups sifted all-purpose flour

1. In large bowl, with portable electric mixer at medium speed, or wooden spoon, beat butter with sugar until light and fluffy.
2. With wooden spoon, stir in flour until smooth and well combined. Dough will be stiff.
3. Refrigerate dough, covered, several hours.
4. Preheat oven to 300F.
5. Divide dough into 2 parts; refrigerate until ready to roll out.
6. On lightly floured surface, roll out dough, one part at a time, 1/3 inch thick.
7. Using 1-1/2- or 2-inch fancy cookie cutters, cut out cookies. Place, 1 inch apart, on ungreased cookie sheets.
8. Bake cookies 25 minutes, or until light-golden. Remove to wire rack; cool.
Makes about 5 dozen.

Old-Fashioned Filled Cookies

Cookie Dough:
3 cups sifted all-purpose flour
1 teaspoon baking powder
1/2 teaspoon salt
3/4 cup butter or regular margarine, softened
1-1/2 cups sugar
2 eggs
1 teaspoon vanilla extract, or 1 tablespoon grated
   lemon peel

Filling:
1 pkg (8 oz) pitted dates, cut up
1/2 cup sugar
1 teaspoon grated lemon peel
1/4 cup lemon juice
1/2 cup coarsely chopped walnuts

1. Sift flour with baking powder and salt; set aside.
2. In large bowl, with wooden spoon, or portable electric mixer at medium speed, beat butter, sugar, eggs, and vanilla until light and fluffy.
3. Gradually stir in flour mixture until smooth and well combined.
4. Using rubber scraper, form dough into a ball. Wrap in waxed paper or foil; refrigerate several hours, or overnight.
5. Divide dough into 4 parts; refrigerate until ready to use.
6. Meanwhile, make Filling: In small saucepan, combine dates and sugar with 1/2 cup water. Cook, stirring and over medium heat, until mixture has thickened—about 5 minutes. Remove from heat. Stir in lemon peel, lemon juice, and walnuts. Cool completely.
7. Preheat oven to 375F. Lightly grease cookie sheets.
8. On lightly floured surface, roll dough, one part at a time, 1/8 inch thick. With floured, 2-1/2-inch, round or scalloped cookie cutter, cut out cookies. Reroll trimmings, and cut.
9. Using spatula, place half the cookies, 2 inches apart, on cookie sheets. Spread 1 teaspoon filling over each cookie; cover with another cookie. With floured fork, seal edges firmly; also prick center of top.
10. Bake 10 to 12 minutes, or until lightly browned. Remove to wire rack; cool.
Makes 3 dozen.

Petit-Four Cookies

3/4 cup butter or regular margarine, softened
2/3 cup granulated sugar
1/4 teaspoon salt
2 egg yolks
1 tablespoon light cream
1 teaspoon vanilla extract
2 cups unsifted all-purpose flour
Confectioners' sugar
Raspberry or apricot jam
Chopped walnuts, pistachios, or pecans
Sliced blanched almonds
Chocolate shot
Candied cherries

1. Measure butter, granulated sugar, and salt into large bowl. With electric mixer at medium speed, beat until mixture is light—this will take about 3 minutes.
2. Add egg yolks, cream, and vanilla. Beat until the mixture is fluffy—2 minutes.
3. Gradually add flour, stirring with wooden spoon until well combined and dough is smooth.
4. With hands or spoon, shape dough into a ball. Place on waxed paper, plastic film, or foil. Flatten; cut in quarters; wrap each quarter.
5. Refrigerate 2 hours. The dough will be firm.
6. Preheat oven to 325F.

Chocolate Glaze:
1/2 cup semisweet-chocolate pieces
2 tablespoons butter or regular margarine
1 tablespoon light cream

7. On lightly floured pastry cloth, with floured rolling pin, roll out one fourth of dough at a time to about 1/4-inch thickness. Gently press together any cracks at edge.

8. Choose shapes, below, and cut as directed. Place cut cookies, 1 inch apart, on ungreased cookie sheets. (If desired, decorate some of the cookies before baking, as directed below.)

9. Bake 12 to 15 minutes, or just until edges of cookies are golden.

10. Remove to wire rack; let cool completely. Decorate, below.

Makes about 6-1/2 dozen.

TO CUT SHAPES
Rounds, Half-Moons, Crescents, Diamonds: Cut dough with a 1-1/2- or 2-inch plain or scalloped round cookie cutter, for round cookies. Cut rounds in half, for half-moons. Cut dough with a 2-inch crescent-shape cutter and with a 2-inch diamond-shape cutter, for crescents and diamonds.

Ribbons: Roll out dough into a long strip 2-1/2 inches wide and 1/4 inch thick. Trim edges evenly. With tines of fork, score dough crosswise. Then, with sharp knife, cut crosswise into 3/4-inch-wide strips.

Sand Tarts: Cut dough as for rounds, above. Cut out centers of half of rounds with small round or other shape aspic cutter. After baking, put one round and one cut-out cookie (lightly dusted with confectioners' sugar) together with raspberry or apricot jam.

Sandwich Cookies: After baking, put two cookies of the same shape together with a little jam.

TO DECORATE
To Decorate before Baking: Sprinkle the unbaked cookies with chopped walnuts, pistachios, or pecans, sliced almonds, chocolate shot, or candied cherries. Press the decorations lightly into cookies.

To Decorate after Baking: Dip ends of cookies in Chocolate Glaze; then dip ends in chopped nuts or chocolate shot.

Or spread or drizzle Chocolate Glaze over cookies; then sprinkle with chopped nuts.

Chocolate Glaze
1. Place semisweet-chocolate pieces, butter, and light cream in top of double boiler. Melt over hot, not boiling, water, stirring occasionally, until smooth.

2. Let stand about 5 minutes. Then use as dip or frosting for cookies. If glaze becomes too stiff to drizzle, place over hot water again.

Old-Fashioned Sugar Cookies

4 cups sifted all-purpose flour
1 teaspoon baking powder
1/2 teaspoon baking soda
1/2 teaspoon salt
1/2 teaspoon nutmeg
1 cup butter or regular margarine, softened
1-1/2 cups sugar
1 egg
1/2 cup dairy sour cream
1 teaspoon vanilla extract

Topping:
1/4 cup sugar
Raisins or blanched almonds (optional)

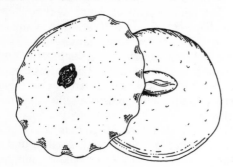

1. Sift flour with baking powder, soda, salt, and nutmeg; set aside.
2. In large bowl of electric mixer, at medium speed, beat butter, sugar, and egg until light and fluffy.
3. At low speed, beat in sour cream and vanilla until smooth.
4. Gradually add flour mixture, beating until well combined.
5. With rubber scraper, form dough into a ball. Wrap in waxed paper or foil; refrigerate several hours, or overnight.
6. Divide dough into 4 parts. Refrigerate until ready to roll out.
7. Meanwhile, preheat oven to 375F. Lightly grease cookie sheets.
8. On well-floured surface, roll dough, one part at a time, 1/4 inch thick.
9. With floured, 2-1/2-inch, round or scalloped cookie cutter, cut out cookies. Using spatula, place, 2 inches apart, on cookie sheets.
10. Sprinkle tops of cookies with sugar. Place a raisin or almond in the center of each, if desired. Reroll trimmings, and cut.
11. Bake 10 to 12 minutes, or until golden. Remove to wire rack; cool. Store in tightly covered tin.
Makes 4 dozen.

Turkish Cookies

1/2 lb sweet butter, softened
1 cup superfine confectioners' sugar
2 cups sifted all-purpose flour
1/4 cup blanched almond halves (about 60)

1. Preheat oven to 350F. Lightly grease several cookie sheets.
2. In large bowl of electric mixer, at medium speed, beat butter until light. Gradually beat in sugar until light and fluffy. At low speed, beat in flour until well combined.
3. On lightly floured pastry cloth, roll out dough to 1/2-inch thickness. Cut into rounds with a 1-inch cookie cutter.
4. Place, 1 inch apart, on cookie sheets. Place an almond half on each. Bake 10 to 15 minutes, until pale golden color.
5. Let cool 1 minute on cookie sheet, then carefully lift to wire rack to cool.
Makes about 5 dozen.

Refrigerator Cookies

Refrigerator (icebox) cookies are made from a stiff dough that must be chilled in the refrigerator until it is firm, so that it can be sliced as thin and even as possible. The great advantage of refrigerator cookies is that the dough, once made, can be kept on hand in the refrigerator almost indefinitely, and the cookies sliced and baked as you need them. Refrigerator cookies are always crisp, buttery, and flavorful—their special taste, of course, depending on the ingredients you use. They're easy to make, convenient to have.

Peanut-Butter Pinwheels

2 cups sifted all-purpose flour
1 teaspoon baking soda
1/2 teaspoon salt
1 cup butter or regular margarine, softened
1 cup light-brown sugar, firmly packed
1 cup chunk-style peanut butter
1 egg
1 teaspoon vanilla extract

Filling:
1 pkg (6 oz) semisweet-chocolate pieces
1 teaspoon butter or margarine

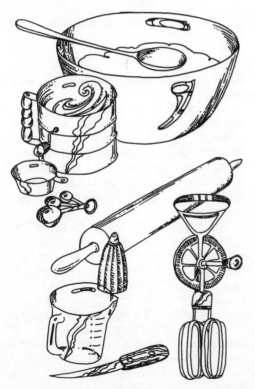

1. Sift flour with soda and salt; set aside.
2. In large bowl, with wooden spoon, or portable electric mixer at medium speed, beat butter until light. Gradually beat in sugar, beating until light and fluffy.
3. Beat in peanut butter, egg, and vanilla.
4. At low speed, gradually add half of flour mixture. Mix in rest, with hands, to form a stiff dough. Refrigerate 30 minutes.
5. Meanwhile, make Filling: Melt chocolate over hot, not boiling, water. Add butter; cool.
6. Divide dough in half. On lightly floured surface, roll each half into an 8-by-10-inch rectangle. Spread each with half the filling.
7. From long side, roll each tightly, jelly-roll fashion. Gently press edge, to seal.
8. Wrap separately, seam side down, in saran or foil. Refrigerate until firm—about 8 hours, or overnight—before slicing and baking. (Rolls may be stored in refrigerator a week or 10 days. Bake fresh as needed.)
9. Preheat oven to 375F. Grease cookie sheets.
10. With sharp knife, cut as many 1/8-inch slices as desired. Rewrap roll; refrigerate.
11. Place slices, 1-1/2 inches apart, on cookie sheets. Bake 6 to 8 minutes, or until lightly browned. Remove to wire rack; cool.
Makes about 9 dozen in all.

Date-and-Walnut-Pinwheel Cookies

Filling:
1 pkg (8 oz) chopped dates
1/4 cup granulated sugar
2 tablespoons lemon juice
1/4 cup chopped walnuts

Cookie Dough:
2 cups unsifted all-purpose flour
1/2 teaspoon salt
1/2 teaspoon baking soda
3/4 cup butter or regular margarine, softened
1/2 cup granulated sugar
1/2 cup dark-brown sugar, packed
1 egg, beaten
1/2 teaspoon vanilla extract

1. Make Filling: In small saucepan, combine dates, 1/4 cup granulated sugar, the lemon juice, and 1/3 cup water. Cook, stirring constantly, 5 minutes, or until thickened. Remove from heat; stir in nuts; cool completely.
2. Make Cookie Dough: Sift flour with salt and baking soda; set aside.
3. In small bowl of electric mixer, at medium speed, cream butter with sugars until light and fluffy. Beat in egg and vanilla.
4. At low speed, beat in flour mixture just until combined. Divide dough in half.
5. Roll out dough, one half at a time, between two sheets of waxed paper, to form 11-by-7-inch rectangle. Spread each rectangle with half of filling.
6. From wide end, roll up rectangles tightly. Wrap each in waxed paper; refrigerate 2 hours or overnight—until firm.
7. Preheat oven to 375F. Slice cookies 1/4 inch thick. Arrange, 1 inch apart, on lightly greased cookie sheets. Bake 8 to 10 minutes, or until golden. Makes 6 dozen.

Oatmeal Icebox Cookies

1 cup sifted all-purpose flour
1/2 teaspoon baking soda
1/2 teaspoon salt
1/2 teaspoon cinnamon
1/2 cup butter or regular margarine, softened
1/2 cup granulated sugar
1/2 cup light-brown sugar, firmly packed
1 egg
2 tablespoons honey
1-1/2 cups rolled oats

1. Sift flour with baking soda, salt, and cinnamon; set aside.
2. In large bowl, with wooden spoon, or portable electric mixer at medium speed, beat butter until light. Gradually beat in sugars. Add egg and honey; continue beating until very light and fluffy.
3. At low speed, gradually add half the flour mixture. Mix in rest, with hands, to form a stiff dough.
4. Add oats, mixing to combine well. Refrigerate 30 minutes.
5. Divide dough in half. On lightly floured surface, shape each half into a roll 7 inches long. Wrap in saran or foil; refrigerate until firm—about 8 hours, or overnight. (Rolls may be stored in refrigerator a week or 10 days. Bake fresh as desired.)
6. Preheat oven to 375F. With sharp knife, cut as many 1/8-inch slices as desired for baking at one time. Rewrap rest of roll; refrigerate.
7. Place slices, 2 inches apart, on ungreased cookie sheets. Bake 8 to 10 minutes, or until lightly browned. Remove to wire rack; let cool.
Makes about 7 dozen in all.

Butterscotch Icebox Cookies

3-1/2 cups sifted all-purpose flour
1 teaspoon baking soda
1/2 teaspoon salt
1 cup butter or regular margarine, softened
2 cups light-brown sugar, firmly packed
2 eggs
1 teaspoon vanilla extract
1 cup finely chopped walnuts or pecans

1. Sift flour with baking soda and salt; set aside.
2. In large bowl of electric mixer at medium speed, beat butter until light. Gradually beat in sugar. Add eggs and vanilla; continue beating until very light and fluffy.
3. At low speed, beat in half the flour mixture until smooth. Mix in rest, with hands, to form a stiff dough. Add nuts, mixing to combine well.
4. Turn out dough onto lightly floured surface. Divide in thirds. With hands, shape each third into a roll 8 inches long.
5. Wrap each in saran or foil. Refrigerate until firm—about 8 hours, or overnight—before slicing and baking. (Rolls may be stored in refrigerator a week or 10 days. Bake fresh as desired.)
6. Preheat oven to 375F. With sharp knife, cut as many 1/8-inch slices as desired for baking at one time. Rewrap rest of roll; refrigerate.
7. Place slices, 2 inches apart, on ungreased cookie sheets. Bake 7 to 10 minutes, or until lightly browned. Remove to wire rack; cool.
Cookies should be crisp.
Makes about 16 dozen in all.

Petticoat Tails

2-1/2 cups sifted all-purpose flour
1/2 teaspoon baking soda
1/4 teaspoon salt
1-1/2 cups soft butter
1-1/2 cups sifted confectioners' sugar
1 teaspoon vanilla extract or rose water

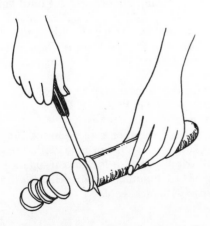

1. Sift flour with soda and salt; set aside.
2. In large bowl, with wooden spoon, or portable electric mixer at medium speed, beat butter, sugar, and vanilla until light and fluffy.
3. Add flour mixture; mix well, with hands, to make a soft dough. Refrigerate 30 minutes.
4. Turn out dough onto lightly floured surface. Divide in half. With hands, shape each into a roll 8 inches long.
5. Wrap each in waxed paper or foil; refrigerate until firm—several hours, or overnight—before baking. (Rolls may be stored in refrigerator a week or 10 days; bake fresh as needed.)
6. Preheat oven to 375F. With sharp knife, cut as many 1/8-inch slices as desired for one baking. Rewrap roll; refrigerate.
7. Place slices, 1 inch apart, on ungreased cookie sheets; bake 8 to 10 minutes, or until lightly browned. Let stand 1 minute. Remove to wire rack; cool.
Makes about 8-1/2 dozen.

Molded Cookies

Molded cookies have somewhat the symmetrical form of rolled cookies but are probably easier to make. The stiff cookie doughs are shaped, sometimes with the palms of the hands, into small balls. Then they are flattened slightly with a floured fork or the bottom of a glass dipped in flour. The more elaborate are forced through a cookie press in many fancy shapes. Most of the doughs should be refrigerated at least an hour before using so they can be handled easily.

Chocolate-Kiss Peanut-Butter Cookies

2-2/3 cups sifted all-purpose flour
2 teaspoons baking soda
1 teaspoon salt
1 cup butter, softened
2/3 cup creamy peanut butter, at room
temperature
Granulated sugar
1 cup brown sugar, firmly packed
2 eggs
2 teaspoons vanilla extract
5 dozen foil-wrapped chocolate kisses

1. Preheat oven to 375F. Sift flour with baking soda and salt. Set aside.
2. In large bowl, with electric mixer at medium speed, beat butter and peanut butter until well blended. Add 1 cup granulated sugar and the brown sugar; beat until light and fluffy.
3. Add eggs and vanilla; beat until smooth. Stir in flour mixture until well combined.
4. Using level tablespoonful for each, shape into 5 dozen balls. Roll each in granulated sugar. Place, 2 inches apart, on ungreased cookie sheets.
5. Bake 8 minutes. Remove from oven. Press an unwrapped chocolate kiss in top of each; bake 2 minutes longer. Remove cookies to wire rack; let cool completely.
Makes 5 dozen.

Finnish Logs

3/4 cup butter or regular margarine, softened
1/3 cup sugar
1 teaspoon almond extract
2 cups sifted all-purpose flour
1/4 teaspoon salt
1 egg, slightly beaten
1/4 cup finely chopped unblanched almonds
1 teaspoon sugar

1. Preheat oven to 350F. Lightly grease cookie sheets.
2. In large bowl, with wooden spoon, beat butter, 1/3 cup sugar, and almond extract until light and fluffy.
3. Add flour and salt; mix well with hands.
4. Turn out dough onto lightly floured surface. With hands, shape into a roll 6 inches long. With sharp knife, cut roll crosswise into 6 parts.
5. With hands, shape each part into a roll 12 inches long and 3/4 inch in diameter. Cut each roll into 6 (2-inch) pieces.
6. Place, 1 inch apart, on cookie sheets. Brush tops lightly with egg; then sprinkle with mixture of almonds combined with 1 teaspoon sugar.
7. Bake 15 to 20 minutes, or until delicately browned. Remove to wire rack; cool.
Makes 3 dozen.

Butter Crisps

3/4 cup sifted all-purpose flour
1/8 teaspoon mace
1/2 cup butter or regular margarine, softened
1/2 teaspoon vanilla extract
1/2 cup confectioners' sugar

1. Preheat oven to 350F. Sift together flour and mace.
2. In small bowl of electric mixer, at medium speed, cream butter with vanilla until light and fluffy. Gradually beat in sugar, then flour mixture; beat just until smooth.
3. Onto ungreased cookie sheet, press dough through cookie press or pastry bag, using star tip. Place cookies 1 inch apart.
4. Bake 15 minutes, or till golden-brown. Cool several minutes; remove to wire racks to cool completely.
Makes about 3 dozen.

Oatmeal-Raisin Cookies

1-1/2 cups sifted all-purpose flour
1 teaspoon baking soda
1 teaspoon salt
1 cup shortening
1 cup granulated sugar
1 cup light-brown sugar, firmly packed
2 eggs
1 teaspoon vanilla extract
3 cups raw, quick-cooking oats
1 cup seedless raisins

1. Preheat oven to 375F. Lightly grease cookie sheets.
2. Sift flour, baking soda, and salt.
3. In large bowl, with electric mixer at medium speed, or wooden spoon, beat shortening, sugars, eggs, and vanilla until light and fluffy.
4. Add flour mixture and oats; beat with wooden spoon until well blended. Stir in raisins.
5. With hands, roll into balls, using a slightly rounded tablespoonful for each. Place, 2 inches apart, on prepared cookie sheets.
6. Bake 12 to 14 minutes, or until golden-brown. Let stand 1 minute; then remove to wire rack; cool.
Makes about 2-1/2 dozen.

Pecan Balls

1 cup sifted all-purpose flour
1/2 cup butter or regular margarine, softened
1 cup finely chopped pecans or hazelnuts
2 tablespoons granulated sugar
1/8 teaspoon salt
1 teaspoon vanilla extract
Confectioners' sugar

1. In large bowl, combine all ingredients except confectioners' sugar. With hands, mix until thoroughly blended. Refrigerate 30 minutes.
2. Meanwhile, preheat oven to 375F. Using hands, roll dough into balls 1-1/4 inches in diameter. Place, 1 inch apart, on ungreased cookie sheets.
3. Bake 15 to 20 minutes, or until cookies are set but not brown. Let stand 1 minute before removing from cookie sheets. Remove to wire rack; cool slightly.
4. Roll in confectioners' sugar while still warm; cool completely. Just before serving, reroll in sugar.
Makes about 20.

Jewel Cookies

1/2 cup butter or regular margarine, softened
1/4 cup light-brown sugar, firmly packed
1 egg yolk
1 teaspoon vanilla extract
1 cup sifted all-purpose flour
1 egg white, slightly beaten
1 cup finely chopped walnuts or pecans
2 tablespoons currant jelly

1. In medium bowl, with wooden spoon, beat butter, sugar, egg yolk, and vanilla until smooth.
2. Stir in flour just until combined. Refrigerate 30 minutes.
3. Meanwhile, preheat oven to 375F. Using hands, roll dough into balls 1 inch in diameter. Dip in egg white; then roll in walnuts.
4. Place, 1 inch apart, on ungreased cookie sheets. With thimble or thumb, press center of each cookie.
5. Bake 10 to 12 minutes, or until a delicate golden-brown. Remove to wire rack; cool.
6. Place 1/4 teaspoon jelly in center of each cookie. (Diced candied fruit may be used, instead of jelly, if desired.)
Makes 24.

Ginger Crinkles

2 cups sifted all-purpose flour
3 teaspoons baking soda
1/4 teaspoon salt
1 teaspoon cloves
1 teaspoon cinnamon
1 teaspoon ginger
1-1/3 cups sugar
3/4 cup shortening
1/4 cup light molasses
1 egg, slightly beaten

1. Preheat oven to 350F.
2. Sift flour with baking soda, salt, cloves, cinnamon, and ginger; set aside.
3. In large bowl of electric mixer, at medium speed, gradually add 1 cup sugar to shortening, creaming until very light and fluffy—about 5 minutes. Blend in molasses and egg.
4. At low speed, beat in flour mixture just until well combined, scraping down side of bowl with rubber scraper. Refrigerate 1 hour.
5. Shape dough into 1-inch balls; roll in remaining 1/3 cup sugar.
6. Place, 2 inches apart, on ungreased cookie sheets. Bake 8 to 10 minutes (no longer), until golden brown. Let stand 1 minute before removing to wire rack to cool.
Makes about 4 dozen.

Almond Lace Wafers

1/2 cup ground blanched almonds
1/2 cup butter or regular margarine
1/2 cup sugar
1 tablespoon flour
2 tablespoons milk

1. Preheat oven to 375F. Grease generously and flour well 2 cookie sheets.
2. Combine all ingredients in a small saucepan. Cook, stirring and over low heat, until butter melts.
3. Drop by teaspoonfuls, 4 inches apart, onto cookie sheets. (Bake only 4 or 5 at a time.)
4. Bake 6 minutes, or until cookies are light-brown and centers are bubbling. Let stand 1 minute.

5. Working quickly, roll each wafer around the handle of a wooden spoon.

6. Gently slide cookie off handle. Place, seam side down, on wire rack; cool. If cookies become too crisp to roll, return to oven for a minute or two.

7. Regrease and reflour cookie sheets before baking each batch.

Makes about 2 dozen.

Peanut-Butter Cookies

1-1/4 cups sifted all-purpose flour
3/4 teaspoon baking soda
1/2 teaspoon baking powder
1/4 teaspoon salt
1/2 cup butter or regular margarine, softened
1/2 cup chunk-style peanut butter
1/2 cup granulated sugar
1/2 cup light-brown sugar, firmly packed
1 egg

1. Preheat oven to 350F.

2. Sift flour with baking soda, baking powder, and salt. Set aside.

3. In large bowl, with portable electric mixer at medium speed, beat butter with peanut butter. Add the sugars gradually; beat until light and fluffy. Beat in egg.

4. Add flour mixture; beat, at low speed, until well combined.

5. Refrigerate dough, covered, until chilled—about 1 hour.

6. With teaspoon, shape dough into balls about 3/4 inch in diameter. Place, 2 inches apart, on ungreased cookie sheets. Flatten with fork, making crisscross pattern.

7. Bake 6 minutes, or until lightly browned. Let stand a few minutes; then remove to wire rack to cool.

Makes about 5 dozen.

Toll House Crunch Cookies

1 cup butter or regular margarine
3/4 cup light-brown sugar, packed
3/4 cup granulated sugar
2 eggs, beaten
2-1/4 cups sifted all-purpose flour
1 teaspoon salt
1 teaspoon baking soda
1 teaspoon hot water
2 pkg (6-oz size) semisweet-chocolate pieces
1 cup chopped walnuts
1 teaspoon vanilla extract

1. In large bowl of electric mixer, at medium speed, cream butter until light. Gradually beat in both kinds of sugar, then eggs, beating until very light and fluffy.

2. Sift flour with salt. Dissolve baking soda in hot water. Add flour to butter mixture alternately with soda. Stir in chocolate, nuts, and vanilla. Refrigerate dough, covered, overnight.

3. Preheat oven to 375F. Lightly grease several cookie sheets.

4. Roll a teaspoon of dough to form balls; place 2 inches apart on cookie sheets. Press flat with fingertips.

5. Bake 10 to 12 minutes, until golden brown. Remove to wire rack to cool.

Makes about 8 dozen.

Date-Nut Rolls

4 tablespoons butter or regular margarine
2 cups sugar
4 eggs
1 cup chopped dates
4 cups crisp rice cereal
1 cup chopped walnuts
2 teaspoons vanilla extract
2 cans (4-oz size) shredded coconut

1. Melt butter in large saucepan. Remove from heat. Stir in sugar, eggs, and dates.
2. Cook over low heat, stirring constantly, until mixture leaves side of pan—about 20 minutes. Remove from heat.
3. Add rice cereal, walnuts, and vanilla; mix until well blended. Let cool. Shape into rolls about 3 inches long. Roll in coconut. Store in refrigerator. Makes about 4 dozen.

Bar Cookies

Bar cookies have a rich, cakelike texture. Easy to make, they store and ship well. They are made in a large pan, cooled, and then cut into squares or bars. Best known, and best loved, of the bar cookies are brownies; we've added some that are less known but equally good.

Chocolate Fudge Brownies

1/2 cup sifted all-purpose flour
1/8 teaspoon baking powder
1/8 teaspoon salt
1/2 cup butter, softened
1 cup sugar
2 eggs
2 squares unsweetened chocolate, melted
1/2 teaspoon vanilla extract
1 cup chopped walnuts

1. Preheat oven to 325F. Lightly grease an 8-by-8-by-2-inch baking pan.
2. Sift flour with baking powder and salt.
3. In small bowl of electric mixer, at high speed, beat butter with sugar until light and fluffy; beat in eggs, one at a time, until very light. Beat in melted chocolate and vanilla.
4. At low speed, blend in flour mixture just until combined. Stir in nuts.
5. Turn into prepared pan, spreading evenly. Bake 30 minutes.
6. Cool 10 minutes. With sharp knife, cut into squares. Let cool completely in pan.
Makes 16.

Scotch Oatmeal Shortbread

3 cups raw quick-cooking oats (not instant)
2/3 cup sugar
1/2 cup sifted all-purpose flour
1/2 teaspoon salt
3/4 cup butter or regular margarine
1 teaspoon vanilla extract

1. Preheat oven to 350F. Lightly grease a 13-by-9-by-2-inch pan.
2. In large bowl, combine oats, sugar, flour, and salt.
3. With pastry blender or 2 knives, cut in butter until mixture resembles coarse cornmeal. Stir in vanilla; mix well.

4. With hands, press mixture evenly into prepared pan.

5. Bake 25 to 30 minutes, or until golden. Cool slightly.

6. Cut into bars while still warm. Let cool thoroughly in pan before removing.

Makes 32.

Dream Bars

Cookie Crust:
1/2 cup butter or regular margarine, softened
1/2 cup light-brown sugar, firmly packed
1 cup sifted all-purpose flour

Filling:
2 eggs
1 cup light-brown sugar, firmly packed
1 teaspoon vanilla extract
3 tablespoons all-purpose flour
1/4 teaspoon salt
1 teaspoon baking powder
1 can (3-1/2 oz) flaked coconut
1 cup coarsely chopped walnuts or pecans

1. Preheat oven to 350F.

2. Make Cookie Crust: In small bowl, cream butter and sugar, with wooden spoon, until smooth.

3. With hands, work in flour until mixture is smooth.

4. Pat into bottom of a 13-by-9-by-2-inch pan; bake 10 minutes, or until golden. Cool on wire rack.

5. Meanwhile, make Filling: In small bowl of electric mixer, at medium speed, beat eggs until light.

6. Gradually beat in sugar. Add vanilla, flour, salt, and baking powder, beating just until combined.

7. Stir in coconut and walnuts.

8. Spread evenly over cooled crust; bake 25 minutes, or until golden and firm to the touch. Cool slightly.

9. With sharp knife, cut into bars while still warm.

Makes 30.

Toffee Crisps

Cookie Crust:
1/2 cup butter or regular margarine, softened
1/2 cup light-brown sugar, firmly packed
1 egg yolk
1 teaspoon vanilla extract
1/2 cup sifted all-purpose flour
1/2 cup raw quick-cooking oats (not instant)

Topping:
3 squares semisweet chocolate
1 tablespoon butter or margarine
1/2 cup coarsely chopped walnuts or pecans

1. Preheat oven to 375F. Lightly grease a 13-by-9-by-2-inch pan.

2. Make Cookie Crust: In large bowl, with wooden spoon, or portable electric mixer at medium speed, beat butter, sugar, egg yolk, and vanilla until smooth.

3. Add flour and oats; stir until well combined.

4. Press mixture evenly in bottom of prepared pan.

5. Bake 15 minutes, or until golden. Cool slightly.

6. Meanwhile, make Topping: Melt chocolate and butter over hot, not boiling, water.

7. Spread over warm cookie crust; sprinkle with nuts.

8. With sharp knife, cut into bars while still warm. Let cool completely in pan before removing.

For teatime, cut each bar in half, to make 48 small bars.

Makes 24.

Filled Oatmeal-Date Bars

Date Filling:
2 pkg (8-oz size) pitted dates, cut up
1/2 cup granulated sugar
1/4 cup lemon juice
1/2 cup coarsely chopped walnuts

Oatmeal Crust:
1-1/2 cups sifted all-purpose flour
1/2 teaspoon baking soda
1/2 teaspoon salt
3/4 cup butter or regular margarine, softened
1 cup light-brown sugar, firmly packed
1-1/2 cups raw quick-cooking oats (not instant)

1. Make Date Filling: In small saucepan, combine dates and sugar with 1 cup water. Over medium heat, cook, stirring constantly, until mixture is thickened—about 5 minutes. Remove from heat. Stir in lemon juice and nuts; cool.

2. Meanwhile, preheat oven to 375F. Lightly grease a 13-by-9-by-2-inch pan.

3. Make Oatmeal Crust: Sift flour with soda and salt; set aside.

4. In medium bowl, with wooden spoon, or portable electric mixer at medium speed, beat butter and sugar until light and fluffy. Add flour mixture and oats. With hands. mix until well combined.

5. Press half oatmeal mixture, evenly, into bottom of prepared pan. Spread with filling. Cover with remaining oatmeal mixture; press lightly with hands.

6. Bake 25 to 30 minutes, or until golden. Cool slightly.

7. Cut into bars while still warm.

Makes 32.

Desserts & Dessert Sauces

The crowning touch to any meal, the most important course of all, according to many people, is the dessert. No matter how good everything else that precedes it, everybody looks forward to what the conclusion will be. Our desserts range from the divinely simple to the simply divine. We've something for everyone—for the traditional, the daring, the sophisticate, the gourmet, the dieter, the kids. In other words, from the simple basic custard to a spectacular creation.

Cheesecakes

True, some of the stars on Broadway have faded away, but Lindy's Famous Cheesecake still lives on for those who would like to bake their own. The recipes for this and others just as fabulous follow.

Lindy's Famous Cheesecake

1 cup sifted all-purpose flour
1/4 cup sugar
1 teaspoon grated lemon peel
1/2 teaspoon vanilla extract
1 egg yolk
1/4 cup soft butter or margarine

Filling:
5 pkg (8-oz size) soft cream cheese
1-3/4 cups sugar
3 tablespoons flour
1-1/2 teaspoons grated lemon peel
1-1/2 teaspoons grated orange peel
1/4 teaspoon vanilla extract
5 eggs
2 egg yolks
1/4 cup heavy cream

Red-Cherry Glaze, page 167, or twice recipe for Strawberry and Pineapple Glazes, pages 167–8

1. In medium bowl, combine flour, sugar, lemon peel, and vanilla. Make well in center; add egg yolk and butter. Mix, with fingertips, until dough cleans side of bowl.
2. Form into a ball, and wrap in waxed paper. Refrigerate about 1 hour.
3. Preheat oven to 400F. Grease the bottom and side of a 9-inch springform pan. Remove the side from the pan.
4. Roll one third of dough on bottom of springform pan; trim edge of dough.
5. Bake 8 to 10 minutes, or until golden.
6. Meanwhile, divide rest of dough into 3 parts. Roll each part into a strip 2-1/2 inches wide and about 10 inches long.
7. Put together springform pan, with the baked crust on bottom.
8. Fit dough strips to side of pan, joining ends to line inside completely. Trim dough so it comes only three fourths way up side of pan. Refrigerate until ready to fill.
9. Preheat oven to 500F. Make Filling: In large bowl of electric mixer, combine cheese, sugar, flour, lemon and orange peel, and vanilla. Beat, at high speed, just to blend.
10. Beat in eggs and egg yolks, one at a time. Add cream, beating just until well combined. Pour mixture into springform pan.
11. Bake 10 minutes. Reduce oven temperature to 250F, and bake 1 hour longer.
12. Let cheesecake cool in pan on wire rack. Glaze top with Red-Cherry Glaze. Refrigerate 3 hours, or overnight.
13. To serve: Loosen pastry from side of pan with spatula. Remove side of springform pan. Cut cheesecake into wedges.
Makes 16 to 20 servings.

Strawberry and Cream Cheesecake

Graham-Cracker Crust:
1 cup graham-cracker crumbs
2 tablespoons sugar
1/3 cup butter or regular margarine, melted

Cheese Filling:
2 env unflavored gelatine
3/4 cup sugar
1/4 teaspoon salt
3 egg yolks
1 cup milk
3 pkg (8-oz size) cream cheese (at room temperature)
2 tablespoons grated lemon peel
2 tablespoons lemon juice
1 teaspoon vanilla extract
3 egg whites (at room temperature)
1/4 cup sugar
1 cup (8 oz) sour cream

Glaze:
1/2 cup sugar
1 tablespoon cornstarch
2 pints fresh strawberries, washed and hulled

1. Make Graham-Cracker Crust: In small bowl, combine crumbs, 2 tablespoons sugar, and the butter; mix well with fork. Reserve 1/4 cup. With back of spoon, press rest of mixture on bottom of a 9-inch springform pan. Refrigerate.

2. Make Filling: In small, heavy saucepan, combine gelatine, 3/4 cup sugar, and the salt. In small bowl, with wire whisk, beat egg yolks with milk until smooth; gradually stir into gelatine mixture; mix well.

3. Cook over medium heat, stirring until gelatine is dissolved and custard is thickened slightly (should form coating on metal spoon)—about 5 minutes. Remove from heat; cool 10 minutes.

4. In large bowl, with electric mixer, at medium speed, beat cream cheese, lemon peel, lemon juice, and vanilla until smooth—3 minutes. Slowly add cooled custard, beating at low speed just to blend. Set in a bowl of ice water to chill, stirring occasionally, until mixture mounds (partially set) when lifted with spoon.

5. Meanwhile, at medium speed and using clean beaters, beat egg whites until soft peaks form when beater is slowly raised. Gradually add 1/4 cup sugar, beating until stiff peaks form.

6. Add beaten egg whites and the sour cream to cheese mixture; beat at low speed just until smooth. Turn into the prepared pan, spreading evenly. Refrigerate until firm and well chilled—at least 4 hours or overnight.

7. Glaze 1 hour before serving: In small saucepan, combine sugar and cornstarch. With fork, crush 2 cups berries. Stir into sugar mixture with 1/4 cup water. Bring to boiling, stirring, until thickened and translucent. Strain; cool.

8. To serve, loosen side of pan with spatula, remove. Arrange some of berries over cake. Top with some of glaze. Sprinkle reserved crumbs around edge. Serve rest of berries in glaze.
Makes 10 to 12 servings.

Glazed Lemon-Cream-Cheese Cake

Crust:
2-1/2 cups packaged graham-cracker crumbs
1/4 cup sugar
1/2 cup butter or regular margarine, softened

Filling:
3 pkg (8-oz size) soft cream cheese
3 tablespoons grated lemon peel
1-1/2 cups sugar
3 tablespoons flour
4 eggs
1/2 cup lemon juice

Blueberry, Strawberry, and Pineapple Glazes,
    pages 167–8
Dairy sour cream

1. Make Crust: In medium bowl, with hands or back of metal spoon, mix graham-cracker crumbs with sugar and butter until well combined.
2. With back of spoon, press crumb mixture to the bottom and sides of a greased 12-by-8-by-2-inch baking dish.
3. Preheat the oven to 350F.
4. Make Filling: In large bowl of electric mixer, at medium speed, beat cream cheese, grated lemon peel, sugar, and flour until they are smooth and well combined.
5. Beat in eggs, one at a time. Then beat in the lemon juice.
6. Pour filling into crust-lined dish. Bake 35 to 40 minutes, or until center of filling seems firm when dish is shaken.
7. Cool completely on wire rack. Refrigerate 4 hours, or overnight—until it is very well chilled.
8. Meanwhile, make Glazes.
9. Lightly mark filling in half crosswise. Then mark each half diagonally, forming 8 sections in all. Spoon glaze evenly over each section. Refrigerate 1 hour before cutting into squares to serve. Pass the sour cream. Wonderful for a large buffet or dessert party.
Makes 12 to 16 servings.

Ratner's Marble Cheesecake

Cookie Crust:
3/4 cup sugar
1/2 cup soft shortening
1-1/4 cups plus 2 tablespoons cake flour
1 tablespoon beaten egg
1/8 teaspoon salt
1/8 teaspoon grated lemon peel
2 tablespoons packaged dry bread crumbs

Cheese Filling:
3-1/2 pkg (8-oz size) cream cheese
1 container (8 oz) skim-milk cottage cheese
   (see Note)
1-1/4 cups sugar
3 eggs
2 tablespoons heavy cream
2 teaspoons vanilla extract
3 squares semisweet chocolate, melted

1. Preheat oven to 350F.
2. Make Cookie Crust: In large bowl, combine 3/4 cup sugar, the shortening, cake flour, egg, 1-1/2 teaspoons water, the salt, and lemon peel. With electric mixer, beat at medium speed until well combined and dough leaves side of bowl.
3. Form dough into a ball. Fit onto bottom of a 9-inch springform pan, rolling lightly with rolling pin to make a smooth surface. Trim pastry 1/8 inch from edge all around. Prick with fork to prevent shrinkage.
4. Bake 10 minutes. Remove from oven; cool on wire rack 15 minutes. Then lightly grease inside of side of springform pan. Sprinkle lightly with bread crumbs, and attach side to bottom of pan with cookie crust. Retrim crust, if necessary.
5. Meanwhile, make Cheese Filling: Increase oven temperature to 400F.

6. In large bowl, with electric mixer, combine cream cheese, cottage cheese, and sugar. Beat at medium speed until mixture is smooth and creamy.

7. Beat in eggs, one at a time, beating well after each addition. Beat in cream and vanilla.

8. Pour half of batter into prepared springform pan. Drizzle 2 tablespoons melted chocolate over batter. With finger, lightly swirl chocolate over surface.

9. Repeat with rest of batter and chocolate.

10. Bake 15 minutes. Remove to wire rack. Let cake cool 45 minutes. Heat oven to 350F.

11. Bake cake 25 minutes longer. Let cool completely on wire rack. Refrigerate several hours or overnight, if possible, before serving.

12. Gently remove side of springform pan before serving.

Makes 8 to 10 servings.

Note: If cottage cheese is moist, drain very well before using.

Red-Cherry Glaze

1 can (1 lb) sour red cherries, packed in water
1/4 cup sugar
1 tablespoon cornstarch
1 tablespoon lemon juice
2 drops red food color

1. Drain cherries, reserving 1/2 cup liquid. Set cherries aside until ready to use.

2. In small saucepan, combine sugar and cornstarch. Add reserved cherry liquid, stirring until mixture is smooth.

3. Bring to boiling, stirring, over medium heat; boil 2 or 3 minutes. The mixture will be thickened and translucent.

4. Remove from heat; let cool slightly. Add lemon juice, cherries, food color. Cool thoroughly before spooning over top of cooled cheesecake.

Makes 2 cups glaze.

Strawberry Glaze

1 pkg (10 oz) frozen strawberry halves, thawed
1 tablespoon sugar
2 teaspoons cornstarch

1. Drain the strawberries, reserving 1/2 cup of the liquid.

2. In a small saucepan, combine sugar and cornstarch. Stir in reserved liquid.

3. Over medium heat, bring to boiling, stirring; boil 1 minute.

4. Remove from heat; cool slightly. Stir in strawberries; cool completely.

Makes 1 cup.

Blueberry Glaze

1 pkg (10 oz) frozen blueberries, thawed
1 tablespoon sugar
2 teaspoons cornstarch

1. Drain blueberries, reserving liquid. Measure liquid; add water, if necessary, to make 1/2 cup.
2. In small saucepan, combine sugar and cornstarch. Stir in reserved liquid.
3. Over medium heat, bring to boiling, stirring; boil 1 minute.
4. Remove from heat; cool slightly. Stir in blueberries. Cool completely.
Makes 2 cups.

Pineapple Glaze

1 tablespoon sugar
2 teaspoons cornstarch
1 can (8-1/4 oz) crushed pineapple, undrained

1. In small saucepan, combine sugar and cornstarch. Stir in pineapple.
2. Over medium heat, bring to boiling, stirring; boil 1 minute. Cool completely.
Makes 1 cup.

Cream Puffs, Crullers, Fritters

To create our wonderful cream puff desserts, begin with a simple chou dough. It's the slight variations in shaping that make all the difference between cream puffs, éclairs, profiteroles, madelons, etc. And when the dough is fried instead of baked, crullers and beignets are the result.

Cream Puffs

Cream-Puff Dough:
1/2 cup water
1/4 cup butter or regular margarine
1/8 teaspoon salt
1/2 cup unsifted all-purpose flour
2 large eggs
Custard Filling, page 171
Chocolate Glaze, page 170
Confectioners' sugar

1. Preheat oven to 400F.
2. In small saucepan, combine water, butter, and salt. Over medium heat, bring to boiling. Remove from heat.
3. Immediately, with wooden spoon, beat in all the flour.
4. Over low heat, beat until mixture leaves side of pan and forms a ball—1 to 2 minutes. Remove from heat.
5. Add 1 egg; with portable electric mixer or wooden spoon, beat until well blended. Then add other egg, and beat until the dough is shiny and satiny—about 1 minute.
6. Drop the dough by rounded tablespoonfuls, 2 inches apart, onto an ungreased cookie sheet.
7. Bake 35 to 40 minutes, or until puffed and golden-brown. Puffs should sound hollow when lightly tapped with fingertip.

8. Meanwhile, make Custard Filling.

9. Carefully remove puffs to wire rack. Let cool completely, away from drafts.

10. Shortly before serving: Cut off tops of cream puffs with sharp knife. With fork, gently remove any soft dough from the inside.

11. Fill puffs with custard; replace tops. Frost tops with Chocolate Glaze, or sprinkle with confectioners' sugar. Serve soon after filling. (Filled puffs become soggy on standing.)

Makes 6 large puffs.

Note: To make double recipe of Cream-Puff Dough: Make as above in medium saucepan, using 1 cup water, 1/2 cup butter or margarine, 1/4 teaspoon salt, 1 cup flour, and 4 eggs.

Miniature Cream Puffs

Drop batter by level teaspoonfuls, 2 inches apart, on ungreased cookie sheet. Bake 20 to 25 minutes at 400F. Proceed as directed above. Fill and frost for dessert, or fill with savory filling for hors d'oeuvres.

Makes 36 miniature puffs.

Madelons

Cream-Puff Dough, page 168
1/2 cup heavy cream
2 tablespoons confectioners' sugar
1/2 teaspoon vanilla extract
3/4 cup cherry preserves
Confectioners' sugar

1. Preheat oven to 400F. Make Cream-Puff Dough.

2. Place dough in pastry bag with number-6 star tip. Pipe, 2 inches apart, onto ungreased cookie sheet, to make 12 S shapes, 3 inches long.

3. Bake 25 to 30 minutes, or until puffed and a deep golden-brown. Remove to wire rack; cool completely.

4. Meanwhile, beat cream with 2 tablespoons sugar and the vanilla until stiff. Refrigerate, covered.

5. To assemble madelons: With sharp knife, cut each S-shape puff in half crosswise. Scoop out any filaments of soft dough.

6. Spoon 1 tablespoon cherry preserves into each bottom half, then a rounded tablespoon of whipped cream; replace top. Sprinkle with confectioners' sugar. Refrigerate if not serving at once.

Makes 12.

Strawberry Profiteroles

Cream-Puff Dough, page 168
1 cup heavy cream
1/4 cup confectioners' sugar
1 tablespoon golden rum
24 large strawberries, washed and hulled
Confectioners' sugar

1. Preheat oven to 400F. Make Cream-Puff Dough.
2. Drop dough by rounded teaspoonfuls, 2 inches apart, onto ungreased cookie sheet, to make 24 puffs.
3. Bake 25 to 30 minutes, or until puffed and golden-brown. Remove to wire rack; let cool completely.
4. Meanwhile, beat cream with 1/4 cup confectioners' sugar until stiff. Stir in rum. Refrigerate, covered.
5. With sharp knife, cut a slice from top of each puff. Fill each with a rounded teaspoonful of whipped cream; press a strawberry into each; replace top. Refrigerate if not serving at once.
6. To serve: On each dessert plate, arrange 4 puffs. Sprinkle with confectioners' sugar.
Makes 6 servings.

Éclairs

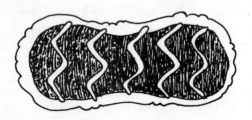

1. Make 1/2 recipe for Cream Puffs.
2. Drop by rounded tablespoonfuls, 3 inches apart, on ungreased cookie sheet.
3. With spatula, spread each ball of dough into a 4-by-1-inch strip.
4. Bake 35 to 40 minutes, or until golden-brown.
5. Let cool completely on wire rack, away from drafts.
6. Slice off tops lengthwise. Scoop out any filaments of soft dough.
7. Fill with sweetened whipped cream, ice cream, or Custard Filling, below. Replace tops.
8. Frost tops with Chocolate Glaze, below.
Makes 6.

Chocolate Glaze

1/2 cup semisweet-chocolate pieces
1 tablespoon shortening
1 tablespoon light corn syrup
1-1/2 tablespoons milk

1. In top of double boiler, combine the chocolate pieces, shortening, corn syrup, and milk.
2. Place over hot, not boiling, water, stirring occasionally, until mixture is smooth and well blended. Let cool slightly before using to frost puffs.
Makes 1/2 cup.

Custard Filling

1 pkg (3-1/4 oz) vanilla-pudding-and-pie-filling
    mix
1-1/2 cups milk
1/2 cup heavy cream
2 tablespoons confectioners' sugar
1/2 teaspoon vanilla extract

1. Make pudding as the label directs, using 1-1/2 cups milk.
2. Pour into medium bowl; place waxed paper directly on surface. Refrigerate until chilled— at least 1 hour.
3. In small bowl, combine heavy cream, sugar, and vanilla; with rotary beater, beat just until stiff. Then fold whipped-cream mixture into pudding until combined.
4. Refrigerate several hours, to chill well before using.
Makes 2 cups; enough filling for 6 large puffs or éclairs or 36 miniature puffs.

Basic Sweet Batter

For Dessert Fritters

1 cup sifted all-purpose flour
1 tablespoon sugar
1 teaspoon baking powder
1 teaspoon salt
2 eggs
1/2 cup milk
1 teaspoon salad oil
1/2 teaspoon vanilla extract
1 teaspoon grated lemon peel

1. Sift flour with sugar, baking powder, and salt.
2. In small bowl, with rotary beater, beat remaining ingredients until mixed.
3. Gradually add flour mixture, beating until smooth.
Makes 1-1/2 cups.

Banana Fritters

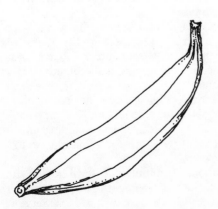

1. Make Basic Sweet Batter.
2. Peel 3 large, not overly ripe bananas; slice on diagonal into 1/2-inch chunks. Sprinkle lightly with lemon juice (1 tablespoon in all) and nutmeg (1/2 teaspoon in all).
3. Meanwhile, in deep skillet or deep-fat fryer, slowly heat salad oil or shortening (at least 2 inches) to 375F on deep-frying thermometer.
4. Roll banana chunks in flour; shake off excess. Then, with fingers, dip into batter, coating evenly.
5. Deep-fry a few at a time, turning once, 3 to 4 minutes, or until golden-brown on both sides. Drain on paper towels.
6. Serve hot, sprinkled with confectioners' sugar, along with slightly thawed frozen sliced strawberries, or with Caramel Sauce, page 216.
Makes about 24 fritters, 6 servings.

Apricot Fritters

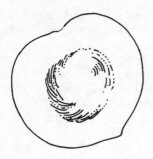

1. Make half of Basic Sweet Batter.
2. On paper towels, drain very well 1 can (1 lb, 13 oz) unpeeled apricot halves.
3. Meanwhile, in deep skillet or deep-fat fryer, slowly heat salad oil or shortening (at least 2 inches) to 375F on deep-frying thermometer.
4. Roll apricot halves in flour; shake off excess. Then, with fingers, dip into batter, coating evenly.
5. Deep-fry a few at a time, turning once, 3 to 4 minutes, or until golden-brown on both sides. Drain on paper towels.
6. Serve hot, sprinkled with confectioners' sugar, with Apricot Sauce, page 215, and whipped cream. Makes about 20 fritters, 5 or 6 servings.

French Crullers and Beignets

Shortening
14 (3-1/2-inch) foil circles
2 tablespoons granulated sugar
1/2 teaspoon salt
1/4 cup butter or regular margarine
1-1/4 cups sifted all-purpose flour
4 eggs
1 teaspoon vanilla extract
Salad oil or shortening for frying
Confectioners' sugar

Apricot Sauce, page 215
Sweetened whipped cream

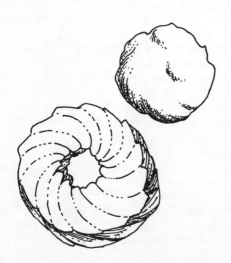

1. Make Crullers: With shortening, grease one side of foil circles very well.
2. In heavy, 2-1/2-quart saucepan, combine sugar, salt, butter, and 1 cup water. Bring to boiling; butter will melt. Remove from heat. Quickly add flour all at once; beat with wooden spoon until flour is moistened.
3. Cook over medium heat, beating until dough forms ball and leaves side of pan. Remove from heat.
4. Add eggs, one at a time, beating with electric mixer at medium speed after each addition. Continue beating until mixture is smooth, shiny, and satiny, and forms strands that break apart. It should hold its shape when beater is slowly raised. Beat in vanilla.
5. To make crullers, turn mixture into a large pastry bag with a number-6 star tip. Press mixture onto greased foil to form circles about 3-1/4 inches in diameter, overlapping ends slightly. Let stand 20 minutes.
6. In electric skillet or large, heavy skillet, slowly heat oil (1-1/2 to 2 inches) to 350F on deep-frying thermometer. Place crullers, including foil, in hot oil, four at a time. Turn each as it rises to top. Lift out foil.
7. Fry about 10 minutes, or until golden, turning several times. Lift out with slotted spoon. Drain on paper towels; remove to wire rack. Serve warm, sprinkled with confectioners' sugar.
8. To make Beignets: Drop batter by rounded table-

spoonfuls into hot oil, six at a time. Fry about 7 minutes, or until golden, turning several times. 9. Lift out; drain. Keep warm in oven, while frying rest. Serve warm beignets with Apricot Sauce and whipped cream.
Makes 14 crullers; 24 beignets.

Custards and Puddings

The old-fashioned custards and puddings, like Floating Island, Blanc Mange, Bread Pudding, Indian Pudding, and all the others so fondly remembered, never go out of style.

Baked Custard

2 eggs
2 cups milk
1/4 cup sugar
Dash salt
1/2 teaspoon vanilla extract
1/2 teaspoon lemon extract
Nutmeg

1. Preheat oven to 350F.
2. Beat eggs and milk together. Add sugar, salt, and extracts.* Mix well.
3. Ladle into 5 ungreased (6-oz) custard cups. Sprinkle with nutmeg.
4. Place in shallow pan. Pour hot water to 1/2-inch level around custard cups.
5. Bake 35 minutes, or until silver knife inserted 1/2 inch into center of custard comes out clean. Be careful not to overbake.
Makes 5 servings.
* Other flavorings can be used: 1/2 teaspoon almond, 1 teaspoon vanilla, etc.

Baked Rice Custard

1/3 cup raw regular white rice
5 cups milk
1 teaspoon salt
3 eggs
3/4 cup sugar
1-1/2 teaspoons vanilla extract

1. In top of double boiler, combine rice, 4 cups milk, and the salt. Cook over boiling water, stirring occasionally, 1 hour, or until rice is tender.
2. Preheat oven to 350F. Grease a 2-quart casserole; place in baking pan.
3. In a large bowl, combine eggs, sugar, vanilla, and remaining milk; beat just until blended. Gradually stir in hot rice mixture.
4. Pour into prepared casserole. Pour hot water to 1-inch depth around casserole.
5. Bake, uncovered, 50 to 60 minutes, or until silver knife inserted in custard 1 inch from edge of casserole comes out clean.
6. Remove from hot water to wire rack, and let cool. Then refrigerate until well chilled—at least 3 hours, or overnight.
Makes 8 servings.

Vanilla Blanc Mange

2-1/4 cups milk
3 tablespoons cornstarch
1/3 cup sugar
1/4 teaspoon salt
1 teaspoon vanilla extract

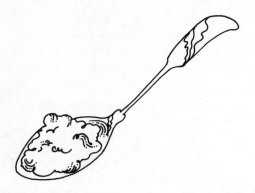

1. In medium saucepan, slowly heat 2 cups milk just until bubbles form around edge of pan.
2. In small bowl, combine cornstarch, sugar, salt, and remaining milk; stir to mix well.
3. Gradually stir cornstarch mixture into hot milk; bring to boiling, stirring. Boil 1 minute, stirring constantly.
4. Remove from heat. Add vanilla.
5. Turn into 6 individual dessert dishes; place piece of waxed paper directly on surface of each. Refrigerate 1 hour before serving. Serve with whipped cream or Strawberry Sauce, page 219, or Quick Chocolate Sauce, page 217.
Makes 6 servings.
Coconut Blanc Mange: Make Vanilla Blanc Mange, adding 1/2 cup flaked coconut to hot milk. Also, use 1/4 teaspoon almond extract, and reduce vanilla extract to 1/2 teaspoon.
Mocha Blanc Mange: Make Vanilla Blanc Mange, adding 1 square unsweetened chocolate, halved, to milk along with 1 teaspoon instant coffee. Heat, stirring, until chocolate is melted. Proceed as directed, increasing sugar to 1/2 cup.
Chocolate Blanc Mange: Make Vanilla Blanc Mange, adding 2 squares unsweetened chocolate, halved, to milk. Heat, stirring, until chocolate is melted. Proceed as directed, increasing sugar to 1/2 cup.

Floating Island

Custard:
2 cups milk
4 egg yolks
1/3 cup sugar
Dash salt
1 teaspoon vanilla extract

Meringue:
4 egg whites
1/4 teaspoon cream of tartar
Dash salt
1/2 cup sugar
1/2 teaspoon vanilla extract
1/3 cup chopped toasted almonds (optional)

1. Several hours before serving, make Custard: In top of double boiler, over direct heat, heat milk until bubbles form around edge.
2. In medium bowl, beat egg yolks with sugar and salt until well blended.
3. Gradually pour hot milk into egg mixture, beating constantly. A wire whisk is handy.
4. Return mixture to top of double boiler; place over hot, not boiling, water. (Water in lower part of double boiler should not touch upper section.)
5. Cook, stirring constantly, until custard coats a metal spoon—about 10 minutes.
6. Pour custard into bowl; press waxed paper right on surface, to prevent formation of skin. When cool, stir in vanilla.
7. Refrigerate, covered, until well chilled—at least 2 hours.

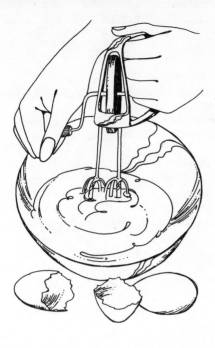

8. Three hours before serving, make Meringue: In large bowl of electric mixer, let egg whites warm to room temperature—about 1 hour. Meanwhile, preheat oven to 350F. Butter generously and coat with sugar 6 (5-oz) custard cups.

9. At high speed, beat egg whites until foamy. Add cream of tartar and salt.

10. Beat, adding sugar gradually, until stiff peaks form when beater is raised.

11. Add vanilla; fold in almonds.

12. Spoon meringue into prepared custard cups, pressing gently to fill air pockets. Place custard cups in shallow pan containing 1 inch hot water.

13. Bake 15 minutes, or until meringue rises and becomes lightly browned.

14. Place on wire rack. Unmold at once into individual serving dishes. Cool; then refrigerate.

15. To serve, spoon custard around meringue. If desired, garnish with additional almonds or whole strawberries.

Makes 6 servings.

Caramel-Custard Mold

Caramelized Sugar:
1 cup sugar

Custard:
1 quart milk
6 eggs
1/2 cup sugar
1/8 teaspoon salt
1 teaspoon vanilla extract

1. Preheat oven to 325F.

2. Make Caramelized Sugar: Place 1 cup sugar in heavy skillet; cook over low to medium heat, without stirring, until sugar has melted and begins to form a light-brown syrup; stir to blend. Use at once to coat a 1-1/2-quart casserole: Hold with pot holder, and slowly pour in hot syrup. Turn and rotate until bottom and side are thoroughly coated.

3. Make Custard: In medium saucepan, over medium heat, heat milk just until bubbles form around edge of pan.

4. In large bowl, with rotary beater, beat eggs slightly. Add 1/2 cup sugar, the salt, and vanilla. Gradually add hot milk, stirring constantly. Pour into prepared dish.

5. Place in shallow pan; pour hot water to 1/2-inch level around dish.

6. Bake 1 hour and 15 minutes, or until silver knife inserted deep into the center of custard comes out clean. Cool; refrigerate overnight.

7. To serve: Run small spatula around edge of dish to loosen. Invert onto shallow serving dish; shake gently to release. The caramel will serve as a sauce.

Makes 8 servings.

Baked Apple Custard

6 small tart baking apples (about 2 lb)
1 tablespoon lemon juice
5 eggs
4 cups milk
3/4 cup sugar
1 teaspoon vanilla extract
1/4 teaspoon nutmeg

1. Preheat oven to 350F.
2. Pare and core apples, leaving apples whole.
3. In medium skillet, bring 1 cup water to boiling; add lemon juice and apples; baste apples. Simmer gently, covered, until apples are just tender, not mushy—5 minutes.
4. With slotted spoon, lift apples to a 2-quart (10-inch) shallow, round baking dish, spacing evenly.
5. In medium bowl, with rotary beater, beat eggs, milk, sugar, vanilla, and nutmeg until combined. Pour over apples.
6. Place baking dish in pan of hot water (water should be 1/2 inch deep). Bake 50 minutes, or until a knife inserted 1/2 inch from edge comes out clean.
7. Cool on wire rack 20 minutes or longer before serving.
Makes 6 to 8 servings.

Caramel Custard

1-1/2 cups sugar
1 quart milk
6 eggs
1/8 teaspoon salt
1 teaspoon vanilla extract

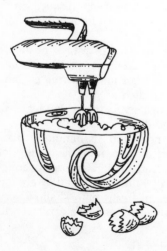

1. Preheat oven to 325F. Place 1 cup sugar in a heavy skillet; cook over low heat, without stirring, until the sugar forms a light-brown syrup. Then stir to blend.
2. Use to coat 1-1/2-quart shallow casserole.* Hold dish with pot holder, and slowly pour in hot syrup, turning to coat bottom and side.
3. Make Custard: In medium saucepan over medium heat, heat the milk just until bubbles form around edge of the saucepan.
4. In large bowl, with rotary beater, beat eggs slightly. Add remaining 1/2 cup sugar, the salt, and vanilla. Gradually pour in hot milk, stirring constantly. Pour into casserole.
5. Set casserole in shallow pan; pour hot water to 1/2-inch level around dish.
6. Bake 1 hour and 35 minutes, or until silver knive inserted in center comes out clean. Let custard cool; then refrigerate overnight.
7. To serve: Run small spatula around edge of casserole, to loosen. Invert on shallow serving dish; shake gently to release. The caramel acts as a sauce.
Makes 8 servings.
*Or use a 1-1/2-quart fluted metal mold, about 7 inches in diameter; bake 1 hour and 15 minutes.

French Custard with Raspberry Sauce

2 cups light cream
3 egg whites
1 teaspoon vanilla extract
1/4 teaspoon salt
1/4 cup sugar
1 pkg (10 oz) frozen raspberries, thawed

1. Preheat oven to 325F.
2. In small saucepan, over medium heat, heat cream just until bubbles form around edge of pan.
3. Meanwhile, in medium bowl, combine egg whites, vanilla, and salt; with portable electric mixer at high speed, beat until frothy. Gradually beat in sugar, 1 tablespoon at a time, beating well after each addition. Continue beating until stiff peaks form when beater is slowly raised.
4. With beater at low speed, gradually add heated cream, beating until well blended.
5. Pour into 6 ungreased (6-oz) custard cups. Place in shallow pan; pour hot water to 1/2-inch level around custard cups.
6. Bake 45 minutes, or until silver knife inserted 1/2 inch into center of custard comes out clean. Cool; then refrigerate until well chilled—several hours.
7. To serve: Run small spatula around edge of each custard cup to loosen. Invert onto 6 serving dishes; shake gently to release. Spoon raspberries around each custard.
Makes 6 servings.

B & B Custard Pudding

5 slices white bread
1/4 cup soft butter or margarine
1/2 cup raisins
1 teaspoon cinnamon
3 cups milk
2/3 cup sugar
4 eggs
1 teaspoon vanilla extract

1. Preheat oven to 350F. Lightly butter 12-by-8-by-2-inch baking dish.
2. Trim crusts from bread, and spread slices generously with butter.
3. Cut each slice into 4 squares. Arrange in prepared baking dish, buttered side up.
4. Sprinkle with raisins and cinnamon.
5. In saucepan, heat milk just until bubbles form around edge of pan. Remove from heat. Add sugar, and stir until sugar is dissolved.
6. Beat eggs in a large bowl. Gradually stir in hot milk mixture. Stir in vanilla. Pour over bread.
7. Set dish in pan of hot water; bake 40 to 50 minutes, or until knife inserted in center comes out clean.
8. Remove pudding from water, and cool at least 10 minutes before serving. Serve warm or cold, with light cream or whipped cream.
Makes 6 to 8 servings.
Baked Pear Bread Pudding: Omit raisins; substitute 1-1/2 cups diced fresh or canned pears. Bake as above.

English Trifle

Custard:
1 cup sugar
1 tablespoon cornstarch
1/2 teaspoon salt
4 cups milk
8 egg yolks
2 teaspoons vanilla extract
1 tablespoon cream sherry

2 (8-inch) bakers' spongecake layers
3/4 cup cream sherry
6 tablespoons raspberry preserves
6 tablespoons toasted slivered almonds
1/2 cup heavy cream, whipped
Candied green and red cherries

1. Make Custard: In a heavy, medium saucepan, combine sugar, cornstarch, and salt. Gradually add milk; stir until smooth.
2. Cook over medium heat, stirring constantly, until mixture is thickened and comes to boil. Boil 1 minute. Remove from heat.
3. In medium bowl, slightly beat egg yolks. Gradually add a little hot mixture, beating well.
4. Stir into rest of hot mixture; cook over medium heat, stirring constantly, just until mixture boils. Remove from heat; stir in vanilla and 1 tablespoon sherry.
5. Strain custard immediately into bowl. Refrigerate until well chilled—several hours or overnight.
6. Split spongecake layers in half crosswise, to make 4 layers in all. Sprinkle each layer with sherry.
7. Spread each of three layers with 2 tablespoons preserves, and sprinkle each with 2 tablespoons almonds. In attractive deep serving bowl, stack prepared layers, jam side up, spreading each with about 1 cup custard. Top with plain layer, then remaining custard.
8. Decorate with whipped cream and candied cherries. Refrigerate until serving time.
Makes 8 to 10 servings.

Creamy Rice Pudding

1/2 cup raw regular white rice
1/2 teaspoon salt
1 quart milk
1/2 cup sugar
1/4 teaspoon vanilla extract
2 (1-inch) cinnamon sticks

1. In medium saucepan, bring 3/4 cup water to boiling. Add rice and salt; cook over low heat, covered and stirring occasionally, 10 minutes, or until water is absorbed.
2. Preheat oven to 325F.
3. Turn rice into lightly buttered 8-1/2-by-1-1/2-inch round baking dish. Stir in milk, sugar, and vanilla. Insert cinnamon sticks in rice.
4. Place in shallow pan. Pour hot water to 1/2-inch depth around baking dish.
5. Bake 2-1/2 hours. Stir rice mixture gently several times during first 2 hours.
Makes 6 servings.

Baked Indian Pudding

1/2 cup yellow cornmeal
4 cups hot milk
1/2 cup maple syrup
1/4 cup light molasses
2 eggs, slightly beaten
2 tablespoons butter or margarine, melted
1/3 cup brown sugar, packed
1 teaspoon salt
1/4 teaspoon cinnamon
3/4 teaspoon ginger
1/2 cup cold milk

1. In double-boiler top, slowly stir cornmeal into hot milk. Cook over boiling water, stirring occasionally, 20 minutes.
2. Preheat oven to 325F. Lightly grease a 2-quart (9-inch round) baking dish.
3. In small bowl, combine rest of ingredients except cold milk; stir into cornmeal mixture; mix well. Turn into prepared dish; pour cold milk on top, without stirring.
4. Bake, uncovered, 50 minutes, or until just set, but quivery on top. Do not overbake. Let stand 15 minutes before serving. Serve warm, with vanilla ice cream or light cream.
Makes 8 servings.

Lemon Pudding Cake

2 tablespoons butter or regular margarine
1/2 cup granulated sugar
2 eggs, separated
3 tablespoons flour
1-3/4 cups milk
1/4 cup lemon juice
2 teaspoons grated lemon peel
Confectioners' sugar

1. Preheat oven to 350F.
2. In large bowl with electric mixer, beat butter with granulated sugar until well blended. Beat in egg yolks until blended.
3. At low speed, blend in flour; add milk, lemon juice and peel.
4. Beat egg whites until soft peaks form when beater is raised. Using a wire whisk or rubber scraper, fold egg whites into lemon mixture.
5. Turn mixture into a shallow, 8-1/2-inch round baking dish. Set dish in pan; pour boiling water into pan to depth of 1 inch.
6. Bake 40 to 45 minutes, or until golden-brown and knife inserted in center comes out clean.
7. Let stand at least 15 minutes before serving. Sprinkle top lightly with confectioners' sugar. Serve warm, with whipped cream, if desired.
Makes 6 servings.

Fruit Desserts

Hostesses are serving lighter, lower-in-calorie desserts these days, which means, of course, more fruit—but served in interesting ways, in unusual combinations. Some cases in point: Pineapple in Crème de Menthe, Strawberries with Raspberry Sauce, Apricot-Glazed Pears, and many more.

Ambrosia Bowl

4 large oranges
1 pkg (12 oz) frozen pineapple chunks, thawed
2 tablespoons Cointreau, white rum, or orange juice
4 medium bananas
4 tablespoons confectioners' sugar
1 can (3-1/2 oz) flaked coconut
6 maraschino cherries

1. Peel oranges; remove white membrane. Cut oranges crosswise into 1/8-inch-thick slices.
2. Drain pineapple, saving syrup. Comine syrup and Cointreau; set aside.
3. Peel bananas. Cut on the diagonal into 1/8-inch-thick slices.
4. In attractive serving bowl, layer half the orange slices; sprinkle with 2 tablespoons sugar. Layer half the banana slices and half the pineapple; sprinkle with half the coconut.
5. Repeat layers of fruit and sugar. Pour syrup mixture over fruit. Sprinkle with remaining coconut.
6. Decorate with maraschino cherries. Refrigerate several hours, until well chilled.
Makes 10 servings.

Fresh Pears in Port

6 fresh pears,* peeled and cored (about 3 lb)
1 cup sugar
1 cup port wine
1/2 cup orange juice
Grated peel of 1 orange
* Or substitute 6 drained canned pear halves; omit water and sugar; add pear halves in step 2.

1. In large saucepan, drop pears into 1/2 cup water and sugar; simmer, covered, until soft, about 30 minutes.
2. Remove from heat and add wine, orange juice, and grated orange peel. Mix gently. Chill, if desired.
Makes 6 servings.

Apricot-Glazed Poached Pears

2 lb ripe Anjou pears (6 to 8)
4 cups sugar
1 teaspoon vanilla extract
1 jar (12 oz) apricot preserves

1. With vegetable peeler, pare pears, leaving them whole, with stems on.
2. In a 3-1/2-quart saucepan, combine sugar and 2 cups water. Heat, stirring until sugar is dissolved. Bring to boiling; boil, uncovered, 10 minutes.
3. Add vanilla. Add pears; simmer, uncovered, over low heat 40 minutes, or just until pears are tender and slightly transparent. Remove pears with slotted spoon; drain on paper towels.
4. In small saucepan, heat preserves, stirring, until melted. Boil 1 minute. Press through sieve. Brush over pears, coating well. Arrange in serving dish; refrigerate several hours.
Makes 6 to 8 servings.

Baked Fruit Flambé

1/2 cup orange marmalade
2 teaspoons grated lemon peel
1/4 cup lemon juice
1-1/2 cups light-brown sugar, firmly packed
1-1/2 teaspoons cinnamon
1 can (1 lb) peach halves, drained
1 can (1 lb, 1 oz) pear halves, drained
1 jar (9-1/2 oz) pineapple sticks, drained
2 bananas, peeled and quartered
1/2 cup white rum

1. Preheat oven to 400F. In small saucepan, combine marmalade, lemon peel, and lemon juice; mix well. Bring just to simmering over low heat. Set aside.
2. Meanwhile, in medium bowl, combine brown sugar and cinnamon; mix well.
3. Dry fruit (except the banana quarters) well on paper towels. Dip all pieces of fruit in marmalade mixture, then in sugar mixture, coating completely.
4. Arrange the fruit in a 13-1/2-by-9-by-2-inch baking dish; bake 15 minutes.
5. Just before serving, slowly heat rum in small saucepan. Ignite; pour flaming over fruit. Nice served over ice cream.
Makes 8 servings.

Oranges Orientale

8 large navel or Temple oranges
1-1/2 cups sugar
1-1/2 cups light corn syrup
Red food color
1/4 cup lemon juice
1/4 cup Cointreau

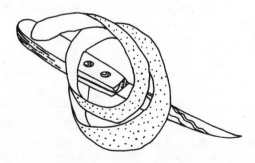

1. With sharp paring knife, remove peel from 4 oranges in 1-1/2-inch-long strips. Remove any white membrane from strips; cut each into 1/8-inch-wide pieces. (Or, if desired, remove peel with a coarse grater.) Makes about 1 cup.
2. Peel remaining oranges; remove any white membrane from all oranges. Place oranges, whole or cut in half, in large bowl; set aside.
3. In small saucepan, combine prepared peel with 2 cups cold water. Bring to boiling, covered. Remove from heat; drain. Reserve peel.
4. In large saucepan, combine sugar and corn syrup with a few drops red food color and 1-1/2 cups water; bring to boiling, over high heat, stirring until sugar is dissolved. Cook, uncovered and over medium heat, 10 minutes. Add reserved peel.
5. Continue cooking 30 minutes longer, or until syrup is slightly thickened. Remove from heat; stir in lemon juice and Cointreau.
6. Pour hot syrup over oranges in bowl. Refrigerate, covered, at least 8 hours; turn oranges occasionally.
7. Serve chilled oranges topped with some of the syrup and candied peel. Decorate, if desired, with candied violets. Serve with dessert forks and fruit knives.
Makes 8 servings.

Baked Apples with Vanilla-Pudding Sauce

Sauce:
1 egg
3-1/2 cups milk
1 pkg (3-1/4 oz) vanilla-pudding-and-pie-filling mix
2 teaspoons vanilla extract

Baked Apples:
1/2 cup light corn syrup
1/2 cup sugar
1/4 cup orange marmalade
1/4 cup butter or margarine
6 baking apples (3 lb)

1. Make Sauce: In medium saucepan, beat egg until fluffy. Add milk; then beat in pudding-and-pie-filling mix.
2. Cook as the label directs. Remove from heat. Stir in vanilla; pour into a bowl. Refrigerate, covered, until well chilled—at least 3 hours.
3. Make Baked Apples: Preheat oven to 375F. In small saucepan, combine corn syrup, sugar, marmalade, and butter. Cook over medium heat, stirring, until well blended.
4. Wash apples, and core; pare at stem end about 1 inch down. Place apples, pared side down, in 12-by-8-by-2-inch baking dish. Pour syrup mixture over apples. Cover dish with foil.
5. Bake, covered, 30 minutes. Remove foil; turn apples pared side up; baste. Bake, uncovered and basting occasionally, 10 to 15 minutes longer, or until tender. Remove from oven. Let cool, basting with syrup from time to time, until just warm.
6. Place apples in individual serving dishes. Serve warm, with vanilla-pudding sauce.
Makes 6 servings.

Macaroon-Stuffed Peaches

12 almond macaroons (1 pkg)
Yolk of 1 egg
2 tablespoons sugar
1/4 cup butter
12 canned peach halves, drained

1. Preheat oven to 350F.
2. Using rolling pin, or blender, make macaroons into crumbs. Combine crumbs, egg yolk, sugar, and butter; mix well.
3. Arrange peach halves, cut side up, in shallow baking dish. Cover peaches with macaroon mixture. Bake 20 minutes. Serve warm with light cream or ice cream, if desired.
Makes 6 servings.

Prune Whip with Custard Sauce

1-1/2 cups pitted cooked prunes
2 teaspoons lemon juice
2 egg whites
Dash salt
2 tablespoons sugar
Pour Custard Sauce, page 217

1. Purée prunes in blender or food mill. Add the lemon juice, and let cool.
2. With mixer at high speed, beat egg whites with salt until frothy. Gradually beat in sugar; beat until stiff peaks form.
3. Add purée, 1/4 cup at a time, beating well. Beat, at high speed, 2 minutes.
4. Chill well. Serve with Pour Custard Sauce.
Makes 6 servings.

Country Applesauce

2 lb tart cooking apples
1/2 to 2/3 cup sugar, depending on tartness of apples

1. Wash, core, and pare apples; cut into quarters. Measure about 7-1/2 cups.
2. In medium saucepan, bring 1/2 cup water to boiling. Add apples; bring to boiling.
3. Reduce heat; simmer, covered, 20 to 25 minutes; stir occasionally. Add water, if needed.
4. Stir in sugar until well combined. Serve warm or cold.

Makes about 3 cups.

Spiced Applesauce: Proceed as with Country Applesauce, but add 1 teaspoon lemon juice, 1/4 teaspoon cinnamon, and 1/8 teaspoon nutmeg to apples along with sugar.

Pears Sabayon

1 cup granulated sugar
4 fresh pears, pared, halved, and cored

Sauce:
4 egg yolks
1 cup confectioners' sugar
1/4 cup sherry
3/4 cup heavy cream

1. In 4-quart saucepan, combine granulated sugar and 3 cups water; heat until sugar dissolves.
2. Add pears; cover; simmer gently until tender— about 30 minutes. Remove from heat.
3. Carefully place pears, with about 1 cup syrup, in bowl; refrigerate several hours.
4. Make Sauce: In top of double boiler, with rotary beater or wire whisk, beat egg yolks, confectioners' sugar, and sherry until light.
5. Place over hot, not boiling, water; water should not touch bottom of double-boiler top. Cook, stirring constantly, 8 to 10 minutes.
6. Refrigerate several hours. Mixture thickens on standing.
7. In medium bowl, beat cream until soft peaks form when beater is raised. Carefully fold in chilled sauce.
8. Drain pears. Serve topped with sauce.

Makes 8 servings.

Strawberries and Pineapple with Sour Cream

1 can (13-1/2 oz) pineapple chunks, drained
1-1/2 cups fresh strawberry halves
3/4 cup dairy sour cream
1/4 cup maple or maple-flavored syrup
Light-brown sugar

1. Divide pineapple and strawberries evenly into 6 dessert dishes.
2. In small bowl, combine sour cream with maple syrup until well blended. Spoon over fruit.
3. Refrigerate until well chilled—at least 1 hour.
4. Just before serving, sprinkle brown sugar over each.

Makes 6 servings.

Fresh Strawberries with Mint

2 pint boxes fresh strawberries
2 tablespoons chopped fresh mint leaves
1 teaspoon grated orange peel
1/2 cup orange juice
1/2 cup confectioners' sugar

1. Gently wash strawberries in cold water; drain; hull.
2. In medium bowl, lightly toss strawberries with mint, orange peel, and orange juice.
3. Turn into serving bowl; sprinkle with confectioners' sugar. Refrigerate at least 1 hour before serving.
4. If desired, top individual servings with sweetened whipped cream.
Makes 6 servings.

Strawberries Romanoff

2 pint boxes fresh strawberries
1 cup confectioners' sugar
1 cup heavy cream
1 teaspoon almond extract
2 tablespoons Cointreau or orange juice

1. Gently wash strawberries in cold water; drain; hull.
2. In medium bowl, sprinkle sugar over berries; toss gently.
3. Refrigerate 1 hour, stirring occasionally.
4. In chilled bowl, with rotary beater, whip cream until stiff. Add almond extract and Cointreau.
5. Fold into strawberries. Serve at once.
Makes 8 servings.

Fresh Strawberries in Port

2 pint boxes fresh strawberries
1/2 cup sugar
1 cup red or white port wine

1. Gently wash strawberries in cold water; drain; and hull.
2. In medium bowl, gently toss strawberries with sugar. Add wine.
3. Refrigerate at least 2 hours, stirring occasionally.
4. If desired, top individual servings with sweetened whipped cream.
Makes 6 servings.

Strawberries with Raspberry Sauce

2 pint boxes fresh strawberries
1 pkg (10 oz) frozen raspberries, partially thawed

1. Gently wash strawberries in cold water; drain; hull.
2. Mound in shallow serving dish. Refrigerate.
3. Make Raspberry Sauce: Press raspberries through sieve, or blend in electric blender, covered, about 1 minute.
4. To serve, spoon sauce over strawberries.
Makes 6 servings.

Baked Spiced Rhubarb

4 cups rhubarb, cut in 1-inch pieces (about 2 lb);
   or 2 pkg (1-lb size) frozen rhubarb in syrup
1 cup sugar
1-inch cinnamon stick
4 whole cloves

1. Preheat oven to 400F.
2. Place rhubarb in a 2-quart casserole. Sprinkle with sugar; add cinnamon and cloves. If using frozen rhubarb, place frozen fruit in a 10-by-8-by-2-inch baking dish. Sprinkle with only 1/4 cup sugar; add spices.
3. Bake, covered, 10 minutes. Stir gently to dissolve sugar, and baste fruit with syrup. Bake 15 minutes longer, or until rhubarb is tender but not mushy.
4. Let stand, covered, on wire rack until cool.
Makes 4 to 6 servings.

Pineapple in Crème de Menthe

2 cans (1-lb, 4-oz size) pineapple chunks
1/2 cup green crème de menthe
1 pkg (12 oz) frozen fresh pineapple chunks

1. Day before serving: Drain 1 can pineapple chunks. In large bowl, combine drained pineapple chunks, 1 can undrained pineapple and crème de menthe. Mix well; refrigerate, covered, overnight. Stir several times while pineapple is marinating.
2. To serve: Turn into attractive serving bowl; mix well. Thaw frozen pineapple chunks as the label directs. Drain; toss lightly with pineapple in bowl.
Makes 8 to 10 servings.

Fresh-Pineapple Luau

4- to 5-lb ripe pineapple
Golden rum
Confectioners' sugar

1. Cut 1-1/2-inch slice from top, including frond, and bottom of pineapple. Set slices aside.
2. With long, narrow, sharp knife, remove pineapple from shell in one piece, leaving shell intact.
3. Cut pineapple lengthwise into 12 spears. Remove core. Roll each spear in rum, then in sugar.
4. Replace spears in shell.
5. Replace bottom and top of pineapple. Stand in shallow dish.
6. Refrigerate until chilled—at least 2 hours.
7. Serve in the shell. Guests help themselves to pineapple spears.
Makes 6 servings.

Fresh Pineapple in Shell

1 medium-size fresh, ripe pineapple
1/4 cup Cointreau
2 tablespoons confectioners' sugar
1 cup fresh strawberries
1 cup seedless green grapes, halved

1. With a long-bladed, sharp knife, cut the pineapple, right through the frond, into quarters. With scissors, snip off the tips of the frond, if desired.
2. Remove pineapple, in one piece, from shells. Refrigerate the shells.
3. Cut core from pineapple, and discard. Cut pineapple into chunks; place chunks in a large bowl. Add the Cointreau and the confectioners' sugar; mix gently.
4. Refrigerate pineapple, covered, 3 hours, or until you are ready to serve.
5. Meanwhile, wash the strawberries; drain. Reserve a few berries for garnish. Hull remaining berries, and slice. Refrigerate all the berries until ready to use. Also refrigerate the green grapes.
6. Just before serving, toss sliced strawberries and halved green grapes with the pineapple chunks. Spoon fruit into chilled pineapple shells. Garnish with reserved whole strawberries.
Makes 4 servings.

Watermelon Basket

1 long (15-inch) watermelon (about 15 lb)
1 honeydew melon
1 cantaloupe
1 pint strawberries
1/4 lb seedless green grapes

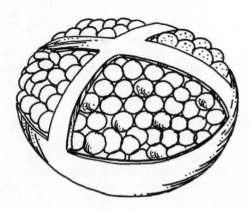

1. On top of watermelon, insert wooden picks to mark 2 diagonal 1-1/2-inch-wide bands, making an X. Cut about 4 inches into watermelon on outer side of markings, leaving uncut diamond in center. Then cut in from sides (being careful not to cut through bands), and remove 4 pieces from top of watermelon.
2. Cut watermelon meat from under bands. With melon-ball cutter, scoop out about 2 cups watermelon balls from pieces and watermelon.
3. Scoop 2 cups balls each from honeydew melon and cantaloupe.
4. Wash and hull strawberries. Wash grapes, and snip stems, to make small bunches.
5. Pile fruits in watermelon. Wrap with plastic film, to hold fruit in place. Refrigerate until well chilled.
6. At serving time, remove wrap; let guests serve themselves.
Makes 8 to 10 servings.

Gelatine Desserts

Fluffy, light, old-fashioned snow puddings, sponges and Bavarians are just as good all-round desserts today as they were years ago. Modern cooks like them especially because they can be made ahead and tucked away in the refrigerator until needed, even a day later.

Cherry-Almond Flip

1 can (1 lb, 1 oz) pitted **Bing cherries**
1 pkg (3 oz) cherry-flavored gelatine
1/2 cup sherry
1/4 cup slivered blanched almonds

1. Drain cherries, reserving liquid. Add cold water to liquid to measure 1-1/2 cups; bring to boiling.
2. Pour hot liquid over gelatine in large bowl, stirring until gelatine is dissolved. Add sherry.
3. Refrigerate until consistency of unbeaten egg white—about 1 hour.
4. Fold in cherries and almonds.
5. Spoon into 4 sherbet glasses; refrigerate until firm—about 1 hour. Serve with light or whipped cream, if desired.
Makes 4 servings.

Mrs. Simmons' Chocolate Whip

1 env unflavored gelatine
1 pkg (6 oz) semisweet-chocolate pieces
1/2 cup milk
1/4 cup sugar
1/8 teaspoon salt
1 teaspoon vanilla extract
4 eggs, separated
1/2 cup heavy cream, whipped

1. Sprinkle gelatine over 1/4 cup cold water in measuring cup, to soften.
2. Combine chocolate pieces, milk, sugar, and salt in top of double boiler. Heat over hot, not boiling, water, stirring occasionally, until chocolate is melted. Stir in softened gelatine; heat until melted. Add vanilla.
3. Beat egg yolks in medium bowl until thick and lemon-colored. Stir into chocolate-gelatine mixture until well blended. Heat 2 minutes.
4. Remove from heat; cool at room temperature 30 to 45 minutes, or until consistency of unbeaten egg white.
5. Beat egg whites until stiff peaks form when beater is raised. Fold into cooled chocolate-gelatine mixture.
6. Gently turn into a 1-quart mold, spreading evenly.
7. Refrigerate several hours, or until firmly set.
8. To unmold: Loosen around edge with small spatula. Invert over serving platter; shake gently to release. If necessary, place a hot, damp dish-cloth over mold; shake again to release. Decorate with whipped cream. Refrigerate until serving time.
Makes 6 servings.

Saint Peter's Pudding

A Holiday Fruit Pudding

2 env unflavored gelatine
2 tablespoons sugar
6 oranges
Orange juice
1/2 cup lemon juice
2 cups sugar
1 cup seedless green grapes, halved
1/2 cup chopped walnuts
1/2 cup light raisins
12 pitted dates, cut in small pieces
12 maraschino cherries, quartered
Whipped cream

1. In small saucepan, combine gelatine and 2 tablespoons sugar; add 1 cup water. Stir, over low heat, until gelatine is dissolved. Set aside.
2. Peel oranges; cut into sections, holding over bowl to catch juice. Measure juice; add enough more juice to make 2 cups.
3. Pour orange juice into large bowl. Add lemon juice, 2 cups sugar, and the gelatine mixture; stir until sugar is dissolved. Refrigerate, stirring occasionally, until consistency of unbeaten egg white.
4. Fold in orange sections, grapes, walnuts, raisins, dates, and cherries. Turn into pretty 12-cup serving bowl. Refrigerate at least 12 hours.
5. Serve, garnished with whipped cream, right from bowl.
Makes 12 to 16 servings.

Strawberry Bavarian Cream

4 pint boxes strawberries
1 tablespoon lemon juice
1 cup sugar
Red food color
2 env unflavored gelatine
2 cups heavy cream
Fresh mint

1. Gently wash strawberries under cold water; drain well. Hull.
2. Crush half the strawberries with potato masher, or blend in electric blender 1 minute. You should have about 2 cups purée.
3. In large bowl, combine crushed strawberries, lemon juice, sugar, and a few drops food color; stir until well blended.
4. In small saucepan, sprinkle gelatine over 1/2 cup cold water, to soften. Heat, over low heat and stirring constantly, until gelatine is dissolved. Stir gelatine into the strawberry mixture.
5. Place bowl in larger bowl of ice and water. Chill, stirring occasionally, until mixture thickens and mounds slightly.
6. Meanwhile, in large bowl, with electric mixer, beat cream until stiff. Carefully fold chilled gelatine mixture into cream.
7. Turn mixture into a 2-quart shallow glass serving bowl; refrigerate at least 4 hours, or until it is firm enough to spoon out.
8. To serve: Mound remaining whole strawberries on Bavarian cream. Decorate with sprigs of fresh mint.
Makes 8 to 10 servings.

Strawberries in May Wine

1 pint box strawberries*
2 env unflavored gelatine
1 cup sugar
1 bottle (3/4 quart) May wine or rosé wine
* You may use 1 pkg (10-oz) frozen strawberries
in quick-thaw pouch instead of fresh strawberries.
Thaw, as directed, 5 minutes; separate, and drain.

1. Gently wash strawberries under cold water; drain well. Turn onto paper towels to dry. Hull.
2. In small saucepan, sprinkle gelatine over 1 cup water, to soften. Heat, over low heat and stirring constantly, until gelatine is dissolved. Stir in sugar until dissolved.
3. In medium bowl, combine gelatine mixture and wine. Place bowl in larger bowl of ice and water. Chill, stirring occasionally, until mixture thickens and mounds slightly; takes about 20 minutes.
4. Gently fold in strawberries. Spoon into stemmed dessert glasses; refrigerate 2 hours, or until gelatine is firm.
Makes 6 servings.

Strawberry Snow with Custard Sauce

3 egg whites
1 pkg (10 oz) frozen strawberry halves, thawed
1 env unflavored gelatine
1/2 cup sugar
1 tablespoon lemon juice
1/8 teaspoon salt
Red food color
Pour Custard Sauce, page 217

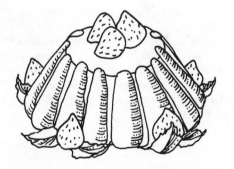

1. In medium bowl, let egg whites stand at room temperature 1 hour.
2. Meanwhile, drain strawberries, reserving syrup. Sprinkle gelatine over syrup in small saucepan, to soften. Place over low heat, stirring until gelatine is dissolved.
3. Turn strawberries, 1/4 cup sugar, the lemon juice, salt, few drops food color, 1/4 cup water, and the gelatine into blender container. Cover; blend at low speed 1 minute.
4. Turn into large bowl. Set in pan of ice and water. Let stand, stirring occasionally, just until beginning to set—about 20 minutes.
5. With electric mixer at high speed, beat egg whites until soft peaks form when beater is slowly raised. Gradually beat in remaining sugar. Continue beating until stiff peaks form.
6. With same beater, at high speed, beat gelatine mixture until light. Fold in beaten egg white until well blended. Turn into 1-quart mold.
7. Refrigerate until firm—at least 3 hours.
8. To serve: Run a small spatula around edge of mold. Invert over serving platter; place a hot, damp dishcloth on bottom of mold; shake gently to release. Serve with Pour Custard Sauce.
Makes 6 servings.

Coffee Jelly with Custard Sauce

3/4 cup sugar
3 env unflavored gelatine
3 cups hot, strong coffee
1 tablespoon lemon juice
Pour Custard Sauce, page 217, or light cream

1. In 2-quart saucepan, combine sugar and gelatine; mix well. Add coffee and 1-1/3 cups water.
2. Heat, stirring, until gelatine and sugar are dissolved. Remove from heat; stir in lemon juice.
3. Pour into a 4-1/2-cup mold. Refrigerate until firm enough to unmold—6 hours, or overnight.
4. To unmold: Run a small spatula around edge of mold. Invert over serving platter; shake gently to release. If necessary, place a hot, damp dishcloth over mold; shake again.
5. Serve with Pour Custard Sauce or light cream. Makes 6 to 8 servings.

Snow Pudding

1 env unflavored gelatine
3/4 cup sugar
Dash salt
3/4 cup boiling water
1 teaspoon grated lemon peel
1/4 cup lemon juice
3 egg whites

1. In large bowl, sprinkle gelatine over 1/2 cup cold water, to soften. Add 1/2 cup sugar, the salt, and boiling water; stir to dissolve gelatine.
2. Add lemon peel and juice, mixing well.
3. Refrigerate until consistency of unbeaten egg white—about 1 hour.
4. Beat egg whites until foamy. Gradually add remaining sugar, beating well after each addition. Continue beating until soft peaks form when beater is raised.
5. Beat gelatine mixture until foamy. With rubber scraper, using an under-and-over motion, gently fold beaten egg whites into gelatine mixture until well combined.
6. Turn mixture into a 1-quart mold; refrigerate until firm.
7. To unmold: Run a small spatula around edge of mold. Invert over serving platter; shake gently to release. If necessary, place a hot, damp dishcloth over mold; shake again to release. Serve with Pour Custard Sauce, page 217.
Makes 6 servings.

Ice Cream Desserts

Ice cream and almost anything in the way of cake, fruit, sauce or pastry were undoubtedly made for one another.
Think of fruit set aflame to spoon over ice cream—

at once, a dessert spectacular. A birthday cake, a pie warm from the oven, strawberries freshly picked—a double treat, with just a spoonful of ice cream.

Brandied Apricots Flambé

1 can (1 lb, 14 oz) whole apricots
6 tablespoons brandy
1/2 cup apricot preserves
1 teaspoon lemon juice
1 quart vanilla ice cream

1. Drain apricots, reserving 1/2 cup syrup. Remove pits from apricots.
2. Pour 2 tablespoons brandy over apricots; refrigerate, covered, 1 hour.
3. In medium saucepan, combine reserved syrup, preserves, and lemon juice; heat to boiling. Add apricots; turn into chafing dish, if desired.
4. In small saucepan, heat remaining brandy just until bubbles form around edge of pan. Ignite with match; pour over hot apricots.
5. Serve flaming apricots and syrup over ice cream.
Makes 6 servings.

Strawberry-Rum Custard Sundaes

1-1/2 cups milk
3 egg yolks
1/4 cup light-brown sugar, firmly packed
1/8 teaspoon salt
1 to 2 tablespoons dark rum
1 pint box fresh strawberries
1 pint vanilla ice cream

1. In small saucepan, slowly heat milk until bubbles form around edge.
2. In top of double boiler, with fork, beat egg yolks, sugar, and salt. Gradually stir in warm milk.
3. Cook, stirring constantly, over hot, not boiling, water about 20 minutes, or until it coats a metal spoon.
4. Pour into bowl; let cool slightly. Stir in rum. Place waxed paper or plastic film directly on surface. Refrigerate until well chilled—about 3 hours.
5. Meanwhile, gently wash strawberries in cold water; drain; hull. Refrigerate until ready to use.
6. To serve: Divide strawberries into 6 dessert dishes. Top each with a scoop of vanilla ice cream. Pour custard sauce over top.
Makes 6 servings.

Cherries Jubilee

1 can (1 lb, 14 oz) pitted Bing cherries
1 tablespoon cornstarch
1/3 cup cherry brandy
1/3 cup brandy or curaçao
3 pints vanilla ice cream

1. Drain cherries, reserving syrup.
2. In 10-inch skillet, combine syrup and cornstarch; stir until smooth. Add cherry brandy; bring to boiling, stirring; boil 2 minutes.
3. Stir in cherries; heat through.
4. In small saucepan, heat brandy until bubbles form around edge of pan. Ignite with match. Pour into cherry mixture.
5. Serve over ice cream.
Makes 8 to 10 servings.

Profiteroles

Cream-Puff Dough, page 168
2 pints strawberry ice cream
Deluxe Chocolate Sauce, page 217
1/2 cup heavy cream, whipped
Chopped pistachios

1. Preheat oven to 400F. Make Cream-Puff Dough.
2. Drop dough by rounded half teaspoonfuls, 1 inch apart, onto ungreased cookie sheet, to make 40 puffs.
3. Bake 20 to 25 minutes, or until puffed and golden-brown. Remove to wire rack; let cool completely.
4. Meanwhile, with large end of a melon-ball cutter or a 1-teaspoon measuring spoon, scoop ice cream into 40 balls. Place immediately in a chilled pan, and store in freezer.
5. Make Deluxe Chocolate Sauce.
6. To assemble profiteroles: With sharp knife, cut a slice from top of each puff. Fill each with an ice-cream ball; replace top. (Place in freezer if not serving at once.)
7. To serve: Mound puffs in serving dish. Spoon chocolate sauce over top. Garnish with whipped cream and pistachios. For individual servings: In each dessert dish, mound 5 puffs. Spoon sauce over top. Garnish with whipped cream and pistachios.
Makes 8 servings.

Banana Split

Fudge Sauce, page 218
Strawberry Sauce, page 219
Marshmallow Sauce, page 219
2 large ripe bananas
Vanilla ice cream
Strawberry ice cream
Chocolate ice cream
Whipped cream
1/4 cup chopped walnuts
Maraschino cherry with stem

1. Make Fudge, Strawberry, and Marshmallow Sauces.
2. Peel bananas; cut one in half lengthwise, and place one half on each side of an oval dish. Cut the other banana in quarters, and place at ends of dish.
3. Using a large, number-6 ice-cream scoop, make one vanilla-, one strawberry-, and one chocolate-ice-cream ball. Place vanilla and strawberry balls in center of dish; place chocolate ball on top.
4. Spoon 2 to 3 tablespoons Fudge Sauce over vanilla ice cream; 2 to 3 tablespoons Strawberry Sauce over strawberry ice cream; 2 to 3 tablespoons Marshmallow Sauce over chocolate ice cream.
5. Decorate with whipped cream in a pastry bag with a number-6 decorating tip. Sprinkle with walnuts; garnish with maraschino cherry.
Makes 1 banana split.
Note: For a party, make ice-cream balls ahead; store in freezer until serving.

Strawberry-Cookie-Shell Sundaes

1 pint fresh strawberries*
1/2 cup granulated sugar

Cookie Shells:
1 egg
1/3 cup sifted confectioners' sugar
2 tablespoons brown sugar
1/4 teaspoon vanilla extract
1/4 cup sifted all-purpose flour
Dash salt
2 tablespoons melted butter or margarine
2 tablespoons chopped pecans

1 quart vanilla ice cream
1/2 cup chopped pecans
* Or use 1 pkg frozen sliced strawberries, thawed.
Omit sugar.

1. Wash strawberries; slice. Add granulated sugar. Refrigerate.
2. Preheat oven to 300F. Grease and flour 2 cookie sheets.
3. Make Cookie Shells: In medium bowl, with electric mixer, beat egg until soft peaks form when beater is raised. Gradually stir in confectioners' sugar and brown sugar, folding until sugars dissolve. Add vanilla.
4. Stir in flour and salt, mixing well. Gradually blend in butter and 2 tablespoons pecans.
5. Spoon about 2 tablespoons batter onto prepared cookie sheet. Spread thin, to make 5-inch round. Make 2 more rounds on cookie sheet and 3 rounds on other cookie sheet.
6. Bake, one sheet at a time, 12 minutes. Remove hot cookies from sheet with broad spatula. Mold each cookie, bottom down, over outside of 6-oz custard cup, to form shell. Cool.
7. To serve: Fill shells with ice cream. Spoon strawberries over ice cream. Top with chopped nuts.
Makes 6 servings.

Peppermint-Ice-Cream-Sundae Pie

3 pints vanilla ice cream, slightly softened
1/4 lb peppermint-stick candy, crushed
2 cups chocolate-wafer crumbs
1/3 cup soft butter or margarine
Fudge Sauce, page 218
1 cup heavy cream, whipped
1/4 cup chopped walnuts

1. Turn ice cream into a large bowl. With spoon, swirl crushed candy into ice cream just enough to give a marbled effect—do not overmix. Return ice cream to containers; freeze.
2. Combine wafer crumbs with butter; mix with fork until thoroughly combined.
3. Press crumb mixture evenly on bottom and side of a 9-inch pie plate. Refrigerate until well chilled—about 1 hour.
4. Meanwhile, make Fudge Sauce.
5. Fill cookie shell with scoops of ice cream, mounding in center.
6. Pour 1/2 cup Fudge Sauce over the top. Store in freezer until serving.
7. Just before serving, garnish with mounds of whipped cream; sprinkle with nuts. Pass rest of Fudge Sauce, if desired.
Makes 8 servings.

Nesselrode-Ice-Cream Cake

3 pkg (4-oz size) ladyfingers (about 36)
1/2 cup light rum or orange juice
1/2 cup apricot preserves
1/2 pint pistachio ice cream
1/4 cup chopped candied fruit
8 candied red cherries, halved
1/2 pint strawberry ice cream
1/2 pint chocolate ice cream
1 cup heavy cream, well chilled
1/4 cup confectioners' sugar
1 teaspoon vanilla extract
8 candied red cherries

1. Lightly grease with butter or margarine a round, 1-1/2-quart baking dish, about 6-1/2 inches in diameter and 4 inches deep.
2. Line bottom and side with split ladyfingers, cut sides inside. Brush ladyfingers lightly with some of rum.
3. Combine 1 tablespoon rum with apricot preserves; mix well; spread over ladyfingers on bottom layer.
4. Cover with more split ladyfingers; brush with rum. Then make a layer of pistachio ice cream; cover with split ladyfingers; sprinkle with rum.
5. Spoon candied fruit and halved cherries over top; sprinkle with a little rum. Make a layer of strawberry ice cream; cover with split ladyfingers; sprinkle with rum.
6. Make a layer of chocolate ice cream; cover with a last layer of split ladyfingers. Cover with plastic film.
7. Freeze in freezer 3 hours or longer.
8. At serving time, with rotary beater, whip cream just until stiff. Gradually beat in confectioners' sugar; add vanilla; beat until stiff enough to hold its shape.
9. To unmold cake: Run a spatula around edge of dish to loosen. Invert on serving platter. Put a hot damp cloth over dish; gently shake out dish. Repeat if necessary.
10. Press whipped cream through pastry bag with decorative tip, making swirls on top and side. Decorate top with cherries. Return to freezer until serving.
Makes 12 servings.

Pineapple Shells Filled with Lemon Ice

1 large ripe pineapple
1/4 cup confectioners' sugar
1 quart lemon or pineapple ice or sherbet
About 1/4 cup green crème de menthe
Fresh mint leaves

1. With a long-bladed, sharp knife, cut pineapple in half, right through the frond. With scissors, snip off the tips of the pineapple frond, if desired.
2. Remove pineapple from shells: With small, sharp knife, cut, on an angle, 1/4 inch from edge of pineapple, to loosen meat. Then cut in half lengthwise, and remove sections. Refrigerate the shells.
3. Cut core from pineapple, and discard. Cut pineapple into small chunks. Place chunks in a medium bowl; stir in confectioners' sugar. Refrigerate until it is well chilled—at least 3 hours.

4. To serve: Fill shells with chilled pineapple. Top with small scoops of ice (these may be prepared ahead and stored in freezer until ready to use). Drizzle 2 tablespoons crème de menthe over ice in each shell. Garnish with mint leaves. Serve at once, spooning from the pineapple shells to serving plates.
Makes 8 servings.

Fresh Strawberries à la Colony

2 pint boxes strawberries
1/2 cup sugar
1/3 cup Cointreau or Grand Marnier
1/2 pint vanilla ice cream
1/2 cup heavy cream
1/4 teaspoon almond extract

1. Gently wash berries in cold water. Drain on paper towels; hull. Turn into large serving bowl; sprinkle with sugar and Cointreau, and toss gently. Refrigerate 1 hour, stirring occasionally.
2. Let the ice cream soften in refrigerator about 1 hour.
3. Beat heavy cream just until stiff. Fold in almond extract.
4. Gently fold whipped cream and softened ice cream into strawberry mixture. Serve at once.
Makes 8 servings.

Homemade Ice Creams and Frozen Desserts

There's probably a whole generation who have grown up and never tasted ice cream made in a crank-type freezer. Unbelievable! We think it's the best in the world. Why not try it sometime and learn how great homemade ice cream can really be.

Strawberry Parfait

1-1/2 pint boxes fresh strawberries
12 marshmallows
1 cup sugar
1 teaspoon lemon juice
2 cups heavy cream
1 tablespoon vanilla extract

1. Gently wash berries in cold water. Drain; hull. Measure 2 cups; refrigerate rest.
2. In medium saucepan, combine 2 cups berries, the marshmallows, 3/4 cup sugar, and the lemon juice. Over low heat, simmer 10 minutes, stirring occasionally. Do not scorch.
3. Remove from heat. Press through a sieve; cool.
4. In large bowl, beat cream until stiff. Stir in vanilla. Blend in strawberry purée. Pour into 2 ice-cube trays.
5. Freeze until mushy; stir thoroughly. Freeze until mushy; stir again. Freeze until firm.
6. To serve: Slice reserved strawberries; toss with remaining sugar. Divide frozen strawberry cream into 6 parfait glasses. Top with sliced berries.
Makes 6 servings.

Basic Vanilla Ice Cream

Crank-freezer Type

1-1/2 cups half-and-half or top milk
3/4 cup sugar
1/4 teaspoon salt
4 egg yolks
1-1/2 to 2 tablespoons vanilla extract
2 cups heavy cream

1. In top of double boiler, heat milk until film forms on surface. Do not boil. Stir in sugar and salt.
2. In medium bowl, beat egg yolks slightly. Gradually beat in small amounts of hot milk mixture until most of it is used.
3. Return to top of double boiler; cook, over boiling water, stirring, until as smooth and thick as mayonnaise—takes about 15 to 20 minutes.
4. Cool custard thoroughly. Stir in vanilla to taste and the heavy cream. Cover, and chill thoroughly.
5. To freeze: Pour custard into freezer container; insert dasher, and close container tightly. Pack freezer with ice and coarse salt in 8-to-1 proportion. Crank until dasher is difficult to turn. (If you use an electric freezer, follow manufacturer's instructions.)
6. Remove dasher (be careful that no salt water gets into ice cream). Replace top, and repack with ice and salt in 8-to-1 proportion. Mellow at least 2 hours.
Makes 1 quart; 6 servings.
Peppermint: Crush coarsely about 1/2 lb peppermint-stripe candy (you'll need 1-1/4 cups crushed candy). Prepare Basic Vanilla Ice Cream. When ice cream is frozen to semihardness, remove dasher. With a long wooden spoon, stir in candy. Pack down ice cream; replace cover, and mellow as in basic recipe.

Homemade Strawberry Ice Cream

4 cups light cream
2 eggs
2 cups sugar
2 pint boxes strawberries
1-1/2 cups heavy cream
1 tablespoon vanilla extract
1/4 teaspoon salt
Red food color

1. In small saucepan, heat 2 cups light cream until bubbles form around edge of pan.
2. In medium saucepan, beat eggs with 1-1/4 cups sugar until well blended. Gradually stir in hot cream. Cook over low heat, stirring constantly, until slightly thickened—15 to 20 minutes. Remove from heat; cool.
3. Meanwhile, wash and hull strawberries. Halve each, placing in large bowl. Add remaining 3/4 cup sugar; with potato masher, mash berries, to make a purée.
4. To cooled egg mixture, add remaining 2 cups light cream, the heavy cream, vanilla, salt, and few drops food color.

5. To freeze in 1-quart crank-type freezer:* Pour half of custard mixture into freezer container; insert dasher, and close container tightly. Pack freezer with ice and coarse salt in 4-to-1 proportion. Crank for 10 minutes. Open container; add half the crushed strawberries; then crank until dasher is difficult to turn.

6. Serve immediately, or spoon into freezer containers, and place in freezer. Then repeat freezing other half of custard and strawberries, to make second quart.

Makes about 2 quarts.

* If using an electric freezer, follow manufacturer's instruction.

Frozen Lemon Cream

Graham-Cracker Crust:
1/4 cup butter or margarine
1 cup packaged graham-cracker crumbs
2 tablespoons sugar

Filling:
1-1/2 cups heavy cream
4 eggs, separated
1 cup sugar
1/2 cup lemon juice
1-1/2 tablespoons grated lemon peel
Yellow food color

1. Make Graham-Cracker Crust: Melt butter in skillet; remove from heat. Stir in graham-cracker crumbs and 2 tablespoons sugar; mix well.

2. Into bottom of each of 12 (5-oz) paper or foil dessert dishes, sprinkle 1 tablespoon crumb mixture, making an even layer. Reserve rest of crumb mixture. Place paper dishes on tray or in shallow pan.

3. Make Filling: Whip cream, and set aside.

4. In medium bowl, with portable electric mixer at high speed, beat egg whites until soft peaks form when beater is slowly raised. Gradually beat in sugar, 2 tablespoons at a time; continue to beat until stiff peaks form.

5. With same beater, at medium speed, beat egg yolks until thick and light. Beat in lemon juice and peel until well combined.

6. Fold egg-yolk mixture, whipped cream, and 3 or 4 drops food color into egg whites. Turn 1/2 cup lemon mixture into each prepared dessert dish. Sprinkle each with about 1 tablespoon reserved crumb mixture.

7. Freeze until firm—about 2 hours.

8. Wrap desserts individually in foil, plastic film, or moisture-vapor-proof freezer paper; seal; label, and return to freezer.

9. To serve: Remove as many desserts as needed from freezer; unwrap. Let thaw in refrigerator 30 minutes. (If desired, remove from dessert to serving dishes by loosening edges with spatula and sliding out.)

Makes 12 servings.

Frozen Maple Mousse

1-1/4 cups maple or maple-blended syrup
2 egg yolks
1/8 teaspoon salt
2 cups heavy cream
Fresh strawberries
Candied violets
Whipped cream (optional)

1. In top of double boiler, over direct heat, heat maple syrup just until it is bubbly around edge of the pan.
2. In small bowl, with electric mixer or rotary beater, beat egg yolks with salt until light-colored. Gradually beat in all the syrup. Return mixture to top of double boiler.
3. Cook over simmering water, stirring constantly, until mixture is slightly thickened and forms a coating on a metal spoon—10 to 15 minutes.
4. Set top of double boiler in ice water; beat mixture until thick and fluffy and well chilled—about 5 minutes.
5. In large chilled bowl, beat cream just until stiff. Fold in syrup mixture. Pour into 2 ice-cube trays.
6. Freeze until firm about 1 inch from edge. Turn into large bowl; beat with wire whisk until smooth. Turn into 6-cup mold, preferably with a tube.
7. Freeze, covered with plastic film, until it is firm —at least 4 hours.
8. To serve: Unmold onto chilled serving plate. Garnish with strawberries, candied violets, and whipped cream.
Makes 8 servings.

Chocolate-Cinnamon Ice Cream

1 vanilla bean
4 cups light cream
4 egg yolks
1 cup sugar
1 tablespoon cornstarch
1/4 teaspoon salt
6 squares (1-oz size) semisweet chocolate
2 tablespoons cinnamon
1-1/2 cups heavy cream

1. Split vanilla bean; with tip of knife, scrape seeds into light cream in a medium saucepan. Heat until bubbles appear around edge of pan.
2. In medium bowl, beat egg yolks with sugar, cornstarch, and salt until well combined. Gradually stir in hot cream. Return to saucepan; cook over medium heat, stirring constantly, until mixture is thickened and just comes to boiling.
3. Add chocolate and cinnamon. Remove from heat; stir until chocolate is melted. Set aside until cool.
4. Stir in heavy cream.
5. To freeze in 1-quart crank-type freezer:* Pour half of chocolate mixture into freezer container; insert dasher, and close container tightly. Pack freezer with ice and coarse salt in 4-to-1 proportion. Crank for 15 minutes, or until dasher is difficult to turn.

6. Serve immediately, or spoon into freezer containers, and place in freezer. Freeze other half. Serve with prepared bittersweet-chocolate sauce. Makes about 2 quarts.

* If using an electric freezer, follow manufacturer's directions.

Floating Heart Ritz

3/4 cup sugar
3 egg yolks
1 cup crumbled almond macaroons
4 ladyfingers, split
2 tablespoons Grand Marnier
1-1/2 cups heavy cream
2 teaspoons vanilla extract
1/2 teaspoon almond extract
Raspberry Sauce, page 220
1/2 cup heavy cream
Chocolate curls

1. Line a 7-inch (6- to 7-cup) heart-shape mold with foil.
2. In small saucepan, combine sugar with 1/3 cup water; bring to boiling over medium heat, stirring until sugar is dissolved. Boil gently, without stirring, to 230F on candy thermometer, or until a little of sugar mixture spins a thread when dropped from spoon.
3. Meanwhile, in medium bowl, with portable electric mixer at medium speed, beat egg yolks and salt until light. Gradually beat in hot syrup, in a thin stream; continue beating until mixture begins to cool—about 2 minutes. Stir in macaroons. Refrigerate 30 minutes.
4. Meanwhile, sprinkle ladyfingers with Grand Marnier; set aside. Combine 1-1/2 cups cream with extracts; beat until stiff.
5. With rubber scraper, fold whipped cream into macaroon mixture. Turn half of mixture into prepared mold; cover with ladyfingers; pour in remaining mixture. Freeze until firm—about 4 hours. Meanwhile, make Raspberry Sauce.
6. At serving time: Beat 1/2 cup cream until stiff. Unmold frozen heart onto chilled shallow serving dish; remove foil. Spoon Raspberry Sauce around base. Decorate top with whipped cream, using pastry bag with decorating tip, if desired. Garnish with chocolate curls.

Makes 8 to 10 servings.

Sherbets

Sherbets with a true-to-the-fruit taste, not artificial, are hard to find. That's the reason for our sherbet recipes that follow. You'll be delighted with their fresh fruit flavor, surprised at the ease with which they're made.

Cranberry Sherbet

2 cups fresh cranberries
1 teaspoon unflavored gelatine
2 tablespoons lemon juice
1 cup orange juice
1-1/2 cups sugar
2 egg whites

1. Wash cranberries, removing stems. Turn into 2-1/2-quart saucepan. Add 1-1/2 cups water; simmer, covered, 10 minutes.
2. Meanwhile, sprinkle gelatine over 2 tablespoons cold water in medium bowl; let stand 5 minutes. Stir in lemon juice, orange juice, and sugar.
3. Then press cranberries and liquid through a sieve, to remove skins and seeds. Add to gelatine mixture, stirring until gelatine and sugar are dissolved.
4. Pour into 2 ice-cube trays; freeze just until mushy—about 1 hour.
5. Then beat egg whites, in small bowl of electric mixer at high speed, just until soft peaks form.
6. Turn cranberry mixture into large bowl of electric mixer; beat, at medium speed, until smooth. With rubber scraper, gently fold egg whites into cranberry mixture till combined.
7. Turn into 3 ice-cube trays; freeze until firm—about 2 hours.
8. Turn into large electric-mixer bowl; beat, at medium speed, until thick and smooth.
9. Return to ice-cube trays; freeze again until firm—30 minutes to 1 hour.
Makes 6 to 8 servings.

Crème-de-Menthe-Sherbet Ring with Strawberries

3 pints lemon sherbet
1/3 cup green crème de menthe
1 quart fresh strawberries
Confectioners' sugar

1. Let sherbet stand in refrigerator 30 minutes, to soften slightly.
2. Turn sherbet into large bowl; beat, with portable electric mixer, just until smooth but not melted.
3. Quickly stir in crème de menthe until well combined.
4. Turn mixture into a 5-1/2-cup ring mold; freeze until firm—several hours or overnight.
5. Meanwhile, wash strawberries; drain. Do not hull. Refrigerate until ready to use.
6. To serve: Invert ring mold over round, chilled serving platter. Place hot, damp cloth over mold; shake to release sherbet.
7. Fill center of ring with strawberries. Dust berries lightly with sugar. Serve at once.
Makes 8 servings.

Pink-Champagne Sherbet

4 pints lemon sherbet
1 bottle (4/5 quart) pink champagne, chilled
1/8 teaspoon red food color

1. Turn sherbet into large bowl; beat just until smooth but not melted. Quickly stir in champagne and food color until well combined.
2. Turn into 12-cup decorative mold. Freeze until firm—overnight, if possible.
3. To serve: Invert mold on serving platter; place hot, damp cloth over mold, and shake to release sherbet. Garnish with fruit, if desired. Serve at once.
Makes 12 servings.

Raspberry Sherbet

2 pkg (10-oz size) frozen raspberries
1/2 cup red-currant jelly
1/3 cup crème de cassis or kirsch
Strawberries (optional)

1. Thaw frozen raspberries as package label directs.
2. Combine raspberries with their juice, jelly, and crème de cassis in electric-blender container. Blend at medium speed 1/2 minute, to make a purée.
3. Turn into ice-cube trays; freeze until firm 1/2 inch from edge all around—about 3 hours.
4. Blend again in blender until mushy, not melted. Turn into 6 tall serving glasses.
5. Keep in freezer until serving. Top with fresh or frozen strawberries.
Makes 6 servings.

Fig Sorbet

2 cans (17-oz size) Kadota figs
1/2 cup honey or light corn syrup
1/3 cup light rum

1. Drain figs, reserving syrup.
2. Put figs in blender, one half at a time. Blend at high speed to form a purée. Combine with 1/4 cup reserved syrup, the honey, and rum. (Or make a purée of figs by pressing through food mill; combine with rest of ingredients and 1/4 cup reserved syrup.)
3. Turn into refrigerator ice-cube trays; freeze until frozen 1 inch from edge—about 3 hours. Turn into large bowl of electric mixer; beat just until mushy, not melted.
4. Turn into serving dishes, piling high. Store in freezer until serving. Garnish with canned figs, if desired.
Makes 4 to 6 servings.

Lime Sherbet with Strawberries

1 env unflavored gelatine
2 cups milk
1-1/3 cups sugar
1/2 teaspoon salt
2 cups light cream
1/2 cup lime juice
1/4 cup lemon juice
2 tablespoons grated lemon peel
Strawberries, washed and hulled

1. In small heavy saucepan, sprinkle gelatine over 1/2 cup milk to soften.
2. In medium bowl combine remaining milk, sugar, salt, and cream. Stir until sugar is dissolved. Stir in lime juice, lemon juice, and peel.
3. Heat gelatine mixture over low heat, stirring constantly until gelatine is dissolved. Remove from heat; slowly stir into mixture in bowl.
4. Turn into ice-cube tray; freeze until frozen 1 inch in from edge.
5. Turn into chilled bowl; with electric mixer or rotary beater beat mixture quickly until smooth but not melted. Return to ice-cube tray.
6. Freeze several hours or until firm.
7. To serve: Spoon into sherbet glasses; top with strawberries.
Makes 6 servings.

Fresh-Orange Sherbet

6 oranges
1/2 cup honey or light corn syrup
2/3 cup sweet orange marmalade
2 cups light cream
1/4 cup Cointreau
1 can (3-1/2 oz) flaked coconut

1. Grate rind from 2 oranges to make 2 tablespoons.
2. Cut all 6 oranges in half and squeeze. (Reserve 8 shells for serving.) Juice should measure 2 cups.
3. In blender container, combine 2 tablespoons grated rind and the juice, honey, marmalade, cream, and Cointreau. Blend 1/2 minute at high speed. Pour into 2 ice-cube trays; freeze until firm 1 inch from edge all around—about 3 hours.
4. Blend again in blender 1/2 minute, until soft but not melted. Turn back into ice-cube trays, or mound in reserved orange shells. Freeze until firm several hours or overnight. (Flavor improves overnight.)
5. Serve in orange shells. Sprinkle with coconut, or decorate with candied orange peel, if desired.
Makes 8 servings.

Soufflés

Best gourmet news yet: Ambrosial, airborne soufflés can now be made hours in advance and simply slid in the oven before mealtime. Our recipe for Orange Soufflé Surprise tells you how.

Orange Soufflé Surprise

8 egg whites
Butter or margarine
Sugar
4 ladyfingers, split
1-1/4 cups orange juice
6 egg yolks
3/4 cup sugar
1/2 teaspoon vanilla extract
3/4 cup sifted all-purpose flour
1 cup milk
2 tablespoons grated orange peel
Chantilly Cream, page 217

1. In large bowl of electric mixer, let egg whites warm to room temperature—about 1 hour.
2. Lightly butter bottom and side of a 1-1/2-quart straight-side soufflé dish (7-1/2-inch diameter). Sprinkle evenly with 2 tablespoons sugar.
3. Fold 26-inch-long piece of waxed paper lengthwise into thirds. Lightly butter one side; then sprinkle evenly with sugar.
4. With string, tie collar (sugar side inside) around soufflé dish, to form a 2-inch rim above top.
5. Place ladyfingers in single layer in shallow dish. Sprinkle with 1/4 cup orange juice; set aside.
6. In medium bowl, beat yolks at high speed until thick. Add 1/4 cup sugar; beat until very thick and lemon-colored—about 3 minutes.
7. Beat in remaining orange juice and the vanilla to combine well. Add flour, blending thoroughly.
8. In large saucepan, heat milk with 1/4 cup sugar, stirring to dissolve sugar, until bubbles form around edge of pan.
9. Stir hot milk mixture into egg-yolk mixture; pour back into saucepan. Cook, over medium heat, stirring constantly, till it thickens and begins to boil—about 10 minutes.
10. Turn mixture into large bowl. Add orange peel; let cool.
11. Meanwhile, at high speed, beat egg whites until foamy. Gradually beat in 1/4 cup sugar. Continue beating until stiff peaks form when beater is slowly raised.
12. Gently fold egg whites into yolk mixture just until well combined.
13. Turn half of mixture into prepared dish. Arrange ladyfingers on top. Pour on the rest of the mixture. Refrigerate until baking time—no longer than 4 hours (see Note).
14. About 1 hour before serving, preheat oven to 375F. Bake soufflé, set in pan of hot water, 45 to 50 minutes, or until golden-brown. It should shake slightly in center.
15. Meanwhile, make Chantilly Cream.
16. Serve soufflé at once. The surprise is soft part in center. Serve as a sauce, with Chantilly Cream. Makes 8 servings.
Note: If desired, soufflé may be baked at once, without refrigerating, 45 to 50 minutes, as directed above, in preheated oven, 375F.

Apricot Soufflé

8 egg whites, unbeaten
2-1/2 cups dried apricots
1/4 teaspoon almond extract
Butter
Granulated sugar
1/4 teaspoon cream of tartar
1/8 teaspoon salt
1/2 cup granulated sugar
1 cup cold heavy cream
2 tablespoons confectioners' sugar
1/8 teaspoon almond extract

1. In large bowl of electric mixer, let egg whites warm to room temperature—about 1 hour. Meanwhile, in 3-1/2 cups water, simmer apricots, covered, about 1/2 hour, or until very tender. Then press apricots, with cooking liquid, through sieve or food mill, or mix in blender, to make purée.
2. To 2 cups apricot purée, add 1/4 teaspoon almond extract; refrigerate.
3. About 1 hour before dessert time, preheat oven to 325F.
4. Butter 2-quart casserole; then sprinkle with a little granulated sugar.
5. Beat egg whites until foamy throughout; add cream of tartar and salt; continue beating to form soft peaks. Gradually add 1/2 cup granulated sugar, 2 tablespoons at a time, beating after each addition until whites form stiff peaks.
6. Gently fold apricot purée into whites until thoroughly combined; turn into prepared casserole; set in pan of hot water. Bake 45 minutes.
7. At dessert time, whip cream until stiff; add confectioners' sugar and 1/8 teaspoon almond extract.
8. Serve soufflé at once with whipped cream. Makes 8 servings.

Cold Caramel Soufflé

6 egg whites (3/4 cup)
3-1/4 cups superfine granulated sugar
English Custard Sauce, page 218

1. In large bowl of electric mixer, let egg whites warm to room temperature—about 1 hour.
2. Meanwhile, place 1-1/2 cups sugar in a heavy, medium skillet. To caramelize, cook over medium heat, stirring, until sugar is completely melted and begins to boil—syrup should be a medium brown.
3. Hold a 1-1/2-quart oven-glassware casserole with pot holder, and pour in hot syrup all at once. Tilt and rotate casserole until bottom and side are thoroughly coated. Set on wire rack, and let cool.
4. Beat egg whites, at high speed, until very stiff—about 5 minutes.
5. While continuing to beat, gradually pour in 1-1/4 cups sugar, in a continuous stream—takes about 3 minutes. Scrape side of bowl with a rubber scraper. Beat 10 minutes.
6. Meanwhile (about 5 minutes before beating time is up), place 1/2 cup sugar in heavy, medium skillet, and caramelize as in Step 2. Remove from heat, and immediately place skillet in pan of cold water for a few seconds, or until syrup is thick; stir constantly.

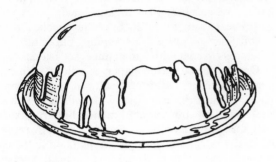

7. With beater at medium speed, gradually pour syrup into beaten egg-white mixture. Scrape side of bowl with rubber scraper. Return to high speed, and continue beating 3 minutes longer.

8. Preheat oven to 250F.

9. Turn egg-white mixture into prepared casserole, spreading evenly. Set in large baking pan; pour boiling water to 1-inch depth around casserole.

10. Bake 1 hour, or until meringue seems firm when gently shaken and rises about 1/2 inch above casserole.

11. Meanwhile, make English Custard Sauce.

12. Remove casserole from water; place on wire rack to cool. Refrigerate until very well chilled—6 hours or overnight.

13. To unmold: Run a small spatula around edge of meringue, to loosen. Hold casserole in pan of very hot water at least 1 minute. Invert onto serving dish.

14. Pour some of the sauce over meringue, and pass the rest.

Makes 8 servings.

Shortcakes and Kuchens

Think of a shortcake made of the biggest, fluffiest biscuit ever, piping hot, split, with butter melting inside it, sweet, juicy strawberries or peaches crowding it, rich whipped cream smothering it.

Apple Cobbler

Filling:
5 cups sliced, peeled tart apples (about 1-1/2 lb)
3/4 cup sugar
2 tablespoons flour
1 tablespoon lemon juice
1 teaspoon vanilla extract
1/2 teaspoon cinnamon
1/4 teaspoon salt
2 tablespoons butter or margarine

Batter:
1/2 cup unsifted all-purpose flour
1/2 cup sugar
1/2 teaspoon baking powder
1/4 teaspoon salt
2 tablespoons butter or regular margarine, softened
1 egg, slightly beaten
Light cream, whipped cream, or ice cream

1. Make Filling: In medium bowl, combine apple, 3/4 cup sugar, 2 tablespoons flour, the lemon juice, vanilla, cinnamon, 1/4 teaspoon salt, and 1/4 cup water. Turn into 8-by-8-by-2-inch baking dish. Dot with 2 tablespoons butter.

2. Preheat oven to 375F.

3. Make Batter: In medium bowl, combine all batter ingredients; beat with wooden spoon until smooth. Drop in 9 portions over filling, spacing evenly. Batter will spread during baking.

4. Bake 35 to 40 minutes, or until apple is tender and crust is golden. Serve warm, with cream.

Makes 9 servings.

Fresh Peach Kuchen

Boiling water
2 lb ripe peaches, peeled and sliced (about 6); or
    2-1/2 pkg (10-oz size) frozen sliced peaches,
    drained
2 tablespoons lemon juice

Kuchen Batter:
1-1/2 cups sifted* all-purpose flour
1/2 cup sugar
2 teaspoons baking powder
1/2 teaspoon salt
2 eggs
2 tablespoons milk
1-1/2 tablespoons grated lemon peel
1/4 cup butter or regular margarine, melted

Topping:
1/4 cup sugar
1/2 teaspoon ground cinnamon
1 egg yolk
3 tablespoons heavy cream

Sweetened whipped cream or soft vanilla ice cream
*Sift before measuring.

1. Pour enough boiling water over peaches in large bowl to cover. Let stand 1 minute to loosen skins; then drain, and plunge into cold water for a few seconds to prevent softening of fruit. With paring knife, pare peaches; place in large bowl.
2. Preheat oven to 400F. Sprinkle peaches with lemon juice to prevent darkening. Slice into the bowl; toss to coat with lemon juice; set aside.
3. Onto sheet of waxed paper, sift flour with the sugar, baking powder, and salt. In large mixing bowl, using fork, beat eggs with milk and lemon peel. Add flour mixture and melted butter, mixing with fork until smooth—1 minute. Do not overmix.
4. Butter a 9-inch springform pan, or a 9-inch round layer-cake pan. (If cake pan is used, kuchen must be served from pan.) Turn batter into pan; spread evenly over bottom. (At this point, kuchen may be refrigerated several hours, or until about 1/2 hour before baking.)
5. Combine sugar and cinnamon; mix well. Drain peach slices; arrange on batter, around edge of pan; fill in center with 5 peach slices. Sprinkle evenly with sugar-cinnamon mixture. Bake 25 minutes. Remove kuchen from oven.
6. With a fork, beat egg yolk with cream. Pour over peaches. Bake 10 minutes longer. Cool 10 minutes on wire rack.
7. To serve, remove side of springform pan. Serve kuchen warm, cut into wedges, with sweetened whipped cream or soft vanilla ice cream. Makes 8 to 10 servings.

Old-Fashioned Strawberry Shortcake

Shortcake:
2 cups unsifted all-purpose flour
1/4 cup granulated sugar
3 teaspoons baking powder
1/2 teaspoon salt
1/2 cup butter or regular margarine
3/4 cup milk

Strawberry Topping:
3 pint boxes fresh strawberries
3/4 cup granulated sugar
1 cup heavy cream
2 tablespoons confectioners' sugar

1. Turn oven to 450F. Lightly grease an 8-by-8-by-2-inch square baking pan.
2. In a sifter placed in a large bowl, sift the flour with granulated sugar, baking powder, and salt.
3. Cut butter into chunks; add to flour mixture. With pastry blender, or two knives used scissors fashion, cut in butter until it is in very small particles, all coated with flour mixture. Mixture will resemble coarse cornmeal.
4. Make a well in center of mixture. Pour in milk all at once; mix quickly, with fork, just to moisten flour. Do not overmix; there will be lumps in the dough.
5. Turn into prepared pan, scraping out bowl with

rubber scraper. With fingers (dipped in a little flour), lightly press out dough so that it fits corners of the pan and is even in the pan.

6. Bake 15 minutes, or until golden and cake tester inserted in center comes out clean. Meanwhile, fix berries.

7. Loosen edges with a sharp knife; then turn out on a wire rack.

8. **Make Strawberry Topping:** Wash strawberries in cold water; drain. Choose several of the nicest berries for garnish, and set them aside.

9. Then remove hulls from rest of berries; slice berries into a bowl. Add granulated sugar; mix well. Set berries aside until shortcake is ready.

10. To serve: Beat cream, with a rotary beater, just until it is stiff. Gently stir in confectioners' sugar.

11. Using serrated-edge knife, carefully cut cake in half crosswise. Put bottom, cut side up, on serving plate. Spoon over half of sliced berries.

12. Set top of cake in place, cut side down. Spoon rest of sliced berries over top of cake. Mound whipped cream lightly in center. Garnish with whole strawberries. Serve at once.

Makes 9 servings.

Peach Shortcake   Made with Biscuit Mix

2 cups pkg buttermilk-biscuit mix
1/4 cup butter or regular margarine
Granulated sugar
2/3 cup milk
1-1/2 lb fresh peaches* (3 cups, sliced)
1/2 cup heavy cream
2 tablespoons confectioners' sugar
* Or use 2 pkg (10-oz size) thawed frozen sliced peaches, undrained. Do not add sugar.

1. Preheat oven to 400F.

2. In large bowl, combine biscuit mix, butter, and 2 tablespoons granulated sugar. Cut in butter with pastry blender until mixture resembles coarse crumbs.

3. Stir in milk, mixing just until flour mixture is moistened.

4. Turn dough onto lightly floured pastry cloth or board. Knead gently 10 times. Roll out to 3/4-inch thickness. With floured 3-inch cutter, cut out 6 biscuits.

5. Place on ungreased cookie sheet; bake 15 minutes, or until lightly browned. Cool completely on wire rack (see Note).

6. Meanwhile, wash peaches; peel; slice into a large bowl. Sprinkle with 1/2 cup granulated sugar.

7. Whip cream with confectioners' sugar until stiff.

8. To serve each shortcake: Split biscuit. Spread with butter, if desired. Spoon 1/4 cup peaches over bottom, then a spoonful of whipped cream. Replace top; spoon on 1/4 cup peaches, and top with a generous tablespoon whipped cream.

Makes 6 servings.

Note: Serve biscuits slightly warm, if you like.

Individual Strawberry Shortcake

3 pint boxes strawberries, washed and hulled
1 cup sugar

Shortcake:
2 cups sifted all-purpose flour
1/4 cup sugar
3 teaspoons baking powder
1/2 teaspoon salt
1/2 cup shortening
1 egg, slightly beaten
1/3 cup milk
1 cup heavy cream
2 tablespoons soft butter or margarine

1. Set aside 6 large berries. Slice remaining berries into medium bowl; gently stir in 1 cup sugar. Refrigerate while making shortcake.
2. Make shortcake: Preheat oven to 450F. Into large bowl, sift flour, 1/4 cup sugar, the baking powder, and salt.
3. With pastry blender or 2 knives, cut in shortening until mixture resembles coarse cornmeal.
4. Add egg, stirring with fork until well combined. Add milk, all at once, stirring until dough cleans side of bowl.
5. Turn out dough onto lightly floured surface; knead gently 8 to 10 times, or until smooth. Roll out about 1/2 inch thick. With lightly floured 3-1/2-inch round cookie cutter, cut out 6 rounds of dough. Arrange, 1 inch apart, on ungreased cookie sheet.
6. Bake 10 to 12 minutes, or until light golden.
7. In small bowl, whip cream until stiff.
8. Split warm shortcakes in half crosswise. Place bottom halves, cut side up, on dessert plates. Spread with butter; spoon on half of sliced strawberries. Top with other shortcake halves, then remaining berries. Garnish with whipped cream and the reserved whole berries. Serve immediately. Makes 6 servings.

Some Special Desserts

Each of these remarkable desserts has earned a reputation that extends far beyond its birthplace— Paris, New York, New Orleans, San Francisco and other cities famous for fine food. Let the Pears Véfour or the Strawberries à la Blue Fox or any of the following be the hit of your next dinner party.

Diplomat Cake

1-1/3 cups orange marmalade
2/3 cup dark rum
3 pkg (3-oz size) ladyfingers
1 cup heavy cream, whipped
Chocolate curls, page 287

1. Line a 1-1/2-quart decorative mold with plastic film.
2. In small bowl, combine orange marmalade with 1/3 cup rum; mix well. Set aside 1/4 cup of mixture, and refrigerate for later use.
3. Split ladyfingers; brush cut sides with remaining 1/3 cup rum.
4. In bottom of mold, arrange two layers of split ladyfingers, cut side up. Spread with 2 tablespoons marmalade mixture.

5. Repeat Step 4.

6. Around side of mold, arrange a row of split ladyfingers, vertically, rounded side against mold. Continue layering ladyfingers and marmalade mixture to fill center of mold, as in Step 4, ending with ladyfingers. Cover top with plastic film; refrigerate several hours or overnight.

7. To unmold, remove plastic film from top; invert mold onto serving plate; gently remove mold and film.

8. Spoon reserved 1/4 cup marmalade-rum mixture over top of cake, letting it drizzle down sides.

9. Using pastry tube with number-5 star tip, make rosettes of whipped cream around base of cake and on top. Arrange chocolate curls on top of rosettes. Refrigerate.

Makes 8 servings.

Blintzes

Cheese, Blueberry, Cherry, or Apple Filling, below

Blintzes:
2 eggs
2 tablespoons salad oil
1 cup milk
3/4 cup sifted all-purpose flour
1/2 teaspoon salt
About 1/4 cup butter or regular margarine

Confectioners' sugar
1 cup dairy sour cream

1. Make one of Fillings.

2. Make Blintzes: In medium bowl, beat eggs, salad oil, and milk until well mixed. Add flour and salt; beat until smooth.

3. Refrigerate, covered, 30 minutes. Batter should be consistency of heavy cream.

4. For each blintz: Melt 1/2 teaspoon butter in a 10-inch skillet. Pour in 3 tablespoons batter, rotating pan quickly, to spread batter evenly. Cook over medium heat until lightly browned on underside; then remove from pan. Stack blintzes, browned side up, as you take them from skillet.

5. Place about 3 tablespoons of filling on browned surface of each blintz. Fold two opposite sides over filling; then overlap ends, covering filling completely.

6. Melt rest of butter in large skillet. Add 3 or 4 blintzes, seam side down; sauté until golden-brown on underside; turn, and sauté other side. Keep blintzes warm in a low oven while cooking rest.

7. Sprinkle with confectioners' sugar. Serve hot, with sour cream.

Makes 10.

Cherry Filling

1 can (1 lb, 4 oz) cherry-pie filling
1/8 teaspoon cinnamon

Combine pie filling and cinnamon in small bowl. Mix well.

Makes 2 cups.

Cheese Filling

1 pkg (3 oz) cream cheese, softened
2 cups (1 lb) dry cottage cheese or ricotta cheese
1 egg yolk
2 tablespoons sugar
1/2 teaspoon vanilla extract

1. In medium bowl, combine cheeses, egg yolk, sugar, and vanilla; beat with electric mixer until smooth.
2. Refrigerate, covered, until ready to use.
Makes about 2-1/2 cups.

Blueberry Filling

1 can (1 lb, 4 oz) blueberry-pie filling
1/8 teaspoon nutmeg

Combine pie filling and nutmeg in small bowl. Mix well.
Makes 2 cups.

Apple Filling

2 lb tart cooking apples, pared, cored, and sliced
1 cup sugar
1 teaspoon cinnamon
1/8 teaspoon nutmeg

1. In medium saucepan, combine apple, sugar, cinnamon, and nutmeg. Cook over low heat, stirring occasionally, 15 minutes, or until apple is very tender.
2. Let cool, covered, about 1/2 hour.
Makes 2 cups.

Heavenly Lemon Meringue

Lemon Filling:
4 egg yolks
1/2 cup granulated sugar
1 tablespoon grated lemon peel
1/4 cup lemon juice
1/2 cup heavy cream
9-inch Baked Meringue Shell, below

1/2 cup heavy cream, whipped
2 tablespoons confectioners' sugar

1. Make Lemon Filling: In top of double boiler, with rotary beater, beat egg yolks with granulated sugar until thick and light.
2. Stir in lemon peel and juice.
3. Cook, over hot, not boiling, water, stirring until thickened and smooth—10 minutes.
4. Remove from heat. Let cool completely, stirring occasionally. (To hasten cooling, place top of double boiler in bowl of ice cubes.)
5. With rotary beater, beat cream in small bowl just until stiff. With rubber scraper, using an under-and-over motion, gently fold into cooled lemon mixture just until smooth.
6. Turn into Meringue Shell, spreading evenly. Cover top loosely with saran or foil; refrigerate overnight.
7. Just before serving, combine whipped cream with confectioners' sugar. Swirl over top.
Makes 6 to 8 servings.

Baked Meringue Shell

3 egg whites
1/4 teaspoon cream of tartar
1/4 teaspoon salt
3/4 cup sugar

1. Lightly butter bottom and side of a 9-inch pie plate.
2. In large bowl of electric mixer, let egg whites warm to room temperature—1 hour.
3. At high speed, beat egg whites with cream of tartar and salt just until very soft peaks form when beater is slowly raised.
4. Gradually beat in sugar, 2 tablespoons at a time, beating well after each addition. Continue beating until very stiff peaks form. Meringue should be shiny and moist.
5. Preheat oven to 275F. Spread two thirds of meringue on bottom of prepared pie plate. Use rest to cover side and mound around rim.
6. Bake 1 hour. Let cool in pan on wire rack.
7. To serve: Fill as directed above, or nice with strawberry ice cream and strawberry sauce.
Makes 6 to 8 servings.

Pear Tatin

2 cans (1-lb, 14-oz size) pear halves
1 cup sugar
1 tablespoon butter or margarine
1/2 pkg piecrust mix (pastry for 1-crust pie)
1 jar (9-1/2 oz) marrons in syrup, drained (optional)
1 cup heavy cream, whipped and sweetened

1. Preheat oven to 450F.
2. Drain pears well. Cut each in half lengthwise; drain on paper towels.
3. To caramelize sugar: Cook sugar in large skillet, over medium heat and stirring occasionally, until sugar melts and becomes a light-brown syrup.
4. Immediately pour into bottom of an 8-1/2-inch round baking dish. Arrange pears, rounded side down, spoke fashion, in caramelized sugar. Top with a second layer of pears, rounded side up, fitting pieces over bottom layer to fill open spaces.
5. Dot with butter. Bake, uncovered, 25 minutes, or just until caramelized sugar is melted.
6. Let stand in baking dish on wire rack until cooled to room temperature—about 1-1/2 hours.
7. Meanwhile, prepare pastry, following package directions. On lightly floured surface, roll out to a 9-inch circle. Place on ungreased cookie sheet; prick with fork. Refrigerate 30 minutes.
8. Bake pastry at 450F for 10 minutes, or until golden-brown. Let stand on cookie sheet on wire rack until ready to use.
9. To serve: Place pastry circle over pears in baking dish. Top with serving plate; invert, and remove baking dish. Mound marrons in center. Serve with whipped cream.
Makes 6 to 8 servings.

Pears Véfour

8 medium-size firm Bartlett or Anjou pears
   (about 3 lb)
1/4 cup lemon juice
1-1/2 cups sugar
1 (1-inch) piece vanilla bean, or 1/4 teaspoon
   vanilla extract
English Custard Sauce, page 218
2 tablespoons Grand Marnier

Pear Filling:
1 cup crushed almond macaroons (4-1/2-oz pkg)
1/4 cup Grand Marnier
1 cup heavy cream
Candied violets
Fresh mint leaves

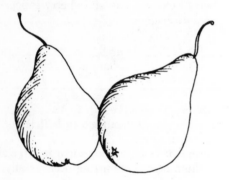

1. Wash pears. Core each from blossom end, leaving pear whole. Remove stem ends; pare. Brush with lemon juice.
2. In a large skillet, combine sugar with vanilla bean or extract and 3 cups water; bring to boiling over medium heat, stirring until sugar is dissolved. Add pears. Reduce heat; simmer, covered, until pears are tender but not soft—about 15 minutes. Remove vanilla bean if used.
3. Turn pears and syrup into large bowl. Refrigerate, covered, until chilled—about 3 hours.
4. Meanwhile, make Custard Sauce.
5. Turn into medium bowl; stir in 2 tablespoons Grand Marnier. Put sheet of waxed paper directly on surface of sauce in bowl. Refrigerate until well chilled and ready to use—at least 3 hours.
6. Make Pear Filling: Combine the crushed macaroons with 2 tablespoons Grand Marnier; mix well.
7. Carefully remove pears from syrup. Fill center of each with a slightly rounded tablespoonful of Pear Filling; brush pears with 2 tablespoons Grand Marnier. Refrigerate.
8. About 1 hour before serving, beat cream until stiff. Stir 1/2 cup whipped cream into chilled custard sauce. Spoon mixture into a large, chilled shallow serving bowl. Arrange 7 pears around edge of bowl and one in the center. Garnish pears with remaining whipped cream, using pastry bag with decorating tip, if desired. Refrigerate until serving time; then garnish with candied violets and mint. Makes 8 servings.

Chocolate Mousse

4 eggs
1 pkg (6 oz) semisweet chocolate pieces
5 tablespoons sweet butter
2 tablespoons Cognac or brandy
Whipped cream
Candied violets

1. One or two days before serving, separate eggs, turning whites into a medium bowl. Let whites warm to room temperature.
2. In top of double boiler, over hot, not boiling, water, melt chocolate and butter; stir to blend. Remove from hot water.
3. Using wooden spoon, beat in egg yolks, one at a time, beating well after each addition. Set aside to cool. Stir in Cognac.
4. When the chocolate mixture has cooled, beat egg whites with rotary beater just until stiff peaks form when beater is slowly raised.

5. With rubber scraper or wire whisk, gently fold chocolate mixture into egg whites, using an under-and-over motion. Fold only enough to combine— there should be no white streaks.

6. Turn into an attractive, 1-pint serving dish. Refrigerate overnight.

7. To serve, decorate with whipped cream and candied violets.

Makes 8 servings.

Chocolate-Nut Torte

Torte Layers:
7 eggs
1/4 teaspoon salt
1 cup granulated sugar
1 teaspoon vanilla extract
1-1/4 cups ground hazelnuts (10 oz unshelled)
1-1/4 cups ground pecans (12 oz unshelled)
1/4 cup packaged dry bread crumbs
1 teaspoon baking powder
1/2 teaspoon salt

Filling:
1 cup heavy cream, chilled
1/2 cup confectioners' sugar
1 teaspoon vanilla extract

Frosting:
4 squares unsweetened chocolate
1/4 cup butter or regular margarine
3 cups sifted confectioners' sugar
1/2 cup hot water or coffee
1-1/2 teaspoons vanilla extract
Whole hazelnuts and pecans

1. Make Torte Layers: Separate eggs, putting whites into large electric-mixer bowl, yolks into small one. Let whites warm to room temperature— about 1 hour. Preheat oven to 375F. Line bottom of 3 (8-inch) round layer-cake pans with circles of waxed paper.

2. With mixer at high speed, beat whites with 1/4 teaspoon salt until soft peaks form when beater is slowly raised. Gradually beat in 1/2 cup granulated sugar (2 tablespoons at a time) beating until stiff peaks form.

3. With same beaters, beat yolks until thick and light. Gradually beat in rest of granulated sugar, beating until thick—3 minutes; beat in 1 teaspoon vanilla.

4. Combine ground nuts, crumbs, baking powder, and salt; turn into yolk mixture. With rubber scraper, mix well; with under-and-over motion, fold into whites just to combine.

5. Divide evenly into prepared pans, smoothing surfaces. Bake 25 minutes, or until surface springs back when gently pressed with fingertip. To cool, hang each pan upside down between 2 other pans —1 hour.

6. Make Filling: In medium bowl, combine the cream, 1/2 cup confectioners' sugar, and 1 teaspoon vanilla. Beat until stiff; refrigerate.

7. Make Frosting: In top of double boiler, over hot water, melt chocolate, butter. Remove from water; mix in sugar, hot water, and vanilla until smooth.

8. Loosen sides of layers from pans with spatula. Turn out of pans; peel off paper. On plate, assemble layers, with half of filling between each two. Put 1 cup frosting in pastry bag with number-2 star tip; refrigerate. Frost and decorate torte. For easier cutting, refrigerate 1 hour.

Makes 12 servings.

Meringue Torte

6 egg whites
1/4 teaspoon salt
1/2 teaspoon cream of tartar
1-1/2 cups sugar
1 teaspoon vanilla extract
1/4 cup light rum
1 cup heavy cream, whipped
Whole strawberries (fresh or frozen)
Canned pineapple slices, drained

1. Day before serving or early in morning: In large bowl of electric mixer, let egg whites warm to room temperature, 1 hour. Lightly butter bottom, not side, of a 9-inch tube pan.
2. Preheat oven to 450F.
3. To egg whites, add salt and cream of tartar; beat until frothy. At high speed, beat in sugar, 2 tablespoons at a time, beating well after each addition. Add vanilla; beat until stiff peaks form when beaters are slowly raised. Turn into tube pan, spreading evenly.
4. Place on middle rack of oven. Immediately, turn off heat. Let stand in oven several hours or overnight.
5. Loosen edge with spatula. Turn out torte on serving plate. Sprinkle surface with rum. Refrigerate until well chilled—at least 4 hours.
6. To serve: Frost top and sides with whipped cream. Decorate top with sliced strawberries; garnish with pineapple.
Makes 10 servings.

Strawberries à la Blue Fox

30 fresh jumbo strawberries

Sherry Cream:
2 egg yolks
2 tablespoons granulated sugar
2 tablespoons sherry, port, or marsala
Confectioners' sugar
1 cup heavy cream

1. Wash strawberries in cold water; drain well; hull. From point, slit each berry into quarters, but don't cut through bottom. Refrigerate.
2. Make Sherry Cream: In top of double boiler, with portable electric mixer at medium speed, beat egg yolks with granulated sugar and sherry until well combined.
3. Place over boiling water; beat at medium speed until mixture is thick and forms soft peaks when beater is slowly raised—about 5 minutes. Remove from heat.
4. Immediately set top of double boiler in bowl of ice; continue beating until mixture is cool—about 2 minutes. Let stand in ice in refrigerator 30 minutes longer.
5. Meanwhile, in medium bowl, combine 1/4 cup confectioners' sugar and the cream. Refrigerate along with electric-beater blades, 30 minutes.
6. Add chilled cooked mixture to chilled cream mixture; beat until stiff.
7. Fill each strawberry with cream mixture—using pastry bag with decorating tip, if desired—bringing mixture to a peak at top. Refrigerate.
8. To serve: Sprinkle filled berries lightly with con-

fectioners' sugar. Arrange on mound of crushed ice.
Makes 8 to 10 servings.

Crêpes Suzette

Crêpes:
1 cup unsifted all-purpose flour
1/4 cup butter or margarine, melted and cooled, or
   1/4 cup salad oil
2 eggs
2 egg yolks
1-1/2 cups milk

Orange Butter:
3/4 cup sweet butter
1/2 cup sugar
1/3 cup Grand Marnier
1/4 cup grated orange peel

Orange Sauce:
1/2 cup sweet butter
3/4 cup sugar
2 tablespoons shredded orange peel
2/3 cup orange juice
2 oranges, peeled and sectioned
1/2 cup Grand Marnier

Butter or margarine
3 tablespoons Grand Marnier

1. Make Crêpes: In medium bowl, combine flour, melted butter, eggs, egg yolks, and 1/2 cup milk: beat with rotary beater until smooth. Beat in the remaining milk until mixture is well blended.
2. Refrigerate, covered, at least 30 minutes.
3. Meanwhile, make Orange Butter: In small bowl, with electric mixer, cream 3/4 cup sweet butter with 1/2 cup sugar until light and fluffy. Add 1/3 Grand Marnier and 1/4 cup orange peel; beat until well blended. Set aside.
4. Make Orange Sauce: In large skillet, melt sweet butter. Stir in sugar, orange peel, and orange juice; cook over low heat, stirring occasionally, until peel is translucent—about 20 minutes. Add orange sections and 1/2 cup Grand Marnier. Keep warm.
5. To cook crêpes: Slowly heat an 8-inch skillet until a drop of water sizzles and rolls off. For each crêpe, brush skillet lightly with butter. Pour in about 2 tablespoons batter, rotating pan quickly, to spread batter completely over bottom of skillet.
6. Cook until lightly browned; then turn, and brown other side. Turn out onto wire rack.
7. Spread each crêpe with Orange Butter, dividing evenly. Fold each in half, then in half again. When all are folded, place in Orange Sauce in chafing dish or skillet; cook over low heat until heated through.
8. To serve: Gently heat 3 tablespoons Grand Marnier in small saucepan just until vapor rises. Ignite with match, and pour over crêpes. Serve flaming.
Makes 6 to 8 servings.

Dessert Sauces

People who love desserts will love them even more dressed up with one of our delicious sauces.

Apricot Sauce

1 jar (12 oz) apricot preserves
2 tablespoons lemon juice
1/2 tablespoon kirsch

Melt preserves in small saucepan with lemon juice; strain. Add kirsch.
Makes 1 cup.

Brandy Sauce

4 egg yolks
1/2 cup sugar
1/3 cup brandy
1/2 cup heavy cream

1. In top of double boiler, beat egg yolks with sugar until very thick and light. Stir in brandy; cook, stirring, over hot, not boiling, water until thickened.
2. Refrigerate until well chilled.
3. Just before serving, pour cream into small bowl; beat until stiff. Fold into brandy mixture until well combined.
Makes 1-1/2 cups.

Butterscotch Sauce

1/3 cup butter or margarine
1 cup light-brown sugar, firmly packed
2 tablespoons light corn syrup
1/3 cup heavy cream

Melt butter in saucepan over low heat. Stir in brown sugar, corn syrup, and cream, cook to boiling point. Then remove from heat, and cool slightly. Serve warm or cold.
Makes 1-1/4 cups.

Caramel Sauce

1-1/2 cups sugar
1 tablespoon butter or margarine
1/8 teaspoon salt
1/2 teaspoon vanilla extract

1. In large, heavy skillet, heat sugar, over very low heat and stirring, until melted and light golden-brown.
2. Remove from heat. Very gradually stir in 1 cup hot water; bring to boiling point. Reduce heat, and simmer until it thickens slightly or reaches 228F on candy thermometer.
3. Remove from heat. Add butter, salt, and vanilla. Let cool.
Makes about 1-1/4 cups.

Cardinal Sauce

3 tablespoons cornstarch
1 pkg (10 oz) thawed frozen raspberries
1 pkg (10 oz) thawed frozen sliced strawberries

1. In saucepan, combine cornstarch with 1-1/4 cups water until smooth. Bring to boiling point; boil, stirring, until thickened and translucent—5 to 8 minutes.
2. Stir in berries. Let cool.
Makes 3-1/4 cups.

Chantilly Cream

1 cup heavy cream
2 tablespoons confectioners' sugar

1. In small bowl, mix cream and sugar. Refrigerate till well chilled.
2. Beat just until stiff with rotary beater. Refrigerate until serving.
Makes 2 cups.

Quick Chocolate Sauce

1 pkg (6 oz) semisweet-chocolate pieces
2/3 cup evaporated milk, undiluted

1. Combine chocolate pieces and milk in medium saucepan. Stir constantly, over low heat, just until chocolate is melted.
2. Serve warm, over ice cream or cakes.
Makes about 1 cup.

Deluxe Chocolate Sauce

1/4 cup sugar
1/3 cup light cream
1 pkg (4 oz) sweet cooking chocolate
1 square (1 oz) unsweetened chocolate

1. In top of double boiler, combine sugar and 2 tablespoons cream; cook, over boiling water, until sugar is dissolved.
2. Cut up both kinds of chocolate. Remove double boiler from heat, but leave top over bottom. Add chocolate to cream mixture, stirring until melted.
3. With spoon, beat in remaining cream. Serve warm.
Makes 1 cup.

Pour Custard Sauce

1-1/2 cups milk
3 egg yolks
1/4 cup sugar
Dash salt
1/2 teaspoon vanilla extract

1. Heat milk in top of double boiler, over direct heat, until tiny bubbles appear around edge of pan.
2. Beat yolks, sugar, and salt to mix well.
3. Very slowly pour hot milk into egg mixture, beating constantly.
4. Return mixture to double-boiler top; place over hot, not boiling, water. Water in lower part of double boiler should not touch upper part.
5. Cook, stirring constantly, until thin coating forms on metal spoon—8 to 10 minutes.
6. Pour custard immediately into bowl; place sheet of waxed paper directly on surface.
7. Set bowl in cold water, to cool. Stir in vanilla. Refrigerate until very cold—several hours or overnight.
Makes 1-1/2 cups.

English Custard Sauce

1/3 cup sugar
1 tablespoon cornstarch
2 cups milk
2 tablespoons butter or margarine
6 egg yolks
1-1/2 teaspoons vanilla extract
1/2 cup heavy cream

1. In medium saucepan, combine sugar and cornstarch. Gradually add milk; stir until smooth. Then add the butter.
2. Cook over medium heat, stirring constantly, until mixture is thickened and comes to boil. Boil 1 minute. Remove from heat.
3. In medium bowl, slightly beat egg yolks. Gradually add a little hot mixture, beating well.
4. Stir into rest of hot mixture; cook over medium heat, stirring constantly, just until mixture boils. Remove from heat; stir in vanilla.
5. Strain custard immediately into bowl. Refrigerate, covered, until cool. Stir in heavy cream. Return to refrigerator until well chilled.
Makes about 2-1/2 cups.

Cinnamon-Ice-Cream Sauce

1 teaspoon cinnamon
1 tablespoon sugar
1-1/2 pints soft vanilla ice cream

Combine cinnamon and sugar. Stir into ice cream until well blended and smooth. Serve immediately. Makes 2 cups.

Fudge Sauce

3 squares unsweetened chocolate
3/4 cup sugar
1/4 teaspoon salt
4-1/2 tablespoons butter or margarine
3/4 teaspoon vanilla extract

1. In small saucepan, combine chocolate with 1/2 cup water. Cook, over low heat and stirring occasionally, until chocolate is melted.
2. Add sugar and salt; cook, stirring, until sugar is dissolved and mixture thickens—about 5 minutes.
3. Remove from heat; stir in butter and vanilla. Let cool.
Makes about 1-1/2 cups.

Hard Sauce

1/4 cup soft butter or margarine
1-1/2 cups sifted confectioners' sugar
2 tablespoons light rum

1. In medium bowl, with portable electric mixer, beat butter until it is light.
2. Add sugar gradually, beating until sauce is smooth and fluffy. Beat in rum.
3. Refrigerate, covered, until ready to use.
4. Let stand at room temperature, to soften slightly, before serving.
Makes about 1 cup.

Nutmeg Hard Sauce

1/3 cup butter or regular margarine, softened
1 cup confectioners' sugar
1 teaspoon vanilla extract
Nutmeg

1. In small bowl, with electric mixer at high speed, beat butter until light.
2. Add sugar and vanilla; beat until fluffy and smooth.
3. Turn into small, attractive bowl. Sprinkle generously with nutmeg. Refrigerate, covered, until serving time.
Makes about 3/4 cup.

Marshmallow Sauce

1 cup prepared creamy marshmallow topping
1/2 teaspoon vanilla extract

In small bowl, with fork, beat marshmallow topping, 2-1/2 teaspoons water, and the vanilla until smooth.
Makes 1 cup.

Pineapple Sauce

1/2 cup sugar
1 tablespoon cornstarch
1 can (6 oz) pineapple juice
1/4 teaspoon grated lemon peel
1 can (8-3/4 oz) crushed pineapple

1. In small saucepan, combine sugar and cornstarch; mix well.
2. Gradually add pineapple juice, stirring until smooth. Add lemon peel and crushed pineapple.
3. Over medium heat, bring to boiling, stirring, and boil until mixture is thickened and translucent.
4. Refrigerate until cold.
Makes about 1-1/2 cups.

Strawberry Sauce

1 pkg (10 oz) frozen sliced strawberries, thawed
1/4 cup sugar
1 tablespoon cornstarch
2 tablespoons strawberry preserves

1. Drain strawberries, reserving syrup. Add water to syrup to measure 1 cup.
2. In small saucepan, combine sugar and cornstarch. Gradually add strawberry syrup, stirring until smooth.
3. Over low heat, slowly bring to boiling, stirring, until mixture is thickened and translucent.
4. Remove from heat. Stir in strawberries and strawberry preserves.
5. Stir until preserves are melted. Refrigerate until cold.
Makes 1-1/3 cups.

Raspberry Sauce

2 pkg (10-oz size) frozen raspberries, thawed
2 tablespoons cornstarch
1/2 cup currant jelly

1. Drain raspberries, reserving liquid. Add enough water to liquid to make 2 cups.
2. In small saucepan, blend liquid with cornstarch. Bring to boiling over medium heat, stirring constantly; boil 5 minutes. Stir in jelly until melted. Remove from heat; add raspberries. Refrigerate, covered, until cold. Serve with Floating Heart Ritz, p. 199.
Makes 2 cups.

Eggs & Cheese

What a perfect invention, the egg! And how very thoughtful of the hen to provide mankind with a food so nutritious, so handy, so inexpensive, so easy to cook and so good in any form: scrambled, boiled, fried, poached—alone or in the company of other foods. We give you recipes that should serve you from the early-morning breakfast hours clear through very late suppers.

All about Eggs

1. Eggs should be refrigerated from the time they are gathered until they are used so that they lose none of their freshness.
2. Since eggs have a natural protective coating that keeps them fresh, do not wash them until ready to use.
3. The contents of eggs, whether white or brown, are exactly the same. They are a good source of protein, fat, Vitamin A and D, iron and riboflavin.
4. The common market sizes of eggs per dozen are:

extra large eggs: 27 ounces
large: 24 ounces
medium: 21 ounces
small: 18 ounces
Buy the size that fits your need, or whatever size happens to be the better buy per pound.
5. Eggs separate best when they are cold.
6. They whip best, attain their greatest volume, at room temperature. In all our recipes calling for beaten egg whites, this is essential.

Know the Eggs You Buy

Nowadays, all eggs on the market have their grade printed clearly on the box. Most markets have three or four grades:

Grade AA: Excellent for table use. When broken from the shell, the white covers only a small area; the yolk stands high; there is a large amount of thick white hugging the yolk and a small amount of thin white at the very edge. When hard-cooked, the yolk may be easily centered. When fried, the yolk is round and upstanding; the white is high and thick around the yolk.
Grade A: Good for table use. When broken from the shell, the white spreads over a larger area; the yolk still stands high; there is a large amount of thick white hugging the yolk and a small amount of thin white at the very edge. When hard-cooked, the yolk is slightly off center. When fried, the yolk

is round and upstanding; the white is somewhat spread out.
Grade B: Fair for table, good for cooking and baking. When broken from the shell, the white spreads out wide; the yolk is somewhat flat; there is a medium amount of thick white around the yolk, but it looks flat; there is a medium amount of thin white. When hard-cooked, the yolk is far off center. When fried, the yolk looks somewhat flat; the white spreads widely and is pretty thin.
Grade C: All right for cooking and baking. When broken from the shell, the white covers a large area, and it is mostly thin; the yolk is very flat and easily broken. When hard-cooked, the yolk is far off center, in a ragged-looking circle. When fried, the white is thin and spreads over a large area; the yolk is very flat.

How to Cook Eggs

A protein food, eggs should be cooked at a low temperature if you want them to retain their tenderness and delicacy. They are so easy to cook that there's no excuse, we think, for not cooking them perfectly. These simple rules will bring success every time.

Soft-Cooked Eggs: Cover eggs with water to an inch above them; bring rapidly to a boil. Take pan off heat; cover, and let stand 2 to 4 minutes, depending on doneness desired. Cool under running water, to prevent further cooking.
Hard-Cooked Eggs: Follow directions for Soft-

Cooked Eggs, letting eggs stand 20 minutes. Cool immediately, in cold water, to prevent dark surface on yolks and so shells can be removed easily.

Scrambled Eggs: Allow 1 teaspoon milk to each egg. Mix well eggs, milk, salt and pepper to taste. Heat fat (enough to cover bottom of skillet) until just hot enough to sizzle a drop of water. Pour in egg mixture, and reduce heat. When eggs have set slightly, stir constantly with a fork. Perfectly scrambled eggs should be soft and creamy. Don't overcook.

Poached Eggs: Bring water (about 1 inch deep) in shallow pan to boiling point. Reduce heat to simmer. Break each egg into a saucer; quickly slip egg into water. Cook, covered, 3 to 5 minutes. Lift out of water with slotted pancake turner or spoon. Drain well.

Fried Eggs: Heat 1 to 2 tablespoons butter or margarine in small skillet until just hot enough to sizzle a drop of water. Break eggs directly into pan. Take pan off heat immediately, and baste eggs with hot fat about 3 or 4 minutes.

Or: Melt 1 tablespoon butter or margarine in small skillet. Break eggs directly into pan. Over low heat, fry gently to desired doneness—about 3 or 4 minutes. Eggs may be covered or turned, to cook yolk.

Deviled Eggs

12 eggs
3/4 cup mayonnaise or cooked salad
   dressing
1 tablespoon white vinegar
1 teaspoon dry mustard
1-1/2 teaspoons Worcestershire sauce
3/4 teaspoon salt
1/8 teaspoon pepper
1/8 teaspoon paprika
Parsley sprigs

1. Hard-cook eggs, as directed in "How to Cook Eggs." Remove shells. Cool eggs completely.

3. Halve eggs lengthwise. Take out yolks, being careful not to break whites.

3. Press yolks through sieve into medium bowl. Add remaining ingredients, except parsley; mix with fork until smooth and fluffy.

4. Lightly mound yolk mixture in egg-whites. Garnish each with parsley sprig.

Makes 12 servings.

Poached Eggs with Ham

1 tablespoon white vinegar
6 eggs
3 (1/4 inch thick) slices boiled ham (1 lb)
1 tablespoon butter or margarine

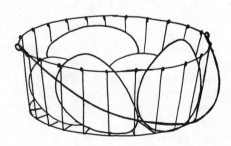

1. To poach eggs: In deep skillet, bring water (1 inch deep) to boiling. Add vinegar; reduce heat to simmer.

2. Break eggs, one by one, into a saucer; quickly slip into water.

3. Poach eggs, uncovered, 5 minutes—until whites are firm but yolks are soft.

4. Meanwhile, cut ham slices in half. In hot butter in skillet, sauté ham until lightly browned on each side. Arrange the ham slices on serving platter.

5. With slotted utensil, carefully remove eggs from skillet. Place an egg on each piece of ham.

Makes 6 servings.

Scrambled Eggs

Should you add water, or milk, or cream to scrambled eggs? Should you add no liquid at all? We belong to the milk-and-cream school, as you can see from our scrambled-egg variations for Sunday brunch or a Saturday-night supper.

Skillet Scrambled Eggs

1-1/2 tablespoons butter or margarine
4 eggs
1/4 teaspoon salt
Dash pepper
2 tablespoons light cream

1. Heat butter in small skillet over low heat.
2. Break eggs into skillet; stir with a fork.
3. Add salt, pepper, and cream; mix well.
4. Cook slowly. As eggs start to set at bottom, gently lift cooked portion, with spatula, to form flakes, letting uncooked portion flow to bottom of pan.
5. When eggs are cooked but still shiny and moist, remove from skillet.
Makes 2 servings.
Bacon Scrambled Eggs: Sauté 4 bacon slices until crisp; drain well. Crumble bacon; stir into eggs as they cook.
Cheese Scrambled Eggs: Stir 1 teaspoon finely chopped onion and 1/4 cup grated mild Cheddar cheese into eggs as they cook.

Mexican-Style Scrambled Eggs

Sauce:
1 tablespoon butter or margarine
1 small white onion, sliced
1 tablespoon flour
1 can (1 lb) stewed tomatoes

3 tablespoons butter or margarine
1/2 cup finely chopped green pepper
1/4 cup finely chopped onion
1 clove garlic, crushed
6 eggs
2 tablespoons milk
1/2 teaspoon salt
1/8 teaspoon pepper

1. Make Sauce: Melt 1 tablespoon butter in small saucepan. Add sliced onion; sauté until soft. Remove from heat. Stir in flour until smooth. Gradually stir in tomatoes; bring to boiling, stirring. Reduce heat, and simmer 3 minutes. Keep warm.
2. In 3 tablespoons hot butter in skillet, sauté green pepper, chopped onion, and the garlic until tender —about 5 minutes.
3. In medium bowl, beat eggs with milk, salt, and pepper until well combined. Add to sautéed vegetables.
4. Cook over low heat. As eggs start to set, lift with spatula to let uncooked portion run underneath.
5. Place on warm serving platter, and surround with tomato sauce.
Makes 3 or 4 servings.

Creamy Scrambled Eggs

14 eggs
1/2 cup milk
1 tablespoon snipped chives
1 teaspoon salt
1/2 teaspoon dried tarragon leaves
1/8 teaspoon pepper
1/4 cup butter or margarine
2 pkg (3-oz size) cream cheese, cubed
4 slices bacon, crisply cooked and crumbled
2 tablespoons chopped parsley

1. In medium bowl, combine eggs, milk, chives, salt, tarragon, and pepper. With rotary beater, beat just until combined but not frothy.
2. Heat butter in large skillet. Pour in egg mixture; cook over low heat. As eggs start to set on bottom, gently lift cooked portion with spatula, to form flakes, letting uncooked portion flow to bottom of pan.
3. Add cream-cheese cubes; continue cooking until eggs are moist and shiny but no longer runny.
4. Sprinkle with bacon and parsley.
Makes 10 servings.

Mushroom Scrambled Eggs

6 eggs
1 tablespoon instant-type flour
1/2 teaspoon salt
Dash pepper
1/3 cup light cream
1 tablespoon sherry
2 tablespoons butter or margarine
1 can (3 oz) sliced mushrooms, drained
2 green onions, sliced

1. In large bowl, with rotary beater, beat eggs until frothy. Sprinkle with flour, salt, and pepper; beat until smooth. Beat in cream and sherry.
2. Melt butter in a 9-inch skillet, over medium heat.
3. Pour egg mixture into skillet; cook slowly. As eggs start to set at bottom, with spatula, gently lift cooked portion to form flakes, letting uncooked portion flow to bottom of skillet. Add mushrooms.
4. When eggs are cooked but still shiny and moist, remove from heat.
5. Turn into serving dish. Sprinkle with onions. Serve with crisp toast slices, if desired.
Makes 3 servings.

Scrambled Eggs à la Suisse

8 eggs
1/2 cup light cream
1/2 teaspoon salt
Dash cayenne
1 cup grated natural Swiss cheese (1/4 lb)
2 tablespoons butter or margarine
Snipped chives or parsley

1. With rotary beater, beat eggs, cream, salt, and cayenne in top of double boiler until well combined.
2. Stir in 3/4 cup Swiss cheese and the butter.
3. Cook, over gently boiling water, stirring occasionally, 12 to 15 minutes, or until eggs are set but still creamy.
4. Serve eggs sprinkled with rest of cheese and the chives.
Makes 4 servings.

Omelets

Reputations and even fortunes have been made by omelets. While we don't promise you'll be able to run a wildly successful omelet restaurant, we will show you how to produce sheer golden perfection, time after time after time. So even if your omelets are runny, or leathery, or thin, or anything a well-behaved omelet should never be, just follow our directions. You'll never have trouble again.

Basic Omelet

3 eggs
1/4 teaspoon salt
1 tablespoon cold water
1 tablespoon butter or margarine

1. In medium bowl, with wire whisk or rotary beater, beat eggs with salt and water just until well mixed. (Mixture should not be too frothy.) Meanwhile, slowly heat a 9-inch heavy skillet or omelet pan. To test temperature, sprinkle a small amount of cold water on skillet; water should sizzle and roll off in drops. Add butter; heat until it sizzles briskly—it should not brown.
2. Quickly turn egg mixture, all at once, into skillet. Cook over medium heat.
3. As omelet sets, run spatula around edge, to loosen. Tilt pan, to let uncooked portion run underneath. Continue loosening and tilting until omelet is almost dry on top and golden-brown underneath.
4. To turn out, loosen edge with spatula. Fold, in thirds, to edge of pan; tilt out onto plate.
Makes 1 serving.

Omelet Fines Herbes

3 eggs
1/4 teaspoon salt
2 tablespoons finely snipped fresh parsley
1 teaspoon finely snipped fresh tarragon leaves
1 teaspoon finely snipped fresh marjoram leaves
1/2 teaspoon finely snipped fresh thyme leaves
1 teaspoon finely chopped shallots
1 tablespoon butter or margarine
Parsley sprig

1. Combine eggs, salt, and 1 tablespoon cold water in small bowl; beat, with rotary beater, just until combined, not frothy.
2. Combine rest of ingredients, except butter and the parsley sprig; stir into eggs, mixing well.
3. Slowly heat a medium-size heavy skillet. It is ready when small amount of cold water sprinkled over surface sizzles and rolls off in drops. Add butter; heat until it sizzles briskly (not browned).
4. Quickly turn egg mixture into skillet; cook over medium heat. As omelet sets, loosen edge with spatula, and tilt skillet, to let uncooked mixture run under set portion.
5. When omelet is dry on top and golden-brown on bottom, fold it over to edge of pan. Tilt out onto hot serving plate. Serve at once, garnished with parsley sprig.

Makes 1 or 2 servings.

Note: Or substitute dried herbs for fresh, using half the quantity.

Cheese Omelet

Filling:
1 tablespoon flour
1/4 teaspoon dry mustard
1/8 teaspoon salt
1/8 teaspoon pepper
1/2 cup milk
2 cups grated sharp Cheddar cheese
1 teaspoon grated onion

4 Basic Omelets
1/2 cup grated sharp Cheddar cheese

1. Make Filling: In top of double boiler, over hot water, combine flour, mustard, salt, pepper, and milk, stirring until smooth.
2. Add 2 cups cheese and the onion; cook, stirring occasionally, 15 to 20 minutes, or until mixture thickens and cheese is melted.
3. Remove from heat; keep warm over hot water.
4. Make 4 omelets, one by one, in omelet pan or skillet with heat-resistant handle.
5. Before pouring into pan, add 1 tablespoon cheese to each.
6. Just before folding each omelet, place 1/4 cup filling in center. Fold over in thirds; sprinkle each with 1 tablespoon cheese.
7. Run under broiler, 6 inches from heat, until the cheese is bubbly and golden—about 1 minute.
8. With spatula, lift out onto serving plate; keep warm until serving.

Makes 4 servings.

Cottage-Cheese-and-Chive Omelet

1 container (8 oz) large-curd
  creamed cottage cheese
2 tablespoons snipped chives
1 teaspoon chopped parsley
6 eggs
1/2 teaspoon salt
1/8 teaspoon dry mustard
1 tablespoon butter or margarine

1. In small bowl, combine cottage cheese, chives, and parsley. Set aside.
2. In medium bowl, combine eggs, 1 tablespoon water, the salt, and mustard; beat with wire whisk until mixed but not foamy.
3. Meanwhile, slowly heat a 10-inch heavy skillet or omelet pan until a little cold water sizzles and rolls off in drops. Add butter; heat until it sizzles-do not brown.
4. Quickly turn egg mixture, all at once, into skillet; cook over medium heat. As mixture sets, run spatula around edge, to loosen; tilt pan, to let uncooked portion run underneath. Continue loosening and tilting until omelet is almost dry on top and golden-brown underneath.
5. Spoon cottage-cheese mixture over half of omelet; fold over other half. Turn out onto serving plate.

Makes 4 servings.

Cecilia's Omelet, Spanish Style

3 tablespoons salad oil
1-1/2 lb potatoes, pared and finely chopped
4 onions, peeled and finely chopped
1-1/2 teaspoons salt
1/4 teaspoon pepper
8 eggs

1. In hot oil in heavy, 9-inch skillet, cook potato and onion, covered, over medium heat 20 to 30 minutes. Stir mixture frequently; it should be soft but not browned. Sprinkle with 1 teaspoon salt and 1/8 teaspoon pepper.
2. In medium bowl, with rotary beater, beat eggs with 1/2 cup water, 1/2 teaspoon salt, and 1/8 teaspoon pepper. Pour egg mixture over potato and onion in skillet, lifting edge of potato mixture all around, to let egg run under. Do this several times.
3. Cook, covered, over medium heat just until eggs are set—about 8 minutes. Loosen edge with spatula.
4. To serve, place a heated serving platter over top of skillet, and invert omelet onto platter.
Makes 8 servings.

Basic Puffy Omelet

6 egg whites
1/8 teaspoon cream of tartar
6 egg yolks
3/4 teaspoon salt
Dash pepper
6 tablespoons milk
2 tablespoons butter or margarine
2 teaspoons salad oil

1. In large bowl of electric mixer, let egg whites warm to room temperature—about 1 hour.
2. Preheat oven to 350F.
3. With mixer at high speed, beat egg whites with cream of tartar just until stiff peaks form when beaters are slowly raised.
4. In small bowl of electric mixer, using same beaters, beat egg yolks until thick and lemon-colored.
5. Add salt, pepper, and milk gradually; beat until well combined.
6. With wire whisk or rubber scraper, using an under-and-over motion, gently fold egg-yolk mixture into egg whites just until combined.
7. Slowly heat a 9- or 10-inch heavy skillet with heat-resistant handle, or an omelet pan. To test temperature: Sprinkle a little cold water on skillet. Water should sizzle and roll off in drops.
8. Add butter and oil; heat until it sizzles briskly—it should not brown. Tilt pan to coat side with butter mixture.
9. Spread egg mixture evenly in pan; cook, over low heat, without stirring, until lightly browned on underside—about 10 minutes.
10. Transfer skillet to oven; bake 10 to 12 minutes, or until top seems firm when gently pressed with fingertip.
11. To serve: Fold omelet in half. Turn out onto heated serving platter. Garnish with parsley sprigs, if desired.

Makes 4 servings.

Puffy Omelet with Cherry Preserves: To serve: Fold Basic Puffy Omelet in half. Turn out on platter. Sprinkle with confectioners' suger. Serve with cherry preserves.

Puffy Spanish Omelet

Basic Puffy Omelet, above

Sauce:
2 tablespoons butter or margarine
1 clove garlic, crushed
1/4 cup chopped onion
1/3 cup thinly sliced celery
1/2 cup chopped green pepper
1/2 teaspoon salt
1/8 teaspoon pepper
1/4 teaspoon paprika
1/4 teaspoon dried oregano leaves
1 can (8 oz) tomato sauce
1 can (3 oz) sliced mushrooms, drained
9 pitted jumbo ripe olives, thickly sliced
1-1/3 cups coarsely chopped fresh tomatoes

Parsley sprigs

1. Make Puffy Omelet as recipe directs; do not fold.
2. Meanwhile, make Sauce: In hot butter in medium skillet, sauté the garlic, onion, celery, and green pepper until they are tender—about 5 minutes.
3. Add salt, pepper, paprika, oregano, and tomato sauce; bring to boiling. Reduce heat; simmer, uncovered, 10 minutes.
4. Add mushrooms, olives, and tomatoes; cook, stirring, until heated through.
5. To serve: Fold half of omelet over other half. Remove to heated serving platter. Pour some of sauce over omelet; pass rest. Garnish with parsley sprigs.
Makes 4 servings.

Special Egg Dishes

Here are such super-elegant egg dishes as Eggs Benedict, so good for any occasion, from extra-special weekend breakfasts and brunches through lunch and supper.

Baked Eggs Gruyère

1 pkg (6 oz) individual Gruyère-cheese wedges
10 crisp-cooked bacon slices
6 eggs
1/2 cup heavy cream
1/8 teaspoon pepper

1. Preheat oven to 350F. Generously butter a 10-by-6-by-2-inch baking dish.
2. Cut each of 5 cheese wedges lengthwise into fourths. Cover bottom of prepared dish with cheese slices.
3. Crumble bacon over cheese in dish. Carefully break eggs over cheese and bacon.
4. Spoon cream over eggs; sprinkle with pepper.
5. Grate remaining cheese wedge; sprinkle over eggs.
6. Bake, uncovered, 20 minutes, or just until eggs are set.
Makes 6 servings.

Eggs Benedict

Hollandaise Sauce, page 22
4 English muffins
8 teaspoons butter or margarine
1 teaspoon salt
8 eggs
4 slices fully cooked ham (1/2 lb)
8 parsley or watercress sprigs

1. Prepare Hollandaise Sauce. Keep warm over hot water.
2. Slice muffins in half, crosswise. Place on cookie sheet. Spread each cut side with 1 teaspoon butter. Toast until golden-brown; cover; keep warm.
3. In large skillet, bring 1 inch water to simmering; add salt.
4. Break one egg at a time into custard cup; slip eggs into water carefully, one by one; poach, covered, 3 to 5 minutes. If possible, use rings to keep shape circular.
5. Meanwhile, in large skillet, sauté the ham about 3 minutes on each side. Cut slices in half.
6. Arrange ham slices on muffins.
7. Remove eggs with slotted utensil; trim if necessary, being careful not to break yolk.
8. Place eggs on ham; top with Hollandaise Sauce. Run under broiler until sauce is golden.
9. With broad spatula, remove to serving plates. Garnish with parsley.
Makes 4 servings.

Ham and Eggs in a Cloud

1 lb sliced Canadian bacon or baked ham
6 slices white bread, toasted, buttered, and halved
10 eggs
Salt
1/2 teaspoon dry mustard
Dash pepper

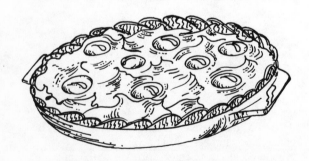

1. Preheat oven to 400F. Lightly grease a 14-by-9-by-2-inch baking dish. Arrange Canadian bacon, overlapping, against sides of dish. Cover bottom with toast, to keep bacon in place.
2. Separate eggs, placing whites in a large bowl and keeping each yolk in its half shell (place half shell back in egg carton for safekeeping). Use 8 yolks.
3. With electric mixer, beat whites with 1/2 teaspoon salt and the mustard until stiff. Turn into baking dish, mounding high. Make 8 depressions, spacing evenly. Bake, uncovered, 1 or 2 minutes, or until slightly set.
4. Place an egg yolk in each depression. Sprinkle each with a little salt and pepper. Bake, uncovered, 8 to 10 minutes, or until whites are slightly golden and yolks are set. Serve at once.
Makes 8 servings.

Cheese

Since cheese is made from milk, it is a concentrated source of the minerals and protein in milk. The many varieties of cheese are due, in part, to the different kinds of milk from which they are made.

The two basic types of cheese are natural and processed. Natural cheese is made from coagulated milk; the curd and whey are separated. Process cheese is made by grinding and mixing natural cheeses and heating and stirring them together; it costs less than the natural cheeses.

Cheese is not only nutritious but delicious in the cheese soufflé and cheese casseroles that follow.

Golden Buck

8 oz Cheddar cheese, coarsely grated (2 cups)
2 eggs
1/2 cup milk
2 tablespoons butter or margarine
2 teaspoons prepared mustard
1/2 teaspoon salt
Dash cayenne
6 eggs
6 slices white bread

1. In top of double boiler, combine cheese, 2 eggs, the milk, butter, mustard, salt, and cayenne. Cook over simmering water, stirring frequently, until cheese is melted and sauce is smooth. Remove from heat, but keep over hot water.

2. Poach the 6 eggs; toast bread.

3. To serve: Spoon about 2 tablespoons sauce on each slice of toast; top with a poached egg. Spoon any remaining sauce over eggs. Garnish with parsley, if desired.

Makes 6 servings.

John Wayne's Cheese Casserole

2 cans (4-oz size) green chiles, drained
1 lb Monterey Jack cheese, coarsely grated
1 lb Cheddar cheese, coarsely grated
4 egg whites
4 egg yolks
2/3 cup canned evaporated milk, undiluted
1 tablespoon flour
1/2 teaspoon salt
1/8 teaspoon pepper
2 medium tomatoes, sliced

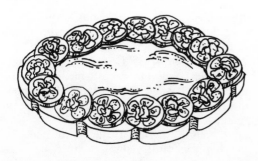

1. Preheat oven to 325F. Remove seeds from chiles, and dice.

2. In a large bowl, combine the grated cheese and green chiles. Turn into a well-buttered, shallow 2-quart casserole (12 by 8 by 2 inches)

3. In large bowl, with electric mixer at high speed, beat egg whites just until stiff peaks form when beater is slowly raised.

4. In small bowl of electric mixer, combine egg yolks, milk, flour, salt, and pepper; mix until well blended.

5. Using a rubber scraper, gently fold beaten whites into egg-yolk mixture.

6. Pour egg mixture over cheese mixture in casserole, and using a fork, "ooze" it through the cheese.

7. Bake 30 minutes; remove from oven, and arrange sliced tomatoes, overlapping, around edge of casserole. Bake 30 minutes longer, or until a silver knife inserted in center comes out clean. Garnish with a sprinkling of chopped green chiles, if desired.

Makes 6 to 8 servings.

Baked Ziti Casserole

Sauce:
1/4 cup olive or salad oil
1 cup finely chopped onion
1 clove garlic, crushed
1 can (2 lb, 3 oz) Italian tomatoes
1 can (6 oz) tomato paste
2 tablespoons chopped parsley
1 tablespoon salt
1 tablespoon sugar
1 teaspoon dried oregano leaves
1/2 teaspoon dried basil leaves
1/4 teaspoon pepper
1 pkg (1 lb) ziti macaroni

Cheese Layer:
2 cartons (15 oz size) ricotta cheese
1 pkg (8 oz) mozzarella cheese, diced
1/3 cup grated Parmesan cheese
2 eggs
1 tablespoon chopped parsley
1 teaspoon salt
1/4 teaspoon pepper

3 tablespoons grated Parmesan cheese

1. Make Sauce: In hot oil in 6-quart kettle, sauté onion and garlic until golden-brown—about 10 minutes. Add undrained tomatoes, tomato paste, 1-l/2 cups water, 2 tablespoons parsley, 1 tablespoon salt, the sugar, oregano, basil, and 1/4 teaspoon pepper; mix well, mashing tomatoes with fork.
2. Bring to boiling; reduce heat; simmer, covered and stirring occasionally, 1 hour.
3. Preheat oven to 350F. Cook ziti as package label directs.
4. Make Cheese Layer: In large bowl, combine ricotta, mozzarella, 1/3 cup Parmesan, the eggs, parsley, salt, and pepper. Beat with wooden spoon until blended.
5. Spoon a little sauce into a 5-quart casserole. Layer a third of ziti, cheese mixture, and remaining sauce. Sprinkle sauce with 1 tablespoon Parmesan. Repeat twice.
6. Bake, uncovered, 45 minutes, or until bubbling in center.
Makes 8 to 10 servings.
Note: If desired, make casserole ahead, and refrigerate. Remove from refrigerator while preheating oven. Bake 60 minutes, or until heated through.

Fabulous Cheese Soufflé

6 eggs
Butter or margarine
Grated Parmesan cheese
6 tablespoons unsifted all-purpose flour
1-1/2 teaspoons salt
Dash cayenne
1-1/4 cups milk
1/2 cup coarsely grated natural Swiss cheese
1/4 teaspoon cream of tartar

1. Separate eggs, placing whites in large bowl, yolks in another large bowl. Set aside until whites warm to room temperature—about 1 hour.
2. Meanwhile, butter a 1-1/2-quart, straight-side soufflé dish (7-1/2 inches in diameter). Dust lightly with Parmesan—about 1 tablespoon.
3. Tear off a sheet of waxed paper, 26 inches long. Fold lengthwise into thirds. Lightly butter one side.
4. Wrap waxed paper around soufflé dish, with buttered side against dish and a 2-inch rim extending above top edge. Tie with string.
5. Preheat the oven to 350F.
6. Melt 5 tablespoons butter in a medium saucepan; remove from heat. Stir in flour, 1 teaspoon salt, and the cayenne until smooth. Gradually stir in the milk.
7. Bring to boiling, stirring. Reduce heat, and simmer, stirring constantly, until mixture becomes very thick and begins to leave the bottom and side of the pan.

8. With wire whisk or wooden spoon, beat egg yolks. Gradually beat in cooked mixture. Add 1/2 cup Parmesan cheese and the Swiss cheese; beat until well combined.

9. Add remaining 1/2 teaspoon salt and the cream of tartar to egg whites. With portable electric mixer at high speed, beat until stiff peaks form when beater is raised.

10. With wire whisk or rubber scraper, fold one third of beaten egg whites into warm cheese mixture until well combined. Carefully fold in remaining egg whites just until combined. Turn into prepared dish.

11. Bake 40 minutes, or until soufflé is puffed and golden-brown. Remove collar. Serve soufflé at once.

Makes 4 servings.

Note: Serve with Lobster Sauce, page 500, for an extra special entrée.

Cheese Lasagna

Tomato Sauce:
1/4 cup olive or salad oil
1 cup finely chopped onion
1 clove garlic, crushed
1 can (2 lb, 3 oz) Italian tomatoes
1 can (6 oz) tomato paste
1 can (8 oz) tomato sauce
2 tablespoons chopped parsley
1 tablespoon salt
1 tablespoon sugar
1 teaspoon dried oregano leaves
1/2 teaspoon dried basil leaves
1/4 teaspoon pepper

1 pkg (1 lb) lasagna noodles

Cheese Layer:
2 cartons (15-oz size) ricotta cheese
1-1/2 pkg (8-oz size) mozzarella cheese, grated coarsely
1/2 cup grated Parmesan cheese
2 eggs
1 tablespoon chopped parsley
1 teaspoon salt
1/4 teaspoon pepper

3 tablespoons grated Parmesan cheese
1/2 pkg (8-oz size) mozzarella cheese, grated

1. Make Tomato Sauce: In hot oil in 6-quart kettle, sauté onion and garlic until golden-brown— about 10 minutes. Add undrained tomatoes, tomato paste, tomato sauce, 2 tablespoons parsley, 1 tablespoon salt, the sugar, oregano, basil, and 1/4 teaspoon pepper; mix well, mashing tomatoes with fork.

2. Bring to boiling; reduce heat, simmer, covered and stirring occasionally, 1 hour.

3. Preheat oven to 350F. Cook lasagna noodles as package label directs. Grease a 14-by-10-by-2-inch baking pan.

4. Make Cheese Layer: In large bowl, combine ricotta, 1-1/2 packages mozzarella, 1/2 cup Parmesan, the eggs, parsley, salt, and pepper. Beat with wooden spoon until all ingredients are blended.

5. Spoon a little tomato sauce into prepared pan. Layer noodles, cheese mixture, and tomato sauce. Repeat until all ingredients are used, ending with tomato sauce. Sprinkle with 3 tablespoons Parmesan and 1/2 package mozzarella.

6. Bake, uncovered, 45 to 50 minutes, or until cheese is melted and top is browned.

Makes 10 to 12 servings.

California Cheese-and-Rice Casserole

1/4 cup butter or margarine
1 cup chopped onion
4 cups freshly cooked white rice
2 cups sour cream
1 cup cream-style cottage cheese
1 large bay leaf, crumbled
1/2 teaspoon salt
1/8 teaspoon pepper
3 cans (4-oz size) green chiles, drained, halved
   lengthwise, leaving seeds
2 cups grated sharp natural Cheddar cheese
Chopped parsley

1. Preheat oven to 375F. Lightly grease a 12-by-8-by-2-inch baking dish (2-quart).
2. In hot butter in large skillet, sauté onion until golden—about 5 minutes.
3. Remove from heat; stir in hot rice, sour cream, cottage cheese, bay leaf, salt and pepper; toss lightly to mix well.
4. Layer half the rice mixture in bottom of baking dish, then half of chiles; sprinkle with half of cheese; repeat.
5. Bake, uncovered, 25 minutes, or until bubbly and hot. Sprinkle with chopped parsley.
Makes 8 servings.

Cheese with Fruit

Europe's favorite dessert is fast becoming America's as well: It's a perfect ending for so many meals, simple or formal, light or rich, luncheon or dinner.

The fruit must be pretty as a picture; the very peak of ripeness, so that it is sweet and juicy; nicely chilled, yet not too cold; served with dainty fruit knives.

Cheese should be ripe and room temperature. Serve several varieties on your cheese board, with crackers or French or Italian bread. Best way to buy cheese is in small amounts.

It's best to serve an assortment of cheeses and fruits, at least three or four, to please a variety of tastes. As a start, choose one from each of the groups listed below, to avoid duplications in texture and flavor.

Except for the fresh, soft cheeses, which should be served slightly chilled, always serve cheeses at room temperature—remove them from the refrigerator 1 to 3 hours before serving. Time depends on the size of the piece of cheese.

Cheeses of the soft, ripened type are at their best when thoroughly "ripe"—very soft and creamy inside. Other firmer cheeses must be adequately aged.

To be certain cheese is of maximum quality, buy it at its best, in small amounts and often.

Wine is also a good accompaniment to cheese: a dry red wine for most cheeses; but Port or Madeira are best with Stilton and other blue-veined cheeses.

Here are some sample fruit-and-cheese arrangements:

On the cheese board: Individual wedges of Petit Suisse, a wedge of Brie, Bel Paese, and Stilton. Serve with plain (not sweet) crackers, French-bread chunks, and sweet butter.

Along with this, a fruit-bowl arrangement of crisp, chilled apples and pears, peaches, fresh figs, and strawberries, hulls on.

Another combination might be: American cream cheese in serving-size chunks, Camembert, Bonbel, and blue cheese. The accompanying fruit: fresh pineapple wedges, crisp chilled pears, peaches or nectarines, green grapes, and raspberries.

Guide to Serving Cheese with Fruit

Soft, Unripened Cheeses — Serve slightly chilled. Use within a few days of purchasing

American cream cheese	Delicate, very mild flavor	Serve these cheeses with all berries (strawberries, raspberries, blueberries, blackberries), nectarines, peaches, and currant, strawberry, or quince jams
Boursin	Creamy, mild flavor (Also with garlic and herbs)	
Crème Danica	Fresh, creamy; buttery flavor	
Swedish Hablé	Soft; delicate in flavor	
French Petit Suisse	Delicate, very mild flavor	
Neufchâtel	Delicate, very mild flavor	

Soft, Ripened Cheeses — Serve at room temperature and optimum ripeness; they should be very soft and creamy inside

Brie	Mild to strong flavor	Eating apples, fresh pears, green grapes, dried fruits
Camembert	Soft and buttery; mild to strong flavor	Fresh pineapple, pears, apples, grapes
Coulommier	Creamy and smooth; mild flavor	Fresh peaches, apricots, pineapple, pears, dried fruit
Liederkranz	Strong odor; a robust flavor	Fresh pears, grapes, apples

Semisoft Cheeses — Serve at room temperature

Port du Salut	Mild	Tart apples, pears, honeydew melon, peaches
Trappist	Mild, aromatic	Same fruits as above
Oka	Mild, aromatic	Same fruits as above
Gruyère	Slightly nutlike flavor	Tart apples, green grapes
Bel Paese	Mild, high flavor; smooth	Apples, pears, dried fruit, as dates, prunes, figs, apricots
Caerphilly	Smooth; slight yoghurtlike flavor	Nice with all berries
Pont-l'Évêque	Rather pungent	Tart apples, pears, green grapes
Bonbel	Mild and smooth	Pears, peaches

Semihard to Hard Cheeses — Serve at room temperature

Edam or Gouda	Mellow, nutty flavor	Apples, green and red grapes
Cheddar	Varies from mild to sharp; sometimes crumbly	Honeydew melon or cantaloupe, apples, plums, pears, grapes, fresh coconut
Double Gloucester	Rich, mellow; robust flavor	Apples, pears, grapes
Fontina	From mild to pungent flavor	Pears, grapes, plums
Cantal	Slight winy flavor	Apples, pears, grapes
Monterey Jack	Mild flavor	Apples, pears, pineapple, melon, peaches

Blue-Veined Cheeses	Serve at room temperature	
Blue or bleu	Semisoft; spicy flavor	Fresh Bartlett pears, apples, orange sections
Roquefort	Semisoft; sharp flavor	Tart apples, pears
Gorgonzola	Rich and creamy; sharp flavor	Pears, orange sections
Stilton	Semisoft; sharp flavor	Pears, fresh figs, melon, bananas, walnuts in the shell

Fish

That gift from the sea, fresh fish, is one of the most nutritious foods that God has provided man. Low in calories and fat, but high in protein and some minerals and vitamins, fish is ideal for weight watchers and budget watchers, too.

Purchasing

In selecting fresh fish, observe these points:

Eyes: Should be clean, clear, bright, full, and bulging. Redness is not an indication of spoilage—the eyes may have been bruised when the fish was caught or in packing.

Gills: Reddish-pink, free from odor, slime, and discoloration.

Scales: Should have a characteristic sheen, adhere tightly to the skin, without slime.

Flesh: Should be firm and elastic and spring back under pressure of your finger. The flesh should not be separated from the bones.

Odor: Fish when it's fresh has a clean, fresh odor, free from objectionable and stale smells.

Amounts to buy: A third to a half pound of fresh fish per serving. If you serve a whole small fish, choose one weighing a pound for one serving.

Storage

Fresh fish should be wrapped in moisture-proof, air-tight material or placed in a covered container and stored in the refrigerator immediately. If you intend to keep it for several days, freeze it in moisture-vapor-proof freezer paper or container. Properly wrapped and frozen, it will not spoil as long as it remains frozen solid. Once it has been thawed, do not refreeze. It should remain packaged and refrigerated while thawing. If you want to thaw it quickly, place it under cold running water.

Salt-Water Fish	Available as	How to Cook
Bass	Whole, steaks	Bake, fry, poach, sauté
Bass, striped	Whole, steaks	Bake, broil, fry
Bluefish	Whole	Broil, bake
Cod	Whole, steaks, fillets; Frozen steaks, fillets	Bake, broil, fry, poach
Flounder or fluke	Whole, fillets; Frozen fillets	Bake, fry, poach
Grouper	Whole	Bake, fry, steam
Haddock	Whole, fillets; Frozen fillets	Broil, bake
Halibut	Steaks, fillets; Frozen steaks	Bake, broil, fry, poach
Mackerel	Whole	Broil, bake, fry
Mullet	Whole	Bake, broil, fry, poach
Perch	Whole	Broil, bake, fry
Pompano	Whole	Broil, bake
Porgy	Whole	Broil, bake, fry
Salmon	Whole, steaks, fillets; Frozen steaks	Poach, bake, broil, sauté
Sea trout	Whole	Broil, bake, sauté, poach
Shad	Whole	Bake
Smelts	Whole	Broil, fry
Snapper	Whole, steaks, fillets	Bake, broil, steam

Salt-Water Fish	Available as	How to Cook
Sole	Frozen fillets	Poach, fry, broil
Sole: Dover	Whole, fillets	Poach, fry, broil
Sole: gray	Whole, fillets	Poach, fry, broil
Sole: lemon	Whole, fillets	Poach, fry, broil
Swordfish	Steaks	Bake, broil, fry
Tuna	Steaks	Bake, broil, fry
Turbot	Whole, fillets	Bake, poach
Whiting	Whole, fillets	Bake, broil, fry

Fresh-Water Fish	Available as	How to Cook
Bass	Whole	Broil
Catfish	Whole	Broil, fry
Perch	Whole, fillets; Frozen fillets	Broil, bake, fry
Pike	Whole, fillets	Broil, bake, fry
Trout: lake	Whole, fillets; Frozen whole	Sauté, bake, broil
Trout: rainbow	Whole; Frozen whole	Sauté, bake, broil
Whitefish	Whole, fillets	Broil, bake, fry

Broiling Fish

Broiling, whether over charcoal or indoors, gives   fish a distinctly different flavor.

Broiled Fish

1. Let frozen fish thaw completely before broiling. Wash fish in cold water; pat dry with paper towels.
2. Lightly brush broiler rack with salad oil; arrange fish on rack. Brush fish with one of basting sauces, below.
3. Broil, 4 inches from heat, as directed in time-table, below, or until fish flakes easily when tested with fork but is still moist.
4. To serve: Remove fish to heated platter. Garnish with lemon wedges and parsley sprigs. Pass one of sauces* for fish, if desired.
* See Sauces.

Herbed Basting Sauce: Combine 2 tablespoons salad oil, 2 tablespoons lemon juice, 1/4 teaspoon paprika, and 1/4 teaspoon dried marjoram, basil, or thyme leaves. Use to brush on fish several times during broiling.

Curried Basting Sauce: Combine 2 tablespoons salad oil, 2 tablespoons lemon juice, and 1/4 teaspoon curry powder. Use to brush on fish several times during broiling.

Lemony Basting Sauce: Combine 3 tablespoons lemon juice with 1/8 teaspoon dry mustard, and 1 bay leaf, crumbled. Use to brush on fish several times during broiling.

Fish: Approximate Broiling Time
Fillets: 5 to 8 minutes on each side
Steaks: 5 to 8 minutes on each side
Dressed Whole: 5 minutes per lb each side
Split: 5 to 8 minutes on each side

Broiled Salmon or Swordfish Steaks, Parsley-Lemon Butter

4 salmon or swordfish steaks, 1/2 inch thick
1/4 cup butter or margarine, melted
1-1/2 teaspoons seasoned salt

Parsley-Lemon Butter:
1/4 cup butter or margarine
2 tablespoons lemon juice
2 tablespoons chopped parsley

1. Rinse salmon steaks under cold running water; drain; pat dry with paper towels.
2. Place salmon on rack of broiler pan. Brush with 2 tablespoons melted butter; sprinkle with 3/4 teaspoon seasoned salt.
3. Broil, 4 inches from heat, 10 minutes. Turn salmon; brush with remaining melted butter, and sprinkle with remaining seasoned salt. Broil 8 minutes longer, or until fish flakes easily when tested with a fork.
4. Meanwhile, make Parsley-Lemon Butter: Melt butter in small saucepan. Stir in lemon juice and parsley. Keep warm.
5. Remove salmon to heated serving platter. Pour lemon butter over salmon.
Makes 4 servings.

Crispy Broiled Salmon Steaks

1/2 cup butter or margarine, melted
1 teaspoon salt
1/8 teaspoon paprika
6(6- to 8-oz size) salmon steaks, 3/4 inch thick
1 cup crushed saltines
1 cup crushed potato chips
6 lemon wedges
6 parsley sprigs

1. Combine butter, salt, and paprika.
2. Wipe steaks with damp cloth. Dip each into butter mixture; then roll in combined saltines and potato chips.
3. Arrange steaks on lightly greased broiler rack in broiler pan. Broil, 6 inches from heat, 5 minutes.
4. Turn; broil 5 to 8 minutes, or until fish flakes easily with fork. Serve each steak with a lemon wedge and parsley sprig.
Makes 6 servings.

The Beauty of Baking

There's always something very impressive about bringing in a whole baked fish on a platter.
Bake fish about eight minutes per pound in a 400F oven. Wrapping the fish "en papillote" (in foil or parchment) will seal in the cooking juices and any fishy smell.
Bacon strips, dots of butter, or clam broth to baste with can be used for additional moisture. Take

care not to overcook or overheat, for fish easily turns tough and dry. The fish is ready when it flakes at a touch of a fork. Serve it with lemon butter.

Baked Stuffed Fish

1 whole red snapper, striped bass, cod, haddock, bluefish, or whitefish, cleaned (2-1/2 to 3 lb)

Stuffing:
1/4 cup butter or margarine
1/2 cup chopped onion
1/2 cup chopped celery
2 tablespoons chopped parsley
1/2 teaspoon salt
1/2 teaspoon dried thyme leaves
1 cup fresh bread cubes (2 slices)
3 slices bacon
Pepper

1. Wash fish inside and out under cold running water. Drain well; pat dry with paper towels.
2. Make Stuffing: In hot butter in medium skillet, sauté onion and celery until tender—about 5 minutes. Add the chopped parsley, 1/2 teaspoon salt, the thyme, and bread cubes; toss to mix well.
3. Preheat oven to 400F.
4. Spoon stuffing into cavity; close opening with skewers or wooden picks.
5. Place fish in large, greased roasting pan. Arrange bacon, not overlapping, lengthwise over top of fish; sprinkle with pepper.
6. Bake 35 to 40 minutes, or until fish flakes easily when tested with a fork and bacon is crisp.
7. To serve: Remove fish to heated serving platter. Sprinkle with additional chopped parsley, if you wish.
Makes 6 to 8 servings.

Baked Striped Bass

4- to 5-lb whole striped bass with head, cleaned
2 teaspoons salt
1 small lemon
Parsley
1 cup thinly sliced onion
1/2 cup thinly sliced carrot
1/2 cup thinly sliced celery
1/2 teaspoon dried thyme leaves
1 bay leaf
1 cup dry white wine
1/4 cup butter or margarine, melted
Lemon Butter, below

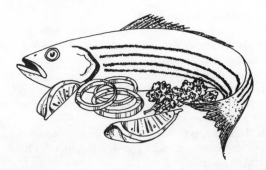

1. Preheat oven to 400F. Lightly grease a shallow roasting pan.
2. Wash fish inside and out under cold running water; pat dry with paper towels. Sprinkle fish inside and out with the salt.
3. Slice lemon thinly; cut slices in quarters. With small, sharp-pointed knife, make deep cuts, about 2 inches apart, along both sides of fish. With fingers, press a piece of lemon and a small sprig of parsley into each cut.
4. Place fish in prepared pan. Add any remaining lemon slices and parsley, along with onion, carrot, celery, thyme, and bay leaf. Pour in wine and 1/2 cup water. Pour butter over fish.
5. Bake, basting frequently with liquid in pan, 30 to 40 minutes, or until fish flakes easily when tested with a fork.
6. With large spatulas, carefully lift fish to heated serving platter. With slotted spoon, lift out vegetables, and place around fish. Vegetables will be on the crisp side. Garnish platter with parsley and lemon, if desired. Serve with Lemon Butter, below. Makes 6 servings.

Lemon Butter

6 tablespoons butter or regular margarine
2 tablespoons lemon juice

1. In a small skillet or saucepan, heat butter over medium heat until it foams and becomes light brown.
2. Remove from heat. Stir in lemon juice. Serve at once.
Makes 1/2 cup.

Baked Haddock, New England Style

1 fresh haddock (3-1/2 lb), cleaned, head and tail removed
1-1/2 teaspoons seasoned salt
Pepper
2 tablespoons lemon juice

Cracker Topping:
1/2 cup crushed unsalted crackers
1/2 cup chopped, washed fresh mushrooms
1/4 cup thinly sliced green onions
2 tablespoons chopped parsley
1-1/2 teaspoons seasoned salt
1/8 teaspoon pepper
1/4 cup butter or margarine, melted
2 tablespoons lemon juice
6 slices bacon

1. Wash fish in cold water; pat dry with paper towels. With sharp knife, carefully remove bones, keeping fish joined down back. (Or have fish boned at market.)
2. Preheat oven to 400F. Line a 13-by-9-by-2-inch baking pan with foil; butter foil.
3. Sprinkle inside of boned fish with 3/4 teaspoon seasoned salt, dash pepper, and 1 tablespoon lemon juice. Fold fish lengthwise. Place in prepared pan. Sprinkle with 3/4 teaspoon seasoned salt, dash pepper, and 1 tablespoon lemon juice.
4. Make Cracker Topping: In medium bowl, combine crushed crackers, mushrooms, green onions, parsley, seasoned salt, and pepper; mix. Pour on butter and lemon juice; toss until well combined.
5. Spoon over fish in a 3-inch-wide layer. Arrange bacon slices diagonally over top.
6. Bake, basting every 10 minutes with pan juices, 30 to 35 minutes, or until fish flakes easily when tested with a fork.
7. Carefully lift fish to heated serving platter. Garnish with parsley and lemon wedges, if desired.
Makes 6 servings.

Fillets of Sole with Tarragon-Chive Butter

2 lb fillets of sole; or 2 pkg (1-lb size) frozen fillets of sole, thawed
1/2 cup butter or margarine, melted
2 tablespoons lemon juice
1 tablespoon coarsely snipped fresh tarragon leaves
1 tablespoon snipped chives
1/4 teaspoon salt

1. Preheat oven to 350F.
2. Brush fillets with 1/4 cup butter. Sprinkle with lemon juice. Arrange in greased 13-by-9-by-2-inch baking dish.
3. Cover dish with foil; bake 20 minutes, or until fish flakes easily with fork.
4. Combine rest of butter with tarragon, chives, and salt; heat slightly.
5. To serve, put fillets on platter; pour warm herb butter, combined with cooking liquid, over them.
Makes 6 servings.

Baked Fillets Thermidor

2 lb sole fillets
5 tablespoons butter or margarine
2 teaspoons salt
1/4 teaspoon pepper
1/2 teaspoon seasoned salt
1-1/4 cups milk
3 tablespoons flour
1 cup grated sharp Cheddar cheese (1/4 lb)
3 tablespoons sherry
Paprika

1. Preheat oven to 350F.
2. Wash fillets, and dry on paper towels.
3. Melt 2 tablespoons butter. Use to brush dark side of fillets. Sprinkle with salt, pepper, and seasoned salt.
4. Roll up fillets, seasonings inside; fasten with wooden picks. Arrange in a 9-by-9-by-1-3/4-inch baking dish. Pour on 1/2 cup milk.
5. Bake, uncovered, 30 minutes.
6. Meanwhile, in medium saucepan, melt rest of butter.
7. Remove from heat. Add flour, stirring until smooth. Gradually stir in remaining milk; bring to boiling, stirring constantly.
8. Reduce heat. Add cheese, stirring until it is melted. Then add sherry.
9. Carefully drain liquid from fish; stir into cheese sauce. Pour sauce over fish. Sprinkle with paprika.
10. Place under broiler, 4 inches from heat, until sauce is golden-brown.
Makes 4 servings.

In Praise of Poaching

For the subtlest of tastes, most gourmets prefer poaching. In the legends of haute cuisine, many a chef's star has risen (or fallen) on simmering fillets in wine. For the beginner, oven-poaching is less tricky than poaching over an open flame. The leftover liquid makes the base for your sauce.

Fillets of Sole Bonne Femme

4 tablespoons butter or margarine
2 shallots, chopped
6 sole, haddock, or flounder fillets (about 2-1/2 lb)
1/2 lb fresh mushrooms, sliced
1 teaspoon salt
1/8 teaspoon pepper
1 cup white wine
1 tablespoon chopped parsley
1-1/2 tablespoons flour

1. Melt 2 tablespoons butter in large skillet. Add shallots, and sauté 2 minutes.
2. Wash fillets; dry on paper towels. Arrange fish over shallots, and top with mushrooms. Sprinkle salt and pepper over all. Add wine.
3. Bring to boiling; reduce heat, and simmer, covered, 10 minutes. Add parsley; cook 5 minutes longer, or until fish flakes easily with fork.
4. Drain fish well, reserving 1 cup liquid. Arrange fish and mushrooms in 12-by-8-by-2-inch baking dish.
5. Melt remaining butter in same skillet; remove from heat. Stir in flour until smooth. Gradually stir in reserved fish liquid.
6. Cook over medium heat, stirring, until thickened. Pour over fish. Run under broiler 3 to 5 minutes, or until top is golden-brown.
Makes 6 servings.

Fillets of Sole Marguery

Hollandaise Sauce, page 22
6 fillets of sole (2-1/2 lb)
1 teaspoon salt
1/8 teaspoon pepper
2 tablespoons butter or margarine
1/4 cup dry white wine
1 small onion, sliced
1 bay leaf
1 pint oysters in liquid
12 cooked shrimp (optional)

Mushroom Sauce:
3 tablespoons butter or margarine
1/2 cup fresh mushrooms, washed and sliced
3 tablespoons flour
Dash cayenne
1-1/4 cups fish stock
1/4 cup light cream

1. Make Hollandaise Sauce. Let cool completely. Preheat oven to 350F.
2. Rinse fillets under cold water; drain. Pat dry with paper towels. Fold crosswise.
3. Arrange fillets in buttered 13-by-9-by-2-inch baking pan. Sprinkle with salt and pepper. Dot with 2 tablespoons butter. Pour wine and 1/2 cup water over all. Top with onion and bay leaf.
4. Bake, uncovered, 15 minutes, or until the fish flakes easily when tested with a fork.
5. Meanwhile, in small saucepan, cook oysters in their liquid until edges begin to curl. Drain; set aside.
6. With slotted spatula, remove fillets, and arrange in buttered 12-by-8-by-2-inch broilerproof dish. Top with oysters. (You may add 12 cooked shrimp, if you wish.) Keep warm. Strain fish stock into 2-cup measure. Reserve 1-1/4 cups.
7. Make Mushroom Sauce: Melt butter in medium saucepan. Add mushrooms, sauté, stirring occasionally, about 5 minutes. Remove from heat; stir in flour and cayenne until smooth. Add reserved 1-1/4 cups fish stock and the cream. Cook over medium heat, stirring constantly, until mixture comes to boiling. Reduce heat; simmer 3 minutes.
8. Pour off any liquid. Pour sauce over fish.
9. Spoon hollandaise sauce over all. Place under broiler, 4 inches from heat, about 3 to 5 minutes, or just until top is golden-brown.
Makes 6 servings.

Fillets of Sole Queen Victoria

8 fillets of sole (2-1/2 lb)
1 egg white
3/4 cup heavy cream
1/2 teaspoon salt
2 tablespoons chopped parsley
3 drops Tabasco
1 cup dry white wine
1 small onion, thinly sliced
3 slices lemon
1 bay leaf
3 whole black peppercorns
1 teaspoon salt
1/4 teaspoon dried tarragon leaves
Newburg Sauce, page 501

1. Rinse fillets under cold water; pat dry with paper towels.
2. Select 6 best fillets; set aside. Cut 2 remaining fillets into 1-inch strips. Place strips in electric-blender container. Add egg white, cream, 1/2 teaspoon salt, the parsley, and Tabasco. Blend, at high speed, 2 minutes, or until mixture is smooth and an even light-green color.
3. Place the 6 reserved fillets, skin side up, on a cutting board. Spoon fish mixture on each, dividing evenly (about 2 rounded tablespoonfuls each). Spread into an even layer, keeping it about half an inch from edges. Starting at narrow end, roll up fillets. Fasten with wooden picks.

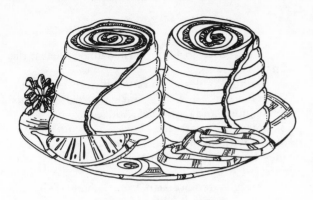

4. Lightly butter a deep medium skillet or Dutch oven. Stand fillets on more even end, barely touching side of pan, to keep upright.

5. Add wine, 1/2 cup water, the onion, lemon, bay leaf, black peppercorns, salt, tarragon. Bring just to boiling; cover; reduce heat to low; simmer 10 to 15 minutes, or till fish mixture in center is firm when tested with fork.

6. Remove with slotted spatula; drain very well. (Reserve stock for sauce.) Place on heated serving platter. Top with some Newburg Sauce; pass remaining sauce.

Makes 6 servings.

Fillets of Sole Florentine

Hollandaise Sauce, page 22
6 fillets of sole (2-1/2 lb)
1/4 cup lemon juice
2 tablespoons finely chopped shallots
2 teaspoons dried tarragon leaves
1 teaspoon salt
1 cup dry white wine
2 pkg (10-oz size) frozen chopped spinach

Wine Sauce:
3 tablespoons butter or margarine
3 tablespoons flour
1/2 teaspoon salt
1/8 teaspoon pepper
1 cup fish-stock
1/3 cup light cream
1/3 cup heavy cream

1. Make Hollandaise Sauce. Let cool completely.

2. Rinse fillets under cool water; pat dry with paper towels. Brush both sides with lemon juice. Fold into thirds, with dark side inside. Arrange in single layer in large skillet. Sprinkle with shallots, tarragon, 1 teaspoon salt. Pour on wine.

3. Bring to boiling; reduce heat; simmer, covered, 5 to 10 minutes, or until fish flakes easily when tested with a fork. Do not overcook.

4. Meanwhile, cook spinach as the label directs. Turn into a sieve; drain well, pressing spinach to remove all liquid. Return to saucepan; cover; keep hot.

5. With slotted spatula, remove fillets to heated platter; set aside; keep warm. Strain liquid from skillet into 2-cup measure. (You should have about 1 cup. Boil down if necessary.)

6. Make Wine Sauce: Melt butter in small saucepan. Remove from heat. Stir in flour, salt, and pepper until smooth. Gradually stir in 1 cup fish stock and the light cream.

7. Bring to boiling, over medium heat, stirring constantly until mixture thickens. Remove from heat.

8. Stir 1/3 cup wine sauce into spinach; toss. Turn into a 12-by-8-by-2-inch broilerproof dish; spread evenly.

9. Arrange fillets in single layer on spinach. Spoon remaining wine sauce over fillets.

10. Beat heavy cream until stiff. Fold into hollandaise sauce. Spoon mixture over wine sauce.

11. Place under broiler 2 to 3 minutes, or until top is golden-brown. Serve right from dish.

Makes 6 servings.

Salmon Steaks Poached in White Wine

6 salmon steaks (2-1/4 lb)
4 tablespoons butter or margarine
1 teaspoon salt
2 shallots, finely chopped
1 tablespoon lemon juice
2 bay leaves, quartered
1/2 cup sauterne
1-1/2 tablespoons flour
2 tablespoons heavy cream
Chopped parsley

1. Preheat oven to 400F. Wash salmon steaks; dry on paper towels.
2. Spread 2 tablespoons butter in medium baking dish. Place fish in dish; sprinkle with salt, shallots, lemon juice, and bay leaves. Add sauterne.
3. Cover dish with foil; bake 15 minutes. Baste steaks with liquid in dish; bake, covered, 10 minutes longer, or just until fish flakes easily with fork.
4. Carefully remove fish from baking dish, and drain well. Strain liquid, and reserve 1 cup.
5. Arrange steaks on heatproof serving platter, or return to baking dish; keep warm.
6. Melt remaining butter in small saucepan; remove from heat. Stir in flour until smooth. Gradually stir in reserved fish liquid; cook over medium heat, stirring, until thickened. Stir in cream.
7. Pour sauce over salmon steaks. Run under broiler 3 to 5 minutes, or until golden-brown. Sprinkle with parsley.
Makes 6 servings.

Fillets of Sole Duglère

6 fillets of sole (about 2-1/2 lb) (see Note)
3 tablespoons lemon juice
3 tablespoons butter or margarine
4 medium fresh mushrooms, washed and sliced
1 teaspoon salt
Dash pepper
1 cup dry white wine
4 medium tomatoes (1-1/2 lb)

Sauce:
1/4 cup butter or margarine
1/4 cup all-purpose flour
1/2 teaspoon salt
Dash cayenne
1-1/2 cups fish stock
3/4 cup grated Parmesan cheese
3 tablespoons dry bread crumbs
2 tablespoons butter or margarine, melted

1. Preheat oven to 350F. Lightly butter 13-by-9-by-2-inch baking dish.
2. Rinse fillets under cold water; pat dry with paper towels. Brush with 2 tablespoons lemon juice. Fold crosswise; place in prepared dish.
3. Melt 3 tablespoons butter in small saucepan. Add mushrooms; sprinkle with 1 tablespoon lemon juice, 1 teaspoon salt, and the pepper; toss. Add wine and 1/4 cup water; bring to boiling. Pour over fish.
4. Lightly butter one side of a double thickness of waxed paper; place, buttered side down, over fish.
5. Bake 15 to 20 minutes, or just until fish flakes easily when tested with a fork.
6. Meanwhile, scald tomatoes, and peel. Cut in quarters; scrape seeds and center pulp into a sieve set over a bowl; press through sieve. (You should have 3/4 cup purée.) Set aside. Dice outer part of tomato. Set aside.
7. Carefully remove fish from baking dish, and arrange, slightly overlapping, in shallow 1-1/2- or 2-quart broilerproof serving dish. Top with the mushrooms. Cover; keep warm.

8. Strain fish stock into a 2-cup measure. Reserve 1-1/2 cups for sauce.

9. Make Sauce: Melt 1/4 cup butter in medium saucepan. Remove from heat; stir in flour, salt, and cayenne. Stir in 1-1/2 cups fish stock and the tomato purée; cook over medium heat, stirring constantly, until mixture thickens and comes to boiling.

10. Stir in 1/2 cup Parmesan. Return to boiling, stirring constantly; reduce heat; simmer 5 minutes. Add diced tomato.

11. Pour off liquid from fish and mushrooms. Spoon sauce over all.

12. In small bowl, toss bread crumbs and melted butter. Sprinkle over sauce; then sprinkle with remaining Parmesan.

13. Run dish under broiler 3 to 5 minutes, or until top is golden-brown.

Makes 6 servings.

Note: If using frozen sole, let thaw completely.

A-Sizzle on the Grill

Close your eyes, inhale, and you're standing on some shore, cooking the early morning's catch over glowing embers. But even if you're just standing over a stove, the smell of fresh fish bubbling in butter is tantalizing. Small whole fish, often tastier than whoppers, are better for sautéing and are unbelievably easy to fix. Dip the fish in milk; then roll them in seasoned flour, and quickly sauté in butter until they're crisp and golden-brown (about five minutes on each side).

Breaded Cod Fillets

2 lb cod fillets
1 egg
1/2 cup dry bread crumbs, or 1/2 cup packaged
   seasoned coating mix for fish
1 teaspoon salt
1/4 teaspoon pepper
6 tablespoons butter or margarine
Parsley
Lemon wedges
Tartar Sauce, page 502

1. Rinse fillets in cold water; pat dry with paper towels. Cut in serving-size pieces.

2. In pie plate, beat egg with a fork until mixed. On waxed paper, mix crumbs, salt, pepper. (Omit salt and pepper if using coating mix.)

3. Dip fish in egg, to moisten both sides; then dip in crumbs, to coat well.

4. In large skillet, heat butter until it sizzles. Add fish pieces in a single layer. Sauté over medium heat until underside is golden-brown—about 5 minutes. Turn with spatula; sauté 5 minutes longer, to brown other side and until fish flakes easily when tested with a fork.

5. Remove to heated serving platter. Garnish with parsley and wedges of lemon. Serve with Tartar Sauce.

Makes 6 servings.

Codfish Cakes

1/2 lb salt codfish
1-1/2 cups diced pared potato
1 egg
2 tablespoons cream
1/8 teaspoon pepper
1/4 cup butter or margarine
Catsup

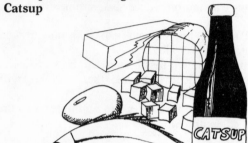

1. Soak codfish in cold water 12 hours, or overnight, or as package label directs.
2. Cut into 1-inch-wide strips or small pieces. Place in small saucepan; add water to cover. Bring to boiling; reduce heat; simmer, uncovered, 5 minutes. Drain.
3. Meanwhile, in medium saucepan, cook potato in unsalted water to cover 10 to 15 minutes, or until tender. Drain.
4. Mash potato in saucepan. Beat in egg, cream, pepper until smooth.
5. With a fork, flake codfish. Add to potato mixture; beat until light and fluffy.
6. Heat butter in large skillet. Spoon cod mixture in 6 mounds into skillet; pat into 1-inch-thick cakes. Cook, over medium heat, 4 or 5 minutes, or until underside is browned. Turn; brown other side 4 or 5 minutes.
7. Serve at once, with catsup.
Makes 6 servings.

Trout Amandine

4 (1/2-lb size) rainbow trout, cleaned, with head and tail on
1/3 cup flour
1/2 teaspoon salt
Dash pepper
1/4 cup milk
Butter or margarine
1/3 cup sliced almonds

1. Wash fish under cold running water. Drain; pat dry with paper towels.
2. On 12-inch square of waxed paper, combine flour, salt, and pepper.
3. Pour milk into 9-inch pie plate. Dip trout in milk; shake off excess; roll in flour mixture until well coated.
4. In large skillet, over medium heat, heat 1/4 cup butter until golden. Add trout; sauté, over medium heat, 5 minutes, or until underside is browned. Turn, being careful not to break fish; sauté 5 minutes, or until fish are browned and flake easily when tested with a fork.
5. Carefully remove fish to heated serving platter.
6. Add 1/4 cup butter to skillet. When melted, add almonds; sauté over low heat until almonds are pale golden. Pour almonds and butter over fish. Serve immediately.
Makes 4 servings.
Note: If you use frozen trout, thaw them completely.

Shellfish

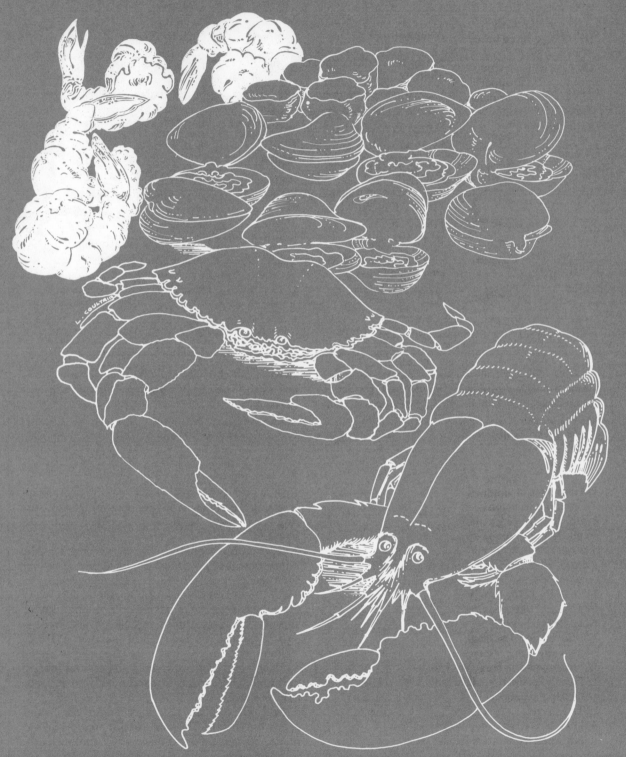

Shellfish, in some form—fresh, frozen or canned—is available all year long. To most people, even fish haters, it's a delicacy. To dieters, a great boon, because it's low in calories but high in protein.

Shellfish	Available as	How to Prepare
Clams	Fresh in shell; Canned whole, minced	Raw, steam, bake
Crabs: blue	Cooked in shell, crabmeat; Canned	Steam, bake, boil
Crabs: Dungeness	Cooked in shell, crabmeat; Canned	
Crabs: king	Frozen legs, crabmeat; Canned	
Lobster	Fresh in shell, lobster meat; Frozen in shell, lobster meat; Canned	Boil, broil
Lobster tails	Frozen in shell	Boil, broil
Oysters	Fresh in shell, shelled in liquid; Frozen; Canned whole or stew	Raw, fry, sauté, poach, bake
Scallops: sea	Fresh; Frozen	Sauté, bake, fry, broil
Scallops: bay	Fresh; Frozen	Sauté, bake, fry, broil
Shrimp	Fresh in shell, shelled; Frozen in shell, shelled	Boil, broil, fry
Squid	Whole	Raw, boil

Clams

There are two general varieties of clams: Soft-shell clams, small and oval in shape, are used primarily for steaming; hard-shell clams, large and rounded, are used for chowder and often served raw on the half shell. They are available all along both seacoasts.

Cioppino

A Hearty Shellfish and Fish Stew

1/3 cup olive or salad oil
1 cup chopped onion
1 cup chopped green onion
1 cup chopped green pepper
3 cloves garlic, crushed
1 dozen fresh littleneck clams, or 1 can (10 oz) whole clams
1 can (1 lb, 12 oz) tomatoes
1 can (8 oz) tomato sauce
1 cup dry red wine
1/4 cup chopped parsley
2 teaspoons salt
1/2 teaspoon dried oregano leaves
1/4 teaspoon dried basil leaves
1/4 teaspoon pepper
1 lb fresh cod
3/4 lb fresh red snapper or striped bass
1/2 lb small frozen rock-lobster tails

1. In hot oil in 6-quart kettle or Dutch oven, sauté onion, green onion, green pepper, and garlic, stirring occasionally, until onion is golden—about 10 minutes.
2. Open clams, reserving liquid; set clams aside. (If you are using canned clams, drain, reserving the liquid.)
3. Add clam liquid, tomatoes, tomato sauce, wine, parsley, salt, oregano, basil leaves, pepper, and 1 cup water to the sautéed vegetables; mix well.
4. Bring to boiling; reduce heat; simmer, covered, 30 minutes.
5. Meanwhile, rinse cod, red snapper, and lobster tails under cold water; drain. Cut cod and snapper in large pieces.
6. Add fish, unthawed lobster tails in shell, and clams to vegetable mixture. Return just to boiling; reduce heat, and simmer, covered, 30 minutes.

7. Serve with hot, crusty Italian bread.
Makes 8 servings.

Fried Clams

1 quart shucked clams
1 egg, slightly beaten
1 teaspoon salt
1/8 teaspoon pepper
Dash paprika
1 cup packaged dry bread crumbs
1/2 cup butter or margarine

1. Drain clams, reserving 2 tablespoons liquid.
2. Combine clam liquid with egg, salt, pepper, and paprika.
3. Dip clams in egg mixture; then roll in bread crumbs, coating completely.
4. In hot butter in medium skillet, sauté clams 3 to 4 minutes on each side, or until golden. Drain well on paper towels.
Makes 4 to 6 servings.

Crabmeat

Because of its delicate flavor, crabmeat is the second most popular shellfish. There are a number of varieties, available fresh, frozen and canned.

Though it is expensive, there is little waste in shelled crabmeat; one pound serves four.

Boiled Crabs

1/4 cup salt
16 live hard-shell crabs

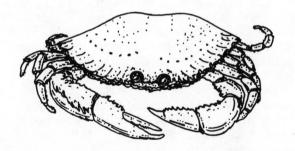

1. In large kettle, bring 4 quarts water and the salt to boiling.
2. Place crabs in colander; wash in cold water until crabs seem clean.
3. Holding crabs by tongs or back feelers, plunge head first into boiling water; return water to boiling. Reduce heat, and simmer, covered, 12 to 15 minutes.
4. Drain; let cool.
5. To remove meat: Twist off claws and legs; crack them with nutcracker or hammer; remove meat.
6. Lay crab on top shell. Insert point of a knife under forward end of the flap that folds under body from rear; break it off, and discard.
7. Pick up crab in both hands; pull upper and lower shells apart. Discard top shell.
8. Hold crab under running water; remove gills and all spongy material.
9. Cut away any hard membrane along outer edge; carefully remove meat with fork.
Makes about 2 cups crabmeat.

Sherried Crabmeat

2 cans (6-1/2-oz size) crabmeat
1/4 cup butter or margarine
3 tablespoons flour
1/2 teaspoon salt
Dash pepper
Dash cayenne
3/4 cup bottled clam juice
1/2 cup heavy cream
1-1/2 tablespoons dry sherry
1 hard-cooked egg, finely chopped
1 tablespoon finely chopped onion
1/2 cup sliced fresh mushrooms
1 tablespoon finely chopped parsley
1 tablespoon finely chopped chives
1/4 cup pkg dry bread crumbs

1. Drain crabmeat, and remove any cartilage.
2. Melt 3 tablespoons butter in medium saucepan. Remove from heat; stir in flour, salt, pepper, and cayenne until smooth. Gradually stir in clam juice and cream.
3. Bring mixture to boiling, stirring; sauce will be thickened and smooth.
4. Stir in sherry, egg, and crabmeat.
5. Heat rest of butter in small skillet; in it, sauté onion, mushrooms, parsley, and chives until mushrooms are tender—about 5 minutes. Stir in bread crumbs.
6. Fill 8 patty shells or toast cups with crabmeat mixture; top each with mushroom mixture.
Makes 8 servings.

Crêpes with Curried Crabmeat

Crabmeat Filling:
5 tablespoons butter or margarine
1/4 cup unsifted all-purpose flour
3/4 teaspoon salt
1-1/2 cups milk
1 can (7-1/2 oz) king-crab meat, drained
1 teaspoon chopped shallots or green onions
1/2 cup dry white wine
1 teaspoon curry powder
1/8 teaspoon pepper
1/4 teaspoon Worcestershire sauce
Dash cayenne

Crêpes:
1 cup milk
3/4 cup sifted all-purpose flour
1/4 teaspoon salt
2 eggs

Salad oil

Topping:
1 egg yolk
1/8 teaspoon salt
4 tablespoons butter or margarine, melted
2 teaspoons lemon juice
1/4 cup heavy cream, whipped

Grated Parmesan cheese

1. Make Crabmeat Filling: For white sauce, melt 4 tablespoons butter in medium saucepan. Remove from heat. Add flour and 1/2 teaspoon salt; stir until smooth. Gradually stir in milk; bring to boiling, stirring constantly. Reduce heat; simmer 5 minutes. Remove from heat, and set aside.
2. Separate crabmeat pieces, removing membrane. In 1 tablespoon hot butter in medium skillet, sauté shallots 1 minute. Add crabmeat; sauté 2 minutes longer. Add wine, curry, 1/4 teaspoon salt, the pepper, Worcestershire, and cayenne; cook over medium heat, stirring, 3 minutes. Stir in 1 cup of the white sauce just until blended. Refrigerate while making crêpes.
3. Make Crêpes: In medium bowl, with rotary beater, beat milk with flour and salt until smooth. Add eggs; beat until well combined.
4. Slowly heat a 5-1/2-inch skillet until a little water sizzles when dropped on it. Brush pan lightly with salad oil. Pour about 1-1/2 tablespoons batter into skillet, tilting pan so batter covers bottom completely.
5. Cook until nicely browned on underside. Loosen edge; turn; cook until browned on other side. Remove from pan; cool on wire rack; then stack on waxed paper. Repeat with rest of batter to make 18 crêpes; lightly brush pan with oil before making each.
6. Preheat oven to 350F. Remove filling from re-

frigerator. Spoon 1 rounded tablespoonful onto each crêpe; fold two opposite sides over filling. Arrange in shallow baking dish; cover with foil. Bake 20 to 25 minutes, or until heated through.

7. Meanwhile, make Topping: In small bowl, with rotary beater, beat egg yolk with salt until foamy; gradually beat in 2 tablespoons melted butter. Mix remaining butter with lemon juice; gradually beat into egg-yolk mixture. With wire whisk or rubber scraper, fold in remaining white sauce just until combined. Fold in whipped cream.

8. Uncover hot crêpes. Spoon topping over them; then sprinkle lightly with grated Parmesan cheese. Broil, 4 to 6 inches from heat, until nicely browned. Makes 6 servings.

To prepare ahead of time: Make and fill crêpes as directed; cover with foil, and refrigerate. Make topping, but do not add whipped cream. Refrigerate. To serve: Bake crêpes as directed. Fold the whipped cream into sauce, ready to spoon over the crêpes. Sprinkle with cheese.

Scalloped Crab

1 lb fresh crabmeat, or 2 cans (7-1/2-oz size)
    crabmeat
1/2 cup dry sherry
1/4 cup butter or margarine
2 tablespoons finely chopped onion
1/4 cup unsifted all-purpose flour
1/2 cup milk
1 cup light cream
1 tablespoon Worcestershire sauce
1 teaspoon salt
Dash pepper
2 egg yolks
2 tablespoons butter or margarine, melted
1/2 cup pkg dry bread crumbs

1. Preheat oven to 350F. Lightly grease 6 or 8 scallop shells or a 1-quart casserole.

2. Drain crabmeat, removing any cartilage. Sprinkle crabmeat with 1/4 cup sherry; toss to mix well.

3. In 1/4 cup hot butter in medium saucepan, sauté onion until tender—5 minutes.

4. Remove from heat. Stir in flour. Gradually stir in milk and cream; bring to boiling, stirring; reduce heat, and simmer until quite thick—8 to 10 minutes.

5. Remove from heat; add Worcestershire, salt, pepper, and rest of sherry. Stir a little of sauce into egg yolks; return to rest of sauce in saucepan; mix well. Stir in crabmeat mixture.

6. Turn into shells or casserole.

7. Toss 2 tablespoons butter with crumbs to mix well. Sprinkle crumbs evenly over crabmeat.

8. Place shells on cookie sheet; bake 20 minutes, or until mixture is bubbly and crumbs are lightly browned. (Bake casserole 25 minutes.)

Makes 6 to 8 servings.

Sautéed Soft-Shell Crabs

6 soft-shell crabs
1 egg
1 teaspoon salt
1/8 teaspoon pepper
1/8 teaspoon paprika
1/2 cup pkg dry bread crumbs
1/4 cup unsifted all-purpose flour
1/2 cup butter or margarine

1. To clean crabs: With sharp knife, cut away segment that folds under body from rear; discard.
2. With scissors, remove head, about 3/4 inch behind eyes; discard.
3. Lift back shell on either side; scrape away lungs and spongy substance under it. Wash crabs well under cold running water.
4. Beat egg slightly with salt, pepper, and paprika. Combine bread crumbs with flour.
5. Dip crabs in egg mixture, then in crumb mixture, coating completely.
6. In hot butter in large skillet, sauté crabs until golden—about 4 minutes on each side.
Makes 3 servings.

Lobster

Two types of lobster are found in our waters: In the south, the spiny or rock lobster, without claws, with the meat concentrated in the tail; in the north, the Maine lobster with the meat concentrated in the claws. Increased demand has made Maine lobster very scarce and expensive. Frozen rock-lobster tails are more available and more reasonably priced.

Boiled Live Lobsters

1 lemon, sliced
1 medium onion, sliced
6 tablespoons salt
2 bay leaves
8 whole black peppercorns
2 (1-lb size) live lobsters
Melted butter or margarine
Lemon wedges

1. In deep, 10-quart kettle, combine 6 quarts water, the lemon, onion, salt, bay leaves, and whole black peppercorns. Bring to boiling; then reduce heat, and simmer, covered, 20 minutes.
2. Holding each lobster by the body with tongs, with claws away from you, plunge it into the boiling water. Return to boiling; reduce heat. Cover kettle; simmer lobsters 12 to 15 minutes.
3. Remove lobsters from kettle; place on back. Split body lengthwise, cutting through thin undershell and lobster meat and back shell. Spread open. Remove and discard dark vein and small sac 2 inches below head. Leave in green liver (tomalley) and any red roe (coral).
4. Crack large claws, to let excess moisture drain off.
5. Serve lobsters at once, with plenty of melted butter and lemon wedges.
Makes 2 servings.

Boiled Rock-Lobster Tails

Boil as directed below in Lobster Thermidor, steps 1 through 5.

Lobster Thermidor

Boiled Rock-Lobster Tails:
1 small onion, peeled and sliced
1/2 lemon, sliced
1 tablespoon salt
5 whole black peppercorns
1 bay leaf
5 (6-oz size) frozen rock-lobster tails
2 tablespoons sherry

Sauce:
1/3 cup butter or regular margarine
1/4 cup unsifted all-purpose flour
1/2 teaspoon salt
Dash mace
1/4 teaspoon paprika
1-1/2 cups light cream
1 tablespoon sherry
1/2 cup grated sharp Cheddar cheese

1. In 6-quart kettle, place 3 quarts water, the onion, lemon, 1 tablespoon salt, the black peppercorns, and bay leaf; bring to boiling.
2. Unwrap frozen lobster tails. With tongs, lower into boiling mixture; return to boiling. Reduce heat, and simmer, covered, 9 minutes.
3. With tongs or slotted spoon, remove lobster tails from kettle. Set aside until cool enough to handle. Discard the cooking liquid.
4. To remove meat from shells: With scissors, carefully cut away thin undershell, and discard. Then insert fingers between shell and meat, and gently pull out meat in one piece. Wash four shells; dry with paper towels, and set aside.
5. Cut lobster meat into bite-size pieces. Place in medium bowl; toss with 2 tablespoons sherry.
6. Preheat oven to 450F.
7. Make Sauce: Melt butter in 2-quart saucepan; remove from heat. Stir in flour, salt, mace, and paprika until smooth. Gradually stir in the light cream.
8. Bring to boiling, stirring constantly. Reduce heat, and simmer 2 to 3 minutes. Add lobster meat and sherry; cook over low heat, stirring frequently, until lobster is heated through. Remove from heat.
9. Spoon into shells, mounding it high. Sprinkle with grated cheese and a little paprika, if desired. Place filled shells on cookie sheet. (Prop up tails with crushed aluminum foil to keep them steady.)
10. Bake 10 to 12 minutes, or until cheese is melted and lightly browned. If desired, garnish with lemon wedges and watercress. Serve with fluffy white rice.
Makes 4 servings.

Lobster Newburg

Boil lobster tails as directed above, steps 1 through 5. Make Newburg Sauce, page 501. Gently heat lobster in sauce. Serve over toast or in patty shells, or over rice. Makes 4 or 5 servings.

Broiled Live Lobsters

2 (1-lb size) live lobsters
Butter or margarine, melted
Salt
Pepper
Paprika
Lemon wedges

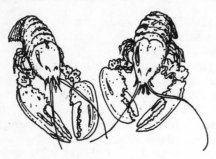

1. Kill lobster: Lay lobster on back on wooden board. To sever spinal cord, insert point of knife through to back shell where body and tail of lobster come together.
2. With sharp knife, split body lengthwise, cutting through thin undershell and lobster meat and back shell. Spread open.
3. Remove and discard dark vein and small sac 2 inches below head. Leave in green liver (tomalley) and any red roe (coral).
4. Crack large claws. Lay lobster, cut side up, on rack of broiler pan. Brush with melted butter. Sprinkle with salt, pepper, and paprika.
5. Broil, 4 inches from heat, 12 to 15 minutes, or until lightly browned.
6. Serve with more melted butter, in a small dish, and lemon wedges.
Makes 2 servings.

Broiled Rock-Lobster Tails

4 (5-oz size) frozen rock-lobster tails, thawed
1/4 cup soft butter or margarine
Salt or garlic salt

Lemon Butter:
1/2 cup butter or margarine
2 tablespoons lemon juice
1 teaspoon salt
Dash cayenne

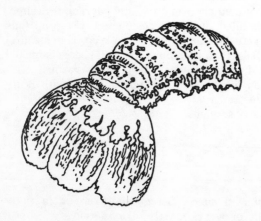

1. With kitchen shears, cut undershells away from lobster. Bend each shell backward until it cracks.
2. Place lobster tails, shell side up, on rack in broiler pan. Broil, 6 inches from heat, 5 minutes.
3. Turn lobster tails; spread with soft butter; sprinkle with salt. Broil 5 to 7 minutes longer, or until tender.
4. Meanwhile, heat all ingredients for Lemon Butter in small saucepan, over low heat, stirring, until butter melts. Serve with lobster.
Makes 4 servings.

Oysters

Oysters are available all year round, but more so in the winter months. They are found in the shallow waters of the Atlantic and Pacific, with most of the catch from the Atlantic. With oyster farming increasing, oysters should be bigger, more plentiful all year, and more reasonable in price.

Oysters Rockefeller

Rock salt
25 oysters in the shell
3/4 cup butter or margarine
1/4 cup finely chopped onion
1/4 cup finely chopped celery
1/4 cup finely chopped parsley
1/4 clove garlic, finely chopped
1/2 cup packaged dry bread crumbs
1/2 cup finely chopped watercress, packed
  (no stems)
1/2 cup finely chopped raw spinach, packed
  (no stems)
Dash anise
1/4 teaspoon salt
1/8 teaspoon liquid hot-pepper seasoning
Lemon wedges (optional)

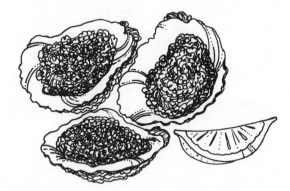

1. Begin by preheating oven to 450F.
2. In each of 5 large ramekins, or in a large, shallow roasting pan, place a layer of rock salt about 1/2 inch deep.
3. Sprinkle the salt lightly with water, to dampen. Place in oven to preheat while preparing oysters and vegetables.
4. Shuck the oysters (or have oysters shucked at fish market). Drain oysters. Place one on the deep half of each of the oyster shells; discard the other half.
5. In 1/4 cup hot butter or margarine in medium skillet, sauté onion, celery, parsley, and garlic until onion is golden and celery is tender—about 5 minutes.
6. Add rest of butter and crumbs; stir, over medium heat, till butter is melted.
7. Add chopped watercress and spinach, anise, salt, and liquid hot-pepper seasoning; cook, stirring, for 1 minute.
8. Pour off any liquid from oysters. Spread each with 1 tablespoon vegetable mixture, covering oysters completely.
9. Arrange 5 oysters on salt in each ramekin, or place all in roasting pan.
10. Bake, uncovered, about 10 minutes, or just until the oysters curl around the edges. Be careful not to overbake.
11. Serve right in ramekins, or remove to serving plates. Garnish with wedges of lemon, if desired. Serve as a first course or a light supper.
Makes 5 servings.

Fried Oysters

Substitute oysters for clams in Fried Clams, page 251.

Scallops

There are two varieties of scallops: The tiny bay scallop, tender and delicately flavored, is caught in the in-shore Atlantic waters; the larger, more available sea scallop is brought in from the deep Atlantic. Each is delicious; one kind or the other is obtainable, fresh or frozen, all year long.

Scallops Brittany Style

1/3 cup butter or margarine, melted
2 teaspoons finely chopped parsley
1/2 clove garlic, crushed
2/3 cup packaged dry bread crumbs
1 lb bay scallops, washed and well drained
Lemon wedges

1. Preheat oven to 325F. Lightly butter 6 scallop shells.
2. Combine the butter, chopped parsley, and garlic. Stir in the bread crumbs.
3. Spread some of bread-crumb mixture in center of each scallop shell. Top with scallops.
4. Sprinkle remaining bread-crumb mixture evenly over scallops. Place shells on cookie sheet.
5. Bake 25 to 30 minutes, or until scallops are done. Serve with lemon wedges.
Makes 6 servings.

Fried Scallops

Salad oil or shortening for frying
1 egg
1/2 teaspoon seasoned salt
1/8 teaspoon garlic powder
1 lb sea scallops, washed and well drained
1/2 cup packaged dry bread crumbs
Tartar Sauce, page 502

1. In deep skillet, heat salad oil (at least 1 inch) to 375F on deep-frying thermometer.
2. In small bowl, beat egg with seasoned salt and garlic powder.
3. Dip scallops in egg mixture; roll in crumbs, coating evenly.
4. Fry, a few at a time, until golden-brown—2 to 3 minutes.
5. Drain on paper towels; keep warm while frying rest. Serve with well-chilled Tartar Sauce and lemon wedges, if desired.
Makes 3 or 4 servings.

Sautéed Scallops

2 lb sea scallops
6 tablespoons butter or margarine
2 tablespoons chopped shallot
3 tablespoons dry vermouth or dry white wine
2 tablespoons chopped parsley
Lemon wedges

1. Rinse scallops gently under cold water; drain. If large, cut in half.
2. In hot butter in large, heavy skillet, sauté shallot 2 minutes. Add scallops in a single layer (do half at a time, if necessary). Sauté, over medium heat and stirring occasionally, until browned and cooked through—5 to 8 minutes.
3. With slotted spoon, remove to heated platter; keep warm.

4. Add vermouth and parsley to skillet; heat, over low heat, stirring to dissolve browned bits, until bubbling—about 1 minute. Pour over scallops.

5. Garnish with lemon wedges and with additional parsley, if desired.

Makes 6 servings.

Fried Scallops, Shrimp, and Sole

1 lb fillets of sole
1 lb sea scallops
3/4 lb shrimp, shelled and deveined
Salad oil or shortening for deep-frying
2 eggs
1-1/2 teaspoons salt
1/4 teaspoon pepper
1/4 teaspoon paprika
1-1/4 cups packaged dry bread crumbs
Tartar Sauce, page 502

1. Wash seafood; dry with paper towels. Cut fillets in half crosswise.

2. In deep skillet, slowly heat salad oil (at least 1 inch deep) to 375F on deep-frying thermometer. Or heat oil in electric skillet at 375F.

3. In pie plate, using a fork, beat eggs with salt, pepper, paprika.

4. Place bread crumbs on waxed paper. Dip seafood in egg mixture, then in crumbs, coating it evenly.

5. Gently place seafood, a few pieces at a time, in hot oil; fry until golden-brown—3 to 5 minutes.

6. Remove, and drain on paper towels. Place in warm oven until all seafood is cooked. Serve with Tartar Sauce and, if desired, lemon wedges.

Makes 4 to 6 servings.

Shrimp

The most popular shellfish is the shrimp. We consume more shrimp than any other country in the world, and about ten times as much shrimp as any other fish. Our chief source of supply is the Gulf Coast. Shrimp are plentiful the year round and are readily available in one form or another.

Boiled Shrimp

1-1/2 to 2 lb unshelled raw shrimp
1 small onion, peeled and thinly sliced
1/2 lemon, thinly sliced
2 sprigs parsley
1 tablespoon salt
5 whole black peppercorns
1 bay leaf
1/4 teaspoon dried thyme leaves

1. Rinse shrimp; remove shells, and devein (using a small, sharp knife, slit each shrimp down back; lift out sand vein).

2. In large skillet, combine 1 quart water, the onion, lemon, parsley, salt, peppercorns, bay leaf, and thyme. Bring to boiling, covered, over medium heat; simmer 10 minutes.

3. Add shrimp; return to boiling. Reduce heat, and simmer, covered, 3 to 5 minutes, or just until tender.

4. Drain; let cool. Refrigerate, covered, until ready to use. Use for shrimp cocktails, in salads, or in any recipe calling for boiled shrimp.

Makes 6 to 8 servings.

Shrimp in Garlic Butter   Scampi

2 lb large, unshelled raw shrimp
1/2 cup butter or margarine
1/2 cup salad or olive oil
1/4 cup chopped parsley
6 cloves garlic, crushed
1 teaspoon salt
Dash cayenne
1/4 cup lemon juice

1. Rinse shrimp; remove shells, leaving tails on. Devein (using a small, sharp knife, slit each shrimp down back; lift out sand vein). Wash under cold running water. Drain; pat dry with paper towels.
2. Melt butter in shallow broiler pan, without rack, or 13-by-9-by-2-inch baking pan. Add salad oil, 2 tablespoons parsley, the garlic, salt, cayenne, and lemon juice; mix well.
3. Add shrimp, tossing lightly in butter mixture to coat well. Arrange in single layer in pan.
4. Broil, 4 to 5 inches from heat, 5 minutes. Turn shrimp; broil 5 to 10 minutes longer, or until lightly browned.
5. Using tongs, remove shrimp to heated serving platter. Pour garlic mixture over all, or pour it into a small pitcher, to pass.
6. Sprinkle shrimp with remaining chopped parsley. Garnish platter with lemon slices, if you wish. Makes 8 servings.
Note: Shrimp may be baked at 400F for 8 to 10 minutes, or just until tender, instead of broiled.

Shrimp Creole with White Rice

1/2 lemon, sliced
4 whole black peppercorns
2 lb raw shrimp, shelled and deveined
4 slices bacon
2 tablespoons butter or margarine
1 clove garlic, finely chopped
1 cup chopped onion
1-1/2 cups chopped green pepper
1/4 cup finely chopped parsley
1-1/2 cups thinly sliced celery
1 can (1 lb, 12 oz) tomatoes
1 can (6 oz) tomato paste
1 tablespoon lemon juice
1 tablespoon sugar
1 teaspoon salt
1/4 to 1/2 teaspoon pepper
1/4 to 1/2 teaspoon crushed red pepper
1 bay leaf
1/2 teaspoon dried thyme leaves
1/2 teaspoon filé powder
Cooked white rice

1. Bring 1 quart water to boiling in large saucepan. Add lemon slices, black peppercorns, and shrimp. Reduce heat; simmer, uncovered, 3 minutes.
2. Drain shrimp, reserving 1 cup cooking liquid.
3. In same saucepan, sauté bacon, over low heat, until crisp. Remove bacon; drain on paper towels; crumble.
4. To bacon fat, add butter, garlic, onion, green pepper, parsley, celery; cook, stirring, about 5 minutes, or until vegetables are tender.
5. Add reserved shrimp liquid, bacon, tomatoes, tomato paste, lemon juice, sugar, salt, pepper, red pepper, bay leaf, and thyme; bring to boiling. Reduce heat; simmer, covered, 30 minutes.
6. Just before serving, stir in filé powder and shrimp; bring to boiling. Reduce heat, and simmer 5 minutes.
7. Serve over hot, cooked white rice.
Makes 6 to 8 servings.
Note: This dish may be made in advance and frozen until ready to use.

Shrimp Gumbo

4 tablespoons butter or margarine
1 tablespoon flour
1 lb raw shrimp, shelled and deveined
2 teaspoons crab or shrimp boil,* tied in a cheesecloth bag
1 teaspoon salt
Dash pepper
1 pkg (10 oz) frozen whole okra, slightly thawed
1/2 cup chopped onion
2 tablespoons chopped green pepper
1 can (8 oz) tomato sauce
1 can (8 oz) tomatoes
2 to 3 cups cooked white rice
Chopped parsley
* A special blend of spices and herbs for boiling
crab and shrimp.

1. In large saucepan or Dutch oven, melt 2 tablespoons butter. Remove from heat; blend in flour
until smooth. Return to heat; add shrimp; cook,
stirring often, 3 to 4 minutes.
2. Add 2 cups water, the crab or shrimp boil, salt,
and pepper. Bring to boiling; reduce heat; simmer,
covered, 15 minutes.
3. Meanwhile, cut okra in 1-inch pieces. Heat remaining butter in medium saucepan. Sauté okra,
onion, and green pepper until tender—about 10
minutes. Stir in tomato sauce and tomatoes.
4. Add tomato mixture to shrimp; simmer 30 minutes longer.
5. Mound 1/2 cup cooked rice in each large soup
plate. Ladle gumbo over rice. Sprinkle with
parsley.
Makes 4 to 6 servings.

Shrimp and Lobster in White Wine

4 (8-oz size) frozen rock-lobster tails
2 lb raw shrimp, shelled and deveined
2 cans (7-1/2-oz size) king-crab meat, drained
10 tablespoons butter or margarine
2/3 cup flour
2 teaspoons salt
1 teaspoon paprika
1/4 teaspoon white pepper
3 cups light cream
1-1/4 cups dry white wine

1. In large kettle, bring 2-1/2 quarts water to boiling. Add lobster tails; return to boiling. Reduce
heat; simmer, covered, 8 minutes. With slotted
utensil, lift out lobster tails, and set aside until
they are cool enough to handle.
2. Return water to boiling. Add shrimp; return to
boiling. Reduce heat, and simmer, covered, 5 minutes, or until shrimp are tender. Drain.
3. Drain crabmeat, leaving pieces as big as
possible.
4. Remove meat from lobster shells; cut into bite-
size pieces. Set all seafood aside.
5. Melt butter in Dutch oven; remove from heat.
Stir in flour, salt, paprika, and pepper until
smooth. Gradually stir in cream, mixing until
smooth.
6. Bring to boiling, stirring constantly; reduce
heat, and simmer 5 minutes.
7. Add wine, lobster, shrimp, and crabmeat; stir
gently just until combined. Cook over low heat just
until heated through—do not let it boil.
8. Serve with parsley-buttered hot rice.
Makes 12 servings.

Shrimp Curry

Curry Sauce:
3 tablespoons butter or margarine
1 cup chopped onion
1 cup chopped pared apple
1 clove garlic, crushed
2 to 3 teaspoons curry powder
1/4 cup unsifted all-purpose flour
1 teaspoon salt
1/4 teaspoon ground ginger
1/4 teaspoon ground cardamom
1/4 teaspoon pepper
2 cans (10-1/2-oz size) condensed chicken broth,
    undiluted
2 tablespoons lime juice
2 teaspoons grated lime peel

2 lb raw shrimp, shelled and deveined (18 to 20 per
    pound)
1 tablespoon salt
1 small onion, peeled and sliced
1/2 lemon, sliced
5 whole black peppercorns
1/4 cup chopped chutney

1. Make Curry Sauce: In hot butter in large skillet, sauté chopped onion, chopped apple, garlic, and curry powder until the onion is tender—will take about 5 minutes.
2. Remove from heat; blend in flour, 1 teaspoon salt, the ground ginger, cardamom, and pepper.
3. Gradually stir in chicken broth, lime juice, and grated lime peel.
4. Bring to boiling, stirring constantly. Reduce heat, and simmer sauce, uncovered, 20 minutes, stirring it occasionally.
5. Meanwhile, cook shrimp: Rinse shrimp under cold running water.
6. In a large saucepan, combine 1 quart water, 1 tablespoon salt, the sliced onion, sliced lemon, and whole black peppercorns; bring to boiling. Add the cleaned shrimp.
7. Return to boiling; reduce heat, and simmer shrimp, uncovered, 5 to 10 minutes, or just until they are tender when tested with a fork.
8. Drain shrimp, discarding cooking liquid. Add shrimp to curry sauce; stir in chopped chutney. Heat gently just to boiling.
9. Serve the Shrimp Curry hot, with Curry Accompaniments and Fluffy White Rice, page 458.
Makes 6 servings.

Curry Accompaniments:
Chutney
Pickled watermelon rind
Chopped green pepper
Chopped green onion
Diced avocado
Cucumber slices
Diced tomato
Salted nuts
Peanuts
Sliced banana
Raisins
Pineapple chunks

International Cooking

In the past few years, Americans have become world travelers. This with the revival of age-old traditions among Americans of all ethnic backgrounds has created a tremendous interest in international cooking and authentic old-world recipes.

What better way to re-create memories of a great trip or a glorious past than to cook and serve the traditional national dishes?

The following have been favorite recipes with our readers.

Chinese

Most of us know Chinese food from the limited experience of dining in Americanized Chinese restaurants. The fact is that the Chinese cuisine is rated, along with the French, as one of the most complex and sophisticated in the world. There's a complete range of different flavorings—from the hot, spicy Szechwan country fare to the delicate Shrimp with Apricot Sauce. Our variety of recipes, all quite authentic, bears this out.

Chinese Cooking Ingredients

All ingredients called for in our recipes can be purchased at Oriental food stores (check your classified directory), some in supermarkets.

Bamboo shoots: Tender shoots of bamboo plants. Buy them fresh—or canned from many supermarkets.

Bean curd: White curd of soybeans pressed into cakes. They're sold dried, but they're better fresh or canned.

Chinese mushrooms: They are larger and more delicate in flavor than the mushrooms we know. Sold dried.

Chinese parsley: Leaves of fresh coriander, or cilantro. Looks like parsley, but flavor is different.

Cloud ears: A kind of dried tree fungus, also known as wood ears. Mushroomlike flavor.

Dow see: Fermented or salted Chinese black beans.

Ginger root: Fresh root of ginger plant. It is aromatic and has a hot bite. Often used grated.

Golden needles. Dried lily buds or stamens.

Hoisin sauce: A thick, dark, brownish-red condiment used in Chinese cooking and as a dip for other dishes.

Hot chili oil: Used in many hot and sour dishes. To make it, soak 2 small dried red chili peppers in 1 cup peanut or salad oil.

Monosodium glutamate: A white crystalline powder used in Chinese cuisine to enhance flavor. We know it as Ac'cent.

Sesame oil: Dark-colored, rich, nutty-flavored oil made from toasted seasame seeds. Some health-food stores carry it, but be sure to get the imported Oriental kind.

Soy sauce: A dark, salty liquid made from soybeans, widely used in Oriental cooking. Most supermarkets carry the Chinese or Japanese kind.

Water chestnuts: Crisp bulblike roots of a vegetable. Sold canned in supermarkets.

Tea Eggs

6 hard-cooked eggs (see Note), shells on
2 teaspoons salt
1-1/2 tablespoons soy sauce
1/4 teaspoon whole anise seed
2 black-tea bags

1. Day before: Roll eggs on hard surface to crack shells, but don't remove shells.
2. In medium saucepan, combine 2 cups cold water, the salt, soy sauce, anise seeds, and tea bags; add eggs. Bring to boiling; reduce heat; simmer, covered, 2 hours, adding water if necessary. Remove from heat; set aside to cool to room temperature. Then refrigerate overnight.

3. To serve: Drain eggs; carefully remove shells. Slice eggs in half, lengthwise, or in quarters. Serve as an hors d'oeuvre.
Makes 12 halves.
Note: To hard-cook eggs: Cover eggs with water to an inch above them; bring rapidly to a boil. Take pan off heat; cover, and let stand 20 minutes. Then cool in cold water.

Shrimp Toast

12 slices white bread
1 lb deveined, shelled shrimp
1/4 cup finely chopped onion
2 teaspoons salt
1 teaspoon sugar
1 tablespoon cornstarch
1/2 teaspoon monosodium glutamate
1 egg, beaten
1 can (5-1/4 oz) water chestnuts, drained and
  finely chopped
Salad oil for frying
Chopped parsley

1. Trim crusts from bread; let slices dry out slightly.
2. Chop shrimp very, very fine (put in blender, if desired, to chop fine); in medium bowl, toss with onion, salt, sugar, cornstarch, and monosodium glutamate; mix well. Stir in beaten egg and water chestnuts; mix well.
3. Spread mixture on bread; cut each slice into quarters (squares or triangles).
4. In a large heavy skillet or saucepan, heat oil (about 1 inch deep) to 375F on deep-frying thermometer.
5. Drop bread pieces, several at a time, shrimp side down, in hot oil. Fry until edges of bread begin to brown; turn on other side; fry until golden-brown.
6. Drain well on paper towels. Sprinkle with chopped parsley. Serve warm, as an hors d'oeuvre.
Makes 48.
Note: These can be made ahead and reheated in 375F oven 10 minutes at serving time.

Five-Flavor Beef

1/4 cup salad oil
4 lb boned chuck or rump pot roast
1 cup soy sauce
1-inch cinnamon stick
2 anise seeds
1/2 cup sugar
1 cup sherry
3 tablespoons cornstarch

1. Slowly heat oil in Dutch oven. In it, brown meat well on all sides—about 15 minutes.
2. Meanwhile, combine soy sauce, 2 cups water, cinnamon stick, anise seeds, and sugar.
3. Pour over meat; simmer, covered, 3 hours, or until meat is tender. After 2 hours, add sherry.
4. Remove meat to heated platter.
5. Reserve 2-1/2 cups liquid in Dutch oven, and discard rest; bring to boil.
6. Meanwhile, in small bowl, make a smooth mixture of cornstarch and 1/2 cup water.
7. Stir into boiling liquid in Dutch oven; simmer, stirring, until thickened and translucent. Serve over beef.
Makes 8 servings.

Egg-Drop Soup

4 cans (13 3/4-oz size) clear chicken broth
3 tablespoons cornstarch
1/2 teaspoon sugar
1 teaspoon salt
1/4 teaspoon pepper
2 eggs, beaten
1 cup chopped green onions (with tops)

1. Heat broth to boiling point in large saucepan.
2. Meanwhile, in small bowl, make a smooth paste of cornstarch and 1/4 cup cold water.
3. Into hot broth, slowly stir cornstarch mixture, with sugar, salt, and pepper. Heat to boiling point, stirring constantly—mixture should be slightly thickened and translucent.
4. Reduce heat. Add eggs, a small amount at a time, stirring to separate them into shreds.
5. Remove from heat; add green onions. Serve at once.
Makes 8 servings.

Fried Rice

1/4 cup salad oil
2 cups cold cooked white rice
3 eggs, beaten
2 cooked bacon slices, crumbled
2 tablespoons soy sauce
1/8 teaspoon pepper
3 green onions with tops, sliced

1. Heat oil in heavy skillet. In hot oil, sauté rice, over medium heat, stirring with metal spoon, about 5 minutes, or until golden.
2. Stir eggs into rice; cook, stirring constantly and over medium heat, until eggs are cooked—about 3 minutes.
3. Then stir in bacon, soy sauce, and pepper; combine well. Garnish with green onions.
Makes 6 servings.

Subgum Fried Rice

4 cups cold cooked rice (see Note)
3 eggs
1 teaspoon salt
3 tablespoons salad oil
1/4 cup chopped scallion
1 cup diced cooked chicken
1 cup diced cooked ham
1/2 cup frozen peas, thawed
1/8 teaspoon pepper
2 tablespoons soy sauce

1. Separate rice with fork.
2. In small bowl, with rotary beater, beat eggs slightly with 1/2 teaspoon salt.
3. Heat 1 tablespoon oil in medium skillet. Pour in eggs. Over high heat, scramble eggs, pushing them with a flat metal spatula to keep from sticking. Cook just until set and no longer runny. Set aside.
4. In remaining hot oil in large skillet, sauté scallion 1 minute; add rice. Fry, stirring quickly with flat metal spatula, until heated through.
5. Add chicken, ham, peas, rest of salt, and the pepper. Heat; stir in eggs with fork. Sprinkle with soy sauce.
Makes 6 to 8 servings.
Note: Cook 1 cup converted raw white rice as package label directs. Refrigerate overnight.

Steamed Rice

1 cup converted raw white rice
2-1/3 cups cold water
1 teaspoon salt
2 tablespoons butter or 1 tablespoon peanut oil

1. In a heavy, 3-quart saucepan with lid, combine rice, water, and salt. Bring to boiling; reduce heat to very low.
2. Fold a kitchen towel in quarters; place over pan; cover with a heavy lid. Cook 25 to 30 minutes. Rice should be tender and water absorbed. Add butter or oil; stir with fork. Turn into heated serving dish. Makes 4 to 6 servings.
Note: Do not double recipe; it is better to make recipe twice.

Sweet-and-Sour Pork

2-3/4 lb pork shoulder, cut into 1/2-inch cubes
3 tablespoons sherry
1-1/2 teaspoons soy sauce
1 teaspoon monosodium glutamate
1/2 teaspoon ground ginger
1 quart salad oil

Batter:
3 eggs
3/4 cup sifted all-purpose flour
3 tablespoons cornstarch

Sauce:
1 can (1 lb 4-oz) pineapple chunks
1 cup sugar
1 cup vinegar
2 large green peppers, cut in 1/2-inch strips
1/2 cup thinly sliced gherkins
2 tablespoons cornstarch
2 teaspoons soy sauce
2 large tomatoes, cut in eighths
1/2 cup slivered crystallized ginger

Cooked white rice

1. In large, shallow dish, toss pork with sherry, soy sauce, monosodium glutamate, and ginger; let stand 10 minutes.
2. Meanwhile, in 3-quart saucepan or deep-fat fryer, slowly heat oil to 375F on deep-frying thermometer.
3. Make Batter: In medium bowl, with rotary beater, beat eggs very well. Add flour and cornstarch; beat until smooth.
4. Drain pork cubes well. Pour batter over them; mix well, to coat evenly.
5. Drop cubes (about one fourth at a time—do not crowd) into hot fat; fry about 5 minutes, turning, until golden on all sides. With slotted spoon, remove pork; drain on paper towels.
6. Keep warm in oven set at very low temperature.
7. Make Sauce: Drain pineapple chunks, reserving juice. Add water to juice to make 1 cup.
8. In large saucepan, combine juice, sugar, and vinegar; heat, stirring, until sugar is dissolved. Then bring to boiling point.
9. Add green peppers and gherkins; boil 2 minutes. Remove from heat.
10. In small bowl, combine cornstarch and 1/4 cup water; stir until smooth. Add to pineapple-juice mixture, with soy sauce, tomatoes, ginger, and pineapple chunks.
11. Cook, stirring and over moderate heat, until thickened and translucent.
12. Arrange pork cubes in serving dish. Pour on the sweet-sour sauce. Serve with hot rice.
Makes 6 to 8 servings.

Chicken with Toasted Almonds

3 (2-lb size) broiler-fryers
5 tablespoons salad oil
2 tablespoons soy sauce
2 teaspoons salt
1-1/2 teaspoons sugar
Dash pepper
1/4 cup cornstarch
1 can (13 3/4-oz) clear chicken broth
1 can (5 oz) water chestnuts, drained and chopped
1/2 cup thawed frozen, or canned, peas, drained
1 cup thinly sliced celery
1 can (4 oz) whole mushrooms, drained
1/2 cup toasted slivered almonds

1. Have meatman bone and skin broiler-fryers. To make them easier to slice, store in freezing compartment until partially frozen. Then slice into long, thin slivers; let thaw completely at room temperature.
2. Heat oil in large skillet. Add chicken slivers, soy sauce, salt, sugar, and pepper; cook, stirring, a few minutes, or just until chicken is no longer pink.
3. In small bowl, make a smooth paste of cornstarch and 1/3 cup water. Stir into chicken mixture, with chicken broth, water chestnuts, peas, celery, and mushrooms; cook, stirring, until slightly thickened and translucent. Sprinkle top with almonds.
Makes 6 servings.

Shrimp with Apricot Sauce

2 lb fresh or thawed frozen uncooked shrimp
2 eggs
1/2 cup milk
3/4 cup sifted all-purpose flour
2 tablespoons cornstarch
1 teaspoon baking powder
1 teaspoon salt
2 teaspoons salad oil
1 quart salad oil
Apricot Sauce, below

1. Leaving shell on tail, remove rest of shell from each shrimp. Devein shrimp; rinse in cold water; drain well on paper towels.
2. In medium bowl, with rotary beater, beat eggs slightly. Add milk, flour, cornstarch, baking powder, salt, and 2 teaspoons oil. Beat until batter is smooth.
3. In deep-fryer or heavy kettle, slowly heat 1 quart oil to 375F on deep-frying thermometer.
4. While oil is heating, make Apricot Sauce.
5. Then dip shrimp in batter, coating thoroughly. Fry, a few at a time, until golden-brown—takes about 4 minutes. Drain on paper towels. Serve shrimp with hot Apricot Sauce.
Makes 6 servings.

Apricot Sauce

1/2 cup pineapple juice
2 to 4 tablespoons dry mustard
2 tablespoons soy sauce
1 cup apricot jam
2 teaspoons grated lemon peel
1/4 cup lemon juice

1. In medium skillet, stir pineapple juice into mustard until mixture is smooth.
2. Add remaining ingredients. Heat, stirring over low heat, until jam is melted.
Makes about 1-3/4 cups.

Lobster Cantonese

Salad oil or peanut oil for frying
1/2 lb ground pork
1/4 cup salted Chinese black beans, mashed
    (fermented black beans)
3 cloves garlic, minced
1/4 teaspoon grated fresh ginger root
1-1/2-lb live lobster (see Note), cut into 2-inch
    pieces, shell and all
1 teaspoon sugar
1-1/2 cups chicken broth
1 teaspoon sherry
1 teaspoon soy sauce
2 tablespoons cornstarch
2 large eggs, slightly beaten
1/4 teaspoon Oriental sesame oil

Garnish:
2 scallions, cut julienne style, or 6 snow peas

1. Heat a large, heavy skillet or wok until hot. Add just enough oil to coat pan; then add 2 more tablespoons; heat.
2. Add pork; stir-fry until pork is almost cooked— about 2 minutes.
3. Add black beans, garlic, and ginger; stir-fry.
4. Add lobster pieces; stir-fry quickly until shell changes to a brilliant orange-red.
5. Sprinkle sugar over top; add chicken broth, sherry, and soy sauce.
6. Combine cornstarch with 6 tablespoons water; stir until smooth.
7. When broth is bubbling, push lobster to one side of pan; in cleared space, slowly stir cornstarch mixture into broth. Cook, stirring, until broth is slightly thickened.
8. Add eggs; let set slightly; then stir into sauce. Stir-fry to coat lobster well with sauce. Remove from heat; drizzle sesame oil over all; toss.
9. Garnish top with scallions or snow peas.
Makes 4 servings.
Note: You may use 3 or 4 (6- to 8-oz size) lobster tails if live lobster is not available. If using frozen, thaw before using. If using live lobster, have fish dealer cut it up if it is to be cooked same day.

Beef and Peppers

1-1/2-lb sirloin steak, 1 inch thick
Boiling water
4 cups thinly sliced green-pepper rings
3 tablespoons salad oil
3 cups thinly sliced onions
3/4 teaspoon salt
2 cloves garlic
5 green onions, with their tops, sliced
2 teaspoons monosodium glutamate
1-1/2 teaspoons sugar
Dash pepper
1/3 cup sherry
1-1/2 teaspoons finely chopped crystallized ginger
3/4 cup canned beef broth
3 tablespoons cornstarch
2 tablespoons soy sauce
Cooked white rice

1. To make beef easier to slice, store in freezing compartment until partially frozen. Slice into 1/8-inch slivers, thaw completely at room temperature.
2. Pour just enough boiling water over green-pepper rings to cover. Let stand about 3 minutes; then rinse in cold water.
3. Heat oil in large skillet. Add green-pepper rings, onion slices, salt, garlic, and green onions; cook, stirring and over high heat, 3 minutes.
4. Then add beef slivers; cook, stirring and over high heat, 2 minutes.
5. Add monosodium glutamate, sugar, pepper, sherry, and ginger; cook, stirring, 1 minute.
6. Add broth, and bring mixture to boiling point.
7. Meanwhile, in small bowl, combine cornstarch, soy sauce, and 3/4 cup water. Stir into skillet; cook, stirring, until sauce is thickened and translucent. Serve with hot rice.
Makes 6 servings.

Sweet-and-Sour Fish

2 (1-1/2- to 2-lb size) whole fish, with head and tail
on, cleaned and scaled (red snapper, sea bass, or
baby striped bass)

Marinade:
1/3 cup Chinese or Japanese soy sauce
1/3 cup sherry
1 tablespoon sugar
1/4 teaspoon finely grated fresh ginger root
1 clove garlic, minced
1/4 teaspoon sesame oil

Sweet-and-Sour Sauce:
1 cup cider vinegar
1 cup sugar
2/3 cup pineapple juice
2/3 cup orange juice
1/3 cup catsup
1/4 teaspoon salt
1 tablespoon cornstarch
Salad or peanut oil for frying

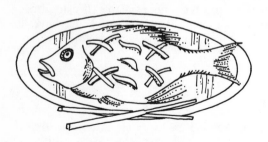

1. Wash fish well; drain on paper towels. With a
sharp knife, make three deep diagonal slashes
across each side of each fish.
2. Make Marinade: In small bowl, combine soy
sauce, sherry, 1 tablespoon sugar, the ginger, garlic, and sesame oil; mix well. Pour into two large
shallow baking dishes. Place each fish in marinade; marinate 15 minutes or longer on each side.
3. Meanwhile, prepare Sweet-and-Sour Sauce: In
medium saucepan, combine vinegar, sugar, pineapple and orange juices, catsup, and salt; mix well;
bring to boiling.
4. In small bowl, combine cornstarch and 2 tablespoons water; stir until smooth. Gradually stir into
boiling liquid; cook, stirring, until slightly thickened and translucent. Reduce heat; keep warm.
5. In a very large heavy skillet, wok, or oval Dutch
oven, heat about 6-1/2 cups oil (1-1/2 inches deep)
to 380F on deep-frying thermometer. Drain fish;
dry well on paper towels.
6. Gently lower each fish, head first, into hot oil,
holding fish by tail and being very careful of
spattering hot oil.
7. Fry until golden-brown on one side—3 to 5
minutes. Carefully turn fish; fry 3 to 5 minutes,
or until golden.
8. Drain on paper towels; arrange on heated oval
platter. Pour warm sauce over fish. Decorate with
matchstick bamboo shoots and scallions, if desired.
Makes 6 servings.

Chinese Fruit Bowl

1 ripe pineapple (3 lb)
1 pint strawberries, washed and hulled
1 can (11 oz) litchi nuts, drained
1 can (11 oz) mandarin-orange sections, drained
1/2 cup preserved whole kumquats
2 bananas, sliced on the diagonal
1/2 cup syrup from preserved kumquats
3/4 cup white rum
2 tablespoons chopped candied ginger (optional)

1. With a long-bladed, sharp knife, cut pineapple
into quarters, right through frond. Remove pineapple, in one piece, from shells. Remove core.
Slice pineapple into wedges, 1/4 inch thick. (Makes
about 4 cups.)
2. In large bowl, gently toss pineapple wedges
with remaining ingredients. Refrigerate, covered,
until well chilled—2 hours or longer.
Makes 12 to 14 servings.

Almond Junket

1 env unflavored gelatine
1-1/2 cups boiling water
Sugar
1/2 cup milk
2 teaspoons almond extract

Garnish:
1/2 cup currant jelly
2 slices canned pineapple, drained
Canned mandarin-orange sections, drained

1. In small bowl, sprinkle gelatine over 1/4 cup cold water; let stand 5 minutes to soften.
2. In medium saucepan, combine boiling water with 3 tablespoons sugar; boil 2 minutes. Remove from heat; stir in milk.
3. Add softened gelatine and almond extract, stirring until gelatine is dissolved.
4. Pour into 13-by-9-by-2-inch pan, to make a layer about 1/4 inch thick. Refrigerate until firm and well chilled—about 1 hour.
5. Make syrup: In small saucepan, combine 1/4 cup sugar with 1/4 cup water. Bring to boiling; reduce heat, and stir until sugar is dissolved. Add 1/2 cup water. Pour into glass serving bowl; refrigerate.
6. At serving time, cut junket into small cubes. Spoon cubes into syrup in serving bowl. Garnish with cubes of currant jelly, pineapple slices, and orange sections.
Makes 6 to 8 servings.

Almond Cookies

3/4 cup butter or regular margarine, softened
3/4 cup sugar
1 egg
2 teaspoons almond extract
1-1/2 cups unsifted all-purpose flour
1/2 teaspoon baking soda
1/4 teaspoon salt
1 egg yolk
18 blanched whole almonds

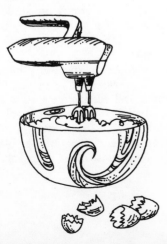

1. Preheat oven to 350F. Lightly grease several cookie sheets.
2. In large bowl, with portable electric mixer at medium speed, beat butter, sugar, whole egg, and almond extract until very light and fluffy.
3. On sheet of waxed paper, sift flour with soda and salt. Beat into butter mixture until well combined.
4. Refrigerate dough one hour; it will be easier to handle.
5. Using hands, form dough into 18 balls about 1-1/4 inches in diameter. Place on prepared cookie sheets, 3 inches apart to allow for spreading; flatten with hands to 1/4-inch thickness.
6. Using a fork, beat egg yolk slightly with 1 tablespoon water. Use to brush over tops of cookies.
7. Press almond into center of each. Brush again with egg yolk.
8. Bake 15 minutes, or until light golden in color. Remove cookies to wire rack to cool slightly.
9. Store in tightly covered glass jar or cookie tin.
Makes 1-1/2 dozen.

English ·

England; its very name conjures up such dishes as steak-and-kidney pie, seed cake, savouries and trifles. Men love its satisfying qualities. You will, too, when you try our recipes.

Baked and Trout and Bacon

3 (3/4-lb size) fresh rainbow trout, cleaned and
    split; or 3 frozen trout, thawed
8 slices bacon
1 teaspoon salt
1/4 teaspoon pepper
2 tablespoons chopped parsley

1. Preheat oven to 375F.
2. Wash trout well under running cold water. Drain; pat dry with paper towels.
3. Line a 13-by-9-by-2-inch baking pan with bacon slices; lay trout on bacon. Sprinkle with salt, pepper, and 1 tablespoon parsley.
4. Cover dish with foil, sealing tightly around edge.
5. Bake 20 to 25 minutes, or just until fish flakes easily when tested with a fork.
6. Gently lift trout and bacon to heated serving platter. Sprinkle with remaining parsley.
Makes 6 servings.

Steak-and-Kidney Pies

2-1/2 pkg (11-oz size) piecrust mix
2 veal kidneys (1 lb)
Salt
3 lb beef chuck, cut into 2-by-1-inch strips
1/3 cup flour
6 tablespoons butter or margarine
4 cans (10-3/4-oz size) beef gravy
1/2 lb fresh mushrooms, sliced
1 cup chopped onion
1/2 bay leaf, crushed
1/2 teaspoon dried thyme leaves
1/4 teaspoon pepper

1. Prepare piecrust mix as the label directs; shape into ball. Refrigerate, covered, until needed.
2. Cover kidneys with cold water; add 1 teaspoon salt. Let stand 30 minutes; drain. Remove outer membrane and excess fat; slice thinly.
3. Coat beef strips with flour.
4. Heat butter in large skillet. Add beef, one third at a time, and brown well on all sides. Remove as it browns; set aside.
5. Stir 1 can gravy into pan drippings; bring to boiling, stirring to loosen browned bits. Pour into large bowl. Add 2 cans gravy, the sliced kidneys, mushrooms, onion, bay leaf, 1 teaspoon salt, the thyme, and pepper. Mix well; set aside.
6. Preheat oven to 350F.
7. Remove one fourth of pastry, and set aside. Divide remaining pastry into 8 pieces. On lightly floured surface, roll each piece into a 5-1/2-inch circle. Cut a 1-inch hole in center of each. Set pastry circles aside.
8. Roll out reserved pastry into a 14-by-9-inch rectangle. Cut lengthwise into 8 strips, about 1 inch wide.

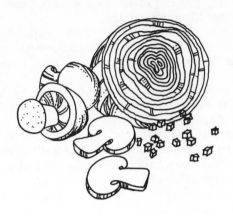

9. Turn beef into 8 (10-oz) baking dishes, dividing evenly. Moisten pastry strips with cold water, and place around inside top edge of each baking dish so pastry stands 1/2 inch above dish. Add 1 cup kidney mixture to each, mounding in center. Top each with a pastry circle; seal edge. Then press edge firmly with tines of fork. If desired, decorate with pastry cutouts. Place on cookie sheet.

10. Bake 1-1/2 to 1-3/4 hours, or until beef is tender. Remove to wire rack. Carefully pour remaining gravy through center hole into meat mixture in each dish (about 2 tablespoons per pie).

11. Let stand until completely cool—1 to 1-1/2 hours. Wrap individually in foil, plastic film, or moisture-vaporproof freezing paper; seal, and label. Place in freezer.

12. To serve: Set the oven at 400F. Remove number of servings desired from freezer. Unwrap; place baking dishes on cookie sheet; cover loosely with foil. Bake about 1 hour, or until the pies are heated through. Garnish with parsley, if desired.

Makes 8 servings.

Welsh Curd Tarts

1 pkg (11 oz) piecrust mix
4 tablespoons butter or regular margarine
1/2 cup sugar
2 egg yolks
1 tablespoon finely grated lemon peel
1-1/2 teaspoons brandy
1/8 teaspoon salt
1 carton (12 oz) pot-style cottage cheese
1 tablespoon light cream
1/4 cup dried currants

1. Prepare piecrust mix as package label directs. Divide in half. On lightly floured surface or pastry cloth, roll out half of pastry to 1/8-inch thickness. With 3-1/2-inch round cutter, cut out 8 circles. Fit each circle into a 3-inch fluted tart pan. Repeat with other half of pastry.

2. Preheat oven to 450F.

3. In medium bowl, with electric mixer, beat butter until soft. Beat in sugar until light and fluffy. Add egg yolks, lemon peel, brandy, and salt; beat until light.

4. Add cottage cheese, cream, and currants; beat at low speed until mixture is almost smooth.

5. Spoon about 2 tablespoons cheese mixture into each pastry-lined pan. Place all on a cookie sheet.

6. Bake 10 minutes; reduce heat to 375F, and bake 15 to 20 minutes longer, or until filling is firm and lightly golden.

7. Set pans on wire rack; let tarts cool completely.

8. Carefully loosen around edges; remove from pans.

Makes 16.

Brussels Sprouts with Chestnut Sauce

1 lb Brussels sprouts
1 teaspoon salt
1/2 lb chestnuts, roasted (see Note) and peeled
1/3 cup butter or margarine

1. Cut off stem end of Brussels sprouts. Soak in cold water 15 minutes; drain.
2. Place in medium saucepan with 3 cups water and the salt; bring to boiling. Lower heat, and simmer, uncovered, 10 minutes, or until tender. Drain.
3. Meanwhile, quarter chestnuts. Sauté in hot butter in saucepan 5 minutes. Toss with drained Brussels sprouts.
Makes 6 servings.
Note: To roast chestnuts: First make a slit in each shell with a sharp knife. Bake at 500F for 15 minutes. Remove shells and skin.

French

The French have a way with food, there's no doubt. A French cook can take the same (nearly the same) ingredients as anyone else and with a dash of something or other—magic, most likely, to judge by the taste of the best French cooking—turn out dishes that will linger lovingly in the memory forever. Here, we give you some great French recipes to let you in on the secret of great French cooking.

Soupe au Pistou

1/2 lb dried white kidney beans
1-1/2 lb zucchini
3 medium white turnips (1 lb)
1 large potato
6 medium carrots (1 lb)
2 celery stalks with leaves
2 red onions
1 red onion studded with 4 cloves
1 whole bay leaf
1 can (1 lb, 1 oz) whole tomatoes, undrained
1 tablespoon dried basil leaves
1/8 teaspoon dried hot red pepper
1-1/2 tablespoons salt
2 tablespoons olive or salad oil
2 tablespoons chopped parsley

1. Day before, soak beans (even though package says otherwise) overnight in cold water to cover.
2. Next day, drain beans in colander; rinse under cold water.
3. Prepare vegetables: Dice zucchini; pare and dice turnips and potato. Pare carrots; slice thinly; slice celery. Coarsely chop 2 onions.
4. Turn beans into a 6-quart Dutch oven with 6 cups water; bring to boiling over medium heat.
5. Add prepared vegetables and rest of ingredients, except oil and parsley. Bring back to boiling; reduce heat, and simmer, covered, 2-1/2 hours, or until beans are tender.
6. To serve, remove and discard onion with cloves and the bay leaf. Stir in oil. Taste for seasoning. Sprinkle with parsley. Flavor is even better the next day.
Makes 4-1/2 quarts.

Potage Printanier

2 tablespoons butter or margarine
2 leeks, chopped (about 1 cup)
1 small onion, chopped
1-1/2 quarts hot water
2 potatoes, pared, quartered, and thinly sliced
2 medium carrots, pared and thinly sliced
2 teaspoons salt
1/4 cup raw regular white rice
8 stalks fresh or frozen asparagus, cut into 1/2-inch pieces
1/2 lb spinach, washed and chopped
1 cup light cream

1. Melt butter in a 3-quart kettle. Add leeks and onion; cook over low heat, covered, about 5 minutes.
2. Add hot water, potato, carrot, and salt; bring to boiling. Reduce heat; simmer, covered, 15 minutes.
3. Add rice and asparagus; simmer, covered, 25 minutes. Add spinach, and simmer 10 minutes longer.
4. Stir in cream; bring just to boiling.
Makes 8 servings.
Note: Flavor is enhanced if soup is refrigerated, covered, overnight and reheated at serving time.

Bouillabaisse

1/4 cup olive or salad oil
1 cup chopped onion
3 cloves garlic, crushed
4 bottles (8-oz size) clam juice
2 cans (1-lb, 12-oz size) whole peeled tomatoes, undrained
1 teaspoon grated orange peel
3/4 teaspoon salt
1/4 teaspoon crumbled saffron
1/4 teaspoon fennel seed
1/8 teaspoon dried thyme leaves
1/8 teaspoon pepper
2 bay leaves
2 pkg (8-oz size) frozen rock-lobster tails
1 lb cod steaks
1 lb halibut steaks
1/2 lb sea scallops
1 loaf French bread, thinly sliced and toasted or fried

1. Heat olive oil in an 8-quart kettle. Add chopped onion and the garlic; sauté until the onion is tender —about 5 minutes.
2. Add clam juice, tomatoes with their liquid, 3/4 cup water, the orange peel, salt, saffron, fennel seed, thyme, pepper, and bay leaves; bring to boiling. Reduce heat, and simmer mixture, covered, 30 minutes.
3. Remove from heat, and let mixture cool. Then refrigerate, covered, overnight.
4. Next day, cut the lobster tails (shell and all) in half crosswise. Wipe the cod and halibut steaks with damp paper towels. Cut into 1-1/2-inch pieces. Rinse the sea scallops in running cold water and drain.
5. About 20 minutes before serving, bring tomato mixture just to boiling. Add the lobster; simmer, covered, 4 minutes. Add the cod and halibut pieces; simmer, covered 10 minutes. Then add the sea scallops, and cook over low heat for 5 minutes, or just until the scallops are tender.
6. Spoon seafood and broth into soup tureen. Serve bouillabaisse with thin slices of toasted French bread.
Makes 8 servings.
Note: Since this dish calls for many fish found only in the Mediterranean, substitutions have been made. These fish and shellfish may be used also: crab; perch; red or gray snappers; rock, calico, or sea bass; flounder.

Moules Marinière

3 dozen mussels
1-1/2 cups chopped onion
1 clove garlic, crushed
1/3 cup butter or margarine
2 cups Chablis
2 tablespoons lemon juice
1/2 cup chopped parsley
1/8 teaspoon pepper
Pinch dried thyme leaves
2 tablespoons soft butter or margarine
1 teaspoon flour

1. Check mussels, discarding any that are not tightly closed. Scrub well under cold running water, to remove sand and seaweed. With a sharp knife, trim off the "beard" around edges. Place mussels in large bowl; cover with cold water. Let soak 1 to 2 hours.
2. Lift mussels from water, and place in a colander. Rinse with cold water; let drain.
3. In 6-quart kettle, sauté onion and garlic in 1/3 cup butter until golden and tender—about 10 minutes. Add wine, lemon juice, 1/4 cup parsley, the pepper, and thyme; bring to boiling. Add mussels; cook over high heat, covered, 5 to 8 minutes, or until shells open. Shake kettle frequently, so mussels will cook uniformly.
4. With slotted utensil, remove mussels to heated serving dish. Cover with hot, damp cloth.
5. Quickly return cooking liquid to boiling; boil, uncovered, until reduced to about 2 cups—about 5 minutes. Mix soft butter with flour until smooth. Stir into boiling liquid, and cook, stirring, 2 minutes longer. Taste, and add salt if needed.
6. Spoon sauce over mussels; sprinkle with remaining parsley. Serve immediately.
Makes 3 or 4 main-dish servings, 6 appetizer servings.

Snails in Garlic Butter

1 can snails with shells (7-1/2-oz can, 1-1/2 dozen shells)
1/2 cup soft butter or margarine
2 or 3 cloves garlic, crushed
1 shallot, finely chopped
1-1/2 tablespoons finely chopped parsley
1 tablespoon lemon juice
3/4 teaspoon salt
3/4 teaspoon dried chervil leaves
1/8 teaspoon nutmeg

1. Prepare several hours before serving. Wash snail shells, and drain well on paper towels. Drain snails thoroughly; set aside.
2. In medium bowl, combine butter with remaining ingredients; mix well.
3. Place a little butter mixture—a generous 1/4 teaspoon—in each shell. Push a drained snail into each shell; cover with more butter mixture.
4. Arrange filled shells carefully, open ends up, in a flat baking dish or special escargot (snail) dishes. Cover, and refrigerate.
5. To serve: Preheat oven to 400F. Bake snails in shells, uncovered, 8 to 10 minutes, or until butter mixture is very bubbly. Serve immediately.
Makes 4 first-course or 6 to 8 hors-d'oeuvre servings.

Beef Bourguignon

Butter or margarine
2-1/2 lb boneless beef chuck, cut into 1-1/2-inch
   cubes
3 tablespoons brandy
1/2 lb small white onions, peeled (about 12)
1/2 lb small fresh mushrooms
2-1/2 tablespoons potato flour
2 to 2-1/2 teaspoons meat-extract paste*
2 tablespoons tomato paste
1-1/2 cups Burgundy
3/4 cup dry sherry
3/4 cup ruby port
1 can (10-1/2 oz) condensed beef broth, undiluted
1/8 teaspoon pepper
1 bay leaf
* Do not use liquid meat extract

1. Slowly heat a 4-quart Dutch oven with tight-fitting lid. Add 2 tablespoons butter; heat—do not burn.
2. In hot butter, over high heat, brown beef cubes well all over (about a fourth at a time—just enough to cover bottom of Dutch oven).
3. Lift out beef as it browns. Continue until all beef is browned, adding more butter as needed. Then return beef to Dutch oven.
4. In small saucepan, heat 2 tablespoons brandy just until vapor rises. Ignite, and pour over beef. As flame dies, remove beef cubes; set aside.
5. Add 2 tablespoons butter to Dutch oven; heat slightly. Add onions; cook over low heat, covered, until onions brown slightly. Then add mushrooms; cook, stirring, 3 minutes. Remove from heat.
6. Stir in flour, meat-extract paste, and tomato paste until well blended. Stir in Burgundy, sherry, port, and beef broth.
7. Preheat oven to 350F.
8. Bring wine mixture just to boiling, stirring; remove from heat. Add beef, pepper, and bay leaf; mix well.
9. Bake, covered and stirring occasionally, 1-1/2 hours, or until beef is tender, adding remaining brandy, little by little. (Nice with Gnocchi Parisienne.)
Makes 6 servings.
Note: This dish is better if made the day before, refrigerated, and reheated gently for serving. (If necessary, add a little more wine, to thin the sauce.)

Steak au Poivre

3-lb boneless sirloin steak
2 tablespoons freshly cracked black pepper
2 tablespoons butter or margarine
1 tablespoon salad oil
1/2 cup dry white or red wine
2 tablespoons brandy
1 teaspoon salt

1. Wipe steak with damp paper towels. Rub 1 tablespoon pepper into each side.
2. Slowly heat a large, heavy skillet until very hot. Add 1 tablespoon butter and the oil, stirring until butter is melted.
3. Add steak; over high heat, brown steak well on each side—about 2 minutes a side. Then reduce heat to medium, and cook 8 to 10 minutes a side for medium rare. Remove steak to a heated serving platter, and keep warm.
4. Add remaining butter, wine, brandy, and salt to skillet; simmer, stirring 3 minutes. Pour over steak.
Makes 6 servings.

Leg of Lamb with White Beans

1 lb dried pea beans
2 cloves garlic
1/4 cup butter or margarine
2 lb onions, thinly sliced
Seasoned salt
1/2 teaspoon salt
1/4 teaspoon pepper
1 teaspoon dried rosemary leaves
2 cans (1-lb size) Italian plum tomatoes, undrained
7-lb leg of lamb
Chopped parsley

1. In 6-quart kettle, combine beans with 6 cups water. Bring to boiling; simmer 2 minutes. Cover; remove from heat; let stand 1 hour.
2. Drain beans, reserving liquid. Add water to liquid to measure 2 quarts. Return beans and liquid to kettle; bring to boiling. Reduce heat; simmer, covered, 1 hour, or until beans are tender. Drain.
3. Preheat oven to 325F. Crush 1 clove garlic.
4. In hot butter in large skillet, sauté onion and crushed garlic until golden—about 10 minutes.
5. In shallow roasting pan, combine cooked beans, onion mixture, 2 teaspoons seasoned salt, the salt, pepper, 1/2 teaspoon rosemary, and the tomatoes; mix well.
6. Split remaining clove garlic; rub over lamb. Sprinkle lamb lightly with seasoned salt and remaining rosemary. Place lamb on beans; insert meat thermometer into meaty part—it should not rest against bone.
7. Roast, uncovered, 3 to 3-1/2 hours, or to 175F on meat thermometer, for well done.
8. To serve: Remove lamb to heated serving platter or carving board. Turn beans into serving dish; sprinkle with parsley.
Makes 10 servings.

Leg of Lamb with Salsify

6-lb leg of lamb
2 carrots, pared and diced
1 cup diced celery with leaves
1 small onion, peeled and diced
3 cloves garlic, crushed
2 bay leaves
Dash dried thyme leaves
1/4 cup butter or margarine
2 jars (14-oz size) salsify strips
1/3 cup finely chopped parsley
Salt
Pepper
3/4 cup red wine

1. Have meatman bone leg of lamb and trim the shank. Do not have it rolled and tied.
2. Preheat oven to 500F. Place leg of lamb, fat side down, without rack, in a shallow roasting pan. Roast, uncovered, 20 minutes.
3. Reduce oven temperature to 400F. Turn lamb fat side up. Sprinkle carrots, celery, onion, 2 crushed cloves garlic, the bay leaves, and thyme leaves over and around the lamb.
4. Roast 35 to 40 minutes longer—lamb will be medium rare. Remove lamb to heated serving platter, and keep warm until serving.
5. Meanwhile, melt butter in skillet. Drain salsify. Add to butter with chopped parsley, 1 crushed clove garlic, 1 teaspoon salt, and 1/8 teaspoon pepper, and toss lightly.
6. Cook over medium heat, covered, until heated through—8 to 10 minutes.
7. Then pour drippings from lamb into a 1-cup

measure, leaving vegetables in the pan. Skim off fat; discard. Return drippings to pan; add 1/2 cup water, the red wine, 1 teaspoon salt, and 1/8 teaspoon pepper.

8. Bring to boiling; reduce heat, and simmer, uncovered, for 3 minutes. Discard the bay leaves. Press the vegetables and liquid through a strainer into a gravy boat.

9. Slice lamb crosswise into thin slices. Arrange lamb slices on a platter with salsify. Pass gravy. Makes 8 servings.

Gnocchi Parisienne

Gnocchi:
1/2 cup butter or margarine
1 teaspoon salt
1 cup unsifted all-purpose flour
4 eggs
1/4 cup grated natural Swiss cheese
1 teaspoon dry mustard

Sauce:
1-1/2 tablespoons butter or margarine
1-1/2 tablespoons flour
1/2 teaspoon salt
Dash cayenne
1 cup light cream
3 tablespoons grated natural Swiss cheese

2 tablespoons grated natural Swiss cheese
1 tablespoon butter or margarine

1. Make Gnocchi: In medium saucepan, combine 1 cup water, 1/2 cup butter, and 1 teaspoon salt; bring to boiling. Remove from heat.

2. With wooden spoon, beat in 1 cup flour. Over low heat, beat mixture until it leaves side of pan and forms a ball—1 to 2 minutes. Remove from heat.

3. Add eggs, one at a time, beating with electric mixer or wooden spoon after each addition until well blended; continue beating until dough is shiny and satiny. Stir in 1/4 cup cheese and the mustard until well blended.

4. In a 4-quart saucepan, bring 2 quarts lightly salted water to boiling. Reduce heat so water is below boiling point.

5. With heated teaspoon (dip spoon into simmering water), remove 1 teaspoon dough; then, with another heated spoon, slide dough into simmering water. Cook about one fourth of dough at a time.

6. Simmer, uncovered, 10 to 12 minutes, or until gnocchi are firm and rise to surface. Remove with slotted spoon; drain well on paper towels. Repeat until all dough is used. Arrange, in single layer, in shallow baking dish; set aside.

7. Make Sauce: In small saucepan, melt 1-1/2 tablespoons butter; remove from heat. Stir in flour, salt, and cayenne until smooth. Gradually stir in cream; bring to boiling, stirring constantly. Reduce heat, and simmer 1 minute. Add 3 tablespoons cheese, stirring until melted.

8. Pour sauce over gnocchi; sprinkle with cheese, and dot with butter.

9. Broil, about 4 inches from heat, about 5 minutes, or until top is golden-brown.
Makes 6 servings.

Duckling with Turnips

5-lb ready-to-cook duckling
1 teaspoon salt
3 tablespoons butter or margarine
1 medium onion, sliced
1 small white turnip, pared and diced
1 sprig parsley
1 can (10-1/2 oz) condensed chicken broth,
    undiluted
1/2 cup white wine
Pinch dried thyme leaves
3 tablespoons flour
Glazed Vegetables, page 285
Chopped parsley

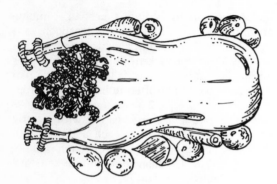

1. Preheat oven to 425F. Sprinkle duckling inside and out with salt. Tie ends of legs together. Prick skin all over with fork. Place, breast side up on a rack in shallow roasting pan.
2. Roast, uncovered, 45 minutes, or until nicely browned.
3. Meanwhile, in 1 tablespoon hot butter, sauté onion, turnip, and parsley sprig until golden—about 10 minutes. Set aside.
4. Remove duckling from oven. Prick skin all over again. Reduce oven temperature to 350F. Pour all fat from pan, and discard. Arrange sautéed vegetables around duckling. Add chicken broth, wine, and thyme. Cover pan with foil.
5. Roast, covered, 1 hour longer, or until tender. Pour off all pan juices, and strain into a 4-cup measure; skim off fat. Add more wine to juices, if necessary, to make 2 cups. Raise oven temperature to 400F. Return duckling to oven, uncovered, for 15 minutes, to crisp skin.
6. Melt 2 tablespoons butter in saucepan; remove from heat. Stir in flour until smooth. Gradually stir in pan juices; bring to boiling, stirring constantly. Reduce heat, and simmer 3 minutes.
7. To serve: Arrange duckling and Glazed Vegetables on heated platter. Garnish with chopped parsley. Pass sauce.
Makes 4 servings.

Cassoulet

1 pkg (1 lb) dried white Great Northern beans
4 cloves garlic
4 cups sliced onion
4 parsley sprigs
Salt
4 whole cloves
1/2 lb sliced bacon, cut into 1-inch pieces
2 lb lean pork, cut into 1-inch pieces
2 cans (10-1/2-oz size) condensed beef broth,
    undiluted
1 can (10-1/2 oz) tomato purée
1 teaspoon dried thyme leaves
3 bay leaves
1 lb Polish sausage
1/2 cup dry white wine

1. In a 4-quart kettle, bring 2 quarts water to boiling. Add beans; return to boiling; boil 2 minutes. Remove from heat, and let stand 1 hour.
2. Crush 2 cloves garlic. Add to beans along with 2 cups onion, the parsley, 1 tablespoon salt, and the cloves; bring to boiling. Reduce heat, and simmer, covered, 1-1/2 hours. Drain. Remove and discard cloves.
3. Meanwhile, in large kettle, sauté bacon until crisp. Remove bacon, and set aside. Pour off drippings; return 2 tablespoons to kettle.
4. In hot drippings, brown pork on all sides. Remove, and set aside. Crush remaining cloves garlic; add, with remaining onion, to kettle, and sauté until golden—about 5 minutes.
5. Return bacon and pork to kettle. Add 1 tablespoon salt, the beef broth, tomato purée, thyme,

and bay leaves; bring to boiling. Reduce heat; simmer, covered, 1-1/2 hours. Remove and discard bay leaves.

6. Meanwhile, cut sausage in half crosswise. Cook in boiling water 30 minutes.

7. Preheat oven to 350F. Add drained beans and the wine to pork mixture. Turn into a 3-quart casserole; top with sausage.

8. Bake, uncovered, 1 hour. (Place foil under casserole to catch any drippings.) Stir the bean mixture before serving.

Makes 8 to 10 servings.

Note: This is delicious prepared the day before and refrigerated. Reheat, covered, in 350F oven until bubbly and hot.

Chicken Basquaise

5-lb roasting chicken
1/4 cup butter or margarine, softened
2 teaspoons dried tarragon leaves
2 teaspoons dried oregano leaves
1 teaspoon salt
1/8 teaspoon pepper
1 teaspoon salt
1/2 teaspoon dried oregano leaves
1/2 teaspoon dried tarragon leaves
1/4 teaspoon crushed dried hot red pepper
Giblets
2 sprigs parsley
2 white onions, peeled
1 shallot, sliced
2 green or red peppers, sliced
2 lb zucchini, thickly sliced
2 tomatoes, quartered
1/4 cup unsifted all-purpose flour
2 tablespoons butter or margarine

1. Preheat oven to 350F.

2. Wash chicken inside and out under cold running water; also wash chicken giblets. Dry on paper towels.

3. Combine 1/4 cup softened butter with 2 teaspoons tarragon and 2 teaspoons oregano. Put half of butter mixture and the liver in cavity of chicken.

4. Rub outside of chicken with rest of butter mixture. Sprinkle with 1 teaspoon salt and the pepper.

5. Place chicken in shallow, 15-by-10-inch roasting pan without rack. Roast 2 hours, basting several times with pan drippings.

6. About 30 minutes before chicken is done, cook vegetables. In 11-inch skillet with tight-fitting cover, bring 2 cups water, the salt, oregano, tarragon, red pepper, giblets, parsley to boiling.

7. Add onions and shallot; cook, covered, over medium heat 15 minutes. Remove and discard giblets, parsley.

8. Layer peppers and zucchini over onions; cook, covered, 10 minutes. Add tomato; cook 5 minutes longer, or just until vegetables are tender. Drain, reserving liquid (about 2 cups).

9. In small saucepan, combine 3/4 cup pan drippings with flour; mix well. Stir in reserved vegetable liquid. Bring to boiling, stirring. Serve as sauce.

10. Return vegetables to skillet, and continue cooking, uncovered, several minutes, to dry out vegetables. Toss with butter.

11. Serve chicken surrounded by vegetables.

Makes 6 servings.

Lobster Soufflé, Plaza Athenée

Lobster Mixture:
3 (1-lb size) live lobsters; or 3 (10- to 12-oz size)
  frozen rock-lobster tails, thawed
1/4 cup salad oil
1/4 cup finely chopped pared carrot
1/4 cup finely chopped onion
1 tablespoon chopped parsley
1 tablespoon chopped chives
1 teaspoon paprika
1 cup heavy cream
1/2 cup sauterne
2 tablespoons cognac

Lobster Sauce:
3 tablespoons butter or margarine
3 tablespoons flour
1 cup milk
1/4 cup heavy cream
1/4 cup dry sherry

Soufflé:
5 tablespoons butter or margarine
6 tablespoons flour
2 teaspoons salt
Cayenne
1-1/4 cups milk
6 egg yolks, beaten
1/2 cup grated Parmesan cheese
6 egg whites, at room temperature
1/2 teaspoon cream of tartar

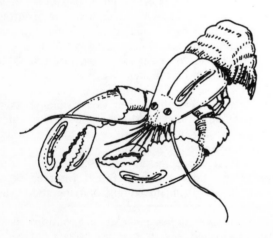

1. To kill lobster: Lay lobster on back on wooden board. Sever spinal cord by inserting point of knife through to back shell where body and tail of lobster come together. Then, with sharp knife, split body down middle, cutting through the under-shell. Discard dark vein and small sac 2 inches below head. Crack large claws with nutcracker.

2. Prepare Lobster Mixture: With sharp knife, cut lobster and shell into large pieces (if using tails, cut into thirds). In hot oil in large skillet, sauté lobster pieces (shell and all), turning occasionally, 5 minutes, or until red. Remove to bowl.

3. In drippings in same skillet, sauté carrot, onion, parsley, and chives until carrot and onion are tender—about 2 minutes.

4. Return lobster to skillet. Add paprika, 1 cup cream, the sauterne, and cognac; cook gently, covered, 10 minutes.

5. Remove lobster; cut away shell, and discard. Slice lobster meat 1/4 inch thick; set aside.

6. Over medium heat, simmer the cream mixture, stirring, to reduce to 1 cup. Force through coarse strainer. Reserve for Lobster Sauce.

7. Make Lobster Sauce: Melt 3 tablespoons butter in small saucepan. Remove from heat; stir in 3 tablespoons flour until smooth. Gradually stir in 1 cup milk.

8. Bring to boiling, stirring. Remove from heat; stir in cream, sherry, and reserved mixture.

9. Combine 1 cup sauce with cut-up lobster. Turn into 1-1/2-quart shallow baking dish. Reserve rest of sauce.

10. Preheat oven to 375F.

11. Make Soufflé: Melt butter in medium sauce-pan. Remove from heat; stir in flour, 1 teaspoon salt, and dash cayenne until smooth. Gradually stir in milk.

12. Bring to boiling, stirring. Then reduce heat; simmer until mixture becomes very thick and leaves bottom and side of pan. Remove from heat.

13. With wire whisk, beat mixture into egg yolks in large bowl; mix well. Beat in cheese.

14. In large bowl, with electric mixer at high speed, beat egg whites with cream of tartar and 1 teaspoon salt just until stiff peaks form when beater is slowly raised.

15. With wire whisk or rubber scraper, fold egg whites, one half at a time, into egg-yolk mixture just until well combined. Pour over lobster in baking dish.

16. Bake 35 to 40 minutes or until puffed and nicely browned. Just before serving, gently reheat reserved lobster sauce. Serve soufflé at once with sauce.

Makes 6 servings.

Omelette Mère Poulard

8 eggs
2 tablespoons heavy cream
Salt and pepper
6 tablespoons butter or margarine

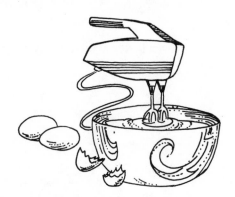

1. Separate eggs, placing the whites in a large bowl and the yolks in a medium bowl.

2. With electric beater at high speed, beat the egg whites until stiff peaks form when the beater is slowly raised.

3. With same beater, beat egg yolks well. Beat in cream, 1/2 teaspoon salt, and dash pepper. Slowly heat an 11-inch skillet. Add butter, and heat until it sizzles—do not brown.

4. Pour in egg-yolk mixture. When it begins to set (5 to 10 seconds), add beaten egg whites; quickly fold into yolk mixture with wire whisk or spatula. Cook over medium heat, shaking skillet gently until omelet is puffy and almost set—takes 3 to 5 minutes.

5. With wide spatula, quickly loosen omelet from side of skillet; tilt skillet, and fold omelet in half. Slip omelet onto serving platter, and serve at once.

Makes 4 servings.

Potatoes Anna

1/2 cup soft butter or margarine
2 lb Idaho potatoes, pared and thinly sliced (about 5 cups)
1 teaspoon salt
1/8 teaspoon pepper

1. Preheat oven to 425F. With 3 tablespoons butter, grease an 8-inch skillet with heat-resistant handle and tight-fitting cover.

2. Gently toss potatoes with salt and pepper. Layer a third of potato slices, circular fashion, around bottom and side of skillet. Dot with butter. Repeat twice.

3. Over high heat, cook potatoes 3 minutes. Then bake, covered, 30 minutes. (Place sheet of foil under skillet to catch any runover.) Remove cover; bake 5 minutes longer. Let stand 5 minutes; invert on platter.

Makes 6 servings.

Potatoes Nicoise

1 clove garlic
3 medium potatoes (about 1 lb)
3 large medium-ripe tomatoes (about 1-1/2 lb)
Boiling water
3 red onions (1 lb)
1/4 teaspoon dried tarragon leaves
1/4 teaspoon dried basil leaves
1-1/2 tablespoons chopped parsley
3 teaspoons salt
1/4 teaspoon nutmeg
2 tablespoons butter or margarine
1/2 cup grated Cheddar or Gruyère cheese

1. Preheat oven to 400F.
2. Rub inside of 12-by-8-inch casserole with cut clove of garlic.
3. Pare potatoes; slice 1/4-inch thick.
4. Scald tomatoes in boiling water; peel skin. Slice tomatoes 1/2 inch thick. Slice onions as thinly as possible.
5. In small bowl, combine tarragon, basil, and parsley; mix well.
6. In prepared casserole, layer potato, then onion, then tomato; repeat layering, ending with tomato. Sprinkle each layer of potato with herbs, salt, and nutmeg. Sprinkle each layer of tomato with salt.
7. Dot top with butter. Bake, covered, 45 minutes, or until potatoes are fork-tender. Sprinkle top with cheese. Bake, uncovered, 5 minutes, to brown top slightly.
Makes 6 servings.
Note: This is even better made the day before and reheated.

Asparagus Quiche

1-1/2 lb fresh asparagus, or 2 pkg (10-oz size) frozen asparagus spears
1 teaspoon salt
1 pkg (11 oz) piecrust mix
8 slices bacon, quartered
1/2 lb natural Swiss cheese, grated
4 eggs
1-1/2 cups light cream
1/8 teaspoon nutmeg
1/8 teaspoon salt
Dash pepper

1. Wash asparagus; break off and discard tough white portion. Scrape ends of asparagus with vegetable parer. Set aside 12 of the best spears for decoration—should be 5 inches long. Cut rest of asparagus into 1/2-inch pieces.
2. In large saucepan, bring 1 quart water to boiling; add salt and asparagus. Bring back to boiling; reduce heat; simmer, covered, 5 minutes. Drain; rinse asparagus under cold water.
3. Prepare piecrust as the label directs. On lightly floured pastry cloth, with a stockinette-covered rolling pin, roll pastry to form a 12-inch circle. Use to line an 11-inch pie plate. Flute edge. Refrigerate.
4. Preheat oven to 375F. Sauté bacon until crisp. Drain on paper towels.
5. Sprinkle bottom of pie shell with bacon, then cheese, cut-up asparagus.
6. In medium bowl, with rotary beater, beat eggs with cream, nutmeg, salt, and pepper just until combined.
7. Pour cream mixture into pie shell. Arrange asparagus spears, spoke fashion, on pie.
8. Bake 40 minutes, or just until puffy and golden. Serve warm.
Makes 12 servings.

Glazed Vegetables

20 small white onions, peeled
4 white turnips, pared and quartered
2 tablespoons butter or margarine
2 teaspoons sugar

1. Cook onions and turnips separately in 1 inch boiling salted water just until tender—15 to 25 minutes for onions, about 10 minutes for turnips. Drain each well.
2. Heat 1 tablespoon butter in large skillet; add onions, and sprinkle with 1 teaspoon sugar. Cook over medium heat, shaking pan often, until onions are golden and glazed—about 5 minutes. Turn into bowl, and keep warm.
3. Heat remaining butter in same skillet. Add turnips, and sprinkle with 1 teaspoon sugar. Cook until golden and glazed. Keep warm.
Makes 4 servings.

Strawberry Flan

Flan Shell:
1/4 cup butter or regular margarine, softened
2 tablespoons granulated sugar
3 tablespoons almond paste
1/2 teaspoon grated lemon peel
1 egg white
3/4 cup sifted all-purpose flour

Rum Cream:
1 teaspoon unflavored gelatine
2 tablespoons granulated sugar
2 tablespoons flour
Salt
1 egg yolk
1/2 cup milk
2 tablespoons rum
1 egg white, stiffly beaten
1/2 cup heavy cream
1 tablespoon confectioners' sugar
1 inch vanilla bean, scraped

1-1/2 pint boxes strawberries, washed and hulled
1/2 recipe Currant-Jelly Glaze, page 431

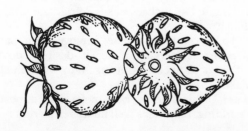

1. Make Flan Shell: Grease and lightly flour an 8-by-1-1/2-inch round layer-cake pan.
2. In a medium bowl, with electric mixer at medium speed, cream butter with 2 tablespoons granulated sugar, the almond paste, and lemon peel until well combined.
3. Add 1 egg white; beat at high speed until smooth. Gradually beat in 3/4 cup flour until well blended. Turn into prepared pan; pat evenly over bottom and side. (If too soft to work with, refrigerate 10 minutes.) Refrigerate 1 hour or longer.
4. Preheat oven to 300F. Bake shell 50 minutes, or until golden-brown. Let cool in pan on wire rack 15 minutes; then gently turn out onto rack, and let cool completely.
5. Make Rum Cream: In small saucepan, mix gelatine, granulated sugar, flour, and dash salt; mix well.
6. Beat egg yolk with milk and rum. Add to gelatine mixture; cook over medium heat, stirring constantly with wire whisk, until mixture is thickened and comes to boiling.
7. Pour into medium bowl; set bowl in pan of ice and water; let stand, stirring occasionally, until mixture begins to set—about 8 to 10 minutes. Fold in beaten egg white.
8. Beat cream with confectioners' sugar; fold into gelatine mixture. Stir in scraped vanilla bean. Spread evenly over flan shell. Refrigerate 30 minutes.
9. Arrange berries on rum cream in shell; brush with Currant-Jelly Glaze. Refrigerate until serving.
Makes 8 servings.

Raspberries Sabayon

Sabayon Sauce:
4 egg yolks
2 tablespoons sugar
1/4 cup Grand Marnier
1/3 cup heavy cream, whipped

2 pint boxes red raspberries, washed and drained;
or 3 pkg(10-oz size) frozen raspberries, thawed
and drained

1. Make Sabayon Sauce: In top of double boiler, with electric mixer at medium speed, beat egg yolks until thick. Gradually beat in sugar; beat until mixture is light and soft peaks form when beater is slowly raised.
2. Place double-boiler top over simmering water (water in bottom should not touch base of top). Slowly beat in Grand Marnier; continue beating until mixture is fluffy and mounds—takes about 5 minutes.
3. Remove double-boiler top from hot water; set in ice water. Beat the custard mixture until cool. Gently fold in whipped cream.
4. Refrigerate sauce, covered, until serving.
5. Place berries in serving bowl or dessert dishes. Stir sauce; pour over fruit.
Makes 6 servings.

Colette's Chocolate Cake

4 eggs
4 bars (4-oz size) German's sweet cooking
chocolate
1/2 cup soft sweet butter
4 teaspoons sugar
4 teaspoons all-purpose flour

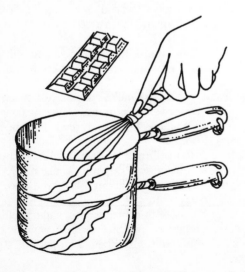

1. Lightly grease a 9-by-5-by-3-inch loaf pan; line with waxed paper. Separate eggs, placing whites and yolks in large bowls. Let whites warm to room temperature—about 1 hour.
2. Preheat oven to 425F.
3. In top of double boiler, melt chocolate over hot, not boiling, water, stirring occasionally. Remove from water; beat in butter with spoon.
4. Meanwhile, with portable electric mixer, beat egg whites until stiff peaks form when beater is slowly raised. Set aside.
5. With same beater, beat yolks until thick and lemon-colored. Slowly add sugar, beating constantly. Add flour; beat just until blended.
6. Stir into chocolate mixture. Then, with rubber scraper or a wire whisk, gently fold chocolate mixture into beaten egg white.
7. Turn into prepared pan. Reduce oven temperature to 350F. Bake 25 minutes.
8. Let cool completely in pan on wire rack. Cake will settle like a cheesecake. Refrigerate until well chilled—about 4 hours.
9. To serve: Loosen cake; remove from pan by inverting on serving plate. If desired, decorate with chocolate curls. Cut cake into 3/4-inch slices. Makes 16 servings.
Note: This is a heavy, rich, moist cake, almost like a pudding, that keeps well under refrigeration.

Pots de Crème

3 cups heavy cream
1/2 cup sugar
1 tablespoon vanilla extract
5 egg yolks
Chocolate curls, below

1. Preheat oven to 325F. Place 8 (5-oz) custard cups or 10 (3-oz) pot-de-crème cups in a baking pan.
2. In medium saucepan, combine cream and sugar; cook over medium heat, stirring occasionally, until sugar is dissolved and mixture is hot. Remove from heat; stir in vanilla.
3. In medium bowl, with wire whisk or rotary beater, beat egg yolks until blended—not frothy. Gradually add cream mixture, stirring constantly.
4. Strain, using fine strainer, into 4-cup measure. (If desired, first line strainer with cheesecloth.) Pour into cups.
5. Set baking pan on oven rack. Pour hot water to 1/2-inch level around cups.
6. Bake 25 to 30 minutes, or until mixture just begins to set around edges.
7. Immediately remove cups from water, and place on wire rack. Let cool 30 minutes; then refrigerate, each covered with plastic film, foil, or lid, till chilled—at least 4 hours.
8. To serve: Top with sweetened whipped cream, if desired. Then garnish with chocolate curls.
Makes 8 to 10 servings.

Chocolate Pot de Crème

3 cups heavy cream
1/2 cup sugar
1-1/2 squares unsweetened chocolate, broken
1 teaspoon vanilla extract
4 egg yolks
Chocolate Curls, below

Make and bake as in Pots de Crème, above, adding chocolate to cream and sugar in step 2. Cook, stirring, until chocolate is melted and mixture is hot.

Chocolate Curls

Let a 1-oz square semisweet or unsweetened chocolate stand in paper wrapper in warm place about 15 minutes, just to soften slightly. For large curls, unwrap chocolate, and carefully draw vegetable parer across broad, flat surface of square. For smaller curls, draw parer across side of square. Lift curls with a wooden pick, to avoid breaking.

Almond Tile Cookies

2 egg whites
1/2 cup sugar
1/4 teaspoon vanilla extract
3 tablespoons butter, melted
3 tablespoons flour
1/2 cup sliced blanched almonds

1. Preheat oven to 400F. Grease a large cookie sheet with salad oil, and dust with flour (omit if using a pan with nonstick coating).
2. In medium bowl, combine egg whites, sugar, and vanilla; beat with wire whisk about 2 minutes, or until sugar is dissolved and mixture is syrupy.
3. Add melted butter and flour; beat until smooth. Stir in almonds.
4. Drop by teaspoonfuls, about 4 inches apart, onto prepared cookie sheet. With small spatula, spread each to a 3-inch circle. Make no more than 8 at a time.
5. Bake 4 to 5 minutes, or until cookies are golden-brown around edge and lightly browned in center.
6. With small spatula, immediately remove cookies carefully, and place over rolling pin, to curve them. (If cookies get too cool, return to oven, just until hot and soft again.)
7. Repeat with remaining batter, oiling and flouring cookie sheet each time.
Makes about 3 dozen.

Baba Au Rhum

3/4 cup warm water (105 to 115F)
2 pkg active dry yeast
1/4 cup sugar
1 teaspoon salt
6 eggs
3-3/4 cups sifted* all-purpose flour
3/4 cup butter, softened
1/2 cup finely chopped citron
1/4 cup currants or seedless raisins

Rum Syrup:
2-1/2 cups sugar
1 medium unpeeled orange, sliced crosswise
1/2 unpeeled lemon, sliced crosswise
1 to 1-1/2 cups light rum

Apricot Glaze:
1 cup apricot preserves
1 teaspoon grated lemon peel
2 teaspoons lemon juice

 * Sift before measuring.

1. Lightly grease a 10-by-4-inch tube pan. If possible, check temperature of warm water with thermometer.
2. Sprinkle yeast over water in large bowl of electric mixer: stir until dissolved.
3. Add 1/4 cup sugar, the salt, eggs, and 2-1/4 cups flour. At medium speed, beat 4 minutes, or until smooth, scraping side of bowl and guiding mixture into beater with rubber scraper.
4. Add butter; beat 2 minutes, or until very well blended.
5. At low speed, beat in rest of flour; beat until smooth—about 2 minutes.
6. Stir in citron and currants. Batter will be thick.
7. Turn batter into prepared pan, spreading evenly. Cover with towel.
8. Let rise in warm place (85F), free from drafts, 1 hour and 10 minutes, or until baba has risen to within 1/2 inch of top of pan.
9. Meanwhile, preheat oven to 400F. Gently place baba on oven rack (do not jar; baba might fall).

10. Bake 40 to 45 minutes, or until it is deep golden-brown and cake tester inserted in center comes out clean.

11. Meanwhile, make Rum Syrup: In medium saucepan, combine sugar with 2 cups water; bring to boiling, stirring until sugar is dissolved. Boil, uncovered, 10 minutes.

12. Reduce heat. Add orange and lemon slices; simmer 10 minutes. Remove from heat. Add rum.

13. With metal spatula, carefully loosen sides of baba from pan. Turn out of pan onto wire rack; let cool 15 minutes. Return baba to pan.

14. Set pan on large sheet of foil. Gradually pour hot syrup, along with fruit slices, over baba. Continue pouring until all syrup is absorbed.

15. Let baba stand 2 hours or longer.

16. Meanwhile, make Apricot Glaze: In small saucepan, over low heat, melt apricot preserves. Stir in lemon peel and juice; strain. Refrigerate 30 minutes, or until ready to use.

17. To serve baba: Discard fruit slices. Turn out baba onto round serving platter. Brush top and side with apricot glaze.

18. If desired, serve with whipped cream.
Makes 12 to 16 servings.

Madeleines

2 eggs
1 cup granulated sugar
1 cup sifted all-purpose flour
3/4 cup butter, melted and cooled
1 teaspoon grated lemon peel
Confectioners' sugar

1. Preheat oven to 350F. Grease and lightly flour madeleine pans.

2. In top of double boiler, over hot, not boiling, water (water in bottom of double boiler should not touch base of pan above), with electric mixer at medium speed, beat eggs and granulated sugar while mixture heats to lukewarm—takes about 2 minutes.

3. Set top of double boiler in cold water. Beat egg mixture, at high speed, 5 minutes, or until very light and fluffy.

4. With wire whisk or rubber scraper, gently fold in flour until well combined. Stir in cooled butter and lemon peel just until blended. Pour into prepared pans, using 1 tablespoon batter for each pan.

5. Bake 12 to 15 minutes, or until golden. Cool 1 minute. Then remove from pans with a small spatula; cool completely on wire racks. Then sprinkle with confectioners' sugar.
Makes 3-1/2 dozen.

Tarte Tatin

Upside-Down Apple Tart

1 cup sugar
1/2 cup butter or margarine
8 medium apples (about 3-1/2 lb)
1/2 pkg (11-oz size) piecrust mix or pastry for
  1-crust pie
Whipped cream

1. Place sugar in 10-inch heavy skillet with heat-resistant handle. Cook over medium heat until it melts and becomes a light-brown syrup. Remove from heat; add butter, stirring until melted.
2. Pare, quarter, and core apples. Arrange in a layer, rounded side down, in sugar mixture. Make a second layer, rounded side up, fitting the pieces between pieces in first layer. If open spaces remain, fill with slices of apple.
3. Preheat oven to 450F.
4. Prepare piecrust mix as the label directs for 1-crust pie. On lightly floured surface, roll pastry to a 10-inch circle. Place over apples.
5. Bake 25 to 30 minutes, or until crust is golden-brown. Invert onto shallow serving dish. Serve luke-warm. Garnish with whipped cream and, if desired, crystallized violets.
Makes 6 to 8 servings.

French Apple Pie

1 pkg (10 or 11 oz) piecrust mix or pastry for
  2-crust pie

Filling:
1/3 cup sugar
2 tablespoons flour
1 cup milk
3 egg yolks
1 tablespoon butter or margarine
1/2 teaspoon vanilla extract

2 lb tart cooking apples
1 tablespoon lemon juice
2 tablespoons butter or margarine
2 tablespoons sugar
Dash nutmeg
3/4 cup apricot preserves
1 egg yolk

1. Prepare piecrust mix as package label directs. Form into a ball. On lightly floured pastry cloth, with a rolling pin covered with a stockinette, roll out two thirds pastry to form a 12-inch circle. Use to line a 9-inch pie plate; refrigerate with rest of pastry.
2. Make Filling: In small saucepan, combine 1/3 cup sugar and the flour; mix well. Stir in milk. Bring to boiling, stirring; reduce heat; simmer, stirring, until slightly thickened—1 minute.
3. In small bowl, beat 3 egg yolks slightly. Beat in a little of hot mixture; pour back into saucepan, beating to mix well. Stir in 1 tablespoon butter and the vanilla. Turn into bowl to cool.
4. Core, pare, and slice apples; sprinkle with lemon juice.
5. In medium skillet, heat butter with sugar and nutmeg. Add apple slices; sauté, stirring occasionally, until partially cooked—about 5 minutes. Remove from heat. Heat apricot preserves just until melted.
6. Preheat oven to 425F.
7. Turn filling into pie shell, spreading evenly. Arrange apple slices on top, mounding slightly in center. Spread with apricot preserves.
8. Roll out rest of pastry to form a 10-inch circle. With knife or pastry wheel, cut into 12 strips 1/2 inch wide.

9. Slightly moisten rim of pie shell with cold water. Arrange 6 strips across filling; press ends to rim of pie shell, trimming off ends if necessary.
10. Arrange rest of strips at right angle to first strips, to form a lattice.
11. Bring overhang of pastry up over ends of strips; crimp edge.
12. Mix yolk with tablespoon water; use to brush lattice strips, not edge.
13. On lowest shelf of oven, bake 35 to 40 minutes, or until pastry is golden. Cool. Serve slightly warm. Makes 8 servings.

Crème Brûlée

3 cups heavy cream
6 egg yolks
1/3 cup granulated sugar
1 teaspoon vanilla extract
1/3 cup light-brown sugar, packed

1. Heat cream in heavy saucepan just until bubbles form around the edge of the pan.
2. In double-boiler top, with electric mixer, beat yolks with granulated sugar until thick and light yellow. Gradually stir in cream.
3. Place over hot, not boiling, water; cook, stirring constantly, until it coats a metal spoon—about 15 minutes. Add the vanilla.
4. Strain custard into a 1-quart, shallow baking dish. Refrigerate 8 hours or overnight.
5. Just before serving, carefully sift brown sugar evenly over surface. Set dish in baking pan; surround with ice. Run under broiler just until sugar melts slightly and caramelizes—it will form a crust.
Makes 8 servings.

German

Americans of German origin have a vast assortment of dishes to call their own—flavorful, satisfying roasts and stews, rich desserts. The following recipes give a good sampling.

Caraway Noodles

1 tablespoon salt
1 pkg (8 oz) medium noodles
1/4 cup melted butter or margarine
1 tablespoon caraway seed

1. In large kettle, bring 3 quarts water and the salt to a rapid boil. Add noodles.
2. Bring back to boiling; cook, uncovered and stirring occasionally, 7 to 10 minutes, or just until noodles are tender.
3. Turn into colander; drain. Return noodles to kettle. Add butter and caraway seed; toss lightly to combine.
Makes 6 servings.

Sauerbraten

1 cup cider vinegar
1 cup Burgundy
2 onions, sliced
1 carrot, sliced
1 stalk celery, chopped
2 whole allspice
4 whole cloves
1 tablespoon salt
1-1/2 teaspoons pepper
4 lb rump or boned chuck pot roast
4 tablespoons unsifted all-purpose flour
1/3 cup salad oil
1 tablespoon sugar
1/2 cup crushed gingersnaps
Caraway Noodles, page 291
Red Cabbage, page 293

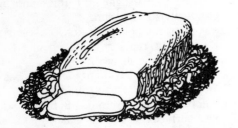

1. In large bowl, combine vinegar, Burgundy, onion, carrot, celery, allspice, cloves, salt, and pepper.
2. Wipe meat with damp paper towels. Put in marinade; refrigerate, covered, 3 days, turning meat occasionally.
3. Remove meat from the marinade. Reserve marinade. Wipe meat dry with paper towels. Coat with 2 tablespoons flour.
4. In hot oil in Dutch oven, over medium heat, brown meat well on all sides.
5. Pour in marinade; simmer, covered, 2-1/2 to 3 hours, or until meat is tender.
6. Remove meat from Dutch oven. Press liquid and vegetables through coarse sieve; skim off fat. Measure 3-1/2 cups liquid (add water, if necessary). Return liquid to Dutch oven.
7. Mix remaining 2 tablespoons flour with 1/3 cup cold water and the sugar. Stir into liquid; bring to boiling, stirring. Stir in gingersnaps.
8. Return meat to the Dutch oven. Spoon gravy over it; simmer, covered, 20 minutes.
9. Remove meat to heated platter. Pour some of gravy over it. Serve meat, thinly sliced, with more gravy. Serve with Caraway Noodles and Red Cabbage.
Makes 6 servings.

Sauerkraut and Pork

2 onions
8 whole cloves
2 carrots, pared
2 lb unsliced bacon, halved
2-lb smoked boneless butt
10 whole black peppercorns
6 juniper berries (optional)
4 cans (1-lb size) sauerkraut (2 qt), drained
1 tablespoon butter or margarine
2 cans (13-3/4-oz size) clear chicken broth
1 cup white wine
1/4 cup lemon juice

1. Stud each onion with 4 cloves. Put onions, carrots, bacon, and smoked butt in large kettle.
2. Add peppercorns and berries, tied in cheesecloth bag. Cover with sauerkraut. Add butter.
3. Combine broth, wine, and lemon juice. Pour over mixture in kettle; bring to boiling point.
4. Reduce heat; simmer, covered, 1-1/2 to 2 hours, or until butt is tender when pierced with fork. Discard onions and cheesecloth bag.
5. To serve: Cut each piece of bacon into 4 slices, butt into 8 slices. Arrange on large platter, with sauerkraut. Slice carrots crosswise, and use as garnish.
Makes 8 servings.

Smoked Loin of Pork

5-lb smoked loin of pork (12 ribs)
2 whole bay leaves
8 whole allspice
6 whole black peppercorns
6 slices bacon, cut into 1/2-inch pieces
1-1/2 cups chopped onion
1-1/2 cups sliced, pared apple
1/4 cup light-brown sugar, packed
1 bay leaf, crushed
2 cans (1-lb, 11-oz size) sauerkraut, drained
1 cup dry white wine

1. Wipe pork loin with damp paper towels.
2. In large kettle, place pork, 2 quarts water, 2 bay leaves, the allspice, and black peppercorns. If necessary, cut pork loin in half to fit in kettle.
3. Bring to boiling; reduce heat, and simmer, covered, 1 hour. Remove from heat. Let pork stand in liquid in kettle until until ready to bake.
4. Preheat oven to 350F.
5. Meanwhile, in 15-1/2-by-10-1/2-by-2-1/4-inch baking pan, cook bacon, onion, apple over medium heat, stirring, until onion is soft—10 minutes.
6. Add brown sugar, crushed bay leaf, sauerkraut, wine, and 1 cup of liquid from pork loin. Cook, uncovered and stirring frequently, over medium heat 20 minutes.
7. Place pork loin in center of baking pan on top of sauerkraut. Baste pork with some of liquid from sauerkraut. Bake, uncovered, 30 minutes, to glaze pork.
8. Baste pork again. Cover pan tightly with foil; bake 40 minutes.
9. To serve: Slice pork loin into chops; serve with sauerkraut and boiled potatoes or Potato Pancakes, page 294.
Makes 8 to 10 servings.
Note: The ingredients for this recipe may be cut in half for fewer servings, but cooking time will be the same.

Red Cabbage

1 medium head red cabbage
2 tablespoons salt
2 tablespoons butter or margarine
1/2 cup cider vinegar
1/2 cup sugar
2 tart red cooking apples
1 tablespoon flour

1. Remove outer leaves from cabbage, and discard. Cut cabbage into quarters; cut out core. Shred cabbage. Measure 10 cups.
2. In large skillet, combine cabbage, salt, butter, vinegar, sugar, and 1/2 cup cold water.
3. Cook, covered, stirring occasionally, over medium heat 15 minutes.
4. Meanwhile, core the apples, but do not pare; slice thinly; add to cabbage. Cook 10 minutes, or until cabbage is tender but still crisp.
5. Sprinkle flour over cabbage mixture; mix gently. Cook, stirring, until mixture thickens.
Makes 6 servings.

Potato Pancakes

4 large potatoes (2 lb), pared
1/4 cup grated onion
2 eggs, slightly beaten
2 tablespoons flour
3/4 teaspoon salt
Dash nutmeg
Dash pepper
Salad oil or shortening for frying
Chilled applesauce or sour cream

1. On medium grater, grate potatoes. Drain very well; pat dry with dish towel; measure 3 cups.
2. In large bowl, combine grated potato with onion, eggs, flour, salt, nutmeg, and pepper.
3. In large, heavy skillet, slowly heat oil, 1/8 inch deep, until very hot but not smoking.
4. For each pancake, drop 2 tablespoons potato mixture at a time into hot fat. With spatula, flatten against bottom of skillet, to make a pancake 4 inches in diameter. Fry 2 or 3 minutes on each side, or until golden-brown.
5. Drain well on paper towels. Serve hot with applesauce or sour cream.
Makes 12.

Apple Kuchen

1-1/4 cups sifted* all-purpose flour
1/4 cup sugar
1-1/2 teaspoons baking powder
1/2 teaspoon salt
1/4 cup butter or margarine
1 egg, beaten
1/4 cup milk
1 teaspoon vanilla extract
5 cups thinly sliced, pared tart apple

Topping:
1/4 cup sugar
1 teaspoon cinnamon
1/4 cup butter or margarine, melted
1/3 cup apricot preserves

Cinnamon-Ice-Cream Sauce, page 218; or whipped cream
* Sift before measuring.

1. Preheat oven to 400F. Lightly grease a 13-by-9-by-2-inch baking pan.
2. Into medium bowl, sift flour with 1/4 cup sugar, the baking powder, and salt. With pastry blender, cut in 1/4 cup butter until mixture resembles coarse crumbs.
3. Add beaten egg, milk, and vanilla extract, stirring with a fork until the mixture is smooth—will take about 1 minute.
4. Spread batter evenly in bottom of prepared pan. Arrange apple slices, thin sides down and slightly overlapping, in parallel rows over the batter.
5. Make Topping: Combine sugar, cinnamon, and melted butter. Sprinkle sugar mixture over the apple slices.
6. Bake 35 minutes, or until apple slices are tender. Remove to wire rack.
7. Mix apricot preserves with 1 tablespoon hot water. Brush over apple. Cut apple kuchen into rectangles, and serve it warm, with Cinnamon-Ice-Cream Sauce or whipped cream, if desired.
Makes 12 servings.

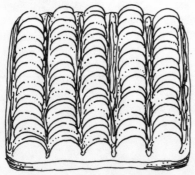

Greek

The food of Greece, like its landscape, has charm, color and a quality of rugged individualism. It may be for that reason that cooking the Greek way is the latest vogue in cooking. Deliciously different; not too complicated; not too expensive; it's great for entertaining. Following are some favorites.

Roast Leg of Lamb Olympia

6-1/2- to 7-1/2-lb leg of lamb
1/2 cup lemon juice
Salt
Pepper
Dried oregano leaves
3 cloves garlic
1/4 cup butter or margarine, melted
Egg-and-Lemon Sauce, below

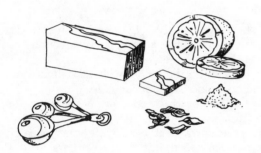

1. Day before serving: Wipe lamb with damp paper towels. Place lamb, fat side down, in shallow roasting pan. Pour 1/4 cup lemon juice over meat; sprinkle with 1 teaspoon salt, 1/4 teaspoon pepper, and 1/2 teaspoon oregano. Turn meat fat side up.
2. Peel garlic, and cut crosswise into thin slices. Using paring knife, cut 20 to 24 small slits, about 3/8 inch deep, in flesh of lamb, and insert garlic slices.
3. Pour remaining lemon juice over meat; sprinkle with 1 teaspoon salt, 1/4 teaspoon pepper, and 1/2 teaspoon oregano. Refrigerate, covered, overnight.
4. Next day: Remove lamb from refrigerator 30 minutes before roasting. Preheat oven to 325F.
5. Uncover lamb; insert meat thermometer in fleshy part, away from bone or fat. Roast 2 hours; brush with melted butter. Roast 1/2 hour longer, or to 175F on meat thermometer, for medium.
6. Let roast stand 20 minutes, for easier carving.
7. Meanwhile, make Egg-and-Lemon Sauce. Pass with lamb.
Makes 8 servings.

Egg-and-Lemon Sauce

2 tablespoons butter or margarine
3 tablespoons flour
3/4 teaspoon salt
1 can (13-3/4 oz) chicken broth
3 tablespoons lemon juice
4 egg yolks
1 tablespoon chopped parsley

1. Melt butter in top of double boiler over direct heat. Remove from heat; stir in flour and salt until smooth. Gradually stir in chicken broth and lemon juice.
2. Cook over low heat, stirring constantly, until mixture boils. Place over hot, not boiling, water.
3. In small bowl, beat egg yolks slightly. Slowly beat in small amount of hot mixture. Slowly add to rest of mixture in double boiler, stirring constantly.
4. Cook over hot water, stirring constantly, until thickened. Remove from heat, and stir in the chopped parsley.

Artichoke Halves

1/2 cup lemon juice
1/2 cup olive oil
1 tablespoon salt
8 large artichokes

1. In large kettle, combine 6 quarts water, the lemon juice, olive oil, and salt; bring to boiling.
2. Meanwhile, trim stems from artichokes; cut a 1-inch slice from tops. Remove discolored leaves; snip off spiny ends of leaves. Cut each artichoke in half lengthwise; wash well.
3. Add to boiling mixture, and return to boiling. Reduce heat, and simmer, covered, 35 to 40 minutes, or until bases of artichokes feel soft.
4. Drain, and serve hot.
Makes 8 servings.
Note: As artichokes discolor quickly, rub cut surfaces with lemon juice if they are not cooked immediately.

Spinach Pie

1/2 pkg (1-lb size) prepared phyllo- or strudel-pastry leaves (16 sheets, 12 by 15 inches)
1/4 cup butter or margarine
1/2 cup finely chopped onion
3 pkg (10-oz size) frozen chopped spinach, thawed and well drained
3 eggs
1/2 lb feta cheese, crumbled
1/4 cup chopped parsley
2 tablespoons chopped fresh dill
1 teaspoon salt
1/8 teaspoon pepper
3/4 cup butter or margarine, melted

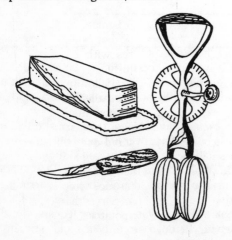

1. Preheat oven to 350F. Let pastry leaves warm to room temperature, according to directions on package label.
2. In 1/4 cup hot butter in medium skillet, sauté onion until golden—about 5 minutes.
3. Add spinach; stir to combine with onion. Remove from heat.
4. In large bowl, beat eggs with rotary beater. With wooden spoon, stir in cheese, parsley, dill, salt, pepper, and spinach-onion mixture; mix well.
5. Brush a 13-by-9-by-2-inch baking pan lightly with some of melted butter. In bottom of baking pan, layer 8 phyllo-pastry leaves (see Note), one by one, brushing top of each with melted butter. Spread evenly with spinach mixture.
6. Cover with 8 more leaves, brushing each with butter; pour any remaining melted butter over top.
7. Using scissors, trim off any uneven edges of pastry. Cut through top pastry layer on diagonal, then cutting in opposite direction, to form about nine 3-inch diamonds.
8. Bake 30 to 35 minutes, or until top crust is puffy and golden. Serve warm.
Makes 8 to 10 servings.
Note: Keep unused pastry leaves covered with damp paper towels, to prevent drying out.

Souvlakia

1/4 cup butter or margarine
1-1/2 lb cubed boneless lamb (for stew)
1 cup sliced onion
1 clove garlic, crushed
1 teaspoon salt
1/8 teaspoon pepper
3 tablespoons tomato paste
1/2 cup red wine
1 teaspoon dried oregano leaves
1/4 teaspoon dried thyme leaves
1/4 teaspoon dried rosemary leaves
1 chicken-bouillon cube
4 loaves Damascus or Arab flat bread

Garnish:
1 small tomato, sliced
4 large onion slices
1 cup shredded lettuce

1. In hot butter in large saucepan, sautè lamb (just enough at a time to cover the bottom of pan) until well browned all over—about 10 minutes. Remove lamb as it browns; continue browning rest.
2. Add 1 cup onion and the garlic; sauté about 5 minutes. Return lamb to saucepan, along with 1/4 cup water and remaining ingredients, except bread and garnish.
3. Bring to boiling; reduce heat, and simmer, covered, 45 minutes, or until meat is tender.
4. Preheat oven to 350F. Heat bread 15 minutes, or until heated through. Split each loaf part way through. Fill with lamb mixture. Garnish with tomato, onion, and lettuce.
Makes 4 servings.

Greek Meatballs with Lemon Sauce

Meatballs:
2 lb ground chuck
1/2 cup finely chopped onion
1/4 cup raw regular white rice
1/4 cup chopped parsley
2 teaspoons salt
1/4 teaspoon pepper
4 beef-bouillon cubes
2 tablespoons butter or margarine

Lemon Sauce:
4 eggs
1/4 cup lemon juice
1/4 teaspoon salt
Chopped parsley

1. Make Meatballs: In medium bowl, combine chuck, onion, rice, parsley, salt, and pepper with 1/4 cup cold water. Using hands, mix well to combine.
2. Shape mixture into meatballs, 1-1/4 inches in diameter.
3. In large kettle, combine bouillon cubes, butter, and 4 cups water; bring to boiling.
4. Drop meatballs, one by one, into boiling liquid. Return to boiling; reduce heat, and simmer, covered, 50 minutes.
5. Meanwhile, make Lemon Sauce: In top of double boiler, over hot, not boiling, water, using rotary beater, beat eggs with 2 tablespoons cold water until light and fluffy.
6. Remove 1/4 cup hot bouillon from kettle; gradually add to egg mixture, beating constantly.
7. Gradually stir in lemon juice. Cook, stirring occasionally, until sauce thickens. Add salt. Remove from heat; let stand over hot water 5 minutes before serving.
8. To serve: With slotted spoon, remove meatballs to serving dish. Pour sauce over. them. Sprinkle with chopped parsley. Serve the meatballs with cooked rice or mashed potatoes, if desired.
Makes 6 to 8 servings.

Baklava

1 pkg (1 lb) prepared phyllo- or strudel-
   pastry leaves (12-by-15-inch)
1 cup finely chopped or ground walnuts
1 cup finely chopped or ground blanched almonds
1/2 cup sugar
1/4 teaspoon ground cinnamon
1/8 teaspoon ground cloves
1-1/2 cups sweet butter, melted

Syrup:
3/4 cup sugar
3/4 cup honey
1-inch cinnamon stick
4 lemon slices
4 orange slices

1. Preheat oven to 325F. Let pastry leaves warm to room temperature, as the label directs.
2. In small bowl, mix walnuts, almonds, 1/2 cup sugar, the ground cinnamon, and cloves.
3. Place 2 leaves of phyllo pastry in a 15-1/2-by-10-1/2-by-1-inch jellyroll pan; brush top leaf with melted butter. Repeat, stacking 14 leaves in all and buttering every other leaf. (Keep rest of pastry leaves covered with damp paper towels, to prevent drying out.)
4. Sprinkle top with one third of nut mixture. Add 6 more leaves, brushing every other one with butter.
5. Repeat Step 4 twice. Stack any remaining pastry leaves on top, brushing every other one with remaining melted butter and buttering top leaf.
6. Bake 60 minutes. Turn off heat, and let baklava remain in oven 60 minutes longer.
7. Meanwhile, make Syrup: In small saucepan, combine sugar, honey, cinnamon stick, lemon and orange slices, and 1-3/4 cups water.
8. Bring to boiling, stirring until sugar is dissolved. Reduce heat; simmer, uncovered, 20 minutes. Strain.
9. As soon as baklava is removed from oven, cut into diamond-shape pieces. (On long side, make 9 crosswise cuts, at 1-1/2-inch intervals. Then, starting at one corner, make 11 cuts on diagonal, at 1-1/2-inch intervals, to form diamonds.) Pour syrup over top. Cool in pan on wire rack 2 hours. Cover with foil; let stand overnight.
Makes about 40 pieces.

Irish

Irish country food is at the opposite end of the scale from Continental cuisine, but in its own way, just as delicious. Plain and hearty, it is simply and beautifully prepared—substantial stews innocent of wine and exotic seasonings; light and fluffy breads and cakes; thick-sliced bacon. We give you here a collection of traditional Irish dishes, which we know you'll enjoy serving.

Cottage Broth

2-1/2 lb neck of lamb, cut crosswise through bone
2-1/2 teaspoons salt
6 whole black peppercorns
2 tablespoons pearl barley
1 cup diced (1/4 inch) peeled potato
1/2 cup diced (1/4 inch) pared carrot
1/2 cup diced (1/4 inch) pared turnip
1/2 cup chopped onion
1/2 cup chopped celery
Chopped parsley

1. Wipe lamb with damp paper towels. In 6-quart kettle or Dutch oven, combine lamb, salt, peppercorns, barley, and 1-1/2 quarts water.
2. Bring to boiling; simmer, covered, 2 hours.
3. Remove lamb from broth. Separate meat from fat and bones. Cut meat in 1/2-inch pieces; set aside.
4. Skim fat from broth. Measure broth (you should have 5 cups. Add water if needed). Return broth to kettle; add meat. Chill overnight.
5. Next day, remove fat from broth; discard. Bring to boiling; add vegetables. Return to boiling; reduce heat; simmer, covered, 1 hour.
6. Sprinkle with chopped parsley.
Makes 8 cups; 8 servings.

Colcannon

2 lb potatoes
Boiling water
3 teaspoons salt
4 cups coarsely shredded green cabbage
1-1/2 cups sliced scallions
1/3 cup milk
1/2 cup butter or margarine
1/4 teaspoon pepper

1. Pare potatoes. Cut each into quarters.
2. In 1/2 inch boiling water, with 1 teaspoon salt, in medium saucepan, cook potato, covered, 15 to 20 minutes, or until fork-tender and completely cooked. Drain. Return pan to low heat, shaking to dry potatoes.
3. Meanwhile, in 1/2 inch boiling water, with 1/2 teaspoon salt, in medium saucepan, cook the cabbage, covered, 8 to 10 minutes, or just until tender. Drain well.
4. Also, heat scallions with milk and 1/2 teaspoon salt. Bring to boiling; reduce heat; simmer 10 minutes.
5. In saucepan, with electric mixer at medium speed, beat potato with 4 tablespoons butter, 1 teaspoon salt, and the pepper. Beat in scallions and hot milk, beating until potato is very light and fluffy.
6. Stir in cabbage, combining well. Heat over low heat 5 minutes.
7. Turn colcannon into heated serving dish. Make depression in center; fill with remaining butter.
Makes 8 servings.

Lamb Stew

3 lb neck of lamb, cut crosswise through bone
8 medium potatoes, peeled
4 large onions
1-1/2 teaspoons salt
1/2 teaspoon dried thyme leaves
1/4 teaspoon pepper
Chopped parsley

1. Wipe meat with damp paper towels. Trim off all fat, and discard.
2. Slice 2 potatoes thinly. Slice onions thinly.
3. Preheat oven to 350F.
4. In Dutch oven or large, heavy saucepan, make a layer of the sliced potato, top with half of sliced onion, then the lamb. Sprinkle with half of salt, thyme, and pepper. Add remaining onion and whole potatoes. Sprinkle with remaining salt, thyme, and pepper.
5. Add 2 cups water; cover Dutch oven with tight-fitting lid; place in oven.
6. Cook for 2-1/2 hours, or until meat is tender. Before serving, sprinkle with chopped parsley.
Makes 6 servings.

Maureen's Soda Bread

2 cups unsifted all-purpose flour
2 tablespoons sugar
2 teaspoons baking powder
1 teaspoon baking soda
1/2 teaspoon salt
3 tablespoons butter or regular margarine, softened
1 cup buttermilk
1 tablespoon butter or regular margarine, melted

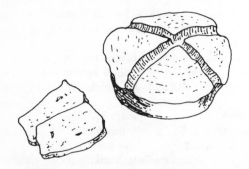

1. Preheat oven to 375F. Lightly grease a small cookie sheet.
2. In large bowl, sift flour, sugar, baking powder, soda, and salt.
3. Cut in softened butter with a pastry blender or fork until mixture looks like fine crumbs.
4. Add buttermilk; mix in with a fork only until dry ingredients are moistened.
5. Turn out on lightly floured pastry cloth or board. Knead gently until smooth—about 1 minute. Shape into a ball. Place on prepared cookie sheet; flatten into a 7-inch circle. (Dough will be about 1-1/2 inches thick.) Press a large floured knife into center of loaf almost through to bottom. Repeat, at right angle, to divide loaf into quarters.
6. Bake 30 to 40 minutes, or until top is golden and loaf sounds hollow when tapped.
7. Remove to wire rack to cool. Brush top with melted butter. Dust with flour, if you wish.
Makes 1 loaf.

Caraway-Raisin Soda Bread

Add 1/2 cup seedless raisins and 1 tablespoon caraway seed to dry ingredients. Proceed as above.

Whole-Wheat Soda Bread

1 cup unsifted all-purpose flour
1 teaspoon baking powder
1 teaspoon baking soda
1/2 teaspoon salt
2 cups whole-wheat flour
1-1/2 cups buttermilk
1 tablespoon butter or margarine, melted

1. Preheat oven to 375F. Grease well a small cookie sheet.
2. Into large mixing bowl, sift together all-purpose flour, baking powder, soda, and salt. Add whole-wheat flour; mix well with a fork.
3. Add buttermilk; mix just until dry ingredients are moistened.
4. Turn out on lightly floured pastry cloth or board. Knead gently until smooth—about 1 minute.
5. Shape dough into a ball. Place on prepared cookie sheet; flatten into a 7-inch circle. (Dough will be about 1-1/2 inches thick.) Press a large floured knife into center of loaf almost through to bottom. Repeat, at right angle, to divide the loaf into quarters.
6. Bake 40 minutes, or until top is golden and loaf sounds hollow when tapped.
7. Remove to wire rack. Brush top with butter. Cool completely.
Makes 1 loaf.

Warm Apple Slices with Custard Sauce

1 cup milk
2 egg yolks
3 tablespoons granulated sugar
Dash salt
1/2 teaspoon vanilla extract
1 can (1 lb, 4 oz) apple slices
1/2 cup granulated sugar
2 tablespoons lemon juice
1/2 cup heavy cream
2 tablespoons confectioners' sugar

1. Make Custard Sauce: Heat milk in top of double boiler, over direct heat, until bubbles form around the edge of the pan.
2. In small bowl, slightly beat egg yolks with 3 tablespoons granulated sugar and the salt. Gradually add hot milk, stirring constantly. Return to double-boiler top.
3. Cook, stirring constantly, over simmering water until mixture coats a metal spoon. Stir in vanilla.
4. Pour into small bowl. Refrigerate, covered, until chilled.
5. Meanwhile, drain apple slices well; discard liquid. Place slices in medium saucepan. Stir in 1/2 cup granulated sugar and the lemon juice. Heat to boiling; reduce heat; cook, uncovered and stirring once or twice, 20 minutes, or until apples are glazed and liquid has evaporated. Keep warm.
6. In small bowl, whip cream and confectioners' sugar until the cream is stiff.
7. To serve: Spoon warm apple slices into 4 dessert dishes, dividing evenly. Pour the chilled custard over each serving. Top with whipped cream.
Makes 4 servings.

Irish Tea Cake

4 eggs
1 cup sifted cake flour
3/4 teaspoon baking powder
1/4 teaspoon salt
1/4 teaspoon cream of tartar
1 cup sugar
1 teaspoon vanilla extract
1 teaspoon lemon juice
1/2 cup red-currant jelly

1. Separate eggs, whites in large bowl, yolks in small bowl. Let whites warm to room temperature —1 hour.
2. Preheat oven to 350F.
3. Sift flour, baking powder, salt.
4. Add cream of tartar to egg whites. With electric mixer at medium speed, beat whites until foamy. Gradually beat in 1/2 cup sugar, a tablespoonful at a time. Continue beating until stiff, glossy peaks form when beater is raised.
5. With same beater, beat egg yolks until thick and lemon-colored. Gradually beat in remaining sugar, a tablespoonful at a time. Beat until thick and light—2 minutes.
6. In measuring cup, combine 1/4 cup water, vanilla, lemon juice.
7. At low speed, blend flour mixture, one third at a time, into egg-yolk mixture alternately with water mixture. Beat 1 minute.
8. With wire whisk or rubber scraper, fold into egg-white mixture.
9. Pour batter into 2 ungreased 8-inch layer-cake pans.
10. Bake 25 to 30 minutes, or just until surface springs back when lightly pressed with fingertip.
11. Invert pans, setting rims on 2 other pans. Cool 1-1/2 hours.
12. Loosen around edge. Tap inverted pan on counter top, to loosen.
13. Spread one layer, crust side down, with currant jelly. Top with other layer, crust side up. Sprinkle top with confectioners' sugar put through a sieve, if desired.
Makes 8 to 10 servings.

Irish Coffee

Sugar
1/2 cup Irish whisky
4 cups hot, strong black coffee
1/2 cup chilled whipped cream

1. Spoon 1-1/2 teaspoons sugar into each of 4 (5-oz) goblets.
2. Add 2 tablespoons whisky to each. Fill with coffee to within 1/2 inch of rim.
3. Float a heaping tablespoonful of whipped cream on coffee in each goblet, by sliding it off a spoon. Serve at once.
Makes 4 servings.

Steamed Raisin Pudding with Irish-Whisky Sauce

1-1/2 cups milk
1-1/2 cups dark raisins, chopped
1-1/2 cups sifted all-purpose flour
2-1/2 teaspoons baking powder
2/3 cup sugar
1/2 teaspoon salt
1 teaspoon nutmeg
1/2 teaspoon cinnamon
3 eggs
1-1/2 cups fresh bread crumbs
1 cup grated suet
Irish-Whisky Sauce, below

1. In the top of double boiler, over hot water, heat milk and raisins 20 minutes. Remove top of double boiler from water; set aside 10 minutes, to cool.
2. Meanwhile, sift flour with baking powder, sugar, salt, nutmeg, and cinnamon.
3. In large bowl, with electric mixer at medium speed, or with rotary beater, beat eggs until light. At low speed, beat in crumbs until well mixed. Beat in suet.
4. At low speed of electric mixer, or with wooden spoon, beat flour ingredients into egg mixture alternately with milk mixture, beating until well combined.
5. Turn into well-greased 2-quart pudding mold with tube; cover tightly. Place on trivet in large kettle; add enough boiling water to come halfway up side of mold.
6. Steam (the water in the kettle should be bubbling), kettle covered, 2 hours.
7. Meanwhile, make Irish-Whisky Sauce.
8. Remove pudding mold from water. Let stand about 10 minutes.
9. With a knife, loosen pudding around edge and tube; turn out of mold. Serve warm, with the sauce. Makes 10 to 12 servings.

Irish-Whisky Sauce

1/4 cup soft butter or regular margarine
2 cups light-brown sugar, firmly packed
1 egg
1 cup light cream
Dash nutmeg
1/4 cup Irish whisky

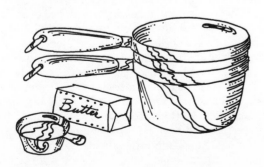

1. In top of double boiler, with electric mixer at medium speed, beat butter with sugar until light and creamy.
2. Beat in egg, cream, and nutmeg; beat until mixture is fluffy.
3. Cook, stirring occasionally, over hot, not boiling, water until mixture is thickened.
4. Remove from heat. Gradually stir in whisky.
5. Serve warm or cold, with the pudding.
Makes 2-1/2 cups.

Italian

Their very names are savory—minestrone, lasagna, zucchini, tortoni. When you taste our wonderful recipes for these and the many others, you'll think of Italy, of tall, dark poplars, of sun-drenched piazzas, of all its warmth and hospitality. Here, we offer a collection of memorable recipes.

Minestrone

3-lb shin of beef
Salt
4 medium carrots, pared
4 sprigs parsley
2 large celery stalks, cut up
1 large onion, quartered
1 bay leaf
1 can (1 lb, 1 oz) Italian tomatoes, undrained
1 can (1 lb, 4 oz) chick peas or kidney beans, undrained
1 pkg (10 oz) frozen cut green beans
1 pkg (10 oz) frozen peas
2 cups chopped cabbage
1/4 lb perciatelli or spaghetti, broken into 1-inch pieces
1/4 teaspoon pepper

1. Place shin of beef, 1 tablespoon salt, and 4 quarts water in large kettle. Bring to boiling, covered; then skim surface.
2. Add carrots, parsley, celery, onion, and bay leaf; simmer, uncovered, 3 hours.
3. Remove beef and carrots; set aside. Strain broth —there should be about 7 cups broth.
4. In kettle, combine broth, tomatoes, chick peas, green beans, peas, cabbage, perciatelli, 2 teaspoons salt, and the pepper; bring to boiling, stirring occasionally. Then reduce heat, and simmer, covered, 45 minutes.
5. Meanwhile, slice carrots, and cut meat from bone into small pieces. Add the meat to the simmering soup.
Makes 3-1/2 quarts.

Pasta e Fagioli

1-1/2 cups dried navy beans
Salt
1/2 pkg (1-lb size) shell macaroni (3 cups)
3 tablespoons olive oil
1 large onion, chopped
2 cups sliced carrot
1 cup chopped celery
1 clove garlic, crushed
2 cups diced, peeled tomato (1 lb)
1 teaspoon dried sage leaves
1/2 teaspoon dried oregano leaves
1/4 teaspoon pepper
Chopped parsley
Grated Parmesan cheese

1. In a large bowl, combine beans with 6 cups cold water. Refrigerate overnight.
2. Next day, turn beans and water into 6-quart kettle. Add 1-1/2 teaspoons salt.
3. Bring to boiling; reduce heat, and simmer, covered, about 3 hours, or until beans are tender. Stir several times during cooking. Drain, reserving liquid (there will be about 2-1/2 cups).
4. Cook macaroni following the label directions.
5. Meanwhile, in hot oil in large skillet, sauté onion, carrot, celery, and garlic, covered, until soft—about 20 minutes. Do not brown. Add tomato, sage, oregano, 1/2 teaspoon salt, and the pepper. Cover; cook, over medium heat, 15 minutes.
6. In large saucepan or kettle, combine beans, macaroni, and sautéed vegetables. Add 1-1/2 cups reserved bean liquid. Bring to boiling; cover; simmer 35 to 40 minutes, stirring several times and adding more bean liquid if needed. Add salt and pepper if needed.

7. Turn into attractive serving dish or casserole. Sprinkle with chopped parsley and grated Parmesan cheese.
Makes 8 servings.

Roman Veal Scallopini

8 tablespoons butter or margarine
3/4 lb mushrooms, sliced
1 small onion, finely chopped
1 clove garlic, peeled
3 cups coarsely chopped, peeled fresh tomatoes (about 2 lb)
2/3 cup dry white wine
Salt
1/4 teaspoon dried tarragon leaves, crushed
12 thin veal scallops (1-1/2 lb)
1/8 teaspoon pepper
Grated Parmesan cheese

1. In 5 tablespoons hot butter in skillet, sauté mushrooms until golden-brown—about 5 minutes. Add onion and garlic, and cook about 5 minutes, or until onion is golden.
2. Add tomatoes, wine, 3/4 teaspoon salt, and the tarragon, stirring until well blended. Reduce heat; simmer, covered and stirring occasionally, 30 minutes.
3. Meanwhile, wipe veal with damp paper towels. Sprinkle with 1/2 teaspoon salt and the pepper.
4. Heat 3 tablespoons butter in another skillet. Add veal, a few pieces at a time, and cook until lightly browned on both sides—about 5 minutes. Remove, and keep warm.
5. Return veal to skillet. Remove garlic from sauce. Pour sauce over veal; simmer, covered, 5 minutes. Sprinkle with Parmesan cheese.
Makes 6 servings.

Chicken Cacciatore with Polenta

2 (2-lb size) ready-to-cook broiler-fryers, cut up
3 tablespoons olive or salad oil
2 tablespoons butter or margarine
1-1/2 cups sliced onion
1 clove garlic, crushed
1 can (1 lb, 1 oz) Italian tomatoes, undrained
2 tablespoons chopped parsley
1-1/2 teaspoons salt
1/2 teaspoon dried basil leaves
1/4 teaspoon pepper
1/2 cup red wine
Polenta, page 460

1. Wash chicken; pat dry with paper towels.
2. Heat oil and butter in Dutch oven. Add chicken, a few pieces at a time, and brown well on all sides. Remove as browned, and set aside.
3. Add onion and garlic to Dutch oven, and sauté until golden-brown—about 5 minutes. Add tomatoes, parsley, salt, basil, and pepper; mix well, mashing tomatoes with fork.
4. Bring to boiling. Reduce heat, and simmer, uncovered, 20 minutes.
5. Add browned chicken and the wine; simmer, covered, 45 to 50 minutes, or until chicken is tender.
6. Meanwhile, make Polenta.
7. To serve, spoon chicken and some of sauce over polenta. Pass rest of sauce. If desired, garnish with chopped parsley.
Makes 6 to 8 servings.

Spaghetti and Meatballs Napoli

Meatballs:
2 eggs
1/2 cup milk
3 slices whole-wheat bread, crumbled
3/4 lb ground beef
1/2 lb ground pork
1/4 lb ground veal
1 medium onion, finely chopped
1/3 cup finely chopped green pepper
2 tablespoons chopped parsley
1 large clove garlic, crushed
1 teaspoon salt
1/2 teaspoon pepper
Dash ground cloves
Dash nutmeg

Sauce:
1/2 lb round steak
1/4 lb salt pork
1 clove garlic
1/4 cup white wine
1 can (1 lb, 12 oz) tomatoes, undrained
1 can (6 oz) tomato paste
2 tablespoons chopped parsley
1 teaspoon salt
1/4 teaspoon pepper
1/4 teaspoon dried basil leaves

1 pkg (1 lb) spaghetti
1/2 cup grated Parmesan cheese

1. Make Meatballs: Preheat oven to 450F. In medium bowl, beat eggs slightly. Add milk and bread; mix well. Let stand 5 minutes.
2. Add rest of meatball ingredients; mix until well blended.
3. Shape into 12 balls—they'll be about 2-1/2 inches in diameter. Place in a well-greased shallow baking pan.
4. Bake, uncovered, 15 minutes. Brush meatballs with pan drippings; bake 15 minutes longer.
5. Meanwhile, make Sauce: Wipe round steak with damp paper towels. Cut into 1/2-inch chunks. Set aside.
6. Chop salt pork in little pieces. Place in Dutch oven with garlic; sauté until well browned. Add beef, and brown on all sides.
7. Add wine; simmer, covered, 10 minutes.
8. Stir in tomatoes, tomato paste, 1/2 cup water, parsley, salt, pepper, and basil; bring to boiling. Reduce heat, and simmer, uncovered, 1/2 hour.
9. Add meatballs; simmer, covered and stirring occasionally, 1 hour longer.
10. Cook spaghetti as the label directs. Drain.
11. To serve: Place spaghetti on serving dish; top with meatballs and sauce, and sprinkle with grated Parmesan cheese.
Makes 6 servings.

Veal Parmigiana

1 lb thin veal scallopini
2 eggs, beaten
1 cup seasoned dry bread crumbs
1/2 cup olive or salad oil
Sauce, recipe below
1 pkg (8 oz) mozzarella cheese, sliced
1/4 cup grated Parmesan cheese

1. Preheat the oven to 350F.
2. Wipe veal with damp paper towels. Dip in egg, then in bread crumbs, coating lightly.
3. In a large skillet, heat about 1/4 cup oil. Add veal slices, a few at a time, and cook until golden-brown on each side—2 to 3 minutes for each side. Add more oil as needed.
4. Place veal in 10-by-6-1/2-by-2-inch baking dish, to cover bottom in a single layer. Add half the Sauce and half the mozzarella and Parmesan cheeses. Repeat the layers, ending with Parmesan cheese.
5. Cover baking dish with foil. Bake 30 minutes, or until bubbly.
Makes 4 to 6 servings.

Sauce for Veal Parmigiana

2 tablespoons olive or salad oil
1/2 cup chopped onion
1 clove garlic, crushed
1 can (1 lb, 1 oz) Italian tomatoes, undrained
2 teaspoons sugar
3/4 teaspoon salt
1/2 teaspoon dried oregano leaves
1/4 teaspoon dried basil leaves
1/4 teaspoon pepper

1. In hot oil in medium saucepan, sauté onion and garlic until golden-brown—about 5 minutes. Add the undrained tomatoes, sugar, salt, oregano, basil, and pepper; mix well, mashing the tomatoes with a fork.
2. Bring to boiling; reduce heat; simmer, covered, 10 minutes. Use in Veal Parmigiana.

Eggplant Parmigiana

2 tablespoons butter or margarine
1/2 cup chopped onion
1 clove garlic, crushed
1 lb ground chuck
1 can (1 lb, 1 oz) Italian tomatoes, undrained
1 can (6 oz) tomato paste
2 teaspoons dried oregano leaves
1 teaspoon dried basil leaves
1-1/2 teaspoons salt
1/4 teaspoon pepper
1 tablespoon brown sugar
1 large eggplant (1-1/2 lb)
2 eggs, slightly beaten
1/2 cup packaged dry bread crumbs
1-1/4 cups grated Parmesan cheese
1/3 cup salad oil
1 pkg (8 oz) mozzarella cheese, sliced

1. In hot butter in large skillet, sauté onion, garlic, chuck until meat is no longer red—about 5 minutes.
2. Add tomatoes, tomato paste, oregano, basil, salt, pepper, sugar, and 1 cup water; bring to boiling.
3. Reduce heat; simmer, uncovered, 20 minutes.
4. Meanwhile, preheat oven to 350F. Lightly grease a 13-by-9-by-2-inch baking dish.
5. Wash eggplant; do not peel. Cut crosswise into slices 1/2 inch thick.
6. In pie plate, combine eggs and 1 tablespoon water; mix well.
7. On a sheet of waxed paper, combine bread crumbs with 1/2 cup Parmesan cheese; mix well.
8. Dip eggplant slices into egg mixture, coating well. Then dip into crumb mixture, coating evenly.
9. Sauté eggplant slices, a few at a time, in 1 tablespoon hot oil until golden-brown and crisp on both sides. Add more oil as needed.
10. Arrange half the eggplant slices in bottom of prepared baking dish. Sprinkle with half of the remaining Parmesan cheese. Top with half the mozzarella cheese. Cover with half the tomato sauce.
11. Arrange remaining eggplant slices over tomato sauce. Cover with rest of Parmesan, tomato sauce, and mozzarella.
12. Bake, uncovered, 25 minutes, or until mozzarella is melted and slightly browned.
Makes 6 servings.

Spinach Frittata

3 tablespoons olive oil
1/2 cup thinly sliced onion
10 eggs
1 cup finely chopped raw spinach (1/2 lb)
1/3 cup grated Parmesan cheese
1 tablespoon chopped parsley
1 small clove garlic, crushed
1 teaspoon salt
1/4 teaspoon pepper

1. Preheat oven to 350F. Heat oil in 10-inch heavy skillet with heat-resistant handle. Add onion; sauté until onion is tender and golden-brown—will take about 5 minutes.
2. In large bowl, combine remaining ingredients; with wire whisk or fork, beat until well blended. Turn into skillet, with onion.
3. Cook over low heat, lifting from bottom with a spatula as the eggs set—3 minutes.
4. Bake, uncovered, 10 minutes, or until top is set. With spatula, loosen from bottom and around edge, and slide onto serving platter. Cut into wedges.
Makes 4 to 6 servings.

Stewed Sweet Peppers

6 or 7 sweet green or yellow peppers (2 lb)
1/2 cup olive or salad oil
1 cup sliced onion
1 clove garlic, peeled
1 can (1 lb, 12 oz) Italian tomatoes, undrained
1-1/2 teaspoons salt
1/8 teaspoon pepper
2 tablespoons chopped parsley

1. Wash peppers. Cut in half lengthwise. Discard cores and seeds. Slice each half into three long strips.
2. In hot oil in large skillet, sauté pepper strips, onion, and garlic, stirring occasionally, 15 minutes.
3. Add tomatoes, salt, and pepper. Bring to boiling; reduce heat, and simmer, uncovered and over medium heat, 45 minutes, or until mixture is like a thick sauce. Remove and discard garlic.
4. Serve hot or cold, garnished with parsley. Nice as an accompaniment to meat.
Makes 8 to 10 servings.

Broccoli, Italian Style

1 bunch broccoli (about 1-1/2 lb)
6 cups boiling water
Salt
1/4 cup olive oil
1/2 clove garlic, finely chopped
2 tablespoons lemon juice

1. Remove large leaves and tough portions of broccoli. Wash thoroughly; drain. Separate, splitting larger stalks into quarters.
2. Place in a 6-quart saucepan; add boiling water and 1 teaspoon salt. Cook, covered, 10 minutes, or until tender. Drain in colander.
3. In same pan, place olive oil and garlic; heat until bubbly. Add broccoli; sprinkle with lemon juice and 1/2 teaspoon salt. Cook, covered, 1 minute, or until broccoli is heated through. Serve hot.
Makes 4 servings.

Artichokes with Lemon Sauce

1/4 cup olive or salad oil
6 lemon slices
2 bay leaves
1 clove garlic, split
1 teaspoon salt
1/8 teaspoon pepper
4 large artichokes (about 3 lb)

Lemon Sauce:
1/4 cup melted butter
2 tablespoons olive oil
2 tablespoons lemon juice

1. In large kettle, combine 3 quarts water with 1/4 cup olive oil, lemon slices, bay leaves, garlic, salt, and pepper; bring to boiling.
2. Meanwhile, trim stalk from base of artichokes; cut a 1-inch slice from tops. Remove discolored leaves; snip off spike ends.
3. Wash the artichokes in cold water; drain.
4. Add to boiling mixture. Reduce heat; simmer, covered, 40 to 45 minutes, or until artichoke bases feel soft. Drain artichokes well.
5. Meanwhile, make Lemon Sauce: In a small bowl, mix the butter, 2 tablespoons olive oil, and the lemon juice until well combined.
6. To serve: Place artichoke and small cup of sauce on individual plates. To eat, pull out leaves, one at a time, and dip in sauce. Discard prickly choke. Makes 4 servings.

Best of All Pizzas

Crust:
1-1/3 cups warm water (105 to 115F)
1 pkg active dry yeast
Salad oil
2 teaspoons salt
4-1/3 cups sifted all-purpose flour

All kinds of fillings, below

1. Prepare Crust: If possible, check temperature of warm water with thermometer. Sprinkle yeast over water in large bowl, stirring until dissolved.
2. Add 2 tablespoons salad oil, the salt, and 4 cups flour; stir, with wooden spoon, until all flour is moistened.
3. Turn out on lightly floured surface. Knead in remaining flour until smooth—this will take about 10 minutes.
4. Place in medium bowl; brush very lightly with salad oil. Cover with towel; let rise in warm place (85F), free from drafts, until double in bulk—about 2 hours. (Or, if desired, refrigerate dough, covered, to rise overnight. Next day, remove from refrigerator; let stand at room temperature 30 minutes.)
5. Punch down dough; divide in half. Pat and stretch each half to fit a 14-inch pizza pan.
6. Move oven rack to lowest position; place cookie sheet on rack to heat. (This ensures a crisp crust.) Preheat oven to 500F.
7. Arrange one of desired fillings over dough, as directed. Let set 10 minutes.
8. Bake pizza, placing pan on cookie sheet, about 20 minutes, or until crust is golden-brown and filling is bubbly.
Makes 2 pizzas.

Meatball and Mozzarella Filling

1 lb ground chuck
1 egg
1/4 cup packaged dry bread crumbs
1 teaspoon salt
1/4 teaspoon pepper
2 tablespoons salad oil
1-1/2 cups Pizza Sauce, below
1 pkg (8 oz) mozzarella cheese, coarsely grated
   (1-1/2 cups)

1. In medium bowl, combine beef, egg, bread crumbs, salt, and pepper; with fork, mix gently until well blended. Shape into 1-inch meatballs—about 30.
2. Heat salad oil in large skillet. Add meatballs, and sauté until browned on all sides—about 5 minutes. Drain on paper towels.
3. Spread sauce over unbaked crust; cover with meatballs. Sprinkle mozzarella over all.
4. Bake as directed.
Makes enough filling for 1 (14-inch) pizza.

Traditional Tomato and Cheese Filling

1-1/2 cups Pizza Sauce, below
2 tablespoons grated Parmesan cheese
1 pkg (8 oz) mozzarella cheese, coarsely grated
   (1-1/2 cups)

1. Spread sauce over unbaked crust.
2. Sprinkle first with Parmesan, then with mozzarella.
3. Bake as directed.
Makes enough filling for 1 (14-inch) pizza.

Salami and Sweet Peppers Filling

1-1/2 cups Pizza Sauce, below
Prepared roasted sweet red or green peppers,
   cut in strips (about 1/2 cup)
1/4 lb sliced salami
1/2 cup onion rings
1/2 pkg (8-oz size) mozzarella cheese, cut in strips

1. Spread sauce over unbaked crust. Arrange peppers, salami, and onion over sauce, as desired.
2. Place mozzarella over all.
3. Bake as directed.
Makes enough filling for 1 (14-inch) pizza.

Pizza Sauce

3 tablespoons olive or salad oil
1 cup sliced onion
1 clove garlic, crushed
2 cans (15-oz size) Italian plum tomatoes,
   undrained
1 tablespoon chopped parsley
1-1/2 teaspoons salt
1 teaspoon dried oregano leaves
1/2 teaspoon sugar
1/4 teaspoon dried basil leaves
1/4 teaspoon pepper

1. In hot oil in medium saucepan, sauté onion and garlic until onion is golden—5 minutes.
2. Add rest of ingredients; bring to boiling. Reduce heat; simmer, uncovered, 25 minutes; stir occasionally.
Makes 3 cups; enough for 2 (14-inch) pizzas.

Spumoni

3 pints chocolate ice cream, slightly soft
1 pint pistachio ice cream, slightly soft
2 pints vanilla ice cream, slightly soft
1/2 cup candied mixed fruits
2 teaspoons rum flavoring
1-1/cups heavy cream, whipped

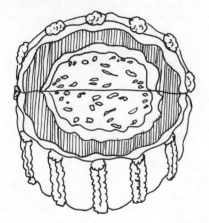

1. Place a 2-1/2-quart fancy mold or melon mold in freezer.
2. In large bowl, with portable electric mixer, beat the chocolate ice cream until smooth but not melted. With spoon, quickly press evenly inside the chilled melon mold, to make a 1-inch-thick layer. Freeze until it is firm.
3. In medium bowl, beat the pistachio ice cream until smooth. Then press evenly over chocolate-ice-cream layer. Freeze until firm.
4. In large bowl, combine the vanilla ice cream, candied fruits, and rum flavoring; beat until well blended but not melted. Press into center of mold. Freeze until firm.
5. **To unmold and decorate spumoni:** Let spumoni stand at room temperature 5 minutes. Invert over serving plate. Hold hot, damp dishcloth over mold, and shake to release. Return to freezer until the surface is firm.
6. Spread three fourths of whipped cream over mold. Place remaining whipped cream in pastry bag with decorating tip, and pipe on mold decoratively. Return to freezer until serving time.
Makes 16 to 20 servings.

Amaretti

Macaroons

2 egg whites
1-1/2 cups blanched almonds, ground
1 cup sifted confectioners' sugar
1/4 teaspoon salt
1 teaspoon almond extract
1/2 teaspoon vanilla extract
Blanched almonds

1. In large bowl of electric mixer, let egg whites warm to room temperature—about 1 hour.
2. Preheat oven to 300F. Lightly grease cookie sheets.
3. In medium bowl, combine the ground almonds with the sugar, mixing well.
4. Beat egg whites with salt until stiff peaks form when beaters are slowly raised. Using a wooden spoon, stir almond mixture into the beaten egg whites, along with the almond and vanilla extracts, just until well combined.
5. Drop by slightly rounded teaspoonfuls, 2 inches apart, onto prepared cookie sheets. Top each with a blanched almond.
6. Bake 20 minutes, or until a light-brown color. With spatula, remove to wire rack to cool completely.
7. Store, covered, overnight.
Makes 2-1/2 to 3 dozen.

Biscuit Tortoni

3 egg whites
3/4 cup sugar
Dash salt
1/4 cup whole blanched almonds
Almond extract
1-1/2 cups heavy cream
3/4 teaspoon vanilla extract
12 candied cherries

1. In small bowl of electric mixer, let egg whites warm to room temperature—about 1 hour.
2. Combine 1/4 cup water with the sugar in a 1-quart saucepan; cook over low heat, stirring, until sugar is dissolved.
3. Bring to boiling over medium heat; boil, uncovered and without stirring, to 236F on candy thermometer, or until syrup spins a 2-inch thread when dropped from a spoon.
4. Meanwhile, at high speed, beat egg whites with salt just until stiff peaks form when beater is slowly raised.
5. Pour hot syrup in thin stream over egg whites, beating constantly until mixture forms very stiff peaks when beater is raised. Refrigerate, covered, 30 minutes.
6. Meanwhile, preheat oven to 350F. Place almonds in shallow pan, and bake just until toasted—8 to 10 minutes. Finely grind almonds in a blender.
7. Turn into a small bowl. Blend in 1-1/2 teaspoons almond extract. Set aside.
8. In medium bowl, beat cream with 1/4 teaspoon almond extract and the vanilla until stiff. With wire whisk or rubber scraper, fold into egg-white mixture until thoroughly combined.
9. Spoon into 12 paper-lined 2-1/2-inch muffin-pan cups. Sprinkle with almond mixture; top with a cherry.
10. Cover with foil; freeze until firm—several hours or overnight. Serve right from freezer.
Makes 12 servings.

Zabaione

6 egg yolks
3 tablespoons sugar
1/3 cup Marsala

1. In top of double boiler, with portable electric mixer at high speed, or with rotary beater, beat egg yolks with sugar until light and fluffy.
2. Gradually add Marsala, beating until well combined.
3. Over hot, not boiling, water, beat at medium speed 8 minutes, or till mixture begins to hold its shape.
4. Turn into 4 dessert glasses. Serve at once, or while still slightly warm. (Zabaione separates on standing.)
Makes 4 servings.

Peaches in Marsala

1 can (1 lb, 14 oz) peach halves
1/2 cup cream Marsala
1-inch cinnamon stick

1. Drain the peach halves, reserving 1 tablespoon of the peach syrup.
2. In medium bowl, combine peaches, Marsala, cinnamon stick, and reserved syrup.
3. Refrigerate, covered, until the peaches are very well chilled—at least 2 hours.
4. To serve: Turn peaches and liquid into individual dessert dishes.
Makes 4 servings.

Anise Toast

2-1/2 cups sifted cake flour
2 teaspoons baking powder
1/4 teaspoon salt
1/4 cup butter or regular margarine, softened
1 cup sugar
3 eggs
1 tablespoon anise extract

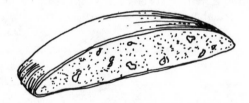

1. Preheat oven to 350F. Grease and flour 2 cookie sheets.
2. Sift flour with baking powder and salt 3 times; set aside.
3. In medium bowl, with portable electric mixer at medium speed, beat butter with sugar until very light. Add eggs, one at a time, beating well after each addition. Beat in anise.
4. Add flour mixture; beat, at low speed, until blended. Divide mixture in half. Spread each half on a cookie sheet to 11-by-5-inch oval.
5. Bake 15 to 20 minutes, or until pale golden-brown. Remove from oven; cut into 1-inch-thick slices. Turn each on its side. Bake 10 to 15 minutes, or until lightly browned.
6. Remove slices to wire rack, and let cool completely.
Makes 18 to 20.

Cannoli

Filling:
3 lb ricotta cheese
2-1/2 cups confectioners' sugar
1/4 cup semisweet-chocolate pieces or grated sweet chocolate
2 tablespoons chopped citron
10 candied cherries, finely chopped
1/2 teaspoon cinnamon

Cannoli Shells, below
Chopped pistachio nuts (optional)
Confectioners' sugar

1. In a large bowl, with portable electric mixer, beat ricotta cheese 1 minute. Add 2-1/2 cups confectioners' sugar, and beat until light and creamy —about 1 minute.
2. Add chocolate, citron, cherries, cinnamon; beat at low speed until well blended. Refrigerate, covered, until well chilled—at least 2 hours. Meanwhile, make Cannoli Shells.
3. Just before serving, with teaspoon or small spatula, fill shells with ricotta mixture. Garnish ends with chopped pistachios; sprinkle tops with confectioners' sugar.
Makes 24.

Cannoli Shells

3 cups sifted all-purpose flour
1 tablespoon sugar
1/4 teaspoon cinnamon
3/4 cup port
Salad oil or shortening for deep-frying
1 egg yolk, slightly beaten

1. Sift flour with sugar and cinnamon onto a board. Make a well in center, and fill with port. With a fork, gradually blend flour into port. When dough is stiff enough to handle, knead about 15 minutes, or until dough is smooth and stiff (if too moist and sticky, knead in a little more sifted flour).
2. Refrigerate dough, covered, 2 hours.
3. In deep-fat fryer, electric skillet, or heavy saucepan, slowly heat salad oil (3 to 4 inches deep), to 400F on deep-frying thermometer.
4. Meanwhile, on lightly floured surface, roll one third of dough to paper thinness, making a 16-inch round. Cut into eight 5-inch circles. Wrap a circle loosely around a 6-inch-long cannoli form or dowel, 1 inch in diameter; seal with egg yolk.
5. Gently drop dough-covered forms, two at a time, into hot oil, and fry 1 minute, or until browned on all sides (turn, if necessary). With tongs or slotted utensil, lift out of oil, and drain on paper towels. Carefully remove forms. Continue until all dough is used.
Makes 24.
Note: Cannoli Shells can be made a day or two ahead and stored, covered, at room temperature, then filled about 1 hour before serving.

Japanese

To the Japanese, the look of food is as important as the taste of it. Japanese meals are planned with texture of foods and contrasts and harmonies of taste in mind. Razor-sharp knives are used to cut the foods into the sheerest slices: small turnips are transformed into chrysanthemums; cucumbers are sliced thin as paper, joined at one end and spread apart to become fans; root vegetables turn into blossoms. Japanese food usually is cut in pieces easy to eat without using table knives. It is served on porcelain, lacquer or china with a soft, dull finish.

Rice with Mushrooms

2 cups raw long-grain white rice
1/4 lb fresh mushrooms, washed and finely chopped
1-1/2 teaspoons salt
1/8 teaspoon pepper
1 tablespoon shoyu or soy sauce

1. Place rice in heavy, 2-1/2-quart saucepan. Add about 1 cup cold water; wash rice well, using fingers.
2. Pour off water, and wash rice again. Repeat until water is clear.
3. Add fresh cold water to cover rice about 1/2 inch—takes about 1-1/2 cups. Let rice soak 1 hour.

4. Add remaining ingredients. Cover saucepan tightly; place over high heat.
5. When steam appears around edge of cover, reduce heat; simmer 15 minutes.
Makes 8 servings.

Tempura

1/2 lb large fresh shrimp, shelled and deveined
1 pkg (10 oz) frozen rock-lobster tails
2 pkg (10-oz size) frozen scallops
6 large parsley sprigs
1/2 small eggplant, cut in 2-by-1/4-inch strips
3/4 lb sweet potatoes, pared and sliced 1/8 inch thick
1 large green pepper, sliced lengthwise in 1/4-inch strips
Salad oil
Batter, below
Sauce, below

1. Drop shrimp into boiling, salted water to cover; bring back to boiling. Reduce heat; simmer, covered, 5 minutes. Then drain, and let cool.
2. Cook lobster tails as the label directs. Drain; cool. With scissors, cut shell away from meat; halve meat crosswise.
3. Drop unthawed scallops into boiling, salted water to cover; bring back to boiling. Reduce heat; simmer, covered, 5 minutes. Then drain, and let cool.
4. On platter, arrange shrimp, lobster, and scallops in attractive pattern with parsley, eggplant, sweet potatoes, and green pepper.
5. Refrigerate, covered, until you are ready to cook Tempura.
6. Tempura is best served immediately, cooked at table. In electric skillet or deep-fryer, heat oil (at least 3 inches deep) to 350F on deep-frying thermometer.
7. With tongs, dip shrimp, lobster, scallops, and vegetables into batter, to coat lightly.
8. Deep-fry, a few pieces at a time, until lightly browned—about 3 minutes.
9. Serve a combination of seafood and vegetables to each guest, along with a small bowl of sauce for dipping.
Makes 6 servings.

Batter for Tempura

3 eggs
2-1/2 teaspoons shoyu or soy sauce
1-2/3 cups sifted all-purpose flour
2 tablespoons sugar
1 teaspoon salt

1. Make batter just before using: Beat eggs, in medium bowl, with rotary beater.
2. Add shoyu and 1-1/4 cups water. Gradually add flour, sugar, and salt, beating until smooth.
Makes 2-1/3 cups.

Sauce for Tempura

1/2 cup sherry
1/2 cup beef bouillon
1 cup shoyu or soy sauce
1 teaspoon monosodium glutamate
Radishes, freshly grated
Horseradish, freshly grated
Ginger root, freshly grated

1. In small saucepan, combine sherry, bouillon, shoyu, and monosodium glutamate; bring to boiling.
2. Divide into 6 individual serving bowls. Place on tray, along with 3 small bowls filled with grated radishes, horseradish, and ginger root.
3. Each guest adds radish, horseradish, or ginger root to dipping sauce to suit his own taste.
Makes enough for 6 servings.

Sukiyaki

To Be Cooked at Table

2 lb boneless sirloin steak, sliced 1/8 inch thick*
2 onions
2 bunches green onions
12 large fresh mushrooms
1 can (5 oz) bamboo shoots, drained
1/2 lb fresh spinach
1/2 small head cabbage
1 can (8-3/4 oz) shirataki, drained (optional)
3/4 cup shoyu or soy sauce
2 tablespoons sugar
2 beef-bouillon cubes, dissolved in 1-1/2 cups
    boiling water
1 teaspoon monosodium glutamate
1/4 lb beef suet or shortening
Cooked white rice
* Have meatman slice on meat slicer.

1. Cut beef into 2-inch strips.
2. Prepare vegetables: Peel onions, and slice very thin. Diagonally slice green onions and tops into 1-inch pieces. Slice mushrooms and bamboo shoots 1/4 inch thick. Cut spinach in 1-inch strips. Shred cabbage.
3. Arrange all these ingredients and the shirataki attractively on a large serving platter.
4. In small saucepan, combine shoyu, sugar, bouillon, and monosodium glutamate; heat, stirring, until sugar is dissolved.
5. Preheat electric skillet to 350F. Fry suet in skillet to lubricate pan; remove.
6. Add onion and green onion slices, sauté, stirring occasionally, until golden. Add remaining vegetables and shirataki.
7. Cover with beef strips, overlapping if necessary. Pour on sauce mixture; simmer, uncovered, 10 minutes.
8. Turn meat; simmer just until vegetables are tender—about 5 minutes.
9. Serve at once, with hot rice.
Makes 6 servings.

Mexican

Hot, spicy food, along with sunshine and siestas, will always be one of Mexico's great attractions. Our south-of-the-Border recipes are not fiery, but of pleasant warmth. Frank adaptations, they nevertheless capture the gay, sunny essence of Mexican cookery.

Tortillas

1-2/3 cups masa harina (see Note)
1/3 cup unsifted all-purpose flour
3/4 teaspoon salt

1. In large bowl, combine masa, flour, and salt.
2. Add 1 cup water, stirring until mixture is completely moistened. Add more water if necessary. Form into a ball.
3. On lightly floured surface, knead or work dough with hands until it is no longer sticky—about 5 minutes. Divide into 12 equal balls. Let balls of dough rest 20 minutes at room temperature.
4. On floured surface, roll out each ball into a 6-inch circle. With paring knife, using a 6-inch saucer as a guide, trim evenly.
5. On a heated, ungreased griddle, bake the tortillas for 1 minute; then turn, and bake 1 minute longer.
Makes 12.
Note: Special corn flour for making tortillas and Mexican dishes; available in Spanish specialty stores.

Eggs Ranchero

Sauce:
2 tablespoons salad or olive oil
1 cup finely chopped green pepper
1/4 cup finely chopped onion
1 cup chili sauce
1 can (8 oz) tomato sauce with tomato pieces
2 tablespoons lemon juice
1 teaspoon Worcestershire sauce
1/4 teaspoon chili powder

Salad oil
6 tortillas
2 tablespoons butter or margarine
6 eggs
1/4 cup grated sharp Cheddar cheese

1. Make Sauce: In 2 tablespoons hot oil in medium saucepan, sauté green pepper and onion just until tender. Add chili sauce, tomato sauce, lemon juice, Worcestershire, and chili powder. Bring to boiling; reduce heat, and simmer, covered and stirring occasionally, 15 minutes.
2. Meanwhile, heat 1/2 inch salad oil in small skillet until very hot. Fry tortillas, one at a time, 15 seconds on each side. Do not let them become crisp. Drain on paper towels. Place the tortillas in a single layer in heated shallow serving dish.
3. In hot butter in large skillet, fry eggs to desired doneness—3 to 4 minutes.
4. To serve: Top each tortilla with a little sauce, then with a fried egg. Spoon remaining sauce around eggs; sprinkle with cheese. If desired, garnish with thin slices of green pepper. Serve immediately.
Makes 6 servings.

Chiles Rellenos

1/4 lb Monterey Jack or process Swiss cheese,
  cut into strips
2 cans (4-oz size) green chiles, drained
3 eggs, separated
3 tablespoons flour

Salad oil or shortening for deep-frying
Flour

Sauce:
1 can (1 lb) stewed tomatoes
2 tablespoons finely chopped onion
1 chicken-bouillon cube
1/2 teaspoon salt
1/4 teaspoon dried oregano leaves
Dash pepper

1/4 cup grated sharp Ceddar cheese

1. Insert a strip of cheese in each chile.
2. In medium bowl, beat egg whites until they form soft peaks. In small bowl, beat egg yolks slightly. Gently fold into egg whites. Add 3 tablespoons flour, and fold just until blended.
3. In electric skillet or heavy saucepan, slowly heat 1-1/2 to 2 inches salad oil to 400F on deep-frying thermometer.
4. Roll the cheese-stuffed chiles in flour. With large, slotted spoon, dip chiles in batter, coating generously. Gently place in hot oil, 2 at a time, and fry until golden on both sides—3 to 4 minutes.
5. Preheat oven to 350F.
6. Make Sauce: In medium saucepan, combine tomatoes, onion, bouillon cube, salt, oregano, and pepper; simmer, stirring sauce occasionally, 10 minutes.
7. Place chiles in shallow baking dish. Spoon sauce over top. Sprinkle with Cheddar cheese.
8. Bake, uncovered, 20 minutes, or until heated through and cheese is melted.
Makes 6 servings.

Beef Tacos with Green-Chile Salsa

Filling:
1 lb ground beef chuck
1 medium onion, chopped
1 clove garlic, crushed
2 tablespoons soy sauce
1 tablespoon Worcestershire sauce
1 can (8 oz) tomato sauce

Salad oil for deep-frying
1 can (11 oz) tortillas
1 medium tomato, coarsely chopped (1 cup)
1 cup shredded lettuce
1 cup grated Monterey Jack or sharp Cheddar
  cheese
Green-Chile Salsa, below

1. Make Filling: In hot skillet, sauté chuck with onion until meat loses red color. Add garlic, soy sauce, Worcestershire, and tomato sauce; simmer about 10 minutes. Keep warm.
2. In heavy saucepan, slowly heat salad oil (at least 3 inches) to 420F on deep-frying thermometer.
3. Use 1 dozen tortillas from can. Gently drop a tortilla into hot oil; when it rises to top, grasp it with two tongs, and bend it into a U shape. Hold in oil until crisp—about 2 minutes. Remove, and drain on paper towels. Continue until the 1 dozen tortillas are used, frying one at a time.
4. Preheat oven to 400F.
5. In each tortilla, arrange, in order, a layer of filling, a little chopped tomato, a small mound of shredded lettuce, and some grated cheese. Place in shallow baking dish.
6. Bake, uncovered, 10 minutes, or just until cheese melts. Serve with Green-Chile Salsa.
Makes 6 servings.

Green-Chile Salsa

1-1/2 cups peeled and chopped tomato
1 cup chopped Bermuda onion
2 canned green chiles, chopped
2 cloves garlic, crushed
1/2 teaspoon salt
1/2 teaspoon monosodium glutamate

1. In medium bowl, combine all ingredients; mix well.
2. Let stand about 15 minutes, to develop flavor, before serving.
Makes about 2-1/2 cups.

Refried Beans

1 pkg (1 lb) dried pinto beans
6 slices bacon
1/4 cup finely chopped onion
1/4 cup finely chopped green pepper
1 clove garlic, crushed
2 teaspoons salt
1 teaspoon chili powder

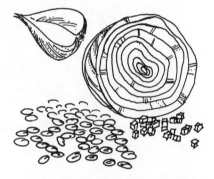

1. Wash beans. Turn into large bowl; cover with 6 cups cold water. Refrigerate, covered, overnight.
2. Next day, turn beans and liquid into a large saucepan. Bring to boiling; reduce heat, and simmer, covered, about 1-1/2 hours, or until tender. Drain beans, reserving liquid. Add water to liquid, if necessary, to make 1 cup.
3. In large skillet, sauté bacon until crisp. Drain on paper towels, and crumble.
4. In bacon drippings in skillet, sauté onion, green pepper, and garlic until tender—about 5 minutes.
5. With wooden spoon, stir in beans, bacon, salt, and chili powder. Cook over medium heat, stirring in reserved bean liquid a little at a time and mashing beans until all are mashed and mixture is creamy.
6. Turn into serving dish. If desired, sprinkle with chopped green pepper, crisp bacon bits, or strips of cheese.
Makes 6 to 8 servings.

Mexican Hot Chocolate

1/4 cup unsweetened cocoa
1/4 cup sugar
3/4 teaspoon cinnamon
Dash salt
1 quart milk
1/4 cup light cream
3/4 teaspoon vanilla extract

1. In small bowl, combine cocoa, sugar, cinnamon, and salt; mix well.
2. In medium saucepan, heat 1 cup milk until bubbling. Stir in cocoa mixture; beat with wire whisk or rotary beater until smooth.
3. Over low heat, bring to boiling, stirring. Gradually stir in rest of milk; return to boiling.
4. Stir in cream and vanilla; heat gently.
5. Before serving, beat with rotary beater until frothy.
Makes 6 servings.

Chili and Enchiladas

Chili con Carne:
2 tablespoons salad oil
1 cup chopped onion
3 lb ground beef chuck
2 pkg chili-seasoning mix (use enough to season 2 lb meat)
1 can (1 lb, 12 oz) tomatoes
1 cup red wine
2 cans (1-lb size) red kidney beans

Enchiladas:
1 pkg (9 oz) frozen tortillas (1 dozen)
3 cups grated Cheddar cheese (3/4 lb)
1 cup chopped onion

1 can (15 oz) tomato sauce with tomato bits
2 tablespoons chopped green chiles

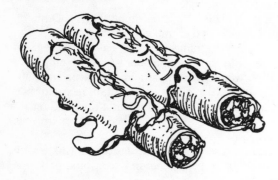

1. Make Chili con Carne: In hot oil in large skillet, sauté 1 cup chopped onion until golden—about 5 minutes. Remove to small bowl.
2. In same skillet, over high heat, cook meat, stirring occasionally, until browned—about 15 minutes.
3. Stir in sautéed onion, chili-seasoning mix, and tomatoes. Bring to boiling; reduce heat; simmer, covered and stirring occasionally, 45 minutes. Add wine; simmer, uncovered, 20 minutes longer, or until mixture is slightly thickened.
4. Spoon into 4-quart, shallow, ovenproof serving dish. Stir in undrained kidney beans.
5. Make Enchiladas: Heat tortillas as the label directs. Preheat oven to 350F.
6. In medium bowl, combine 2 cups grated cheese and the onion. Place a rounded tablespoon cheese mixture on each tortilla. Roll up. Arrange, seam side down, on chili in serving dish.
7. Combine tomato sauce and chopped green chiles; spoon over tortillas. Sprinkle with remaining cheese.
8. Bake 30 to 35 minutes, or until sauce bubbles and cheese melts.
Makes 8 servings.
Note: Chili con Carne may be made early in the day through Step 4, and refrigerated. Remove from refrigerator while preheating oven, and continue with Step 5.

Brandied Caramel Flan

3/4 cup sugar

Custard:
2 cups milk
2 cups light cream
6 eggs
1/2 cup sugar
1/2 teaspoon salt
2 teaspoons vanilla extract
1/3 cup brandy
Boiling water

1 tablespoon brandy

1. Place 3/4 cup sugar in a large, heavy skillet. Cook, over medium heat, until sugar melts and forms a light-brown syrup; stir to blend.
2. Immediately pour syrup into a heated 8-1/4-inch round, shallow baking dish; holding dish with pot holders, quickly rotate, to cover bottom and side completely. Set aside.
3. Preheat oven to 325F.
4. Make Custard: In medium saucepan, heat milk and cream just until bubbles form around edge of pan.
5. In large bowl, with rotary beater, beat eggs slightly. Add sugar, salt, and vanilla. Gradually stir in hot milk mixture and 1/3 cup brandy. Pour into prepared dish.

6. Set dish in shallow pan; pour boiling water to 1/2-inch level around dish.

7. Bake 35 to 40 minutes, or until silver knife inserted in center comes out clean. Let custard cool; refrigerate 4 hours or overnight.

8. To serve: Run small spatula around edge of dish, to loosen. Invert on shallow serving dish; shake gently to release. The caramel acts as sauce. Warm 1 tablespoon brandy slightly; ignite and quickly pour over flan.

Makes 8 servings.

Mexican Cinnamon Cookies

1 cup butter or regular margarine, softened
1/2 cup confectioners' sugar
2-1/4 cups sifted all-purpose flour
1 teaspoon cinnamon
1 teaspoon vanilla extract
1/4 teaspoon salt
1/2 cup granulated sugar or 3/4 cup confectioners' sugar
1/2 teaspoon cinnamon

1. In large bowl, with electric mixer at high speed, beat butter until light and fluffy.

2. At low speed, beat in 1/2 cup confectioners' sugar, the flour, 1 teaspoon cinnamon, the vanilla, and salt just until combined—dough will be rather stiff.

3. Shape into a ball; wrap in waxed paper. Refrigerate 30 minutes.

4. Preheat oven to 400F.

5. To make ball cookies, roll dough into 3/4 inch balls. To make flat cookies, roll in 1-inch balls; flatten with fingers to about 1/4-inch thickness. Place 1-1/2 inches apart on ungreased cookie sheets.

6. Bake 10 minutes, or until a delicate golden-brown.

7. Combine sugar and cinnamon. Roll hot cookies in this mixture. Place on wire rack to cool; sprinkle with any remaining cinnamon-sugar.

Makes about 5 dozen ball cookies or 3 dozen flat cookies.

Margaritas

1/2 cup lemon juice
Coarse salt
1 cup plus 2 tablespoons tequila
1/3 cup Cointreau
1/4 cup superfine sugar
2 cups cracked ice

1. Before squeezing lemons for juice, twirl rims of 8 cocktail glasses on cut lemon surface. Then dip rims of glasses in salt. Refrigerate glasses about 1 hour.

2. Combine lemon juice, tequila, Cointreau, sugar, and ice in electric blender; cover, and blend at high speed 1/2 minute.

3. Pour into chilled glasses.

Makes 8 servings.

Note: Or use a margarita-cocktail mix. Some have all the necessary ingredients and are ready for serving. Others just require the tequila.

Spanish

The food of Spain—gentle, well seasoned and tasty—does not burn the tongue. It takes its character, better savored than described, from the lemon, olives, garlic, herbs and other natural seasonings.

Cream-of-Chicken Soup

3 egg yolks
1 can (12-1/2 oz) chicken consommé, undiluted
1-1/4 cups heavy cream
1 teaspoon salt
1/4 teaspoon pepper
3 tablespoons dry sherry
1 tablespoon coarsely chopped watercress

1. In top of double boiler, combine egg yolks and chicken consommé; mix well.
2. Cook, over hot water and stirring constantly, until mixture thickens and forms coating on metal spoon—about 10 minutes.
3. Remove from heat. Stir in cream, salt, and pepper.
4. Cook, over hot water and stirring occasionally, about 5 minutes, or until very hot. Stir in sherry.
5. Serve at once. Garnish each serving with a little watercress.
Makes 3 cups—4 servings.

Paella

Rice with Clams and Shrimp

1 dozen small clams, in shell
2 lb shrimp, shelled and deveined
4 tablespoons olive or salad oil
1 tablespoon butter or margarine
1 cup raw long-grain white rice
1 teaspoon salt
1 bay leaf
1 chicken-bouillon cube
2 cloves garlic, finely chopped
2 medium onions, peeled and finely chopped
2 green peppers, seeded and finely chopped
2 large tomatoes, peeled
1/2 cup pimiento-stuffed olives, sliced
2 teaspoons paprika
1/8 teaspoon cayenne
1-1/2 cups grated Cheddar cheese (6 oz)

1. Wash clams and shrimp thoroughly. Place clams in saucepan with 6 cups water; bring to boiling. Add shrimp; cook over high heat, covered, 5 minutes. Remove from heat.
2. Pour off enough shellfish liquid to make 2-1/4 cups. Set aside clams and shrimp, in remaining broth; keep warm.
3. Heat 2 tablespoons olive oil and the butter in 3-quart saucepan. Add rice, and stir to coat well. Add reserved 2-1/4 cups liquid, the salt, bay leaf, and bouillon cube. Bring to boiling; lower heat, and simmer, covered and without stirring, 25 minutes.
4. Preheat oven to 375F. Meanwhile, in 2 tablespoons hot oil in 6-quart Dutch oven, sauté garlic, onion, and green pepper until green pepper is tender—about 10 minutes.
5. Chop tomatoes. Add to sautéed vegetables with olives, paprika, and cayenne; cook 5 minutes longer. Keep warm.
6. Drain shellfish, and add with rice to tomato mixture; stir gently to blend. Turn into paella pan or shallow 4-quart casserole.
7. Sprinkle cheese over top of all. Bake 10 to 15 minutes, or until cheese is melted and bubbly.
Makes 6 to 8 servings.

Arroz con Pollo

3-lb broiler-fryer, cut in 8 pieces
1/2 cup olive oil
2 cups chopped onion
1 clove garlic, crushed
1/2 teaspoon crushed red pepper
2-1/2 teaspoons salt
1/2 teaspoon pepper
2 cups raw converted white rice
1/4 teaspoon saffron threads
1 can (1 lb, 12 oz) tomatoes, undrained
1 canned green chile pepper, chopped
1 can (10-1/2-oz) condensed chicken broth,
    undiluted
1/2 pkg (10-oz size) frozen peas
1/2 cup pimiento-stuffed green olives, sliced
1 can (4-oz) pimientos, drained and sliced

1. Wipe chicken pieces with damp paper towels.
2. In heavy, 6-quart Dutch oven, heat olive oil. Brown chicken, a few pieces at a time, until golden-brown all over. Remove chicken as it browns.
3. Preheat oven to 325F.
4. Add chopped onion, garlic, and red pepper to Dutch oven; sauté, stirring, over medium heat until golden—about 3 minutes.
5. Add salt, pepper, rice, and saffron to Dutch oven; cook, stirring, until rice is lightly browned— 10 minutes.
6. Add tomatoes, chile pepper, and chicken broth to rice mixture. Add chicken pieces. Bring just to boiling.
7. Bake, covered, 1 hour.
8. Add 1/2 cup water. Sprinkle peas, olives and pimiento strips over top; do not stir. Bake, covered, 20 minutes longer, or until chicken is tender and peas are cooked.
9. Serve hot right from Dutch oven.
Makes 6 servings.

Spanish Doughnuts

Churros

4 tablespoons butter or margarine, cut into small
    pieces
1/8 teaspoon salt
1-1/4 cups sifted all-purpose flour
3 eggs
1/4 teaspoon vanilla extract
Salad oil for deep-frying
1/2 teaspoon cinnamon
1/2 cup sugar

1. In medium saucepan, combine butter with 1/2 cup water; cook over low heat, stirring, until butter is melted and mixture just comes to boil. Add salt, and remove from heat.
2. Add flour all at once; beat very hard with wooden spoon. Return to low heat, and beat until very smooth—about 2 minutes.
3. Remove from heat; let cool slightly. Beat in eggs, one at a time, beating well after each addition. Add vanilla. Continue beating until mixture has satinlike sheen.
4. Meanwhile, in deep skillet or deep-fat fryer, slowly heat oil (at least 1-1/2 inches) to 380F on deep-frying thermometer.
5. Press doughnut mixture through a large pastry bag with a large, fluted tip, 1/2 inch wide. With wet scissors, cut batter into 2-inch lengths as it drops into hot oil.
6. Deep-fry, a few at a time, 2 minutes on a side, or until golden-brown. Lift out with slotted spoon; drain well on paper towels.
7. Combine cinnamon and sugar in medium bowl. Add drained doughnuts, and toss to coat well. Serve warm.
Makes about 2-1/2 dozen.

Caramel Custard Flan

1-1/4 cups sugar
4 eggs
1 can (14-1/2 oz) evaporated milk, undiluted
1 teaspoon vanilla extract
Whole blanched almonds
Whipped cream

1. Preheat oven to 350F.
2. Spread 1/2 cup sugar evenly over bottom of an 8-inch round baking dish. Heat in oven 30 to 35 minutes, or until sugar is melted to a golden-brown syrup.
3. Remove from oven; let cool 10 minutes, or until hardened.
4. Meanwhile, in medium bowl, with rotary beater, beat eggs well. Add 3/4 cup sugar, the evaporated milk, 1-1/2 cups water, and the vanilla; stir until sugar is dissolved.
5. Pour into prepared baking dish. Place in shallow pan; pour hot water to 1-inch level around dish.
6. Bake 1 hour, or until silver knife inserted in center of custard comes out clean. Cool; then refrigerate until well chilled.
7. To serve: Run small spatula around edge of dish to loosen. Invert onto shallow serving dish. Decorate with almonds and whipped cream.
Makes 6 servings.

Scandinavian

Though the Scandinavian countries each have their own individual cuisines, they serve many dishes in common. The smorgasbord, a stunning array of delicacies that can precede a meal or serve as one; the colorful open sandwiches, the unique breads and the delicious, flaky pastries are found everywhere with slight national variations. Here, a sampling of our favorite recipes.

Yellow-Pea Soup with Pork

1 lb quick-cooking dried split yellow peas, washed (2-1/4 cups)
1 bay leaf
2-1/2-lb pork shoulder, bone in
1 cup finely chopped onion
3 teaspoons salt
1 teaspoon dried marjoram leaves
1/2 teaspoon ginger
1/4 teaspoon dried thyme leaves
1/4 teaspoon pepper
Lemon slices

1. In deep, 8-quart kettle, combine peas, bay leaf, and 2 quarts water; bring to boiling. Reduce heat, and simmer, covered and stirring occasionally, 1 hour.
2. Add pork shoulder, onion, salt, marjoram, ginger, thyme, and pepper; bring to boiling. Reduce heat, and simmer, covered and stirring occasionally, 2 hours, or until pork is tender. (If soup seems too thick, stir in a little water—about 1/2 cup.)
3. Turn into soup tureen, and garnish with lemon slices.
4. When serving, lift pork out of soup. Cut into slices. Serve with mustard and dark bread.
Makes about 2 quarts; 6 to 8 servings.
Note: Flavor is improved if soup is made one day, refrigerated, then reheated and served next day.

Glögg

2 cups claret
2 cups dry sherry
1/2 cup cognac
2/3 cup sugar
1/3 cup light raisins
1/3 cup blanched whole almonds
10 whole cloves
2 (3-inch) cinnamon sticks

1. In large saucepan, combine all ingredients. Heat over medium heat, stirring, just until vapor starts to rise.
2. Ignite with a match; stir until sugar is dissolved. Heat 10 minutes, stirring occasionally.
3. Ladle immediately into punch cups, spooning some of the raisins and almonds into each cup. Makes 8 servings.

Stuffed Eggs

6 hard-cooked eggs
4 oz smoked salmon, finely chopped (1/2 cup)
1/4 cup mayonnaise or cooked salad dressing
1 tablespoon chopped parsley
2 teaspoons prepared mustard
1/4 teaspoon salt
Dash pepper
Black olives, drained
Pimiento, drained

1. Halve eggs lengthwise. Remove yolks to a small bowl. Reserve whites.
2. Mash yolks with fork. Add salmon, mayonnaise, parsley, mustard, salt, and pepper; mix well.
3. Fill each white with yolk mixture, mounding it high. Garnish with crescent-shape pieces of olive and bits of pimiento.
4. Refrigerate, covered, at least 1 hour before serving.
Makes 12.

Swedish-Style Brown Beans

2 cups dried Swedish brown beans
2 teaspoons salt
3/4 cup cider vinegar
3/4 cup dark corn syrup
1/4 cup light-brown sugar, firmly packed

1. Wash beans; turn into 3-quart saucepan with 6 cups water. Refrigerate, covered, overnight.
2. Next day, bring to boiling. Reduce heat; simmer, covered, 1 hour.
3. Add remaining ingredients; simmer, covered, about 4 hours, or until beans are tender and mixture is thick; stir occasionally.
Makes 6 to 8 servings.

Scandinavian Cabbage

2 quarts (2 lb) coarsely shredded green cabbage
3 cups boiling water
1 cup dairy sour cream
1 teaspoon caraway seed
1-1/2 teaspoons salt
1/4 teaspoon pepper

1. Cook cabbage in boiling water, covered, 6 to 8 minutes, or until tender but still quite crisp. Drain very well.
2. In top of double boiler, toss cabbage with rest of ingredients; cook, covered, over boiling water, 15 minutes (cabbage will still be slightly crisp).
Makes 6 servings.

Norwegian Fish Balls

1 lb haddock
2 egg whites, beaten
1 cup heavy cream
1 teaspoon cornstarch
Salt
1/8 teaspoon nutmeg
1 bay leaf
2 lemon slices

1. Remove skin and bones from fish. Wash and dry on paper towels.
2. Cut fish into chunks; put through food grinder using fine blade, twice.
3. Beat egg whites until they form soft peaks; fold into fish. Put through grinder again; turn into medium bowl.
4. In small bowl combine cream, cornstarch, 1 teaspoon salt and the nutmeg; mix well. Gradually add to fish mixture, beating with electric or rotary beater. Shape into 1-1/2-inch balls.
5. Meanwhile in a large skillet, place water (1-1/2-inch depth), 1 teaspoon salt, the bay leaf and lemon; bring to boiling.
6. Gently drop fish balls, eight at a time, into boiling water; simmer, uncovered, 10 minutes or until firm. Remove with slotted spoon to serving dish. Keep hot. Serve with a savory parsley, tomato, or Hollandaise sauce.
Makes 6 servings.

Waffles

2 cups sifted all-purpose flour
1/2 teaspoon baking soda
1/2 teaspoon salt
4 eggs
1/4 cup sugar
2 cups dairy sour cream

1. Preheat waffle iron. Sift flour with baking soda and salt.
2. In medium bowl, with portable electric or rotary beater, beat eggs and sugar until thick and lemon colored.
3. Fold in flour (in thirds) alternately with sour cream (in halves) mixing just until blended.
4. For each waffle, pour about 1 cup batter in middle of lower half of waffle iron.
5. Lower cover on batter; cook as manufacturer directs or until waffle iron stops steaming. Do not raise cover during baking.
6. Carefully loosen edge of waffle with fork; remove. Serve hot with fresh berries and ice cream.
Makes 4 large waffles.

Jams, Jellies & Preserves

Preserved Perfection

There is such a wide variety of all kinds of jams, jellies, preserves and relishes available on the market that we have limited our recipes to very special ones. These are no simple fruit preserves to be spread on breakfast toast. No, indeed. Nor are our relishes run-of-the-mill. All are destined to become proud recipes of the house, to serve at special occasions and to give as special gifts.

Directions for Sterilizing Glasses and Jars

Examine tops and edges of glasses and jars. Wash glasses, jars, lids and caps in hot, soapy water. Rinse in scalding water. Invert on rubber tray or towels to drain. Keep out of draft.

If making jelly without added pectin, leave glasses in boiling water until jelly has cooked about 5 to 10 minutes. Remove glasses from hot water using tongs. Invert on rubber tray or towels to drain. Keep out of draft. If making jelly with pectin, remove glasses from boiling water just before putting jelly on to cook. Invert on rubber tray or towels to drain. Keep out of draft.

Test for Jellying Point

Dip a large metal spoon into boiling syrup; tilt spoon so syrup runs off edge. Syrup is at jellying point when it doesn't flow, but divides into two drops that run together and sheet from the spoon.

Apricot-Sherry Jelly

3-1/2 cups sugar
1 cup apricot nectar
1 cup dry sherry
1/2 bottle (6-oz size) liquid fruit pectin

1. Sterilize 6 medium jelly glasses (see Directions for Sterilizing).
2. Measure sugar into top part of double boiler. Add apricot nectar and sherry; mix well. Place over rapidly boiling water; stir to dissolve sugar. Remove from heat; stir in pectin.
3. With metal spoon, skim foam from surface. Pour quickly into sterilized glasses.
4. Cover jelly at once with 1/8 inch hot paraffin. Makes 6 glasses.

Port-Wine Festival Jelly

2 cups port wine
3 cups sugar
1/8 teaspoon cinnamon
1/8 teaspoon cloves
1/2 bottle (6-oz size) liquid fruit pectin

1. Sterilize 4 (8-oz) jelly glasses (see Directions for Sterilizing); leave in hot water until ready to fill.
2. In top of double boiler, combine port, sugar, cinnamon, and cloves. Place over rapidly boiling water; heat 2 minutes, stirring constantly.
3. Then, over direct heat, bring to a full, rolling boil. Stir in pectin.
4. Again bring to a full, rolling boil; boil 1 minute—stir constantly.

5. Remove pan from heat. Skim off any foam from liquid.

6. Ladle jelly into hot, sterilized jelly glasses. Immediately cover with 1/8 inch hot paraffin.

7. Let cool; then cover with lid. Looks beautiful on a buffet table.

Fills about 4 (8-oz) jelly glasses.

Tropical Jam

3 pt boxes fresh strawberries
1 can (1 lb, 4 oz) crushed pineapple, drained
2 tablespoons lemon juice
7-1/2 cups sugar
1 bottle (6 oz) liquid fruit pectin

1. Sterilize 10 (6-oz) jelly glasses (see Directions for Sterilizing); keep in hot water until ready to fill.

2. Wash berries gently in cold water. Drain; hull. In large bowl, with potato masher, crush berries. Measure 3-2/3 cups.

3. In large kettle, combine berries, pineapple, lemon juice, and sugar; stir to combine well. Place over high heat; stirring constantly, bring to a full rolling boil. Boil hard for 1 minute.

4. Remove from heat. Stir in pectin. With metal spoon, stir and skim 5 minutes, to cool slightly and prevent fruit's floating.

5. Ladle quickly into hot, sterilized jelly glasses. Top with 1/8 inch hot paraffin. Cool.

Makes 10 (6-oz) jelly glasses.

Tarragon-Wine Jelly

1 cup fresh tarragon leaves, packed
1/2 bay leaf
1 cup boiling water
1-1/2 cups dry white wine
4 cups sugar
1 bottle (6 oz) liquid fruit pectin
1 drop green food color
2 drops yellow food color
5 fresh tarragon sprigs

1. Sterilize 5 (6-oz) jelly glasses with lids and 5 forks (see Directions for Sterilizing).

2. Wash and dry tarragon leaves; chop finely. Turn into small bowl with bay leaf. Add boiling water. Let stand, covered, 5 minutes.

3. In 3-quart saucepan, combine tarragon mixture, wine (we used American Sauterne), and sugar. Heat, stirring until sugar is dissolved. Bring mixture to a rolling boil; stir in liquid pectin; boil 1 minute, stirring constantly. Add food color.

4. Pour through strainer lined with eight thicknesses of cheesecloth and suspended over a bowl.

5. In bottom of each hot jelly glass, place a sprig of tarragon. Hold in place with sterilized forks. Pour hot jelly into hot glasses.

6. Let jelly stand 10 minutes; then carefully remove forks; do not dislodge tarragon sprigs.

7. Cover jelly at once with 1/8 inch hot paraffin. Store in refrigerator to make jelly firm. Serve very cold with meats.

Makes 5 glasses.

Rhubarb Jelly

3 lb rhubarb
3 lb sugar (about 7 cups)
1 bottle (6 oz) liquid pectin

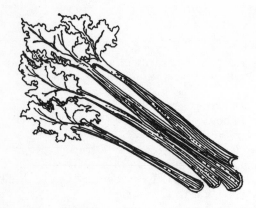

1. Sterilize 11 (8-oz) jelly glasses with lids (see Directions for Sterilizing).
2. Wash rhubarb; slice crosswise, 1/4 inch thick.
3. Measure 6 cups; turn into medium saucepan. Add 1 cup water; bring to boiling; reduce heat, and simmer 10 minutes, stirring once or twice.
4. Place 36-inch square of cheesecloth (in 4 thicknesses) in a colander in a large bowl. Pour rhubarb into cheesecloth, twisting corners together; press with potato masher to extract all liquid. Juice should measure 4 cups.
5. Pour juice into large saucepan (at least 6-quart); add sugar. Over high heat, bring to full rolling boil. Add pectin. Continue boiling hard, stirring constantly, 1 minute.
6. Remove from heat. Using a large metal spoon, quickly skim foam from surface.
7. Pour into prepared glasses. Immediately cover with a thin layer (1/8 inch) paraffin. Cool; then cover. Jelly should be firm in 3 to 4 hours, a shorter time if refrigerated.
Makes 11 (8-oz) glasses.

Crème-de-Menthe and Crème-de-Cassis Jelly

4 lb tart apples
Sugar
2 tablespoons green crème de menthe
2 tablespoons lemon juice
4 drops red food color
2 tablespoons crème de cassis

1. Wash apples; cut into quarters. Do not pare or core.
2. Place in large saucepan or kettle; add 4 cups water. Bring to boiling; cover; reduce heat, and cook gently 25 minutes.
3. Line a large colander with 3 thicknesses of cheesecloth; set over a large bowl or kettle.
4. Turn apple and liquid into prepared colander. Cover loosely with foil. Let drain 12 hours or overnight. Do not press apple pulp. (You should have 4-2/3 cups juice.)
5. Next day, sterilize 6 jelly glasses and lids (see Directions for Sterilizing). Leave in hot water until ready to fill. Lift out with tongs.
6. In medium saucepan, combine 2 cups apple juice and 1-1/2 cups sugar.
7. Heat to boiling, stirring constantly until sugar dissolves. Cook over medium heat, without stirring, about 20 minutes, or until candy thermometer registers 220F.
8. Remove from heat. Quickly stir in crème de menthe.

9. Pour immediately into hot, sterilized glasses. Let stand until set—about 15 minutes. Then carefully float 1/8 inch hot paraffin on top. Let cool completely. Cover with lids.

10. Repeat, using 2 cups apple juice, 1-1/2 cups sugar, the lemon juice, food color, and crème de cassis.

Makes about 3-1/2 cups; enough to fill 6 jelly glasses.

Spiced Pear Butter

12 fresh pears (about 6 lb)
1/4 cup cider vinegar
4 cups sugar
1/2 cup orange juice
1/4 cup lemon juice
1-1/2 teaspoons whole allspice, tied in a cheesecloth bag

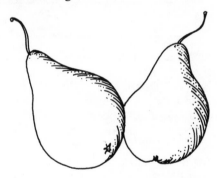

1. Pare and core pears; cut into 1-inch cubes, to make 3 quarts. Place in 5-quart kettle with vinegar and 1/4 cup water; cook, covered, until soft—about 30 minutes.

2. Mash with potato masher, or put through food mill. Measure pulp—there should be about 7 cups. Return to kettle.

3. Add sugar, orange juice, lemon juice, and allspice; cook over medium heat, stirring frequently, until mixture is very thick—about 60 minutes. Remove allspice.

4. Meanwhile, sterilize 6 or 7 (8-oz) jelly glasses (see Directions for Sterilizing). Leave in hot water until ready to fill. Lift out with tongs.

5. Ladle pear butter into hot, sterilized jars, filling to within 1/2 inch of top. Cover immediately with about 1/8 inch hot paraffin; cool. Cover with metal lids.

Makes 6 or 7 (8-oz) glasses.

La Velle's Plum Chutney

5 lb unpeeled purple plums, halved and pitted
2 lb yellow onions, coarsely chopped
4 lb McIntosh apples, peeled, cored, coarsely chopped
3 cups white vinegar
2 lb granulated sugar
2 lb dark-brown sugar
1 tablespoon allspice
1 tablespoon cloves
1 tablespoon ginger
3 tablespoons salt
1 teaspoon cayenne

1. In very large kettle, combine plums, onions, apples, and vinegar; bring to boiling point. Stir in remaining ingredients.

2. Again bring to boiling point. Reduce heat; simmer, uncovered, 1-1/2 hours. Stir occasionally, to prevent scorching.

3. Meanwhile, sterilize 10 pint jars (see Directions for Sterilizing); keep in hot water until ready to fill.

4. Ladle into hot, sterilized jars. Cap immediately as manufacturer directs.

Makes about 10 pints.

Cranberry Conserve

4 cups fresh cranberries (1 lb)
3 cups sugar
1 medium orange, peeled and finely chopped
   (1 cup)
1/2 cup coarsely chopped walnuts or pecans
1/3 cup seeded raisins

1. Wash cranberries, removing stems. Turn into 3-1/2-quart saucepan; add 3/4 cup water. Simmer, covered, until skins pop— 6 to 8 minutes.
2. Press cranberries and liquid through food mill or coarse sieve. Turn into 6-quart kettle; add sugar, orange, nuts, raisins, and 3/4 cup water.
3. Bring to boiling, stirring constantly until sugar is dissolved. Boil gently, uncovered, 30 minutes, or until thickened.
4. Meanwhile, sterilize 5 or 6 (8-oz) jars (see Directions for Sterilizing); keep in hot water until ready to fill.
5. Immediately ladle conserve into hot, sterilized jars. Cover at once with 1/8 inch hot paraffin. Let cool; cover with lids.
Makes 5 or 6 (8-oz) jars.

Tomato Marmalade

2-1/2 lb ripe tomatoes (about 6)
1 lemon, thinly sliced
1/2 teaspoon ground ginger
2 lb sugar

1. Sterilize 5 half-pint jars (see Directions for Sterilizing).
2. Peel tomatoes; chop coarsely. Place in 3-quart saucepan; add lemon and ginger. Bring to boiling; reduce heat, and simmer, uncovered, 1 hour.
3. Stir in sugar; boil, uncovered and stirring frequently, until thick—25 to 30 minutes, or until candy thermometer registers 221F.
4. Ladle marmalade into hot jars. Immediately cover with 1/8 inch hot paraffin.
Makes 5 half pints.

Rumtopf

1 can (1 lb, 14 oz) whole, peeled apricots,
   drained
1 can (1 lb, 13-1/2 oz) sliced pineapple, drained
1 can (1 lb, 14 oz) peach halves, drained
2 cans (1-lb, 14-oz size) Bartlett pears, drained
1 container (16 oz) frozen whole strawberries,
   thawed and drained
2 cups sugar
4/5 quart light rum

1. Cut apricots in half; remove pits. Cut pineapple slices into 1-inch pieces. Cut peach and pear halves in half.
2. In large container, layer fruits, topping with strawberries. Add sugar and rum. Stir to mix. Cover with plastic film.
3. Let stand in a cool, dark place about 1 week; then store in refrigerator to mellow.
4. Store a month or two. Serve, well chilled, as a deluxe fruit compote or as a sauce over ice cream or sherbet.
Makes 3-1/2 quarts.

A Harvest of Pickles and Relishes

For a harvest of Pickles and Relishes, gather the last of the cucumbers, the corn, the tomatoes; pickle them or spice them for a crop of crunchy, old-fashioned delicacies like crisp Icicle Pickles; Dilled Whole Carrots, Coleslaw-Stuffed Peppers; chunky Pickled Corn on the Cob; Zucchini Bread-and-Butter Pickles; and others just as good, just as easy.

Rules for Making Pickles and Relishes

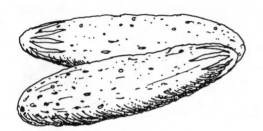

1. Use fresh vegetables as soon as possible after they are picked.
2. Use vegetables free of blemishes. Sort for size. Immature vegetables are best.
3. Wash vegetables very thoroughly, being sure to remove blossoms.
4. Use fresh, whole spices for best flavor and color. Iodized salt may cause cloudiness and darkening.
5. Use the right equipment: an aluminum or stainless-steel kettle, large enough to keep food from boiling over.
6. Since types of lid and closure vary, be sure to follow manufacturer's directions for sterilizing and sealing.
7. Fill and seal one jar at a time. Make certain that the liquid covers the food completely.
8. Check seals; then store jars in a cool, dry place. Discard any pickles that have a bad color or are moldy or mushy when opened. Do not taste.

Sour Green-Tomato Pickles

2-1/2 lb green tomatoes (6 medium)
2 cups white vinegar
1/4 cup salt
1 clove garlic, split in half
4 sprigs fresh tarragon, or 1 teaspoon dried
   tarragon leaves

1. Wash tomatoes; remove stems. Cut each tomato into 4 wedges.
2. Sterilize two 1-quart jars or a 2-quart jar (see Directions for Sterilizing); leave in hot water until ready to fill.
3. In medium saucepan, combine vinegar with salt and 2 cups water. Bring mixture to boiling, and boil 5 minutes.
4. Meanwhile, pack tomatoes into sterilized jars. Add garlic and tarragon. Completing one jar at a time, ladle boiling vinegar mixture over tomatoes to within 1/2 inch of top, but covering tomatoes completely. Cap at once as manufacturer directs. Makes 2 quarts.

Our Best Zucchini Bread-and-Butter Pickles

5 lb zucchini
1-1/2 lb yellow onions
1 quart cider vinegar
2 cups sugar
1/2 cup salt
2 teaspoons celery seed
2 teaspoons mustard seed
1/2 teaspoon turmeric

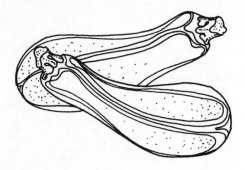

1. Scrub zucchini well with a stiff brush. Slice about 1/4 inch thick. (Makes about 4 quarts.)
2. Slice onions thinly. (Makes about 1 quart.)
3. In large kettle, combine vinegar, sugar, salt, celery seed, mustard seed, and turmeric. Cook over moderate heat, stirring, until sugar is dissolved and mixture comes to boil. Remove from heat.
4. Stir in sliced zucchini and onion. Cover; let stand 1 hour.
5. Meanwhile, sterilize seven 1-pint jars (see Directions for Sterilizing); leave in hot water until ready to fill.
6. Heat zucchini mixture to boiling. Reduce heat; simmer, uncovered, 3 minutes. Remove from heat.
7. With slotted spoon, immediately ladle zucchini and onion slices into sterilized jars, completing one jar at a time. Fill with vinegar mixture to within 1/2 inch of top, but covering mixture completely. Cap at once as manufacturer directs.
Makes 7 pints.

Mrs. Lamb's Watermelon Pickle

3 lb watermelon rind
2 teaspoons salt
3-inch cinnamon stick
2 tablespoons whole cloves
7 cups sugar
2 cups vinegar

1. Remove and discard green skin and pink flesh from rind. Cut rind in 1-inch cubes. (You should have 10 cups cubes.)
2. In kettle, combine rind, salt, and 3 quarts water; bring to boiling; boil gently, uncovered, just until tender—about 10 minutes.
3. Tie cinnamon stick and cloves in a small bag made of several thicknesses of cheesecloth.
4. In large saucepan, combine sugar, vinegar, and spice bag. Bring to boiling, stirring until sugar is dissolved; boil gently 5 minutes. Remove from heat; add, if desired, a little red or green food color.
5. Drain rind well; place in a 4-quart bowl. Pour syrup over rind; weigh down with a plate, so all pieces are covered with syrup.
6. Refrigerate overnight.
7. Next day, drain syrup into a large saucepan; bring to boiling. Pour over rind; weigh down, and refrigerate overnight.
8. On the third day, drain syrup, and bring to boiling. Place rind in 5 or 6 pint jars; cover with hot syrup. Let cool; store in refrigerator, covered. It will keep several weeks.

9. To keep longer, sterilize 6 pint jars (see Directions for Sterilizing); leave in hot water until ready to fill. Bring rind and syrup to boiling point; remove from heat. Immediately ladle into hot, sterilized jars; cover with hot syrup; cap as manufacturer directs.

Makes 5 or 6 pints.

Old-Fashioned Icicle Pickles

4 large cucumbers, about 8 inches long (2-1/2 lb)
Ice water
1 quart white vinegar
1 cup sugar
2 teaspoons salt
1 stalk celery, washed well
3 small onions, peeled
1 teaspoon mixed pickling spice

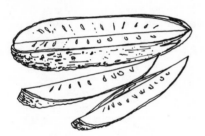

1. Wash cucumbers; do not pare. Cut lengthwise into 6 to 8 strips, depending on size of cucumbers. Place in shallow baking dish; add enough ice water to cover cucumber strips. Let stand 3 hours.
2. Sterilize a quart jar (see Directions for Sterilizing); leave in hot water until ready to fill.
3. In medium saucepan, combine vinegar with sugar and salt; cook over moderate heat, stirring, until sugar is dissolved and mixture boils.
4. Drain cucumbers. Pack into sterilized jar with celery stalk, onions, and pickling spice. Ladle boiling vinegar mixture over cucumbers to within 1/2 inch of top, but covering cucumbers completely. Cap at once as manufacturer directs.

Makes 2 quarts.

Note: If you prefer to use two 1-quart jars, use 2-1/2 lb medium-size cucumbers instead of large ones. Complete one quart at a time.

Pickled Corn on the Cob

5 or 6 medium ears of corn
1 tablespoon salt
3 cups white vinegar
1 cup sugar
1 tablespoon mixed pickling spice
2 bay leaves
1 (1-inch) cinnamon stick

1. Husk corn. Trim ends from each ear; then cut each ear into 4 pieces (about 1-1/2 inches long). Wash corn; cover with water; add salt. Refrigerate.
2. Sterilize two 1-quart jars (see Directions for Sterilizing); leave in hot water until ready to fill.
3. In large kettle, combine vinegar, sugar, pickling spice, bay leaves, and cinnamon stick. Cook over moderate heat, stirring, until sugar is dissolved and mixture comes to boiling.
4. Drain corn; rinse in cold water. Add to boiling vinegar mixture. Bring back to boiling; reduce heat, and simmer, covered, 10 minutes. Remove cinnamon stick.
5. With slotted spoon, pack corn into sterilized jars, completing one quart at a time. Fill with boiling vinegar mixture to within 1/2 inch of top, but covering corn completely. Cap at once as manufacturer directs.

Makes 2 quarts.

Coleslaw-Stuffed Peppers

6 medium red or green peppers (about 1-3/4 lb)
1 cup salt

Coleslaw:
6 cups (about 2 lb) finely shredded cabbage
1/2 cup finely chopped onion
1 teaspoon salt
1 teaspoon mustard seed

3 cups cider vinegar
1/2 cup sugar

1. Wash peppers; cut each in half lengthwise; remove ribs and seeds.
2. In large bowl, combine 1 cup salt with 2 quarts cold water; stir until salt is dissolved. Add pepper halves; cover bowl with plate to keep peppers immersed in salt water. Refrigerate overnight.
3. Next day, make Coleslaw: In medium bowl, combine cabbage with onion, 1 teaspoon salt, and the mustard seed; mix well. Cover; refrigerate.
4. Sterilize two 1-quart jars (see Directions for Sterilizing); leave in hot water until ready to fill.
5. In large saucepan, combine vinegar with sugar and 1 cup water. Cook over moderate heat, stirring, until sugar is dissolved and mixture boils; boil 5 minutes.
6. Meanwhile, drain pepper halves. Fill each with 1/2 cup coleslaw. Pack 6 pepper halves in each sterilized jar, completing one jar at a time. Immediately ladle boiling vinegar mixture over peppers to within 1/2 inch of top, but covering peppers completely. Cap at once as manufacturer directs.
7. Cool; then store in refrigerator or cool dry place.
Makes 2 quarts.

Old-Fashioned Chili Sauce

Boiling water
8 lb ripe red tomatoes
4 medium green peppers (1 lb)
4 medium sweet red peppers (1 lb)
3 cups coarsely chopped celery
3 cups coarsely chopped onion
2 cups granulated sugar
1 cup light-brown sugar, firmly packed
2 tablespoons salt
2 (3-inch) cinnamon sticks
2 hot-pepper pods, crushed
2 teaspoons whole cloves
1 tablespoon mustard seed
1 tablespoon celery seed
3 cups cider vinegar

1. Pour boiling water over tomatoes to cover; let stand several minutes. Peel; remove stems. Chop tomatoes. (They should measure about 3 quarts.)
2. Wash and drain peppers well. Halve, and remove seeds and ribs. Chop peppers coarsely.
3. In 12-quart kettle, combine chopped tomato, pepper, celery, and onion with both kinds of sugar and the salt. With long-handled wooden spoon, stir, over medium heat, until sugar is dissolved.
4. Bring to boiling; boil, uncovered, 45 minutes.
5. Tie spices in a bag (several thicknesses of cheesecloth or muslin). Add bag of spices to vegetable mixture.
6. Boil, uncovered and stirring occasionally, 30 minutes longer.
7. Add vinegar; boil 1 hour longer, or until of desired consistency.
8. Meanwhile, sterilize six 1-pint jars (see Directions for Sterilizing); leave in hot water until ready to fill.
9. Remove and discard spice bag. Completing one

jar at a time, ladle hot chili sauce into jars to within 1/2 inch of top. Cap at once as manufacturer directs.

Makes 6 pints.

Sweet Corn Relish

8 large ears of corn
Boiling water
1-1/2 lb yellow onions (4 large)
2 lb green tomatoes (5 medium)
2 lb sweet red peppers (8 medium)
1/2 cup salt
3 tablespoons mixed pickling spice
1 teaspoon celery seed
1 teaspoon mustard seed
1 quart cider vinegar
2 cups light-brown sugar, firmly packed
1 cup granulated sugar
1/2 teaspoon ground cinnamon

1. Drop corn into boiling water in large kettle; boil 3 minutes. Drain; cool. Cut corn from cob. (Makes about 1 quart.)
2. Coarsely chop onions, tomatoes, and red peppers.
3. In large bowl, combine corn, chopped vegetables, salt, and 2 quarts cold water; mix well. Cover; refrigerate overnight.
4. Next day, sterilize six 1-pint jars (see Directions for Sterilizing); leave in hot water until ready to fill.
5. Drain chilled vegetables. Tie pickling spice, celery seed, and mustard seed in bag made of cheesecloth or muslin.
6. In large kettle, combine vinegar with both kinds of sugar, cinnamon, and bag of spices; cook over moderate heat, stirring, until sugar is dissolved and mixture boils.
7. Add vegetables; return to boiling. Reduce heat; simmer, uncovered and stirring occasionally, until relish is thick—about 40 minutes. Remove and discard bag of spices.
8. Completing one jar at a time, immediately ladle into sterilized jars to within 1/2 inch of top. Cap at once as manufacturer directs.

Makes 5 or 6 pints.

Iowa Corn Relish

15 ears sweet corn, or 6 cans (12-oz size) whole-kernel corn, undrained
1 cup chopped green pepper
1 cup chopped sweet red pepper, or 2 cans (4-oz size) pimientos, drained and chopped
1-1/4 cups chopped onion
1 cup chopped celery
1-1/2 cups sugar
1-1/2 tablespoons mustard seed
1 tablespoon salt
1 teaspoon celery seed
1/2 teaspoon turmeric
2-2/3 cups white vinegar

1. Sterilize six pint jars with lids (see Directions for Sterilizing).
2. Boil fresh corn for 5 minutes; drain. Plunge into cold water; let stand until cool enough to handle. Cut kernels from cobs; measure—you should have 2-1/2 quarts cut corn.
3. In a 6-quart Dutch oven, combine corn, 2 cups water, and all remaining ingredients. Bring to boiling; reduce heat, and simmer, uncovered, 20 minutes.
4. Bring to a full boil. Pack, boiling hot, into sterilized jars, leaving 1/8 inch head space. Seal.

Makes 6 pints.

Dilled Whole Carrots

4 lb slender carrots (about 6 inches long)
Boiling water
2 tablespoons mixed pickling spice
2 teaspoons dill seed
1 quart white vinegar
1-1/2 cups sugar
2 garlic cloves, halved
Fresh dill sprigs

1. Wash carrots; trim ends. Place in large saucepan; add boiling water to cover. Bring to boiling; reduce heat, and simmer, covered, for 10 minutes, or just until skins can be easily scraped off. Do not overcook.
2. Drain carrots; let cool. Then, with paring knife, scrape off skins. Wash and drain carrots again; turn into large bowl.
3. Meanwhile, tie pickling spice and dill seed in a bag made of muslin or several layers of cheesecloth. Place in medium saucepan with vinegar and sugar. Bring to boiling, stirring until sugar is dissolved; reduce heat, and simmer 5 minutes. Remove and discard spice bag.
4. Pour hot syrup over carrots. Refrigerate, covered, overnight.
5. Next day, sterilize two 1-quart jars (see Directions for Sterilizing); leave in hot water until ready to fill.
6. Turn carrots and syrup into large kettle. Bring to boiling; boil, uncovered, 3 minutes.
7. Using tongs, carefully pack carrots in jars, completing one quart at a time. Ladle boiling vinegar mixture over carrots to within 1/2 inch of top, but covering carrots completely. Add garlic and dill sprigs to each jar. Cap at once as manufacturer directs.
Makes 2 quarts.
Dilled Carrot Sticks: Prepare 3 lb carrots as above, but cut peeled, cooked carrots into strips 3 inches long and 1/4 inch wide. Continue as directed, but do not boil carrots the next day. Instead, remove carrots, and boil the syrup only. Pack as directed, using three or four 1-pint jars instead of quart jars.

Jerusalem-Artichoke Relish

2 lb Jerusalem artichokes
1 lb yellow onions (4 medium)
1 lb red peppers (3 medium)
1 cup salt
1 quart cider vinegar
2 cups sugar
1 tablespoon mustard seed
1 tablespoon celery seed

1. Scrub artichokes well, with a stiff brush; pare, and chop coarsely.
2. Coarsely chop onions, peppers.
3. In large bowl, combine chopped vegetables, salt, and 2 quarts cold water; mix well. Cover; refrigerate overnight.
4. Next day, sterilize two 1-quart jars (see Directions for Sterilizing); leave in hot water until ready to fill.

5. Drain chilled vegetables; place in large kettle. Add vinegar, sugar, mustard seed, and celery seed; cook over moderate heat, stirring, until sugar is dissolved and mixture boils. Reduce heat; simmer, uncovered and stirring occasionally, until relish is thick—about 30 minutes.

6. Completing one quart at a time, immediately ladle into sterilized jars to within 1/2 inch of top. Cap at once as manufacturer directs.
Makes 2 quarts.

Dilly Vegetables

1 lb onions, peeled
1/4 cup coarse salt
2 lb carrots
3 lb small Brussels sprouts, or 4 pkg (10-oz size) frozen Brussels sprouts
1 teaspoon salt
2 tablespoons mixed pickling spice
2 teaspoons dill seed
2 quarts white vinegar
4 cups sugar
1 large clove garlic, peeled and quartered
Dill sprigs

1. Slice onions 1/4 inch thick; separate into rings. Sprinkle with coarse salt; toss to mix well. Let stand 1 hour.

2. Pare carrots; trim ends; slice, on the diagonal, 1/4 inch thick. Let stand in ice water until ready to use.

2. Wash Brussels sprouts; trim stems; removing any discolored outer leaves. Bring 2 cups water to boiling; add 1 teaspoon salt and the Brussels sprouts. Simmer, covered, 15 to 20 minutes, or until tender; drain. (Cook frozen Brussels sprouts as the label directs.)

4. Meanwhile, tie pickling spice and dill seed in a small bag of several thicknesses of cheesecloth. Place in a medium saucepan with vinegar, sugar, and 1 cup water. Bring to boiling, stirring until sugar is dissolved; reduce heat, and simmer 5 minutes. Discard spice bag.

5. Drain carrots. Pour half of hot syrup over carrots and other half over Brussels sprouts. Refrigerate, covered, overnight.

6. Also, add water to onions to cover; refrigerate, covered, overnight.

7. Next day, sterilize three (1-quart) jars (see Directions for Sterilizing); leave in hot water until ready to fill.

8. Turn carrots, Brussels sprouts, and syrup into large kettle. Bring to boiling; boil, uncovered, 3 minutes. Meanwhile, drain onions, and rinse well under cold water.

9. Using tongs, carefully layer carrot slices, Brussels sprouts, and onion into jars. Place a garlic quarter and 4 dill sprigs in each jar. Cover with hot syrup. Cap immediately.
Makes 3 quarts.

Aunt Cal's Garden Relish

1-1/2 lb small white onions
2 medium red peppers
1 medium green pepper
2 medium cucumbers
1/2 cup salt
1 lb baby lima beans, shelled
1 lb green beans, cut into 1-inch pieces
1/2 lb wax beans, cut into 1-inch pieces
2 medium carrots, pared and cubed
1 head cauliflower (about 2 lb), cut into flowerets
1 quart cider vinegar
4 cups sugar
1 teaspoon turmeric
1 teaspoon celery seed
1 tablespoon mustard seed
1 cinnamon stick (about 1 inch)
1 can (15 oz) red kidney beans, drained

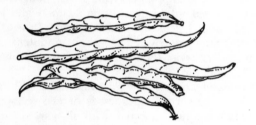

1. Peel onions. Coarsely chop peppers. Wash and thinly slice unpared cucumbers.
2. In large bowl, combine onions, peppers, cucumbers, salt, and 2 quarts cold water; mix well. Cover; refrigerate overnight.
3. Next day, cook lima beans, green beans, wax beans, carrots, and cauliflower separately in boiling water just until tender-crisp—8 to 10 minutes; do not overcook. Drain.
4. Drain chilled onions, peppers, and cucumbers.
5. Sterilize three 1-quart jars or six 1-pint jars (see Directions for Sterilizing); leave in hot water until ready to fill.
6. In large kettle, combine vinegar with sugar, turmeric, celery seed, mustard seed, and cinnamon stick. Cook over moderate heat, stirring, until sugar is dissolved and mixture boils.
7. Stir in kidney beans, drained chilled vegetables, and the cooked vegetables. Cover; return to boiling. Reduce heat; simmer, uncovered, 25 minutes. Remove and discard cinnamon stick.
8. Using slotted spoon, immediately spoon vegetables into sterilized jars, completing one jar at a time. Fill with boiling vinegar mixture to within 1/2 inch of top, but covering mixture completely. Cap at once as manufacturer directs.
Makes about 3 quarts.

Spiced Peaches

4 lb peaches
4-1/2 cups sugar
1-1/2 cups cider vinegar
1 tablespoon whole allspice
2 teaspoons whole cloves
2 (3-inch) cinnamon sticks

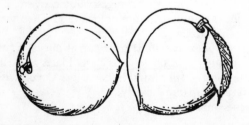

1. Peel peaches, placing them as they are peeled in slightly salted water, to prevent discoloring.
2. In 5-quart kettle, combine sugar, vinegar, 3/4 cup water, and spices tied in a cheesecloth bag.
3. Bring to boiling. Add peaches, return to boiling; reduce heat; simmer 10 minutes, or until tender.
4. Turn into a large bowl. Refrigerate, covered, overnight.
5. Spoon peaches into 4 pint jars.
6. Remove spice bag. Bring syrup to boiling. Pour over peaches, filling jars to 1/2 inch from top.
7. Place on lids, and process in a boiling-water bath, following manufacturer's directions for peaches.
Makes 4 pints.

Quick and Easy Relishes

Walnut Cranberry Relish

1 pkg (1 lb) fresh cranberries
1-1/2 cups sugar
1 cup coarsely chopped walnuts
1 cup orange marmalade
Juice of 1 lemon or lime (about 3 tablespoons)

1. Preheat oven to 350F. Wash cranberries; drain. Place in shallow baking pan with sugar; mix well. Cover pan with foil.
2. Bake 1 hour.
3. Meanwhile, spread nuts in shallow baking pan. Place in oven with cranberries, about 10 minutes, or until lightly toasted.
4. In medium bowl, combine baked cranberries, toasted nuts, marmalade, and lemon juice; mix well.
5. Refrigerate, covered, until well chilled—at least 6 hours.
Makes about 4 cups, or 8 to 10 servings.

Pickled Garden Relish

1/2 small head cauliflower, cut in flowerets and sliced
2 carrots, pared, cut in 2-inch strips
2 stalks celery, cut in 1-inch pieces (1 cup)
1 green pepper, cut in 2-inch strips
1 jar (4 oz) pimiento, drained, cut in strips
1 jar (3 oz) pitted green olives, drained
3/4 cup wine vinegar
1/2 cup olive or salad oil
2 tablespoons sugar
1 teaspoon salt
1/2 teaspoon dried oregano leaves
1/4 teaspoon pepper

1. In large skillet, combine ingredients with 1/4 cup water. Bring to boil; stir occasionally. Reduce heat; simmer, covered, 5 minutes.
2. Cool; then refrigerate at least 24 hours.
3. Drain well.
Makes 6 servings.

Jellied Cranberry Mold

2 cups boiling water
1 pkg (6 oz) or 2 pkg (3-oz size) lemon-flavored gelatine
2 cans (1-lb size) whole-cranberry sauce
1/2 cup chopped celery
1/2 cup coarsely chopped walnuts
Crisp lettuce

1. Pour boiling water over gelatine in large bowl; stir until gelatine dissolves. Add cranberry sauce; stir with fork until well blended.
2. Refrigerate until consistency of unbeaten egg white—about 1 hour.
3. Fold in celery and walnuts. Turn into 1-1/2-quart mold. Refrigerate until firm enough to unmold—overnight.
4. To serve: Run a small spatula around edge of mold. Invert over platter; place a hot, damp dishcloth over inverted mold, and shake gently to release. Garnish with lettuce.
Makes 6 to 8 servings.

Pepper Relish

4 lb medium red peppers (about 12)
4 lb medium green peppers (about 12)
6 hot peppers (optional)
3 lb onions
Boiling water
2 cups white vinegar
2 cups sugar
3 tablespoons salt

1. Wash and dry vegetables. Remove seeds and cores from peppers; peel onions. Chop all coarsely.
2. Turn into 10-quart kettle; cover with boiling water; let stand 5 minutes; drain.
3. To vegetables in kettle, add vinegar, sugar, and salt. Bring mixture to boiling; boil 5 minutes; let cool.
4. Store, covered, in refrigerator. Serve with hamburgers and hot dogs.
Makes 5 quarts.

Salsa Fria

4 medium tomatoes, (1-1/4 lb)
1 large onion, (8 oz)
1 can (4 oz) green chiles
2 tablespoons olive oil
2 tablespoons vinegar
1/2 teaspoon salt
1/8 teaspoon seasoned pepper
1/4 teaspoon dried oregano leaves

1. Peel tomatoes and chop coarsely. Also peel onion and chop. Drain chiles and chop.
2. In medium bowl, combine chopped vegetables, oil, vinegar, salt, pepper, and oregano; mix well.
3. Refrigerate, covered, until well chilled—at least 3 hours.
Makes 6 servings.
Note: This is a delicious raw relish to serve with grilled or fried fish or hamburgers.

Cranberry-Tangerine or -Orange Relish

3 medium-size tangerines, or 2 large navel oranges
4 cups (1 lb) fresh cranberries
1-1/2 cups sugar

Peel tangerines; reserve half of the peel. Remove white membrane and seeds. Then chop the tangerines coarsely.
2. Wash cranberries; drain; remove stems. Put cranberries and reserved peel through coarse blade of food chopper.
3. Add tangerines and sugar; mix well.
4. Refrigerate until serving.
Makes 4 cups.

Cranberry-Apple Relish

1 large orange
2 cups cranberries
1 cup sugar
1 lb red apples

1. Grate orange peel on coarse grater, to make long shreds—about 2 tablespoons.
2. Peel orange. Cut orange into 1/2-inch cubes.
3. Wash and drain cranberries; remove any stems. Chop cranberries very coarsely.
4. In medium bowl, combine the grated orange peel, cubed orange, cranberries, and sugar; mix well.

5. Refrigerate until well chilled—several hours.

6. Meanwhile, wash and core apples. Do not pare. Refrigerate. Just before serving, chop apples coarsely; you should have about 3 cups.

7. Add to cranberry-orange mixture; mix well. Makes 5 cups.

Mushroom Relish

1 lb medium-size fresh mushrooms
2 teaspoons chopped parsley
1/4 teaspoon salt
1/8 teaspoon pepper
1/2 teaspoon dried oregano leaves
1/4 teaspoon dried basil leaves
2 tablespoons grated onion and juice
1 clove garlic, pressed
1/3 cup chopped pimiento-stuffed olives
1 teaspoon sugar
1/4 cup salad oil
1/4 cup white-wine vinegar

1. Wash and dry mushrooms. Slice thinly lengthwise, through stems.

2. In large saucepan, combine mushrooms with 2 cups water. Bring to boiling; reduce heat, and simmer 5 minutes, or until almost tender. Drain. Arrange in large, shallow baking dish.

3. Combine rest of ingredients; mix very well; pour over mushrooms. Refrigerate, covered and stirring gently occasionally, at least 12 hours.

Makes about 8 servings.

Quick Corn Relish

1 can (12 oz) whole-kernel corn
1 teaspoon mustard seed
1/2 teaspoon dry mustard
1/4 teaspoon salt
1/4 teaspoon pepper
1/3 cup cider vinegar
1 tablespoon salad oil
2 tablespoons light-brown sugar
1/2 cup chopped onion
2 canned pimientos, drained and chopped
1/4 cup chopped green pepper

1. Drain liquid from corn into a small saucepan. Stir in mustard seed, mustard, salt, pepper, vinegar, oil, and brown sugar. Bring to a full boil.

2. Combine corn, onion, pimiento, and green pepper in medium bowl. Pour hot liquid over corn mixture; toss lightly until well combined.

3. Refrigerate, covered, at least 1 hour before serving. Nice to serve with meat.

Makes 2-1/2 cups.

Pickled Beets

2 cans (1-lb size) whole beets
1 cup white-wine vinegar
1/2 cup sugar
1 teaspoon salt
3 whole cloves
4 whole black peppercorns
1 small bay leaf
2 medium onions, peeled and thinly sliced

1. Drain beets, reserving 1-1/4 cups liquid. Place beets in 1-1/2- to 2-quart jar.

2. In medium saucepan, combine vinegar, sugar, salt, cloves, peppercorns, bay leaf, and reserved liquid; bring to boiling. Reduce heat, and simmer, uncovered, 5 minutes.

3. Add onion slices to jar. Pour hot liquid over beets and onions. Refrigerate, covered, several hours.

Makes 6 cups.

Pickled Vegetables

2 pints white vinegar
1-1/2 cups sugar
Dash salt
4 carrots, pared and cut in strips
3 green peppers, cut in strips
3 celery stalks, cut in strips
1/2 cup thinly sliced onion rings
1 cup cauliflowerets
2 cloves garlic
2 teaspoons dried oregano leaves
3 dill pickles

1. In large kettle, combine vinegar, sugar, salt, and 2 cups water. Bring to boiling, stirring; remove from heat; let cool completely. Add all the rest of ingredients.
2. Pack in quart jars with tight-fitting lid. Refrigerate, covered, at least 2 weeks before serving. Makes 3 quarts.

Pickled Pears

1 can (1 lb, 14 oz) pear halves
Whole cloves
1 cup apple cider
3 tablespoons cider vinegar
1 (3-inch) cinnamon stick
1/4 cup sugar
Currant jelly

1. Drain pears well, reserving 1/4 cup syrup.
2. Stud each pear half with 2 or 3 cloves.
3. In medium saucepan, combine reserved pear syrup, cider, vinegar, cinnamon, and sugar; bring to boiling, slowly.
4. Add pear halves; simmer pears gently about 5 minutes. Remove from heat.
5. Refrigerate, covered, until well chilled—at least 1 hour.
6. Serve, as garnish for lamb, with centers filled with currant jelly.
Makes 6 servings.

Roasted Peppers

8 medium sweet red peppers (2-1/2 lb)
1 cup olive or salad oil
1/4 cup lemon juice
2 teaspoons salt
3 small cloves garlic
3 anchovy fillets

1. Preheat the oven to 450F.
2. Wash red peppers, and drain them well.
3. Place peppers on cookie sheet; bake about 20 minutes, or until the skin of the peppers becomes blistered and charred. Turn the peppers every 5 minutes, with tongs.
4. Place hot peppers in a large kettle; cover kettle, and let peppers stand 15 minutes.
5. Peel off charred skin with sharp knife. Cut each pepper into fourths. Remove the ribs and seeds, and cut out any dark spots.
6. In large bowl, combine olive oil, lemon juice, salt, and garlic. Add the peppers, and toss lightly to coat with oil mixture.
7. Pack pepper mixture and anchovy fillets into a 1-quart jar; cap. Refrigerate several hours or overnight. Serve as an appetizer, or in a tossed salad.
Makes 1 quart.

Meats

Since meat is the costliest item on the food budget, it makes good sense to know how to buy it to get the best for the money; how to store it; and how to cook it to get the most in flavor and nutrition.

What to Look For

Beef should have fat that is firm and creamy white. Lean meat should be red, well marbled with fat, firm, with a fine grain.
Veal has little fat; the fat should be firm, clear, and white, not watery. Lean meat should be grayish-pink, firm, fine grained, not marbled with fat.
Lamb should be well covered with clear, white, firm fat. Lean meat is pinkish-red and marbled with fat.
Pork is well covered with fat that is firm, white, free from moisture. Lean meat is grayish-pink to rose; firm, fine grained, well marbled with fat.

AMOUNTS TO BUY
Boneless meat: Buy 1/4 pound per serving; e.g., lean ground beef, liver.
Bone-in meat: Buy 1/2 pound per serving; e.g., leg of lamb, steaks, chops.
Bony meat: Buy 3/4 to 1 pound per serving; e.g., spareribs, short ribs.

Storage of Meat

Fresh Meat: Cover or wrap loosely, and place in the coldest part of the refrigerator. Fresh meat that has been prepackaged (as it is in self-service markets) should have the wrapping loosened before storing. Proper circulation of air is important in storing fresh meats; the slight drying effect retards bacterial action. Most fresh meat can be stored 2 to 3 days; but ground beef and variety meat should be used within a day or two, or wrapped and frozen.
Cured Meat: Lightly cover or wrap; place in the refrigerator. It will keep longer than fresh meat.

Cooked Meat: Keep lightly covered in refrigerator. It can be held 4 to 5 days safely.
Frozen Meat: Properly packaged in moisture- and vaporproof wrap or in an airtight container, it should be maintained at 0F or lower. *The ice-cube compartment of a standard refrigerator is not adequate.* Meat should be kept wrapped while it is defrosting.
Canned Meat: Store in a cool place. After you open it, refrigerate what you don't use.

Basic Meat Cookery

For all meat cookery, regardless of method, the best results are obtained with low to moderate heat. Three basic methods are dry-heat, moist-heat, and cooking with fat.

COOKING WITH DRY HEAT
Dry-Heat Roasting: This is done in an oven, with heat circulating around the meat placed, fat side up, on a rack in a shallow, open pan. The meat thermometer is placed in the thickest part, not resting on bone or fat. The pan is uncovered, without water or basting. Seasoning is not necessary; salt does not penetrate more than half an inch, anyway. Roast at 325F. See timetables.
Broiling and Grilling: This is cooking by direct heat, over charcoal, under gas flame or electric unit. Low temperatures are obtained by the distance the meat is placed from the source of heat (2 to 5 inches, depending on the meat's thickness). Preheating a broiler pan is not necessary. The fat on chops and steaks should be scored, to prevent curling. Seasoning is done *after* browning. This helps prevent the loss of juices. Broiled meats should be served at once. See timetable.

Pan-Broiling: Meat is placed in a heavy skillet, uncovered, without fat or liquid. This is good for thinly cut steaks and chops, as well as meat patties. The cooking is done slowly; occasionally, the meat is turned. Fat is poured off as it is accumulated. Cook to the desired doneness.

COOKING WITH MOIST HEAT

Braising: This is top-of-range cooking, in a heavy skillet or Dutch oven. Chops, steaks, or roast may be done by this method. The meat can be coated with flour, if you wish. It should be well browned, slowly, in a small amount of fat. Add seasonings and a small amount of liquid. Cover tightly, to allow the formation of steam, and simmer slowly until the meat is tender. The time depends on the cut of meat. This method is often referred to as "pot-roasting."

Simmering in Water and Stewing: This is cooking on the top of the range in a large quantity of liquid. The meat can first be floured and then browned, if you wish; then liquid is added. It is never boiled, but simmered, covered, at low temperature. Seasonings can be added with the liquid. Vegetables are added toward the end of the cooking time and should never be overcooked. This method is best for the less-tender cuts of meat.

COOKING WITH FAT

Pan-Frying: This is similar to pan-broiling, with the addition of fat. Meat is often coated with flour or with egg and crumbs. Pan-frying is done uncovered, at moderate heat.

Deep-Fat Frying: Enough fat must be used to cover the meat. A deep-frying thermometer should be used. The fat should be heated to 350 to 360F before the meat is added. Temperature drops with the addition of the meat, so adjust the heat to maintain the proper temperature. Variety meats and croquettes are best done by this method. Cooking time depends on the size of the piece of meat. After meat is cooked, drain on paper towels.

Beef

The great plains of America and the know-how of its cowboys and cattlemen produce some of the world's best beef. Although it tastes so good you'd never guess it, beef, like all meat, is simply loaded with nutrition. No need to discuss it at the dinner table, but it should reassure you to know that beef contains all the essential amino acids a young body requires for growth and an older one to repair tissues, regenerate blood, and build resistance to infection. Also, like all meat, beef is strong on vitamins of the B-complex group, including riboflavin and niacin, and further provides essential minerals, such as iron, copper, and phosphorus, in the forms the body can most readily use.

All these hidden pluses exist in all cuts of beef, the cheapest as well as the costliest. There are cuts and recipes for any budget. On the pages that follow are facts on beef, and delicious fancies, that will take you from the supermarket to the table. We've included ABC instructions for the four principal ways to cook the many cuts—roasting, simmering, braising, and broiling. For the truly practiced, knowledgeable cook, we've sprinkled exotic dishes liberally through the pages. So let's start with Sunday dinner and a great big beautiful roast.

Roast Beef

Large, tender cuts of beef lend themselves especially well to roasting. The standing rib roast, rolled rib roast, sirloin roast (silver tip), and eye-of-round roast all take particularly kindly to this method of cooking. In all cases, the actual cooking procedure is the same:

Begin by seasoning with salt and pepper if that's your style. Some people prefer to season all meats after cooking. As for us—we like roasts cooked either way.

Next, put the meat, with the fat side up, on a rack in an open, shallow roasting pan. The rack will hold the roast above the drippings as fat from the top trickles down in a self-basting operation. (Roasts like a standing rib form a natural rack.) Insert a meat thermometer into the roast so the tip is in the center of the thickest part. Be sure the tip is not touching a bone or resting in fat.

Don't add any water, and don't cover the pan. Roasting is a dry-heat method of cooking; if you add liquid or a cover, your roast will turn into a pot roast.

Roast in a 325F oven unless the recipe specifically calls for another setting. Your own taste dictates how long the roasting should take. The meat thermometer will be your clue to when the roast is rare,

medium, well done. (See Timetable for Roasting Beef.)

Take the roast out of the oven 15 or 20 minutes before you're ready to serve it—it will carve much more easily that way. Actually, the meat continues to cook even after it's out of the oven.

Note: Sirloin and eye-of-round roasts can be roasted if of high quality (Prime or Choice) and/or tenderized. These two cuts should be roasted only until rare and should be thinly sliced on the diagonal.

Timetable for Roasting Beef—at 325F

Cut	Weight	Approx. Roasting Time	Internal Temperature
Rib roast, standing (bone in)*	4 lb	1-3/4 hours	140F (rare)
		2-1/4 hours	160F (medium)
		3 hours	170F (well done)
	6 lb	3-1/4 hours	140F (rare)
		3-3/4 hours	160F (medium)
		4-1/4 hours	170F (well done)
	8 lb	3-1/2 hours	140F (rare)
		4-1/2 hours	160F (medium)
		5 hours	170F (well done)
Rib roast, boned and rolled**	4 lb	2-3/4 hours	140F (rare)
		3-1/4 hours	160F (medium)
		3-1/2 hours	170F (well done)
	6 lb	3-1/2 hours	140F (rare)
		4-1/4 hours	160F (medium)
		4-3/4 hours	170F (well done)
Sirloin-tip roast (Prime or Choice)	3–5 lb	1-3/4–2-1/2 hours	140F (rare)
		2-1/4–3 hours	160F (medium)
		2-1/2–3-1/2 hours	170F (well done)

* Ribs that measure approximately 6 inches from chine bone to tip of ribs. If ribs are cut longer, allow less roasting time.

** Diameter of roasts: 4 pounds—4-1/2 to 5 inches; 6 pounds—5-1/2 to 6 inches. Thinner roasts of same weight require less roasting time.

It is advisable to use a meat thermometer as an extra precaution since roasts vary in size and shape, in amount of meat to bone, etc.

Roast Prime Ribs of Beef

3-rib roast of beef (about 7 lb)
1 tablespoon flour
1 teaspoon dry mustard
1 teaspoon salt
1/2 teaspoon pepper

1. Preheat oven to 325F. Wipe the roast of beef with damp paper towels.

2. Combine flour, mustard, salt, and pepper. Rub all over beef.

3. Place roast, fat side up, with the ribs as rack, in

roasting pan. Insert meat thermometer through fat into center of roast.

4. Roast, uncovered, 3-1/4 hours, or until meat thermometer registers 140F, for rare; or 4-1/4 hours, 160F, for medium. (See timetable.)

5. Let roast stand 20 minutes, for easier carving.

6. Serve au jus or with Brown Gravy, page 503.

Makes 8 servings.

Savory Roast Beef with Yorkshire Pudding

1/2 teaspoon salt
1/4 teaspoon dried marjoram leaves
1/4 teaspoon dried thyme leaves
1/4 teaspoon dried basil leaves
1/4 teaspoon rubbed savory
1/8 teaspoon pepper
Standing 3-rib roast beef, bone in (8 to 9 lb)*
1 teaspoon liquid gravy seasoning
1/2 cup Burgundy
Yorkshire Pudding, below
Burgundy Gravy, page 504
* Ribs that measure approximately 6 inches from chine bone to tip of the ribs. If ribs are cut longer, allow less roasting time. Diameter of roasts: 4 lbs, 4-1/2 to 5 inches; 6 lbs, 5-1/2 to 6 inches. Thinner roasts of same weight will require less roasting time.

1. Preheat oven to 325F. Mix salt with the herbs and pepper.

2. Stand roast, fat side up, in a shallow roasting pan. Rub salt mixture into the beef on all sides. Insert meat thermometer through the outside fat into the thickest part of muscle (the point should not rest on fat or bone).

3. Mix gravy seasoning with Burgundy. Spoon some of mixture over the beef.

4. Roast, uncovered, basting several times with remaining Burgundy mixture, to desired doneness: rare (140F), 3-1/2 hours; medium (160F), 4-1/2 hours; well done (170F), 5 hours.

5. Get ready Yorkshire Pudding ingredients to assemble and bake when the roast is done.

6. Remove roast to heated platter. Pour drippings into a 2-cup measure. Let roast stand in warm place while pudding is baking and you're making Burgundy Gravy. The roast will be easier to carve after standing 20 to 30 minutes.

Makes 8 to 10 servings.

Yorkshire Pudding

2 eggs
1 cup milk
1 cup sifted all-purpose flour
1/2 teaspoon salt
2 tablespoons roast-beef drippings

1. As soon as the roast beef has been removed from the oven, increase oven temperature to 425F.

2. In a medium bowl, with a rotary beater, beat eggs, milk, flour, and salt to make a smooth batter.

3. Pour drippings into a 10-inch pie plate; tilt to coat bottom and side of pie plate. Pour in batter.

4. Bake 23 to 25 minutes, or until the pudding is deep golden-brown. Serve immediately with the Roast Beef.

Makes 8 servings.

Filet of Beef Burgundy

6-lb whole filet of beef*
1-1/2 teaspoons salt
1/4 teaspoon pepper
1 teaspoon dried rosemary leaves
10 slices bacon
1 cup Burgundy
1/2 cup butter or margarine
2 lb large mushrooms
Bordelaise Sauce, page 497
Chopped parsley
Watercress sprigs
* Because the whole filet or tenderloin is such a tender cut of beef, it does not have to be Prime or even Choice quality.

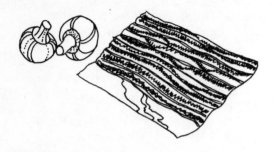

1. Trim excess fat from beef. Sprinkle beef all over with salt, pepper, and rosemary.
2. Tuck narrow end of roast under, to make uniformly thick; fasten with a skewer.
3. Arrange bacon slices over top of beef; secure with twine.
4. Place beef on rack in shallow roasting pan. Place roasting pan on rack in broiler pan, so meat is 4 inches from heat. Broil 45 minutes, turning meat every 10 minutes.
5. Remove meat, in roasting pan, from broiler; discard the twine and bacon slices. Reduce oven temperature to 300F.
6. Pour Burgundy over beef. Roast, basting occasionally with pan juices, 30 minutes for rare.
7. Meanwhile, in hot butter in large skillet, sauté mushrooms, stirring occasionally, until tender— about 20 minutes. Remove from heat, and keep warm.
8. Remove roast to serving platter. Cover, and keep warm while making Bordelaise Sauce.
9. To serve: Cut meat into slices 3/4 inch thick. Surround slices with mushrooms, sprinkled with parsley. Garnish with watercress sprigs. Pass Bordelaise Sauce.
Makes 10 to 12 servings.

Beef Wellington

Filet of Beef in Brioche

Brioche Dough, below

6-lb filet of beef
1 teaspoon salt
1/4 teaspoon pepper
1 can (7/8 oz) truffles
1 egg

Truffle Sauce:
1-1/2 cups Burgundy or claret
2 tablespoons flour
1/2 cup canned condensed beef broth, undiluted
1 teaspoon meat-extract paste
1/2 teaspoon salt
Watercress

1. Day before, make Brioche Dough.
2. Early the next day, roast filet of beef: Preheat oven to 450F. Remove most of surface fat from filet. Wipe with damp paper towels.
3. Place filet on rack in shallow, open roasting pan, tucking narrow end under, to make roast uniformly thick. Sprinkle with salt and pepper.
4. Insert meat thermometer into thickest part. Roast 40 to 50 minutes, or to 140F on meat thermometer, for rare; about 60 minutes, or to 160F, for medium rare.
5. Let roast cool in pan. Reserve pan drippings for Truffle Sauce.
6. About 3 hours before serving, lightly grease large cookie sheet. Turn out Brioche Dough onto lightly floured pastry cloth. Roll into a 16-by-15-inch rectangle. Trim 1 inch dough from short side, and set aside for decoration.

7. Drain truffles, reserving liquid for sauce; chop truffles. Sprinkle 1 tablespoon truffles over dough; press gently into surface. Set remaining truffles aside for sauce.

8. Center filet lengthwise on dough. Bring long sides of dough over filet, one at a time, pressing edges to seal. Pinch ends together.

9. Reroll dough trimmings 1/8 inch thick. Using pastry wheel, cut into four strips, 1/2 inch wide. Arrange strips over top of dough.

10. Transfer filet to prepared cookie sheet. Cover with towel; let rise in warm place (85F), free from drafts, until dough doubles in bulk—about 1 hour.

11. Preheat oven to 400F. Beat egg with 1 teaspoon water. Gently brush over dough.

12. Bake 20 minutes, or until deep golden-brown. Cover top lightly with foil; bake 10 minutes longer.

13. Let stand on cookie sheet on wire rack 20 minutes before slicing.

14. Meanwhile, make Truffle Sauce: Add wine to reserved drippings in roasting pan. Over medium heat, bring to boiling, stirring to dissolve brown bits. Reduce heat; simmer gently, uncovered, 10 minutes. Strain if necessary, and skim off excess fat. Turn into small saucepan.

15. Combine flour with 2 tablespoons cold water and the beef broth; stir into wine mixture with meat-extract paste and salt. Bring to boiling, stirring. Reduce heat; simmer 1 minute, or until mixture is thickened.

16. Add reserved truffles and truffle liquid; stir well.

17. Cut filet crosswise into 1-inch slices, and arrange on serving platter. Garnish with watercress. Pass sauce.

Makes 12 to 14 servings.

Brioche Dough

1/2 cup warm water (105 to 115F)
1 pkg active dry yeast
1/4 cup sugar
2 teaspoons salt
1 cup soft butter
6 eggs, at room temperature
4-1/2 cups sifted all-purpose flour

1. If possible, check temperature of water with thermometer. Sprinkle yeast over water in large bowl of electric mixer; stir until dissolved.

2. Add sugar, salt, butter, eggs, and 3 cups flour. Beat at medium speed 4 minutes, occasionally scraping side of bowl with rubber scraper.

3. Add remaining flour. Beat at low speed 2 minutes longer, or until smooth.

4. Cover bowl with waxed paper, then with a damp cloth. Let rise in warm place (85F), free from drafts, until double in bulk—1 to 1-1/2 hours. Then refrigerate, covered, overnight.

5. Next day, use as directed.

Roast Eye-Round Provencale

5-lb beef eye-round or sirloin (silver tip) roast*
1 clove garlic, cut in 8 slivers
1 teaspoon salt
1/2 teaspoon pepper
1 teaspoon dried thyme leaves

Marinade:
1/2 cup Italian-style dressing
1 cup red wine
1 bay leaf, crumbled

Sauce:
2 tablespoons flour
1 cup red wine
1/4 teaspoon salt
Dash pepper

* If possible, use Prime quality.

1. Day before: Wipe roast with damp paper towels.
2. Make 8 slits, 1 inch deep, across top of meat. Insert a sliver of garlic into each slit. Rub entire surface of meat with 1 teaspoon salt, 1/2 teaspoon pepper, and the thyme. Place the meat in a shallow baking dish.
3. Make Marinade: In small bowl, combine dressing, 1 cup wine, and the bay leaf. Pour over meat. Cover well with plastic film. Refrigerate overnight; turn meat in the marinade once or twice.
4. Next day: Preheat oven to 450F.
5. Place roast in shallow, open roasting pan. Insert meat thermometer into thickest part. Reserve marinade.
6. Roast 25 minutes. Pour marinade over roast; roast 25 minutes longer, or until meat thermometer registers 140F, for rare; or 60 minutes, 160F, for medium rare.
7. Remove roast to heated serving platter; keep warm. Let stand 15 minutes, for easy carving.
8. Make Sauce: Pour off fat from roasting pan. Reserve 2 tablespoons drippings in pan; stir in flour to make a smooth paste. Stir in 1/2 cup water, the wine, salt, and pepper. Bring to boiling, stirring. Simmer 3 minutes, until slightly thickened.
9. To serve: Slice meat thinly, on the diagonal. Pass sauce.
Makes 8 to 10 servings.

Broiling and Pan-Broiling

Steak is the most ordered meat in good restaurants and the most demanded at home when there is something to celebrate. And although some steaks are admittedly rather luxuriously priced, there are several cuts in the distinctly budget class that need only a few hours of marinating or a bit of meat tenderizer to make them into party fare. But whether you're splurging on filet, porterhouse, T-bone, club or sirloin, or serving less costly chuck, flank or round, the preferred method of cooking the steak is to broil it. Because it involves cooking under very high direct heat, broiling in general has the advantage of being the quickest way to cook beef. A steak, for example, can go from the refrigerator to the table in under half an hour. But for the same reason, broiling also requires the most precise timing. Even as little as an extra minute's cooking can turn rare to medium. So when you're broiling, *do* use a timer. The best method of broiling anything from hamburger to London broil is to follow these steps:

First, set the oven regulator for broiling. You may or may not preheat the broiler, as you prefer.

Place the meat on the rack of the broiler pan, two to five inches from the heat. (Usually two to three inches is best for steaks or patties that are an inch or less thick, three to five inches for those between one and two inches in thickness.) Broil until top is brown. The meat should be half, or perhaps slightly more than half, done by the time it is brown on top. (See timetable below.) Season the top with salt and pepper if you like. Broiled meats should not be seasoned before browning, since salt tends to bring moisture to the cut surface and delay browning. Then turn the meat, and brown it on the other side.

The timetable is a good guide for broiling any beef. But if a steak is especially thick, you may want to use a meat thermometer. Some of these, designed especially for broiler cooking, can be inserted and left in the meat throughout the broiling period. You can also test the degree of doneness by cutting a slit near the bone to check the interior of the meat. Pan-broiling is a top-stove method of broiling, best for thin (minute) steaks. Heat a heavy skillet. Brown meat on both sides, adding a small amount of fat, if necessary, to prevent sticking. Reduce heat, and continue cooking until meat is done to your taste. Pour off fat as it accumulates. Season before serving.

Timetable for Broiling Steaks

Cut	Thickness	Approximate Minutes per Side		
		Rare	Medium	Well Done
Filet	1 inch	3 min	5 min	6–7 min
	1-1/2 inches	8 min	9 min	11 min
Porterhouse	1 inch	6 min	8 min	11 min
	1-1/2 inches	8 min	10 min	14 min
T-bone	1 inch	6 min	8 min	11 min
	1-1/2 inches	9–10 min	11–12 min	14–15 min
Rib	1 inch	5–6 min	7 min	8–9 min
	1-1/2 inches	9–10 min	11–12 min	14–15 min
Club	1 inch	5–6 min	7 min	8–9 min
	1-1/2 inches	9 min	11 min	14–15 min
Delmonico	1 inch	5 min	7 min	8–9 min
	1-1/2 inches	9 min	11–12 min	14–15 min
Shell or strip	1 inch	5 min	7 min	8–9 min
	1-1/2 inches	9 min	10–11 min	14–15 min
Sirloin	1 inch	8–9 min	10 min	12 min
	1-1/2 inches	12–14 min	14–15 min	17–18 min
Sirloin butt*	1 inch	4 min	6 min	
	1-1/2 inches	12 min	14 min	
Sirloin tip*	1 inch	10 min	11–12 min	
	1-1/2 inches	12 min	14 min	
Flank*	3/4 inch	2 min	3 min	
	1 inch	3 min	4 min	
Butterfly* (eye of round)	1 inch	4 min	6 min	
	1-1/2 inches	8–9 min	10 min	
Ground sirloin, round, or chuck patties	3/4 inch	4 min	6 min	7 min

For steaks at room temperature in preheated broiler
Broil 1-inch-thick steaks (flank steak, 3/4 inch) 3 inches from heat.
Broil 1-1/2-inch-thick steaks (flank steak, 1 inch) 4 inches from heat.
* Use unseasoned instant meat tenderizer as label directs.

Sirloin Steak with Red Wine

4-1/2- to 5-lb sirloin steak,* about 1-1/2 inches
  thick
1 clove garlic, split
1/3 cup olive or salad oil
1-1/2 teaspoons salt
1/2 teaspoon coarsely cracked pepper
1-1/4 teaspoons dried rosemary leaves
1/2 cup dry red wine
1 tablespoon butter or margarine
* Have steak at room temperature.

1. Preheat oven to 350F.
2. Wipe steak with damp paper towels. Rub each side with garlic; reserve garlic.
3. Heat oil in a large, heavy skillet until very hot.
4. Over high heat, brown steak very well on both sides—3 to 5 minutes per side.
5. Place steak on rack in shallow roasting pan. Sprinkle with salt, pepper, and rosemary; add garlic. Insert meat thermometer in side of steak, making sure point is as close to center of meat as possible.
6. Bake in top part of oven 25 to 30 minutes, or or until meat thermometer registers 130 degrees, for medium rare. Remove thermometer; place steak on hot platter.
7. Pour fat from roasting pan; discard garlic. Add wine to pan, and bring to boiling, stirring to loosen brown particles. Stir in butter. Pour 2 tablespoons sauce over steak; pass the rest.
8. To serve, slice thinly on the diagonal.
Makes 6 to 8 servings.

London Broil

1 flank steak (about 2 lb), or see Note
1 tablespoon salad oil
2 teaspoons chopped parsley
1 clove garlic, crushed
1 teaspoon salt
1 teaspoon lemon juice
1/8 teaspoon pepper
Maître d'Hôtel Sauce, page 500

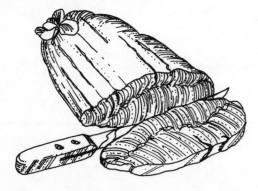

1. With sharp knife, trim excess fat from steak. Wipe with damp paper towels. Lay steak on cutting board.
2. Combine salad oil, parsley, garlic, salt, lemon juice, and pepper. Brush half of mixture over steak; let stand about 45 minutes.
3. Place steak, oil side up, on lightly greased broiler pan. Broil, about 4 inches from heat, 5 minutes. Turn steak; brush with remaining oil mixture; broil 4 to 5 minutes longer. The steak will be rare, the only way London broil should be served.
4. Remove steak to board or platter. Slice very thinly, on the diagonal across the grain. Serve with Maître d'Hôtel Sauce.
Makes 4 servings.
Note: In many areas, in self-service meat departments, a cut of beef labeled London Broil (round steak) is sold. To prepare: While steak is still moist after being wiped with damp paper towels, sprinkle with instant unseasoned meat tenderizer, as label directs. Then proceed as above, but omit salt.

Steak with Mustard and Herbs

1/4 cup butter or margarine
1 teaspoon dried marjoram leaves
1 teaspoon dried basil leaves
1 teaspoon dried thyme leaves
1 teaspoon cracked black pepper
4-1/2- to 5-lb sirloin steak, 1-1/2 inches thick
6 tablespoons dry mustard
3 tablespoons dry white wine
1 to 2 tablespoons finely chopped fresh tarragon
1-1/2 to 2-1/2 tablespoons finely chopped parsley
1 to 2 tablespoons finely chopped chives
Béarnaise Sauce, page 22

1. In small bowl, combine soft butter with marjoram, basil, and thyme, rubbing dried herbs between fingers while blending in. Add 1/4 teaspoon pepper.
2. With point of sharp knife, make 1/2-inch-deep cuts in steak, 1-1/2 inches apart.
3. Fill each cut with 1/4 teaspoon herb butter, reserving the rest of the herb butter.
4. In small bowl, combine mustard, remaining pepper, and the wine to form a paste.
5. Spread mustard paste smoothly on both sides of steak. Place steak on waxed paper; allow to stand, uncovered, at room temperature 1 to 1-1/2 hours before broiling.
6. Place steak, herb-butter side down, on broiler rack. Broil steak, 2 to 3 inches from heat, 8 minutes on first side, or until mustard paste is brown and crusty. Turn steak, and broil 3 minutes.
7. Remove steak from broiler; spread surface with remaining herb butter, and sprinkle with 1 tablespoon fresh tarragon combined with 1-1/2 tablespoons parsley and 1 tablespoon chives. Return steak to broiler, and continue to broil about 4 minutes longer, or until steak is cooked rare to medium.
8. To serve, place on steak board. Sprinkle with remaining fresh herbs, if desired. Slice steak on the diagonal, 1/4 inch thick. Serve with Béarnaise Sauce.
Makes 6 to 8 servings.

Florentine Chuck Steak

4-1/4- to 5-lb beef round-bone chuck steak,
  about 2 inches thick
Unseasoned instant meat tenderizer
1/4 cup olive or salad oil
1/4 cup lemon juice
1/2 teaspoon salt
1/2 teaspoon coarsely ground black pepper

1. Wipe steak with damp paper towels. Sprinkle with meat tenderizer, as label directs. Combine olive oil, lemon juice, salt, and pepper; mix well.
2. Place steak on rack in broiler pan; brush with about 2 tablespoons oil mixture. Broil, 5 inches from heat, 20 minutes. Turn steak, and brush with more of the oil mixture. Broil 20 minutes longer, for rare.
3. To serve: Slice thinly. Drizzle with any remaining oil mixture. Garnish with lemon wedges, if desired.
Makes 8 to 10 servings.

Steak with Marrow Sauce

2-1/2 lb round steak, 1-1/2 inches thick*
  or 3 lb boneless sirloin steak
Freshly ground pepper

Marrow Sauce:
2 large marrowbones (about 1-1/2 lb)
3 tablespoons butter or margarine
6 shallots, chopped
1-1/2 tablespoons flour
1-1/2 cups red wine
1 tablespoon chopped parsley
1/2 teaspoon dried thyme leaves
1/2 teaspoon salt

2 tablespoons butter or margarine
1 shallot, chopped
1 teaspoon chopped parsley
1/2 teaspoon salt
Watercress

***Use Prime or Choice quality meat. If desired, you
may use unseasoned meat tenderizer as package label directs on round steak.**

1. Wipe steak with damp paper towels. Sprinkle both sides with pepper, pressing in well. Let stand 30 minutes.
2. Make Marrow Sauce: In large saucepan, bring 1 quart water to boiling. Add marrowbones; bring back to boiling; reduce heat; simmer, uncovered, 10 minutes. Remove bones; cool. Scoop out marrow; chop finely.
3. In 3 tablespoons hot butter in small saucepan, sauté 6 chopped shallots, stirring, until transparent—about 5 minutes. Remove from heat; stir in flour. Cook over low heat, stirring 1 minute. Slowly add wine, stirring constantly. Add 1 tablespoon parsley, the thyme, and 1/2 teaspoon salt. Simmer gently 10 minutes. Stir in marrow. Keep warm over very low heat while cooking steak.
4. In 2 tablespoons hot butter in heavy skillet, sauté 1 shallot and the parsley about 1 minute. Add steak; cook over medium heat 10 minutes, turning once. Steak will be quite rare. Cook 5 minutes longer for medium rare. Place on hot serving platter; sprinkle with salt.
5. Pour about 1/4 cup marrow sauce into skillet; bring to boiling, stirring to loosen brown particles. Add to rest of sauce. Spoon a little of hot marrow sauce over steak. Garnish platter with watercress. Pass rest of sauce. To serve, slice steak very thinly, on the diagonal.
Makes 8 servings.

Braising

Braising is a method of cooking beef that consists of browning a less tender cut, such as top and bottom round, rump, chuck and flank, in a small amount of fat—often its own—and then simmering for several hours until it is deliciously tender. Begin by browning the meat slowly on all sides in a heavy pan or Dutch oven. If the meat has a fair amount of fat, you won't have to add any. However, if it is lean or if the particular recipe calls for coating with flour or crumbs, a small amount of fat should be added. After browning, pour off all drippings, and season with salt, pepper, herbs or spices, as you like. Be sure, though, to wait until after browning to add seasonings. Then pour a lit-

tle liquid (water, vegetable juice or broth) into the pan, and cover tightly. A tight-fitting lid is essential to hold in the steam necessary for softening connective tissues and making the meat tender.
Cook at a low temperature so the liquid does not boil, merely simmers. The cooking may be done on top of the range or in a slow oven (300 to 325F). Allow 2 to 2-1/2 hours for steak and 3 to 4 hours for pot roasts, depending on thickness. Vegetables can be added during the last 45 minutes of cooking. When the meat is cooked, don't overlook the gravy possibilities. A rich, savory gravy, made from the stock the meat has cooked in, is half the pleasure of many braised dishes.

Beef à la Mode

4 tablespoons chopped parsley
1 teaspoon seasoned salt
1/4 lb salt pork
4- or 5-lb beef top- or bottom-round roast
Flour
1-1/2 teaspoons salt
1/4 teaspoon pepper
1/4 cup salad oil
1/2 cup chopped onion
1 clove garlic, crushed
2 whole cloves
1 bay leaf
1 teaspoon dried thyme leaves
1 can (10-1/2 oz) condensed beef consommé,
    undiluted
1 cup dry red wine
1/2 lb carrots, pared and cut in 1-inch pieces
1/2 lb white turnips, pared and cut in 1-inch cubes
1 pkg (10 oz) frozen peas

1. Combine parsley and seasoned salt on waxed paper. Cut salt pork into strips 3 inches long and 1/4 inch thick. Roll in parsley mixture.
2. Wipe roast with damp paper towels. Make cuts 3 to 4 inches deep, 1-1/2 inches apart. Push salt-pork strips into cuts.
3. Mix 1/4 cup flour, the salt, and pepper; use to coat roast. Save any remaining flour mixture.
4. In hot oil in Dutch oven, over medium heat, brown roast well on all sides—about 20 minutes in all. Add onion, garlic, cloves, bay leaf, thyme, consommé, and 1/2 cup wine.
5. Bring to boiling; reduce heat, and simmer, covered and turning roast several times, 2-1/2 hours. Add carrots and turnips; simmer 20 minutes. Add peas; simmer 20 minutes longer, or until meat and vegetables are tender.
6. Remove roast to heated serving platter. Using slotted spoon, remove vegetables, and place around roast. Keep warm. Skim fat from pan juices.
7. Add enough flour to remaining flour mixture to make 6 tablespoons. Mix, in small bowl, with remaining wine until smooth. Stir into pan juices; bring to boiling, stirring. Reduce heat, and simmer 3 minutes. Pass with meat.
Makes 8 servings.

Swedish Pot Roast

5-lb lean boneless chuck pot roast
6 tablespoons butter or margarine
1-1/2 cups chopped onion
2 cloves garlic, crushed
1/3 cup flour
1/4 cup wine vinegar
1 tablespoon anchovy paste
2 tablespoons honey or corn syrup
2 cans (10-1/2-oz size) condensed beef broth,
    undiluted
2 bay leaves
4 sprigs parsley
1 teaspoon whole black peppercorns

1. Wipe roast with damp paper towels.
2. In hot butter in 6-quart Dutch oven, brown roast well over medium heat, turning on all sides with wooden spoons—about 20 minutes. Remove roast; set aside. Preheat oven to 325F.
3. Add onion and garlic to drippings in Dutch oven; cook over low heat about 5 minutes, or until tender.
4. Remove from heat; stir in flour until smooth. Add vinegar, anchovy paste, honey, broth; stir to mix well.
5. Tie bay leaves, parsley, and black peppercorns in cheesecloth bag; add to Dutch oven. Bring to boiling, covered.
6. Place in oven; roast 3 to 3-1/2 hours, or until meat is fork-tender. Remove and discard cheesecloth bag.
7. Remove pot roast to heated platter. Serve with sauce from Dutch oven.
Makes 8 to 10 servings.

Brisket Pot Roast

6- to 7-lb brisket of beef
1/2 teaspoon salt
1/8 teaspoon pepper
2 medium onions
2 medium carrots
2 celery stalks
1 large tomato

1. Preheat oven to 350F.
2. Sprinkle beef with salt and pepper; place in large skillet. Brown meat on fat side only, over high heat.
3. While meat is browning, prepare vegetables. Slice onions very thin. Pare carrots; cut carrots and celery in 1-inch pieces. Peel tomato, and cut it in chunks.
4. When meat is well browned, remove from skillet; place in roasting pan or large Dutch oven.
5. Add onions to skillet; sauté until golden.
6. Spoon onions over meat; surround meat with prepared vegetables. Add 1 cup water.
7. Roast, covered, 2-1/2 to 3 hours, or until meat is tender.
8. Remove roast to serving platter; keep warm while preparing gravy.
9. Make gravy: Strain pan juices to remove vegetables. Press vegetables through food mill. Skim fat from pan juices.
10. Add vegetables to pan juices; heat thoroughly. Pass along with roast.
Makes 10 to 12 servings.

Herbed Pot Roast with Vegetables

4-lb beef rump roast
2 tablespoons salad oil
1 env (1-3/8 oz) dried-onion-soup mix
1 clove garlic, crushed
1/2 teaspoon dried thyme leaves
1/2 teaspoon dried marjoram leaves
1/4 teaspoon salt
1/4 teaspoon pepper
1/2 cup chopped celery
3 sprigs parsley
8 carrots, pared (about 1 lb)
8 small white onions, peeled
Boiling water
3 medium white turnips, pared and quartered
   (about 1 lb)
3 tablespoons flour

1. Wipe roast with damp paper towels.
2. In hot oil in Dutch oven, over medium heat, brown roast well on all sides—about 20 minutes in all. Turn fat side up. Sprinkle with soup mix, garlic, thyme, marjoram, salt, and pepper. Add 1 cup water, the celery, and parsley.
3. Bring to boiling. Reduce heat, and simmer, covered, 2-1/2 hours. Add carrots and onions; simmer about 40 minutes longer, or until meat and vegetables are tender.
4. Meanwhile, in 1 inch boiling water in medium saucepan, simmer turnips, covered, about 30 minutes, or until tender. Drain.
5. Remove roast to serving platter, along with carrots, onions, and turnips. Keep warm. Skim excess fat from pan juices.
6. Mix flour with 1/4 cup water until smooth. Stir into pan juices; bring to boiling, stirring. Reduce heat, and simmer 3 minutes. Pass with meat.
Makes 8 servings.

Country Pot Roast with Noodles

5- to 6-lb beef blade-bone chuck roast
Flour
1-1/2 teaspoons salt
1/4 teaspoon pepper
1/4 cup salad oil
1/2 cup chopped onion
1/2 cup chopped celery
1 clove garlic, crushed
1 cup tomato juice
2 tablespoons Worcestershire sauce
1 teaspoon dried oregano leaves
6 carrots, pared (about 1 lb)
1 pkg (8 oz) wide noodles

1. Wipe roast with damp paper towels. Combine 1/4 cup flour, the salt, and pepper; use to coat roast.
2. In hot oil in a large skillet, over medium heat, brown roast well on all sides—about 20 minutes in all.
3. Add onion, celery, and garlic; sauté until golden.
4. Add tomato juice, 1/4 cup water, the Worcestershire, and oregano; bring to boiling. Reduce heat, and simmer, covered and turning meat once, 2 hours. Add carrots; simmer 30 minutes longer, or until meat and carrots are tender.
5. Meanwhile, cook noodles as package label directs. Drain.
6. Remove roast and carrots to heated serving platter. Surround with noodles. Keep warm.
7. Pour pan drippings into 2-cup measure. Skim off fat, and discard. Add water to liquid to make 1-1/2 cups. Return to pan.
8. In small bowl, stir 2 tablespoons flour with 2 tablespoons water until smooth. Stir into pan juices; bring to boiling, stirring. Reduce heat, and simmer 3 minutes. Serve with roast.
Makes 6 servings.

Savory Braised Short Ribs

4 lb beef short ribs, in serving-size pieces
1 cup coarsely chopped onion
1 clove garlic, crushed
4 whole black peppercorns
1 bay leaf
2 teaspoons Worcestershire sauce
1/2 teaspoon dried marjoram leaves
1 can (10-1/2 oz) condensed beef broth, undiluted

Horseradish Cream:
1/2 cup heavy cream
1/4 cup dairy sour cream
2 tablespoons prepared horseradish
1 teaspoon prepared mustard
1/8 teaspoon salt

3 tablespoons flour

Tomato wedges
Parsley sprigs

1. Wipe short ribs with damp paper towels. If necessary, trim excess fat.
2. Slowly heat a Dutch oven. Add short ribs, fat side down; over medium heat, brown well on all sides—about 30 minutes. Discard drippings.
3. Add onion, garlic, peppercorns, bay leaf, Worcestershire, marjoram, broth, and 1 cup water; bring to boiling. Reduce heat, and simmer, covered and turning meat once, 1-1/2 to 2 hours, or until tender.
4. Meanwhile, make Horseradish Cream: In small bowl, beat heavy cream until stiff. Stir in sour cream, horseradish, mustard, and salt. Refrigerate, covered, until needed.
5. Remove short ribs to serving platter; keep warm. Skim fat from pan juices.
6. Mix flour with 1/2 cup water until smooth. Stir into pan juices; bring to boiling, stirring. Reduce heat, and simmer 3 minutes. Strain, and pour over short ribs. Garnish with tomato wedges and parsley. Pass Horseradish Cream.
Makes 8 servings.

Braised Chuck Steak with Vegetables

3-1/2- to 4-lb chuck steak, 1-1/2 inches thick
1/4 cup unsifted all-purpose flour
1 tablespoon shortening
2 teaspoons salt
1/8 teaspoon pepper
1/8 teaspoon ginger
1/2 cup chopped onion
1/2 cup chopped celery
1/4 teaspoon liquid gravy seasoning (optional)
4 carrots, pared and quartered
1 rutabaga, pared and cut up (4 cups)

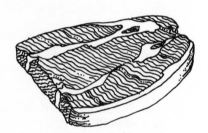

1. Wipe steak with damp paper towels. Roll in 2 tablespoons flour, coating evenly on both sides.
2. Slowly heat large, heavy skillet or Dutch oven. Add shortening; heat. In it, brown steak well on both sides, turning with tongs—15 to 20 minutes in all.
3. Add salt, pepper, ginger, onion, celery, and 1 cup water; bring to boiling. Reduce heat; simmer, covered, 1-1/2 hours, or until meat is fork-tender.
4. Add gravy seasoning, carrots, and rutabaga; bring to boiling. Reduce heat; simmer, covered, 30 minutes, or until vegetables are tender.
5. Remove steak and vegetables to heated platter; keep warm.
6. Pour pan liquid into bowl; skim off fat from surface; measure liquid. For each cup liquid, combine 2 tablespoons flour and 1/4 cup water, stirring to make a smooth paste; then stir into liquid to combine well.
7. Return to skillet; bring to boiling. Reduce heat; simmer 2 minutes. Pour over steak.
Makes 4 servings.

Pot Roast with Vegetables

3-1/2-lb top- or bottom-round beef pot roast
All-purpose flour
Salt
Pepper
2 tablespoons salad oil
1 cup sliced onion
1 bay leaf
1 beef-bouillon cube
1 can (8 oz) tomato sauce
6 medium potatoes, pared (2 lb)
6 small white turnips, pared
6 carrots, pared and halved crosswise

1. Wipe roast well with damp paper towels. Combine 2 tablespoons flour, 1 teaspoon salt, and 1/8 teaspoon pepper. Sprinkle over entire roast, and rub into surface.
2. Heat salad oil in Dutch oven over high heat. Add roast, and cook, over medium heat, until well browned on all sides; turn with wooden spoons— takes 15 to 20 minutes.
3. When roast is partially browned, add onion, and brown very well. This is the secret of good flavor and color.
4. Add bay leaf, bouillon cube, 1 cup water. Reduce heat; simmer, covered, 1-1/2 hours.
5. Turn roast. Add tomato sauce and vegetables, pressing them down into liquid. Simmer, covered, 1-1/2 hours longer, or until roast and vegetables are tender.
6. Carefully lift out vegetables and roast, and arrange attractively on heated serving platter. Remove string. Keep warm.

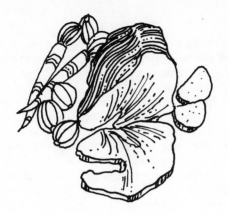

7. For gravy: Strain pan liquid through a coarse sieve into a 4-cup measure, pressing any remaining vegetables through sieve. Tilt liquid; with tablespoon, skim off all fat.

8. Measure liquid, adding water, if necessary, to make 2-1/2 cups. Return the liquid to the Dutch oven.

9. Measure 1/4 cup flour into small bowl. Gradually add 1/2 cup water, stirring until smooth. Slowly stir into liquid in Dutch oven. Add 1/2 teaspoon salt and dash pepper. Bring to boiling, stirring constantly; reduce heat, and simmer 5 minutes.

10. Ladle some of gravy over meat. Pass rest, in gravy boat, with the roast and vegetables.

Makes 6 servings.

Sauerbraten with Gingersnap Sauce

1 cup cider vinegar
1 cup Burgundy
2 onions, sliced
1 carrot, sliced
1 stalk celery, chopped
2 whole allspice
4 whole cloves
1 tablespoon salt
1-1/2 teaspoons pepper
4 lb rump or boned chuck pot roast
4 tablespoons unsifted all-purpose flour
1/3 cup salad oil
1 tablespoon sugar
1/2 cup crushed gingersnaps
Caraway Noodles, page 291
Red Cabbage, page 293

1. In large bowl, combine vinegar, Burgundy, onion, carrot, celery, allspice, cloves, salt, and pepper.

2. Wipe meat with damp paper towels. Put in marinade; refrigerate, covered, 3 days, turning meat occasionally.

3. Remove meat from the marinade. Reserve marinade. Wipe meat dry with paper towels. Coat with 2 tablespoons flour.

4. In hot oil in Dutch oven, over medium heat, brown meat well on all sides.

5. Pour in marinade; simmer, covered, 2-1/2 to 3 hours, or until meat is tender.

6. Remove meat from Dutch oven. Press liquid and vegetables through coarse sieve; skim off fat. Measure 3-1/2 cups liquid (add water, if necessary). Return liquid to Dutch oven.

7. Mix remaining 2 tablespoons flour with 1/3 cup cold water and the sugar. Stir into liquid; bring to boiling, stirring. Stir in gingersnaps.

8. Return meat to the Dutch oven. Spoon gravy over it; simmer, covered, 20 minutes.

9. Remove meat to heated platter. Pour some of gravy over it. Serve meat, thinly sliced, with more gravy. Serve with Caraway Noodles and Red Cabbage.

Makes 6 servings.

Beef Stroganoff

2-lb filet of beef or boneless beef sirloin, 1/2 inch
  thick*
6 tablespoons butter or margarine
1 cup chopped onion
1 clove garlic, finely chopped
1/2 lb fresh mushrooms, sliced 1/4 inch thick
3 tablespoons flour
2 teaspoons meat-extract paste
1 tablespoon catsup
1/2 teaspoon salt
1/8 teaspoon pepper
1 can (10-1/2 oz) condensed beef broth, undiluted
1/4 cup dry white wine
1 tablespoon snipped fresh dill, or 1/4 teaspoon
  dried dillweed
1-1/2 cups dairy sour cream
1-1/2 cups cooked wild rice tossed with 4 cups
  cooked white rice
2 tablespoons snipped fresh dill or parsley
* If using sirloin, sprinkle with instant unseasoned
meat tenderizer, as package label directs.

1. Trim fat from beef. Cut crosswise into 1/2-inch-thick slices. Cut each slice across grain into 1/2-inch-wide strips.
2. Slowly heat large, heavy skillet. In it, melt 2 tablespoons butter. Add just enough beef strips to cover skillet bottom. Over high heat, sear quickly on all sides. With tongs, remove beef as it browns. (It should be browned outside, rare inside.) Brown rest of beef; set aside.
3. In remaining hot butter in same skillet, sauté onion, garlic, and mushrooms until onion is golden —about 5 minutes. Remove from heat. Add flour, meat-extract paste, catsup, salt, and pepper; stir until smooth. Gradually add beef broth; bring to boiling, stirring. Reduce heat; simmer 5 minutes.
4. Over low heat, add wine, snipped dill, and sour cream, stirring until well combined. Add beef; simmer just until sauce and beef are hot.
5. Serve Stroganoff with rice. Sprinkle dill or parsley over top.
Makes 6 servings.

Braised Swiss Steak, Family Style

2-1/2-lb beef round steak, 1-1/2 inches thick*
1/2 cup flour
1-1/2 teaspoons salt
1/2 teaspoon pepper
1/3 cup salad oil
2 cups sliced onion
1 can (1 lb) tomatoes
1/2 teaspoon dried thyme leaves
1 bay leaf
* A 3-1/2-lb blade-bone chuck steak, 1-1/2 inches
thick, may be used instead of round steak. Prepare
as above, braising about 15 minutes longer. After
removing steak to platter, pour pan liquid into
2-cup measure. Pour off excess fat—there should
be about 1 cup liquid left. Thicken if desired.

1. Wipe steak with damp paper towels. Combine flour, salt, pepper.
2. Spread half of flour mixture on a wooden board. Place steak on flour mixture, and sprinkle with remaining flour mixture. Pound it into both sides of steak, using a wooden mallet or rim of a heavy saucer or plate, until all the flour mixture has been pounded in.
3. In hot oil in large skillet, over medium heat, brown steak well on both sides—about 20 minutes in all. Sauté onion with steak during last 5 minutes.
4. Add tomatoes, 1/2 cup water, the thyme, and bay leaf; bring to boiling. Reduce heat, and simmer, covered, 1 hour. Turn steak, and simmer 1 hour longer, or until tender. Remove steak to heated platter.
5. Bring sauce in skillet to boiling, stirring to loosen any browned bits in pan.
6. Arrange onion on steak. Pour sauce around it.
Makes 6 servings.

Flank Steak Stroganoff

2-1/4-lb flank steak
6 tablespoons butter or margarine
1 clove garlic, halved
1 cup chopped onion
2 cans (6-oz size) button mushrooms, drained
3 tablespoons flour
1/2 teaspoon salt
1/8 teaspoon pepper
3 beef-bouillon cubes, crumbled
1 can (10-1/2 oz) condensed beef broth, undiluted
1/4 cup dry white wine
1 tablespoon snipped fresh dill, or 1-1/2 teaspoons
   dried dillweed
1 cup dairy sour cream

1. Place steak in freezer 15 minutes; it will be easier to slice.
2. Trim off excess fat. Slice steak, 1/4 inch thick, across the grain. Cut long strips into 2-1/2-inch pieces.
3. In large skillet, heat 2 tablespoons butter until very hot. Add sliced steak (just enough to cover bottom of pan); brown quickly on both sides. Remove from pan as it browns; continue browning the rest of the beef.
4. Add remaining butter to skillet. Sauté garlic, onion, and mushrooms 5 minutes. Remove from heat. Discard garlic.
5. Stir in flour, salt, and pepper until smooth; add bouillon cubes. Gradually stir in beef broth. Bring to boiling, stirring until thickened; reduce heat; simmer 5 minutes.
6. Over low heat, stir in wine, dill, and sour cream. Add the browned beef; heat slowly until thoroughly hot.
Makes 6 to 8 servings.

Simmering

Less expensive and less tender cuts such as beef brisket, corned beef and stew meat are prepared by cooking in liquid usually for a fairly long time. Although this means they must be started earlier, simmering requires little attention during the cooking, and the dish will usually not suffer if dinner is delayed and the cooking time is extended a few minutes. Simmer-cooking, which is also the method used to make meat soups, involves these steps: For stews, cut the meat into uniform pieces, usually one- to two-inch cubes. Brown the cubes on all sides. The browning brings out flavor and makes the meat more appetizing-looking. Exception: Corned beef should never be browned. If the meat is dredged with flour, add some fat to the pan for browning. Dredging in flour also makes the meat come out a deeper brown. After all sides of the beef are browned, cover the meat with water or stock. The liquid can be either hot or cold, but make sure it completely covers the meat throughout the simmering, to produce uniform cooking without your turning the meat. Season with salt, pepper, herbs, spices, vegetables in any combination that appeals to you. Again, corned beef is the exception; it should not be salted. In all other cases, though, seasonings artfully used add a delicious extra fillip to meats cooked in liquid. Literally dozens of spices and herbs are available everywhere today. Some of the most popular for seasoning stewed meats are bay leaves, thyme, marjoram, parsley, green pepper, celery and onion salts or flakes, garlic cloves, peppercorns and allspice.

When the meat is browned and liquid and seasonings poured over it, cover the kettle, and simmer until the meat is tender. The time required varies with the size of the piece or pieces of meat and, to some degree, with the particular type of meat. A stew, for example, may take from one to three hours, depending on whether the beef is chuck, round or shank. During cooking, *never* let the liquid boil. Boiling makes the meat shrink, dries it, and detracts from flavor and texture. With larger pieces, it also makes the meat difficult to slice.

If the beef is to be served cold, as is often the case with corned beef, let the cooked meat cool, and then refrigerate it in the stock it was cooked in. Beef retains more flavor and juice and shrinks less if cooled in its stock.

When vegetables are to be cooked with the meat, they can be added whole or in pieces at the appropriate time.

Beef and Vegetable Stew

3 lb beef for stew
6 tablespoons salad oil
1 cup chopped onion
1 cup chopped green pepper
1 cup sliced celery
1 can (10-1/2 oz) condensed beef broth, undiluted
1 can (8 oz) tomato sauce
2 tablespoons chopped parsley
1 clove garlic, finely chopped
1 tablespoon salt
1/4 teaspoon pepper
1/8 teaspoon dried thyme leaves
1 bay leaf
6 small potatoes, pared and halved (about 2 lb)
6 medium carrots, pared (about 3/4 lb)
6 small white onions, peeled
1 to 2 tablespoons flour
1 tomato, cut in wedges (optional)

1. Cut beef into 1-inch pieces. In hot oil in Dutch oven, over medium heat, brown one third meat at a time (just enough to cover bottom of pan) until browned on all sides. Remove as browned.
2. Add chopped onion, green pepper, and celery to Dutch oven, and sauté until tender—about 8 minutes. Return beef to pan.
3. Add 1/2 cup water, the beef broth, tomato sauce, parsley, garlic, salt, pepper, thyme, and bay leaf; bring to boiling. Reduce heat; simmer, covered and stirring several times, 1-1/4 hours.
4. Add potatoes, carrots, and onions. Simmer, covered, 1 hour longer, or until meat and vegetables are tender. Remove from heat; skim off fat.
5. Mix flour with 2 tablespoons water. Stir into beef mixture. Arrange tomato wedges, skin side up, on top; simmer, covered, 10 minutes.
Makes 6 servings.

Beef Ragout

2/3 cup flour
1 tablespoon salt
1/8 teaspoon pepper
3 lb beef chuck, cut in 1-1/2-inch cubes
1/3 cup salad oil
1 cup chopped onion
1 cup chopped celery
1/2 cup chopped green pepper
2 cloves garlic, crushed
2 cans (10-1/2-oz size) condensed beef consommé, undiluted
1 can (1 lb) tomatoes, undrained
1 can (6 oz) tomato paste
2 tablespoons chopped parsley
2 teaspoons paprika
2 teaspoons Worcestershire sauce
12 new potatoes, scrubbed (about 1 lb)

1. On waxed paper, combine flour, salt, and pepper; use to coat beef cubes. Reserve remaining flour mixture.
2. In 3 tablespoons hot oil in Dutch oven, brown beef cubes, a third at a time. Remove as they are browned. Add more oil as needed.
3. Add onion, celery, green pepper, and garlic to drippings in Dutch oven; sauté until tender—about 5 minutes. Remove from heat.
4. Stir in reserved flour mixture, stirring until well blended. Gradually stir in consommé. Add tomatoes, tomato paste, parsley, paprika, Worcestershire, and browned beef.
5. Bring to boiling, stirring occasionally. Reduce heat, and simmer, covered, 1-3/4 hours. Add potatoes, and cook, covered, 45 minutes longer, or until the potatoes and meat are tender. Sprinkle with more chopped parsley, if desired, before serving.
Makes 6 to 8 servings.

Boiled Beef Brisket

4-lb beef brisket
1 large onion, peeled and quartered
1/2 cup coarsely chopped celery
2 parsley sprigs
1-1/2 teaspoons salt
4 whole cloves
4 whole black peppercorns
1 bay leaf, crumbled
8 medium potatoes, pared (about 3 lb)
6 medium carrots, pared (about 3/4 lb)
1 medium head cabbage, cut in 6 wedges
  (optional)
Horseradish Sauce, page 496

1. Wipe beef with damp paper towels.
2. Slowly heat Dutch oven. Add brisket, fat side down; over medium heat, brown well on both sides —about 20 minutes in all. Discard drippings.
3. Turn brisket fat side up. Add onion, celery, parsley, salt, cloves, peppercorns, bay leaf, and 2 cups water.
4. Bring to boiling; reduce heat, and simmer, covered, 2-1/4 hours. Add potatoes and carrots; simmer 10 minutes. Add cabbage wedges; simmer about 20 minutes longer, or until meat and vegetables are tender.
5. Meanwhile, make Horseradish Sauce. Keep warm.
6. Remove meat and vegetables to heated serving platter. Serve with Horseradish Sauce.
Makes 6 to 8 servings.

Hungarian Goulash

1/4 cup salad oil
3-lb boneless beef chuck, cut in 1-inch cubes
1 lb onions, peeled and sliced (3 cups)
1 tablespoon paprika
1-1/2 teaspoons salt
1/8 teaspoon pepper
1 can (10-1/2 oz) condensed beef broth, undiluted
3 tablespoons flour
1 cup dairy sour cream
Poppyseed Noodles, page 463

1. In Dutch oven, heat oil over high heat. Add the beef cubes, in a single layer at a time, and cook, over medium heat, until cubes are well browned on all sides. As they brown, remove to a bowl. This will take about 15 to 20 minutes in all.
2. Add onion to drippings; sauté until tender and golden-brown—about 10 minutes.
3. Return meat to Dutch oven. Add paprika, salt, and pepper, stirring until well blended with meat. Stir in 3/4 cup beef broth.
4. Bring to boiling; then reduce heat, and simmer, covered, for 2 hours, or until the beef cubes are fork-tender.
5. In small bowl, combine flour and remaining beef broth, stirring until smooth. Gradually add to beef mixture, stirring constantly. Simmer, uncovered and stirring occasionally, 15 minutes longer.
6. Just before serving, place sour cream in small bowl. Slowly add 1/2 cup hot gravy. Slowly add to beef mixture, stirring until well blended. Heat, but do not boil. Serve the goulash with Poppyseed Noodles.
Makes 6 servings.

New England Boiled Dinner

4- to 5-lb corned-beef brisket
1 clove garlic
2 whole cloves
10 whole black peppercorns
2 bay leaves
8 medium carrots, pared
8 medium potatoes, pared
8 medium yellow onions, peeled
1 medium head cabbage, cut in 8 wedges
2 tablespoons butter or margarine
Chopped parsley
Mustard Sauce, page 499

1. Wipe corned beef with damp paper towels. Place in large kettle; cover with cold water. Add garlic, cloves, black peppercorns, and bay leaves.
2. Bring to boiling; reduce heat, and simmer 5 minutes. Skim surface; then simmer, covered, 3 to 4 hours, or until meat is fork-tender.
3. Add carrots, potatoes, and onions during last 25 minutes. Add cabbage during last 20 minutes. Cook just until vegetables are tender.
4. To serve: Slice corned beef thinly across the grain. Arrange on one side of serving platter. Place cabbage wedges beside meat. Brush potatoes with butter, and place in serving dish; sprinkle with parsley. Arrange carrots and onions in another dish. Pass Mustard Sauce.
Makes 8 servings.

Perfect Corned-Beef Hash

4 medium potatoes (1-1/2 lb), cooked and peeled*
1 can (12 oz) corned beef
1/2 cup chopped onion
1 teaspoon salt
1/4 teaspoon pepper
1 teaspoon monosodium glutamate
1/4 cup butter or margarine
Catsup or chili sauce
*Use either boiled or baked potatoes.

1. Finely chop potatoes, corned beef, and onion together.
2. In large bowl, combine mixture with salt, pepper, and monosodium glutamate; mix well.
3. Slowly heat butter in large skillet.
4. Turn hash mixture into skillet, patting down firmly with spatula or pancake turner.
5. Over medium heat, cook hash, uncovered, about 15 minutes, or until a brown crust forms on bottom.
6. Loosen edges; fold in half, like an omelet. Turn out on serving platter. Serve with catsup.
Makes 4 servings.

Ground Beef

Ground beef has the same quality protein, B vitamins and iron that you'd find in a roast of beef or a sirloin steak. Proteins are proteins and nutrition is nutrition, no matter what price you pay for the meat you buy. It's what you do with it that distinguishes the low-cost dish from the festive, elegant company one. Our recipes show you how to go grand at low prices.

Beef Balls Stroganoff

1-3/4 lb ground chuck
1 teaspoon salt
1/4 teaspoon pepper
4 teaspoons bottled steak sauce
1/3 cup packaged dry bread crumbs
1 egg
2 tablespoons butter or margarine

Sauce:
2 tablespoons butter or margarine
1/2 lb mushrooms, sliced
2 tablespoons flour
1 teaspoon catsup
1 can (10-1/2 oz) condensed beef broth, undiluted
1/2 pkg (1-5/8 oz) dry onion-soup mix
1 cup dairy sour cream

Oven-Steamed Rice, page 459

1. Make beef balls: In large bowl, lightly toss ground chuck with salt, pepper, steak sauce, crumbs, and the egg until well combined.
2. Using hands, gently shape the chuck mixture into 18 balls, each about 2 inches in diameter.
3. In 2 tablespoons hot butter in large skillet, brown beef balls well all over. Reduce heat; cook gently about 10 minutes. Remove beef balls.
4. Make Sauce: To drippings in skillet, add 2 tablespoons butter. Sauté mushrooms 5 minutes, stirring. Then remove from heat. Stir in flour and catsup.
5. Gradually stir in broth. Add the onion-soup mix; bring to boiling, stirring. Then reduce heat, and simmer for 2 minutes.
6. Add beef balls; simmer gently 5 minutes, or until heated through.
7. Stir in sour cream; heat gently, over low heat. Serve over Oven-Steamed Rice.
Makes 6 servings.

Bobotie

2 tablespoons butter or margarine
2 medium onions, sliced
2 lb ground chuck
1 egg
1/4 cup milk
2 slices white bread, cubed
1/4 cup dried apricots, finely chopped
1/4 cup dark raisins
12 blanched almonds, chopped
2 tablespoons sugar
1 tablespoon curry powder
2 tablespoons lemon juice
2 teaspoons salt
1/4 teaspoon pepper
5 bay leaves

Topping:
1 egg
3/4 cup milk
1/4 teaspoon turmeric

Hot cooked rice
Chutney

1. In hot butter in large skillet, sauté onion until golden—about 5 minutes. Add chuck, and sauté until browned. Remove from heat.
2. Preheat oven to 350F.
3. In large bowl, combine 1 egg, 1/4 cup milk, and the bread cubes, mashing bread with fork. Add apricots, raisins, almonds, sugar, curry, lemon juice, salt, and pepper; mix until well blended.
4. Add meat mixture; mix lightly with fork. Turn into 2-quart casserole, spreading evenly. Press bay leaves into mixture.
5. Bake, uncovered, 30 minutes.
6. Meanwhile, make Topping: In small bowl, beat egg with milk and turmeric just until blended. Set aside.
7. Remove casserole from oven; discard bay leaves. Pour topping over meat mixture.
8. Bake 10 to 15 minutes, or just until topping is set. Serve with rice and chutney.
Makes 8 servings.

Beef Balls Bourguignon

2-1/2 lb ground chuck
1 teaspoon salt
1/4 teaspoon pepper
1 tablespoon butter or margarine
3 tablespoons brandy
1/2 lb small fresh mushrooms
1/2 lb small white onions, peeled
2 tablespoons flour
1/2 cup canned condensed beef broth, undiluted
1 cup Burgundy
1/2 cup ruby port
1 teaspoon meat-extract paste
2 tablespoons tomato paste
1 bay leaf

1. Lightly mix beef with salt and pepper. Shape into 24 meatballs, about 2 inches in diameter. In hot butter in Dutch oven, brown meatballs well all over.
2. Heat brandy in small saucepan until bubbles form around edge of pan. Ignite with match, and pour over meatballs. When flame dies out, remove meatballs from Dutch oven with slotted spoon.
3. Add mushrooms to drippings in Dutch oven; sauté until lightly browned—about 5 minutes. Remove mushrooms, and add to meatballs.
4. Add onions to Dutch oven; sauté until lightly browned—about 5 minutes. Remove from heat. Stir in flour, then beef broth, wines, meat-extract paste, tomato paste, bay leaf.
5. Cook, stirring frequently, until thickened. Reduce heat; simmer, covered, 10 minutes. Add meatballs and mushrooms to mixture; simmer, covered and stirring occasionally, 30 minutes longer.
6. Serve with noodles.
Makes 8 servings.

Madras Curried Meatballs

Meatballs:
1 cup soft white-bread crumbs
2 lb ground chuck
2 teaspoons curry powder
1-1/2 teaspoons salt
1/2 teaspoon ginger
1/4 teaspoon pepper
2 tablespoons butter or margarine
2 tablespoons salad oil

Sauce:
1/2 cup chopped onion
1 clove garlic, crushed
1 cup chopped pared tart apple
4 teaspoons curry powder
3/4 teaspoon ginger
1/2 teaspoon salt
Dash pepper
1/4 cup unsifted all-purpose flour
1 can (1 lb, 1 oz) fruits for salad
1 can (10-1/2 oz) condensed chicken broth, undiluted
2 tablespoons lemon juice
4 cups cooked white rice

1. Make Meatballs: In large bowl, combine bread crumbs, 1/2 cup water, the chuck, 2 teaspoons curry powder, 1-1/2 teaspoons salt, 1/2 teaspoon ginger, and 1/4 teaspoon pepper; mix lightly with fork. With hands, lightly shape into 16 meatballs (1/4 cup each).
2. In hot butter and oil in Dutch oven, brown meatballs all over, half at a time. Remove as they are browned.
3. Make Sauce: In hot drippings in Dutch oven, sauté onion, garlic, apple, curry powder, ginger, salt, and pepper until onion is tender—about 5 minutes.
4. Remove from heat, stir in flour until smooth.
5. Drain fruit, reserving 2/3 cup juice. Gradually stir juice, then chicken broth into mixture in Dutch oven. Return to heat; cook, stirring, until mixture boils.
6. Add meatballs; simmer, covered, 25 minutes. Add fruit and lemon juice; heat 5 minutes.
7. Meanwhile, cook rice as package label directs.
8. To serve: Spoon rice onto large heated platter; mound meatballs with fruit and some of sauce in center. Pass rest of sauce.
Makes 4 to 6 servings.

Roast Meat Loaf

2 eggs
1 cup milk
3/4 cup raw quick-cooking oats
1 tablespoon salt
1 teaspoon monosodium glutamate
1/2 teaspoon dried savory leaves
1/4 teaspoon pepper
1 tablespoon chopped parsley
1 tablespoon butter or margarine
1/2 cup coarsely chopped onion
2-1/2 lb ground chuck

Glaze:
1/2 cup chili sauce
2 tablespoons brown sugar
1/4 teaspoon dry mustard
1/2 teaspoon liquid gravy seasoning

1. In large bowl, beat eggs slightly with fork. Stir in milk, oats, salt, monosodium glutamate, savory, pepper, and parsley; set aside.
2. In hot butter in skillet, sauté onion until tender —about 5 minutes.
3. Add to egg mixture along with chuck; mix until well combined, using hands if necessary.
4. Line a 9-by-5-by-3-inch loaf pan with waxed paper. Turn meat mixture into pan, packing down well; refrigerate, covered, at least 2 hours.
5. Preheat oven to 350F.
6. Run spatula around edge of meat loaf, to loosen. Carefully turn out into shallow baking pan, keeping original shape as much as possible; bake 30 minutes.
7. Meanwhile, make Glaze: In small bowl, combine all ingredients, mixing well. Brush top and sides of meat loaf with glaze.
8. Bake 45 minutes, brushing several times with glaze. Remove to platter.
Makes 8 to 10 servings.

Hamburger Roulade

Stuffing:
3 tablespoons butter or margarine
1/3 cup chopped onion
1/3 cup chopped celery
1 cup packaged herb-seasoned stuffing

Meat Mixture:
1 egg
1-1/2 lb ground chuck
1/2 cup milk
1/3 cup raw quick-cooking oats
1/4 cup finely chopped onion
1 tablespoon chopped parsley
1-1/2 teaspoons salt
1/2 teaspoon monosodium glutamate
1/8 teaspoon pepper

4 cooked carrots, halved lengthwise
6 slices bacon
1/4 cup chili sauce
2 tablespoons dark corn syrup

1. Make Stuffing: In hot butter in small saucepan, sauté 1/3 cup onion and the celery until tender— about 5 minutes. Add stuffing and 1/3 cup water; mix well. Set aside.
2. Preheat oven to 350F.
3. Make Meat Mixture: In medium bowl, beat egg slightly with fork. Add chuck, milk, oats, onion, parsley, salt, monosodium glutamate, and pepper; mix lightly with fork until well combined.
4. Turn onto large sheet of waxed paper. With moistened hands, pat into 12-by-9-inch rectangle. Spread evenly with stuffing. Arrange carrots lengthwise down center.
5. Starting from long side, roll up like a jelly roll, peeling off waxed paper while rolling. Place, seam side down, in 12-by-8-by-2-inch baking dish. Arrange bacon slices close together over top; wrap around roll.
6. Bake 45 minutes. Mix chili sauce with corn syrup; brush over top of meat roll between bacon slices. Bake 5 minutes longer.
7. Let stand in baking dish 5 minutes; then carefully remove to serving platter. Serve immediately.
Makes 6 servings.

Tamale Casserole

2 tablespoons salad or olive oil
1 cup chopped onion
2 cloves garlic, crushed
1-1/2 lb ground chuck
3 to 5 teaspoons chili powder
2 teaspoons salt
1 can (8 oz) tomato sauce
1 can (12 oz) Mexican-style corn, undrained
1 can (15-1/4 oz) red kidney beans, undrained
1/2 cup pitted ripe olives, quartered
1/2 pkg (6-1/4-oz size) tortilla chips
1 cup grated Cheddar cheese

1. In hot oil in Dutch oven, sauté onion and garlic until golden—about 3 minutes. Add ground chuck, breaking up with fork.
2. Cook, stirring occasionally, over medium heat until browned—about 10 minutes. Drain off excess fat.
3. Add chili powder, salt, tomato sauce, corn, and kidney beans. Bring to boiling, stirring; reduce heat; simmer, uncovered and stirring occasionally, 20 minutes.
4. Preheat oven to 375F.
5. Turn meat mixture into 10-inch round, shallow casserole. Sprinkle with olives. Arrange tortilla chips around edge; sprinkle chips with cheese. Bake 10 minutes, or until cheese is melted.
Makes 6 servings.

Italian Spaghetti and Meatballs

Sauce:
1/4 cup butter or margarine
1 cup chopped onion
2 cloves garlic, crushed
1/2 cup chopped celery
1 teaspoon salt
1/2 teaspoon pepper
1/2 cup chopped green pepper
1/2 cup dry white wine
2 cans (1-lb, 3-oz size) tomatoes, undrained
1 can (6 oz) tomato paste
1/4 teaspoon dried oregano leaves

Meatballs:
1 lb ground chuck
1/2 lb ground veal
1/2 lb lean ground pork
1/4 cup pkg dry, flavored bread crumbs
2 cloves garlic, crushed
2 teaspoons salt
1/2 teaspoon pepper
2 eggs, slightly beaten
1/2 cup milk
1 teaspoon dried basil leaves
1/2 cup chopped parsley
1/4 cup olive or salad oil

1 pkg (1 lb) spaghetti
Grated Parmesan cheese

1. Make Sauce: In hot butter in 6-quart Dutch oven or kettle, sauté onion, garlic, and celery, stirring, 5 minutes.
2. Add remaining sauce ingredients; mix well. Bring to boiling, stirring. Reduce heat; simmer, covered, 2 hours, stirring occasionally.
3. Make Meatballs: In large bowl, combine all ingredients, except oil. Mix well with hands to combine.
4. With moistened hands, shape mixture into meatballs, 1-1/2 inches in diameter.
5. In hot oil in medium skillet, sauté meatballs (just enough at one time to cover bottom of skillet), until browned all over. Remove from skillet as they brown.
6. Add meatballs to sauce; simmer, covered, 30 minutes longer.
7. Meanwhile, cook spaghetti as package label directs; drain.
8. To serve: Mound meatballs in center of large, round platter; surround with spaghetti. Pour sauce over all. Sprinkle with cheese.
Makes 6 to 8 servings.

Stuffed Cabbage Rolls

1 large head green cabbage (about 3-1/2 lb)
1 lb ground chuck
1/2 cup raw regular white rice
1 small onion, grated
2 eggs, beaten
1 teaspoon salt
1/4 teaspoon pepper
1/8 teaspoon allspice
1 large onion, sliced

Sauce:
2 cans (8-oz size) tomato sauce
1 can (1 lb, 12 oz) tomatoes
1/3 cup lemon juice
1 teaspoon salt
1/8 teaspoon pepper
1/4 cup light-brown sugar

1. In large kettle, bring 3 quarts water to boiling. Add cabbage; simmer 2 to 3 minutes, or until leaves are pliable. Remove cabbage; drain.
2. Carefully remove 12 large leaves from cabbage; trim thick rib. If leaves are not soft enough to roll, return to boiling water for a minute.
3. Preheat oven to 375F.
4. In large bowl, combine chuck, rice, grated onion, eggs, 1 teaspoon salt, 1/4 teaspoon pepper, the allspice, and 1/4 cup water. Mix with fork until well blended.
5. Place about 1/4 cup meat mixture in hollow of each of the 12 cabbage leaves. Fold sides of leaf over stuffing; roll up from the thick end of the leaf.
6. In Dutch oven, place a few of the remaining cabbage leaves. Arrange rolls, seam side down, on leaves. Top with onion slices.
7. Make Sauce: In large bowl, combine tomato sauce, tomatoes, lemon juice, 1/4 cup water, the salt, and pepper. Pour over cabbage rolls.
8. Bring to boiling over medium heat. Sprinkle with sugar; cover, and place in oven.
9. Bake 1-1/2 hours. Uncover; bake 1-1/2 hours longer.
Makes 6 to 8 servings.

Upside-Down Chili Pie

1 tablespoon salad or olive oil
1-1/2 lb ground chuck
1/2 cup chopped onion
1 clove garlic, crushed
1 tablespoon chili powder
1-1/4 teaspoons salt
1 teaspoon dried oregano leaves
1/2 teaspoon dried basil leaves
1 can (8-1/4 oz) tomatoes, undrained
1 can (8-1/2 oz) kidney beans, undrained
1/2 cup red wine or beef broth
1 pkg (12 oz) corn-muffin mix
1 can (8-3/4 oz) cream-style corn
1 egg
1/4 cup milk
Grated Cheddar cheese
Chopped parsley
Catsup

1. In hot oil in heavy, 10-inch skillet, sauté chuck, onion, and garlic until chuck is browned—about 5 minutes.
2. Add chili powder, salt, oregano, basil, and tomatoes; mix well. Cook over low heat, covered, 30 minutes. Stir in kidney beans and wine; cook 10 minutes longer.
3. Preheat oven to 400F.
4. In medium bowl, combine corn-muffin mix, corn, egg, and milk; mix just until muffin mix is moistened.
5. Skim fat from meat mixture in skillet, and discard. Spread the muffin mixture over the meat mixture evenly.
6. Bake 25 minutes, or until top is golden-brown. Let stand in skillet 2 minutes; then invert onto serving platter. Garnish with grated cheese and parsley. Serve with catsup.
Makes 8 servings.

Stuffed Eggplant Creole

2 small eggplants (about 2 lb)
Salt
2 tablespoons bacon fat or salad oil
1/2 lb ground beef
1 clove garlic, crushed
1/4 cup finely chopped onion
1/4 cup finely chopped green pepper
1/4 cup finely chopped celery
1 can (1 lb) tomatoes, undrained
1/4 teaspoon dried thyme leaves
1/2 teaspoon Tabasco
1/2 cup Grapenuts
1/2 cup pkg dry bread crumbs
1/4 cup butter or margarine, melted

1. Wash eggplants; cut in half lengthwise. Add with 1/2 teaspoon salt to 1 inch boiling water in kettle; simmer, covered, 15 minutes. Drain; cool.
2. Preheat oven to 375F. Carefully scoop out pulp from eggplant halves, leaving 1/4-inch-shell. Dice pulp; set aside with shells.
3. In bacon fat in large skillet, sauté beef with garlic until brown. Add onion, green pepper, and celery; cook over low heat about 5 minutes.
4. Stir in tomatoes, 1-1/2 teaspoons salt, the thyme, and Tabasco; remove from heat. Add diced eggplant and the Grapenuts.
5. Spoon meat mixture into eggplant shells. Place in shallow baking pan. Combine bread crumbs and butter; sprinkle over stuffed eggplants.
6. Bake, uncovered, about 45 to 50 minutes, or until hot and bubbly.
Makes 4 servings.

Hamburgers

1 lb chuck, coarsely ground (only once)

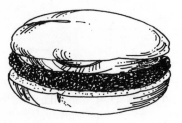

1. Shape gently into 4 thick patties.
2. To Broil: Preheat broiler. Arrange patties on cold broiler rack. Broil, 3 inches from heat, turning once, 8 to 10 minutes, or until of desired doneness.
Or Pan-Broil: Heat heavy skillet until sizzling. Brush lightly with a little oil. Brown patties on both sides, cook 5 to 8 minutes longer, or until of desired doneness.
Makes 4 servings.

Frankfurters

Frankfurters may be all beef or a combination of beef and pork. They come in different sizes and styles. They are great budget foods, very popular with children.

How to Store Frankfurters

Leave them in their original package, or wrap them loosely in waxed paper, plastic wrap or foil. Keep in refrigerator. Use within 3 to 4 days, for peak flavor.

How to Heat Frankfurters

Simmered: Drop frankfurters into a kettle of boiling water. Cover. Remove from heat, or keep heat so low the water never boils. Heat 5 to 8 minutes. Remove with tongs. Never break skins with a fork.

Pan-Broiled: Melt a tablespoon of fat in skillet or griddle. Add frankfurters, and heat, over low temperature, until brown. Use tongs to turn.

Broiled: Rub each frankfurter with butter, margarine or salad oil. Arrange on broiler rack, and broil, 3 inches from heat, until evenly browned.

Campfire Grilled: Let the fire burn down to glowing coals. Put frankfurters on long forks or green sticks, and grill over coals until brown.

Franks and Sauerkraut in Beer

10 large frankfurters (5 or 6 per lb)
1 can (12 oz) light beer
1 can (1 lb, 11 oz) sauerkraut, drained
2 teaspoons caraway seed

1. Slash frankfurters, on the diagonal, in several places. Place in large skillet with beer.
2. Cook over medium heat, covered, until hot—about 10 minutes. Remove frankfurters.
3. Stir sauerkraut and caraway into liquid in skillet; place frankfurters on top. Cook, covered, 10 minutes, or until sauerkraut is heated through.
4. Arrange sauerkraut and frankfurters on heated platter. Serve with buttered new potatoes, hot mustard.

Makes 5 or 6 servings.

Frankfurter Goulash

1-1/2 lb frankfurters
2 tablespoons butter or margarine
2 cups chopped onion
1 clove garlic, finely chopped
1 tablespoon paprika
1 teaspoon dried dill weed
1 teaspoon caraway seed
1 beef-bouillon cube
1 cup boiling water
1 can (1 lb, 11 oz) sauerkraut, drained
2 cups dairy sour cream

1. Cut frankfurters in half crosswise.
2. In hot butter in Dutch oven or heavy kettle, sauté onion, garlic, and paprika until onion is soft. Add frankfurters, dill, caraway, bouillon cube, and boiling water.
3. Bring to boiling; reduce heat, and simmer, covered, 15 minutes.
4. Add sauerkraut; simmer, covered, 15 minutes longer.
5. Stir in sour cream; heat but do not boil. Serve with boiled or mashed potatoes.

Makes 8 servings.

Pork

Whenever pork is in abundance, it is one of the best buys in the market. It provides as much high-quality protein as other meats, and the new variety of pork is leaner, has less fat. Remember: Pork must be thoroughly cooked.

Timetable for Roasting Fresh Pork—at 325F

Cut	Weight	Internal Temperature	Approx. Roasting Time
Fresh Ham	10 to 14 lb	185F	6 to 7 hours
Fresh Ham (half)	5 to 6 lb	185F	3-1/2 to 4 hours
Loin	4 to 5 lb	185F	3-1/4 to 3-1/2 hours
Loin End	2-1/2 to 3 lb	185F	2-1/4 to 2-1/2 hours
Shoulder Butt	4 to 6 lb	185F	3-1/2 to 4 hours

Roast Pork with Herb Gravy

3-1/2-lb loin of pork
1 tablespoon finely chopped onion
2 tablespoons flour
1 teaspoon salt
1/8 teaspoon pepper
1 teaspoon dried sage leaves
1/4 teaspoon dried thyme leaves
1/4 teaspoon dried oregano leaves
1/4 teaspoon liquid gravy seasoning

1. Preheat oven to 325F.
2. Wipe pork with damp paper towels. Place pork, fat side up, in shallow roasting pan. (Omit rack; pork will rest on bones.) Insert meat thermometer into center of meaty part of pork; it should not rest against bone.
3. Roast 2-1/2 to 3 hours, or to 185F on meat thermometer. Remove to heated platter; keep warm.
4. Pour off fat from pan (leaving any meat juices in pan). Return 1 tablespoon fat to pan.
5. Add onion; sauté, stirring and over direct heat, about 3 minutes, or until onion is golden. Remove from heat.
6. Stir in flour, to form a smooth mixture. Stir in rest of ingredients.
7. Gradually add 1-1/2 cups water; bring to boiling, stirring—mixture will be thickened and smooth.
8. Reduce heat; simmer 2 minutes. Serve gravy with pork.
Makes 6 to 8 servings.

Roast Fresh Ham

10-lb bone-in fresh ham
1 teaspoon salt
1/4 teaspoon pepper
2 cups sliced onion
1 can (10-3/4 oz) condensed chicken broth, undiluted
1 can (8-3/4 oz) crushed pineapple, drained
1/4 cup honey
1/4 teaspoon cinnamon
1/8 teaspoon ginger
6 tablespoons flour

1. Preheat oven to 375F.
2. Wipe ham with damp paper towels. Remove skin and excess fat from ham. Rub with salt and pepper. Place, fat side up, in shallow, open roasting pan.
3. Roast, uncovered, 1-1/2 hours. Remove from oven. Reduce oven temperature to 350F.
4. Drain drippings from pan, and discard. Arrange onion slices around ham; pour chicken broth into pan. Insert meat thermometer into thickest part of meat; it should not rest on bone or fat. Cover with foil.
5. Roast, covered, 2 hours. Remove from oven. Pour drippings into medium saucepan, and set aside.

6. In small bowl, combine pineapple, honey, cinnamon, and ginger. Spread evenly over ham. Roast, uncovered, 45 minutes longer, or until meat thermometer registers 185F. Remove ham to heated platter.

7. Skim off excess fat from drippings in saucepan. Measure 4 cups liquid; return to saucepan. Mix flour with 1/4 cup water until smooth. Stir into drippings; bring to boiling, stirring constantly. Reduce heat, and simmer 3 minutes. Serve with ham. Makes 8 to 10 servings.

Roast Pork with Sautéed Peppers

5-lb loin of pork
Salt
Dried rosemary leaves
Dried oregano leaves
Dried thyme leaves
Dried sage
Pepper
Nutmeg
1 cup thinly sliced onion
1 cup thinly sliced carrot
Sautéed Sweet Peppers, below

Herb Gravy:
1/4 cup pan drippings
1/4 cup unsifted all-purpose flour
Boiling water

1. Preheat oven to 325F. Wipe pork with damp paper towels.

2. In small bowl, combine 2 teaspoons each salt and rosemary; 1-1/2 teaspoons each oregano, thyme, and sage; and 1/4 teaspoon each pepper and nutmeg. With paring knife, make 1/2-inch-deep slits on back of roast between ribs and on fat side of meat. Press half of herb mixture into slits; rub remaining herb mixture on surface of meat.

3. Insert meat thermometer in center of roast, away from bone. Place roast, fat side up, in shallow roasting pan without rack. (Roast will rest on bones.) Scatter onion and carrot around roast.

4. Roast about 3 hours, or until meat thermometer registers 185F.

5. Meanwhile, prepare Sautéed Sweet Peppers.

6. Remove roast to heated platter. Surround roast with peppers; keep warm in low oven.

7. Make Herb Gravy: Pour pan drippings with onion and carrot mixture through strainer. Reserve 1/4 cup drippings; discard onion and carrot.

8. In 1-quart saucepan, combine reserved pan drippings and the flour; mix until smooth; set aside. Pour 2-3/4 cups boiling water into roasting pan. Return to boiling, loosening brown particles and brown drippings from pan. Continue boiling about 2 minutes.

9. Slowly pour boiling liquid into flour mixture, stirring briskly with wire whisk. Stir in 1/2 teaspoon salt, 1/4 teaspoon rosemary, 1/8 teaspoon oregano, 1/8 teaspoon thyme, 1/8 teaspoon sage, 1/8 teaspoon pepper, and dash nutmeg. Bring to boiling, stirring constantly.

10. Reduce heat, and simmer, covered, 5 minutes. Stir with wire whisk just before serving. (You should have about 2-1/2 cups.) Serve with roast. Makes 8 servings.

Sautéed Sweet Peppers

6 or 7 green and red peppers (2 lb)
1/2 cup salad oil
1 cup sliced onion
1 clove garlic, crushed
1 teaspoon salt
1/8 teaspoon pepper

1. Wash peppers. Slice into 3/4-inch-wide strips, removing ribs and seeds.
2. In hot oil in large skillet, sauté onion and garlic, stirring occasionally, 5 minutes. Add peppers; sauté, stirring occasionally, 10 minutes. Sprinkle with salt and pepper.

Glazed Smoked Shoulder Butt

3 lb fully cooked smoked boneless shoulder butt, sliced 1 inch thick
1 can (9 oz) crushed pineapple, undrained
1/4 cup light-brown sugar, firmly packed
1/4 teaspoon cinnamon
1/8 teaspoon cloves
1/4 teaspoon dry mustard
2 tablespoons vinegar
3 maraschino cherries, quartered

1. Preheat oven to 375F.
2. Place butt slices, overlapping, in a 12-by-8-by-2-inch baking dish.
3. Add 1/2 cup water; bake, uncovered, 30 minutes. Drain off liquid.
4. Meanwhile, combine rest of ingredients in small saucepan; bring to boiling. Reduce heat, and simmer 2 minutes, stirring.
5. Pour over meat; bake 30 minutes. Serve pork slices with the glaze spooned over.
Makes 6 to 8 servings.

Party Crown Roast of Pork with Apple Stuffing

4-3/4-lb crown roast of pork
2-1/4 teaspoons salt
1/2 teaspoon pepper
4-1/2 tablespoons flour
1 cup diced, unpared tart apple
2-1/2 cups toasted bread cubes
1/4 cup seedless raisins, soaked
1/4 cup chopped cooked prunes
1/4 cup butter or margarine, melted
2 tablespoons light-brown sugar
1 teaspoon grated lemon peel
1/4 teaspoon paprika
1/4 teaspoon cinnamon
1/4 cup apple juice
1/2 teaspoon liquid gravy seasoning

1. Preheat oven to 325F.
2. Wipe meat well with damp paper towels.
3. Combine 1 teaspoon salt, 1/4 teaspoon pepper, and 2 tablespoons flour; rub meat well with mixture.
4. Insert meat thermometer into center of fleshy part of meat, away from fat and bone. Place roast in shallow roasting pan, without rack; roast 1 hour and 15 minutes.
5. Meanwhile, prepare stuffing. In large bowl, toss apple, bread cubes, raisins, prunes, butter, sugar, lemon peel, paprika, cinnamon, apple juice, and 1/2 teaspoon salt.
6. Remove roast from oven. Spoon stuffing lightly into center cavity, mounding it. Cover stuffing with 10-inch square of foil.
7. Return roast to oven; roast 1 hour and 25 minutes, or until meat thermometer registers 185F. Place roast on heated platter; keep warm while making gravy.
8. In small saucepan, blend 2 tablespoons pan drippings with 2-1/2 tablespoons flour.

9. Stir in 1-1/2 cups water, gravy seasoning, 3/4 teaspoon salt, and 1/4 teaspoon pepper; cook, over medium heat and stirring constantly, until mixture boils and thickens. Serve with roast.
Makes 8 servings.

Glazed Smoked Pork with Buttered Carrots and Cabbage

3-lb boneless smoked pork shoulder butt
4 whole black peppercorns
2 whole cloves
1 bay leaf
1/2 cup apricot preserves

Buttered Carrots:
4 large carrots, pared and cut on diagonal into
    1/8-inch-thick slices
1/2 teaspoon salt
1 tablespoon sugar
2 tablespoons butter or margarine

Buttered Cabbage:
2-1/4 teaspoons salt
3 quarts shredded cabbage (2-1/2 lb)
1/4 cup butter or margarine
1 tablespoon cider vinegar
1/4 teaspoon pepper

1. Remove wrapping from pork butt. Place butt in 6-quart kettle or Dutch oven; cover with water. Add peppercorns, cloves, and bay leaf; bring to boiling. Reduce heat, and simmer 2-1/4 hours (45 minutes per pound), or until pork is fork-tender. Remove from heat; let meat cool in water about 2 hours.
2. Preheat oven to 375F. Remove meat from cooking liquid, and place in shallow roasting pan. Spread apricot preserves over top.
3. Bake, uncovered, 40 minutes.
4. Meanwhile, prepare Buttered Carrots: In 1 inch boiling water, cook carrots with 1/2 teaspoon salt and the sugar 10 minutes, or until tender. Drain; add 2 tablespoons butter. Cover, and keep warm.
5. Also prepare Buttered Cabbage: In 1 quart boiling water with 1 teaspoon salt, cook cabbage 5 minutes, or just until tender. Drain well, and toss with butter, vinegar, remaining salt, and the pepper.
6. To serve: Arrange cabbage in center of large platter. Cut pork butt into 1-inch slices, and place on cabbage. Arrange carrots around edge of platter.
Makes 8 servings.

Pork-and-Sauerkraut Goulash

2-lb boneless pork-shoulder roast, trimmed
2 cups chopped onion
1 clove garlic, finely chopped
1 teaspoon dried dill weed
1 teaspoon caraway seed
1 tablespoon salt
1 beef-bouillon cube
1/2 cup boiling water
1 tablespoon paprika
1 can (1 lb, 11 oz) sauerkraut, drained
2 cups dairy sour cream

1. Cut pork into 2-inch cubes.
2. In large Dutch oven or heavy kettle, combine pork, onion, garlic, dill, caraway seed, salt, bouillon cube, and boiling water.
3. Bring to boiling. Reduce heat, and simmer, covered, 1 hour.
4. Add paprika; stir until dissolved. Add sauerkraut; mix well.
5. Simmer, covered, until meat is tender—1 hour longer.
6. Stir in sour cream; heat thoroughly.
Makes 6 servings.

Orange-Braised Pork Chops

6 loin pork chops, 1 inch thick
2 tablespoons flour
1/2 teaspoon salt
2 tablespoons salad oil or shortening
1 tablespoon light-brown sugar
1/8 teaspoon ginger
1 tablespoon grated orange peel
1 cup orange juice
1 cup orange sections

1. Wipe chops with damp paper towels. Coat with mixture of flour and salt.
2. In hot oil in large skillet, brown chops well on both sides—about 10 minutes per side. Drain fat.
3. Combine remaining ingredients, except orange sections. Pour over chops; cover.
4. Reduce heat; simmer 45 to 50 minutes, or until chops are fork-tender.
5. Add orange sections just before serving.
Makes 6 servings.

Fresh-Ham Hocks, Country Style

5 lb fresh-ham hocks
1 quart apple cider
1/4 cup cider vinegar
1/4 cup butter or margarine
3 cups sliced onion
1 teaspoon sugar
Salt
Pepper
4 cups cubed (1-inch) yellow turnip or
    rutabaga (1-1/2 lb)
1 bay leaf
1 jar (1 lb) applesauce

1. Preheat oven to 350F. Wash ham hocks; dry with paper towels. Arrange in 15-by-10-by-2-inch roasting pan. Pour cider and vinegar over ham hocks. Cover pan with foil; bake 1-1/2 hours, basting several times with liquid.
2. Meanwhile, in hot margarine in medium skillet, sauté onion with sugar until onions are lightly browned. Sprinkle with 1/2 teaspoon salt and 1/8 teaspoon pepper; set aside.
3. Remove ham hocks from oven; skim off fat, and discard. Add turnip; sprinkle with 1-1/2 teaspoons salt and 1/2 teaspoon pepper. Add browned onion and bay leaf; bake, covered, 1-1/2 hours.
4. Remove foil; spoon applesauce around ham hocks; bake, uncovered, 1/2 hour longer, or until ham hocks are very tender. Serve with turnips and pan liquid spooned over all.
Makes 6 servings.

Baked Pork Chops and Apples

6 rib pork chops, 1 inch thick (2-1/2 lb)
1-1/2 teaspoons sage
1-1/2 teaspoons salt
1/4 teaspoon pepper
1 lb carrots, pared
2 cups sliced onion
1 lb tart cooking apples, pared and quartered
1/4 cup light-brown sugar

1. Preheat oven to 350F.
2. Wipe pork chops with damp paper towels. Trim off fat.
3. On waxed paper, combine sage, salt, and pepper. Dip both sides of chops in seasoning.
4. Slice carrots diagonally 1/2 inch thick. Layer in 3-quart casserole or baking dish. Top with half of onion. Then add chops, slightly overlapping; sprinkle with any remaining seasoning. Cover chops with remaining onion. Arrange apple quarters over all; sprinkle with brown sugar.

5. Bake, covered, 2-1/2 hours. Remove cover; baste with pan juices. Bake 30 minutes, or until tender.
6. Let stand for 5 minutes, and then skim off fat.
Makes 6 servings.

Swiss Pork Chops with Mustard Sauce

6 loin or rib pork chops, about 1 inch thick
    (2-1/4 lb)
2 tablespoons flour
1 teaspoon salt
1/4 teaspoon pepper
2 tablespoons butter or margarine
1/4 cup white wine
1 tablespoon lemon juice

Mustard Sauce:
1-1/2 tablespoons flour
1 cup light cream
2 tablespoons Dijon-style prepared mustard
Dash cayenne

1. Wipe pork chops with damp paper towels. Trim off fat, if necessary. Mix 2 tablespoons flour, the salt, and pepper; use to coat chops.
2. In hot butter in large skillet, brown chops well on both sides—about 20 minutes in all.
3. Add wine and lemon juice; simmer, covered, 45 to 50 minutes, or until chops are tender. Remove chops to warm serving platter.
4. Make Mustard Sauce: Stir flour into drippings in skillet until smooth. Stir in cream, mustard, cayenne. Boil, stirring, 1 minute.
5. Serve chops with sauce.
Makes 6 servings.

Baked Stuffed Pork Chops

4 rib pork chops, cut 2 inches thick, each with
    a pocket

Savory Stuffing:
2 tablespoons butter or margarine
1/3 cup finely chopped onion
1/2 cup chopped celery
1-1/2 cups soft bread cubes
1/4 cup dark raisins
2 tablespoons chopped parsley
1 teaspoon salt
1/2 teaspoon dried marjoram leaves
1/8 teaspoon pepper
3 tablespoons apple juice
1 teaspoon seasoned salt

1. Preheat oven to 350F. Wipe pork chops well with damp paper towels.
2. Make Savory Stuffing: In hot butter in skillet, cook onion and celery until tender—about 8 minutes. Add bread cubes, and brown slightly. Remove from heat.
3. Add raisins, parsley, salt, marjoram, pepper, and apple juice; toss mixture lightly, to combine.
4. Fill pockets in chops with Savory Stuffing. Stand chops on rib bones on rack in a shallow roasting pan; sprinkle with seasoned salt. Pour water to 1/2-inch depth in roasting pan—water should not touch the rack. Cover chops and pan with foil.
5. Bake chops 45 minutes. Remove the foil, and bake, uncovered, 45 to 55 minutes longer, or until the chops are tender and brown.
Makes 4 servings.

Maple-Barbecued Spareribs

1-1/2 cups maple syrup
2 tablespoons chili sauce
2 tablespoons cider vinegar
1-1/2 tablespoons finely chopped onion
1 tablespoon Worcestershire sauce
1 teaspoon salt
1/2 teaspoon dry mustard
1/8 teaspoon pepper
3 lb spareribs, cut in serving-size pieces

1. Preheat oven to 350F.
2. In medium bowl, combine maple syrup with rest of ingredients, except spareribs; mix well.
3. Wipe spareribs with damp paper towels. Brush on both sides with maple basting sauce.
4. Place ribs, in single layer, on rack in shallow, open roasting pan. Roast 1-1/2 hours, or until tender, brushing frequently with sauce and turning occasionally, to glaze evenly.
Makes 4 servings.

Ham

A beautifully glazed baked ham is perfect to serve at an informal summer buffet, or a holiday cocktail party, certainly a must for Easter Sunday. Use up the leftovers, hot or cold—in casseroles, salads, sandwiches—until nothing's left but the bone for pea soup.

Timetable for Baking Ham—at 325F

Type	Weight	Internal Temperature	Approx. Baking Time
Fully Cooked Ham:			
Bone-in whole ham	8 to 12 lb	130F	2-1/4 to 2-3/4 hours
Bone-in whole ham	14 to 18 lb	130F	3 to 3-1/2 hours
Bone-in half ham	6 to 8 lb	130F	2 to 2-1/4 hours
Boneless whole ham	8 to 10 lb	130F	2-1/2 to 3 hours
Boneless quarter or half ham	2-1/2 to 5 lb	130F	1-1/2 to 1-3/4 hours
Cook-before-Eating-Ham:			
Bone-in whole ham	8 to 12 lb	155F	2-3/4 to 3-1/4 hours
Bone-in whole ham	14 to 18 lb	155F	3-1/2 to 4 hours
Bone-in half ham	6 to 8 lb	155F	2 to 2-1/2 hours

Baked Ham in Crust with Cumberland Sauce

Pastry:
2 pkg (11-oz size) piecrust mix
1-1/2 tablespoons dry mustard
1-1/2 teaspoons dried sage leaves
1/2 cup ice water
12-lb fully cooked bone-in whole ham
1 egg yolk

Cumberland Sauce, page 499

1. Preheat oven to 375F.
2. Make Pastry: In medium bowl, combine piecrust mix, mustard, and sage; mix well. Blend in ice water as the label directs. Shape into a ball.
3. On lightly floured surface, roll out pastry to about 1/8-inch thickness. Trim to make a 22-by-17-1/2-inch rectangle. Save trimmings.
4. Remove rind from ham. Place ham near one end of rectangle, covering about one third of the pastry,

and mold short end of pastry to ham. Bring long end of pastry over ham, and mold around top and sides of ham, pressing firmly. Moisten edges with cold water, and press together firmly, to seal.

5. Roll out trimmings, and cut with leaf cookie cutter.

6. Beat egg yolk with 1 teaspoon cold water; brush some of egg over pastry. Arrange leaf cutouts decoratively on top; brush with egg. Place ham on cookie sheet or in jelly-roll pan.

7. Bake 1-1/2 hours, or until pastry is a deep golden-brown. (If pastry breaks, tuck a piece of foil under ham, to keep it level.)

8. For buffet serving, cut a lengthwise slice from thin underside; then stand ham on cut side. Serve with Cumberland Sauce.

Makes 24 servings.

Ham Baked in Cider

10- to 12-lb fully cooked bone-in ham
1/2 cup sliced onion
1 bay leaf, crumbled
4 cups apple cider
1/2 cup light-brown sugar, packed
1 tablespoon lemon juice
1/4 cup sliced onion
Whole cloves
Apple-Cider Sauce, page 498

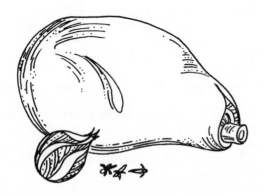

1. Preheat oven to 325F.

2. Wipe ham with damp paper towels. Place in shallow roasting pan without rack. Arrange 1/2 cup onion slices on ham; sprinkle with bay leaf.

3. Insert meat thermometer in center of thickest part of ham, away from bone. Pour 2 cups cider into pan. Cover pan tightly with foil.

4. Bake ham 2-1/2 to 3 hours, or until meat thermometer registers 130F. Remove ham from oven; drain liquid.

5. Meanwhile, in medium saucepan, combine remaining 2 cups cider, the brown sugar, lemon juice, and onion; bring to boiling, boil, uncovered, 5 minutes; strain.

6. Return ham to roasting pan. With sharp knife, make diagonal cuts in fat (be careful not to cut into meat), 1/4 inch deep and 1 inch apart. Stud the center of each diamond shape with a whole clove.

7. Pour cider mixture over ham. Bake, uncovered and basting every 15 minutes, until meat thermometer registers 140F—about 40 minutes.

8. Remove ham to serving platter. Let stand 20 minutes before carving.

9. Serve with Apple-Cider Sauce.

Makes 20 servings.

Baked Ham and Scalloped Potatoes

6-lb fully cooked bone-in half ham
3 lb potatoes, pared and thinly sliced
4 medium onions, thinly sliced
Salt
3 tablespoons butter or margarine
2 tablespoons flour
1/8 teaspoon pepper
1/8 teaspoon paprika
2-1/4 cups milk
1 tablespoon brown sugar
1/2 teaspoon dry mustard

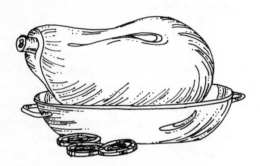

1. Preheat oven to 325F. Wipe ham with damp paper towels. Place the ham on rack in a shallow roasting pan.
2. Bake, uncovered, 1-1/4 hours.
3. Place potato, onion, and 2 teaspoons salt in large saucepan; cover with water. Bring to boiling; boil gently 5 minutes, or until potato is just tender. Drain.
4. Melt butter in small saucepan; remove from heat. Stir in flour, 1 teaspoon salt, the pepper, and paprika until smooth. Gradually stir in milk. Bring to boiling, stirring constantly; boil gently 3 minutes. Set sauce aside.
5. Remove ham from oven. Increase oven temperature to 400F. Mix brown sugar and mustard; pat mixture on ham. Insert meat thermometer in center of ham, away from bone.
6. Place ham in center of 3-quart shallow baking dish or shallow casserole. Spoon drained potato mixture around ham. Pour sauce over potato mixture.
7. Bake 25 to 30 minutes, or until meat thermometer registers 130F and sauce is bubbling.
Makes 6 to 8 servings.

Maple-Glazed Baked Ham

8- to 10-lb fully-cooked boneless ham
Whole cloves
3/4 cup light-brown sugar, firmly packed
1 cup dark corn syrup
2 tablespoons prepared mustard
1 tablespoon maple flavoring

1. Preheat oven to 325F.
2. Place ham, fat side up, on rack in shallow, open roasting pan. Insert meat thermometer in center. Bake, uncovered, 2-1/2 to 3 hours, or until internal temperature is 130F. Remove from oven.
3. To glaze: Turn oven temperature to 450F. Take out meat thermometer; carefully remove rind from ham.
4. With tip of knife, cut fat into diamond pattern; do not cut into ham. Insert a clove in each diamond.
5. In bowl, mix rest of ingredients. Spread half of glaze over ham; bake 10 minutes.
6. Put on rest of glaze; bake 10 minutes.
7. For easy slicing, let ham stand 20 minutes.
Makes about 20 servings.

Fruit-Glazed Baked Ham

10- to 12-lb fully cooked, bone-in ham
1/2 cup light-brown sugar, firmly packed
3/4 cup light corn syrup
1/2 cup prepared brown mustard
1 teaspoon dry mustard
1 can (1 lb, 4-1/2 oz) sliced pineapple, drained
1 can (1 lb, 1 oz) pear halves, drained
8 to 10 preserved kumquats, drained
8 to 10 maraschino cherries
1 small lime, thinly sliced

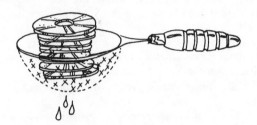

1. Preheat oven to 325F. Place ham, fat side up, on rack in roasting pan. Insert meat thermometer in thickest part of ham, away from bone.
2. Bake, uncovered, 2-1/2 hours.
3. Meanwhile, combine brown sugar, syrup, mustard. Cook over low heat, stirring occasionally, until sugar is dissolved and mixture comes to boil.
4. In medium bowl, combine fruit with mustard mixture. Let stand at room temperature, basting the fruit several times, about 2 hours.
5. Remove any skin from ham; then score fat into 1-inch diamonds. Brush about 1/4 cup syrup from fruit over ham; bake 15 minutes. Arrange 3 each pineapple slices, pears, kumquats, cherries on ham; secure with wooden picks. Brush ham with about 1/4 cup more syrup; bake 15 minutes, or until nicely glazed and meat thermometer registers 130F. Place a slice of lime, curled up, in center of each pineapple slice. Pass remaining mustard fruit.
Makes 16 to 18 servings.

Glazed Ham Loaf

1/2 cup milk
1 egg
1 tablespoon catsup
1 tablespoon prepared mustard
1/8 teaspoon pepper
1 cup soft white-bread crumbs
1 lb ground ham
1/2 lb ground veal
2 tablespoons finely chopped onion
1 tablespoon chopped parsley

Fruit Glaze:
1 can (8-3/4 oz) fruits for salad
1/4 cup light-brown sugar, firmly packed
2 tablespoons cider vinegar

Mustard Sauce, page 499

1. Preheat oven to 350F. In large bowl, combine milk, egg, catsup, mustard, and pepper; beat until well blended. Stir in bread crumbs; let mixture stand several minutes.
2. Add ham, veal, onion, and parsley; mix well. In shallow baking pan, shape meat into loaf about 8 inches long and 4 inches wide. Bake ham loaf, uncovered, for 30 minutes.
3. Meanwhile, make Fruit Glaze: Drain syrup from fruit into a small saucepan. Add brown sugar and vinegar; bring to boiling, stirring. Add fruit; reduce heat, and simmer 5 minutes. Remove saucepan from heat.
4. Remove ham loaf from oven. Pour glaze over loaf, arranging the fruit attractively on top. Then bake ham loaf 30 minutes longer.
5. Meanwhile, prepare Mustard Sauce.
6. With wide spatula, remove ham loaf to a warm platter. Spoon glaze from pan over top of the loaf. Serve with cabbage wedges, if desired, and pass Mustard Sauce separately
Makes 6 servings.

Baked Virginia Ham

10- to 12-lb country-style Virginia ham
Whole cloves
1 cup dark-brown sugar, firmly packed
1 teaspoon dry mustard
3 tablespoons pineapple juice
1 tablespoon cider vinegar

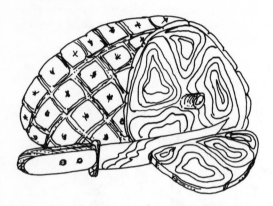

1. Cover ham completely with cold water; let stand 24 hours.
2. Next day, scrub ham with stiff brush. Rinse well in cold water.
3. In large kettle, cover ham with cold water; bring to boiling. Reduce heat; simmer, covered, 4 to 5 hours, or until ham is almost tender.
4. Remove from heat; let cool in liquid.
5. Meanwhile, preheat oven to 325F.
6. Remove cooled ham from liquid; carefully remove skin and excess fat.
7. With tip of knife, cut fat into diamond pattern; do not cut into ham. Insert a clove in each diamond.
8. Place ham on rack, in shallow roasting pan. Insert meat thermometer in center, away from bone.
9. Bake, uncovered, 2-1/2 hours.
10. Combine remaining ingredients; spread over ham.
11. Bake 15 minutes longer, or until internal temperature is 155F. For easy slicing, let stand 20 minutes.
Makes about 24 servings.

Ginger-Glazed Baked Ham

7- to 8-lb fully cooked, bone-in ham butt
6 cups unsifted all-purpose flour
2 tablespoons ginger
1 tablespoon ground cloves
1/2 teaspoon salt

Glaze:
1 cup ginger ale
1 cup orange juice
1/2 cup light-brown sugar, firmly packed
1 tablespoon ginger
1 tablespoon grated orange peel
About 24 whole cloves

1. Preheat oven to 325F.
2. Wipe ham with damp paper towels.
3. In large bowl, combine flour, ginger, cloves, and salt; mix well. Gradually add 2 cups cold water, mixing well with fork.
4. On lightly floured board, mold dough around top and side of ham until they are evenly covered.
5. Place on rack in shallow roasting pan; insert meat thermometer in center away from bone. Bake until internal temperature is 130F—about 2 hours.
6. Meanwhile, make Glaze: Combine ingredients in small saucepan; bring to boiling, stirring.
7. Reduce heat; simmer, uncovered and stirring occasionally, 40 to 60 minutes. (Glaze should measure 1 cup.)
8. Remove pastry covering from ham, and discard.
9. With sharp knife, lift off skin. In outside fat layer, make diagonal cuts, 1-1/4 inches apart, to form a diamond pattern. Stud center of each diamond with a whole clove.
10. Brush ham well with glaze; bake 25 minutes, brushing twice more.
Makes 12 servings.

Upside-Down Ham Loaf—Family Favorite

1 tablespoon butter or margarine
1/2 cup dark-brown sugar, firmly packed
1 can (13-1/2 oz) crushed pineapple
3 maraschino cherries, quartered
Milk
1 egg
1 cup soft white-bread crumbs
2 tablespoons prepared mustard
1 teaspoon salt
1/8 teaspoon pepper
1-1/2 lb fully cooked smoked ham, ground
1/2 lb pork, ground

1. Preheat oven to 350F.
2. Slowly melt butter in an 8-by-8-by-2-inch pan, over low heat. Stir in sugar until smooth; remove from heat.
3. Drain pineapple well, reserving liquid. Spread pineapple evenly over sugar mixture in pan.
4. Arrange cherries in a pretty design on pineapple; set aside.
5. Combine pineapple liquid with enough milk to measure 1 cup.
6. In large bowl, beat egg slightly with fork. Stir in milk mixture, bread crumbs, mustard, salt, and pepper.
7. Add ham and pork; mix until well combined, using hands if necessary.
8. Spoon meat mixture evenly over pineapple in pan; bake 1 hour.
9. Drain off excess liquid. Invert loaf on platter, so pineapple is on top.
Makes 8 servings.

Baked Ham Steak with Hot Mustard Fruit

1/4 cup light-brown sugar, firmly packed
1/4 teaspoon ground allspice
2-1/2-lb fully cooked ham steak, 1-1/2 inches thick
Whole cloves
1 can (6 oz) apricot nectar
Hot Mustard Fruit, below

1. Preheat oven to 325F.
2. Combine sugar and allspice; spoon mixture evenly over top of ham steak. Press cloves into ham, all around side.
3. Place ham in shallow baking dish. Pour apricot nectar around ham.
4. Bake, uncovered, 1 hour, basting occasionally with pan liquid.
5. To serve: Place ham on serving platter. Spoon pan liquid over ham. Cut crosswise into slices. Serve with Hot Mustard Fruit.
Makes 6 servings.

Hot Mustard Fruit

1/4 cup butter or margarine, melted
1/2 cup light-brown sugar, firmly packed
2 tablespoons prepared brown mustard
1 teaspoon dry mustard
1 can (1 lb) sliced peaches, well drained
1 can (13-1/2 oz) pineapple chunks, well drained
2 large, medium-ripe bananas, peeled and sliced on diagonal in 1-inch chunks

1. Preheat oven to 325F.
2. In small bowl, combine butter, sugar, and mustard, mixing well. Remove 1/4 cup for topping.
3. In a shallow 1-quart casserole, combine fruits with remaining sugar mixture; toss lightly to combine. Spoon reserved sugar mixture over top.
4. Bake, uncovered, 40 minutes. Serve warm, with Baked Ham Steak.

How to Cook Bacon

Pan-Fried: Start bacon in cold skillet. Cook, over moderate heat, turning frequently. Remove bacon from pan when desired doneness is reached. Drain on paper towels.

Baked (an ideal method for large quantities): Start oven at 400F, or hot. Use broiling pan and rack, or cake rack over a shallow baking pan. Put bacon on rack over drip pan. (No need to separate slices now.) Bake 5 minutes; then pull slices slightly apart, if necessary, and bake 5 minutes longer. (No need to watch or turn.) Drain on paper towels if crispness is desired.

Broiled: Separate slices; arrange on rack. Broil, 6 inches from heat, 3 to 4 minutes. Turn; broil 1 minute. Drain on paper towels.

Lamb

Comes spring, comes lamb. But this light, tender meat is available all year round, although we'll admit it is especially appealing when the days turn warmer. Broiled, braised, roasted, stewed, served hot, or served in cold, thin slices, lamb has more than taste and texture to recommend it, for it abounds in precious vitamins and minerals.

Timetable for Roasting Lamb — at 325F

Cut	Weight	Internal Temperature	Approx. Roasting Time
Leg (whole)	6 to 7 lb	175 to 180F	3-1/2 to 3-3/4 hours
Leg (half)	3 to 4 lb	175 to 180F	3 to 3-1/2 hours
Boned Rolled Shoulder	4 to 6 lb	175 to 180F	3 to 4 hours
Bone-in, Stuffed	4 to 5 lb	175 to 180F	2-1/2 to 2-3/4 hours

Roast Leg of Lamb

6-lb leg of lamb
1 clove garlic, slivered
1/2 cup salad oil
2 cups dry red wine
3 onions, sliced
1/4 teaspoon cloves
2 teaspoons dried oregano leaves
2 teaspoons salt
1 carrot, sliced
3 sprigs parsley

1. Wipe lamb with damp paper towels. Using paring knife, make several small pockets in flesh, and insert garlic slivers.
2. Combine remaining ingredients, to make marinade. In large, shallow glass baking dish, arrange lamb as flat as possible. Pour marinade over it.
3. Refrigerate, covered, at least 24 hours, turning lamb occasionally.
4. Preheat oven to 325F.
5. Place lamb, fat side up, on rack in shallow roasting pan. In fleshy part, away from bone or fat, insert meat thermometer.
6. Roast, uncovered and basting occasionally with marinade, about 2-1/2 hours, or to 175F on meat thermometer, for medium.
7. Let roast stand 20 minutes before carving, for easier slicing. If desired, some of the marinade may be heated, to pass with roast.
Makes about 10 servings.

Roast Leg of Lamb en Croûte with Mushroom Stuffing

6-lb leg of lamb, bone in
1 clove garlic, slivered
1/2 teaspoon dried thyme leaves
1/2 teaspoon dried rosemary leaves
1 teaspoon salt
1/4 teaspoon pepper
1 pkg (11 oz) piecrust mix

Mushroom Stuffing:
1/4 cup butter or margarine
1/2 lb fresh mushrooms, washed and finely
chopped
1/4 cup finely chopped onion
1/2 teaspoon salt
1/8 teaspoon pepper
1/4 cup Madeira

1 egg yolk
2 tablespoons butter or margarine
2 tablespoons flour
1/4 cup Madeira
1 teaspoon currant jelly

1. Preheat oven to 325F. Wipe lamb with damp paper towels; trim off most of fat. Using paring knife, make 6 small slits in flesh; insert garlic slivers in each. Sprinkle with thyme, rosemary, 1 teaspoon salt, and 1/4 teaspoon pepper.
2. Place on rack in shallow roasting pan. Insert meat thermometer into thickest part of meat.
3. Roast, uncovered, until thermometer registers 150F, for rare—about 2 hours.
4. About 1/2 hour before roasting time is up, prepare piecrust mix as the label directs. Set aside.
5. Also, make Mushroom Stuffing: In 1/4 cup hot butter in medium skillet, sauté mushrooms and onion until tender—about 5 minutes. Add salt, pepper, and 1/4 cup Madeira; cook, stirring, over medium heat until juices are evaporated and mixture is thick enough to spread—10 to 15 minutes. Spread over surface of lamb.
6. Increase oven temperature to 450F. Remove roast to shallow baking pan without rack; remove thermometer. Reserve drippings in roasting pan.
7. On lightly floured surface, roll pastry to form a 16-by-14-inch oval; trim edges; reserve for decoration.
8. Lay pastry over roast, pressing against meat and tucking underneath, to cover completely. Beat yolk with 1 tablespoon water; brush over pastry.
9. Reroll trimmings 1/4 inch thick. Cut strips 1/4 inch wide for stems. Cut leaf pattern with cutter. Press into pastry top. Brush again with egg-yolk mixture.
10. Bake 20 to 25 minutes, or until pastry is golden.
11. Meanwhile, add 1 cup water to reserved drippings in roasting pan; heat, stirring to loosen browned bits. Strain into 2-cup measure; skim off fat. There should be 1 cup drippings.
12. Melt butter in small saucepan. Stir in flour, and cook, stirring constantly, until slightly golden. Gradually add strained drippings; cook over medium heat, stirring constantly, until thickened; boil gently 1 minute. Stir in wine and jelly. Keep warm.
13. To serve: Place roast on heated platter. Arrange vegetables around roast, if desired. Carve lamb in thin slices right through crust. Serve lamb with crust, along with sauce.
Makes 6 to 8 servings.

Braised Pot Roast of Lamb

5-1/2-lb boned shoulder of lamb*
1/4 cup chopped parsley
1 clove garlic, crushed
1 teaspoon salt
1/2 teaspoon dried basil leaves
1/2 teaspoon dried marjoram leaves
1/4 teaspoon pepper
2 tablespoons butter or margarine
1/2 cup chopped onion
1/2 cup chopped celery
1/2 cup chopped carrot
1 can (10-1/2 oz) condensed beef broth, undiluted
1/2 cup red wine
1 bay leaf
2 lb medium potatoes, peeled and halved
2 tablespoons flour
1/4 cup chopped fresh mint
* Weight after lamb shoulder is boned. Have butcher flatten lamb to 1-1/2-inch thickness.

1. Wipe lamb with damp paper towels. Trim off fat; spread meat flat.
2. In small bowl, combine parsley, garlic, salt, basil, marjoram, and pepper.
3. Spread parsley mixture evenly over lamb. Starting from one end, roll up, jelly-roll fashion, as tightly as possible. Tie with twine in 3 or 4 places.
4. In hot butter in Dutch oven, brown roast well on all sides—about 20 minutes. Remove roast.
5. In same pan, sauté onion, celery, and carrot until soft and lightly golden. Drain off fat.
6. Return roast to pan. Add beef broth, wine, and bay leaf; bring to boiling. Reduce heat, and simmer, covered and turning meat once, 1-1/2 hours.
7. Add potatoes; simmer, covered, 40 minutes longer, or until lamb and potatoes are tender.
8. Remove lamb and potatoes to heated serving platter. Remove string from lamb. Keep warm. Skim fat from pan liquid. Boil liquid, uncovered, about 8 minutes, to reduce it. (Liquid should measure 1-3/4 cups.)
9. Mix flour with 1/4 cup cold water until smooth. Stir into pan liquid; bring to boiling, stirring. Add chopped mint. Reduce heat, and simmer 3 minutes. Spoon some of mint gravy over meat. Pass the rest.
Makes 8 servings.

Roast Leg of Lamb, Swedish Style

4- to 4-1/2-lb leg of lamb
2 teaspoons salt
1/4 teaspoon pepper
3/4 cup black coffee
1 tablespoon light cream
2 teaspoons sugar
2 tablespoons flour
About 1-1/2 cups milk
2 teaspoons currant jelly

1. Preheat oven to 350F.
2. Wipe lamb with damp cloth; rub with salt and pepper.
3. Place lamb, fat side up, on rack in shallow roasting pan. Insert meat thermometer in fleshy part, away from bone or fat. Roast, uncovered, 1-1/2 hours.
4. Combine coffee, cream, and sugar; pour over lamb. Roast, basting occasionally, about 1 hour, or to 175F on thermometer, for medium.
5. Remove lamb to heated platter. For easier slicing, let stand in warm place 20 minutes before carving.

6. Meanwhile, make gravy: Strain pan drippings. Skim off fat, and measure 2 tablespoons fat into roasting pan.

7. Stir in flour until smooth; cook, stirring, over low heat about 1 minute, to brown flour.

8. Pour pan drippings into 2-cup measure. Add milk to make 2 cups. Gradually stir into flour mixture; bring to boiling, stirring.

9. Remove from heat; add currant jelly. Serve gravy hot, with lamb.

Makes 6 to 8 servings.

Crown Roast of Lamb, Filled with Sautéed Mushrooms

5-1/2-lb crown roast of lamb (3 racks tied together)
2 teaspoons salt
1/4 teaspoon pepper
1/8 teaspoon garlic powder

Sautéed Mushrooms:
2 lb fresh mushrooms
1/2 cup butter or margarine
2 tablespoons lemon juice
2 teaspoons salt
1/2 teaspoon pepper

Paper frills
Fresh mint sprigs
Mint-Jelly Sauce, page 499

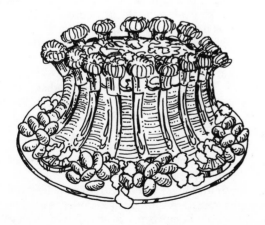

1. Preheat oven to 300F. Wipe lamb with damp cloth.

2. Combine 2 teaspoons salt, 1/4 teaspoon pepper, and the garlic powder. Rub meat well with mixture.

3. Insert meat thermometer into center of fleshy part of meat, away from fat and bone. Place roast, rib ends down, in shallow roasting pan without rack; roast 1 hour.

4. Remove from oven. Turn roast so rib ends are up. Return to oven; roast 1 hour and 30 minutes, or until meat thermometer registers 180F.

5. About 20 minutes before lamb is done, prepare Sautéed Mushrooms: Wash mushrooms; trim ends of stems. Slice 1/4 inch thick, through caps and stems.

6. In large skillet, sauté mushrooms in hot butter, stirring, until tender—about 5 minutes. Add lemon juice, salt, and pepper; toss lightly.

7. Place roast on heated platter; spoon mushrooms into center cavity, mounding them. Place paper frills on rib ends. Garnish with mint.

8. Serve with Mint-Jelly Sauce.

Makes 10 servings.

To carve Crown Roast of Lamb: Steady roast by inserting fork firmly between ribs. Start carving at one of the two ends where ribs are tied together. Cut down between the ribs, allowing two ribs for each serving. Using the fork to steady the slice, lift it on the knife blade to the serving plate.

Leg of Lamb, French Style

6- to 7-lb leg of lamb
3 lb new potatoes, pared
1/4 cup butter or margarine
2 carrots, pared, diced
1 cup diced celery, with leaves
1 small onion, peeled and diced
Dash thyme
2 bay leaves
2 cloves garlic, peeled and crushed
3/4 cup red wine
1 teaspoon salt
1/8 teaspoon pepper

1. Have your meatman bone the leg of lamb and trim the shank. Do not have it rolled and tied.
2. Preheat oven to 500F. Place lamb flat, fat side down, in a shallow roasting pan. Arrange potatoes around meat; dot with butter. Roast, uncovered, 20 minutes.
3. Reduce oven temperature to 400F. Turn lamb fat side up; turn potatoes. Sprinkle carrots, celery, onion, thyme, bay leaves, and garlic over and around lamb. Roast, turning potatoes occasionally, 35 to 40 minutes longer—lamb will be medium rare.
4. Remove lamb and potatoes to serving platter. Keep warm.
5. Pour drippings into 1-cup measure, leaving vegetables in pan. Skim off all fat; discard. Return remaining drippings to pan. Add 1/2 cup water, the wine, salt, and pepper.
6. Bring to boiling; lower heat; simmer, uncovered, 3 minutes. Discard bay leaves. Press vegetables and juice through strainer into gravy boat.
7. To serve: Slice the leg of lamb crosswise. Pass the gravy.
Makes 8 servings.

Broiled Leg-of-Lamb Slices with Sauce Maître d'Hôtel

7-lb leg of lamb, boned

Marinade:
1/2 cup salad oil
1/4 cup lemon juice
1 teaspoon salt
1/4 teaspoon pepper
1 teaspoon dried oregano leaves
1/2 teaspoon dried basil leaves
2 bay leaves
2 cloves garlic, crushed

Maître d'Hôtel Sauce, page 500

1. Place leg of lamb fat side down. With sharp knife, make gashes in thick sections of lamb, to make it as uniformly thick as possible.
2. Remove any excess fat. Wipe lamb with damp paper towels.
3. Make Marinade: In jar with tight-fitting lid, combine all marinade ingredients; shake vigorously to combine.
4. Place lamb in large, shallow baking dish. Pour marinade over lamb. Refrigerate, covered, overnight; turn lamb occasionally.
5. Place meat, fat side down, on broiler rack; broil, 4 inches from heat, 20 minutes.
6. Turn with tongs; brush with marinade; broil 20 minutes longer, or until desired doneness.
7. To serve: Remove to carving board or heated serving platter. Slice thinly, on the diagonal. Serve with Sauce Maître d'Hôtel.
Makes 8 servings.

Broiled Lamb Chops, Savory Mushroom Stuffing

Maître d'Hôtel Butter:
1/4 cup soft butter or margarine
1 tablespoon chopped parsley
1 tablespoon lemon juice
1/2 teaspoon salt
Dash cayenne

Savory Mushroom Stuffing:
3 tablespoons butter or margarine
2 tablespoons finely chopped green pepper
2 tablespoons finely chopped onion
1/2 lb mushrooms, chopped
3/4 cup soft white-bread cubes
1/4 teaspoon salt
Dash pepper
Dash cayenne

6 loin or shoulder lamb chops, 1-1/2 inches thick, with pocket

1. Make Maître d'Hôtel Butter: In small bowl, beat 1/4 cup soft butter with the parsley, lemon juice, 1/2 teaspoon salt, and dash cayenne until well blended. Refrigerate.
2. Make Savory Mushroom Stuffing: In hot butter in large skillet, sauté green pepper, onion, and mushrooms until golden—about 5 minutes. Remove from heat. Stir in bread cubes, salt, pepper, and cayenne.
3. Wipe chops with damp paper towels. Trim excess fat. Stuff each pocket with a heaping tablespoonful of mushroom mixture; fasten with wooden picks. Place any remaining stuffing on tail; roll, and secure with wooden picks.
4. Broil, 4 inches from heat, 8 to 10 minutes; turn, and broil 8 to 10 minutes longer for medium rare. Or cook to desired degree of doneness.
Serve with Maître d'Hôtel Butter.
Makes 6 servings.

Barbecued Lamb Riblets

10 lb lamb riblets
1/2 lemon, sliced
2 stalks celery, broken
1 onion, halved
1/4 cup cider vinegar
1 teaspoon salt
4 whole black peppercorns

Barbecue Sauce:
1 bottle (14 oz) catsup
1/2 cup honey
1/4 cup dark-brown sugar, packed
1/4 cup cider vinegar
1/8 teaspoon Tabasco
1/2 teaspoon salt
1/4 cup salad oil
1 slice lemon

1. In large 8- to 10-quart kettle, place lamb riblets, sliced 1/2 lemon, the celery, onion, 1/4 cup vinegar, 1 teaspoon salt, the black peppercorns, and 5 quarts water. Bring to boiling; reduce heat, and simmer, covered, 45 minutes, or until riblets are very tender. Remove from heat; let riblets cool in broth.
2. Meanwhile, make Barbecue Sauce: In 2-quart saucepan, combine all barbecue-sauce ingredients, along with 1 cup water. Bring to boiling; reduce heat, and simmer, uncovered, 20 minutes.
3. When ready to broil, drain riblets, and discard broth. Arrange riblets on broiler rack, bone side up. Brush with some of barbecue sauce.
4. Place rack in broiler, 4 to 5 inches from heat. Broil riblets 10 minutes; brush with sauce, and broil 5 minutes longer. Turn with tongs; brush with sauce. Broil 10 minutes; brush with sauce, and continue broiling 10 to 15 minutes longer, or until riblets are browned and glazed.
5. To serve: Cut riblets into serving-size pieces, and pile on large serving platter. Garnish with celery tops and lemon slices, if desired.
Makes 6 to 8 servings.

Broiled Lamb-Chop Grill

6 tablespoons soft butter or margarine
3 tablespoons grated Parmesan cheese
3 firm tomatoes
1-1/2 teaspoons dried oregano leaves
1/4 cup lemon juice
1/2 cup salad oil
1 teaspoon dried tarragon leaves
6 loin lamb chops, 1-1/2 inches thick
1 can (1 lb) cling-peach halves
1/4 teaspoon cloves
Dash cinnamon
1/3 cup currant jelly, melted
Parsley or watercress

1. Combine butter with cheese.
2. Slice tomatoes in half. Sprinkle with oregano, and spread cut side with cheese mixture. Arrange on cold broiler rack.
3. Mix lemon juice, salad oil, and tarragon. Brush part of mixture on chops, and arrange chops on broiler rack.
4. Place broiling pan 4 inches from heat (chops will be about 2 inches from heat). For medium chops: Broil 5 to 6 minutes on first side; then turn; baste with more lemon-juice mixture, and broil 4 to 5 minutes. For well-done chops: Broil 6 to 8 minutes on first side; then turn, basting as above, and broil 5 to 7 minutes.
5. Meanwhile, drain peach halves, reserving 1/3 cup syrup. Add cloves and cinnamon.
6. When chops are turned, place peach halves, cut side up, on broiler rack. Brush generously with currant jelly and peach syrup.
7. Serve, garnished with parsley or watercress, on a heated platter. Heat any remaining lemon-juice mixture, and pour it over chops.
Makes 6 servings.

Mixed Grill

4 loin lamb chops, 1-1/2 inches thick
4 Bermuda-onion slices, 1/2 inch thick
Melted butter or margarine
Salt
Pepper
Paprika
2 tomatoes, halved
2 tablespoons grated sharp Cheddar cheese
1/4 teaspoon curry powder
4 fresh mushroom caps
4 bacon slices

1. Wipe chops with damp paper towels. Arrange chops and onion slices on broiler pan. Brush with butter; sprinkle with salt and pepper. Sprinkle onion slices with paprika.
2. Broil, 4 inches from heat, 15 minutes.
3. Brush tomato halves with butter; sprinkle with salt and pepper. Top each with some of Cheddar cheese combined with curry powder.
4. Arrange tomatoes on broiler rack. Turn chops and onion slices; broil 10 minutes.
5. Brush mushroom caps with butter; sprinkle with salt and pepper. Place on broiler rack.
6. Broil 6 minutes.
7. Place bacon slices on broiler rack. Broil, turning bacon once, 4 minutes longer, or until bacon is crisp.
8. On each of 4 heated plates, arrange a chop, onion slice, tomato half, mushroom cap, and bacon slice.
Makes 4 servings.

Spring-Lamb Stew with Dill

2-1/2 lb boneless lamb
2 tablespoons salad oil
12 small white onions, peeled
3/4 cup tomato juice
2 teaspoons salt
1/4 teaspoon pepper
6 medium carrots
6 new potatoes
1/4 cup flour
1 pkg (10 oz) frozen peas
Fresh dill

1. Cut lamb in 1-inch pieces; trim off fat. In hot oil in Dutch oven, over medium heat, brown one third of meat at a time until browned on all sides. Remove as browned.
2. Add onions, and brown on all sides. Remove; set aside. Pour all fat from pan.
3. Return lamb to pan. Add 2 cups water, the tomato juice, salt, and pepper; bring to boiling. Reduce heat; simmer, covered, 30 minutes.
4. Meanwhile, scrape carrots, and cut in half. Pare a band of skin, about 1/2 inch wide, around center of each potato.
5. Add onions, carrots, and potatoes to lamb mixture. Simmer, covered, 40 minutes longer, or until meat and vegetables are tender. Remove from heat; skim off fat.
6. Mix flour with 6 tablespoons water. Stir into lamb mixture. Add peas and 3 tablespoons snipped dill. Simmer, covered, 10 to 15 minutes longer, or until peas are tender.
7. Remove from heat; let stand 5 minutes; skim off any fat. Ladle stew into heated serving dish. Garnish with a fresh dill sprig.
Makes 6 servings.

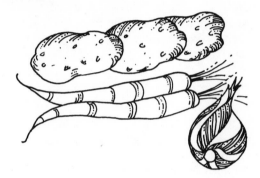

Rack of Lamb

2-lb rack of lamb
1 teaspoon salt
1/4 cup orange marmalade
1/4 cup lemon juice

1. Preheat oven to 300F.
2. Cover tip of each rib bone with aluminum foil, to prevent scorching. Rub lamb with salt. Insert meat thermometer in fleshy part, away from bone or fat.
3. Place lamb, fat side up, on rack in shallow roasting pan; roast, uncovered, 30 minutes.
4. Mix marmalade with lemon juice. Brush half of glaze on lamb.
5. Roast lamb, uncovered, 30 minutes; then brush with rest of glaze. For medium lamb: Roast 15 minutes more, or until meat thermometer reads 175F. For well-done lamb: Roast 30 minutes more, or until thermometer reads 180F.
6. To serve, replace foil tips with paper frills.
Makes 2 or 3 servings.

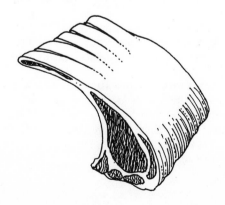

Rack of Lamb, Provençale

4- to 5-lb rack of lamb (12 chops)
1 cup fresh bread crumbs
1/4 cup chopped parsley
1 clove garlic, crushed
1 teaspoon salt
1/4 teaspoon pepper
2 tablespoons Dijon mustard
1/4 cup butter or margarine, melted

1. Preheat oven to 375F. Wipe lamb with damp paper towels; trim off all fat. Place lamb, using ribs as rack, in shallow, open roasting pan.
2. Roast, uncovered, 15 minutes for each pound.
3. Remove roast from oven; let cool about 15 minutes.
4. Combine bread crumbs, parsley, garlic, salt, and pepper.
5. Spread mustard over top of lamb. Pat crumb mixture into mustard, pressing firmly. Drizzle with butter. Insert meat thermometer into center of middle chop.
6. Roast 20 minutes, or until thermometer registers 175F. Garnish with parsley, if desired.
Makes 6 servings.

Lamb Pie with Dill

3 lb boneless lamb for stew
1-1/2 teaspoons salt
1/4 teaspoon pepper
1 large carrot, pared and sliced
1 medium onion, chopped
1/2 cup chopped celery
1 pkg (11 oz) piecrust mix
2 teaspoons flour
1 tablespoon vinegar
2 teaspoons sugar
2 egg yolks
1/2 cup heavy cream
3/4 cup chopped fresh dill or 6 tablespoons dried
   dill weed

1. Trim excess fat from lamb; cut meat into 1-inch cubes. Sprinkle with salt and pepper.
2. In 4-quart Dutch oven, combine lamb, carrot, onion, and celery with 2-1/2 cups water. Bring to boiling; reduce heat; simmer, covered and stirring occasionally, 1 hour, or till lamb is tender. Skim off fat, if necessary.
3. Meanwhile, prepare pastry as the label directs; roll out to form 12-inch circle. Preheat oven to 350F.
4. Drain lamb and vegetables, pouring liquid into a medium saucepan. Liquid should measure 2 cups.
5. Combine flour and 1 tablespoon water; stir into liquid; cook, stirring, until slightly thick. Add vinegar, sugar.
6. In medium bowl, beat egg yolks slightly; beat in cream, then a small amount of hot sauce; pour back into rest of sauce. Add lamb mixture and dill; mix well.
7. Turn lamb mixture into 10-inch shallow casserole (about 2 inches deep). Make slits in pastry for steam vents, and adjust over top of casserole; crimp edges. Bake 45 minutes, or until top is golden.
Makes 6 to 8 servings.

Veal

Try a welcome change of pace with savory, sophisticated veal, subtle in flavor. Cooked properly, it can be fork-tender, delicate and juicy. A word of caution: Because veal is less available than it once was, it is higher in price and much more of a luxury.

Timetable for Roasting Veal—at 325F

Cut	Weight	Internal Temperature	Approx. Roasting Time
Leg (center cut)	7 to 8 lb	170F	3 to 3-1/2 hours
Loin	4-1/2 to 5 lb	170F	2-1/2 to 3 hours
Boned Rolled Shoulder	5 to 6 lb	170F	3-1/2 to 4 hours
Boned Rolled Shoulder	3 lb	170F	3 hours

Roast Veal Florentine

Florentine Stuffing:
1 pkg (10 oz) frozen chopped spinach
1/4 cup butter or margarine
1 cup chopped onion
1 clove garlic, crushed
1-1/2 cups soft white-bread crumbs
1 tablespoon chopped parsley
1 tablespoon grated Parmesan cheese
1 teaspoon salt
1/2 teaspoon dried oregano leaves
1/8 teaspoon pepper

5- to 6-lb leg of veal, boned, not rolled and tied
4 slices bacon

1. Make Florentine Stuffing: Cook spinach as the label directs. Drain well.
2. In hot butter in large skillet, sauté onion and garlic until onion is tender—about 5 minutes. Remove from heat.
3. Add spinach, bread crumbs, parsley, Parmesan, salt, oregano, and pepper; stir until well combined.
4. Preheat oven to 325F.
5. Wipe veal with damp paper towels. Place, skin side down, on board. If necessary, pound with mallet to about 1-inch thickness.
6. Place stuffing lengthwise down center of veal. Bring long sides of meat over stuffing, and overlap. Fasten with skewers, and lace with twine.
7. Place, laced side up, in shallow, open roasting pan. Arrange bacon over top. Insert meat thermometer in thickest part of veal; do not rest it in stuffing.
8. Roast, uncovered, about 2-1/2 hours, or until thermometer registers 170F. Serve hot or cold.
9. Cool 1/2 hour; refrigerate, covered, 1 to 2 hours, or until serving.
10. To serve: Remove skewers and twine from roast. Cut crosswise into 1/4-inch-thick slices.
Makes 8 servings.

Roast Stuffed Veal en Gelée

3/4 lb fresh spinach, or 1 pkg (10 oz) frozen
   spinach

Stuffing:
1 lb ground veal
3 tablespoons flour
1-1/2 teaspoons chopped fresh savory, or
   1/2 teaspoon dried savory
1 teaspoon salt
1/8 teaspoon pepper
1 egg
2 tablespoons Madeira wine
3/4 cup milk

4- to 5-lb boned breast of veal
2 tablespoons lemon juice
3 teaspoons chopped fresh rosemary, or 1 teaspoon
   dried rosemary leaves
1 teaspoon salt
1/8 teaspoon pepper
2 cups grated raw carrot
1/2 cup dry white wine

Glaze:
2 env unflavored gelatine
2 cans (12-oz size) chicken consommé
1/4 cup Madeira wine
1/2 cup mayonnaise or cooked salad dressing

1. Wash spinach; remove large stems. Place leaves in saucepan with just the water clinging to them. Cook, covered, over medium heat and turning once with a fork, 5 minutes, or until spinach is tender. (If using frozen spinach, cook as the label directs.) Drain very well. Set aside.

2. Make Stuffing: In large bowl, combine ground veal, flour, savory, 1 teaspoon salt, and 1/8 teaspoon pepper; with a fork, mix well. Mix in egg and 2 tablespoons Madeira. Add milk, 2 tablespoons at a time, beating well after each addition until mixture is smooth. Set aside. Preheat oven to 375F.

3. Wipe veal with damp paper towels. Trim off fat. Spread meat flat, skin side down, on board. Sprinkle with lemon juice, rosemary, salt, and pepper.

4. Spread carrot in an even layer over meat, 1 inch from edges. Top with an even layer of stuffing, then spinach in an even layer.

5. Starting at shortest side, roll up jelly-roll fashion. Fasten with skewers; tie with string at 1-1/2-inch intervals. Place, seam side down, in shallow roasting pan. Brush surface with salad oil.

6. Roast, uncovered, 1 hour. Pour white wine over roast. Roast, basting several times, 1-1/2 hours longer, or until meat is tender when tested with a fork. Serve hot, if desired.

7. Remove roast to platter; let cool. Wrap well in plastic film; refrigerate overnight.

8. Next day, make Glaze: In small saucepan, sprinkle gelatine over 3/4 cup consomme, to soften. Heat, over low heat and stirring constantly, until gelatine is dissolved. Pour into medium bowl; stir in remaining consommé.

9. Remove 2 cups consommé mixture to 11-by-7-by-2-inch pan. Stir in Madeira. Refrigerate.

10. Add mayonnaise to remaining consommé mixture; beat until smooth. Set bowl in larger bowl of ice and water; chill, stirring occasionally, until as thick as unbeaten egg white.

11. Meanwhile, remove skewers and string from cold veal roll. Set roll on wire rack on a pan or small tray.

12. Spoon thickened mayonnaise glaze over roll. Refrigerate roll, on rack, 10 to 15 minutes.

13. Scrape glaze from pan; melt, and rechill. Spoon over roll. Repeat, if necessary, to coat roll completely and evenly.

14. To decorate, press thin slices cooked carrot and sprigs of dill into last coat of glaze. Refrigerate at least 1 hour, or until glaze is firm.

15. To serve: Place roast on serving platter. Carve a few slices, 1/4 inch thick. Cut jellied Madeira consommé into 1/2-inch cubes. Spoon around meat.

Makes 8 to 10 servings.

Roast Leg of Veal in White Wine

4 slices bacon
7-lb boned leg of veal* (do not have tied)
Salt
Pepper
1/2 teaspoon dried rosemary leaves
2 large cloves garlic, finely chopped
1/3 cup chopped parsley
1/2 cup white wine
2 tablespoons butter or margarine
2 tablespoons flour
* Veal weighs 9 pounds before boning.

1. Cut bacon in 1/2-inch pieces. Fry until crisp; drain. Set bacon drippings aside to cool.

2. Preheat oven to 350F. Wipe veal with damp paper towels. On waxed paper, combine 1 teaspoon salt, 1/2 teaspoon pepper, and the rosemary.

3. Spread veal flat, skin side down, on work surface. Cut four slits, about 1-1/2 inches deep, in thickest part of meat.

4. Rub half of salt mixture over top of veal and into slits; then spread veal evenly with bacon drippings, garlic, and parsley; sprinkle with bacon bits. Carefully bring ends together, and tie with twine securely into a well-shaped roll.

5. Rub remaining salt mixture over veal roll. Place on rack in shallow, open roasting pan. Insert meat thermometer into the thickest part of veal.

6. Roast, uncovered, 30 minutes. Pour wine over veal. Roast, basting frequently with pan drippings, 2 to 2-1/2 hours longer, or until meat thermometer registers 170F. Add 1/2 cup water to pan if necessary. Remove veal to serving platter.

7. Pour drippings into a 2-cup measure. Skim off excess fat, and discard. Add water to drippings to measure 1-1/2 cups. Return to roasting pan; bring to boiling, stirring to dissolve all browned bits in pan. Boil 1 minute; remove from heat, and strain, if desired.

8. Melt butter in medium saucepan; remove from heat. Stir in flour until smooth; cook 3 minutes. Remove from heat. Gradually stir in hot liquid; bring to boiling. Reduce heat, and simmer 3 to 5 minutes. Season with salt and pepper to taste. Serve with veal, thinly sliced.

Makes 12 to 14 servings.

Veal Pot Roast

4-1/2-lb veal rump roast
1 tablespoon dry mustard
1 teaspoon poultry seasoning
2 tablespoons light-brown sugar
1 tablespoon salt
1/4 teaspoon pepper
1 tablespoon flour
3 tablespoons salad oil
1 bay leaf
3 tablespoons cider vinegar
2/3 cup sliced onion

1. Wipe roast with damp paper towels.
2. In small bowl, combine mustard, poultry seasoning, sugar, salt, pepper, and flour. Rub well into roast.
3. Heat oil in medium Dutch oven. In it, brown roast well on all sides.
4. Add remaining ingredients and 1/4 cup water.
5. Cover; simmer 2-1/2 hours, or until fork-tender, turning twice during cooking. Serve with pan juices.
Makes 6 servings.

Veal Pot Roast with Mushroom Sauce

4-lb rolled boned shoulder of veal
1 tablespoon paprika
2 teaspoons salt
4 tablespoons salad oil
1/2 cup chopped onion
1 can (10-1/2 oz) condensed mushroom soup,
  undiluted
3 tablespoons flour
1/2 cup dairy sour cream

1. Wipe veal with damp paper towels. Rub with paprika and salt.
2. Preheat oven to 350F.
3. In hot oil in Dutch oven, brown veal well; then remove.
4. Add onion to pan drippings; sauté until golden —about 5 minutes. Stir in soup. Return veal to pan.
5. Bake, covered, 2-1/2 hours, or until veal is tender. Remove veal to serving platter; keep warm.
6. Skim fat from liquid in Dutch oven. Mix flour with 2 tablespoons water. Gradually stir into liquid in Dutch oven; bring to boiling, stirring. Reduce heat; simmer 3 minutes.
7. In a small bowl, gradually stir a little hot gravy into sour cream; then stir into rest of gravy. Pour into gravy boat, and serve with veal.
Makes 8 servings.

Braised Veal Chops

6 veal chops, cut 1-1/2 inches thick
1-1/2 teaspoons salt
1/4 teaspoon pepper
1/3 cup salad oil
1/2 cup chopped onion
3/4 cup sliced raw carrots
1 can (8 oz) tomatoes, undrained
1/3 cup dry sherry or chicken broth
1 can (6 oz) sliced mushrooms, drained
2 tablespoons chopped parsley

1. Wipe chops with damp paper towels. Sprinkle with salt and pepper.
2. In large skillet, over medium heat, heat oil. Brown chops on both sides, with onion.
3. Add carrots, tomatoes, and sherry. Reduce heat; simmer, covered, 1 hour, or until meat is fork-tender.
4. Remove cover. Add mushrooms and parsley; heat 5 minutes. Serve chops with sauce.
Makes 6 servings.

Veal Chops with Mushrooms

4 veal loin chops, 1-1/4 inches thick
  (about 2-1/2 lb)
1/3 cup butter or margarine
1/2 lb fresh mushrooms, sliced; or 1 can (6 oz)
  sliced mushrooms, drained
2 tablespoons lemon juice
1/2 cup sliced onion
1/2 clove garlic, crushed
1/4 cup flour
1 teaspoon salt
1/8 teaspoon pepper
1 can (10-1/2 oz) condensed beef broth, undiluted
2/3 cup dry white wine
1 teaspoon chopped fresh tarragon leaves
1 teaspoon liquid gravy seasoning
1/2 teaspoon snipped chives
1/8 teaspoon pepper

1. Wipe chops with damp paper towels. Trim excess fat. Roll up ends of chops, and secure with wooden picks.
2. In hot butter in Dutch oven or deep skillet, brown chops on both sides. Remove chops, and set aside.
3. Sprinkle mushrooms with lemon juice. Add with onion and garlic to drippings in Dutch oven; sauté until golden—about 5 minutes. Remove from heat. With slotted spoon, remove sautéed vegetables, and set aside with chops.
4. Stir flour, salt, and pepper into pan drippings until well blended. Gradually stir in beef broth and wine. Add tarragon, gravy seasoning, chives, and pepper.
5. Bring to boiling, stirring occasionally. Add chops and sautéed vegetables; reduce heat, and simmer, covered, 30 minutes, or until chops are tender.
6. To serve: Remove chops to heated serving platter, and remove picks. Spoon vegetables and some of gravy over chops. Pass rest of gravy.
Makes 4 servings.

Veal Rolls, Marsala

1-1/2 lb thin veal scallops (8)
4 thin slices boiled ham (about 1/4 lb)
1/2 pkg (8-oz size) Mozzarella cheese, sliced
1/4 cup butter or margarine
1 tablespoon flour
Dash pepper
1/2 cup Marsala wine
Chopped parsley

1. Have meatman pound veal very thin.
2. Place 1/2 slice of ham and 1 slice of cheese on each veal scallop. Roll up; secure with wooden picks.
3. In hot butter in large skillet, over medium heat, lightly brown veal rolls on all sides. Reduce heat to low; cover skillet; cook 10 minutes, or until veal is fork-tender.
4. Remove from heat. Remove veal rolls to platter; keep warm.
5. Combine flour and pepper with 1/4 cup water to make a smooth paste. Add to drippings, stirring.
6. Bring to boiling; reduce heat, and simmer, stirring, 3 minutes. Add wine; simmer, stirring, 1 minute.
7. Pour sauce over veal rolls. Sprinkle with chopped parsley.
Makes 4 servings.

Veal Roulades

5 tablespoons butter or margarine
1/4 cup sliced green onion
1 cup white-bread crumbs
1 tablespoon chopped fresh tarragon, or
  1 teaspoon dried tarragon leaves
1 tablespoon chopped fresh basil leaves, or
  1 teaspoon dried basil leaves
1 tablespoon chopped fresh parsley
8 veal scallops (about 2 lb), pounded to
  1/4-inch thickness
Salt
1/4 lb thinly sliced prosciutto
2 tablespoons brandy
1 bay leaf
1/2 cup dry white wine
1 cup chicken broth
3 tablespoons flour

1. In 2 tablespoons hot butter in medium skillet, sauté onion until soft—2 minutes. Remove from heat. Add bread crumbs, tarragon, basil, and parsley; toss until well combined.
2. Arrange pieces of veal in a single layer on board. Sprinkle with salt. Place 2 tablespoons crumb mixture on each; top each with prosciutto. Roll up from short side; tie with string.
3. In remaining hot butter in large, heavy skillet or Dutch oven, brown veal rolls on all sides. Remove from heat.
4. Warm brandy slightly; ignite, and pour flaming over the veal rolls. Add bay leaf, wine, and chicken broth.
5. Bring to boiling; reduce heat; simmer, covered, 30 to 40 minutes, or until veal is tender. Remove veal to heated serving platter; keep warm.
6. Measure pan liquid; you should have 1-3/4 cups (add water if necessary). Return to skillet.
7. In small bowl, mix flour with 1/4 cup cold water until smooth. Stir into liquid in skillet. Bring to boiling, stirring constantly, until mixture thickens; reduce heat; simmer 2 minutes. Pour over veal. Sprinkle with additional chopped parsley, if desired.
Makes 4 to 6 servings.

Hungarian Veal Casserole for a Crowd

1 cup butter or margarine
8 lb boneless veal, cut in 1-inch cubes
1 teaspoon salt
1/4 teaspoon pepper
6 cans (10-1/2-oz size) condensed cream-of-mushroom soup, undiluted
6 cups sliced onion
1/2 teaspoon seasoned salt
1/4 teaspoon Tabasco
1/2 cup sherry
2 cups dairy sour cream
1/4 teaspoon cracked black pepper

1. Heat 1/2 cup butter in large skillet. Add veal, one third at a time, and brown well on all sides. Remove as browned to large, deep roasting pan with tight-fitting cover.
2. Sprinkle veal with salt and 1/4 teaspoon pepper. Spoon mushroom soup over top.
3. Preheat oven to 375F.
4. Heat remaining butter in same skillet. Add onion, and sauté until golden. Place on meat mixture in roasting pan.
5. Add 1/2 cup water, the seasoned salt, and Tabasco to skillet; bring to boiling, stirring to dissolve the browned bits in the pan. Pour over onion.
6. Bake, covered, 45 minutes. Remove cover; pour sherry over mixture. Bake, uncovered, 35 minutes.
7. Add sour cream; sprinkle with cracked pepper; stir gently just until blended. Bake, uncovered, 10 minutes longer. Serve over rice.
Makes 24 servings.

Baked Stuffed Breast of Veal

Salt
Pepper
4 tablespoons unsifted all-purpose flour
5-lb breast of veal, with pocket for stuffing
1/4 cup salad oil
2-1/2 cups rye-bread cubes (1/2-inch)
1 can (10-1/2-oz) condensed beef consommé,
    undiluted
2 eggs, beaten
1 clove garlic, crushed
2 tablespoons chopped parsley
3/4 cup finely chopped onion
1 teaspoon caraway seed
3 teaspoons prepared mustard
1 tablespoon Worcestershire sauce
1 teaspoon liquid gravy seasoning

1. Preheat oven to 325F.
2. On large sheet of waxed paper, blend 1 teaspoon salt, 1/8 teaspoon pepper, and 2 tablespoons flour. Coat veal on all sides with flour mixture.
3. Heat oil in 12-inch skillet, and brown veal. Remove veal from skillet, and let cool. Discard any fat in pan.
4. In medium bowl, combine bread cubes, 1/2 cup undiluted consommé, the eggs, garlic, parsley, onion, caraway seed, 1 teaspoon prepared mustard, 1/2 teaspoon salt, and 1/4 teaspoon pepper; mix well.
5. Spoon mixture into veal pocket, pushing mixture well into cavity. Place veal, meaty side up, in a 15-by-10-by-2-inch roasting pan. Add remaining consommé, 1/2 cup water, 1/4 teaspoon salt, and 1/8 teaspoon pepper. Cover pan with foil, securing edges tightly. Bake 2 to 2-1/2 hours, or until tender. Remove veal to platter; keep warm.
6. Meanwhile, make sauce: Measure drippings from pan; strain; add water, if necessary, to make 2 cups; pour into small saucepan. Mix 2 tablespoons flour and 1/4 cup water together smoothly; stir into pan liquid, along with remaining mustard, the Worcestershire, and gravy seasoning. Bring mixture to boiling, stirring, until mixture is slightly thickened and smooth.
7. To serve, cut veal in slices; pass sauce in heated sauceboat.
Makes 6 to 8 servings.

Baked Veal Loaf

2 eggs
3/4 cup milk
1/2 cup catsup
1 cup packaged cracker meal
1/2 cup chopped stuffed olives
2 teaspoons salt
1 teaspoon monosodium glutamate
1/4 teaspoon pepper
1 tablespoon butter or margarine
1/4 cup coarsely chopped onion
1-1/2 lb veal, ground
1/2 lb pork, ground

1. Preheat oven to 350F.
2. In large bowl, beat eggs slightly with fork. Stir in milk, catsup, cracker meal, olives, salt, monosodium glutamate, and pepper; set aside.
3. In hot butter in skillet, sauté onion until tender —about 5 minutes.
4. Add to egg mixture along with veal and pork. Mix just until well combined, using hands if necessary.
5. With moistened hands, shape into loaf in 2-quart flat baking dish; bake, uncovered, 1-1/4 hours. Remove to platter. Serve with Mushroom Sauce, page 497.
Makes 6 to 8 servings.

Veal Birds with Bread Stuffing

6 tablespoons butter or margarine
1 cup finely chopped onion
3 cups soft bread crumbs
1 teaspoon salt
1/8 teaspoon pepper
1/4 teaspoon dried dill weed
12 thin veal scallops (1-1/2 lb)
2 tablespoons flour
1 can (10-1/2 oz) condensed beef broth, undiluted

1. Melt 4 tablespoons butter in large skillet. Add onion, crumbs, salt, pepper, and dill; cook, over medium heat, stirring, about 2 minutes.
2. Place about 2 tablespoons stuffing on each veal slice; roll up; secure with wooden pick. Roll in flour.
3. Heat remaining butter in skillet; brown veal birds well on all sides.
4. Add beef broth; simmer, covered, 30 to 35 minutes, or until tender.
5. Remove wooden picks. Spoon pan juices over birds.
Makes 4 servings.

Cold Roast Veal Loaf

2 eggs
1/2 cup packaged dry bread crumbs
2 tablespoons prepared mustard
1 teaspoon dried basil leaves
1-1/2 teaspoons salt
1/2 teaspoon pepper
Dash Tabasco
1/2 cup finely chopped onion
1/2 cup finely chopped green pepper
1 cup chopped parsley
1-1/2 lb ground veal
1/2 lb lean ground pork
1 lemon, thinly sliced
6 slices bacon

1. Preheat oven to 350F.
2. In large bowl, combine eggs, bread crumbs, mustard, basil, salt, pepper, Tabasco, onion, green pepper and parsley; beat with fork until well combined. Let stand 5 minutes.
3. Add veal and pork; mix well with fork.
4. Line a 13-by-9-by-1-3/4-inch pan with foil (use piece long enough to hang over ends of pan). Turn meat-loaf mixture into pan; shape with hands to form a loaf 8 inches long and 4 inches wide. Overlap lemon slices on top; place bacon slices lengthwise on top.
5. Bake, uncovered, 1 hour and 15 minutes.
6. Let cool in pan on wire rack 30 minutes. Lifting with foil, remove meat loaf to serving platter; refrigerate several hours, covered, to chill well.
7. Serve with mustard and garnished with salad greens and sliced tomatoes, if desired.
Makes 8 servings.

Variety Meats

In Europe the so-called variety meats are much more appreciated than they are here. Kidney, sweetbreads, calves' liver and the others, well prepared and interestingly seasoned, are a gourmet's delight. We hope our recipes will make many converts. And a good thing, because these meats are very high in food value and usually low in price. Let variety meats give variety to your table.

Broiled Liver

1 lb calves' or lambs' liver, sliced 1/2 inch thick
Melted butter or margarine
Salt
Pepper

1. Brush liver with melted butter; sprinkle with salt and pepper.
2. Broil, 3 inches from heat, 3 minutes on each side.
Makes 4 servings.

Pan-Fried Liver

2 tablespoons flour
1/2 teaspoon salt
1/8 teaspoon pepper
1 lb calves' or lambs' liver, sliced 1/2 inch thick
2 tablespoons butter or margarine

1. Combine flour, salt, and pepper on sheet of waxed paper. Roll liver in mixture, coating well.
2. Melt butter in large skillet. Sauté liver until nicely browned—about 5 minutes on each side. Serve with crisp bacon.
Makes 4 servings.

Sautéed Chicken Livers

1 lb chicken livers
3 tablespoons butter or margarine
1/2 lb mushrooms, sliced
1/2 cup sliced onion
1 teaspoon flour
1 can (8 oz) tomatoes
1/2 cup dry white wine
2 teaspoons chopped parsley
1/2 teaspoon salt
1/2 teaspoon Worcestershire sauce
Toast points

1. Wash chicken livers; drain on paper towels. Cut each in half.
2. In hot butter in large skillet, quickly brown chicken livers—about 5 minutes. Remove as browned.
3. Add mushrooms and onion to skillet; sauté until golden—about 5 minutes. Remove from heat.
4. Stir in flour, tomatoes, wine, parsley, salt, and Worcestershire; simmer, stirring frequently, about 5 minutes. Add chicken livers; simmer 5 minutes longer.
5. Turn into serving dish. Surround with toast points. Sprinkle with chopped parsley, if desired.
Makes 4 servings.

Calves' Liver Venetian Style

1-1/2 lb calves' liver, sliced 1 inch thick
1/4 cup flour
1-1/2 teaspoons salt
1/4 teaspoon pepper
1/4 cup butter or margarine
1/4 cup olive or salad oil
2 lb onions, thinly sliced
1/2 teaspoon dried sage leaves
1/4 cup dry white wine
1 tablespoon lemon juice
2 tablespoons chopped parsley

1. With paper towels, pat liver dry. Cut into strips 1/8 inch wide (see Note).
2. On sheet of waxed paper, combine flour, salt, and pepper. Roll liver in mixture, coating well.
3. In large skillet, heat butter and 2 tablespoons oil. Sauté liver strips, turning frequently, until lightly browned on all sides—about 5 minutes. Remove, and set aside.
4. Add remaining oil to skillet. Sauté onion slices, stirring frequently, until golden—about 10 minutes. Add sage. Cook, covered, over low heat 5 minutes.
5. Combine liver with onion, tossing lightly. Cook, covered, over low heat 5 minutes. Remove liver and onion to serving dish.
6. To drippings in skillet, add white wine and lemon juice; bring to boiling, stirring. Pour over liver and onion. Sprinkle with chopped parsley. Nice served with slices of hot polenta.
Makes 6 to 8 servings.
Note: To make liver easier to slice thinly, place in freezer long enough to chill thoroughly.

Veal Kidneys Provencale

2 (1/2-lb size) veal kidneys
1/4 cup unsifted all-purpose flour
1 teaspoon salt
1/8 teaspoon pepper
1/2 lb fresh mushrooms
1/4 cup butter or margarine
1 tablespoon olive or salad oil
1 tablespoon chopped shallot
2 tablespoons chopped parsley
1-1/4 cups dry white vermouth
Dash lemon juice
Chopped parsley

1. Wash kidneys; cut in half; remove white center part. Slice thinly 1/4 inch thick.
2. On waxed paper, combine flour, salt, and pepper; mix well. Roll sliced kidneys in flour mixture, coating well.
3. Wipe mushrooms with damp cloth; trim stems; slice lengthwise through cap and stem.
4. In hot butter and oil in large skillet, sauté kidneys, turning kidneys and shaking skillet, about 10 minutes, or until nicely browned on both sides. Add shallot and 2 tablespoons parsley; cook 5 minutes more.
5. Add mushrooms and 1/4 cup vermouth; cook 5 minutes longer. Add rest of vermouth; cook gently, covered, 15 more minutes, or until kidneys are tender.
6. To serve, sprinkle with lemon juice and parsley. Serve with rice or toast points, if desired.
Makes 6 servings.

Braised Lamb Kidneys

8 lamb kidneys (1 lb)
1/4 cup butter or margarine
1 cup sliced green pepper (about 1)
1/2 cup sliced onion
1/2 cup beef broth
1/2 teaspoon salt
1/8 teaspoon pepper
1 can (3 oz) sliced mushrooms
1 tablespoon flour
1/4 cup sherry
Cooked white rice

1. Remove fat and white veins from kidneys; cut each in 4 or 6 pieces. Rinse well, and dry with paper towels.
2. In hot butter in large skillet, sauté green pepper and onion until tender—about 5 minutes. Remove; set aside.
3. In same skillet, sauté kidneys until nicely browned—about 5 minutes. Remove from heat. Stir in beef broth, salt, and pepper.
4. Drain mushrooms, reserving liquid. Add mushrooms, green pepper, and onion to skillet; simmer, uncovered, 15 minutes.
5. Add reserved mushroom liquid to flour, stirring until smooth. Add to mixture in skillet, mixing well. Bring to boiling, stirring; boil 2 minutes.
6. Remove from heat; stir in sherry. Serve over rice.
Makes 4 servings.

Boiled Tongue

3- to 4-lb smoked beef tongue
1 large onion, quartered
10 whole black peppercorns
1/4 teaspoon mustard seed
2 bay leaves
4 whole cloves

1. Wash tongue; pat dry with paper towels.
2. In 6-quart kettle, combine tongue and remaining ingredients with water to cover—about 3 quarts.
3. Bring to boiling. Reduce heat; simmer, covered, 2-1/2 to 3 hours, or until tongue is tender.
4. Drain tongue. (If desired, reserve stock for use in sauce.) Plunge tongue into cold water.
5. To remove skin: With sharp knife, gently slit skin on underside from thick end to tip. Peel off skin, and remove and discard root.
6. To serve: Slice tongue thinly, and serve hot or cold with Gingersnap or Sour-Cream Horseradish Sauce, page 498.
Makes 7 or 8 servings.

Game

If the hunter in your family should return home triumphantly bearing gifts of partridge, quail or venison, please him; prepare it according to one of our special recipes.

Braised Partridges

2 (3/4-lb size) ready-to-cook partridges*
1/4 cup butter or margarine
1/3 cup sliced onion
1 can (10-1/2 oz) condensed cream-of-mushroom
  soup, undiluted
1/3 cup sauterne
* Grouse may be substituted for partridge and
cooked as directed above.

1. Rinse partridges; dry with paper towels.
2. In hot butter in heavy skillet or Dutch oven,
sauté partridges until nicely browned—about 10
minutes.
3. Add onion; cook, stirring occasionally, until
tender—about 5 minutes.
4. Add soup and sauterne, mixing well; bring to
boiling. Reduce heat, and simmer, covered, 25 to
30 minutes, or until partridges are fork-tender.
Serve with sauce spooned over.
Makes 2 servings.

Brandied Partridges

2 (3/4-lb size) ready-to-cook partridges
1/4 cup butter or margarine
1 tablespoon finely chopped onion
1/2 cup chicken broth or consommé
1/2 teaspoon salt
1 cup seedless grapes
1/4 cup brandy
2 teaspoons cornstarch

1. Rinse partridges; dry with paper towels.
2. In hot butter in large skillet, sauté partridges
until nicely browned—10 minutes.
3. Add onion, broth, and salt; bring to boiling. Reduce heat, and simmer, covered, 25 to 30 minutes,
or until partridges are almost tender.
4. Add grapes; simmer 10 minutes longer. Remove
from heat.
5. In small bowl, combine brandy and cornstarch,
mixing well. Add to mixture in skillet, blending
well. Bring to boiling, stirring; boil 1/2 minute.
Serve partridges with sauce.
Makes 2 servings.

Roast Wild Duck

1-1/2-lb ready-to-cook wild Mallard duck
1/2 teaspoon salt
1/8 teaspoon pepper
3 onion slices, 1/4 inch thick
1 celery stalk
1 medium carrot, pared
3 juniper berries (optional)
2 bacon slices
1/2 cup dry white wine

1. Rinse duck well; pat dry with paper towels.
Sprinkle surface and body cavity with salt and
pepper. Preheat oven to 450F.
2. Stuff duck cavity with onion, celery, carrot,
and juniper berries.
3. Fasten skin of neck to back, with poultry pin.
Fold wing tips under body, to secure wings close
to it. Then close body cavity with poultry pins.
Lace with twine. Tie ends of legs together.
4. Place duck on rack in shallow roasting pan.
Secure bacon slices across top; baste with wine.
Roast 30 minutes, basting frequently with wine.
(Roast longer if a well-done duck is desired.)
5. When duck is done, remove poultry pins and
twine. Cut into serving-size pieces, and arrange
on platter.
Makes 2 servings.

Smothered Quail

4 ready-to-cook quail (1-1/2 lb)
1/4 cup butter or margarine
1/2 cup sliced shallots
1/4 cup cider vinegar
1 tablespoon sugar
1/2 teaspoon salt

1. Rinse quail well; pat dry with paper towels.
2. In hot butter in large skillet, sauté quail until nicely browned—about 10 minutes.
3. Add shallots; cook, stirring occasionally, until tender—about 5 minutes.
4. Add vinegar, sugar, and salt, mixing well; bring to boiling. Reduce heat, and simmer, tightly covered, 20 to 30 minutes, or until quail are tender.
5. Serve quail with pan juices spooned over.
Makes 2 servings.

Squab in Sour Cream

2 (3/4-lb size) ready-to-cook squab
1/4 cup unsifted all-purpose flour
2 tablespoons butter or margarine
1/2 cup sliced onion
1/2 cup tomato juice
1 teaspoon salt
1/2 teaspoon paprika
1/2 teaspoon dried basil leaves
1/4 teaspoon pepper
1 can (3 oz) sliced mushrooms, undrained
1/2 cup dairy sour cream

1. Rinse squab well; pat dry with paper towels. Coat well with flour.
2. In hot butter in large skillet, sauté squab until nicely browned—10 to 15 minutes.
3. Add onion; cook, stirring occasionally, until tender—about 5 minutes.
4. Combine tomato juice, salt, paprika, basil, pepper, and mushrooms. Pour over squab; bring to boiling. Reduce heat, and simmer, covered, 20 to 30 minutes, or until squab is tender.
5. Remove squab to heated platter; keep warm.
6. Gradually add sour cream to mixture in skillet, stirring constantly. Reheat gently. Pour over squab. Nice served with rice.
Makes 2 servings.

Roast Venison with Wine

7-1/2-lb boned leg-of-venison roast
9 bacon slices
1 teaspoon salt
1/4 teaspoon dried thyme leaves
1/4 teaspoon pepper
2 tablespoons chopped onion
1 clove garlic, crushed
1/4 cup lemon juice
1 cup beef broth
1 cup Burgundy

1. Preheat oven to 500F. Wipe roast with damp paper towels. Arrange 6 bacon slices on inside surface of roast; roll up, and tie securely. Place 3 bacon slices across top.
2. Place roast on rack in shallow roasting pan. Sear, in oven, 10 to 15 minutes.
3. Remove roast from oven. Lower oven temperature to 425F.
4. Combine remaining ingredients; pour over roast. Cover with foil.
5. Roast, basting occasionally with pan drippings, 2-1/2 to 3 hours, until meat is tender.
6. Remove to heated serving platter. Strain pan drippings, and pass with roast.
Makes 15 to 20 servings.

Venison Pot Roast

7-lb boned leg-of-venison roast
3 to 6 bacon slices
2 cups Burgundy
1/2 cup cider vinegar
2 celery tops
1 medium onion, sliced
4 lemon slices
1 large carrot, pared and sliced
1 tablespoon salt
10 whole black peppercorns
2 bay leaves
1 clove garlic, crushed
1/4 cup unsifted all-purpose flour
2 tablespoons salad oil

1. Wipe roast with damp paper towels. Arrange bacon slices over inside surface of meat; roll up, and tie securely.
2. Combine Burgundy, vinegar, celery tops, onion, lemon slices, carrot, salt, black peppercorns, bay leaves, and garlic with 1 cup water.
3. Pour over roast in large bowl. Refrigerate, covered, 24 hours, turning occasionally.
4. Remove roast from marinade; reserve 2 cups marinade.
5. Coat roast well with flour. Slowly heat oil in Dutch oven. Add roast; cook, over medium heat, until browned all over—about 20 minutes.
6. Add 1 cup reserved marinade; bring to boiling. Reduce heat, and simmer, covered, 4 hours, or until roast is fork-tender. Baste meat occasionally with pan liquid, adding rest of marinade as needed.
7. Remove to heated serving platter.
Makes 15 to 20 servings.

Pies & Small Pastries

One of the oldest tests of a good cook is being able to make a really good pie with a crisp, golden crust that literally melts in your mouth. Of all the culinary procedures, pastry making requires the most skill and experience. We give precise directions for making and handling your own pastry, of course; but, a word about the packaged piecrust mixes.

They're so good today that one can scarcely improve on them. We especially advise the novice cook to start with one of these. Our recipes include a list of pies as long as your arm—fruit pies, cream pies, chiffon pies, very special pies, deep-dish pies, dumplings, tarts and turnovers. What wonderful treats await your family and lucky guests!

Tips for Pie Bakers

1. Our pastry recipes were tested using sifted all-purpose flour, unless stated otherwise. This means that flour must be sifted before measuring.
2. If using a pastry cloth, rub flour well into surface, with palm of hand, then brush off any excess, so that no additional flour is rolled into pastry.
3. Tracing a circle on pastry cloth or waxed paper is a helpful guide in rolling pastry to desired circumference. Or cut a sheet of waxed paper to desired circumference, to use as a guide.
4. A stockinette cover for the rolling pin should be floured to keep pastry from sticking and tearing.
5. Another rolling trick: Roll pastry between two sheets of waxed paper to desired circumference. Chill in waxed paper in refrigerator while preparing pie filling. Waxed paper peels easily from chilled pastry. No additional flour is used, making a more flaky pastry.
6. For well-baked, browned bottom crust, select pie plates of heat-resistant glass. Shiny metal pans do not bake bottom crusts as well; use aluminum pans with dull finish.
7. When baking a two-crust fruit pie, place a square of foil on bottom of oven, directly under pie plate, to catch any juices that might bubble through crust.

TO FREEZE PIE SHELLS

Unbaked Pie Shells: Prepare pie shell as recipe directs. Prick pie shell that is going to be baked without filling. Freezer-wrap; label, and freeze.
Baked Pie Shells: Prepare and bake pie shell as recipe directs. Let cool completely on wire rack. Freezer-wrap; label, and freeze.

TO USE FROZEN PIE SHELLS

Unbaked Pie Shells: Preheat oven to 450F. Remove freezer-wrap. Immediately bake frozen pie shell about 20 minutes, or until golden-brown. Let cool completely on wire rack. Fill as desired.
If pie shell is going to be baked along with filling: Remove freezer-wrap. Let stand in refrigerator or at room temperature to thaw. Then fill as desired, and bake as specific recipe directs.
Baked Pie Shells: Preheat oven to 375F. Remove freezer-wrap. Heat solidly frozen pie shell 10 minutes, or until thawed. Cool completely on wire rack. Fill as desired.
Or remove freezer-wrap. Let stand at room temperature until completely thawed.
All Other Pie Shells: Let stand at room temperature to thaw. If necessary to bake pie shell, bake as specific recipe directs.

TO FREEZE PIES

Kinds to Freeze: Fruit pies, baked or unbaked, freeze best. You may also freeze chiffon pies, although filling may toughen slightly. Cream and custard pies do not freeze well.
Unbaked Fruit Pies: Prepare pie as recipe directs. Do not make slits in upper crust. Freeze pie, unwrapped, until firm.
Then wrap pie in freezer-wrap; label, and freeze.
Baked Fruit Pies: Prepare and bake pie as recipe directs. Cool completely on wire rack. Freezer-wrap; label, and freeze.
Chiffon Pies: Prepare pie as recipe directs; omit whipped-cream topping. Freeze pie, unwrapped, until filling is firm. Then wrap in freezer-wrap; label, and freeze.

TO SERVE FROZEN PIES

Unbaked Fruit Pies: Preheat oven to 425F. Remove freezer-wrap. Make slits in upper crust for steam vents. Bake about 1 hour, or until fruit is tender and crust is golden-brown.
If lightweight-aluminum-foil pie pans are used, place on cookie sheet during baking.
Baked Fruit Pies: Preheat oven to 375F. Remove freezer-wrap. Bake solidly frozen pies about 40 minutes, or until filling bubbles through slits in upper crust.
Chiffon Pies: Remove freezer-wrap. Let stand in refrigerator, to thaw, about 1-1/2 hours. Then top as desired.

Flaky Pastry for 1-Crust Pie

1 cup sifted* all-purpose flour
1/2 teaspoon salt
1/3 cup plus 1 tablespoon shortening or 1/3
 cup lard
2 to 2-1/2 tablespoons ice water
* Sift before measuring.

1. Sift flour with salt into medium bowl.
2. With pastry blender, or 2 knives, using a short, cutting motion, cut in shortening until mixture resembles coarse cornmeal.
3. Quickly sprinkle ice water, 1 tablespoon at a time, over all of pastry mixture, tossing lightly with fork after each addition and pushing dampened portion to side of bowl; sprinkle only dry portion remaining. (Pastry should be just moist enough to hold together, not sticky.)
4. Shape pastry into a ball; wrap in waxed paper, and refrigerate until ready to use. Flatten with palm of hand.
Makes enough pastry for an 8- or 9-inch pie shell, or top of 1-1/2-quart casserole.

Unbaked Pie Shell

1. On lightly floured surface, roll out Flaky Pastry for 1-Crust Pie to an 11-inch circle, rolling with light strokes from center to edge and lifting rolling pin as you reach edge. As you roll, alternate directions, to shape an even circle.
2. If rolled piecrust is too irregular in shape, carefully trim off any bulge and use as patch. Lightly moisten pastry edge to be filled in. Gently press patch in place. Smooth seam with several light strokes of the rolling pin.
3. Fold rolled pastry in half; carefully transfer to 9-inch pie plate, making sure fold is in center.
4. Unfold pastry, and fit carefully into pie plate, pressing gently with fingertips toward center of plate. This eliminates air bubbles under crust and helps reduce shrinkage.
5. Fold under edge of crust, and press into upright rim. Crimp decoratively.
6. Refrigerate until ready to fill and bake.

Unbaked Graham-Cracker Pie Shell

1-1/4 cups graham-cracker crumbs (about 18
 crackers, crushed with a rolling pin)
1/3 cup butter or regular margarine, softened
1/4 cup sugar
1/4 teaspoon cinnamon

1. Combine all ingredients in medium bowl; blend with fingers, fork, or pastry blender.
2. Press evenly on bottom and side of 9-inch pie plate, not on rim. Refrigerate until ready to fill.
Makes 9-inch shell.

Baked Pie Shell

1. Prepare Flaky Pastry for 1-Crust Pie; then make pie shell as directed in Unbaked Pie Shell.
2. Prick entire surface evenly with fork.
3. Refrigerate 30 minutes.
4. Meanwhile, preheat oven to 450F. Bake pie shell 8 to 10 minutes, or until golden-brown.
5. Cool completely on wire rack before filling.

Flaky Pastry for 2-Crust Pie

2 cups sifted* all-purpose flour
1 teaspoon salt
3/4 cup shortening or 2/3 cup lard
4 to 5 tablespoons ice water
* Sift before measuring.

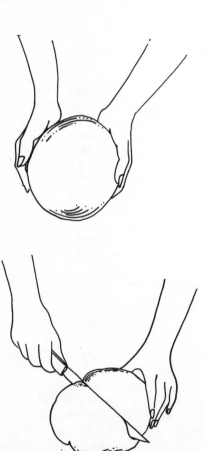

1. Sift flour with salt into medium bowl.
2. With pastry blender, or 2 knives, using a short, cutting motion, cut in shortening until mixture resembles coarse cornmeal.
3. Quickly sprinkle ice water, 1 tablespoon at a time, over all of pastry mixture, tossing lightly with fork after each addition and pushing dampened portion to side of bowl; sprinkle only dry portion remaining. (Pastry should be just moist enough to hold together, not sticky.)
4. Shape pastry into a ball; wrap in waxed paper, and refrigerate until ready to use. Divide in half; flatten each half with palm of hand.
5. To make bottom crust: On lightly floured surface, roll out half of pastry to an 11-inch circle, rolling with light strokes from center to edge and lifting rolling pin as you reach edge. As you roll, alternate directions, to shape an even circle.
6. If rolled piecrust is too irregular in shape, carefully trim off any bulge and use as patch. Lightly moisten pastry edge to be filled in. Gently press patch in place. Smooth seam with several light strokes of the rolling pin.
7. Fold rolled pastry in half; carefully transfer to pie plate, making sure fold is in center.
8. Unfold pastry, and fit carefully into pie plate. Do not stretch pastry. Trim bottom crust even with edge of pie plate.
9. Turn prepared filling into bottom crust.
10. To make top crust: Roll out remaining half of pastry to an 11-inch circle.
11. Fold in half; make several gashes near center for steam vents.
12. Carefully place pastry on top of filling, making sure fold is in center; unfold.
13. Trim top crust 1/2 inch beyond edge of pie plate. Fold top crust under bottom crust; press

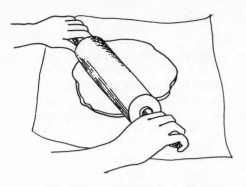

gently together, to seal. Crimp edges decoratively.
14. For a shiny, glazed top, brush top crust with 1 egg yolk beaten with 1 tablespoon water, or with 1 slightly beaten egg white, or with undiluted evaporated milk.
15. To prevent edge of crust from becoming too brown, place 1-1/2-inch strip of foil around crust; bake as recipe indicates. Remove foil last 15 minutes of baking.
Makes enough pastry for an 8- or 9-inch 2-crust pie.

Fruit Pies

When the bloom is on the apple and the peach and the pear, when dried fruits are newly appealing and nuts simply beg to be cracked, then it's high time for our fruit-pies-plus. Eat them warm, as though they'd recently been taken from the oven; serve them with heavy cream, whipped or poured; or sharp Cheddar cheese; or with vanilla ice cream that melts down into the fruit; or with any of the sauces we'll tell you about.

Fresh-Apple Flan

Pastry for 2-crust pie
1-1/4 cups sugar
1/3 cup unsifted all-purpose flour
1-1/4 teaspoons cinnamon
Dash salt
3 lb tart cooking apples

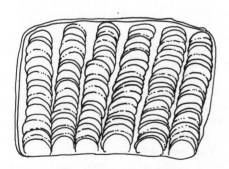

1. Line a 13-by-9-by-2-inch baking pan with foil, letting it extend about 2 inches above each end of pan.
2. On lightly floured surface, roll out pastry into an 18-by-14-inch rectangle. Fold in half. Carefully lift and fit into prepared pan; fold edges over, to make shell 1-1/2 inches high. Refrigerate.
3. Preheat oven to 425F.
4. In large bowl, combine sugar, flour, cinnamon, and salt; mix well.
5. Pare, quarter, core, and slice apples—you should have 9 cups. Add to sugar mixture. Toss lightly to coat well.
6. Place some of apple slices in pastry-lined pan. Arrange remaining slices in parallel rows across pan.
7. Bake 45 minutes, or until pastry is golden-brown and apple is tender. If desired, sprinkle 2 tablespoons sugar over apple slices the last 5 minutes of baking.
8. Let flan stand in pan on wire rack 20 minutes. Carefully lift out of pan (foil and all), onto serving plate; remove foil. Serve warm.
Makes 9 servings.

Upside-Down Apple Pie

Pastry:
1-1/4 cups unsifted all-purpose flour
1/2 teaspoon salt
1/3 cup shortening
1 egg
1 tablespoon lemon juice

Filling:
3 cooking apples (1 lb)
1/2 cup granulated sugar
2 tablespoons flour
1/2 teaspoon cinnamon
1/4 teaspoon nutmeg
1/4 teaspoon salt

2 tablespoons butter or margarine, melted
1/2 cup walnut halves
1/3 cup light-brown sugar, firmly packed

1. Make Pastry: Combine flour and salt in medium bowl. With pastry blender, cut in shortening until mixture resembles coarse cornmeal.
2. In cup, slightly beat egg with lemon juice. With fork, stir into flour mixture until pastry holds together. Form pastry into ball, and wrap in waxed paper or plastic film. Refrigerate until ready to use.
3. Make Filling: Pare, core, and thinly slice apples —there should be 3 cups. In large bowl, combine the apples, granulated sugar, flour, cinnamon, nutmeg, and salt.
4. Pour melted butter over bottom of 9-inch pie plate. Place walnuts, flat side up, in plate. Sprinkle with brown sugar.
5. Preheat oven to 375F.
6. Divide pastry in half. On lightly floured surface, roll out half of pastry to an 11-inch circle. Prick all over with fork. Fit into pie plate on top of sugar and nuts. Fill with apple mixture.
7. Roll out remaining pastry to a 10-inch circle; place on top of filling. Fold edge of top crust under bottom crust; press together, and crimp edge decoratively. Prick top crust in several places.
8. Place a sheet of foil under pie plate to catch juice. Bake 30 to 35 minutes, or until pastry is nicely browned. Cool in pie plate 5 minutes. Then invert on serving plate, and lift off pie plate. Serve warm.
Makes 6 to 8 servings.
To do ahead: Complete Steps 1 through 7. Refrigerate. Bake the pie about 45 minutes before serving.

Fresh-Berry Pie

Pastry for 2-crust pie
2 pint boxes fresh blackberries, raspberries, or blueberries
1 tablespoon lemon juice
1 cup sugar
1/4 cup all-purpose flour
1/4 teaspoon cinnamon
1/8 teaspoon nutmeg
Dash ground cloves
2 tablespoons butter or margarine
1 egg yolk

1. Shape pastry into a ball; divide in half. On lightly floured surface, roll out half of pastry into an 11-inch circle. Use to line a 9-inch pie plate. Refrigerate with rest of pastry until ready to use.
2. Preheat oven to 400F.
3. Gently wash berries; drain well. Place in large bowl; sprinkle with lemon juice.
4. Combine sugar, flour, cinnamon, nutmeg, and cloves. Add to berries, and toss lightly to combine. Turn into pastry-lined pie plate, mounding in center. Dot with butter.
5. Roll out remaining pastry into an 11-inch circle. Make several slits near center, for steam vents.

Adjust over filling; fold edge of top crust under bottom crust; press together, and crimp decoratively.

6. Beat egg yolk with 1 tablespoon water. Brush lightly over top crust.

7. Bake 45 to 50 minutes, or until juices start to bubble through steam vents and crust is golden-brown.

8. Cool on wire rack at least 1 hour. Serve slightly warm.

Makes 8 servings.

Note: Or use 2 packages (10-oz size) frozen unsweetened blueberries, thawed.

Peach-and-Blueberry Pie

2 tablespoons lemon juice
3 cups sliced, pitted, peeled peaches (2-1/4 lb)
1 cup blueberries
1 cup sugar
2 tablespoons quick-cooking tapioca
1/2 teaspoon salt
Pastry for 2-crust pie
2 tablespoons butter or margarine

1. Sprinkle lemon juice over fruit in large bowl.

2. Combine sugar with tapioca and salt. Add to fruit, tossing lightly to combine. Let stand 15 minutes.

3. Meanwhile, preheat oven to 425F.

4. On lightly floured surface, roll out half of pastry into an 11-inch circle. Use to line 9-inch pie plate; trim.

5. Turn fruit mixture into pastry-lined pie plate, mounding in center; dot with butter.

6. Roll out remaining pastry into an 11-inch circle. Make several slits near center, for steam vents; adjust over filling; trim.

7. Fold edge of top crust under bottom crust; press together with fingertips. Crimp edge decoratively.

8. Bake 45 to 50 minutes, or until fruit is tender and crust is golden-brown.

9. Cool partially on wire rack; serve slightly warm.

Makes 6 to 8 servings.

Open-Face Plum Pie

9-inch Kuchen Pie Shell (recipe follows)
1-1/2 lb Italian plums
2 tablespoons granulated sugar
1-1/2 teaspoons grated orange peel
Confectioners' sugar

1. Prepare pie shell; refrigerate until ready to fill.

2. Preheat oven to 400F.

3. Wash plums. Cut into quarters; remove pits. Arrange plums, in tight circular rows, in pie shell. Sprinkle with granulated sugar and orange peel.

4. Bake 15 minutes. Reduce oven temperature to 350F; bake 45 minutes longer.

5. Sprinkle with confectioners' sugar. Cool partially on wire rack; serve warm, with light cream, vanilla ice cream or whipped cream.

Makes 6 to 8 servings.

Kuchen Pie Shell

1-1/2 cups sifted* all-purpose flour
1/4 teaspoon baking powder
1/2 cup butter or regular margarine, softened
1 egg
1/3 cup sugar
Dash salt
*Sift before measuring.

1. Sift flour, baking powder into medium bowl.
2. With portable electric mixer, or back of spoon, blend in butter until smooth.
3. In small bowl, beat egg until frothy. Gradually beat in sugar and salt, beating until mixture is thick and lemon-colored.
4. Add to flour mixture, mixing until smooth.
5. Turn dough into center of greased 9-inch pie plate. Press dough evenly over bottom and side, not on rim, of pie plate.
6. Refrigerate until ready to fill.
Makes 9-inch shell.

Peach Streusel Pie

1/2 cup light brown sugar, packed
1/2 cup unsifted all-purpose flour
1/2 cup butter or regular margarine
2 lb ripe peaches (see Note)
9-inch unbaked pie shell
1/2 cup granulated sugar
1/4 teaspoon nutmeg
1 egg
2 tablespoons light cream
1 teaspoon vanilla extract

1. In bowl, combine brown sugar and flour; mix well. With pastry blender, cut in butter until mixture is like coarse crumbs. Preheat oven to 400F.
2. Wash peaches; peel; quarter; discard pits. Measure 4 cups peaches.
3. Sprinkle 1/2 cup crumb mixture over bottom of pie shell. Add peaches. Sprinkle with granulated sugar and nutmeg.
4. Beat together the egg, light cream and vanilla. Pour over peaches. Cover with the remaining crumb mixture.
5. Bake 40 to 50 minutes, or until top is golden brown all over. Cool slightly. Serve warm, with cream, if desired.
Makes 6 servings.
Note: Or use 4 packages (12-oz size) frozen sliced peaches, thawed and drained. Sprinkle with 1 tablespoon granulated sugar (not 1/2 cup) and 1/4 teaspoon nutmeg.

Rhubarb Lattice Pie

Pastry for 2-crust pie
1-1/2 cups sugar
1/3 cup unsifted all-purpose flour
1-3/4 lb rhubarb, cut into 1-inch pieces (4 cups)
1 tablespoon butter or margarine
Milk
Sugar

1. Shape pastry into a ball; divide in half.
2. On lightly floured surface, roll out half of pastry into a 12-inch circle. Use to line 9-inch pie plate. Refrigerate, with remaining pastry, until ready to use.
3. Preheat oven to 400F.
4. In large bowl, combine 1-1/2 cups sugar and the flour. Add rhubarb, tossing lightly to combine.

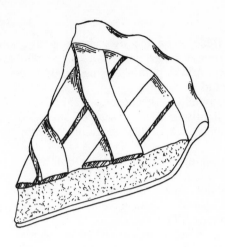

5. Roll out remaining half of pastry into a 10-inch circle. With knife or pastry wheel, cut into 9 1-inch-wide strips.

6. Turn rhubarb mixture into pastry-lined pie plate, mounding in center. Dot with butter.

7. Moisten rim of pastry slightly with cold water. Arrange 5 pastry strips, 1/2 inch apart, over filling; press ends to pastry rim. Place remaining strips across first ones at right angle, to make a lattice, and press to rim. Fold overhang of bottom crust over ends of strips, and crimp decoratively. Brush lattice top, but not rim, lightly with milk, and sprinkle with sugar.

8. Bake 50 minutes, or until crust is golden and juice bubbles through lattice.

9. Cool on wire rack. Serve warm, with ice cream, if desired.

Makes 6 to 8 servings.

Best Cherry Pie

Pastry for 2-crust pie
2 cans (1-lb size) tart red cherries, packed in water
1 cup sugar
1/3 cup unsifted all-purpose flour
1/8 teaspoon salt
2 tablespoons butter or margarine
1/4 teaspoon almond extract
1/4 teaspoon red food color
1 egg yolk

1. Preheat oven to 425F. Make pastry. Wrap in waxed paper, and refrigerate until ready to use.

2. Drain cherries, reserving 1 cup liquid.

3. Combine sugar, flour, and salt; stir into cherry liquid in saucepan. Bring to boiling, stirring.

4. Reduce heat, and simmer 5 minutes. Mixture will be thickened. Stir in butter.

5. Add almond extract and food color. Add cherries; refrigerate, covered.

6. Roll half of pastry, on lightly floured surface, into an 11-inch circle. Fit into 9-inch pie plate; trim. Roll other half of pastry into an 11-inch circle. With knife or pastry wheel, cut eight 1/2-inch wide strips.

7. Pour cooled cherry filling into pie shell.

8. Moisten edge of pie shell with cold water. Arrange 4 pastry strips across filling; press ends to rim of shell.

9. Place 4 pastry strips across first ones at right angles, to make lattice. Press ends to rim of shell.

10. Fold overhang of lower crust over ends of strips, to make a rim; crimp decoratively.

11. Lightly brush top, not edge, with egg yolk beaten with 1 tablespoon water.

12. Bake 30 to 35 minutes, or until pastry is nicely browned. Cool partially on wire rack; serve slightly warm.

Makes 6 to 8 servings.

Spiced Plum Pie

2 tablespoons lemon juice
4 cups sliced, pitted, unpeeled purple plums (3 lb)
1 cup sugar
2 tablespoons quick-cooking tapioca
1/2 teaspoon cinnamon
1/2 teaspoon nutmeg
Pastry for 2-crust pie
2 tablespoons butter or margarine

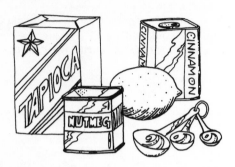

1. Sprinkle lemon juice over plums in large bowl.
2. Combine sugar with tapioca, cinnamon, and nutmeg. Add to plums, tossing lightly to combine. Let stand 15 minutes.
3. Meanwhile, preheat oven to 425F.
4. On lightly floured surface, roll out half of pastry into an 11-inch circle. Use to line 9-inch pie plate; trim.
5. Turn plum mixture into pastry-lined pie plate, mounding in center; dot with butter.
6. Roll out remaining pastry into an 11-inch circle. Make several slits near center, for steam vents; adjust over filling; trim.
7. Fold edge of top crust under bottom crust; press together with fingertips. Crimp edge decoratively.
8. Bake 45 to 50 minutes, or until plums are tender and crust is golden-brown.
9. Cool partially on wire rack; serve slightly warm. Makes 6 to 8 servings.

Very Special Pies

Here we have the marvelous old favorites like the nut pies and the cheese pies, as well as the newer ones like Blum's Coffee-Toffee pie and the super Chocolate Mousse pie.

Southern Pecan Pie

9-inch unbaked pie shell

Filling:
4 eggs
1 cup sugar
1 cup light corn syrup
1/2 tablespoon flour
1/4 teaspoon salt
1 teaspoon vanilla extract
1/4 cup butter or margarine, melted
2 cups pecan halves

Whipped cream

1. Prepare the pie shell, and refrigerate.
2. Preheat oven to 350F.
3. Make Filling: In a medium bowl, with a rotary beater, beat the eggs well.
4. Add the sugar, corn syrup, flour, salt, and vanilla; beat until well combined.
5. Stir in butter and pecans, mixing well.
6. Turn into unbaked pie shell. Bake 50 minutes, or until the filling is set in the center when the pie is shaken gently.
7. Cool pie completely on a wire rack. Then chill it slightly before serving.
8. Just before serving, decorate pecan pie with whipped cream.
Makes 8 servings.

Blum's Coffee-Toffee Pie

Pastry Shell:
1/2 pkg piecrust mix or pastry for a 1-crust pie
1/4 cup light-brown sugar, firmly packed
3/4 cup finely chopped walnuts
1 square unsweetened chocolate, grated
1 teaspoon vanilla extract

Filling:
1/2 cup butter, softened
3/4 cup granulated sugar
1 square unsweetened chocolate, melted and
    cooled
2 teaspoons instant coffee
2 eggs

Topping:
2 cups heavy cream
2 tablespoons instant coffee
1/2 cup confectioners' sugar
Chocolate curls

1. Preheat the oven to 375F.
2. Make Pastry Shell: In medium bowl, combine piecrust mix with brown sugar, walnuts, and grated chocolate. Add 1 tablespoon water and the vanilla; using fork, mix until well blended. Turn into well-greased 9-inch pie plate; press firmly against bottom and side of pie plate. Bake for 15 minutes. Cool pastry shell in pie plate on wire rack.
3. Meanwhile, make Filling: In small bowl, with electric mixer at medium speed, beat the butter until it is creamy.
4. Gradually add granulated sugar, beating until light. Blend in cool melted chocolate and 2 teaspoons instant coffee.
5. Add 1 egg; beat 5 minutes. Add remaining egg; beat 5 minutes longer.
6. Turn filling into baked pie shell. Refrigerate the pie, covered, overnight.
7. Next day, make Topping: In large bowl, combine cream with 2 tablespoons instant coffee and the confectioners' sugar. Refrigerate mixture, covered, 1 hour.
8. Beat cream mixture until stiff. Decorate pie with topping, using pastry bag with number-6 decorating tip, if desired. Garnish with chocolate curls. Refrigerate the pie at least 2 hours.
Makes 8 servings.

Favorite Cheese Pie

4 pkg (3-oz size) cream cheese, softened
2 eggs
1/2 cup sugar
1/2 teaspoon vanilla extract
2 teaspoons grated lemon peel
Unbaked Graham Cracker Pie Shell, page 411
1 cup dairy sour cream

1. Preheat oven to 350F.
2. In small bowl of electric mixer, at medium speed, beat cheese, eggs, sugar, vanilla and lemon peel until smooth and creamy.
3. Turn into crust; bake 35 minutes. Spread with sour cream while still warm.
4. Let cool on wire rack; serve slightly warm or well chilled—refrigerate several hours or overnight.
Makes 8 servings.
Glazed Cream Cheese Pie: Bake pie as above, omitting sour cream. Spread with one of the Glazes for Cheesecake, pages 167–8. Refrigerate 1 hour before serving.

Cherry Cheese Pie Supreme

9-inch unbaked pie shell
1 can (1 lb, 5 oz) cherry-pie filling
4 pkg (3-oz size) cream cheese, softened
1/2 cup granulated sugar
2 eggs
1/2 teaspoon vanilla extract
1 tablespoon grated lemon peel
1/2 cup heavy cream
2 tablespoons confectioners' sugar

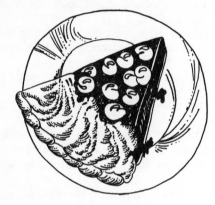

1. Preheat oven to 425F. Prepare pie shell.
2. Set aside 3/4 cup cherry-pie filling. Spread remaining filling in unbaked pie shell.
3. Bake 15 minutes, or just until crust is golden-brown; remove to wire rack. Reduce oven temperature to 350F.
4. Meanwhile, in medium bowl, with electric mixer at medium speed, beat cheese with granulated sugar, eggs, and vanilla until smooth. Stir in lemon peel. Pour over hot cherry filling in pie shell.
5. Bake 25 to 30 minutes. Filling will be set in center.
6. Remove to wire rack; let cool completely. Spread reserved cherry filling on pie, leaving 1-inch margin around edge. Refrigerate until well chilled—about 1-1/2 hours.
7. To serve: Beat cream with confectioners' sugar until stiff. Place in pastry bag with number-6 star tip. Pipe swirls around edge of pie.
Makes 8 servings.
Blueberry Cheese Pie Supreme: Follow above recipe, substituting 1 can (1 lb, 5 oz) blueberry-pie filling for cherry-pie filling.

Almond Tart

Pastry:
1 cup sifted all-purpose flour
1/4 cup sugar
2 teaspoons grated lemon peel
1/3 cup butter or margarine
1 egg yolk

Filling:
3 egg yolks, slightly beaten
3/4 cup sugar
1 tablespoon grated orange peel
1/2 teaspoon almond extract
1-1/3 cups heavy cream
1 cup blanched almonds, ground
1/4 cup crushed almond macaroons

Whipped cream
Citron or angelica

1. Make Pastry: In medium bowl, combine flour with 1/4 cup sugar and the lemon peel.
2. With pastry blender or two knives, cut in butter until mixture resembles coarse cornmeal. Stir in egg yolk; with hands, knead into a ball.
3. Press evenly onto bottom and side, not on rim, of 9-inch pie plate. Refrigerate 1 hour.
4. Preheat oven to 350F.
5. Make Filling: In medium bowl, combine egg yolks with 1/3 cup water, 3/4 cup sugar, the orange peel, almond extract, heavy cream, almonds, and macaroons. With rotary beater, beat until well combined.
6. Turn into chilled pie shell; bake 1 hour, or just until filling is set in center when pie is gently shaken.
7. Cool completely on wire rack; then refrigerate until chilled—at least 2 hours.
8. To serve: Decorate with rosettes of whipped cream, and garnish with strips of citron or angelica.
Makes 8 servings.

Fresh Peach and Green-Grape Pie

9-inch baked pie shell
7 or 8 small fresh peach halves, peeled
1 cup seedless green grapes

Glaze:
1-1/2 teaspoons unflavored gelatine
1 cup apricot jam
1/4 cup sherry
Dash salt

1/2 cup heavy cream, whipped

1. Let baked pie shell cool.
2. Place peaches, cut side down, in bottom of cooled shell. Arrange grapes between peaches.
3. Make Glaze: Sprinkle gelatine over 2 tablespoons cold water; let stand, to soften.
4. In small saucepan, gently heat apricot jam; remove from heat.
5. Add gelatine mixture, stirring to dissolve gelatine. Stir in sherry and salt.
6. Pour glaze over peaches and grapes in pie shell.
7. Refrigerate pie until the glaze is set—about 2 hours.
8. Before serving, decorate pie with rosettes of whipped cream.
Makes 6 to 8 servings.

Fresh-Strawberry Glacé Pie

9-inch baked pie shell

Glaze:
1 pint box fresh strawberries
1 cup granulated sugar
2-1/2 tablespoons cornstarch
1 tablespoon butter or margarine

Filling:
2 pint boxes fresh strawberries
2 tablespoons Cointreau or orange juice

1 cup heavy cream, whipped
2 tablespoons sifted confectioners' sugar

1. Prepare and bake pie shell; let cool.
2. Make Glaze: Wash strawberries gently in cold water. Drain; hull. In medium saucepan, crush strawberries with potato masher.
3. Combine sugar and cornstarch; stir into crushed strawberries. Add 1/2 cup water.
4. Over low heat, stirring constantly, bring to boiling. Mixture will be thickened and translucent.
5. Strain; add butter. Cool.
6. Meanwhile, make Filling: Wash strawberries gently in cold water. Drain; hull. Measure 3 cups; reserve rest for garnish.
7. In medium bowl, gently toss strawberries with Cointreau; let stand about 30 minutes. Then arrange in baked pie shell.
8. Pour cooled glaze over strawberries. Refrigerate until well chilled—about 2 hours.
9. Just before serving, whip cream until stiff; fold in confectioners' sugar. To serve, garnish pie with reserved strawberries and whipped cream.
Makes 6 to 8 servings.
Strawberry Devonshire Glacé Pie: Combine 1 package (3 oz) soft cream cheese with 1 tablespoon light cream. Spread over bottom of cooled pie shell before adding strawberries.

Chocolate Mousse Pie

8- or 9-inch baked pie shell
1 bar (1/2 lb) vanilla sweet chocolate, or 1-1/3
   cups semisweet-chocolate pieces
2 tablespoons sugar
4 eggs, separated
Whipped cream

1. Prepare and bake pie shell. Let cool.
2. In top of double boiler, combine chocolate, sugar, and 1/4 cup water. Cook over hot, not boiling, water, stirring frequently, until chocolate is melted.
3. Remove from hot water; let cool slightly. Add egg yolks; stir until well combined.
4. Beat egg whites just until stiff. Fold into chocolate mixture until well combined. Turn into pie shell.
5. Refrigerate until well chilled—at least 6 hours. At serving time, decorate top with whipped cream. Makes 6 to 8 servings.

Cream Pies, Chiffon Pies

These delectable, creamy pies make super desserts. Whether it's chocolate cream or coconut cream, or lemon, hidden under a fluffy meringue, do be sure to follow our recipes to the letter. Cream pies must be smooth, but firm enough to slice neatly; a cream pie that does not hold its shape defeats its purpose as a tempting dessert. Pies with creamy fillings (meringue pies are the exception) are usually served well chilled.

Chocolate Cream Pie

3/4 cup sugar
1/3 cup cornstarch
2 squares unsweetened chocolate, cut up
1/2 teaspoon salt
2-1/2 cups milk
3 egg yolks, slightly beaten
1/2 teaspoon vanilla extract
9-inch baked pie shell

Cream Topping:
1 cup heavy cream
2 tablespoons confectioners' sugar
1/2 teaspoon vanilla extract

1. In top of double boiler, combine the sugar, cornstarch, chocolate, and salt; mix well. Then gradually stir in the milk.
2. Cook, over boiling water, stirring, until the mixture is thickened—about 10 minutes. Cook, covered, stirring occasionally, 10 minutes longer.
3. Gradually stir half of the hot mixture into beaten egg yolks. Return to rest of mixture in double boiler; cook over boiling water, stirring occasionally, 5 minutes. Remove from heat; stir in vanilla. Pour chocolate filling into baked pie shell.
4. Refrigerate until well chilled—at least 3 hours.
5. Make Cream Topping 1 hour before serving. With rotary beater, beat cream with confectioners' sugar and vanilla until stiff. Spread over pie. Refrigerate.
Makes 6 to 8 servings.

Lemon Meringue Pie

Lemon Filling:
1/4 cup cornstarch
3 tablespoons flour
1-3/4 cups sugar
1/4 teaspoon salt
4 egg yolks, slightly beaten
1/2 cup lemon juice
1 tablespoon grated lemon peel
1 tablespoon butter

9-inch baked pie shell

Meringue:
4 egg whites
1/4 teaspoon cream of tartar
1/2 cup sugar

1. Make Lemon Filling: In medium saucepan, combine cornstarch, flour, sugar, and salt, mixing well. Gradually add 2 cups water, stirring until smooth.
2. Over medium heat, bring to boiling, stirring occasionally; boil 1 minute.
3. Remove from heat. Quickly stir some of hot mixture into egg yolks. Return to hot mixture; stir to blend.
4. Return to heat; cook over low heat 5 minutes; stirring occasionally.
5. Remove from heat. Stir in lemon juice, lemon peel, and butter. Pour into pie shell.
6. Preheat oven to 400F.
7. Make Meringue: In medium bowl, with mixer at medium speed, beat egg whites with cream of tartar until frothy.
8. Gradually beat in sugar, 2 tablespoons at a time, beating after each addition. Then beat at high speed until stiff peaks form when beater is slowly raised.
9. Spread over lemon filling, carefully sealing to edge of the crust and swirling top decoratively.
10. Bake 7 to 9 minutes, or until the meringue is golden-brown. Let pie cool completely on wire rack —2-1/2 to 3 hours.
Makes 8 servings.

Old-Fashioned Pumpkin Pie

3 eggs
1 can (1 lb) pumpkin
1/2 cup light-brown sugar, packed
1/2 cup granulated sugar
1 teaspoon cinnamon
1/2 teaspoon ginger
1/4 teaspoon nutmeg
1/8 teaspoon cloves
1/2 teaspoon salt
3/4 cup milk
1/2 cup heavy cream
9-inch unbaked pie shell
Whipped-Cream Lattice (recipe follows)

1. Preheat oven to 350F. In large bowl, beat eggs slightly. Add pumpkin, sugars, spices, salt; beat until well blended. Slowly add milk and cream.
2. Pour into shell; bake 60 to 70 minutes, or until knife inserted in center comes out clean. Cool on rack. Just before serving, decorate pie with Whipped-Cream Lattice.
Makes 6 to 8 servings.

Whipped-Cream Lattice

1/2 cup heavy cream
1 tablespoon confectioners' sugar
1/4 teaspoon vanilla extract

1. Whip cream with sugar and vanilla until stiff.
2. Using cream in pastry bag with number-3 (large rosette) decorating tip, pipe cream in lattice design over top of pumpkin pie.

Slipped Coconut-Custard Pie

9-inch baked pie shell
4 eggs
1-1/2 cups heavy cream
1-1/3 cups milk
1 can (4 oz) shredded coconut
1/2 cup granulated sugar
1 teaspoon vanilla extract
1/4 teaspoon coconut flavoring
1/4 teaspoon salt
2 tablespoons confectioners' sugar

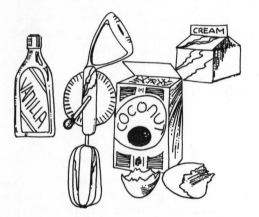

1. Prepare and bake pie shell. Cool.
2. Preheat oven to 350F. Butter a 9-inch pie plate.
3. In medium bowl, with wire whisk or rotary beater, beat eggs slightly. Add 1 cup cream, the milk, 1 cup coconut, the granulated sugar, vanilla, coconut flavoring, and salt; beat until well mixed.
4. Pour into prepared pie plate. Place in shallow pan; pour cold water to about 1/2 inch around pie plate.
5. Bake 40 to 45 minutes, or until silver knife inserted in center comes out clean.
6. Remove pan from water. Let custard cool completely on wire rack; then refrigerate until well chilled—several hours or overnight.
7. Loosen custard from pie plate by carefully running a small spatula around edge and shaking plate gently. Holding plate just above rim of baked shell, carefully slip custard into shell.
8. Whip remaining cream with confectioners' sugar. Use to decorate edge of pie. Sprinkle cream with remaining coconut. (Toast coconut, if desired.)
Makes 6 to 8 servings.
Custard Pie: Make as above, omitting coconut.

Lemon Chiffon Pie

1 env unflavored gelatine
4 eggs
1/2 cup lemon juice
1 cup sugar
1/4 teaspoon salt
1 tablespoon grated lemon peel
Yellow food color
Unbaked Graham-Cracker Pie Shell, page 411
1 cup heavy cream

1. Sprinkle gelatine over 1/4 cup cold water in measuring cup; set aside to soften.
2. Separate eggs, placing whites in large bowl of electric mixer, yolks in double-boiler top. Set whites aside to warm to room temperature.
3. Beat yolks slightly with wooden spoon. Stir in lemon juice, 1/2 cup sugar, and salt.
4. Cook over hot, not boiling, water (water should not touch bottom of double-boiler top), stirring constantly, until mixture thickens and coats metal spoon—about 12 minutes.

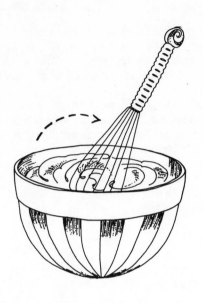

5. Add gelatine mixture and lemon peel, stirring until gelatine is dissolved. Add 2 drops food color; mix well. Remove pan from hot water. Refrigerate, stirring occasionally, until cool and the consistency of unbeaten egg white—about 35 minutes.

6. Meanwhile, make Graham-Cracker Pie Shell.

7. At high speed, beat egg whites just until soft peaks form when the beater is slowly raised— peaks bend slightly.

8. Gradually beat in remaining 1/2 cup sugar, 2 tablespoons at a time, beating well after each addition. Continue beating until stiff peaks form when beater is raised.

9. With rubber scraper or wire whisk, gently fold gelatine mixture into egg-white mixture just until combined.

10. Gently turn into the pie shell, mounding high. Refrigerate until firm—3 to 6 hours.

11. To serve: Whip cream until stiff. Spread about half of it over pie. Put remaining cream in pastry bag with number-30 decorating tip, and pipe rosettes around pie edge.

Makes 6 to 8 servings.

Honolulu Coconut Pie

Filling:
3/4 cup granulated sugar
3 tablespoons cornstarch
Dash salt
2 cups milk
3 egg yolks
3/4 teaspoon vanilla extract
1/4 teaspoon almond extract

9-inch baked pie shell

1 cup heavy cream
2 tablespoons confectioners' sugar
2 cans (3-1/2-oz size) flaked coconut, or 2 cups grated fresh coconut

1. Make Filling: In top of double boiler, combine granulated sugar, cornstarch, and salt. Gradually stir in milk until smooth.

2. Cook over boiling water, stirring constantly, until mixture thickens. Cover, and cook 15 minutes, stirring several times.

3. In small bowl, beat egg yolks slightly. Stir 1/2 cup hot cornstarch mixture into egg yolks, mixing well. Pour back into top of double boiler; cook mixture 2 minutes longer, stirring constantly. Remove from heat.

4. Stir in extracts; turn into small bowl; cover. Cool to room temperature—about 1 hour.

5. Refrigerate until well chilled—at least 1 hour.

6. Meanwhile, make, bake, and cool pie shell. Also, whip cream with confectioners' sugar until stiff. Refrigerate, covered.

7. To assemble pie: Turn filling into pie shell. Sprinkle with half the coconut. Cover with whipped cream. Sprinkle remaining coconut over top. Serve at once, or refrigerate no longer than 1 hour.

Makes 8 servings.

Banana Coconut Pie: Slice two bananas; arrange in pie shell to cover bottom; cover with filling, as in Step 7.

Maple Squash Pie

Filling:
3 eggs, slightly beaten
1/2 cup sugar
1/2 cup maple or maple-flavored syrup
1/2 teaspoon cinnamon
1/2 teaspoon ginger
1/2 teaspoon salt
2 pkg (12-oz size) frozen squash, thawed, un-
drained
1 cup light cream

9-inch unbaked pie shell

1/2 cup heavy cream, whipped
Maple syrup

1. Preheat oven to 400F.
2. Make Filling: In large bowl, combine eggs, sugar, maple syrup, spices, salt, squash, and light cream. Beat, with rotary beater, until mixture is smooth.
3. Turn most of filling into unbaked pie shell. Place on lowest shelf of oven; pour in rest of filling. Bake 55 to 60 minutes, or until filling is set in center when pie is gently shaken.
4. Let cool on wire rack. Serve pie slightly warm or cold. Garnish with whipped cream rosettes, drizzled with maple syrup.
Makes 8 servings.

Deep-Dish Pies, Dumplings, and Tarts

These pastries go something like this: The **deep-dish pie** is a fruit pie with a crust on the top, not on the bottom. It is usually more juicy than the average pie and is served warm with cream or à la mode. The **dumpling** is a pastry sack containing a whole fruit. It may have a glaze of its own juices as they run into the pan, and it may be served with a separate sauce or poured cream. The **tart** is a miniature open-face pie, and it is usually filled with fruit.

Apple Dumplings

Pastry for 2-crust pie
3 tablespoons butter or regular margarine,
softened
3 tablespoons sugar
1 tablespoon dark raisins
2 tablespoons chopped walnuts
3/4 teaspoon cinnamon
4 medium baking apples (about 2 lb)
1/2 cup maple-blended syrup
Cinnamon-Ice-Cream Sauce, page 218

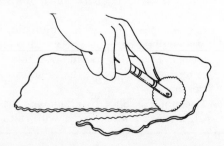

1. Form pastry into a ball; wrap in waxed paper. Place in refrigerator.
2. In small bowl, combine butter, sugar, raisins, chopped walnuts, and cinnamon; mix until they are well blended.
3. Pare and core apples. Fill each with raisin-walnut mixture.
4. Preheat oven to 375F. Generously grease a 13-by-9-by-2-inch baking dish.
5. Divide pastry into fourths. On lightly floured surface, roll out each part, from center to edge, to make a 7-inch square. Trim edges, using pastry wheel for decorative edge, if desired. Reserve trimmings.
6. Place an apple in center of each square. Bring each corner of square to top of apple, and pinch edges of pastry together firmly, to cover apple completely.

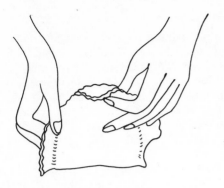

7. Reroll trimmings. With leaf-shaped cookie cutter, cut out as many leaves as possible. Brush leaves with cold water, and press on top of the dumplings.

8. Arrange dumplings in prepared baking dish. Brush the top and sides of each with some of the maple-blended syrup.

9. Bake, brushing occasionally with syrup, 40 minutes, or until pastry is a rich golden-brown and apples seem tender when tested with wooden pick. With broad spatula, immediately remove dumplings to serving dish. Serve with light cream, soft vanilla ice cream, or Cinnamon Ice Cream Sauce. Makes 4 servings.

Deep-Dish Pear Pie

2-1/4 to 2-1/2 lb fresh pears
3/4 cup light-brown sugar, packed
3 tablespoons flour
1/8 teaspoon salt
Dash ground cloves
Dash nutmeg
1/3 cup heavy cream
2 tablespoons lemon juice
2 tablespoons butter or margarine
Pastry for 1-crust pie
1 egg yolk
Heavy cream or vanilla ice cream

1. Halve pears lengthwise; scoop out core; cut a V shape to remove stems. Pare and slice to make 6 cups.

2. In small bowl, combine brown sugar, flour, salt, cloves, and nutmeg. Stir in 1/3 cup cream.

3. Place sliced pears in an 8-1/4-inch round, shallow baking dish or 9-inch deep-dish-pie plate (about 1-3/4 inches deep). Sprinkle with lemon juice; add cream mixture. With wooden spoon, stir gently until well mixed. Dot with butter.

4. Preheat oven to 400F.

5. On lightly floured surface, roll out pastry to an 11-inch circle. Fold in half; make slits for steam vents.

6. Place over fruit in baking dish, and unfold. Press pastry to edge of dish. For decorative edge, press firmly all around with thumb.

7. Lightly beat egg yolk with 1 tablespoon water. Brush over pastry.

8. Place a piece of foil, a little larger than baking dish, on oven rack below the one on which pie bakes, to catch any juices that may bubble over edge of dish. Bake pie 35 to 40 minutes, or until crust is golden and juice bubbles through steam vents.

9. Let pie cool on wire rack about 30 minutes. Serve warm, with heavy cream or ice cream.

Makes 6 to 8 servings.

Note: To make pie with canned pears, use 2 cans (1-lb, 13-oz size) sliced pears. Drain, reserving 2 tablespoons syrup. Make as above, reducing sugar to 1/2 cup and decreasing flour to 2 tablespoons. Add reserved syrup with the cream.

Deep-Dish Apple-Cider Pie

Filling:
1-1/2 cups apple cider
1 to 1-1/4 cups sugar
3 lb tart cooking apples
2 tablespoons lemon juice
2 tablespoons butter or margarine

Pastry for 1-crust pie
1 egg yolk

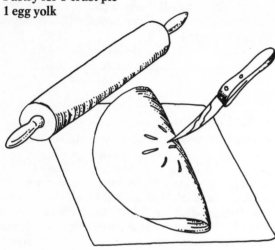

1. Make Filling: In large saucepan, combine cider and sugar; bring to boiling, stirring until sugar is dissolved. Boil, uncovered, 10 minutes.
2. Meanwhile, pare and core apples; slice thinly into large bowl. Sprinkle with lemon juice. Add to cider mixture; return to boiling over moderate heat, stirring several times. Lower heat; simmer, uncovered, 5 minutes, or just until apples are partially cooked.
3. With slotted spoon, lift apples out of syrup and into a round, 8-1/4-inch, shallow baking dish, mounding slices in center.
4. Return remaining syrup to boiling; boil, uncovered, 5 minutes. (Syrup should measure 1/2 cup.) Pour over apple slices; dot with butter.
5. Preheat oven to 400F.
6. On lightly floured surface, roll out pastry into an 11-inch circle. Fit over top of baking dish; flute edge. Make several slits in center for vents.
7. Beat egg yolk with 1 tablespoon water; brush over pastry. Bake 40 to 45 minutes, or until pastry is golden-brown and juice bubbles through slits.
8. Serve warm, with ice cream, light cream, or hard sauce.
Makes 6 to 8 servings.

Deep-Dish Peach Pie

4 to 4-1/2 lb fresh peaches
1/4 cup lemon juice
1-1/2 cups light-brown sugar
1/4 cup unsifted all-purpose flour
1/8 teaspoon cloves
1/8 teaspoon cinnamon
1/2 cup heavy cream
1/4 cup butter or margarine
Pastry for 2-crust pie
1 egg yolk

1. Peel and slice enough peaches to make 9 cups. Turn into large bowl. Add lemon juice; toss gently.
2. In small bowl, mix well sugar, flour, cloves, and cinnamon. Sprinkle over peaches; stir until combined. Stir in cream. Turn into a 12-by-8-by-2-inch shallow baking dish. Dot with butter.
3. Preheat oven to 425F.
4. On lightly floured pastry cloth or board, roll out pastry to a 12-inch square. Cut into 1-inch-wide strips.
5. Arrange 4 strips lengthwise over peaches; arrange remaining strips across them, slightly on diagonal. Trim strips, pressing ends to edge of dish. If you wish, arrange leftover pastry strips, end to end, around edge of dish, to make a border.
6. Mix egg yolk with 1 tablespoon cold water; brush over pastry.
7. Bake 35 to 40 minutes, or until pastry is golden-brown and juice bubbles.

8. Let pie cool on wire rack about 30 minutes.
Makes 8 to 10 servings.

Note: To make pie with canned peaches, use 3 cans (1-lb, 14-oz size) sliced peaches. Drain peaches, reserving syrup. Reduce sugar to 1 cup and use 1/2 cup reserved syrup in place of cream.

Fluted Tart Shells

1. Prepare pastry for 2-crust pie.
2. Divide pastry in half; divide each half into 5 parts.
3. On lightly floured surface, roll each part into a 5-inch circle. Use each circle to line a 3-1/2-inch fluted tart pan, pressing pastry evenly to bottom and side of each pan; trim.
4. Prick each tart shell well with fork; refrigerate 30 minutes.
5. Meanwhile, preheat oven to 450F.
6. Bake shells, on large cookie sheet, 10 to 12 minutes, or until golden-brown.
7. Cool completely on wire racks; then carefully remove shells from pans. Fill as desired.

Note: For thicker shells, divide pastry in half; divide each half into 4 parts. Proceed as above. Makes 8 or 10.

Pear-Marmalade Tarts

1 can (1 lb, 1 oz) pear halves
1/2 cup sugar
1-1/2 teaspoons lemon peel
2 teaspoons lemon juice
1/8 teaspoon cloves
12 (3-inch) baked tart shells
1/2 cup heavy cream, whipped

1. Drain pear halves; measure liquid. If necessary, add water to make 1 cup. In 3-quart saucepan, combine pear liquid and sugar.
2. Bring to boiling, stirring, until sugar is dissolved. Boil gently, uncovered, until syrup is thickened—about 10 minutes.
3. Meanwhile, chop pears finely in bowl. To syrup, add pears, lemon peel, juice, and the cloves. Cook, uncovered and stirring occasionally, over medium heat until consistency of marmalade—about 5 minutes.
4. Turn into bowl; refrigerate, covered, until cold, or until ready to use. (Can be made a day or two ahead of time.)
5. To serve: Fill tart shells with pear marmalade, 1 heaping tablespoonful for each. Top each with a spoonful of whipped cream.
Makes 12.

Fruit Tarts

Tart Shells:
1/2 cup butter or regular margarine, softened
1/4 cup sugar
1/4 teaspoon salt
1 egg white
1-1/2 cups sifted all-purpose flour

Rum Cream, below

Fruits: whole strawberries, blueberries, red
raspberries, sliced bananas, seedless green grapes,
apricot halves, black cherries (fresh, frozen, or
canned), canned small pineapple rings or tidbits

Apricot Glaze or Currant-Jelly Glaze, below

1. Make Tart Shells: In medium bowl, with fork,
blend butter, sugar, salt, and egg white until
smooth and well combined.
2. Gradually stir in flour, mixing until smooth.
3. For each tart, use 2 teaspoons dough. Press
evenly into 2-1/2- to 3-inch tart pans of assorted
shapes and sizes. Set pans on cookie sheet.
4. Refrigerate 30 minutes.
5. Preheat oven to 375F. Bake tart shells 12 to 15
minutes, or until light golden. Cool in pans on wire
rack a few minutes; then turn out, and cool completely before filling.
6. To fill tarts: Spoon several teaspoons of Rum
Cream into each shell. Refrigerate.
7. Top with fruit. (Drain fruit very well before
using.) Brush yellow or light fruit with warm
Apricot Glaze and red or dark fruit with Currant-
Jelly Glaze.
8. Refrigerate until ready to serve.
Makes 1-1/2 dozen.
Note: If desired, make Tart Shells and Rum Cream
day before. Then assemble tarts several hours before serving.

Rum Cream

1 teaspoon unflavored gelatine
2 tablespoons granulated sugar
2 tablespoons flour
Salt
1 egg yolk
1/2 cup milk
2 tablespoons rum
1 egg white, stiffly beaten
1/2 cup heavy cream
1 tablespoon confectioners' sugar
1 inch vanilla bean, scraped, or 1/2 teaspoon
    vanilla extract

1. In small saucepan, mix gelatine, granulated
sugar, flour, and dash salt; mix well.
2. Beat egg yolk with milk and rum. Add to gelatine mixture; cook over medium heat, stirring constantly with wire whisk, until mixture is thickened
and comes to boiling.
3. Pour into medium bowl; set bowl in pan of ice
and water; let stand, stirring occasionally, until
mixture begins to set—about 8 to 10 minutes. Fold
in beaten egg white.
4. Beat cream with confectioners' sugar; fold into
gelatine mixture. Stir in vanilla. Refrigerate until
ready to use—at least 30 minutes.
Makes about 1-1/2 cups.

Apricot Glaze

1/2 cup apricot preserves

1. In small saucepan, over medium heat, stir apricot preserves until melted. (If preserves seem too thick, thin with 1/2 to 1 tablespoon hot water.)
2. Strain. Use warm, on tarts.
Makes about 1/2 cup.

Currant-Jelly Glaze

1/2 cup red-currant jelly
1 tablespoon kirsch

1. In small saucepan, over moderate heat, stir currant jelly until melted. Remove from heat.
2. Stir in kirsch. Use warm, on tarts. (If glaze becomes too thick, reheat gently, and add a little hot water.)
Makes about 1/2 cup.

Lemon Sandbakels

1/2 cup butter or regular margarine, softened
1 cup unsifted all-purpose flour
1/4 cup sugar
1 egg yolk
2 tablespoons ground blanched almonds
1/2 teaspoon almond extract

Lemon Filling:
1 egg
1 egg yolk
1/2 cup sugar
1/4 cup butter or regular margarine
1 tablespoon grated lemon peel
1/4 cup lemon juice

1. Preheat oven to 400F.
2. In medium bowl, with pastry blender, cut 1/2 cup soft butter into the flour and 1/4 cup sugar until mixture resembles coarse crumbs.
3. Add 1 egg yolk, the almonds, and almond extract; stir with fork until well blended. Press tablespoonful of mixture into each of 18 (2-inch) fluted tart pans.
4. Bake 10 to 12 minutes, or until golden. Remove to wire rack. Let cool about 5 minutes. Loosen around side with small spatula, and turn out of pans. Let cool on wire rack.
5. Meanwhile, make Lemon Filling: In top of double boiler, combine egg and egg yolk; beat with spoon just until blended. Add sugar, butter, lemon peel, and lemon juice.
6. Cook over hot, not boiling, water, stirring constantly, until consistency of mayonnaise—about 10 minutes. Turn into small bowl; place waxed paper directly on surface. Refrigerate until well chilled.
7. Just before serving, fill each tart shell with 2 teaspoonfuls of lemon filling. Decorate each with a little whipped cream, if desired.
Makes 1-1/2 dozen.

Glazed Tartlets Triumphant

Praline Paste, below
Tartlet Shells, below
Pastry Cream, below
Assorted fruits (fresh, frozen, or canned)
Apricot Glaze, page 431

1. Spoon 1/4 teaspoon Praline Paste into each shell.
2. Add 1/2 teaspoon Pastry Cream to each shell; top with fruit of your choice. (Drain frozen or canned fruit.)
3. Spoon 1/2 teaspoon Apricot Glaze over fruit in each shell.
Makes 65.

Frosted Tartlets Triumphant

Praline Paste, below
Tartlet Shells, below
Pastry Cream, below
Drained whole maraschino cherries (optional)
Chocolate or Vanilla Frosting, below

1. Spoon 1/4 teaspoon Praline Paste into each shell.
2. Add 1/2 teaspoon Pastry Cream; top with cherry. (If cherry is omitted, increase amount of cream to 1 teaspoon.)
3. Spoon about 1 teaspoon warm frosting over each tartlet. Decorate as desired.
Makes 65.

Pastry Cream for Tartlets

1/4 cup sugar
Dash salt
1 tablespoon cornstarch
1 cup milk
2 egg yolks, slightly beaten
1/2 teaspoon vanilla extract
1/4 teaspoon almond extract

1. In small saucepan, mix sugar, salt, and cornstarch. Stir in milk.
2. Cook, stirring constantly, over medium heat, until mixture thickens and begins to boil; boil 1 minute. Remove from heat.
3. Add a little hot mixture to egg yolks, mixing well. Return to saucepan.
4. Cook, stirring constantly, until mixture is thick and bubbly.
5. Stir in extracts. Let cool to room temperature—about 1 hour.
Makes about 1-1/4 cups.

Praline Paste for Tartlets

1/4 cup sugar
1/2 cup coarsely chopped pecans or hazelnuts
2 squares semisweet chocolate, melted

1. Lightly butter an 8-by-1-1/2-inch round layer-cake pan or small cookie sheet.
2. Melt sugar in small, heavy skillet, over low heat, shaking pan from side to side. Continue to cook, stirring, until syrup turns light golden.
3. Remove from heat. Add nuts, stirring until just coated with syrup.

4. Working quickly, turn mixture into prepared pan. (Mixture will harden almost immediately.)
5. When cool, break into 2-inch pieces. Blend in food blender, to grind pieces finely.
6. In small bowl, combine ground nut mixture with chocolate, mixing well.
Makes 1/2 cup.

Tartlet Shells

1/2 cup butter, softened
1/4 cup sugar
1/4 teaspoon salt
1 egg white
1/4 teaspoon almond extract
3/4 cup blanched almonds, ground
1 cup sifted all-purpose flour

1. In medium bowl, with spoon, blend butter, sugar, salt, egg white, and almond extract until smooth and well combined.
2. Add ground almonds and flour; mix until smooth. (If dough is very stiff, mix with hands.)
3. Wrap dough in waxed paper; refrigerate 1 hour.
4. Preheat oven to 375F.
5. For each tartlet, use 1 teaspoon dough. Press dough evenly into 2-by-1/2-inch tartlet pans.
6. Set tartlet pans on cookie sheet; bake about 10 minutes, or until golden-brown.
7. Let cool on wire rack 10 minutes. With small spatula, gently remove tartlets from pans. Let cool completely before filling.
Makes 65.
Note: Tartlet Shells may be made day before and stored in an air-tight container.

Chocolate Frosting for Tartlets

2 tablespoons butter or margarine
1/3 cup sugar
2 squares unsweetened chocolate
1 teaspoon vanilla extract

1. In small saucepan, combine butter, sugar, chocolate, and 1/4 cup water.
2. Stir, over medium heat, until chocolate melts and mixture is smooth and starts to boil.
3. Add vanilla. Spoon while still warm over tartlets.
Makes 2/3 cup.

Vanilla Frosting for Tartlets

2-1/2 cups sifted confectioners' sugar
2 tablespoons light corn syrup
1 teaspoon vanilla extract
1/4 teaspoon almond extract
Few drops red or green food color (optional)

1. In top of double boiler, combine all ingredients with 2 tablespoons water.
2. Cook, stirring, over hot water, just until frosting is smooth and shiny and coats a wooden spoon. Spoon while still warm over tartlets.
3. If frosting thickens on standing, thin it with a little water.
Makes about 1 cup.

Miniature Coconut Tarts

Pastry:
1-1/3 cups sifted*all-purpose flour
1/3 cup sugar
1/4 teaspoon salt
3/4 cup butter or margarine
1 egg, slightly beaten

Filling:
1 egg
1 can (3-1/2 oz) flaked coconut
2/3 cup sugar
*Sift before measuring.

1. Make Pastry: Sift flour with sugar and salt into medium bowl. With pastry blender or 2 knives, cut in butter until mixture is like coarse cornmeal. With fork, stir in egg.
2. Knead slightly, with hands, until mixture holds together. Wrap in waxed paper; refrigerate several hours, or until firm.
3. Then preheat oven to 375F. Make Filling: With fork, beat egg in small bowl. Add coconut and sugar; mix well.
4. For each tart: Pinch off about 1 teaspoon chilled dough. Press into 2-by-1/2-inch tartlet pan, to make a lining 1/8 inch thick.
5. Fill each tart with 1 teaspoon filling.
6. Bake tarts (about 24 at a time), set on cookie sheet, 12 minutes, or until coconut filling is golden-brown.
7. Place pans on wire rack; cool slightly. With small spatula, gently remove tarts.
Makes about 47.

Lemon-Curd Tarts

Filling:
3 eggs
2 tablespoons grated lemon peel
1/2 cup lemon juice
3/4 cup butter, softened
1 cup plus 2 tablespoons sugar

8 (3-inch) baked tart shells
1/2 cup heavy cream

1. Make Filling: In top of double boiler, beat eggs well with a fork. Add lemon peel and juice, butter, and 1 cup sugar; mix well till combined.
2. Place over simmering water (water should not touch bottom of double-boiler top); cook egg-lemon mixture, stirring constantly, about 15 to 20 minutes, or until mixture forms a thick coating on a metal spoon and mounds slightly.
3. Remove mixture from heat, and turn it into a bowl. Refrigerate the filling, covered, several hours, or until it is well chilled.
4. To serve: Divide the lemon filling into 8 tart shells.
5. In a small bowl, using a rotary beater, beat heavy cream with 2 tablespoons sugar until stiff. Decorate tarts with whipped cream, using a spoon or a pastry bag with decorating tip. Sprinkle whipped cream with grated lemon peel, if desired. Makes 8 tarts.
Lime-Curd Tarts: Substitute 1 tablespoon grated lime peel for the grated lemon peel, and 1/2 cup lime juice for the lemon juice. Tint a pale green by adding 2 drops green food color.

Poultry

Poultry, especially chicken and turkey, is a good buy any time of the year. It's company food at family prices, a good thing to remember if you have to do much entertaining on a limited budget.

Buying and Storage

How much should you buy?
For each serving allow:
1/2 of one 1-1/2-pound broiler
3/4 pound for frying
3/4 pound for roasting
3/4 pound for stewing
Remember these amounts are per serving, not per person served. Gauge your needs by appetites—whether or not you expect people to take seconds. Also, if yours is a dark-meat family, take advantage of legs and thighs sold separately. One whole chicken plus several legs will give each his choice. The most economical way to buy chicken is whole, rather than cut up.

Often, fresh ready-to-cook poultry arrives at the market in a plastic wrapping. If so, leave it in this wrapping and keep it in the refrigerator until you are ready to cook it. It should keep several days. If your butcher cuts up your chicken or wraps it whole in his own wrappings, or if you buy parts, remove the wrappings when you get home. Rewrap loosely in foil, waxed paper or plastic wrap and refrigerate until used. Use within a few days.
If you buy a frozen chicken or packaged frozen parts, keep frozen until 24 hours before cooking. Then unwrap, and leave it on your refrigerator shelf overnight. Or for quicker defrosting, unwrap and thaw in running cold water for 1 or 2 hours.

Test Your Terminology

Broiler or broiler-fryer: Chicken about 9 weeks old, weighing 1-1/2 to 3-1/2 pounds. Tender, with smooth-textured skin and flexible breastbone cartilage. Of all chickens sold, 70 to 80 percent are broiler-fryers.
Roaster: Tender chickens of 3-1/2 to 5 pounds, about 12 weeks old.
Stewing chicken: Mature female chickens, less tender than roasters. Can be broiler chickens allowed to grow old or hens past ideal age for laying eggs.

Capon: Desexed (through surgery) male chicken, weighing 4 to 8 pounds. Very tender, with large amount of white meat.
Ready-to-cook or oven-ready: All commercially produced birds are now sold ready to cook. Pinfeathers are removed, hair singed, bird thoroughly cleaned inside and out; giblets cleaned, wrapped and placed in cavity; bird shipped to market in iced wooden crates in refrigerated trucks.

Chicken

Chicken is always a good choice. Everybody likes it, and it's economical for serving a large group.

If your chicken repertoire runs to the tried and true, turn the page. These recipes are for you.

Roast Stuffed Chicken

1 whole roasting chicken (4 lb)
Bread Stuffing, page 455
2 tablespoons butter or margarine, melted
2 cups canned chicken broth

1. Wash chicken well under cold running water; dry with paper towels. Remove excess fat.
2. Preheat oven to 350F.
3. Make Bread Stuffing.

4. Fill body cavity with stuffing. Close with poultry pins. Tie legs together with twine. Tuck wings under body.

5. Place chicken on rack in shallow roasting pan. Brush with melted butter. Roast, uncovered, 1-3/4 to 2 hours, or until leg joints move easily; baste occasionally with pan drippings.

6. Remove chicken to heated serving platter; remove poultry pins and twine. Let stand 15 minutes before carving.

7. Skim fat from drippings. Add chicken broth to pan. Cook over medium heat, stirring to dissolve browned bits; simmer until reduced to 1 cup. Strain into gravy boat.

Makes 4 servings.

Timetable for Roasting Stuffed Chicken—at 325F

Chicken	Ready-To-Cook Weight	Approximate Roasting Time
Broiler-fryer	3 lb	1-1/2* hours
Roaster	4 lb	3-1/2 hours
Capon	5 lb	2-1/2 hours
	8 lb	4-1/2 hours

Chicken and dressing should be at room temperature.

* Broiler-fryers are roasted at 375F for 30 minutes per pound.

Broiled Chicken with Parsley Butter

3 broiler-fryers, split (2 to 2-1/2 lb each)
3 teaspoons salt
1 teaspoon dried oregano leaves
1 teaspoon dried thyme leaves
3 tablespoons butter or margarine, melted
Parsley Butter, page 500

1. Wash chicken; pat dry with paper towels.
2. Combine salt, oregano, thyme, and pepper.
3. Brush both sides of chicken halves with butter. Place, skin side down, in broiler pan without rack; sprinkle with salt mixture.
4. Broil, 8 inches from heat, 25 minutes; brush with pan drippings two or three times.
5. Turn halves skin side up; brush with pan drippings. Broil, brushing with pan drippings two or three times, 15 minutes, or until chicken is golden-brown and well done. (When done, drumstick will move easily at joint.)
6. Remove to heated platter. Top each chicken half with a piece of Parsley Butter.

Makes 6 servings.

Chicken Cacciatore

2 (2-lb size) broiler-fryers, cut up
3 tablespoons olive or salad oil
2 tablespoons butter or margarine
1 can (15 oz) tomato sauce
1 can (1 lb, 12 oz) whole tomatoes, undrained
3/4 cup dry red wine
1 teaspoon dried basil leaves
1 teaspoon dried oregano leaves
1/4 teaspoon minced garlic
2 tablespoons chopped parsley
3/4 teaspoon salt
1/4 teaspoon pepper
3 tablespoons flour
1 can (6 oz) whole mushrooms, drained

1. Wash chicken; pat dry with paper towels.
2. Heat oil and butter in 6-quart Dutch oven. Add chicken, a few pieces at a time, and brown well on all sides. Remove as browned.
3. Return chicken to Dutch oven; add tomato sauce, tomatoes, wine, basil, oregano, garlic, parsley, salt, and pepper. Simmer, covered 45 to 50 minutes, or until chicken is tender.
4. Combine flour with 3 tablespoons water; stir into sauce. Add mushrooms; cook 10 minutes longer, or until sauce is thickened.
Makes 6 servings.

Poached Chicken with Vegetables

4- to 5-lb ready-to-cook roasting chicken, with giblets
Salt
1/8 teaspoon pepper
1/4 cup butter or margarine
8 leeks
1-1/2 to 2 lb small carrots, pared
1-1/2 lb small new potatoes, pared
1/4 cup butter or margarine, melted
4 teaspoons flour
1/2 cup dry white wine
1/2 cup canned chicken broth
2 bunches chives
Chopped parsley

1. Remove giblets from chicken; rinse giblets, and set aside on paper towels. Rinse chicken well; dry with paper towels. Sprinkle inside with 1-1/2 teaspoons salt and the pepper. Tuck wings under body; tie legs together. If necessary, fasten skin at neck with a skewer.
2. In 1/4 cup hot butter in Dutch oven, brown chicken well all over—takes about 30 minutes. Turn chicken carefully with two wooden spoons; do not break skin.
3. Meanwhile, coarsely chop giblets. Wash leeks well; cut off roots, and discard. Remove some of top leaves, and add to giblets. Then halve leeks crosswise, and set aside.
4. Place giblet-leek mixture under browned chicken. Cover tightly, and simmer over low heat 30 minutes.
5. Arrange carrots (halved, if necessary) around the chicken; simmer, covered, 40 minutes longer, or until chicken and carrots are tender. Remove from heat.
6. Meanwhile, cook potatoes in 1 inch boiling salted water in medium saucepan, covered, 20 to 25 minutes, or until tender. Drain; then drizzle with 2 tablespoons melted butter.
7. Also, cook halved leeks in 1 inch boiling water in medium saucepan, covered, 10 minutes, or until tender. Drain, and drizzle with 2 tablespoons melted butter.
8. Carefully remove chicken and carrots to heated platter; keep warm.

9. Strain drippings; return to Dutch oven. Stir in flour until smooth. Gradually stir in wine and chicken broth; bring to boiling. Reduce heat, and simmer 3 minutes. Taste, and add salt, if needed.

10. To serve: Arrange potatoes, leeks, and bunches of chives around chicken and carrots. Sprinkle potatoes with parsley. Pass gravy.

Makes 4 to 6 servings.

Chicken Tetrazzini

2 lb whole chicken breasts, split
3 lb chicken legs and thighs
3 celery tops
3 parsley sprigs
2 medium carrots, pared and sliced
1 onion, quartered
2 teaspoons salt
10 whole black peppercorns
1 bay leaf

Sauce:
3/4 cup butter or margarine
3/4 cup all-purpose flour
3 teaspoons salt
1/8 teaspoon nutmeg
Dash cayenne
1 quart milk
4 egg yolks
1 cup heavy cream
1/2 cup dry sherry

1 pkg (1 lb) thin spaghetti
2 cans (6-oz size) whole mushrooms, drained
2 pkg (8-oz size) sharp Cheddar cheese, grated
   (4 cups)

1. In the morning, wash chicken. Place in 6-quart kettle with 3 cups water, the celery, parsley, carrots, onion, salt, peppercorns, and bay leaf. Bring to boiling; reduce heat, and simmer, covered, 1 hour, or until chicken is tender.

2. Remove chicken from stock to bowl; set aside. Strain stock; return to kettle. Bring to boiling; boil gently, uncovered, until reduced to 2 cups—about 30 minutes.

3. Remove chicken meat from bones in large pieces—there should be about 6 cups. Set the chicken meat aside.

4. Make Sauce: Melt butter in large saucepan. Remove from heat. Stir in flour, salt, nutmeg, and cayenne until smooth. Gradually stir in milk and the 2 cups stock; bring to boiling, stirring constantly. Boil gently, stirring constantly, 2 minutes, or until slightly thickened.

5. In small bowl, beat egg yolks with cream. Gently beat in a little of the hot mixture. Return to saucepan; cook over low heat, stirring constantly, until sauce is hot—do not let it boil. Remove from heat. Add sherry.

6. Cook spaghetti as package label directs; drain. Return spaghetti to kettle. Add 2 cups sauce, and toss until well blended.

7. Remove another 2 cups sauce, and refrigerate, covered. To remaining sauce, add cut-up chicken and the mushrooms.

8. Divide spaghetti into two 12-by-8-by-2-inch baking dishes, arranging it around edges. Spoon half of chicken mixture into center of each. Sprinkle 2 cups cheese over spaghetti in each dish. Cover with foil; refrigerate.

9. About 1 hour before serving, preheat oven to 350F. Bake, covered, 30 to 45 minutes, or until piping hot.

10. Just before serving, reheat reserved sauce, and spoon over spaghetti in baking dishes.

Makes 12 servings.

Golden-Fried Chicken

3- to 3-1/2-lb broiler-fryer, cut up
1/3 cup all-purpose flour
1-1/2 teaspoons salt
1/4 teaspoon pepper
Salad oil or shortening (about 1-1/4 cups)

1. Wash chicken pieces under cold running water. Thoroughly dry with paper towels. Fold under wing tips.
2. In clean bag, combine flour, salt, and pepper. Add chicken to bag, a few pieces at a time, and shake to coat evenly with flour mixture.
3. In electric skillet, pour in salad oil, or melt shortening, to measure one fourth inch; heat at 375F. (Or slowly heat oil or shortening in large skillet with tight-fitting cover.)
4. Add chicken, a few pieces at a time, starting with meatiest pieces; brown on all sides, turning with tongs. Remove pieces as they are browned. It takes about 20 minutes to brown all the chicken.
5. Carefully pour off all but 2 tablespoons fat from skillet.
6. Using tongs, return chicken to skillet, placing pieces skin side down. Reduce temperature to 300F, or turn heat low. Cook, covered, 30 minutes. (If using electric skillet, leave steam vent open.) Then turn chicken skin side up, and cook, uncovered, 10 minutes, or until meat is fork-tender and skin is crisp.
7. Remove chicken to heated platter, or place in napkin-lined basket. Serve at once.
Makes 4 servings.

Chicken Paprikash

1 (4-lb) ready-to-cook roasting chicken
2-1/4 teaspoons salt
1/4 teaspoon pepper
1/4 cup butter or margarine
Paprika
1 can (10-1/2 oz) condensed chicken broth, undiluted
Giblets (gizzard, heart) and neck
8 small white onions, peeled
8 small carrots, pared
1/4 cup unsifted all-purpose flour
1 cup dairy sour cream
1 tablespoon chopped parsley

1. Rinse chicken well; dry with paper towels. Sprinkle inside and out with 1-1/2 teaspoons salt and the pepper. Tuck chicken wings under body; then tie legs together at ends, with twine. If necessary, fasten skin at neck, with a skewer.
2. In hot butter in Dutch oven, brown chicken well on all sides—about 30 minutes. Turn chicken carefully with two wooden spoons—do not break skin.
3. When bird is browned, sprinkle with 1 tablespoon paprika. Slip a small rack under the bird.
4. Heat chicken broth; add 1 tablespoon paprika, stirring until dissolved. Add to Dutch oven along with giblets and neck.
5. Arrange onions and carrots around chicken in Dutch oven.
6. Boil gently, covered, about 1 hour, or until chicken and vegetables are tender; baste with liquid frequently.

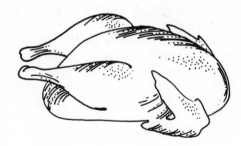

7. Remove chicken and vegetables to heated serving platter; cover loosely with foil; keep warm.

8. Remove rack from Dutch oven. Remove giblets; chop fine; set aside. Discard neck.

9. In small bowl, blend flour with 1/4 cup water to make a smooth paste. Stir into hot liquid in Dutch oven until smooth. Add remaining 3/4 teaspoon salt.

10. Bring to boiling, stirring; reduce heat, and simmer 2 minutes.

11. Remove from heat. Slowly stir in chopped giblets and sour cream; heat gently, but do not boil.

12. To serve: Sprinkle vegetables with parsley. Pass sauce.

Makes 4 to 6 servings.

Chicken Curry

4 whole chicken breasts (about 3-1/4 lb), split
1/4 cup butter or margarine
1 can (13-3/4 oz) chicken broth

Curry Sauce:
3 tablespoons butter or margarine
1 clove garlic, crushed
1 cup chopped onion
2 to 3 teaspoons curry powder
1 cup chopped pared apple
1/4 cup unsifted all-purpose flour
1/4 teaspoon ground cardamom
1 teaspoon ginger
1 teaspoon salt
1/4 teaspoon pepper
2 teaspoons grated lime peel
2 tablespoons lime juice
1/4 cup chopped chutney
Saffron Rice, page 459

Curry Accompaniments:
Chopped green pepper
Chutney
Whole salted peanuts
Flaked coconut
Sliced banana, dipped in lemon juice
Raisins
Kumquats
Sliced green onions
Chopped unpared cucumber
Yoghurt
Pineapple chunks
Coconut chips

1. Skin chicken; wipe with damp paper towels. Brown chicken, a few pieces at a time, in 1/4 cup hot butter in large skillet—5 minutes per side.

2. Return all chicken to skillet. Add chicken broth; bring to boiling. Reduce heat; simmer, covered, 20 minutes, or until tender.

3. Remove chicken pieces; keep warm. Measure liquid in skillet; add water to make 3 cups; reserve.

4. Make Curry Sauce: In 3 tablespoons hot butter in large skillet, sauté garlic, onion, curry powder, and apple until onion is tender—about 5 minutes.

5. Remove from heat. Stir in flour, cardamom, ginger, salt, and pepper; mix well.

6. Gradually stir in reserved liquid; add lime peel and juice.

7. Bring to boiling, stirring. Reduce heat; simmer, covered, 20 minutes, stirring occasionally.

8. Stir in cooked chicken and the chopped chutney. Heat gently just to boiling.

9. Serve with Saffron Rice and Curry Accompaniments.

Makes 8 servings.

Sweet-and-Sour Chicken

2 whole chicken legs and 2 whole chicken breasts
1/3 cup flour
1/3 cup salad oil or shortening
1 teaspoon salt
1/4 teaspoon pepper

Sauce:
1 can (13-1/2 oz) pineapple chunks
1 cup sugar
2 tablespoons cornstarch
3/4 cup cider vinegar
1 tablespoon soy sauce
1/4 teaspoon ginger
1 chicken-bouillon cube
1 large green pepper, cut in 1/2-inch-wide strips

1. Wash chicken; pat dry with paper towels. Coat chicken with flour.
2. Heat oil in large skillet. Add chicken, a few pieces at a time, and brown on all sides. Remove as browned to shallow roasting pan, arranging pieces skin side up. Sprinkle with salt and pepper.
3. Meanwhile, preheat oven to 350F.
4. Make Sauce: Drain pineapple chunks, pouring syrup into 2-cup measure. Add water to make 1-1/4 cups.
5. In medium saucepan, combine sugar, corn-starch, pineapple syrup, vinegar, soy sauce, gin-ger, and bouillon cube; bring to boiling, stirring constantly. Boil 2 minutes. Pour over chicken.
6. Bake, uncovered, 30 minutes. Add pineapple chunks and green pepper; bake 30 minutes longer, or until chicken is tender.
Makes 4 servings.

Coq au Vin with New Potatoes

2-1/2-lb broiler-fryer, quartered
6 bacon slices, diced
2 tablespoons butter or margarine
8 small white onions, peeled
8 small whole mushrooms
2/3 cup sliced green onions
1 clove garlic, crushed
2 tablespoons flour
1 teaspoon salt
1/8 teaspoon pepper
1/4 teaspoon dried thyme leaves
2 cups Burgundy
1 cup canned chicken broth
8 small new potatoes, scrubbed
Chopped parsley

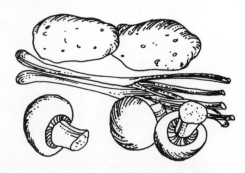

1. Day before, wash the chicken, and pat it dry with paper towels.
2. In a 3-quart Dutch oven, over medium heat, sauté the diced bacon until crisp. Remove bacon from the Dutch oven, and drain it on paper towels.
3. Add the butter to bacon drippings; heat. In hot fat, brown the chicken quarters well on all sides. Remove the chicken when it has browned; set aside.
4. Pour off all but 2 tablespoons fat from Dutch oven. Add the white onions, mushrooms, green onions, and garlic to the Dutch oven. Over low heat, cook, covered, and stirring occasionally, for 10 minutes.
5. Remove from heat; stir in the flour, salt, pepper, and thyme leaves. Gradually add the Burgundy and chicken broth; bring mixture to boiling, stir-ring.
6. Remove from heat. Add the potatoes, chicken, and bacon to Dutch oven; mix well. Cover, and refrigerate overnight.
7. The next day, about 2 hours before serving time, preheat oven to 400F.
8. Bake Coq au Vin, covered, about 1 hour and 50 minutes, or until chicken and potatoes are tender.
9. Sprinkle with chopped parsley before serving.
Makes 4 servings.

Picnic Chicken

Prepare Golden-Fried Chicken. Remove from skillet; let cool about 10 minutes; then refrigerate, covered, until well chilled. Place individual servings in small plastic bags. Carry to picnic in a portable cooler or an insulated bag.

Crispy Chicken Drumsticks

12 broiler-fryer legs (2-1/2 to 3 lb)
3/4 cup unsifted all-purpose flour
3/4 cup packaged cornflake crumbs
2 teaspoons salt
1/2 teaspoon poultry seasoning
1/4 teaspoon pepper
2 eggs, beaten
1/2 cup butter or margarine, melted

1. Preheat oven to 400F. Wipe chicken legs with damp paper towels.
2. In a clean paper bag, combine flour, cornflake crumbs, salt, poultry seasoning, and pepper.
3. Dip chicken legs, a few at a time, into beaten egg; then shake in bag, to coat with flour mixture.
4. Arrange in single layer in greased shallow baking pan. Brush chicken with melted butter. Cover pan with foil; bake 30 minutes.
5. Remove foil. Increase oven temperature to 450F, and bake 25 to 30 minutes, or until golden-brown. Makes 12 servings.

Crusty Chicken Wrap-Ups

8 chicken drumsticks
1/4 cup margarine
1/2 cup bottled barbecue sauce with onions
1 pkg (8 oz) refrigerator crescent dinner rolls
1 egg, beaten
2 teaspoons Italian seasoning
2 teaspoons grated Parmesan cheese
2 teaspoons sesame seed

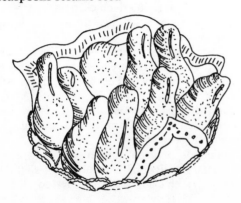

1. Wash chicken; dry on paper towels. (If desired, remove skin.)
2. In hot margarine and barbecue sauce, sauté chicken, turning, until lightly browned.
3. Over medium heat, cook, covered and turning occasionally, 25 minutes, or until tender. Remove chicken from pan; let cool slightly—5 minutes.
4. Preheat oven to 375F. Unroll crescents; separate into triangles.
5. Brush each triangle lightly with egg; then sprinkle lightly with Italian seasoning and grated cheese.
6. Place a chicken leg on long side of each triangle; bring sides up over chicken; press together with fingers. Twist end of crescent around bone.
7. Arrange seam side down on ungreased cookie sheet. Brush tops with egg; sprinkle with sesame seed.
8. Bake 15 to 20 minutes, or until golden. Serve warm or cold.
Makes 8 servings.

Breast of Chicken in Madeira Sauce

1-1/2 cups raw long-grain white rice
Salt
4 whole chicken breasts (about 3 lb)
1/4 cup butter or margarine
2 shallots, sliced
1/2 lb fresh mushrooms, washed and cut in half
   lengthwise
1 teaspoon dried thyme leaves
Dash pepper
1-1/2 cups dry Madeira wine
1 teaspoon cornstarch
1 cup light cream
1/2 cup heavy cream
1 cup grated natural Swiss cheese
2 tablespoons chopped parsley

1. Cook rice with 1/2 teaspoon salt and 3-1/3 cups water as package label directs.
2. Wipe chicken breasts with damp paper towels. Cut breasts in half; with sharp knife, carefully remove skin and bone, keeping chicken breast intact.
3. In hot butter, in large skillet, cook shallots several minutes. Add chicken breasts; brown well over medium heat, about 10 minutes on each side.
4. Add mushrooms, thyme, 1-1/2 teaspoons salt and pepper; cook about 3 minutes.
5. Preheat oven to 375F.
6. Turn rice into a lightly buttered, 2-quart shallow casserole. Arrange chicken breasts, overlapping slightly, down center of casserole. Arrange mushrooms around chicken.
7. In same skillet, pour wine into drippings; stir to dissolve browned bits in pan.
8. Meanwhile, dissolve cornstarch in 2 tablespoons light cream.
9. Add heavy cream, rest of light cream and cornstarch to wine mixture; bring just to boiling, stirring. Remove from heat; add cheese.
10. Spoon half of sauce over chicken; bake in oven 10 to 12 minutes; then run under broiler several minutes to brown slightly. Sprinkle with parsley. Reheat rest of sauce; serve along with casserole. Makes 8 servings.

Pâté-Stuffed Chicken Breasts

1 medium onion, sliced
1 celery stalk, sliced
1 carrot, sliced
1 parsley sprig
1 teaspoon salt
1/4 teaspoon dried thyme leaves
1 small bay leaf
1 can (10-3/4 oz) condensed chicken broth,
   undiluted
4 (12-oz size) whole chicken breasts, split
2 cans (4-3/4-oz size) liver pâté

Glaze:
1 envelope unflavored gelatine
1 cup heavy cream
Pitted black olives, cut into diamond shapes
Pimiento-stuffed olives, sliced

Watercress sprigs

1. In 6-quart kettle, combined sliced onion, sliced celery, sliced carrot, parsley sprig, salt, thyme leaves, bay leaf, undiluted chicken broth, 1-1/3 cups water, and the split chicken breasts; bring mixture to boiling.
2. Reduce heat, and simmer, covered, 30 minutes, or just until the chicken breasts are fork-tender.
3. Remove kettle from heat. Let the chicken breasts cool in the broth.
4. Remove the chicken breasts from the broth; reserve broth. Remove skin and bone from chicken breasts; trim edges evenly.
5. On underside of each chicken breast, spread about 1 tablespoon liver pâté, mounding it slightly. Refrigerate the chicken breasts, covered, for 1 hour.

6. Meanwhile, strain broth; skim off the fat. Reserve 2 cups of the broth.

7. Make glaze: In medium saucepan, bring reserved broth to boiling. Reduce heat; simmer broth, uncovered, 30 minutes, or until the liquid is reduced to 1 cup.

8. In 1/4 cup cold water in medium bowl, let the gelatine stand 5 minutes, to soften. Add hot broth, stirring to dissolve the gelatine.

9. Add the heavy cream, mixing until it is well combined with gelatine mixture.

10. Set bowl with gelatine mixture in ice water; let stand about 20 minutes, or until well chilled but not thickened. Stir occasionally. Remove from ice water.

11. Place chicken breasts, pâté side down, on a wire rack; set rack on a tray. Spoon glaze over chicken breasts.

12. Refrigerate, on the tray, for 30 minutes, or until the glaze is set.

13. Scrape glaze from the tray; reheat it, and set it, in the saucepan, in ice water again to chill. Spoon the glaze over the chicken breasts, coating them completely.

14. Press both kinds of olive into glaze, to decorate. Refrigerate until the glaze is set—about 1 hour.

15. To serve: Arrange chicken breasts, in a single layer, in a large, shallow serving dish. Garnish the stuffed chicken breasts with sprigs of watercress before serving.

Makes 8 servings.

Roast Cornish Hens with Walnut Stuffing and Wine Sauce

Stuffing:
3 tablespoons bacon drippings
1 cup chopped onion
1 cup chopped green pepper
6 cooked bacon slices, crumbled
3 cups small dry white-bread cubes
1 cup coarsely chopped walnuts
1-1/2 teaspoons salt
1/2 teaspoon dried thyme leaves
1/2 teaspoon rubbed sage

6 (1-lb size) frozen Rock Cornish hens, thawed
Basting Sauce, below
Wine Sauce, below
Watercress sprigs

1. Make Stuffing: In hot bacon drippings in a medium skillet, sauté chopped onion and green pepper, stirring, until tender.

2. Add vegetables to rest of stuffing ingredients; toss lightly with fork, to mix. Use mixture to stuff hens. Close openings in hens with wooden picks; tie legs together.

3. Arrange hens, breast side up, in a shallow roasting pan without a rack.

4. Preheat oven to 400F. Make Basting Sauce. Brush some over the hens.

5. Roast hens 1 hour, brushing occasionally with rest of sauce, until golden.

6. Discard string, wooden picks. Arrange hens on round platter; keep warm. Make Wine Sauce.
Garnish hens with watercress.
Makes 6 servings.

Basting Sauce

1/2 cup butter or margarine
1/2 cup white wine
1 clove garlic, crushed
1-1/2 teaspoons salt
1/2 teaspoon rubbed sage

1. Melt the 1/2 cup butter in a small skillet. Then remove the skillet from heat.
2. Add rest of ingredients to butter in skillet, mixing well.

Wine Sauce

3 tablespoons flour
1 cup white wine
1 cup currant jelly
1 teaspoon dry mustard
1 teaspoon salt

1. Pour off drippings in roasting pan; return 2/3 cup drippings to pan. Gradually add the 3 tablespoons flour to the drippings, and stir to make the mixture smooth.
2. Add white wine, currant jelly, dry mustard, and salt. Bring mixture to boiling, stirring to loosen any brown bits in the roasting pan.
3. Reduce heat, and simmer the sauce, stirring occasionally, until it thickens. Pass wine sauce along with hens. Makes about 2-1/3 cups sauce; 6 generous servings.

Roast Stuffed Goose

Sausage Stuffing:
1 lb sausage meat
2 cups finely chopped onion
1 pkg (8-oz) herb-seasoned stuffing mix
1 teaspoon salt
1/4 teaspoon pepper

10-lb ready-to-cook goose
1 tablespoon lemon juice
1 teaspoon salt
1/8 teaspoon pepper
White-Wine Sauce, below
Glazed Apples, below

1. Make Stuffing: In large skillet, cook sausage about 5 minutes, breaking up with fork into 1-inch chunks. As sausage is cooked, remove it to a large bowl. Pour fat from skillet, reserving 2 tablespoons.
2. In the 2 tablespoons hot fat, sauté onion until tender—5 minutes.
3. Add to sausage with stuffing, salt, and pepper, tossing lightly to mix well.
4. Preheat oven to 325F. Remove giblets and neck from goose; reserve for White-Wine Sauce. Wash goose inside and out; dry well with paper towels. Remove all fat from inside, and discard. Rub cavity with lemon juice, salt, and pepper.
5. Spoon stuffing lightly into neck cavity; bring skin of neck over back, and fasten with poultry pins. Spoon stuffing lightly into body cavity; close with poultry pins, and lace with twine. Bend wing tips under body; tie ends of legs together.
6. Prick skin only (not meat) over thighs, back, and breast very well. Place, breast side up, on rack in large roasting pan.

7. Roast, uncovered, 2 hours. Remove goose from oven.

8. Pour fat from pan, and discard. Roast goose, uncovered, 1 hour longer. Remove goose to platter; keep warm. Make White-Wine Sauce.

9. To serve, garnish with Glazed Apples, Pass White-Wine Sauce.

Makes 8 to 10 servings.

White-Wine Sauce

Goose giblets and neck
1 celery stalk, cut up
1 medium onion, peeled and quartered
1 medium carrot, pared and cut up
1 teaspoon salt
4 whole black peppercorns
1 bay leaf
Dry white wine
2 tablespoons flour

1. While goose is roasting, wash giblets and neck well. Refrigerate liver until ready to use. Place rest of giblets and neck in 2-quart saucepan; add 2-1/2 cups water, the celery, onion, carrot, salt, peppercorns, and bay leaf.

2. Bring to boiling. Reduce heat; simmer, covered, 2-1/2 hours, or until giblets are tender; add liver; simmer 15 minutes. Discard neck. Chop giblets coarsely; set aside.

3. Strain cooking broth, pressing vegetables through sieve with broth. Measure broth; add enough dry white wine to make 3 cups; set aside.

4. Remove goose to platter; pour drippings into 1-cup measure. Skim fat from surface, and discard. Return 2 tablespoons drippings to roasting pan.

5. Stir in flour until smooth. Over very low heat, stir to brown flour slightly. Remove from heat; gradually stir in broth.

6. Bring to boiling, stirring. Reduce heat; simmer, stirring, 5 minutes, or till thick and smooth. Add chopped giblets, salt to taste; simmer 5 minutes. Makes about 3 cups.

Glazed Apples

1/4 cup butter or margarine
1/4 cup lemon juice
1/2 cup sugar
1/4 teaspoon salt
2 large red apples

1. In large skillet, melt butter; stir in lemon juice, sugar, salt, and 1/2 cup water. Bring to boiling, stirring, until sugar is dissolved. Reduce heat; simmer, uncovered, 5 minutes.

2. Wash apples; cut crosswise into 1/2-inch-thick slices, leaving skin on; remove cores. Place in simmering syrup, turning to coat both sides.

3. Cook apple slices, uncovered, 1 to 2 minutes on each side, or just until tender. Remove from syrup. Use as garnish around goose.

Duckling à l'Orange

5-lb ready-to-cook duckling*
1 teaspoon salt
1 clove garlic, chopped
3 whole black peppercorns
2 unpeeled oranges, quartered
1/4 cup Burgundy
1/2 cup orange marmalade
Orange Sauce, below

* If using frozen duckling, let it thaw completely before stuffing it.

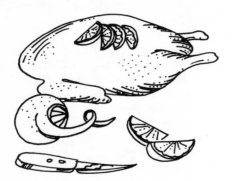

1. Preheat the oven to 425F.
2. Remove giblets and neck from duckling; set liver aside for Orange Sauce. Wash duckling well under running water; drain; dry.
3. Bring skin of neck over back; fasten with poultry pins. Sprinkle inside of duckling with salt. Then stuff body cavity with the garlic, black peppercorns, and orange quarters. Truss duckling: Close cavity with poultry pins; lace with twine. Tie ends of the legs together, and bend the wing tips under the body.
4. Place duckling, breast side up, on a rack in a shallow roasting pan. Pour the Burgundy over duckling.
5. Roast, uncovered, 30 minutes. Reduce oven temperature to 375F, and roast 1-1/2 hours, removing fat from the roasting pan with a baster every 1/2 hour.
6. Spread duckling with orange marmalade. Roast 10 minutes longer.
7. Remove poultry pins and twine from duckling. With long-handled fork or spoon, carefully remove orange quarters from cavity, and discard. Place duckling on heated platter. Cut into quarters, and serve with Orange Sauce.
Makes 4 servings.

Orange Sauce

3 large oranges
3 tablespoons butter or margarine
Liver from duckling, above
3 tablespoons brandy
3/4 teaspoon minced garlic
2 tablespoons flour
2 teaspoons catsup
1-1/2 teaspoons meat-extract paste*
1/8 teaspoon pepper
1 can (10-3/4 oz) condensed chicken broth, undiluted
1/3 cup Burgundy
1/4 cup orange marmalade

* Do not use liquid meat extract.

1. Grate peel from 1 orange, and reserve 2 tablespoons. Holding oranges over bowl to catch juice, peel with sharp knife; remove sections; set aside. Reserve 1/4 cup orange juice.
2. In 2 tablespoons hot butter in medium skillet, brown duckling liver well. Remove pan from heat.
3. Heat brandy slightly in small saucepan. Ignite; slowly pour over liver. When flames subside, remove liver; set aside.
4. Add remaining butter, reserved grated peel, and garlic to skillet; sauté 3 minutes. Remove from heat. Stir in flour, catsup, meat-extract paste, and pepper until well blended. Gradually stir in chicken broth, Burgundy, marmalade, and reserved orange juice.

5. Bring to boiling, stirring constantly. Reduce heat, and simmer, stirring occasionally, 15 minutes.
6. Meanwhile, chop liver. Add to sauce along with orange sections. Heat gently.
Makes 2 cups.

Roast Capon with Herbs

5-1/2- to 6-lb ready-to-cook capon
Salt
Pepper
1/2 cup butter or margarine, softened
1 tablespoon lemon juice
1 tablespoon chopped chives
1 tablespoon chopped parsley
1 clove garlic, crushed
1-1/2 teaspoons chopped fresh tarragon, or
   1/2 teaspoon dried tarragon leaves
3/4 teaspoon chopped fresh rosemary, or
   1/4 teaspoon dried rosemary leaves
3/4 teaspoon chopped fresh thyme, or
   1/4 teaspoon dried thyme leaves
1 onion, sliced
2 carrots, pared and sliced
1 stalk celery, sliced
1 can (10-3/4 oz) condensed chicken broth,
   undiluted
1/2 cup dry white wine
3 tablespoons flour
Fresh tarragon sprigs

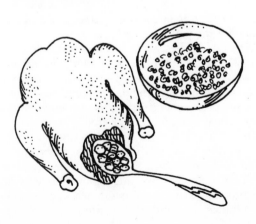

1. Preheat over to 400F.
2. Wash capon well, inside and out, under cold water. Pat dry, inside and out, with paper towels. Sprinkle inside with 1 teaspoon salt and 1/4 teaspoon pepper. Rinse giblets; set aside.
3. In small bowl, with electric mixer or wooden spoon, beat butter with lemon juice, chives, parsley, garlic, chopped tarragon, rosemary, thyme, 1/2 teaspoon salt, and 1/8 teaspoon pepper until well blended.
4. With fingers, carefully loosen skin from breast meat. Spread 2 tablespoons butter mixture over breast meat, under skin, on each side. Tie legs together; fold wing tips under back. Spread 1 tablespoon butter mixture over capon. Insert meat thermometer inside thigh at thickest part.
5. Place onion, carrot, celery, and giblets (except liver) in shallow roasting pan. Set capon on vegetables.
6. Roast, uncovered, 1 hour. Reduce oven temperature to 325F; roast 1-1/4 to 1-1/2 hours, basting occasionally with remaining butter mixture, until meat thermometer registers 185F and leg moves easily at joint.
7. Remove capon to heated platter. Remove string. Let stand 20 minutes.
8. Meanwhile, make gravy: Pour undiluted chicken broth into roasting pan; bring to boiling, stirring to dissolve brown bits. Strain into a 4-cup measure; skim off fat, and discard.
9. In small saucepan, stir wine into flour until flour is dissolved. Stir in chicken broth. Bring to boiling, stirring constantly, until mixture thickens; reduce heat; simmer 5 minutes. Add salt and pepper, if necessary.
10. Garnish capon with tarragon sprigs. Pass gravy.
Makes 6 servings.

Turkey

When it's time to think of Thanksgiving dinner and what you will serve—though you know perfectly well, and so do we—you'll be grateful for the section on turkeys that follows. Your planning will start with a plump, full-breasted turkey, done to a crisp-skinned gold. Our step-by-step instructions show you how.

No need to think of turkey for holidays only. Serve our Turkey au Vin or Turkey Flambé for special occasions year round.

Turkey au Vin

8-1/2 to 9-lb ready-to-cook turkey
6 tablespoons soft butter or margarine
6 slices bacon, cut in 1-inch pieces
1/2 cup chopped onion
1 clove garlic, crushed
2 tablespoons brandy
2-1/2 cups red Burgundy
1 can (10-3/4 oz) condensed chicken broth, undiluted
2 teaspoons salt
1/2 teaspoon dried thyme leaves
1/2 teaspoon pepper
2 bay leaves
4 large sprigs parsley
Tops from 2 celery stalks
16 small white onions, peeled
12 medium mushrooms
16 small new potatoes
1/3 cup flour
2 tablespoons chopped parsley

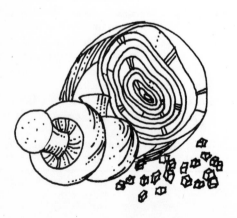

1. Remove giblets and neck from turkey; wash; set aside. Wash turkey inside and out. Pat dry with paper towels. Remove, discard excess fat.

2. Preheat oven to 400F.

3. Place heart and cut-up gizzard inside turkey; discard liver. Bring skin of neck over back; fasten with poultry pin. Bend wing tips under body, or fasten to body with poultry pins. Tie ends of legs together.

4. Place turkey, breast side up, in shallow roasting pan without rack. Brush 2 tablespoons butter over turkey.

5. Roast, uncovered, 40 minutes; brush well with pan drippings; roast 10 minutes longer, or until browned. Remove from oven.

6. Meanwhile, in 8-quart Dutch oven (about 10 inches wide, 13 inches long), sauté bacon until crisp. Remove bacon; reserve. Pour fat into a cup. Return 2 tablespoons fat to Dutch oven; add 2 tablespoons butter.

7. To butter mixture, add chopped onion and garlic; sauté until golden. Place turkey, breast side up, in Dutch oven. In large cooking spoon, warm brandy; ignite and pour over turkey.

8. When flame dies, turn turkey breast side down. Add 2 cups Burgundy, the cooking liquid with browned particles scraped from roasting pan, chicken broth, salt, thyme, pepper, bay leaves, parsley sprigs, and celery tops; bring to boiling. Reduce heat, and simmer, covered, 30 minutes.

9. In medium skillet, in 2 tablespoons hot butter, brown whole onions. Remove as browned; set aside. Add mushrooms to skillet, and sauté.

10. Turn turkey breast side up. Add onions and mushrooms to Dutch oven; simmer, covered, 45 to 50 minutes, or until turkey and vegetables are tender.

11. Meanwhile, scrub potatoes; pare a narrow band of skin around center of each. In 1-inch boiling salted water in medium skillet, cook potatoes,

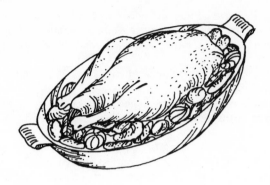

covered, 20 to 25 minutes, or until tender. Drain. Keep warm.

12. Remove turkey and vegetables to heated serving platter. Sprinkle bacon over vegetables. Keep warm.

13. Remove and discard celery, parsley, and bay leaves. Measure liquid in Dutch oven; it should measure 4 cups. (If more, reduce by boiling.)

14. Blend flour with remaining Burgundy. Stir into pan liquid; bring to boiling, stirring; boil until sauce thickens; simmer 5 minutes.

15. Spoon some sauce over turkey and vegetables; pass rest. Sprinkle chopped parsley over vegetables.

Makes 8 servings.

Note: If desired, make day ahead. Cool completely before storing, covered, in refrigerator. Reheat slowly, covered, in 350F oven 1 to 1-1/4 hours.

Turkey Ragout

Butter or margarine
1 large onion, sliced
2 medium zucchini, sliced (about 3 cups)
1/2 cup sliced celery
4 cups cooked turkey, in large chunks
  (about 1-1/2 inch)
1/2 lb small fresh mushrooms
  1 can (1 lb) whole carrots, drained
2/3 cup dry white wine
2/3 cup canned condensed chicken broth
1 can (10-1/2 oz) condensed cream-of-celery soup
1 can (10-1/2 oz) condensed cream-of-chicken soup
1/4 teaspoon dried thyme leaves
1/4 teaspoon dried marjoram leaves
Chopped parsley

1. Preheat oven to 350F.

2. In 4 tablespoons hot butter in large, heavy skillet, sauté onion, zucchini, and celery until almost tender and lightly browned—about 10 to 15 minutes. Combine with turkey in a 3-quart casserole.

3. In same skillet, brown mushrooms, adding more butter if needed. Add to turkey mixture in casserole. Add carrots.

4. Stir wine into drippings in skillet, then undiluted chicken broth, celery soup, chicken soup, thyme, and marjoram. Bring to boiling, stirring to loosen browned bits in pan. Pour wine mixture over turkey and vegetables in casserole, and mix lightly with a fork.

5. Bake, covered, 1 hour, or until bubbling in center. Sprinkle with chopped parsley.

Makes 6 servings.

Timetable for Roasting Turkey

Weight of unstuffed, ready-to-cook turkey (pounds)	Cooking time in uncovered pan, at 325F (hours)	Internal temperature (leg joint moves freely)
6 to 8	3 to 3-1/2	180 to 185F
8 to 12	3-1/2 to 4-1/2	180 to 185F
12 to 16	4-1/2 to 5-1/2	180 to 185F
16 to 20	5-1/2 to 6-1/2	180 to 185F
20 to 24	6-1/2 to 7	180 to 185F

Golden Roast Turkey

14- to 16-lb ready-to-cook turkey
Choice of Dressings, pages 454–6
1 cup butter or margarine, melted
Salt
Pepper
Giblet Gravy, page 504

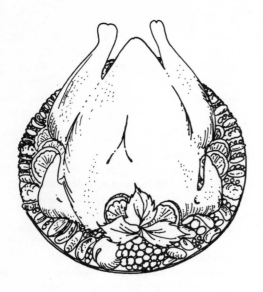

1. Remove giblets and neck from turkey; wash, and set aside. Wash turkey thoroughly inside and out. Pat dry with paper towels. Remove and discard any excess fat.

2. Prepare your choice of dressing. Preheat oven to 325F.

3. Spoon some of dressing into neck cavity of turkey. Bring skin of neck over back; fasten with poultry pin.

4. Spoon remaining dressing into body cavity; do not pack, Insert 4 or 5 poultry pins at regular intervals. Lace cavity closed, with twine, bootlace fashion; tie.

5. Bend wing tips under body, or fasten to body with poultry pins. Tie ends of legs together. Insert meat thermometer in inside of thigh at thickest part.

6. Place turkey on rack in shallow roasting pan. Brush with some of butter; sprinkle with salt and pepper.

7. Roast, uncovered and brushing occasionally with remaining butter and pan drippings, about 4-1/2 hours, or until meat thermometer registers 185F. Leg joint should move freely. When turkey begins to turn golden, cover with a square of butter-soaked cheesecloth or a loose tent of foil, to prevent too much browning.

8. While turkey roasts, cook giblets and neck as directed in Giblet Gravy.

9. Place turkey on heated serving platter. Remove cheesecloth or foil, twine, and poultry pins. Let stand 20 to 30 minutes before carving. Meanwhile, make gravy.

Makes 14 to 16 servings.

Turkey Breast Marsala

4 to 6 tablespoons butter or margarine
8 slices (1/4 inch thick) cooked turkey breast
** (about 1-1/4 lb)**
Dash pepper
8 thin slices prosciutto
1 pkg (8 oz) mozzarella cheese, cut in 8 slices
1/2 cup Marsala
Chopped parsley

1. Heat 4 tablespoons butter in large, attractive skillet. Sauté turkey slices, in single layer, until golden on both sides—1 minute on each side. Add more butter as needed. Remove turkey slices as browned, and keep warm.

2. Return all slices to skillet, overlapping. Sprinkle with pepper. Place a slice of ham and one of cheese on each slice of turkey. Pour Marsala over all.

3. Cook, covered, 3 to 5 minutes, or until heated through and cheese is melted. Sprinkle with

chopped parsley. Garnish with watercress, if desired. Serve in skillet.
Makes 4 servings.

Roast Turkey Flambé with Oyster-and-Pecan Dressing

12-to 14-lb ready-to-cook turkey, with giblets and neck
Sausage-Oyster-and-Pecan Dressing, page 456
1/4 cup soft butter or margarine
1-1/2 teaspoons seasoned salt
1 celery stalk, cut up
1 large onion, peeled and halved
1 bay leaf
4 whole black peppercorns
1/3 cup all-purpose flour
1/2 cup canned condensed chicken broth, undiluted
2 or 3 chicken-bouillon cubes
1/2 teaspoon liquid gravy seasoning
1/2 cup brandy (for flaming)

1. Remove giblets and neck from turkey; wash; set aside. Wash turkey inside and out; pat dry with paper towels. Remove and discard excess fat.
2. Make Sausage-Oyster-and-Pecan Dressing. Preheat oven to 350F.
3. Spoon some of dressing into neck cavity of turkey. Bring skin of neck over back; fasten with poultry pin.
4. Spoon rest of dressing into body cavity; do not pack. Insert 3 or 4 poultry pins at regular intervals; lace cavity closed with twine, bootlace fashion; tie. Bend wing tips under body. Tie ends of legs together. Brush skin all over with butter; sprinkle with salt.
5. Place turkey inside a brown-in-bag (17 by 22 inches), along with celery, onion, bay leaf, black peppercorns, neck, and giblets. Place turkey in bag on rack in large, shallow roasting pan.
6. Insert meat thermometer, right through bag, in inside of thigh at thickest part. Close bag with twist tie, placing tie near turkey. Cut off excess bag. With tip of paring knife or fork, puncture six holes in top of bag (see brown-in-bag package instructions).
7. Roast about 3 hours, or until meat thermometer registers 185F; leg joint should move freely.
8. Remove turkey from oven. Let stand 20 minutes in bag; then slit bag; remove turkey to a warm, large serving platter. Remove twine, poultry pins.
9. Make gravy: Remove giblets; chop coarsely. Discard neck. Strain broth left in pan and bag; pour into medium saucepan. Bring to boiling; boil, uncovered, to reduce broth to 2-1/2 cups—about 20 minutes.
10. In small bowl, combine flour with chicken broth, mixing until smooth. Stir flour mixture into broth mixture in saucepan, along with bouillon cubes. Bring to boiling, stirring until smooth. Add chopped giblets and gravy seasoning; simmer 5 minutes.
11. To serve: If desired, garnish with watercress and orange slices. Flame turkey at table just before serving: In saucepan, warm brandy. Ignite with match; pour, blazing, over turkey.
Makes 12 to 14 servings.

Stuffing

Exactly as important as the chicken or the turkey is the stuffing, and we have provided a great variety that will add a special elegance, appreciated by family and guests alike. Elsewhere in this book you will find suggestions for sauces, conserves, and relishes that go well with poultry.

Cornbread-Dressing Balls

1 pkg (10- or 12-oz) cornbread mix
1/2 cup butter or margarine, melted
1-1/2 cups chopped celery
1 cup chopped onion
1/4 cup chopped parsley
1/2 teaspoon rubbed sage
1/2 teaspoon dried thyme leaves
1 teaspoon salt
1/4 teaspoon pepper
1 egg
1/2 cup canned condensed chicken broth, undiluted

1. Make and bake cornbread as the label directs. Cool in pan, on wire rack, 25 minutes; then crumble into medium mixing bowl.
2. Preheat oven to 325F.
3. Heat 1/4 cup butter in medium skillet. Add celery, onion, and parsley; sauté, stirring, until celery and onion are tender—about 5 minutes.
4. Add to crumbled cornbread, along with seasonings, egg, and chicken broth; mix well.
5. With hands, lightly form mixture into balls, using about 1/2 cup for each. Arrange in greased shallow baking dish.
6. Brush with rest of butter; bake, covered, 30 minutes.
7. Remove cover; bake 15 minutes longer, or until browned on top.
Makes 10 servings.
Note: Dressing balls may be baked in the oven with the turkey.

Cranberry-Orange Dressing

1/2 cup butter or margarine
1/2 cup chopped onion
1/2 cup chopped celery
1 cup chopped walnuts or Brazil nuts
2 cups fresh cranberries, washed
1/2 cup sugar
1/2 cup orange juice
1 tablespoon grated orange peel
2 loaves (1-lb size) raisin bread
1-1/2 teaspoons salt
1/2 teaspoon poultry seasoning
1/2 teaspoon dried savory leaves
1/8 teaspoon pepper

1. Preheat oven to 350F.
2. In hot butter in medium skillet, sauté onion, celery, and Brazil nuts about 5 minutes.
3. Add cranberries, sugar, and orange juice and peel; cook over medium heat, stirring constantly, until cranberries start to pop. Remove from heat; let stand 20 minutes.
4. Cut bread slices into 1/2-inch cubes, to measure 10 cups. Spread the bread cubes on a cookie sheet. Place in oven 5 minutes, or until lightly toasted.
5. Turn cubes into large bowl. Add salt, poultry seasoning, savory, and pepper; toss to mix.
6. Add cranberry mixture; toss lightly until well mixed.
7. Use to fill prepared turkey.
Makes 12 cups, enough to stuff a 16-lb turkey.

Chicken-Liver-Mushroom Dressing

1/2 cup butter or margarine
2 pkg (8-oz size) herb-seasoned stuffing mix
1 lb chicken livers
1 cup chopped onion
2 cups chopped fresh mushrooms (1/2 lb)
1/4 cup chopped parsley
1 teaspoon dried marjoram leaves

1. In 6-quart Dutch oven or kettle, heat 1/2 cup water and 1/4 cup butter until butter is melted. Remove from heat.
2. Add stuffing mix; toss to mix well.
3. Wash chicken livers; pat dry with paper towels.
4. In remaining butter in large skillet, sauté livers 5 minutes, or until no longer pink. Remove from skillet, and chop coarsely. Then add to stuffing mixture.
5. In same skillet, sauté onion and mushrooms until onion is golden—5 to 7 minutes. Add parsley, marjoram.
6. Add to stuffing mixture; toss lightly until well mixed.
7. Use to fill prepared turkey.
Makes 12 cups, enough to stuff a 16-lb turkey.

Cornbread-Oyster Dressing

1-1/2 cups butter or margarine
2 pkg (8-oz size) cornbread-stuffing mix
1-1/2 pints fresh oysters; or 3 cans (7-oz-size)
　frozen oysters, thawed
1/2 cup chopped onion
1/2 cup chopped green pepper
1/2 cup chopped celery
1 teaspoon salt
1/2 teaspoon dried rosemary leaves
1/4 teaspoon pepper

1. In 6-quart Dutch oven or kettle, heat 1 cup water and 1 cup butter until butter is melted. Remove from heat.
2. Add stuffing mix; toss to mix well.
3. Drain oysters; cut in half.
4. In remaining butter in medium skillet, sauté oysters, onion, green pepper, and celery until onion is golden—5 to 7 minutes. Stir in salt, rosemary, and pepper.
5. Add to stuffing mixture; toss lightly until well mixed.
6. Use to fill prepared turkey.
Makes 12 cups, enough to stuff a 16-lb turkey.

Bread Stuffing

2 tablespoons butter or margarine
1/3 cup chopped onion
1 chicken liver, chopped
3 slices white bread, cubed
2 tablespoons chopped parsley
1/2 teaspoon dried thyme leaves
1/2 teaspoon salt
Dash pepper
1/4 cup milk

1. In 2 tablespoons hot butter in medium skillet, sauté onion until golden. Add liver, sauté 1 minute.
2. Remove from heat; stir in bread cubes, parsley, thyme, salt, and pepper. Add milk, tossing mixture with a fork.
3. Use to fill prepared chicken.
Makes enough to stuff a 4-lb roasting chicken.

Old-Fashioned Dressing

12 cups fresh white-bread cubes
1/2 cup chopped parsley
1 tablespoon poultry seasoning
2 teaspoons salt
1/2 teaspoon pepper
1/2 cup butter or margarine
3 cups chopped celery
1 cup chopped onion

1. In large bowl, combine bread cubes, parsley, poultry seasoning, salt, and pepper; toss to mix well.
2. In hot butter in medium skillet, sauté celery and onion until golden—7 to 10 minutes.
3. Add to bread mixture; toss lightly until well mixed.
4. Use to fill prepared turkey.
Makes 12 cups, enough to stuff a 16-lb turkey.

Sausage-Oyster-and-Pecan Dressing

1/2 lb pork-sausage meat
1/2 cup butter or margarine
1 cup chopped onion
1 cup chopped celery
2 tablespoons chopped parsley
1 teaspoon salt
1/4 teaspoon white pepper
1/2 tablespoon Worcestershire sauce
3 cups fresh oysters, drained; or 3 cans
   (8-oz size) oysters, drained; or 3 cans (7-oz size)
   frozen oysters, thawed, drained
1 cup coarsely chopped pecans
6 cups day-old bread cubes, crusts removed

1. In 6-quart Dutch oven or kettle, sauté sausage until golden—about 5 minutes. Remove sausage; add butter to sausage fat. In hot fat, sauté onion, celery, parsley until onion is golden—about 5 minutes. Remove from heat.
2. Add salt, pepper, Worcestershire, oysters, cooked sausage, pecans, and bread cubes to Dutch oven. Toss lightly to mix well.
3. Use to fill prepared turkey.
Makes 10 cups, enough to stuff a 12- to 14-lb turkey.

Rice, Grains & Pasta

Rice

One of the oldest foods known to man, rice goes back to the centuries before recorded history. Thrifty housewives have known for ages that rice is ideal as an extender of casseroles and main dishes. But even gourmet cooks would favor rice at any price because it adapts itself so gracefully to any main dish made with a sauce.

Rice is sold in a number of forms today. Following are those commonly found in the markets, which we use in our recipes:

Regular white rice has the outer coating of bran removed. It comes in long-, medium- or short-grain forms, polished or unpolished. It is usually enriched; that is, vitamins and minerals lost in processing are replaced. We often call for the long-grain form when rice is to be served with meat dishes because it's fluffier than the short-grain rice, which is best used in puddings. Regular white rice triples in size in cooking.

Converted or processed white rice is long-grain rice especially processed to retain vitamins and minerals. It is very dry and fluffy; for this reason it is most popular with gourmets. This type swells to four times its original size in cooking.

Packaged precooked white rice is processed so that it can be cooked very quickly. This type doubles in cooking.

Brown rice is the whole unpolished form of rice. It is highest in natural vitamins and minerals. It has a nutty flavor and is prized by natural-food lovers. This type triples its original size in cooking.

Wild rice is not a rice but the seed of a grass that grows wild. It is very expensive and prized for its nutty, unusual flavor.

In addition there are a variety of packaged, seasoned rices on the market.

Fluffy White Rice

1-1/2 cups raw long-grain white rice
1-1/2 teaspoons salt
1-1/2 tablespoons butter or margarine

1. In heavy, medium-sized saucepan with tight-fitting cover, combine 3 cups cold water with the rice, salt, and butter.
2. Bring to boiling, uncovered.
3. Reduce heat; simmer, covered, 15 to 20 minutes, or until rice is tender and water is absorbed.
4. Fluff up with fork.
Makes 4-1/2 cups.

Old-Fashioned Fluffy White Rice

1 tablespoon salt
1 cup raw long-grain white rice
2 tablespoons butter or margarine

1. In large saucepan over high heat, bring to boiling 2 quarts cold water and the salt.
2. Slowly add rice; boil, uncovered, about 20 minutes, or until rice is tender.
3. Drain well. Fluff up with fork; add butter.
Makes 4 cups.

Wild Rice

3/4 cup wild rice
3/4 teaspoon salt
1 tablespoon butter or margarine

1. Wash rice several times; drain.
2. In heavy, medium-sized saucepan with tight-fitting cover, bring 3 cups cold water and salt to boiling.

3. Add rice very slowly. Boil, covered, stirring occasionally, 45 minutes, until rice is tender and water absorbed. Add butter.
Makes about 2 cups.
Wild and White Rice: Combine 2 cups cooked wild rice and 4 cups cooked white rice; toss lightly with fork.

Oven-Steamed Rice

1-1/2 cups raw converted white rice
1-1/2 teaspoons salt
Dash pepper
2 tablespoons butter or margarine
3-1/2 cups boiling water

1. Preheat oven to 350F.
2. In 2-quart, ungreased casserole with tight-fitting lid, mix rice, salt, and pepper. Dot with butter.
3. Pour boiling water over rice; stir, with fork, to melt butter.
4. Bake, covered, 45 minutes (do not lift the lid). To serve, fluff up rice lightly, with a fork, to mix well.
Makes 6 servings.
White Rice with Onions: Add 1/4 cup sliced green onions to cooked rice just before serving.

Saffron Rice

1/4 teaspoon saffron, crumbled
2 tablespoons olive or salad oil
2 tablespoons butter or margarine
1-1/2 cups raw long-grain white rice
1-1/2 teaspoons salt

1. Mix saffron with 1 tablespoon hot water; set aside.
2. In medium saucepan, heat oil and butter. Add rice and salt; cook, stirring occasionally, 5 minutes.
3. Add saffron mixture and 3 cups water; bring to boiling. Reduce heat; simmer, covered, 15 to 20 minutes, or until liquid is absorbed.
Makes 8 servings.

Rice and Spinach Ring Mold

5 cups cooked white rice
3/4 cup finely chopped fresh spinach
3 tablespoons butter or margarine, melted

1. Preheat the oven to 350F. Butter a 4- or 5-cup ring mold.
2. In large bowl, combine rice, spinach, and melted butter; toss to combine. Pack lightly into mold, smoothing top.
3. Bake 10 minutes, or till heated.
4. To serve: Run small spatula around edge of mold; turn out on warm serving platter. Serve with fish or veal dishes with sauces.
Makes 6 to 8 servings.
Note: Rice Ring is nice for a party. You may also serve Spinach Rice from a casserole.

Rice Pilaf

1/2 cup butter or margarine
1 large onion, thinly sliced
1 cup sliced fresh mushrooms; or 1 can (6 oz)
   sliced mushrooms, drained
1/4 cup finely chopped green pepper
1 cup raw long-grain white rice
Dash dried thyme leaves
2 cups canned chicken broth or chicken bouillon

1. Preheat oven to 350F.
2. In 1/4 cup hot butter in skillet, cook onion over medium heat until golden.
3. Add mushrooms and green pepper; cook until tender. Remove vegetables, and set aside.
4. In same skillet, heat remaining butter. Add rice, and brown slightly, stirring, over low heat.
5. Then stir in vegetables and thyme.
6. Meanwhile, heat chicken broth to boiling point. Stir into rice-vegetable mixture; then turn into 1-quart casserole.
7. Cover, and bake 30 to 40 minutes, or until liquid is absorbed and rice is tender.
Makes 6 servings.

Mushroom Rice Pilaf

1/4 cup butter or margarine
1-1/2 cups raw converted white rice
2 chicken-bouillon cubes, crumbled
3/4 teaspoon salt
1/4 teaspoon pepper
1 cup chopped mushroom stems
3-1/2 cups boiling water
Chopped parsley

1. Preheat oven to 375F.
2. Melt butter in flameproof casserole. Add rice, and sauté, stirring, until lightly browned—about 10 minutes.
3. Add bouillon cubes, salt, pepper, mushroom, and boiling water; mix well.
4. Bake, tightly covered, 40 minutes, or until rice is tender and liquid is absorbed.
5. To serve: Fluff up pilaf with a fork, and turn out on serving platter. Sprinkle with the chopped parsley.
Makes 6 to 8 servings.

Grains and Cereals

Grains and cereals ranging from breakfast foods to dinner pasta are one of the most economical and nutritious kinds of food available.

Our recipes will be appreciated by natural-food advocates and gourmets alike. Here are some great dishes to make menus more varied and interesting.

Polenta

1 tablespoon salt
2 cups yellow cornmeal

1. In a 9- or 10-inch skillet, bring 4 cups water and the salt to a full, rolling boil.
2. Slowly add cornmeal, stirring constantly with wire whisk—mixture will get very thick. With spatula, smooth top.

3. Turn heat very low, and cook, uncovered and without stirring, until thick crust forms around edge and mixture is firm—about 20 minutes.

4. To serve: With spatula, loosen around edge and underneath. Invert on large round platter. Serve with hearty Italian veal and chicken dishes with sauces.

Makes 6 to 8 servings.

Gnocchi

3 cups milk
1 cup farina
4 tablespoons butter or margarine
2 eggs, beaten
1/2 cup grated Parmesan cheese
1/2 teaspoon salt
Dash nutmeg

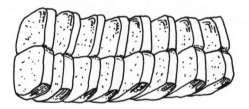

1. Lightly butter a 13-by-9-by-2-inch baking pan. Heat the milk slightly in a 3-1/2-quart heavy saucepan; do not boil.

2. Sprinkle in farina. Cook, over medium heat and stirring, until mixture is thick—about 5 minutes. Remove from heat.

3. Stir in half of butter, the eggs, 1/4 cup Parmesan, the salt, and nutmeg; beat until smooth. Spread evenly in prepared baking pan. Refrigerate until firm—about 3 hours.

4. To serve: Cut the chilled mixture into 24 pieces. Arrange pieces, overlapping, in shallow baking pan. Melt remaining butter, and sprinkle over top with remaining Parmesan.

5. Broil, 4 inches from heat, until hot and golden— about 5 minutes.

Makes 8 servings.

Barley Pilaf

1/2 cup butter or margarine
1/2 lb mushrooms, thinly sliced
1/2 cup coarsely chopped onion
1-1/3 cups pearl barley
6 chicken-bouillon cubes, dissolved in 5 cups
   boiling water; or 5 cups canned chicken broth

1. Preheat oven to 350F.

2. In 2 tablespoons hot butter in medium skillet, sauté mushrooms until tender—4 to 5 minutes. Lift out mushrooms with slotted spoon, and set aside.

3. Heat remaining butter in same skillet. Add onion; sauté until golden—about 5 minutes.

4. Add barley; cook over low heat, stirring frequently, until barley is golden-brown—about 5 minutes.

5. Remove from heat. Stir in mushrooms and 2 cups bouillon.

6. Turn into 2-quart casserole; bake, covered, 30 minutes.

7. Stir in 2 more cups bouillon; bake, covered, 30 minutes, or until barley is tender.

8. Finally, stir in remaining cup bouillon; bake 20 minutes. Serve with veal or chicken.

Makes 8 servings.

Hot Buttered Grits

1-1/3 cups grits
6-2/3 cups boiling water
1-1/2 teaspoons salt
3 tablespoons butter or margarine

1. Pour grits into boiling water in medium sauce-pan, stirring constantly. Add salt. Reduce heat; cook, stirring, till it thickens—2 or 3 minutes.
2. Cover, and cook, over low heat, stirring once or twice, 25 minutes.
3. Pour into serving dish; dot with butter.
Makes 8 servings.
Note: Or use quick-cooking or instant grits as the label directs.

Fried Cornmeal Mush

1-1/4 cups yellow cornmeal
1 teaspoon salt
3 tablespoons butter or regular margarine

1. Mix 1 cup cornmeal and the salt. Stir in 1 cup of cold water.
2. Bring 3 cups water to boiling in medium sauce-pan. Gradually stir in cornmeal mixture. Cook over low heat, stirring constantly, until thick; cook, covered and stirring occasionally, 10 minutes. Pour into 9-by-5-by-3-inch loaf pan; place waxed paper directly on surface.
3. Refrigerate until well chilled—at least 4 hours.
4. Remove cornmeal mush from pan; cut into 16 slices. Dip in remaining cornmeal, coating each side.
5. Fry in butter until golden-brown and crisp—about 4 minutes per side.
Makes 8 servings.

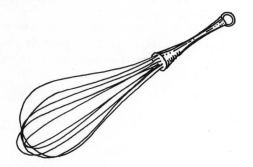

Pasta

Macaroni, Spaghetti and Noodles

Whether it comes in the form of bows, shells, alphabets, numbers, spirals, stars, fluted ribbons, ridged tubes, or toy hats, pasta is a general term for macaroni products (macaroni, spaghetti and noodles). These are made of hard wheat flour and water. (Exception: Noodles, which have eggs, and occasionally spinach, added to the dough.)

Basic Directions for Cooking Macaroni, Spaghetti, Noodles

1 tablespoon salt
3 quarts boiling water
1 pkg (7 or 8 oz) macaroni, spaghetti, or noodles (3 cups)

1. In large kettle, bring salted water to a rapid boil. Add macaroni, breaking long pieces into short ones. You may leave long spaghetti whole; place one end in boiling water, and gradually coil in rest as it softens.

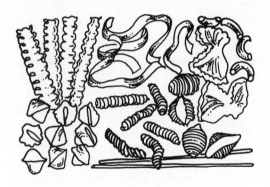

2. Bring back to boiling. Cook, uncovered, stirring occasionally with long fork to prevent sticking, just until tender—about 7 to 10 minutes. Do not overcook.

3. Drain in colander or sieve. Do not rinse.

Makes 4 to 6 servings.

Poppy-Seed Noodles: Cook 8-oz pkg noodles as directed above. Toss drained, hot noodles with 1/4 cup melted butter and 1 tablespoon poppy seed.

Caraway Noodles: Cook 8-oz pkg noodles as directed above. Toss drained, hot noodles with 1/4 cup melted butter and 1 tablespoon caraway seed.

Parmesan Noodles

1 pkg (8 oz) medium egg noodles
1/4 cup butter or margarine
1 cup grated Parmesan cheese
1/4 teaspoon salt
Dash pepper
1/2 cup light cream
Finely chopped parsley

1. Cook noodles in boiling salted water as package label directs.

2. Meanwhile, melt butter in medium saucepan. Add cheese, 1/4 teaspoon salt, the pepper, and cream. Cook over low heat, stirring constantly, until blended and fairly smooth.

3. Drain noodles well. Immediately add to cheese mixture, and toss until noodles are well coated.

4. Turn into heated serving dish. Sprinkle with parsley and a little more grated cheese, if you wish.

Makes 6 servings.

Baked Noodles Romanoff

1 pkg (8 oz) noodles
1 cup cottage cheese
1-1/2 cups dairy sour cream
1 teaspoon Worcestershire sauce
1 teaspoon salt
1/8 teaspoon pepper

1. Preheat oven to 350F.

2. Cook noodles as package label directs; drain.

3. In large bowl, blend cottage cheese, sour cream, and seasonings. Toss gently with noodles.

4. Turn into 2-quart casserole; cover.

5. Bake 15 to 20 minutes, or until thoroughly hot.

Makes 4 to 6 servings.

Buttered Linguine Parmesan

1 pkg (1 lb) linguine
3/4 cup butter or margarine
2 tablespoons finely chopped onion
1 small clove garlic, crushed
2 tablespoons chopped parsley
1/2 cup grated Parmesan cheese

1. Cook linguine as package label directs.

2. Meanwhile, melt butter in small saucepan. Add onion and garlic; simmer 5 minutes. Keep warm.

3. Drain linguine, and place on serving platter. Pour sauce over all; sprinkle with parsley; toss gently. Sprinkle with Parmesan, and serve immediately.

Makes 10 servings.

Our Favorite Lasagna

1 lb sweet or hot Italian sausage (5 links)
1/2 lb ground beef
1/2 cup finely chopped onion
2 cloves garlic, crushed
2 tablespoons sugar
1 tablespoon salt
1-1/2 teaspoons dried basil leaves
1/2 teaspoon fennel seed
1/4 teaspoon pepper
1/4 cup chopped parsley
4 cups canned tomatoes, undrained; or 1 can
   (2 lb, 3 oz) Italian-style tomatoes
2 cans (6-oz size) tomato paste
1 tablespoon salt
12 curly lasagna noodles (3/4 of 1-lb pkg)
1 container (15 oz) ricotta or cottage cheese,
   drained
1 egg
1/2 teaspoon salt
3/4 lb mozzarella cheese, thinly sliced
1 jar (3 oz) grated Parmesan cheese (3/4 cup)

1. Remove sausage meat from outer casings; chop the meat. In 5-quart Dutch oven, over medium heat, sauté sausage, beef (break up beef with wooden spoon), onion, and garlic, stirring frequently, until well browned—20 minutes.
2. Add sugar, 1 tablespoon salt, the basil, fennel, pepper, and half the parsley; mix well. Add tomatoes, tomato paste, and 1/2 cup water, mashing tomatoes with wooden spoon. Bring to boiling; reduce heat; simmer, covered and stirring occasionally, until thick—1-1/2 hours.
3. In 8-quart kettle, bring 3 quarts water and 1 tablespoon salt to boiling. Add lasagna, 2 or 3 at a time. Return to boiling; boil, uncovered and stirring occasionally, 10 minutes, or just until tender. Drain in colander; rinse under cold water. Dry lasagna on paper towels.
4. Preheat oven to 375F. In medium bowl, combine ricotta, egg, remaining parsley, and salt; mix.
5. In bottom of 13-by-9-by-2-inch baking dish, spoon 1-1/2 cups sauce. Layer with 6 lasagna, lengthwise and overlapping, to cover. Spread with half of ricotta mixture; top with third of mozzarella. Spoon 1-1/2 cups sauce over cheese; sprinkle with 1/4 cup Parmesan. Repeat layering, starting with 6 lasagna and ending with 1-1/2 cups sauce sprinkled with Parmesan. Spread with remaining sauce; top with rest of mozzarella and Parmesan. Cover with foil, tucking around edge.
6. Bake 25 minutes; remove foil; bake, uncovered, 25 minutes longer, or until bubbly. Cool 15 minutes before serving.

Makes 8 servings.

Noodles Alfredo

Homemade Noodles:
3 cups unsifted all-purpose flour
Salt
3 eggs
3 tablespoons lukewarm water

Alfredo Sauce:
1/2 cup butter or margarine
2/3 cup heavy cream
1-1/4 cups grated Parmesan cheese
1/4 teaspoon salt
Dash pepper
Chopped parsley

1. Make Homemade Noodles: In medium bowl, combine flour and 1/2 teaspoon salt. Make well in center. Add eggs and water; beat with fork until ingredients are combined. Dough will be stiff.
2. Turn out on lightly floured surface, and knead until smooth and elastic—about 15 minutes. Cover with bowl; let rest 10 minutes. Then divide dough into 4 parts. Keep covered until ready to roll out.
3. Roll out each part to paper thinness, a 12-inch square. Sprinkle lightly with flour. Then roll loosely around rolling pin, as for jelly roll. Slip out rolling pin. With sharp knife, cut into 1/8-inch-wide strips for fine noodles, 1/3-inch-wide strips for broad noodles. Arrange the dough strips on an ungreased cookie sheet.

4. In large kettle, bring 4 quarts water with 1 tablespoon salt to boiling. Add noodles; return to boiling. Boil, uncovered, stirring occasionally, until tender—about 20 minutes. Drain; keep warm.

5. Make Alfredo Sauce: Heat butter and cream in saucepan until butter is melted. Remove from heat. Add 1 cup Parmesan cheese, salt, pepper. Stir until sauce is blended and fairly smooth.

6. Add to drained noodles, and toss until they are well coated. Sprinkle with remaining Parmesan cheese and the chopped parsley. Serve at once.
Makes 6 servings.

Baked Macaroni and Cheese

1 pkg (8 oz) elbow macaroni
1/4 cup butter or margarine
1/4 cup all-purpose flour
1 teaspoon salt
1/8 teaspoon pepper
2 cups milk
8 oz Cheddar cheese, grated (2 cups)

1. Preheat oven to 375F. Cook macaroni as the package label directs; drain.

2. Meanwhile, melt butter in a medium saucepan; remove from heat. Stir in the flour, salt, and pepper until smooth. Gradually stir in milk. Bring to boiling, stirring. Reduce heat, and simmer mixture 1 minute. Remove from heat.

3. Stir in 1-1/2 cups cheese and the macaroni. Pour into a 1-1/2-quart casserole, and sprinkle remaining cheese over top.

4. Bake 15 to 20 minutes, or until cheese is golden-brown.
Makes 4 to 6 servings.

Spaghetti Sauces

If desired, prepare spaghetti sauces a day ahead, and refrigerate, covered. Before serving, let warm to room temperature, and mix well, then reheat slowly.

Spaghetti with Marinara Sauce

1/3 cup olive or salad oil
2 or 3 cloves garlic, crushed
1/3 cup chopped parsley
1 can (1 lb, 12 oz) Italian tomatoes, undrained
1 teaspoon dried oregano leaves
1/2 teaspoon salt
Dash pepper
1 pkg (8 oz) cooked spaghetti

1. In hot oil in large skillet, sauté garlic and parsley about 3 minutes. Add the undrained tomatoes, oregano, salt, and pepper; mix well, mashing the tomatoes with a fork.

2. Bring the mixture to boiling. Then reduce heat, and simmer, uncovered and stirring occasionally, for 30 minutes, or until the sauce is thickened.

3. Serve hot over spaghetti.
Makes 2-1/2 cups.

Spaghetti with Pesto Sauce

1/4 cup butter or margarine, softened
1/4 cup grated Parmesan cheese
1/2 cup finely chopped parsley
1 clove garlic, crushed
1 teaspoon dried basil leaves
1/2 teaspoon dried marjoram leaves
1/4 cup olive or salad oil
1/4 cup finely chopped walnuts or pine nuts
1 pkg (8 oz) cooked spaghetti or noodles

1. With wooden spoon, cream butter, Parmesan, parsley, garlic, basil, and marjoram until well blended.
2. Gradually add oil, beating constantly. Add walnuts; mix well.
3. Add to spaghetti in heated serving dish, and toss until well coated.
Makes about 4 servings.

Spaghetti with White Clam Sauce

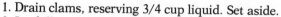

2 cans (7-1/2-oz size) minced clams
1/4 cup olive or salad oil
1/4 cup butter or margarine
2 or 3 cloves garlic, crushed
2 tablespoons chopped parsley
1-1/2 teaspoons salt
1 pkg (8 oz) cooked spaghetti
Grated Parmesan cheese

1. Drain clams, reserving 3/4 cup liquid. Set aside.
2. In skillet, slowly heat oil and butter. Add garlic, and sauté until golden. Remove from heat.
3. Stir in clam liquid, parsley, salt; bring to boiling. Reduce heat; simmer, uncovered, 10 minutes.
4. Add clams; simmer 3 minutes.
5. Serve hot over spaghetti, with Parmesan cheese. Makes 4 to 6 servings.

Salads & Salad Dressings

A salad is much more than a chunk of head lettuce with a spoonful of dressing poured over it. Today, the markets are full of the most tempting greens, from the palest, almost white Belgian endive to crisp, tangy dark-green watercress. A salad can open a meal or close it. It can give a fresh, clean taste to complement a hearty dinner. It can serve as the main course of a summer luncheon or supper. And it can also serve as a dessert.

Green Salads
Know Your Salad Greens

Curly Endive, or Chicory, has a maze of narrow, thin, twisted leaves, shading from dark green at the edges to a pale-yellow heart. It is often used with grapefruit and orange sections or tomatoes. It has an almost bitter tang.

Belgian Endive can be sliced lengthwise or crosswise into a salad. Although it is a member of the chicory and escarole family, it is a straight, pale, slender leaf, six inches or more in length. Endive can be eaten alone or served with greens. Some people enjoy eating it as they do celery.

Escarole. This green tastes a little like Belgian endive, though not as bitter. It is often called the broad-leaf endive. It resembles chicory, but its leaves are broader and not as curly. They are dark green, edging into yellow.

Bibb Lettuce, or Limestone Lettuce, is smaller and more delicate than Boston lettuce, but has something of the same shape and delicious flavor. Use the whole leaf in a salad. This lettuce gets its name from Jack Bibb, of Frankfort, Kentucky, who introduced it to his friends shortly after the Civil War. Still fairly expensive, it is growing less so, now that it has begun to reach the markets in greater quantity.

Boston Lettuce, also known as "butterhead" and "big Boston," has velvety, spreading leaves, which can be easily separated. This tender lettuce will do much for a salad. It is available throughout most of the year. However, its distribution is rather limited.

Head Lettuce, or Iceberg Lettuce, or Simpson Lettuce is the most familiar of lettuces. It is the firm, tight, compact head of light-green leaves. Separated, the leaves make a lettuce cup as a container for potato salad, fruit salad, and so on. Cut in wedges, it is a favorite of men, particularly those who like to pour blue-cheese dressing over it.

Leaf Lettuce is a favorite with the home gardener. It is crisp and has a curly edge. It is a lovely green and has a good flavor, and it grows in large, leafy bunches.

Oak-Leaf Lettuce. So-called because of the deeply notched leaves, which look so much like true oak leaves. Its flavor is delicate. Bronze Beauty is another variety of this plant, with reddish-tinted leaves instead of green.

Romaine Lettuce is more strongly flavored than several other varieties of lettuce. It can be recognized by its long head and spoonshape leaves, coarser and crisper than head lettuce. Good served with tomatoes and avocados.

Spinach is not a lettuce; but the tender young leaves of spinach give an interesting taste and color to a tossed green salad.

Watercress. This dark-green, leafy plant, with the unexpected bite in its taste, grows along the edges of brooks and springs. It gives an interesting color and taste contrast to a tossed green salad, adds a bright-green note as a garnish, and looks particularly attractive with the contrast of red tomatoes sliced over it.

Mixing Salad Greens

Greens should be clean, cold, crisp and dry. Tear into bite-size pieces. Turn into bowl large enough for tossing. Keep refrigerated if not using at once. Just before serving, add dressing in small amounts, toss gently, adding more dressing as needed. Better to use too little than too much and add more dressing if necessary.

Care of Salad Greens

Prepare greens as soon as they are brought home.
1. Discard any wilted or discolored leaves.
2. Wash under cold running water. To separate iceberg lettuce into leaves, cut out core with pointed knife. Hold cut part under running water to separate leaves. Drain as well as possible on paper towels.

3. Store in plastic bags in crisper or store in plastic container with tight-fitting lid.
4. Wash and drain parsley and watercress as above. Stand upright in shallow plastic container in very small amount of water. Refrigerate, tightly covered.

Caesar Salad

1 large head romaine
1 clove garlic
1/2 cup salad oil
1 cup French-bread cubes (1/2-inch), crusts removed
3/4 teaspoon salt
1/4 teaspoon dry mustard
1/4 teaspoon freshly ground black pepper
1-1/2 teaspoons Worcestershire sauce
6 anchovy fillets, drained and chopped
1/4 cup crumbled blue cheese
2 tablespoons grated Parmesan cheese
1 egg
Juice of 1/2 lemon (2 tablespoons)

1. Trim core from romaine. Separate head into leaves, discarding any that are wilted or discolored. Place in wire salad basket; rinse under cold running water; then shake well to remove excess moisture. (If you do not have a salad basket, wash greens under running water; drain; dry on paper towels.)
2. Now wrap in plastic film, and store in vegetable crisper in refrigerator until crisp and cold—several hours or overnight. Or put cleaned, drained greens in a plastic bag, and store on bottom shelf of refrigerator.
3. Several hours before serving, halve garlic. Set one half aside. Crush remaining half, and combine with salad oil in a jar with a tight-fitting lid. Refrigerate oil mixture at least 1 hour.
4. Heat 2 tablespoons oil-garlic mixture in medium skillet. Add bread cubes; sauté until brown all over. Set aside.
5. To remaining oil-garlic mixture in jar, add salt, mustard, pepper, Worcestershire, and anchovies. Shake vigorously. Refrigerate until needed.
6. Bring 2-inch depth of water to boiling in a small saucepan. Turn off heat. Carefully lower egg into water; let stand 1 minute; then lift out. Drain, and set aside to cool.
7. Just before serving, rub inside of large wooden salad bowl with reserved 1/2 clove garlic; discard the garlic.
8. Cut out coarse ribs from large leaves of romaine. Tear in bite-size pieces into salad bowl.
9. Shake dressing well, and pour over romaine. Sprinkle with cheeses. Toss until all romaine is coated with dressing.
10. Break egg over center of salad. Pour lemon juice directly over egg; toss well.
11. Sprinkle bread cubes over the salad, and quickly toss it again. Serve salad at once.
Makes 4 to 6 servings.

Fresh-Spinach Salad

White-Wine French Dressing:
2 tablespoons white-wine vinegar
2 tablespoons lemon juice
1/2 cup salad oil
1 teaspoon salt
1/4 teaspoon pepper
1 teaspoon sugar
1/2 teaspoon dry mustard
1 clove garlic (optional)

Salad:
3/4 lb tender young spinach
6 green onions, thinly sliced (1/4 cup)
1/2 cup sliced radishes
1 small cucumber, pared and thinly sliced

1. Make White-Wine French Dressing: Combine all dressing ingredients in jar with tight-fitting lid; shake vigorously. Refrigerate until ready to use.
2. Make Salad: Wash spinach, and remove stems. Tear leaves in bite-size pieces into salad bowl.
3. Arrange the other vegetables in groups on spinach. Refrigerate, covered, about 2 hours.
4. To serve: Remove garlic from dressing, and shake vigorously. Pour dressing over salad; toss until spinach is well coated. Serve at once.
Makes 4 to 6 servings.

French Green Salad

1 small head Boston lettuce
1 small head Bibb lettuce
1/2 small head romaine
1 Belgian endive
1/2 clove garlic
6 tablespoons olive oil
3 tablespoons tarragon vinegar
1 teaspoon salt
Freshly ground black pepper

1. Prepare salad greens: Wash lettuce, romaine, and endive, and separate into leaves, discarding discolored or bruised leaves. Drain well, shaking in salad basket or placing on paper towels, to remove excess moisture.
2. Place cleaned greens in plastic bag, or wrap in plastic film. Refrigerate until crisp and cold—several hours. Also refrigerate salad bowl.
3. At serving time, rub inside of salad bowl with garlic; discard garlic. Tear greens in bite-size pieces into bowl; leave small leaves whole.
4. In jar with tight-fitting lid, combine oil, vinegar, salt, and dash pepper; shake until well combined.
5. Pour half of dressing over greens. With salad spoon and fork, toss greens until they are well coated and no dressing remains in bottom of bowl. Add more dressing, if desired.
Makes 6 to 8 servings.

Old-Fashioned Lettuce Salad Bowl

2 quarts Boston or leaf lettuce, in bite-size pieces
1/2 cup sliced green onion
1/2 cup light cream
1/4 cup lemon juice
4 teaspoons sugar
1/2 teaspoon salt
Dash white pepper

1. Place lettuce and green onion in salad bowl.
2. In small bowl, combine cream, lemon juice, sugar, salt, and pepper; mix well. Pour over lettuce, and toss well. Serve immediately.
Makes 6 to 8 servings.

Garden Salad Bowl

1 medium head Boston lettuce
1/2 lb young spinach
1/2 small head chicory
1 small cucumber
4 radishes
1/2 bottle (8-oz size) Italian-style or 1/2 cup
Oil and Vinegar Dressing, page 492
1 tablespoon lemon juice

1. Wash greens thoroughly; drain well. Core lettuce; break leaves in bite-size pieces into large salad bowl. Remove stems from spinach, and discard; break leaves into salad bowl. Break chicory to measure 2 cups, and add.
2. Thinly slice cucumber and radishes; add to greens. Cover bowl; refrigerate until serving time.
3. In jar with tight-fitting lid, combine dressing and lemon juice. Refrigerate.
4. Just before serving, shake dressing well; pour over salad. Toss until greens are well coated.
Makes 8 servings.

Main-Dish Salads
Chef's Salad

Creamy Dressing:
1 bottle (8 oz) herb-garlic salad dressing
1/4 cup mayonnaise or cooked salad dressing
1/4 teaspoon sugar

Salad:
1-1/2 quarts bite-size pieces crisp salad greens
2 tablespoons snipped chives
2 cups slivered cooked ham (1/2 lb)
1-1/2 cups slivered cooked chicken (1/2 lb)
1/2 lb natural Swiss cheese, slivered
2 medium tomatoes, cut in wedges

1. Make Creamy Dressing: In small bowl, combine all dressing ingredients; with wire whisk or rotary beater, beat well. Refrigerate, covered, until ready to use.
2. Just before serving, make Salad: Place greens and chives in salad bowl. Add ham, chicken, and cheese.
3. Stir dressing well; pour over salad. Toss to coat meat and greens.
4. Garnish with tomato wedges.
Makes 6 servings.

Cobb Salad with Russian Dressing

2 cup crisp iceberg lettuce in bite-size pieces
2 cups crisp romaine in bite-size pieces
2 cups crisp chicory in bite-size pieces
2 medium tomatoes, cut in eighths
2 medium avocados, peeled and sliced
3 cups slivered cooked chicken, chilled
6 crisp-cooked slices bacon, cut in 1/2-inch pieces
1 hard-cooked egg
2 tablespoons snipped chives
Watercress
Russian Dressing, page 490

1. Just before serving, assemble salad: Place lettuce, romaine, and chicory in salad bowl. Arrange tomato and avocado around edge of bowl. Mound chicken in center, and sprinkle with bacon. Chop egg white and egg yolk separately; sprinkle decoratively, along with chives, over top of salad. Garnish with watercress.
2. To serve: At the table, pour half the dressing over salad; toss well. Pass rest of dressing.
Makes 8 to 10 servings.

Chicken Salad

5- to 5-1/2-lb ready-to-cook roasting chicken
2 large carrots, pared and cut into 1-inch pieces
2 stalks celery, cut into 1-inch pieces
1 large onion, sliced
6 whole black peppercorns
2 teaspoons salt
1 bay leaf
1 cup mayonnaise or cooked salad dressing
2 tablespoons lemon juice
2 tablespoons milk or light cream
1-1/2 teaspoons salt
Dash pepper
3 or 4 crisp large celery stalks
Crisp lettuce
Watercress
Tomato wedges

1. Remove giblets and neck from chicken. Then rinse chicken well under cold water. Place, breast side down, in an 8-quart kettle.
2. Add carrot, cut-up celery, onion, whole peppercorns, 2 teaspoons salt, the bay leaf, and 1 quart water.
3. Bring to boiling over high heat. Reduce heat, and simmer, covered, about 2 hours, or until chicken is tender. (After 1 hour, carefully turn chicken with wooden spoons.) Remove kettle from heat.
4. Let stand, uncovered, and frequently spoon broth in kettle over chicken, 1 hour, or until cool enough to handle. Lift out chicken. Strain broth, and refrigerate, covered, to use as desired.
5. Cut legs, thighs, and wings from chicken. Remove skin. Then remove meat from bones in as large pieces as possible. Set aside.
6. Pull skin from remaining chicken. With sharp knife, cut between the breastbone and meat, removing breast meat in large piece. Then check carefully, and remove any additional meat. Refrigerate, covered, to chill—about 1-1/2 hours.
7. Make salad: In large bowl, combine mayonnaise, lemon juice, milk, salt, pepper; stir until blended.
8. Cut celery, on the diagonal, into thin slices, to measure 2 cups. Add to dressing in bowl.
9. Cut large pieces of chicken meat into 1-inch pieces; there should be almost 5 cups. Add all meat to dressing. Toss lightly, to coat well.
10. Refrigerate, covered, until serving time—at least 1 hour.
11. To serve: Spoon salad into attractive bowl; garnish with lettuce, watercress, and tomato wedges.
Makes 6 to 8 servings.

Chicken Pineapple Salad

Chicken Salad, above
1 cup coarsely diced pared cucumber
1 can (13-1/2 oz) frozen pineapple chunks, thawed and drained
1/4 cup toasted slivered almonds (optional)

Prepare Chicken Salad, reducing sliced celery to 1 cup. Add diced cucumber with celery. Just before serving, add pineapple chunks. Garnish bowl with lettuce and watercress. Sprinkle with almonds.
Makes 8 servings.

Chicken Waldorf Salad

Chicken Salad, above
2 cups coarsely diced red apple
3/4 cup broken walnut meats

Prepare Chicken Salad, reducing sliced celery to 1 cup. Add apple to dressing as soon as it is cut, to prevent darkening. Add walnuts, celery; toss lightly. Garnish with lettuce leaves and watercress. Makes 8 servings.

Green-Goddess Salad

Green-Goddess Dressing:
1 cup mayonnaise or cooked salad dressing
1/4 cup tarragon vinegar
6 anchovy fillets, chopped
1/4 cup finely chopped parsley
2 tablespoons finely chopped green onion
2 tablespoons snipped chives
1/2 teaspoon dry mustard
1/4 teaspoon salt
1/8 teaspoon pepper

Salad:
2 quarts bite-size pieces crisp salad greens
3 cups cubed cooked chicken, chilled

2 medium tomatoes, sliced

1. Make Green-Goddess Dressing: In small bowl, conbine all dressing ingredients; mix well. Refrigerate, covered, several hours or overnight, to let flavors blend. (Or use bottled green-goddess dressing.)
2. Just before serving, make Salad: Place greens in salad bowl.
3. Place chicken in center of greens. Add dressing; toss to coat chicken and greens well.
4. Garnish with tomato slices.
Makes 8 servings.

Salade Niçoise

Dressing:
1/2 cup olive oil
1/4 cup salad oil
1/4 cup red-wine vinegar
1 teaspoon sugar
3/4 teaspoon salt
1/4 teaspoon cracked pepper

Salad:
1 lb fresh green beans, trimmed and washed; or
   2 pkg (9-oz size) frozen whole green beans
1 medium red onion, thinly sliced
2 medium tomatoes, cut in wedges
1/2 cup pitted ripe olives
1 can (2 oz) anchovy fillets
2 cans (7-oz size) solid-pack tuna, drained and
   broken into chunks
2 hard-cooked eggs, sliced

1. Make Dressing: In jar with tight-fitting lid, combine oil, vinegar, sugar, salt, and pepper; shake vigorously until well combined.
2. Cook whole fresh beans in small amount of boiling salted water, covered, 17 to 20 minutes, or until tender. Cook frozen beans, as package label directs, 5 minutes, or just until tender. Drain well; turn into shallow dish. Add 1/2 cup dressing; toss until beans are well coated.
3. Refrigerate beans, covered. Also refrigerate remaining dressing and the salad ingredients until well chilled—at least 2 hours.
4. To serve: Turn green beans into salad bowl. Add all but a few onion slices, tomato wedges, olives, and anchovy fillets; toss gently. Then add tuna chunks, egg slices; toss again.
5. Garnish with reserved onion, tomato, olives, and anchovy. Drizzle remaining dressing over all.
Makes 6 servings.

Curried-Chicken Salad

3 whole chicken breasts, split (about 3 lb in all)
2 carrots, pared and cut up
2 stalks celery, cut up
1 small onion, peeled and sliced
6 whole black peppercorns
Salt
1 bay leaf
3 cups boiling water
1/2 cup thinly sliced celery, cut on the diagonal
1-1/2 cups diced, unpared, tart apple
1/2 cup coarsely chopped green pepper
2 teaspoons grated onion
3/4 cup mayonnaise or cooked salad dressing
3 tablespoons light cream
1/2 to 1 teaspoon curry powder
1/2 teaspoon white pepper
Watercress sprigs

1. In a 4-quart kettle, combine chicken breasts, carrot, cut-up celery, sliced onion, black peppercorns, 1-1/2 teaspoons salt, the bay leaf, and the 3 cups boiling water.
2. Bring to boiling; reduce heat, and simmer, covered, for about 30 minutes, or until the chicken is tender.
3. Remove chicken from broth; cool; refrigerate until well chilled. (Refrigerate broth, for use another time.)
4. Remove and discard skin from chicken; cut meat from bones in large pieces.
5. In large bowl, combine chicken, sliced celery, apple, green pepper, and grated onion.
6. In small bowl, combine mayonnaise, cream, curry powder, 3/4 teaspoon salt, and the white pepper; mix well.
7. Add to chicken mixture; toss lightly to combine. Refrigerate until serving time—at least 1 hour.
8. Spoon chicken salad onto large platter. Garnish with watercress.
Makes 6 to 8 servings.

Shrimp and Roasted Peppers

Salad:
2 tablespoons salt
1 lb large raw shrimp (18 to 20)
2 sweet red peppers
2 sweet green peppers
2 medium tomatoes
1 head Boston lettuce

Dressing:
1 tablespoon prepared brown mustard
3 tablespoons lemon juice
1/8 teaspoon pepper
5 tablespoons olive or salad oil

8 large pitted ripe olives, quartered

1. In large saucepan, bring 2 cups water to boiling; add salt. Add shrimp; boil 5 minutes; drain, and cool slightly. Shell and devein shrimp; refrigerate to chill well.
2. Prepare roast peppers: Preheat oven to 450F. Wash peppers; remove seeds and ribs. Cut peppers into lengthwise strips, 1/4 inch wide. Arrange in single layer on cookie sheet. Roast 10 minutes, or until slightly browned. Let cool. Refrigerate.
3. Halve tomatoes; remove seeds; cut into wedges. Refrigerate. Wash and dry lettuce. Store in refrigerator crisper until ready to use.
4. Make Dressing: Combine all ingredients in a jar with a tight-fitting lid. Shake well. Refrigerate until serving.
5. At serving time: Line salad bowl with half of lettuce. Coarsely shred rest into bowl. Arrange shrimp and peppers alternately on top. Sprinkle with olives and tomato wedges.
6. Shake dressing well; pour over salad, and toss.
Makes 4 to 6 servings.

Fresh-Salmon-and-Cucumber Salad

Salad:
3-1/2-lb piece fresh salmon
1/2 lemon, sliced
1-1/2 tablespoons salt
6 whole black peppercorns
1 bay leaf
Tops from 2 stalks celery

Dressing:
1-1/4 cups mayonnaise or cooked salad dressing
1-1/2 tablespoons lemon juice
3 tablespoons snipped fresh dill
1-1/2 cups diced pared cucumber

Boston or iceberg lettuce, washed and crisped
Tomato wedges
Lemon wedges
Cucumber slices

1. Wash salmon. Place in a large kettle or fish poacher. Add just enough water to cover salmon. Add sliced lemon, salt, black peppercorns, bay leaf, and celery tops.
2. Slowly bring to boiling; reduce heat, and simmer, covered, 30 to 35 minutes, or until fish flakes when tested with a fork.
3. With slotted utensils, carefully lift salmon out of water onto a plate. Let stand until cool enough to handle. Remove and discard skin and bones (there should be about 2-1/2 lb meat). Break salmon in large chunks into large bowl. Chill several hours.
4. Make Dressing: In medium bowl, combine mayonnaise, lemon juice, dill, and diced cucumber; mix well. Refrigerate at least 1 hour.
5. Just before serving, toss the salmon with dressing. Taste, and add salt if needed.
6. To serve: Line a large serving plate with lettuce. Mound salad in center. Garnish with tomato and lemon wedges and cucumber slices.
Makes 12 servings.

Pacific Coast Summer Salad

7 medium potatoes (about 2-1/4 lb)
1 medium onion
1 bottle (8 oz) Italian-style salad dressing
1 can (7 oz) solid-pack tuna
1 can (7-3/4 oz) salmon
1 tablespoon chopped fresh dill
Boston lettuce, washed and chilled

1. Scrub potatoes. Cook in boiling, salted water, covered, just until tender—about 30 minutes. Drain, and let cool slightly.
2. Peel potatoes; then cut into slices 1/4 inch thick. Peel onion; slice, and separate into rings.
3. In shallow baking dish, arrange potato slices and onion rings in alternate layers. Pour 3/4 cup salad dressing over all. Refrigerate, covered, 3 hours.
4. Meanwhile, drain tuna and salmon. Break into large chunks; remove any bone and skin from salmon. Place in small bowl; toss with remaining dressing. Refrigerate, covered.
5. To serve: In shallow serving dish or bowl, arrange potato slices and onion rings in layers alternately with fish mixture. Sprinkle dill over top. Garnish with lettuce.
Makes 6 servings.

Tuna-Macaroni Supper Salad

1 pkg (8 oz) elbow macaroni
1 cup mayonnaise or cooked salad dressing
1/2 cup Italian-style dressing
1 tablespoon prepared mustard
2 cups thin, pared cucumber slices
1-1/2 cups diced tomato
1/2 cup diced green pepper
1/4 cup coarsely chopped green onion
1 teaspoon salt
1/8 teaspoon pepper
2 cans (7-oz size) solid-pack tuna, drained
1 hard-cooked egg, chopped
Chicory
Chopped parsley

1. Cook macaroni as the label directs. Drain; rinse with cold water.
2. In large bowl, combine mayonnaise, Italian-style dressing, and mustard; mix well.
3. Add cucumber, tomato, green pepper, green onion, salt, pepper, tuna in large pieces, and macaroni; toss to mix well. Turn into salad bowl.
4. Refrigerate, covered, until well chilled—about 4 hours.
5. Just before serving, garnish with hard-cooked egg, chicory, and parsley.
Makes 8 to 10 servings.

Vegetable Salads
Marinated-Mushroom Salad

1 lb small whole mushroom caps

Marinade:
3/4 cup salad oil
3/4 cup red-wine vinegar
1/4 cup finely chopped onion
1/4 cup finely chopped parsley
2 cloves garlic, crushed
1 teaspoon salt
1 teaspoon sugar

Boston-lettuce leaves
Watercress sprigs

1. Wash mushroom caps well. Dry on paper towels.
2. Make Marinade: In large bowl, combine all marinade ingredients.
3. Toss mushroom caps with marinade, coating well.
4. Refrigerate, covered, at least 1-1/2 hours.
5. To serve: Arrange lettuce and watercress on large platter or in wooden salad bowl. With slotted spoon, remove mushroom caps from marinade; mound in center of platter. Pour over remaining marinade, if desired.
Makes 6 to 8 servings.

Fresh Asparagus Vinaigrette

2 to 2-1/2 lb fresh asparagus
Boiling water
Salt
3 tablespoons cider vinegar
1/4 cup salad oil
2 tablespoons olive oil
1/2 teaspoon sugar
Dash pepper
1 hard-cooked egg, chopped
2 sweet gherkins, chopped

1. Break or cut off tough ends of asparagus stalks. Wash asparagus well with cold water; if necessary, use a soft brush to remove grit. With vegetable parer or paring knife, remove scales and skin from lower part of stalks.
2. Tie stalks into a bunch with string. Stand upright in deep saucepan. Add boiling water, to depth of 2 inches, and 1-1/2 teaspoons salt.
3. Bring to boiling; cook, covered, 15 to 20 minutes, or just until tender. Drain well. Lay stalks in shallow baking dish.

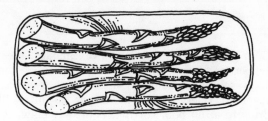

4. In jar with tight-fitting lid, combine vinegar, oils, 2 teaspoons salt, the sugar, and pepper; shake well.

5. Pour dressing over asparagus. Refrigerate 1 hour, turning stalks several times.

6. Arrange asparagus on platter. Sprinkle with egg and pickle.

Makes 6 servings.

Garbanzo-Bean Salad

2 cups diced potato
1 cup thinly sliced carrot
1 large red onion, thinly sliced
1/4 cup salad or olive oil
2 cans (1-lb size) garbanzo beans
1/2 cup bottled Italian-style dressing
1 or 2 cloves garlic, crushed
2 teaspoons salt
1-1/2 teaspoons sugar
Chopped parsley

1. In large saucepan, in 1 inch salted boiling water, cook potato and carrot until tender—about 10 minutes. Drain; turn into large bowl.

2. In medium, heavy skillet, sauté onion in oil until soft but not brown. Add to potato and carrot.

3. Drain garbanzos. Add to potato mixture.

4. In small bowl, combine dressing, garlic, salt, and sugar; mix well. Pour over vegetable mixture.

5. Toss gently until well mixed. Serve warm. Or refrigerate 2 hours, or until well chilled. Sprinkle with chopped parsley.

Makes 8 servings.

Kidney-Bean Salad

2 cans (1-lb size) kidney beans, drained
1/3 cup vinegar
2 tablespoons salad oil
1 teaspoon salt
Dash pepper
1/4 teaspoon dry mustard
2 large onions
Few sprigs parsley
1 clove garlic
1 jar (4 oz) pimientos

1. Mix beans with vinegar, oil, salt, pepper, and mustard.

2. Chop onions, parsley, and garlic fine; chop pimientos coarsely.

3. Add chopped vegetables to bean mixture; chill about 1 hour before serving.

Makes 6 servings.

Three-Bean Salad Bowl

1/2 bottle (8 oz size) Italian-style salad dressing
1 tablespoon Worcestershire sauce
3/4 cup sweet-pickle relish, drained
1 can (1 lb) cut wax beans, drained
1 can (1 lb) cut green beans, drained
1 can (15 oz) kidney beans, drained
1/2 cup sliced red onion
1 quart torn salad greens (optional)

1. In large bowl, combine salad dressing, Worcestershire, pickle relish and all the beans; toss lightly to combine.

2. Refrigerate, covered, until well chilled—about 4 hours.

3. Just before serving, add onion and salad greens; toss to combine.

4. Turn into salad bowl.

Makes 8 servings.

Harvey House Slaw

1 head green cabbage, slivered (10 cups)
1 large green pepper, cut in rings
2 medium Spanish onions, cut in rings
1 cup sugar
1 teaspoon dry mustard
2 teaspoons sugar
1 teaspoon celery seed
1 tablespoon salt
1 cup white vinegar
3/4 cup salad oil

1. In large bowl, make layers of cabbage, green pepper, and onion; sprinkle 1 cup sugar over top.
2. In saucepan, combine mustard, 2 teaspoons sugar, the celery seed, salt, vinegar, oil; mix well. Bring to a full boil, stirring; pour over slaw. Refrigerate, covered, at least 4 hours.
3. To serve, toss salad to mix well.
Makes 8 servings.

Sour-Cream Coleslaw

1-1/2 cups dairy sour cream
2 egg yolks
2 tablespoons lemon juice
3 tablespoons prepared horseradish, drained
1/4 teaspoon paprika
1 teaspoon sugar
1 teaspoon salt
2 quarts (2 lb) finely shredded green cabbage

1. Combine sour cream and egg yolks in medium bowl; mix well. Blend in remaining ingredients, except cabbage.
2. Pour dressing over cabbage; toss until it is well coated.
3. Refrigerate at least 30 minutes.
Makes 6 to 8 servings.

Sliced Cucumbers in Sour Cream

2 large cucumbers, pared and very thinly sliced
1-1/2 teaspoons salt
1 cup dairy sour cream
2 tablespoons lemon juice
1 tablespoon finely chopped onion
1/4 teaspoon sugar
Dash pepper
1-1/2 teaspoons finely chopped parsley

1. Lightly toss cucumber with 1 teaspoon salt. Chill well.
2. Meanwhile, combine sour cream, lemon juice, remaining salt, the onion, sugar, and pepper.
3. Drain cucumber. Toss with sour-cream mixture; refrigerate until well chilled—about 2 hours.
4. To serve: Turn cucumber mixture into shallow serving bowl; sprinkle with chopped parsley.
Makes 4 to 6 servings.

Pickled Cucumbers

4 large cucumbers (2-1/2 lb)
2 tablespoons salt
1 cup white vinegar
1/4 cup sugar
1/2 teaspoon white pepper
2 tablespoons snipped fresh dill or parsley

1. Scrub cucumbers with vegetable brush; wipe dry with paper towels. Do not pare. Cut cucumbers into very thin slices.
2. In medium bowl, lightly toss cucumber with salt. Cover with a plate, and weigh down with a heavy can. Let stand at room temperature 2 hours.
3. Drain cucumber well; pat dry with paper towels. Place in medium bowl.

4. In small bowl, combine vinegar, sugar, and pepper; mix well. Pour over cucumber slices. Refrigerate, covered, until well chilled—overnight.
5. To serve: Drain cucumber slices well. Turn into serving dish. Sprinkle with dill.
Makes 8 to 10 servings.

Creamy Coleslaw

Dressing:
2 cups mayonnaise or cooked salad dressing
1/4 cup prepared horseradish
1 tablespoon sugar
1 tablespoon lemon juice
1 tablespoon grated onion
2 teaspoons salt
1/2 teaspoon paprika

3 quarts finely shredded green cabbage (3 lb)
1-1/2 cups shredded carrots (1/2 lb)
1/2 cup shredded radishes

Green-pepper strips
Shredded radishes

1. In large bowl, combine mayonnaise, horse-radish, sugar, lemon juice, onion, salt, and paprika; mix well.
2. Add cabbage, carrots, and 1/2 cup radishes; toss until vegetables are well coated with dressing.
3. Refrigerate, covered, until well chilled—several hours, or overnight.
4. To serve: Garnish with green-pepper strips and shredded radishes.
Makes 12 servings.

Cold Leeks and Endives Vinaigrette

Dressing:
1/2 cup salad or olive oil
2 tablespoons tarragon vinegar
1 tablespoon snipped chives
1 teaspoon salt
1 teaspoon sugar
1/4 teaspoon pepper
1/4 teaspoon dry mustard

2 bunches leeks (about 8)
1 teaspoon salt
3 Belgian endives, washed and crisped, leaves separated
Watercress sprigs

1. In small bowl or tightly covered jar, combine oil, vinegar, chives, 1 teaspoon salt, the sugar, pepper, and mustard. Stir or shake until well blended. Refrigerate until needed.
2. Trim leeks: Cut off root ends and green stems—leeks should be about 7 inches long after trimming. Cut each in half lengthwise, being careful not to cut all the way through the root end. Wash thoroughly.
3. In 4-quart kettle, bring 2 quarts water to boiling. Add leeks and salt; simmer, covered, 15 minutes, or just until tender. Drain leeks; cool 30 minutes.
4. Arrange leeks in shallow dish. Shake dressing well; pour over leeks. Refrigerate, covered, until well chilled—about 4 hours.
5. To serve: Remove leeks from dressing with slotted utensil, and arrange in center of chilled serving dish. Place endives, spoke fashion, at each end, and drizzle with dressing. Garnish with watercress.
Makes 8 servings.

Delicatessen Deluxe Potato Salad

6 lb medium potatoes

Dressing:
3 cups mayonnaise or cooked salad dressing
1-1/2 cups finely chopped onion
1-1/2 cups cubed pared cucumber
1 cup coarsely chopped green pepper
1 can (4 oz) pimientos, drained and diced
2/3 cup sliced sweet gherkins
1/3 cup pickle juice
3 tablespoons cider vinegar
2 tablespoons salt

Celery leaves
Cherry tomatoes
Ripe olives

1. In boiling salted water to cover, cook unpared potatoes, covered, just until tender—about 30 minutes. Drain; refrigerate until cold.
2. In large bowl, combine mayonnaise, onion, cucumber, green pepper, pimientos, gherkins, pickle juice, vinegar, and salt; mix well.
3. Peel potatoes; cut into 1-inch cubes. Add to dressing; toss until potatoes are well coated. Refrigerate, covered, until well chilled—several hours, or overnight.
4. To serve: Garnish with celery leaves, cherry tomatoes, and ripe olives.
Makes 12 servings.
Note: For 6 servings, cut recipe in half; follow directions above.

German Potato Salad

3-1/2 lb medium potatoes (10)
1 cup chopped onion
1/2 lb bacon, diced
2 tablespoons flour
1/4 cup sugar
2 tablespoons butter or margarine
1-1/2 teaspoons salt
1/4 teaspoon pepper
1/2 cup cider vinegar
1 cup dairy sour cream
Chopped parsley

1. Cook potatoes, covered, in salted boiling water to cover 35 to 40 minutes, until fork-tender. Peel warm potatoes; slice; add onion.
2. In large skillet, cook bacon; remove from heat. Lift out with slotted spoon, and set aside. Pour off fat; return 1/4 cup to skillet.
3. Stir flour into fat in skillet. Add sugar, butter, salt, pepper, vinegar, 1 cup water. Bring to boil, stirring. Remove from heat; add sour cream.
4. Add potatoes, onion, half of bacon; toss gently. Sprinkle with rest of bacon, parsley. Serve warm.
Makes 10 servings.

Marinated Rice Salad

2/3 cup raw long-grain white rice
1/2 cup thinly sliced celery
2 tablespoons chopped green pepper
2 tablespoons chopped green onion
2 tablespoons chopped parsley
2 tablespoons dark raisins
1/2 cup bottled oil-and-vinegar dressing
Crisp salad greens
8 cherry tomatoes, halved

1. Cook rice as the label directs. Let cool 15 minutes.
2. In large bowl, combine rice, celery, green pepper, onion, parsley, and raisins. Pour dressing over top; toss until thoroughly blended.
3. Refrigerate, covered, until well chilled—at least 2 hours.
4. To serve: Line shallow serving dish with salad greens. Fill with rice salad. Arrange tomato around edge.
Makes 4 servings.

French Potato Salad

3 lb waxy or new potatoes
1/4 cup wine vinegar
1-1/2 teaspoons salt
1 teaspoon freshly ground pepper
3 tablespoons canned condensed consommé,
    undiluted
1/3 cup dry white wine
1 tablespoon chopped fresh tarragon or 1 teaspoon
    dried tarragon leaves
2 teaspoons chopped fresh chervil or 1/2 teaspoon
    dried chervil leaves
1-1/2 tablespoons chopped parsley
1 tablespoon chopped chives
3/4 cup salad or olive oil

1. Cook potatoes, covered, in enough boiling, salted water to cover, 30 minutes, or just until fork-tender.
2. Drain; peel; slice while still warm into 1/4-inch-thick slices into salad bowl.
3. In bowl or jar with tight-fitting lid, combine vinegar and rest of ingredients; mix very well.
4. Pour over warm potatoes; toss gently to coat with liquid. Serve warm, or let cool and refrigerate. Before serving, toss gently again.
Makes 8 servings.

Gazpacho Salad Bowl

Dressing:
1/3 cup olive or salad oil
1/3 cup red-wine vinegar
1 tablespoon snipped chives
1 clove garlic, crushed
1 teaspoon salt
1/8 teaspoon cracked black pepper
Few drops liquid hot-pepper seasoning

Salad:
2 large tomatoes (1 lb)
1 large cucumber
1 medium green pepper, sliced in rings
1/2 cup sliced onion, separated into rings
Snipped chives (optional)
Croutons (optional)

1. Make Dressing: In jar with tight-fitting lid, combine all dressing ingredients; shake vigorously to combine.
2. Peel tomatoes; slice; cut each slice in half. Score unpared cucumber with fork; slice thinly.
3. In salad bowl or shallow glass serving bowl, combine tomato, cucumber, green pepper, onion, and dressing; toss until vegetables are well coated.
4. Refrigerate, covered, until well chilled—about 2 hours.
5. Just before serving, toss salad. Sprinkle with chives and croutons.
Makes 6 to 8 servings.

Old-Fashioned Sliced Tomatoes

4 large tomatoes (about 2 lb)
2 tablespoons sugar
1 teaspoon salt
1/8 teaspoon pepper
1/4 cup tarragon vinegar

1. Wash tomatoes; cut out cores. Cut into 1/4-inch-thick slices.
2. Arrange half the slices in a large, shallow serving dish; sprinkle with half the sugar, salt, and pepper. Top with remaining slices; sprinkle with rest of sugar, salt, and pepper. Drizzle vinegar over top.
3. Refrigerate, covered, at least 1 hour before serving.
Makes 6 to 8 servings.

Marinated Sliced Tomatoes

4 large tomatoes (1-1/2 lb)
1/4 cup salad oil
1 tablespoon lemon juice
1/2 teaspoon minced garlic
1/2 teaspoon salt
1/2 teaspoon dried oregano leaves

1. Peel and slice tomatoes. Arrange in shallow dish.
2. Combine oil, lemon juice, garlic, salt, and oregano; mix well.
3. Pour over tomatoes. Refrigerate, covered, several hours, until well chilled.
Makes 6 servings.

Guacamole-and-Tomato Salad

6 medium tomatoes (2 lb)
Salt
1/2 cup finely chopped onion
1 or 2 canned green chiles, finely chopped
2 teaspoons lemon juice
2 very ripe medium avocados
3 slices bacon, crisp-cooked and crumbled
Crisp lettuce

1. Cut 1/2-inch-thick slice from stem end of each tomato. Scoop out centers, and chop finely. Sprinkle the insides of tomato cups lightly with salt; turn upside down on paper towels, to drain. Refrigerate.
2. Stir chopped onion and chile, lemon juice, and 1-1/2 teaspoons salt into chopped tomato. Refrigerate, covered.
3. Just before serving, peel and pit avocados; mash. Stir in chopped-tomato mixture.
4. Spoon guacamole into tomato cups; top with crumbled bacon. Arrange on lettuce leaves on serving platter. Pass any remaining guacamole.
Makes 6 servings.

Macaroni Salad

1 pkg (1 lb) elbow macaroni
1 jar (9-1/2 oz) sweet-pepper relish
1 can (4 oz) pimientos, drained and chopped
1/2 cup diced green pepper
1 tablespoon chopped parsley
2 teaspoons grated onion
1-1/2 teaspoons salt
1-1/2 cups mayonnaise or cooked salad dressing
1/2 cup dairy sour cream
1/2 cup milk
Crisp salad greens

1. Cook macaroni as the label directs. Drain, and rinse with cold water.
2. In large bowl, combine relish, pimiento, green pepper, parsley, onion, salt, 1 cup mayonnaise, the sour cream, and 1/4 cup milk; blend well. Add macaroni; toss lightly until well combined.
3. Refrigerate, covered, until well chilled—several hours or overnight.
4. To serve: Combine remaining mayonnaise and milk; stir into salad. Turn into salad bowl; garnish with salad greens.
Makes 12 servings.

Fruit Salads

Apple and Sour Cream Slaw

4-1/2 cups thinly sliced, cored, unpared red
    apples (about 1-1/2 lb)
3 cups finely shredded green cabbage
1 cup dairy sour cream
3 tablespoons lemon juice
1 tablespoon sugar
3/4 teaspoon salt
1/8 teaspoon pepper
1 tablespoon poppy seed

1. In large bowl, lightly toss all ingredients until well combined.
2. Refrigerate at least 1 hour before serving.
Makes 6 to 8 servings.

Pink-Grapefruit-and-Avocado Salad Platter

2 heads Boston lettuce
1 small head romaine
2 ripe medium avocados, peeled and halved
2 large pink grapefruit, peeled and sectioned
1 cup thinly sliced celery
2 tablespoons snipped chives
Watercress sprigs
Special French Dressing, page 493

1. Wash salad greens; trim ends; discard with any discolored leaves. Crisp in crisper several hours.
2. In large bowl, place avocado halves and grapefruit sections, spooning grapefruit juice over avocado to prevent discoloration. Refrigerate, covered, until serving.
3. To serve: Arrange greens in shallow square serving dish. Slice each avocado half into 8 lengthwise slices. Reassemble halves, cut side down, and place one in each corner. Arrange grapefruit sections in center. Sprinkle celery and chives over all. Garnish with watercress. Refrigerate, covered, if not serving at once.
4. Serve with Special French Dressing.
Makes 10 servings.

Fresh-Fruit Dessert Salad

Dressing:
1 cup dairy sour cream
3 tablespoons maple-blended syrup
Dash salt

2 navel oranges
2 bananas
1 medium pear
1 medium apple
1/2 lb grapes
1 can (1 lb, 4 oz) pineapple slices
1/2 cup pitted date halves

1. In small bowl, combine sour cream, syrup, and salt; mix well. Refrigerate until ready to use. Also refrigerate all fruits until well chilled.
2. Just before serving, peel oranges, and cut into 1/4-inch-thick slices. Cut bananas in half crosswise, then lengthwise. Cut pear and apple into wedges; core. Cut grapes into small clusters. Drain pineapple well.
3. Place dressing, in attractive bowl, in center of large, round platter. Arrange banana, pear, apple, grapes, and orange and pineapple slices in groups around dressing. Garnish platter with date halves.
Makes 8 servings.

Green-and-White Fruit Salad

2 large grapefruit
2 large avocados
1/2 large honeydew melon
1/2 head romaine
Sour-Cream Dressing, page 490
3/4 lb seedless green grapes, washed
Mint sprigs

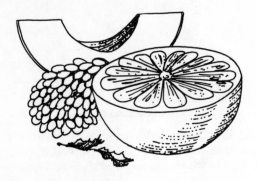

1. With sharp knife, peel grapefruit, removing white membrane; section carefully into a large bowl.
2. Cut avocados in half lengthwise; discard peel and pits. Add to grapefruit. Mix gently, to coat avocado with grapefruit juice.
3. Scrape seeds and stringy pulp from melon. Cut melon lengthwise into 4 pieces; peel. Add to grapefruit mixture. Refrigerate, covered, 2 hours, or until well chilled.
4. To serve: Line a platter with romaine. Set bowl of Sour-Cream Dressing in center. Then arrange fruit around bowl, alternating avocado halves, each cut lengthwise into 4 slices; honeydew-melon pieces, each cut crosswise into 6 slices; small clusters of grapes; and mounds of grapefruit sections. Garnish with sprigs of mint. Serve with the dressing.

Makes 8 to 10 servings.

Orange-and-Onion Salad

4 small oranges
1 small onion, peeled
1/4 cup olive or salad oil
2 tablespoons red-wine vinegar
1 clove garlic, split
1/4 teaspoon salt
Dash freshly ground pepper
1 quart crisp salad greens
1/2 cup pitted green olives, sliced (optional)

1. Peel oranges; remove white membrane. With sharp knife, cut oranges and onion in thin slices. Place in shallow dish.
2. In measuring cup, combine olive oil with vinegar, 2 tablespoons water, the garlic, salt, and pepper; stir well with fork. Pour over oranges and onion.
3. Refrigerate, covered, until well chilled—at least 2 hours. Remove garlic.
4. To serve: Place greens and olives in salad bowl. Add oranges and onions (separated into rings), with the dressing, and toss well.

Makes 6 servings.

Gelatine Salads

Tomato Aspic

1 can (1 qt, 14 oz) tomato juice
12 whole black peppercorns
8 whole cloves
2 bay leaves
1/4 teaspoon salt
3 env unflavored gelatine

1. In medium saucepan, combine 5 cups tomato juice, the peppercorns, cloves, bay leaves, salt. Bring to boiling; reduce heat, and simmer 5 minutes.
2. Sprinkle gelatine over remaining tomato juice, to soften. Add to hot mixture; stir until gelatine is dissolved. Remove from heat.

3. Strain mixture. Pour into 12 individual molds or 1-1/2-quart mold.

4. Refrigerate until firm—at least 3 hours.

5. To unmold: Run a small spatula around edge of mold. Invert on a serving plate; place a hot, damp dishcloth on bottom of mold; shake gently to release. Garnish as desired—with sliced olives, green pepper, cucumber, or salad greens. Serve with mayonnaise.

Makes 8 servings.

Guacamole Salad Mold

1 env unflavored gelatine
5 medium garden-ripe tomatoes
2 ripe avocados (about 1-1/2 lb)
2 tablespoons white vinegar
1/4 cup finely chopped onion
2 tablespoons finely chopped green chile pepper
1 teaspoon salt
Oil and Vinegar Dressing, page 492

1. Sprinkle gelatine over 1/2 cup cold water in small custard cup; let stand 5 minutes, to soften.

2. Bring to boiling 1 inch water in small skillet or saucepan. Set custard cup in water; stir gelatine until dissolved.

3. Peel 1 tomato; slice into medium bowl; mash with a fork.

4. Cut avocados in half; discard peel and pits. Slice into tomato; mash avocado and tomato until well blended.

5. Add vinegar, onion, chile pepper, and salt. Mix in dissolved gelatine until well combined.

6. Turn mixture into a 1-quart bowl. Refrigerate until firm—at least 4 hours.

7. To unmold: Loosen around edge with small spatula. Invert over serving platter; place a hot-damp dishcloth over bowl; shake to release; lift off bowl.

8. Slice remaining tomatoes. Arrange around guacamole mold. Drizzle tomatoes with about 2 tablespoons dressing. Nice for a summer buffet table.

Makes 8 servings.

Cranberry Salad Mold

4 cups (1 lb) fresh cranberries
1 cup sugar
1 env unflavored gelatine
1/2 cup orange juice
1 cup chopped celery
1 cup chopped pared apple
1 cup chopped pecans or walnuts

1. Wash cranberries; drain, and remove stems. Put through food chopper, using coarse blade. Add sugar; let stand 15 minutes, stirring occasionally.

2. Sprinkle gelatine over orange juice in small saucepan, to soften. Place over low heat, stirring until gelatine is dissolved.

3. Add gelatine mixture, celery, apple, and nuts to cranberries; mix well. Turn into 1-quart mold.

4. Refrigerate until firm—6 to 8 hours. Serve with salad dressing or whipped cream.

Makes 8 servings.

Molded Gazpacho Salad

2 env unflavored gelatine
1 can (1 pt, 2 oz) tomato juice
1/3 cup red-wine vinegar
1 teaspoon salt
Tabasco
2 small tomatoes, peeled and diced (1 cup)
1 medium cucumber, pared and diced (1 cup)
1/2 medium green pepper, diced (1/2 cup)
1/4 cup finely chopped red onion
1 tablespoon chopped chives
Avocado Dressing, page 492

1. In medium saucepan, sprinkle gelatine over 3/4 cup tomato juice to soften. Place over low heat, stirring constantly, until gelatine is dissolved. Remove from heat.
2. Stir in remaining tomato juice, the vinegar, salt, and few drops Tabasco. Set in bowl of ice, stirring occasionally, until mixture is consistency of unbeaten egg white—about 15 minutes.
3. Fold in tomato, cucumber, green pepper, onion, and chives until well combined. Pour into 1-1/2-quart mold that has been rinsed in cold water.
4. Refrigerate until firm—at least 6 hours.
5. To unmold: Run a small spatula around edge of mold. Invert over serving platter; place a hot, damp dishcloth over inverted mold, and shake gently to release. Refrigerate salad, if not serving at once. Serve with Avocado Dressing.
Makes 6 to 8 servings.

Crisp Cucumber Aspic

2 cups boiling water
1 pkg (6 oz) or 2 pkg (3-oz size) lemon-flavored gelatine
1/3 cup white-wine vinegar
1/4 teaspoon salt
Green food color
2 medium cucumbers, pared and grated (2 cups)
1/2 cup finely chopped celery
1 to 2 tablespoons prepared horseradish
1 tablespoon grated onion
2 teaspoons snipped fresh dill
About 20 paper-thin slices cucumber
1 pint box cherry tomatoes, washed (optional)
Crisp salad greens
1/2 pint dairy sour cream

1. In medium bowl, pour boiling water over gelatine; stir until dissolved. Stir in vinegar, salt, and few drops green food color.
2. Set in bowl of ice, stirring occasionally, until mixture is consistency of unbeaten egg white—about 35 minutes.
3. Fold in grated cucumber, celery, horseradish, onion, and dill until well blended. Turn into 5-1/2-cup ring mold that has been rinsed in cold water and lined with the thin cucumber slices.
4. Refrigerate until firm—at least 3 hours.
5. To unmold: Run a small spatula around edge of mold. Invert over platter; place a hot, damp dishcloth over inverted mold, and shake gently to release.
6. Fill center with tomatoes. Garnish edge with salad greens. Pass sour cream.
Makes 8 servings.

Perfection Salad

2 env unflavored gelatine
1/2 cup sugar
1 teaspoon salt
1 can (12 oz) apple juice
1/2 cup lemon juice
2 tablespoons vinegar
1 cup shredded carrot
1 cup sliced celery
1 cup finely shredded cabbage
1/2 cup chopped green pepper
1 can (4 oz) chopped pimiento

1. In small saucepan, mix gelatine, sugar, and salt well.
2. Add 1 cup water. Heat over low heat, stirring constantly, until sugar and gelatine are dissolved. Remove from heat.
3. Stir in apple juice, lemon juice, vinegar, and 1/4 cup cold water. Pour into medium bowl. Refrigerate 1 hour, or until mixture is consistency of unbeaten egg white.
4. Add carrot, celery, cabbage, green pepper, and pimiento; stir until well mixed.
5. Turn into a 9-by-5-by-3-inch loaf pan. Refrigerate 4 hours, or until firm.
6. To unmold: Run a sharp knife around edge of pan. Invert over serving plate. Place a hot, damp dishcloth over pan; shake gently to release. Lift off pan. Serve with mayonnaise.
Makes 8 servings.

Ginger-and-Fresh-Fruit Salad Mold

1 cup boiling water
2 pkg (3-oz size) or 1 pkg (6 oz) orange-flavored
    gelatine
3 bottles (7-oz size) or 2-1/2 cups ginger ale
1 pint strawberries
1/4 lb seedless green grapes
1 cup cantaloupe balls
1 cup honeydew balls
Ginger Dressing, page 491

1. In large bowl, pour boiling water over gelatine; stir until gelatine is dissolved. Stir in ginger ale.
2. Refrigerate, stirring occasionally, until consistency of unbeaten egg white—about 1 hour.
3. Meanwhile, wash strawberries. Hull and halve enough to make 1 cup. Set aside the rest for garnish. Wash and drain grapes, to use for garnish.
4. Fold melon balls and halved strawberries into thickened gelatine. Carefully turn mixture into a decorative 6-cup mold.
5. Refrigerate until firm—at least 4 hours.
6. To unmold: Run a small spatula around edge of mold. Invert onto serving plate. Place a hot, damp dishcloth over mold; shake gently to release. Repeat, if necessary. Lift off mold.
7. Refrigerate until ready to serve. Garnish with grapes and reserved strawberries. Serve with Ginger Dressing. This is delicious as a dessert salad.
Makes 6 to 8 servings.

Bing-Cherry Salad

1 can (1 lb, 14 oz) pitted Bing cherries
1 cup boiling water
1 pkg (3 oz) cherry-flavored gelatine
3/4 cup cream sherry
1 cup chopped pecans
1 pkg (3 oz) cream cheese, chilled
Crisp greens

1. Drain cherries, reserving liquid.
2. Pour boiling water over gelatine in medium bowl; stir until gelatine dissolves. Stir in sherry or 3/4 cup liquid from cherries.
3. Refrigerate until consistency of unbeaten egg white—about 1 hour.
4. Add drained cherries and nuts. Cube cream cheese, and add to gelatine mixture; mix well. Turn into 8-inch square pan or 5-cup mold.
5. Refrigerate until firm—several hours. Unmold on crisp greens. Nice to serve as a dessert salad. Makes 6 to 8 servings.

Creamy Dressings

Mayonnaise can be rather tricky to make, which is one of the reasons that most homemakers use a commercially prepared mayonnaise. The ingredients are similar to those in French dressing—oil, an acid, as vinegar or lemon juice, and egg. The oil is beaten into the egg and vinegar, drop by drop, to form a permanent emulsion.

A boiled or cooked salad dressing is similar to mayonnaise, but is easier and less expensive to make. A white sauce forms the base rather than the high proportion of oil in mayonnaise.

Mayonnaise

2 egg yolks, or 1 whole egg
1 teaspoon salt
Dash cayenne
1 cup salad or olive oil
2 tablespoons lemon juice or vinegar

1. In small bowl, with portable electric mixer at medium speed, beat egg yolks, salt, and cayenne until thick and lemon-colored.
2. Add 1/4 cup oil, one drop at a time, beating until thick.
3. Gradually add 1 tablespoon lemon juice, beating after each addition. Then add 1/2 cup oil, in a steady stream, beating constantly.
4. Slowly add remaining lemon juice and then remaining oil, beating constantly.
5. Refrigerate, covered, until ready to use. Makes 1-1/4 cups.

Lemon Mayonnaise

1/3 cup mayonnaise
1 tablespoon cream
1 teaspoon lemon juice

1. In small bowl, combine mayonnaise, cream, and lemon juice. Stir until well blended. Refrigerate.
Makes 1/3 cup.

Boiled Dressing

1 tablespoon flour
2 tablespoons sugar
1 teaspoon salt
1-1/4 cups milk
3 egg yolks, slightly beaten
1/4 cup cider vinegar
1 tablespoon prepared mustard
2 tablespoons butter or margarine

1. In small, heavy saucepan, stir flour with sugar and salt. With wire whisk, gradually stir in milk.
2. Cook, stirring, over medium heat until mixture starts to boil. Boil 1 minute; remove from heat.
3. Gradually stir the hot flour-milk mixture, a little at a time, into the beaten egg yolks in small bowl. Pour back into saucepan.
4. Add vinegar and prepared mustard. Cook, stirring constantly, until mixture starts to boil. Remove from heat. Stir in butter. Cool; then refrigerate, covered.
Makes 1-1/2 cups.

Creamy Blue Cheese or Roquefort Salad Dressing

1/4 lb Roquefort cheese
1 cup dairy sour cream
1/4 cup mayonnaise or cooked salad dressing
1/4 cup sherry
1/4 cup wine vinegar
1 tablespoon grated onion
1/2 teaspoon salt
1/2 teaspoon garlic salt
1/4 teaspoon paprika
Generous sprinkle freshly ground pepper

1. Coarsely crumble cheese into a medium bowl. Add remaining ingredients, stirring until well blended.
2. Refrigerate, covered, until well chilled—at least 1 hour. Serve on favorite combination of crisp greens, garnished with tomato and avocado slices if desired.
Makes about 2 cups.

Curry Dressing

1 cup mayonnaise or cooked salad dressing
1/2 cup dairy sour cream
1 tablespoon lemon juice
2 teaspoons curry powder

1. In small bowl, combine all ingredients, mixing well. Refrigerate, covered, several hours, or until needed.
2. Turn into attractive dish. Serve with cold chicken or shrimp.
Makes 1-1/2 cups.

Golden-Gate Dressing

2 eggs, slightly beaten
1/4 cup honey
1/4 cup canned pineapple juice
1/2 cup orange juice
1 tablespoon grated orange peel
1/2 cup heavy cream, whipped

1. Combine all ingredients, except cream, in top of double boiler. Cook, stirring, over hot, not boiling, water 15 minutes, or until thickened.
2. Refrigerate, covered, until well chilled.
3. Just before serving, fold in whipped cream until well combined. Delicious for fruit salad.
Makes 1-1/4 cups.

Russian Dressing

1/2 cup mayonnaise or cooked salad dressing
1 tablespoon chili sauce
2 tablespoons milk
2 tablespoons finely chopped stuffed olives
1 tablespoon finely chopped onion
1 tablespoon finely chopped green pepper
2 tablespoons lemon juice
1/4 teaspoon salt
1 tablespoon prepared horseradish

1. In small bowl, combine mayonnaise with rest of ingredients; mix well.
2. Refrigerate, covered, until ready to use.
Makes 3/4 cup.

Sour-Cream Dressing

1 tablespoon flour
1 tablespoon sugar
1-1/2 teaspoons salt
1/2 teaspoon dry mustard
2 tablespoons salad oil
3 tablespoons cider vinegar
1 egg, slightly beaten
1/2 teaspoon celery seed
1/4 cup dairy sour cream

1. In top of double boiler, combine flour, sugar, salt, mustard, oil, and 1/2 cup water. Bring to boiling, stirring, over medium heat. Mixture will be smooth and thickened.
2. In small bowl, gradually stir vinegar into egg; then stir in hot mixture, a little at a time.
3. Pour back into double-boiler top; cook, stirring, over hot, not boiling, water (water should not touch bottom of top part), until thickened—about 5 minutes. Remove from heat.
4. Stir in celery seed and sour cream. Refrigerate, covered, until ready to use.
Makes 1 cup.

Sour-Cream Dressing for Fruit

1/2 cup mayonnaise or cooked salad dressing
1/2 cup dairy sour cream
2 tablespoons lemon juice
1/3 cup apricot preserves
Dash salt

1. In small bowl, combine all ingredients.
2. Refrigerate until well chilled.
Makes about 1 cup.

Thousand Island Dressing

2 tablespoons chopped pickle
2 tablespoons finely chopped green pepper
2 tablespoons chopped red pepper or pimiento
2 tablespoons finely chopped onion
1 cup mayonnaise or cooked salad dressing
2 tablespoons chili sauce
2 tablespoons milk

1. Combine all ingredients in small bowl; stir until well blended.
2. Refrigerate, covered, at least 2 hours before serving.
Makes 1-3/4 cups.

Ginger Dressing

1/2 cup heavy cream
1/4 cup mayonnaise or cooked salad dressing
1 tablespoon chopped preserved ginger in syrup
1 tablespoon syrup from ginger

1. In small bowl, whip cream until stiff. Fold in mayonnaise, ginger, and syrup.
2. Refrigerate until serving time. Nice for fruit salad.
Makes 1-1/3 cups.

Honey-Lime Dressing

1 cup mayonnaise or cooked salad dressing
1/2 cup honey
1 cup heavy cream, whipped
1/4 cup lime juice

1. In small bowl, combine all ingredients well.
2. Refrigerate, covered, until ready to use. Delicious on fruit salad.
Makes 2-1/2 cups.

Green Mayonnaise

1 cup mayonnaise or cooked salad dressing
2 tablespoons lemon juice
2 tablespoons chopped parsley
1 tablespoon chopped chives
1 tablespoon chopped watercress

1. In small bowl, combine mayonnaise, lemon juice, parsley, chives, and watercress; mix well.
2. Refrigerate, covered, overnight.
Makes 1-1/4 cups.

Poppy-Seed Dressing

3/4 cup sugar
1 teaspoon dry mustard
1 teaspoon salt
1/3 cup cider vinegar
1 tablespoon onion juice
1 cup salad oil
1-1/2 tablespoons poppy seed

1. In medium bowl, combine sugar, mustard, salt, vinegar, and onion juice.
2. Using portable electric mixer or rotary beater, gradually beat in oil until mixture is thick and smooth. Stir in poppy seed.
3. Store, covered, in refrigerator. This dressing is good with any fruit salad.
Makes 1-2/3 cups.

Cucumber Yoghurt Dressing

1 large cucumber
1 cup plain yoghurt
2 tablespoons finely chopped fresh mint
1/2 teaspoon salt

1. Pare cucumber; quarter lengthwise. Cut each quarter crosswise into thin slices.
2. In medium bowl, combine yoghurt, cucumber, mint, and salt; mix well.
3. Refrigerate, covered, 1 hour, to blend flavors.
4. Serve over mixed salad greens.
Makes 1-3/4 cups.

Avocado Dressing

1 large ripe avocado (about 1 lb)
1/2 cup sour cream
1/2 cup light cream
1 tablespoon grated onion
1-1/2 teaspoons salt
Dash cayenne
1/8 teaspoon sugar
1 clove garlic, crushed
1 tablespoon lemon juice

1. Peel avocado; cut into chunks. Blend in electric blender with sour cream, light cream, and rest of ingredients until smooth—several minutes.
2. Refrigerate, covered (see Note), until well chilled—several hours.
Makes 2 cups.
Note: Place plastic film directly on surface.

Salad Dressings

The soul of a salad is its dressing. And though literally hundreds of bottled dressings are available in the market, many of them excellent, a home-made dressing has the extra something that family and guests appreciate.

French Dressing

French dressing, also known as oil and vinegar dressing, is the simplest and most widely used of all the salad dressings. It is a temporary emulsion of an oil and an acid with seasonings. It separates on standing and must be mixed well just before using.

The oil may be corn, olive, peanut, etc. The acid may be lemon juice, plain vinegar, wine vinegar, or any of the flavored vinegars. Seasonings may vary from salt, pepper, paprika, mustard, catsup, Worcestershire, Tabasco, etc.

Basic French or Oil and Vinegar Dressing

1/3 cup vinegar* or lemon juice
2/3 cup salad or olive oil
1-1/2 teaspoons salt
1/4 teaspoon pepper
1 teaspoon sugar (optional)
1 clove garlic (optional)

1. Combine all ingredients in jar with tight-fitting lid; shake vigorously to blend.
2. Refrigerate, covered, at least 2 hours before using.
3. Remove garlic; shake just before using.
Makes 1 cup.
* You may use white, cider, wine, or herb-flavored vinegar.

Roquefort or Blue-Cheese Dressing

1. Crumble a package (about 3 oz) Roquefort or blue cheese into a small bowl.

2. Add 2 tablespoons Basic French Dressing, page 492; mix well with fork. Add rest of dressing
3. Store, covered, in refrigerator. Mix again just before using.
Makes 1-1/4 cups.

Best French Dressing

1 cup salad oil
1/2 cup olive oil
1/4 cup dry white wine
1/2 cup red-wine vinegar
2 teaspoons salt
1/2 teaspoon pepper
1/2 teaspoon dry mustard
1/2 teaspoon dried basil leaves
1/2 cup chopped parsley
1 clove garlic, finely chopped

1. Combine all ingredients in medium bowl; beat, with rotary beater, until well blended.
2. Pour into jar with tight-fitting lid. Refrigerate at least 2 hours. Shake well just before serving.
Makes 2-1/2 cups.

Vinaigrette Dressing

1 cup olive or salad oil
1/3 cup red-wine vinegar
1 teaspoon salt
1/8 teaspoon pepper
2 tablespoons chopped capers
2 tablespoons chopped chives

1. Combine all ingredients in jar with tight-fitting lid. Shake vigorously.
2. Refrigerate the dressing until ready to use. Shake it again just before using.
Makes 1-1/2 cups.

Special French Dressing

2/3 cup salad or olive oil
1/3 cup cider vinegar
2 teaspoons salt
1/8 teaspoon pepper
1/4 teaspoon paprika
Dash celery salt
1 teaspoon sugar
1-1/2 teaspoons chili sauce
1-1/2 teaspoons catsup
1/2 teaspoon prepared mustard
1 tablespoon lemon juice
1-1/4 teaspoons Worcestershire sauce
1/2 teaspoon prepared horseradish
Dash Tabasco
1 clove garlic, peeled

1. Combine all ingredients, except garlic, in a medium bowl. With wire whisk, beat until smooth and well blended.
2. Turn into a jar with a tight-fitting lid. Add garlic. Refrigerate several hours. Before serving, shake well; remove garlic. Refrigerate leftover dressing for later use.
Makes 1-1/3 cups.

White-Wine French Dressing

1 cup salad oil
1/2 cup olive oil
1/4 cup dry white wine
1/2 cup red-wine vinegar
2 teaspoons salt
1/2 teaspoon pepper
1/2 teaspoon dry mustard
1/2 teaspoon dried basil leaves
1/2 cup chopped parsley
1 clove garlic, finely chopped

1. Combine all ingredients in medium bowl; beat, with rotary beater, until well blended.
2. Pour into jar with tight-fitting lid. Refrigerate at least 2 hours. Shake well just before serving. Makes 2-1/2 cups.

Zesty French Dressing

1/2 cup finely chopped onion
1 clove garlic, finely chopped
1/4 cup sugar
1 cup red-wine vinegar
1 cup olive oil
1 cup catsup
2 teaspoons salt
1 teaspoon dry mustard
1 teaspoon paprika
1 teaspoon dried oregano leaves

1. Combine all ingredients in jar with tight-fitting lid; shake to mix well.
2. Refrigerate, covered, at least 2 hours, to blend flavors.
3. Strain, to remove onion and garlic. Shake well just before using. Makes 2-3/4 cups.

Lime Salad Dressing

3/4 cup salad oil
2 tablespoons cider vinegar
3 tablespoons lime juice
1/4 cup orange juice
2 tablespoons sugar
1/2 teaspoon salt
1/8 teaspoon paprika
3 tablespoons chopped fresh mint

1. Combine all ingredients in pint jar with tight-fitting lid. Shake vigorously to combine well.
2. Refrigerate until ready to use. Shake well just before serving. Nice for fruit salad. Makes 1-1/3 cups.

Fresh Mint Dressing

1/2 cup tarragon vinegar
2/3 cup salad oil
1/4 cup sugar
1/2 teaspoon salt
1/8 teaspoon pepper
1/4 cup chopped fresh mint leaves

Combine vinegar, oil, sugar, salt, pepper, and chopped mint in a jar with tight-fitting lid. Shake, vigorously, to mix well. Makes 1-1/2 cups.

Sauces & Gravies

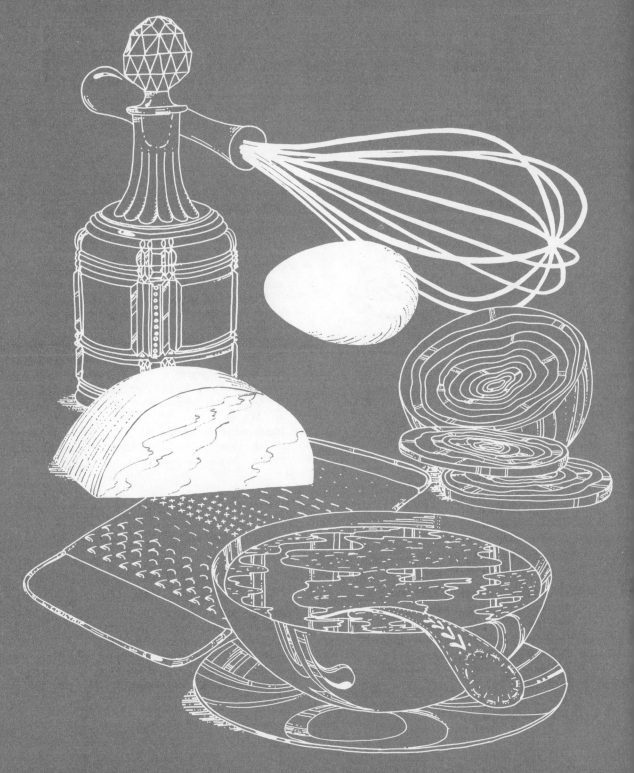

It's the sauce, the absolutely right sauce, that lifts a dish from the routine to the spectacular. If you want to win a reputation as a gourmet cook, this chapter is a good place to start.

A basic white sauce is one of the first lessons given in cooking class—for good reason, too.

The trick in making a really smooth white sauce lies in melting the butter and taking the pan *off the range* before blending in the flour; then, gradually, blending in the milk. The sauce is *then* returned to the heat. (When flour is blended in over heat, it tends to cook in lumps, which no amount of stirring will remove afterward.)

When white sauce—or, for that matter, almost any other sauce—is made in advance, it is best reheated in a double boiler, to prevent sticking and scorching. Cover it, to prevent the formation of a skin on the surface.

When you add wine to a sauce, be careful not to let the sauce boil—you might ruin the delicate flavor of the wine. Nor should it be subjected to prolonged heating after the wine has been added.

Basic White Sauce

1/4 cup butter or margarine
1/4 cup unsifted all-purpose flour
1/2 teaspoon salt
1/8 teaspoon pepper
2 cups milk or light cream

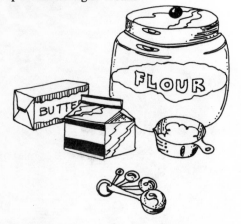

1. In medium saucepan, slowly heat butter just until melted and golden, not browned, stirring all the while. Remove from heat.
2. Add flour, salt, and pepper; stir until smooth. Add milk, a small amount at a time, stirring after each addition. Return to heat.
3. Over medium heat, bring to boiling, stirring constantly. Reduce heat; simmer 3 minutes. Makes 2 cups.

Thin White Sauce: Reduce butter and flour to 2 tablespoons each. Proceed as in Basic White Sauce. Use for soups.

Parsley Sauce: Add 1/2 cup chopped parsley and 1/4 cup lemon juice to Basic White Sauce. Makes 2-1/2 cups.

Horseradish Sauce: Add 1/3 cup prepared horseradish, 1 tablespoon lemon juice and dash cayenne to Basic White Sauce. Makes 2-1/3 cups.

Béarnaise Sauce, page 22

Blender Béarnaise Sauce

2 tablespoons dry white wine
1 tablespoon tarragon vinegar
1 teaspoon dried tarragon leaves
2 teaspoons chopped onion or shallots
1/4 teaspoon pepper
3/4 cup Hollandaise Sauce, page 499

1. In medium skillet, combine wine, vinegar, tarragon, onion, and pepper.
2. Over moderate heat, bring to boiling. Cook until most of liquid is evaporated.
3. In blender container, combine cooked mixture with Hollandaise. Cover; blend at high speed 4 seconds. Serve warm, with steak. Makes 3/4 cup.

Bordelaise Sauce

1/4 cup butter or margarine
2 shallots, finely chopped
2 cloves garlic, finely chopped
2 slices onion
2 slices carrot
2 sprigs parsley
10 whole black peppercorns
2 whole cloves
2 bay leaves
3 tablespoons flour
1/2 teaspoon meat-extract paste*
1 can (10-1/2 oz) condensed beef broth, undiluted
1 cup Burgundy
1/4 teaspoon salt
1/8 teaspoon pepper
2 tablespoons finely chopped parsley
* Do not use liquid meat extract.

1. In hot butter in medium skillet, sauté shallots, garlic, onion, carrot, parsley, peppercorns, cloves, and bay leaves until onion is golden—about 3 minutes.
2. Remove from heat; stir in flour smoothly. Cook, stirring, over very low heat, until flour is lightly browned—about 5 minutes. Remove from heat. Add meat-extract paste.
3. Stir beef broth and 3/4 cup Burgundy into flour mixture.
4. Over medium heat, bring just to boiling, stirring constantly. Reduce heat; simmer, uncovered, 10 minutes, stirring occasionally.
5. Strain sauce, discarding vegetables and spices. Return sauce to skillet. Add salt, pepper, parsley, and remaining 1/4 cup Burgundy; reheat gently—do not boil.
6. Taste; add more meat extract, if desired. Serve with filet of beef, steak, or hamburger.
Makes about 2 cups.

Mushroom Sauce

1. Prepare Bordelaise Sauce as directed.
2. Meanwhile, in small skillet, sauté 2 cups thickly sliced fresh mushrooms in 2 tablespoons hot butter, stirring, until tender—about 5 minutes.
3. Add to Bordelaise Sauce; reheat gently.
Makes about 3 cups.

Lemon-Chive Sauce

1/3 cup butter or margarine
2 tablespoons finely chopped chives
1 tablespoon lemon juice
1 teaspoon grated lemon peel
1/2 teaspoon salt
Dash pepper

1. Melt butter in small saucepan. Add remaining ingredients.
2. Beat thoroughly. Serve sauce hot. Delicious served over boiled potatoes, asparagus, broccoli, carrots, or baked fish.
Makes about 1/2 cup.

Cheese Sauce

Basic White Sauce
1/2 teaspoon dry mustard
2 cups grated sharp Cheddar cheese (1/2 lb)

1. Make Basic White Sauce.
2. Add mustard and grated cheese; stir, over low heat, just until cheese is melted and sauce is hot.
3. Serve over such vegetables as broccoli and asparagus; or use in casseroles.
Makes about 3 cups.

Apple-Cider Sauce for Ham

1 quart cider
2 lb McIntosh apples, pared and quartered
1/2 cup sugar

1. In a 4-quart saucepan, bring cider to boiling. Boil gently over medium heat about 20 minutes, or until cider is reduced to 1 cup.
2. Add quartered apples and sugar; toss gently to combine. Gently simmer apples, covered, until apples are soft—about 20 minutes. Stir once.
3. Serve warm with ham.
Makes 3-1/2 cups.

Sour-Cream Horseradish Sauce

1/2 cup dairy sour cream
2 tablespoons prepared horseradish
1/8 teaspoon salt

1. In small bowl, combine sour cream, horseradish, salt; mix well.
2. Refrigerate, covered, until serving time.
Makes 2/3 cup.

Creole Sauce

2 tablespoons bacon fat or salad oil
1/2 cup chopped onion
1 clove garlic, finely chopped
1/4 cup chopped green pepper
1 can (1 lb, 12 oz) tomatoes, undrained
1 teaspoon celery seed
1 bay leaf
1 teaspoon salt
2 teaspoons sugar
1/2 teaspoon chili powder
1 tablespoon chopped parsley

1. In hot bacon fat in medium saucepan, sauté onion, garlic, and pepper until tender—about 5 minutes.
2. Add remaining ingredients; simmer, uncovered, 45 minutes, or until mixture is thickened; stir occasionally.
Makes about 3 cups.

Gingersnap Sauce

2 bacon slices
1/4 cup finely chopped onion
1/3 cup gingersnap crumbs
  (about 6 gingersnaps)
1/4 cup red-wine or cider vinegar
1/4 cup light-brown sugar,
  firmly packed
1 can (10-1/2 oz) condensed beef broth,
  undiluted

1. In medium saucepan, sauté bacon until crisp. Drain on paper towels. Crumble, and set aside.
2. Drain off all but 1 tablespoon drippings from skillet. In drippings, sauté onion, stirring, until tender.
3. Add gingersnap crumbs, vinegar, brown sugar, and beef broth.
4. Bring to boiling, stirring. Reduce heat, simmer 5 minutes, stirring occasionally.
5. Remove from heat. Add bacon. Serve hot, over tongue or ham.
Makes about 1-1/2 cups.

Cumberland Sauce

2 cups ruby port
1/3 cup slivered orange peel
2/3 cup orange juice
2 tablespoons lemon juice
1 cup red-currant jelly
Dash cayenne

1. In medium saucepan, combine port and orange peel; cook over medium heat, uncovered, until reduced to 1-1/3 cups—10 to 15 minutes.
2. Stir in orange juice, lemon juice, currant jelly, and cayenne until well blended.
3. Bring to boiling; reduce heat, and simmer, uncovered, 10 minutes, or until jelly is melted. Serve hot or cold with ham or chicken.
Makes about 2-1/2 cups.

Hollandaise Sauce, page 22

Blender Hollandaise Sauce

3 egg yolks
2 tablespoons lemon juice
1/4 teaspoon salt
Dash cayenne
1/2 cup hot, melted butter or margarine

1. In blender container, combine egg yolks, lemon juice, salt, and cayenne. Cover; turn motor on and off; remove cover.
2. Turn motor to high speed; gradually add butter in steady stream. Turn off motor.
3. Serve immediately, or keep warm by placing blender container in 2 inches of hot (not boiling) water.
Makes 1 cup.

Mustard Sauce

2 tablespoons butter or margarine
1-1/2 tablespoons flour
1/2 teaspoon salt
1/8 teaspoon pepper
1 cup milk
1/4 cup prepared mustard
1 tablespoon sugar
1 tablespoon cider vinegar
1 teaspoon Worcestershire sauce

1. Melt butter in small saucepan; remove from heat. Stir in flour, salt, and pepper until smooth. Stir in milk. Bring to boiling over medium heat, stirring, until thick.
2. Gradually stir in mustard, sugar, vinegar, Worcestershire. Reduce heat, and simmer the mixture, stirring, 2 minutes. Serve warm.
Makes about 1-1/4 cups.

Mint-Jelly Sauce

1 jar (12 oz) mint jelly
1/2 cup coarsely chopped fresh mint

1. Melt jelly in small saucepan, over low heat, stirring occasionally.
2. Remove from heat. Stir in chopped mint. Serve warm, with lamb.
Makes about 1 cup.

Lobster Sauce

Salt
2 (6-oz size) frozen lobster tails
3 tablespoons butter or margarine
1-1/2 tablespoons flour
Dash paprika
1-1/4 cups light cream
2 egg yolks, slightly beaten
1/4 cup dry sherry

1. In medium saucepan, bring 4 cups water with 1/2 teaspoon salt to boiling. Add lobster tails; boil gently 5 minutes. Drain.
2. Remove lobster meat from shells. Cut meat into pieces—there should be about 1-1/4 cups. Set aside.
3. Melt butter in medium saucepan. Remove from heat. Stir in flour, 1/2 teaspoon salt, and the paprika. Gradually stir in cream.
4. Bring to boiling over medium heat, stirring until mixture thickens.
5. Stir a little hot mixture into egg yolks; return to saucepan.
6. Add sherry and lobster; bring just to boiling. Keep warm.
Makes 2 cups.

Maître d'Hôtel Butter Sauce

1/4 cup butter or margarine, melted
1 tablespoon lemon juice
1/2 teaspoon salt
1 tablespoon finely chopped parsley

1. Melt butter, stirring, in small skillet over low heat.
2. Remove from heat. Then stir in the remaining ingredients. Serve hot or cold with London broil, lamb chops, steaks.
Makes 1/3 cup.

Quick Mustard Sauce

1/2 cup mayonnaise or cooked salad dressing
1 teaspoon chopped onion
1/2 cup prepared mustard

1. Combine all the ingredients; mix well.
2. Refrigerate, covered, until ready to use. Serve with corned beef or ham.
Makes about 1 cup.

Parsley Butter

1/4 cup butter or regular margarine
2 tablespoons chopped parsley
1 tablespoon snipped chives

1. In small bowl, let butter soften slightly. Beat until smooth.
2. Mix in parsley and chives until well blended.
3. Turn out onto waxed paper; shape into a bar about 6 by 3/4 by 3/4 inches. Refrigerate or place in freezer 1 hour, or until hard.
4. Cut into 6 pieces. Serve on chicken, chops, steaks, hamburgers.
Makes 6 servings.

Red-Wine Steak Sauce

1 tablespoon minced shallot
3/4 cup dry red wine
1/2 cup soft butter or margarine
2 teaspoons chopped parsley
Salt
Pepper

1. Cook shallot in wine in small saucepan until liquid is reduced to 1/4 cup. Remove the saucepan from heat; cool.
2. With electric mixer, cream butter with parsley. Gradually beat in wine-shallot mixture. Season to taste with salt and pepper.
2. Serve at room temperature, with broiled steak. Makes about 3/4 cup.

Spanish Sauce

2 tablespoons butter or margarine
2/3 cup chopped onion
2 tablespoons chopped green pepper
1 clove garlic, finely chopped
2 cans (8-oz size) tomato sauce
1/4 cup chopped mixed sweet pickles
1 tablespoon sugar
1/4 teaspoon dried oregano leaves
1 teaspoon salt
1/8 teaspoon pepper

1. In hot butter in medium saucepan, sauté onion, green pepper, and garlic until tender—about 5 minutes.
2. Stir in remaining ingredients; bring to boiling.
3. Reduce heat; simmer gently 15 minutes, stirring occasionally.
4. Serve with omelet, or over meat loaf.
Makes 2 cups.

Seafood-Cocktail Sauce

1/2 cup chili sauce
1 tablespoon prepared horseradish
1 tablespoon lemon juice
2 teaspoons Worcestershire sauce
1/4 teaspoon salt
Dash cayenne

1. In small bowl, combine all ingredients; mix well. Refrigerate, covered, at least 3 hours.
2. Serve with cold boiled shrimp, crabmeat, or lobster.
Makes 2/3 cup.

Newburg Sauce

3 tablespoons butter or margarine
2 tablespoons flour
1/4 teaspoon salt
1/8 teaspoon paprika
3/4 cup light cream
1/2 cup fish stock*
2 egg yolks
2 tablespoons dry sherry
* Use liquid from cooking fish or bottled clam broth.

1. Melt butter in medium saucepan. Remove from heat; stir in flour, salt, and paprika until blended. Gradually stir in cream and fish stock.
2. Cook, over medium heat and stirring constantly, until mixture thickens and comes to boiling; boil 1 minute. Remove from heat.
3. In medium bowl, beat egg yolks well. Stir in about 1/2 cup hot sauce; then stir egg-yolk mixture into sauce in saucepan. Add sherry.
4. Cook over low heat, stirring, until heated through. Do not boil.
Makes 1-1/2 cups.

Rémoulade Sauce for Seafood

1 cup mayonnaise
1 tablespoon chopped onion
1 tablespoon chopped parsley
1 tablespoon chopped celery
2 tablespoons Dijon mustard
1 tablespoon prepared horseradish
1 teaspoon paprika
1/2 teaspoon salt
Dash Tabasco
1/4 cup salad oil
1 tablespoon vinegar
1/2 teaspoon Worcestershire sauce

1. Combine all ingredients in small bowl; mix until well blended.
2. Refrigerate several hours or overnight.
3. Serve with cold boiled shrimp, crabmeat, lobster, or with tomatoes.
Makes 1-1/2 cups.

Tartar Sauce

1 cup mayonnaise or cooked salad dressing
1/3 cup drained sweet-pickle relish
1 tablespoon lemon juice
1 tablespoon drained capers
1 tablespoon chopped parsley
1 teaspoon grated onion
1/8 teaspoon salt

1. Combine all ingredients; mix well.
2. Refrigerate, covered, until well chilled—at least 2 hours.
Makes 1-1/3 cups.

Sour-Cream Tartar Sauce

1 cup dairy sour cream
2 tablespoons sweet-pickle relish, drained
1/2 teaspoon salt
Dash Tabasco
1 teaspoon grated onion

1. Thoroughly combine all ingredients in a small bowl.
2. Refrigerate until well chilled. Serve with shrimp or clam fritters.
Makes about 1 cup.

Tarragon–Sour-Cream Sauce

2 egg yolks
1/4 teaspoon dried tarragon leaves
1 cup dairy sour cream
1 bay leaf, crumbled
1/4 teaspoon finely chopped garlic
1/2 teaspoon salt
1 teaspoon bottled capers, drained

1. In small bowl, with rotary beater, beat egg yolks with tarragon until thick and lemon-colored.
2. In saucepan, slowly heat sour cream, bay leaf, and garlic just until bubbles form around edge.
3. Strain; discard garlic and bay leaf. Pour sour cream back into saucepan.
4. Pour a little hot sour cream into egg yolks, stirring; return to saucepan.
5. Over low heat, bring just to boiling point, stirring constantly. Add salt and capers. Delicious served with salmon or chicken.
Makes 1 cup.

Don's Barbecue Sauce

1/3 cup vinegar
3 tablespoons brown sugar
1 tablespoon prepared mustard
1/2 teaspoon pepper
2 teaspoons salt
1/4 teaspoon cayenne
2 thick lemon slices
1 medium onion, sliced
1/3 cup butter or margarine
2/3 cup catsup
3 tablespoons Worcestershire sauce

In medium saucepan, combine vinegar, 1/3 cup water, the brown sugar, mustard, pepper, salt, cayenne, lemon slices, onion, and butter; stir to mix well. Simmer, uncovered, 20 minutes. Add catsup and Worcestershire, bring just to boiling. For spareribs, chicken, frankfurters.
Makes 2 cups.

Barbecue Sauce, California Style

1/3 cup cider vinegar
1/4 cup chili sauce
1 can (8 oz) tomato sauce
1/4 cup chopped onion
2 tablespoons brown sugar
1 tablespoon Worcestershire sauce
1 teaspoon dry mustard

In medium saucepan, combine all of sauce ingredients. Bring to boiling; reduce heat, and simmer, uncovered and stirring occasionally, 30 minutes. For chicken, spareribs, hamburgers, steak.
Makes 1-1/3 cups.

Gravy

Today's low-temperature methods of roasting meats have reduced the amount of drippings in the roast pan. For this reason, bottled gravy flavorings are frequently used to make the flavor richer.

The use of beef broth in cans or bouillon cubes helps enrich the taste. A wire whisk is an invaluable tool in stirring up a smooth gravy. Be careful to *stir* it with a flat, circular motion.

Brown Gravy

1/4 cup meat drippings
3 tablespoons flour
1 can (10-1/2 oz) condensed beef broth
1/2 teaspoon salt
Dash pepper

1. Lift roast from pan, and place on heated platter. Let stand 20 minutes.
2. Pour off drippings in roasting pan. Skim fat from surface and discard. Return 1/4 cup drippings to pan.
3. Stir in flour, to make a smooth mixture; brown it slightly over low heat, stirring to loosen any brown bits in pan.
4. Add water to beef broth to measure 2 cups; gradually stir into flour mixture; add salt and pepper.
5. Bring to boiling, stirring gravy until smooth, and bubbly.
Makes 2 cups.

Giblet Gravy

Turkey giblets and neck, washed
1 celery stalk, cut up
1 medium onion, peeled and quartered
1 medium carrot, pared and cup up
1 teaspoon salt
4 whole black peppercorns
1 bay leaf
1 can (10-1/2 oz) condensed chicken broth,
   undiluted
1/3 cup flour

1. Refrigerate liver until ready to use.
2. Place rest of giblets and neck in a 2-quart saucepan. Add 3 cups water, the celery, onion, carrot, salt, peppercorns, and bay leaf.
3. Bring to boiling; reduce heat; simmer, covered, 2-1/2 hours, or until giblets are tender. Add liver; simmer 15 minutes longer. Discard neck. Remove giblets from broth, and chop coarsely. Set aside.
4. Strain cooking broth, pressing vegetables through sieve with broth. Measure broth; add enough undiluted canned broth to make 2-1/2 cups. Set aside.
5. When turkey has been removed from roasting pan, pour drippings into a 1-cup measure. Skim fat from surface, and discard. Return 1/3 cup drippings to roasting pan.
6. Stir in flour until smooth. Stir, over very low heat, to brown flour slightly. Remove from heat. Gradually stir in broth.
7. Bring to boiling, stirring; reduce heat; simmer, stirring, 5 minutes, or until gravy is thickened and smooth. Add giblets; simmer 5 minutes.
Makes about 3 cups.

Chicken Gravy

3 tablespoons roast-chicken drippings
3 tablespoons flour
1-1/2 cups canned chicken broth, undiluted
1/2 teaspoon salt
1/8 teaspoon pepper
1 teaspoon coarsely snipped fresh marjoram
   leaves, or 1/2 teaspoon dried marjoram
   leaves (optional)

1. Pour off drippings from roasting pan. Return 3 tablespoons drippings to pan.
2. Add flour; stir to make a smooth paste. Gradually stir in broth; add rest of ingredients.
3. Bring to boiling, stirring. Mixture will be thickened and smooth. Simmer, stirring, 1 minute longer. Serve hot, with roast chicken.
Makes 1-1/2 cups.

Burgundy Gravy

6 tablespoons roast-beef drippings
1/4 cup unsifted all-purpose flour
1/2 teaspoon salt
Dash pepper
2 cans (10-1/2-oz size) condensed beef broth,
   undiluted
1/2 cup Burgundy

1. Return the 6 tablespoons reserved drippings to the roasting pan. Stir in the flour, salt, and pepper to make a smooth mixture.
2. Gradually add the beef broth and Burgundy to the flour mixture, stirring until it is smooth and browned bits in pan are dissolved.
3. Bring to boiling, stirring. Reduce heat, and simmer, stirring, 5 minutes longer. Taste, and add more salt and pepper, if necessary.
Makes 3 cups.

Soups

Whether it's a chowder, bouillon, broth, or "cream of"—whether it's served as a first course, a meal in itself, or even dessert—a really good soup is great! And most soups are even better, made one day and served the next.

Serve one of these first-course soups by the fire right in your own living room as a convivial way to start dinner.

Hot Tomato Consommé

2 cans (1-lb size) tomatoes, undrained
2 cans (10-1/2-oz size) condensed chicken broth,
    undiluted
1/2 cup celery tops, cut up
4 sprigs parsley
12 whole black peppercorns
1 bay leaf
1 tablespoon sugar
Salt
Red food color
Chopped parsley

1. Place tomatoes in large saucepan; crush with potato masher. Add chicken broth, 1 cup water, the celery, parsley sprigs, peppercorns, bay leaf.
2. Bring to boiling, stirring occasionally. Reduce heat, and simmer about 30 minutes.
3. Strain through a fine sieve. Add sugar, salt to taste, and a few drops food color. Keep hot.
4. At serving time, pour into mugs or soup bowls. Sprinkle with parsley.
Makes 6 servings.

French Onion Soup

1/4 cup butter or margarine
4 cups thinly sliced onion
4 cans (10-1/2-oz size) condensed beef broth,
    undiluted
1 teaspoon salt
6 slices French bread, 1 inch thick
2 tablespoons grated Parmesan cheese
2 pkg (1-oz size) process Gruyere cheese, grated

1. In hot butter in large kettle, sauté onion until golden—about 8 minutes.
2. Add beef broth and salt; bring to boiling. Reduce heat, and simmer, covered, 30 minutes.
3. Meanwhile, toast bread on both sides in broiler. Sprinkle one side with Parmesan and Gruyère cheese; broil just until cheese is bubbly—about 1 minute.
4. To serve: Pour soup into tureen or individual soup bowls. Float toast, cheese side up, on soup.
Makes 6 servings.

Royal Consommé Madrilène

Royal Custard:
1 egg
1/3 cup light cream
1/4 teaspoon salt
Dash white pepper

2 cans (13-oz size) consommé madrilène
1/2 cup dry sherry or Madeira
1 tablespoon lemon juice

1. Preheat oven to 300F. In small bowl, with rotary beater, beat egg, cream, salt, and pepper until well blended but not foamy.
2. Strain into a buttered 2-cup custard cup. Set custard cup in shallow pan on oven rack. Pour hot water into pan to 1/2-inch level. Cover custard cup with piece of waxed paper.
3. Bake 25 to 30 minutes, or until knife inserted in center comes out clean. Remove custard cup from water. Cool; then refrigerate until well chilled.
4. Just before serving: In medium saucepan, heat madrilène just to boiling.

5. Cut chilled custard into 1/3-inch cubes. Place cubes in 6 consommé cups, dividing evenly.
6. Stir sherry and lemon juice into madrilene. Ladle over custard cubes in consommé cups.
Makes 6 servings.

Cream Soups

For just the thing to set off a special occasion or a holiday dinner, try one of these cream soups like the Winter Squash or Pumpkin Soup, the Clam Broth with Tarragon or the Cheddar Cheese Soup.

Green Cabbage Soup

4 cups shredded green cabbage
2 tablespoons butter or margarine, melted
1 cup grated pared raw potato
1/2 cup finely chopped onion
2 tablespoons flour
1 teaspoon salt
1/4 teaspoon pepper
1/2 teaspoon mace
3 cups milk
1/2 cup crumbled crisp-cooked bacon
1/4 cup grated Parmesan cheese
2 tablespoons finely chopped parsley

1. In 1/2 inch boiling water in large saucepan, cook cabbage, covered, 5 minutes; drain well.
2. Add butter, potato, onion, and flour. Cook, stirring, over low heat, 3 to 4 minutes—do not brown.
3. Add salt, pepper, mace, milk, and 2 cups water; bring to boiling, stirring constantly. Reduce heat; simmer, covered, 20 minutes, or until vegetables are very tender.
4. Blend soup, a third at a time, in electric blender, covered and at high speed, 1-1/2 minutes. Remove soup to saucepan after each blending (or serve soup unblended).
5. Reheat gently, stirring. Add bacon, cheese, and parsley.
Makes about 1-1/2 quarts.

Clam Broth with Tarragon

1/4 cup butter or margarine
3 white onions, chopped
1 teaspoon dried tarragon leaves
2 tablespoons flour
1/2 cup dry white wine
1 bottle (8-oz) clam juice
1-1/2 cups light cream
1/2 teaspoon sugar
2 egg yolks

1. In hot butter in medium saucepan, sauté onion until tender—about 5 minutes. Add tarragon; cook, stirring, over low heat 1 minute.
2. Add flour; cook, stirring with wire whisk, over low heat 1 minute.
3. Slowly add wine and clam juice, stirring constantly with wire whisk. Bring just to boiling; strain into saucepan to remove onion.
4. Stir in 1-1/4 cups light cream. Cook, stirring, over low heat several minutes; add sugar.
5. Meanwhile, in small bowl, combine egg yolks with remaining light cream; mix well. Strain through small sieve into hot cream mixture. Cook, stirring, 1 more minute, or until slightly thickened. Serve hot.
Makes 3 cups; 6 to 8 servings.

Cheddar Cheese Soup

4 tablespoons butter or margarine
1/4 cup finely chopped onion
1/2 cup finely chopped green pepper
1/2 cup finely chopped carrot
5 tablespoons flour
3 cans (10-1/2-oz size) condensed chicken broth, undiluted
3 cups grated sharp natural Cheddar cheese (3/4 lb)
2 cups milk
1/4 teaspoon salt
Dash pepper
1/2 cup croutons (optional)
Chopped parsley

1. In hot butter in 3-quart saucepan, cook onion, green pepper, and carrot 10 minutes, stirring occasionally.
2. Remove from heat; stir in flour, and mix well. Cook one minute, stirring constantly.
3. Add chicken broth to vegetable mixture. Bring to a boil, stirring constantly.
4. Gradually stir in cheese; cook, over medium heat and stirring, until cheese has melted. Gradually add milk. Season with salt and pepper. Bring just to boiling, but do not boil.
5. Serve with croutons, and sprinkle with the parsley.
Makes 6 to 8 servings.

Cream-of-Peanut Soup

1/4 cup butter or margarine
1 cup finely chopped celery
1/3 cup finely chopped onion
1 tablespoon flour
1 cup chunk-style peanut butter
3 cans (13-3/4-oz size) chicken broth
2 cups heavy cream

1. In hot butter in 4-quart saucepan, sauté celery and onion until tender—about 5 minutes.
2. Remove from heat. Add flour and peanut butter, stirring until peanut butter is melted. Gradually stir in chicken broth.
3. Bring to boiling; reduce heat, and simmer, uncovered, 10 minutes, stirring occasionally.
4. Stir in heavy cream; heat a few minutes longer, until heated through.
Makes 2-1/4 quarts; 8 to 10 servings.

Cream-of-Pumpkin Soup

2 tablespoons butter or margarine
1/2 lb yellow onions, thinly sliced
1/2 tablespoon flour
1 can (10-1/2 oz) condensed chicken broth, undiluted
1 can (1 lb) pumpkin
2 cups milk
1 cup light cream
1 teaspoon salt
1/8 teaspoon pepper
1/4 teaspoon ginger
1/8 teaspoon cinnamon

1. In hot butter in 6-quart Dutch oven, sauté onion, stirring occasionally, 10 minutes, or until tender. Remove from heat.
2. Stir flour into onion; gradually stir in chicken broth. Bring to boiling; reduce heat; simmer, covered, 10 minutes.
3. Ladle mixture into electric blender. Blend, covered, at high speed one minute, or until completely smooth.
4. Return to Dutch oven; blend in pumpkin smoothly with wire whisk. Add milk, cream, 2 cups water, and the seasonings; beat with wire whisk to blend.
5. Heat soup slowly over medium heat just to boiling; reduce heat, and simmer, covered, 15 minutes, stirring occasionally. Serve hot.
Makes 2 quarts; 6 to 8 servings.

Lobster Bisque

1 small carrot, sliced
1 medium onion, peeled and quartered
1 teaspoon salt
2 whole black peppercorns
1 bay leaf
Pinch dried thyme leaves
1 sprig parsley
3/4 cup dry white wine
3 (5-oz size) frozen rock-lobster tails, unthawed
1/2 cup butter or margarine
3 tablespoons flour
2 cups heavy cream
1 to 2 tablespoons sherry (optional)
Paprika

1. In 4-quart saucepan, combine carrot, onion, salt, peppercorns, bay leaf, thyme, parsley, and 6 cups water.
2. Add wine and lobster tails; bring just to boiling. Reduce heat; simmer, covered, 5 minutes.
3. Remove lobster tails from cooking liquid; cool. Continue to cook liquid, uncovered, about 45 minutes, to reduce to about half of original volume. Strain; liquid should measure 2 cups.
4. Melt butter in same saucepan. Remove from heat; stir in flour to make a smooth mixture.
5. Gradually add reserved cooking liquid, stirring until smooth. Bring to boiling, stirring; reduce heat; simmer 10 minutes, stirring occasionally.
6. Meanwhile, remove meat from shells; cut into very small pieces.
7. Gradually add cream, then lobster and sherry. Reheat gently—do not boil. Sprinkle with paprika before serving.
Makes 5 cups; 6 servings.

Cream-of-Winter-Squash Soup

1 butternut squash* (about 3 lb)
2 cans (10-1/2-oz size) condensed chicken broth, undiluted
1/4 teaspoon salt
Dash white pepper
1 cup heavy cream
1/4 teaspoon nutmeg
* Or use 3 pkg (12-oz size) frozen squash, partially thawed.

1. Preheat oven to 400F. Bake whole squash about 1 hour, or until tender when pierced with a fork.
2. Let squash cool slightly. Cut in half lengthwise; discard seeds. With a spoon, scoop squash pulp from the skin.
3. In electric blender, combine half of squash pulp and 1 can broth; blend at low speed until well combined, then at high speed until smooth. Turn into bowl. Repeat with remaining squash and broth. Stir in salt and pepper.
4. Refrigerate soup, covered, overnight.
5. At serving time, heat squash mixture just to boiling. Gradually stir in 1/2 cup cream; cook slowly until heated through. Taste for seasoning, adding more salt and pepper if necessary.
6. Meanwhile, beat remaining cream just until stiff.
7. Serve soup very hot. Garnish each serving with a spoonful of whipped cream; sprinkle with nutmeg.
Makes 6 servings.

Spring Lettuce Soup

2 medium heads iceberg lettuce, or 1 large head
    romaine, shredded (about 8 cups)
1-1/2 cups chicken broth
1-1/2 cups light cream
1/4 cup butter or margarine
1 teaspoon sugar
1/2 teaspoon salt
1/8 teaspoon nutmeg
Dash pepper

1. In 4-quart kettle, combine shredded lettuce and chicken broth; bring to boiling over medium heat. Reduce heat, and simmer, covered, 10 minutes, or just until lettuce is soft.
2. In electric-blender container, place one half lettuce and liquid; cover, and blend at high speed 1 minute. Pour into bowl. Repeat with remaining lettuce and liquid. Pour back into kettle.
3. Add cream, butter, sugar, salt, nutmeg, and pepper to mixture in kettle. Cook over medium heat, stirring, until butter is melted and soup is hot.
4. Beat mixture with a rotary beater, to make very smooth. Serve soup at once.
Makes 8 to 10 servings.

Hearty Soups

Nothing is as soul-satisfying on a wintry day as a pot of hearty, meal-in-itself soup simmering on the stove. And there are few such soul-satisfying occupations on such a day as putting one together from scratch. Here, a collection of substantial soups and chowders from all over the world: a real hot Russian borsch, an Indian mulligatawny, and a number of American favorites, such as the New England clam chowder and the Beef-and-Vegetable Soup.

Hearty Beef-and-Vegetable Soup

2 lb shin of beef
Large marrowbone
1 tablespoon salt
4 cups thinly sliced cabbage (1 lb)
1-1/2 cups chopped onion
6 carrots, pared and cut in 3-inch pieces (1/2 lb)
3/4 cup chopped celery
1/4 cup chopped green pepper
1 can (1 lb, 12 oz) tomatoes, undrained
1/2 pkg (10-oz size) frozen lima beans
1/2 pkg (9-oz size) frozen cut green beans
1/2 pkg (10-oz size) frozen peas
1 can (12 oz) whole-kernel corn, drained
1 pared potato, cubed (1 cup)
2 tablespoons chopped parsley
1 can (6 oz) tomato paste
1/2 teaspoon ground cloves
1 teaspoon sugar
2 teaspoons salt
1/2 teaspoon pepper

1. Place beef, marrowbone, 1 tablespoon salt, and 4 quarts water in very large kettle. Cover; bring to boiling. Skim surface.
2. Add cabbage, onion, carrot, celery, green pepper, and tomatoes.
3. Bring to boiling; simmer, covered, 30 minutes.
4. Add remaining ingredients; simmer, covered, 3-1/2 hours.
5. Remove meat and bone; discard bone.
6. Let meat cool. Cut into cubes; add to soup. Refrigerate overnight.
7. Next day: Remove all fat from surface, and discard. Before serving, slowly heat soup to boiling. (Store leftover soup, covered, in refrigerator.)
Makes 6-1/2 quarts.

Beef Borsch with Sour Cream

4-lb shin of beef
1 large marrowbone
Salt
1 can (1 lb) tomatoes, undrained
1 medium onion, peeled and quartered
1 stalk celery, cut up
3 parsley sprigs
6 whole black peppercorns
1 bay leaf
2 cups shredded pared beets (4 medium)
3 cups coarsely shredded cabbage (1 lb)
1-1/2 cups thickly sliced pared carrots (4 medium)
1 cup chopped onion
2 tablespoons snipped fresh dill
1/4 cup cider vinegar
2 tablespoons sugar
Dairy sour cream

1. Day before serving: In a deep, 8-quart kettle, place beef, marrowbone, 1 tablespoon salt, and 2 quarts water. Cover, and bring to boiling; skim surface. Reduce heat, and simmer, covered, 1 hour.
2. Add tomatoes, quartered onion, celery, parsley, black peppercorns, and bay leaf; simmer, covered, 2 hours longer. Remove from heat.
3. Lift out beef, and set aside. Remove marrowbone, and discard. Strain soup; skim off fat. (You should have about 9 cups liquid.) Return soup and beef to kettle.
4. Add beets, cabbage, carrots, chopped onion, dill, vinegar, sugar, and 1 teaspoon salt; bring to boiling. Reduce heat, and simmer, covered, 30 minutes, or until beef and vegetables are tender. Remove from heat. Refrigerate overnight.
5. Next day, remove beef from soup; cut into cubes; return beef to soup.
6. Heat gently to boiling. Turn into tureen. Top with spoonfuls of sour cream. If desired, garnish with snipped dill.
Makes about 3 quarts; 8 to 10 servings.

Calcutta Mulligatawny Soup

4- to 5-lb roasting chicken, cut up
1/3 cup unsifted all-purpose flour
1/3 cup butter or margarine
1-1/2 cups chopped onion
2 cups chopped carrot
2 cups chopped celery
1-1/2 cups chopped, pared tart apple
1-1/2 tablespoons curry powder
4 teaspoons salt
3/4 teaspoon mace
1/2 teaspoon pepper
1/4 teaspoon chili powder
3/4 cup canned flaked coconut
1 cup apple juice
1 cup light cream
1-1/2 cups hot cooked white rice
1/2 cup chopped parsley

1. Wash chicken; pat dry with paper towels. Roll chicken in flour, coating completely. Reserve any remaining flour.
2. In hot butter in large kettle or Dutch oven, sauté chicken until well browned on all sides. Remove chicken from kettle, and set aside.
3. Add to kettle the onion, carrot, celery, apple, and any remaining flour; cook, stirring, 5 minutes.
4. Add curry powder, salt, mace, pepper, chili powder, coconut, chicken, and 6 cups cold water; mix well. Bring to boiling; reduce heat, and simmer, covered, 2 hours. Stir occasionally. Remove from heat.
5. Skim fat from soup. Remove skin and bone from chicken. Cut chicken meat into large pieces; set aside.
6. Put soup through blender. Return to kettle, with chicken. Stir in apple juice and light cream; reheat.
7. To serve: Place 1 heaping tablespoon rice in each of 6 to 8 bowls. Add soup. Sprinkle each serving with parsley.
Makes 2-1/2 quarts; 6 to 8 servings.

Old-Fashioned Split-Pea Soup

1-1/2 cups quick-cooking split green peas
2-1/2 lb fully cooked ham shank
2/3 cup coarsely chopped onion
1/4 cup cut-up carrot
1/2 cup coarsely chopped celery
2 parsley sprigs
1 clove garlic
1 bay leaf, crumbled
1/2 teaspoon sugar
1/4 teaspoon salt
1/8 teaspoon dried thyme leaves
1/8 teaspoon pepper
2 cans (13-3/4-oz size) clear chicken broth

1. In 3-1/2-quart kettle, combine peas and 1 quart water; bring to boiling. Reduce heat; simmer, covered, 45 minutes. Add more water if necessary.
2. Add ham shank and rest of ingredients; simmer, covered, 1-1/2 hours.
3. Remove ham shank from soup; cool; cut ham from bone; dice.
4. Press vegetables and liquid through coarse sieve.
5. Return to kettle. Add ham; reheat slowly, uncovered, until thoroughly hot, 15 minutes.
Makes 8 servings.

Oyster Stew

2 pints fresh oysters in liquid, or 2 dozen oysters and 2/3 cup liquid
1/4 cup butter or regular margarine
1/2 teaspoon salt
1/2 teaspoon celery salt
1/8 teaspoon pepper
2 cups light cream
1 cup milk
Paprika
Chopped parsley
Oyster crackers

1. Drain oysters, reserving liquid.
2. Heat butter in 3-quart saucepan. Add oysters; cook 3 to 5 minutes, or until edges begin to curl.
3. Add salt, celery salt, pepper, cream, milk, and oyster liquid. Heat, over medium heat, just until bubbles form around edge of pan. Do not boil.
4. Sprinkle with paprika and the chopped parsley. Serve with oyster crackers.
Makes 4 to 6 servings.

Corn-and-Clam Chowder

3 slices bacon, cut up
1-1/2 cups chopped onion
2 tablespoons butter or margarine
2 tablespoons flour
2 cans (8-oz size) minced clams or 1-1/2 dozen fresh clams
1 can (12 oz) whole-kernel corn
2 cups diced, pared potato
1 teaspoon salt
1/8 teaspoon black pepper

1. In 6-quart Dutch oven or kettle, sauté bacon slightly. Add onion and butter, and sauté until onion is golden—about 5 minutes. Remove from heat. Add flour, stirring until smooth.
2. Drain canned or fresh clams, reserving liquid. Chop fresh clams coarsely. Drain corn, reserving liquid.
3. Add clams, corn, potato, salt, pepper to Dutch oven. Combine clam and corn liquids; add water to measure 4 cups. Add to Dutch oven.
4. Bring to boiling; reduce heat, and simmer, covered, 25 to 30 minutes, or until potato is tender. Serve hot.
Makes 7 cups; 6 to 8 servings.

Corn Chowder

4 slices bacon, finely chopped
1 medium onion, thinly sliced
4 cups cubed, pared potatoes (about 4 medium)
4 cups fresh corn kernels,* cut from cob
1 cup heavy cream
1 teaspoon sugar
1/4 cup butter or margarine
2-1/2 teaspoons salt
1/4 teaspoon white pepper
2 cups milk
* Or use 2 pkg (10-oz size) frozen whole kernel
  corn, thawed.

1. In large saucepan with cover, sauté bacon, over moderate heat, until golden.
2. Add onion, potatoes, and 1 cup water. Cover; bring to boiling, and simmer about 10 minutes, or until potatoes are tender but not mushy.
3. Remove cover, and set saucepan aside.
4. In medium saucepan with cover, combine corn, cream, sugar, and butter. Simmer, covered and over low heat, 10 minutes.
5. Add to potato mixture with remaining ingredients. Cook, stirring occasionally and over low heat, until heated through—do not boil.
Makes 8 to 10 servings.

Manhattan Clam Chowder

4 bacon slices, diced
1 cup sliced onion (about 4)
1 cup diced carrots (about 4)
1 cup diced celery
1 tablespoon chopped parsley
1 can (1 lb, 12 oz) tomatoes
2 jars (11-1/2-oz size) clams
2 teaspoons salt
4 whole black peppercorns
1 bay leaf
1-1/2 teaspoons dried thyme leaves
3 medium potatoes, pared and diced (3-1/2 cups)

1. In large kettle, sauté bacon until almost crisp.
2. Add onion; cook until tender—about 5 minutes.
3. Add carrots, celery, and parsley; cook over low heat 5 minutes, stirring occasionally.
4. Drain tomatoes; reserve liquid in 1-quart measure. Add tomatoes to vegetables in kettle.
5. Drain clams; set clams aside. Add clam liquid to tomato liquid. Add water to make 1-1/2 quarts liquid. Pour into kettle. Add salt, peppercorns, bay leaf, and thyme.
6. Bring to boiling. Reduce heat; cover, and simmer 45 minutes.
7. Add potatoes; cover, and cook 20 minutes.
8. Chop clams; add to chowder. Simmer, uncovered, 15 minutes. Serve hot.
Makes 8 large servings.

New England Clam Chowder

2 slices bacon
1 cup finely chopped onion
2 cups cubed pared potato
1 teaspoon salt
Dash pepper
1 pint shucked fresh clams, or 2 cans (10-1/2-oz
  size) minced clams
2 cups half-and-half
2 tablespoons butter or margarine

1. Chop bacon coarsely. Sauté in large kettle until almost crisp. Add onions; cook about 5 minutes.
2. Add cubed potato, salt, pepper, and 1 cup water. Cook, uncovered, 15 minutes, or until potato is fork-tender.
3. Meanwhile, drain clams, reserving clam liquid. Chop clams coarsely.
4. Add clams, 1/2 cup clam liquid, the half-and-half, and butter to kettle; mix well. Heat about 3 minutes; do not boil.
Makes 4 servings.

New England Fish Chowder

2 lb halibut fillets
2-1/2 teaspoons salt
3 cups cut-up pared potatoes
6 bacon slices, chopped
1 cup chopped onion
2 cups milk
2 cups light cream
1/4 teaspoon pepper

1. Place halibut, with 2 cups water, in large saucepan; bring to boiling.
2. Reduce heat; simmer, covered, 15 minutes, or until fish flakes easily with fork. Remove fish; set aside.
3. To fish broth, add 1 teaspoon salt and the potatoes; boil, covered, about 8 minutes, or until potatoes are almost tender.
4. Meanwhile, sauté bacon until crisp; remove, and drain on paper towels.
5. Sauté onion in bacon fat until tender—about 5 minutes.
6. Flake fish. Add, along with bacon, onion, remaining salt, and rest of ingredients, to potatoes; slowly bring to boiling.
7. Reduce heat; simmer, uncovered, 15 minutes.
Makes 3 quarts; 8 large servings.

Lentil Soup with Ham

2-1b fully cooked ham shank*
1-1/2 cups dried lentils
3 tablespoons butter or margarine
1/2 cup chopped celery
1/2 cup chopped leek
1/2 cup chopped onion
1 small clove garlic, crushed
1-3/4 teaspoons salt
1/4 teaspoon dried thyme leaves
1/4 teaspoon coarsely ground black pepper
1 cup sliced frankfurters (about 3)
Dairy sour cream
Chopped parsley
* Lightly smoked, if desired.

1. Trim excess fat from ham shank.
2. In large kettle, combine ham shank and lentils with 5 cups cold water; bring to boiling.
3. Reduce heat; simmer, covered, 1 hour.
4. Meanwhile, melt butter in medium skillet. Add celery, leek, onion, and garlic; sauté 5 minutes.
5. Add sautéed vegetables, salt, thyme, and pepper, along with 2 cups water, to ham shank and lentils. Simmer, covered, until lentils are tender—about 30 minutes.
6. Remove ham from soup; cool. Then cut ham from bone, and dice.
7. With potato masher, mash vegetables, right in kettle; leave some lentils whole.
8. Add diced ham to soup, along with frankfurters; simmer, covered, 30 minutes longer. (For a very thick soup, simmer uncovered.)
9. Serve topped with sour cream and parsley.
Makes 8 cups; 8 servings.

Meatballs-and-Sauerkraut Soup

Meatballs:
1-1/2 lb ground chuck
1 egg, slightly beaten
1/2 cup soft bread crumbs (1 slice)
1/4 teaspoon salt
2 tablespoons chopped parsley
2 tablespoons butter or margarine

1 can (10-1/2 oz) condensed beef broth, undiluted
1 can (14 oz) sauerkraut, undrained
1 can (1 lb, 12 oz) tomatoes, undrained
1 env (1-3/8 oz) dry onion-soup mix
1 cup sliced pared carrots (2 or 3 medium)
1/2 cup chopped celery tops
1 teaspoon salt
1/8 teaspoon pepper
1 bay leaf
1 tablespoon sugar
2 tablespoons chopped parsley

1. Make Meatballs: In medium bowl, combine chuck, egg, 3 tablespoons water, the bread crumbs, 1/4 teaspoon salt, and 2 tablespoons parsley, mix lightly. With hands, lightly shape into 28 balls, using 1 rounded tablespoon for each.
2. In hot butter in Dutch oven or 4-1/2-quart kettle, sauté meatballs, a single layer at a time, until browned all over. Drain off fat. Set meatballs aside.
3. In same kettle, combine 2 cups water, the beef broth, sauerkraut, tomatoes, onion-soup mix, carrots, celery, salt, pepper, bay leaf, and sugar; bring to boiling. Reduce heat, and simmer, covered and stirring occasionally to break up tomatoes, 30 minutes. Add meatballs; simmer 20 minutes longer.
4. Serve in tureen or individual bowls. Garnish with chopped parsley.
Makes 2-1/2 quarts; 8 servings.
Note: This soup is even better made day before and reheated.

Cold Soups

Our refreshing cold soups take the heat off any warm-weather meal. On a hot summer evening, serve tall goblets of icy-cold avocado or tomato frappé as a buffet first course or serve the Gazpacho, if it's a small dinner party. Try the Cantaloupe Soup for brunch; it's a great dessert too.

Jellied Consommé with Red Caviar

1 env unflavored gelatine
4 cans (10-1/2-oz size) condensed beef consommé,
    undiluted (not chilled)
1/2 cup heavy cream, whipped
1 jar (4 oz) red caviar

1. In small saucepan, sprinkle gelatine over 1 cup consommé, to soften—2 to 3 minutes. Heat over low heat, stirring constantly, until gelatine is dissolved.
2. Turn into a 13-by-9-by-2-inch baking pan or 3-quart shallow baking dish. Add remaining consommé, stirring until well mixed.
3. Refrigerate until firm—at least 4 hours.
4. At serving time, cut consommé into about 1/2-inch cubes. Remove from pan with spatula, and place in bouillon cups or sherbet glasses. Spoon a heaping tablespoonful whipped cream on each serving. Sprinkle red caviar over cream. If desired, serve consommé in a large bowl set in ice.
Makes 8 to 10 servings.

Cream-of-Artichoke Soup

2 (1-1/2- to 2-lb size) artichokes
1 can (10-1/2 oz) condensed chicken broth,
    undiluted
2 tablespoons lemon juice
1/4 cup chopped onion
1/4 teaspoon dried thyme leaves
1/8 teaspoon pepper
1 cup light cream

1. Trim stalks from base of artichokes; remove tough outer leaves. Wash artichokes under cold running water; drain.
2. Cut artichokes lengthwise into quarters. Remove inner purple leaves and chokes.
3. In 3-1/2-quart saucepan, combine artichokes, chicken broth, lemon juice, 1 cup water, the onion, thyme, and pepper. Bring to boiling; reduce heat, and simmer, covered, 30 minutes, or until artichokes are tender.
4. Remove artichokes from liquid, reserving liquid. Remove leaves; cut up hearts. With back of knife or spoon, scoop flesh from artichoke leaves.
5. In blender, combine strained cooking liquid, artichoke flesh and hearts, and cream. Blend, at high speed, 2 minutes, or until smooth. Refrigerate, covered, several hours or overnight, or until well chilled.
Makes 4 cups; 6 servings.

Chilled Cream-of-Asparagus Soup

1 pkg (10 oz) frozen cut asparagus
1 can (10-1/2 oz) condensed cream-of-asparagus
    soup, undiluted
1-1/4 cups milk
1/4 cup dairy sour cream
1/2 teaspoon salt
1/8 teaspoon pepper
1/4 teaspoon dried basil leaves

1. In medium saucepan, bring 1/2 cup water to boiling. Add frozen asparagus; simmer, covered, 5 minutes.
2. In electric blender, combine remaining ingredients; add asparagus and cooking liquid. Blend, at high speed, 2 minutes, or until mixture is smooth.
3. Refrigerate, covered, until very cold—several hours or overnight. To serve, garnish with a spoonful of sour cream or asparagus spears, if desired.
Makes 3 cups; 4 servings.

Avocado Frappé

2 ripe avocados (1-1/2 lb)
1 tablespoon grated orange peel
1/8 teaspoon ginger
1 teaspoon salt
Dash pepper
3 cups milk

1. Peel avocados; remove pits. Cut flesh into chunks. Put in electric-blender container with orange peel, ginger, salt, and pepper. Blend, adding milk a little at a time, until mixture is smooth.
2. Refrigerate, covered (see Note), several hours or overnight, or until well chilled. To serve, garnish with avocado slices, if desired.
Makes 4 cups; 5 or 6 servings.
Note: Place plastic film directly on surface of soup to prevent darkening.

Senegalese Soup

1 medium onion, chopped
1 medium carrot, pared and diced
1 stalk celery, sliced
3 tablespoons butter or margarine
2 tablespoons curry powder
1-1/2 tablespoons flour
1 tablespoon tomato paste
2 cans (10-1/2-oz size) condensed chicken broth
1 tablespoon almond paste
1 tablespoon red-currant jelly
10 whole cloves
1 cinnamon stick
1-1/2 cups heavy cream
2 tablespoons shredded coconut

1. In large saucepan, sauté onion, carrot, and celery in hot butter until golden—about 5 minutes. Remove from heat.
2. Stir in curry powder and flour until well blended. Add tomato paste; cook, stirring, 1 minute.
3. Gradually stir in undiluted chicken broth and 2 cups water; bring to boiling, stirring constantly. Stir in almond paste and jelly; add cloves and cinnamon stick; simmer, uncovered and stirring occasionally, 1/2 hour.
4. Strain; cool. Then refrigerate until very well chilled—several hours or overnight.
5. When ready to serve, skim off any fat from surface. Blend in cream. Serve in bouillon cups. Top each serving with coconut.
Makes 8 to 10 servings.

Frozen Tomato Frappé

1 tablespoon butter or margarine
1/3 cup finely chopped onion
2 teaspoons sugar
1 teaspoon lemon juice
1/2 teaspoon Worcestershire sauce
1 can (1 qt, 14 oz) tomato juice
Lemon wedges
Crackers

1. In hot butter in small skillet, sauté onion until golden. Turn into blender container; add sugar, lemon juice, Worcestershire, and half of tomato juice.
2. Blend, at high speed, 1 minute, or until smooth. Turn into 13-by-9-by-2-inch baking dish. Stir in remaining tomato juice. Cover with foil or plastic film; freeze overnight.
3. One hour before serving, remove from freezer. Let stand at room temperature until it begins to melt.
4. Break up with a fork, and beat until no large pieces remain. Blend half at a time, at high speed, until smooth, not melted. Turn into sherbet glasses. Serve at once, with lemon wedges and crackers.
Makes 8 to 10 servings

Chilled Cantaloupe Soup

1 (3 lb) ripe cantaloupe
1/2 cup dry sherry
1/4 cup sugar
1 tablespoon lime juice

1. Cut melon in half; scoop out seeds. Scoop out cantaloupe meat.
2. In blender, combine cantaloupe and rest of ingredients. Blend until smooth—several times if necessary. Refrigerate, covered, until very cold.
Makes 4 cups; 5 servings.

Cold Cucumber Soup

1-1/2 cucumbers (about 1 lb)
1-1/2 tablespoons butter or margarine
1 tablespoon flour
1/4 teaspoon salt
3/4 cup chicken broth
1/2 cup milk
1/2 cup light cream

1. Pare cucumbers; cut in half lengthwise. With teaspoon, scoop out and discard seeds. Cut cucumber into 1/4-inch pieces.
2. In large saucepan, sauté cucumber in hot butter 5 minutes, or until transparent. Remove from heat. Stir in flour and salt until blended. Gradually add chicken broth and milk.
3. Cook over medium heat, stirring constantly, until mixture boils. Reduce heat; simmer, covered, 15 minutes.
4. Turn into electric-blender container; blend, at high speed, 1 minute. (Or put mixture through a sieve, pressing cucumber through.) Turn into a bowl.
5. Stir in cream. Refrigerate, covered, until very well chilled—at least 4 hours.
6. Serve in bouillon cups. Garnish with a slice of cucumber, if you wish.
Makes 4 or 5 servings.

Gazpacho

2 large tomatoes, peeled (1-3/4 lb)
1 large cucumber, pared and halved
1 medium onion, peeled and halved
1 medium green pepper, quartered, seeded
1 pimiento, drained
2 cans (12-oz size) tomato juice
1/3 cup olive or salad oil
1/3 cup red-wine vinegar
1/4 teaspoon Tabasco
1-1/2 teaspoons salt
1/8 teaspoon coarsely ground black pepper
2 cloves garlic, split
1/2 cup packaged croutons
1/4 cup chopped chives

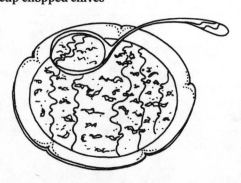

1. In electric blender, combine one tomato, half the cucumber, half the onion, a green-pepper quarter, the pimiento, and 1/2 cup tomato juice. Blend, covered and at high speed, 30 seconds, to purée the vegetables.
2. In a large bowl, mix the puréed vegetables with remaining tomato juice, 1/4 cup olive oil, the vinegar, Tabasco, salt, and black pepper.
3. Refrigerate mixture, covered, until it is well chilled—about 2 hours. At the same time, refrigerate 6 serving bowls.
4. Meanwhile, rub inside of small skillet with garlic; reserve garlic. Add rest of oil; heat. Sauté the croutons in oil until they are browned. Set aside until serving time.
5. Chop separately remaining tomato, cucumber, onion, and green pepper. Place each of these, and the croutons, in separate bowls. Serve as accompaniments.
6. Just before serving time, crush reserved garlic. Add to chilled soup, mixing well. Sprinkle with chopped chives. Serve the gazpacho in chilled bowls. Everyone helps himself to the accompaniments.
Makes 6 servings.

Cold Shrimp Bisque

1 can (10-1/2 oz) condensed cream-of-shrimp
   soup, undiluted
1 cup light cream
1/2 cup tomato juice
1/3 cup dry sherry

1. In medium saucepan, combine shrimp soup, cream, and tomato juice; mix well. Bring to boiling, stirring. Add sherry; reduce heat, and simmer gently 5 minutes.
2. Set aside to cool; refrigerate, covered, until well chilled—several hours or overnight.
3. Stir very well just before serving. Garnish each serving with chopped parsley or dill and a whole shrimp, if desired.
Makes 3 cups; 4 servings.

Strawberry-Rhubarb Soup

1 lb rhubarb
2 pints strawberries
3/4 cup sugar
Red food color
1/4 cup white port
Whipped cream

1. Wash rhubarb; cut it in 1-inch pieces. You should have 3 cups. Wash and hull strawberries.
2. In medium saucepan, combine rhubarb, 2 cups water, and the sugar. Bring to boiling over low heat; simmer, covered, about 10 minutes, or until rhubarb is soft.
3. Strain into medium bowl; discard pulp. Add a few drops red food color, if needed, to tint deep pink.
4. Combine 1 cup of the rhubarb juice and 2 cups strawberries in electric-blender container; blend, at high speed, 15 to 20 seconds. Pour into rest of rhubarb juice in bowl; mix well. Refrigerate, covered, until well chilled—3 or 4 hours.
5. Slice remaining strawberries. Refrigerate, covered.
6. Just before serving, stir wine and sliced strawberries into rhubarb mixture. Add a little sugar, if needed.
7. Serve in bouillon cups or sherbet glasses. Pass whipped cream in a bowl. Nice as a first course, instead of a fruit cup; or serve as dessert.
Makes 6 servings.

Orange-Apricot-Yoghurt Soup

2 cartons (8-oz size) apricot-flavored yoghurt
1 cup milk
1/2 cup orange juice
6 thin slices orange
6 sprigs mint

1. In medium bowl, combine yoghurt, milk, and orange juice; stir to mix well.
2. Refrigerate until well chilled—at least 1 hour.
3. Serve in bouillon cups or sherbet glasses. Float a thin slice of orange and a sprig of mint on each serving.
Makes 6 servings.

Lemon-Buttermilk Soup

4 egg yolks
1/2 cup sugar
1 tablespoon lemon juice
2 teaspoons grated lemon peel
2 teaspoons vanilla extract
1 quart buttermilk
Thin lemon slices

1. In electric blender, blend egg yolks with sugar until mixture is very thick and lemon-colored. Blend in lemon juice, peel, and vanilla.
2. At low speed, gradually blend in buttermilk.
3. Refrigerate, covered, several hours or overnight —until well chilled. Pour into individual serving dishes. Garnish each serving with lemon slices. Makes 6 cups; 8 servings.

Cold Plum Soup

2 cans (17-oz size) purple plums
1/8 teaspoon ground cinnamon
Dash ground cloves
1/3 cup lime juice
2/3 cup light rum

1. Drain plums, reserving syrup. Remove pits from plums.
2. Combine plums, reserved syrup, and remaining ingredients. Blend in blender, about one third at a time.
3. Refrigerate, covered, until well chilled (see Note) —4 hours or overnight.
4. Serve in chilled glasses or individual dishes set in ice. Garnish with a dab of whipped cream sprinkled with cinnamon, if desired.
Makes 5 cups; 6 servings.
Note: Place in freezer an hour or two to chill more quickly, if desired.

With Canned Soups

Starting with canned soups as a base, you can quickly and easily make delicious versions of many traditional soups which otherwise would take hours to prepare. The quick Cape Cod Chowder and Beet Soup with Dill are two cases in point.

Black-Bean Soup with Rum

2 cans (10-1/2-oz size) condensed black-bean soup
1 can (10-1/2 oz) condensed beef broth
1/4 teaspoon Worcestershire sauce
1/3 cup golden rum
6 lemon slices
Chopped parsley

1. In medium saucepan, combine undiluted bean soup, undiluted beef broth, and Worcestershire. Stir in 1-3/4 cups water. Bring to boiling over medium heat, stirring occasionally; reduce heat; simmer, covered, 5 minutes.
2. Remove from heat; stir in rum. Serve in mugs. Garnish each serving with a slice of lemon and parsley.
Makes 6 servings.

Beet Soup with Dill

2 cans (1-lb size) julienne-style beets, undrained
2 cans (10-1/2-oz size) condensed beef broth,
   undiluted
1 tablespoon snipped fresh dill
2 tablespoons instant minced onion
1 cup chopped raw cabbage
1 clove garlic, crushed
1-1/2 teaspoons salt
6 tablespoons lemon juice
3 tablespoons light-brown sugar
Dairy sour cream

1. In a 6-quart saucepan, combine beets, broth, dill, onion, cabbage, garlic, salt, lemon juice, sugar, and 1-1/2 cups water.
2. Over medium heat, bring to boiling. Reduce heat; simmer, uncovered, 15 minutes.
3. Serve hot, each serving topped with a spoonful of sour cream.
Makes about 8 cups; 6 servings.

Quick Cape Cod Clam Chowder

2 bacon slices, diced
1/3 cup chopped onion
2 cans (7-1/2-oz size) minced clams
1 can (10-1/2 oz) condensed cream-of-chicken
   soup, undiluted
1-1/3 cups light cream
1 can (8 oz) small whole potatoes, drained and
   cubed
1/4 teaspoon salt
Dash pepper
Oyster crackers

1. In large saucepan, sauté bacon until crisp. Remove bacon; drain on paper towels.
2. Pour off bacon drippings from saucepan; return 1 tablespoon. In bacon drippings, sauté onion 5 minutes. Remove from heat.
3. Drain clams, reserving liquid. Add clam liquid to sautéed onion, along with chicken soup, cream, potatoes, salt, and pepper.
4. Bring to boiling, stirring. Reduce heat; simmer, covered, 5 minutes.
5. Add clams; simmer 3 minutes longer. Just before serving, add bacon. Serve crackers with the chowder.
Makes 5 cups; about 6 servings.

Lentil Soup with Frankfurters

3 slices bacon, diced
4 frankfurters, thinly sliced (1/2 lb)
1 teaspoon instant minced onion
1/8 teaspoon dried thyme leaves
2 cans (1-lb, 4-oz size) lentil soup
Dairy sour cream
Chopped parsley

1. In 3-quart saucepan, sauté bacon until almost crisp. Pour drippings into a cup; return 1 tablespoon to saucepan; discard rest.
2. Add frankfurters, onion, and thyme; cook over high heat until frankfurters are browned—2 to 3 minutes. Remove from heat.
3. Add soup; bring to boiling. Reduce heat; simmer, covered, 5 minutes.
4. Top each serving with a spoonful of sour cream and bacon. Sprinkle with parsley.
Makes 6 cups; 6 servings.

Quick Split-Pea Soup with Ham

2 cans (11-1/4-oz size) condensed split-pea-and-
  ham soup, undiluted
1 can (11-1/4 oz) condensed green-pea soup,
  undiluted
2 cups diced cooked ham
2 teaspoons instant minced onion
Salt
Pepper

1. In 3-quart saucepan, combine soups, ham, and onion with 3 cups water; mix well.
2. Bring to boiling, stirring. Reduce heat; simmer, covered, 15 minutes.
3. Add salt and pepper to taste.
Makes 6 cups; about 6 servings.

Quick Vichyssoise

2 cans (10-1/4-oz size) condensed cream-of-
  potato soup
2 soup cans (10-1/4-oz size) milk
1/4 cup snipped chives
1 cup dairy sour cream

1. Combine soup, milk, and chives in medium saucepan.
2. Heat slowly, stirring, until soup boils.
3. With rotary beater, beat until smooth (or blend in electric blender, covered and at high speed, until smooth—about 1 minute).
4. Then beat in (or blend in) sour cream.
5. Refrigerate until very well chilled—about 4 hours.
Makes 6 to 8 servings.

Vegetables

Properly cooked and well-seasoned vegetables can change a vegetable hater to a vegetable eater. Our collection of recipes following combines vegetables in a variety of ways, with sauces, spices and herbs to turn the most ordinary vegetables into interesting and exciting dishes.

In menu planning, choose vegetables that contrast in color, texture and flavor; for example, broccoli and sweet potatoes, or cauliflower and peas. There should be no more than one strongly flavored vegetable, like cauliflower, broccoli or Brussels sprouts, in a menu.

We depend on vegetables as a major source of vitamins and many minerals. But the water-soluble vitamins B and C and some of the minerals can be lost, to some degree, in the cooking. To ensure minimum loss of nutrients, cook all vegetables in the least possible amount of water, and, whenever you can, in their skins. There's a taste dividend, too — vegetables cooked quickly until just tender, using a little water, are much more flavorful. Ideally, when vegetables are cooked, the water will be cooked away. If any is left, save it, because the missing nutrients are still in it — as they are also in the liquid from canned vegetables. Add this liquid to soups, stews and gravies, or boil down and pour over vegetables.

Our Vegetable Chart that follows tells when vegetables are in season and how to prepare and cook them, from artichokes to zucchini.

Vegetable Chart

Vegetable	Buying Guide	Preparation	Basic Cookery
All vegetables	Best buys are in season	Wash all vegetables before cooking	Approximate number of servings per pound and cooking time. Simmer, tightly covered, in 1 inch boiling water with 1/2 to 1 teaspoon salt per pound. Vegetables are done when tender-crisp
Artichokes (French or Italian)	Compact, firm, heavy globes; free from brown blemishes. Good green color. Fleshy, tightly closed leaf scales. Season: All year	Cut 1 inch from top. Cut stem close to base. Remove lower tough outer leaves. With scissors, cut thorny tip of each leaf	1 per serving 20 to 45 minutes, standing upright in saucepan
(Jerusalem)	Free from blemishes	Pare thinly. Leave whole, dice, or slice	3 or 4 servings 15 to 35 minutes
Asparagus	Green, firm stalk with close, compact tips; tender stalk is brittle and easily punctured. Should not be woody. Free from blemishes. Season: March–June	Break off woody end of stalk. Pare and remove scales. Leave stalk whole, or cut into 1-inch lengths	3 or 4 servings 10 to 20 minutes
Beans, Green or Wax	Clean, firm, crisp, tender pods. Should snap when broken. Free from blemishes Season: All year Peak: May–August	Remove ends. Cut, into lengthwise strips, for French-style. Cut on diagonal, into 1-inch pieces; or serve whole	4 to 6 servings French style: 10 to 20 minutes Cut or whole: 15 to 30 minutes

Vegetable	Buying Guide	Preparation	Basic Cookery
Beans, Lima	Unshelled limas should be well filled, clean, free from blemishes; dark-green, firm pods. Shelled limas are very perishable; should be light-green or green-white; plump, with tender skins. Season: July–November	Shell just before cooking	2 servings 20 to 25 minutes
Beets	Sold in bunches. Smooth, free from blemishes or cracks; fairly clean, firm roots with green tops. Small to medium in size. Season: All year	Remove tops (use as green vegetable); leave 1-inch stems. Scrub well. Peel and slice after cooking	3 servings Cover with cold water. Cook, covered, 30 to 45 minutes (Cook greens just with water that clings to leaves, 5 to 15 minutes)
Broccoli	Firm, tender stems with compact cluster of flower buds. Dark-green or purple-green (depending on variety) free from bruises or yellow. Season: All year Peak: October–March	Trim stem end; split heavy stalks. (Entire stalk is edible)	3 servings 10 to 15 minutes
Brussels Sprouts	Firm, compact, bright-green. Avoid yellow or worm-eaten leaves. Season: November–January	Cut off stem end. Soak in cold water 15 minutes	4 servings 10 to 20 minutes
Cabbage	Firm, heavy heads: crisp, tender leaves. Avoid yellowing or worm-eaten leaves. Season: All year Peak: October–March	Remove outer leaves; wash. Cut into wedges and remove most of core; or shred	3 or 4 servings Green, in wedges: 10 to 15 minutes Shredded: 3 to 10 minutes; Red, shredded: 8 to 12 minutes
Carrots	Firm, clean, smooth, well-shaped, with good color. Free from bruises and cracks. Season: All year	Remove tops. Scrape or pare thinly, or scrub well with brush. Cook whole or cut	4 servings Whole: 15 to 25 minutes Cut: 10 to 20 minutes
Cauliflower	Clean, heavy, compact head. White flowerets with green, crisp leaves. Avoid bruises or brown spots. Season: All year Peak: October–December	Remove outer leaves. Leave whole, removing stem, or cut into flowerets.	3 or 4 servings Whole: 15 to 20 minutes Flowerets: 8 to 15 minutes
Corn on Cob	Plump, firm, milky kernels with bright color. Husks should be green; dried-out, yellow discolorations indicate stale corn. Immature corn lacks flavor. Season: All year	Just before cooking, remove husks and silk	1 or 2 per serving 5 to 10 minutes

Vegetable	Buying Guide	Preparation	Basic Cookery
Eggplant	Heavy, firm, free from blemishes; shiny, smooth purple skin. Season: All year	Pare, if necessary. Do not soak in salted water. Cut as desired	4 or 5 servings Cook as directed in recipes
Greens (Collards, Dandelions, Kale, Spinach)	Young, tender, crisp leaves. Free from bruises, excess dirt, and coarse stems. Season: Some type available all year round	Cut off root ends. Wash several times, lifting out of water, letting sand sink to bottom of vessel	3 or 4 servings Thin leaf greens are cooked just with water that clings to leaves. Thick leaf greens need only 1/2 inch water
Onions, Small, White	Firm, clean, white, dry skins, free from sprouts. Season: All year	Remove outer skins under cold, running water.	4 servings 15 to 25 minutes
Parsnips	Smooth, firm, clean, well-shaped, free from rot. Small to medium in size. Season: August–May	Scrape or peel. Cut as desired, or leave whole	3 or 4 servings Cut: 10 to 20 minutes Whole: 20 to 40 minutes
Peas	Bright-green, filled pods, free from yellow or mildew, moisture or bruises. Season: All year Peak: May–August	Shell just before cooking	2 servings 8 to 20 minutes
Potatoes, Sweet (or yams)	Firm, plump, free from soft spots. Purchase small quantities; perishable. Sweets: skins are pale to deep yellow. Flesh is light orange. Yams: skins are white to reddish. Flesh is deep orange. Season: All year	Remove bruised spots and root ends. Do not pare	2 or 3 servings Cover with boiling water. Cook, covered, 25 to 35 minutes, or until tender
Potatoes, White (mature or new)	Firm, uniform in shape (medium-size). Free from cuts and blemishes. Color varies with variety. Eyes should be shallow	Pare; remove eyes; leave whole. Pare; cut into quarters. Pare; cut into 1-inch cubes; or slice 1/8 inch thick. Whole, small new potatoes. Pare or scrape. Unpared, whole potatoes (medium size)	2 or 3 servings 35 to 40 minutes 20 to 25 minutes 20 to 25 minutes 20 to 25 minutes Cover with boiling water. Cook, covered, 35 to 40 minutes
Squash, Acorn	Dark-green, ribbed. Hard rind. Season: All year Peak: October–December	Cut in half, lengthwise. Remove seeds. Do not peel	2 servings (1 large) 20 to 30 minutes (Cook cut side down)
Squash, Summer (Zucchini included)	Heavy for size, free from blemishes. Thin, tender skin. Season: May–August	Remove stem and blossom ends. Paring not necessary. Cut as desired	2 or 3 servings 10 to 20 minutes
Squash, Winter	Heavy for size, free from blemishes and bruises. Hard rind. Season: Oct.–December	Cut as desired. Remove seeds. Remove rind, if desired	2 servings 25 to 30 minutes

Vegetable	Buying Guide	Preparation	Basic Cookery
Turnips (Rutabagas)	Firm, smooth, clean, free from bruises with few fibrous roots. Heavy for size Season: All year Peak: October–November	Peel thinly just before cooking. Cut as desired	3 or 4 servings 20 to 30 minutes
Turnips, White	Firm, smooth, clean, free from bruises, with few fibrous roots. Small to medium in size. Season: All year Peak: October–November	Peel thinly just before cooking. Leave whole, or cut	3 or 4 servings Whole: 20 to 30 minutes Cut: 10 to 20 minutes

Artichokes with Tarragon Butter

1/4 cup olive or salad oil
6 lemon slices
2 bay leaves
1 clove garlic, split
1 teaspoon salt
1/8 teaspoon pepper
4 large artichokes (about 3 lb)

Tarragon Butter:
1/2 cup melted butter
2 tablespoons olive oil
2 tablespoons lemon juice
1 tablespoon dried tarragon leaves

1. In large kettle, combine 3 quarts water with 1/4 cup olive oil, lemon slices, bay leaves, garlic, salt, and pepper; bring to boiling.
2. Meanwhile, trim stalk from base of artichokes; cut a 1-inch slice from tops. Remove discolored leaves; snip off spike ends.
3. Wash the artichokes in cold water; drain.
4. Add to boiling mixture. Reduce heat; simmer, covered, 40 to 45 minutes, or until artichoke bases feel soft. Drain artichokes well.
5. Meanwhile, make Tarragon Butter: In a small bowl, mix butter, olive oil, lemon juice, and tarragon until well combined.
6. To serve: Place artichoke and small cup of sauce on individual plates. To eat, pull out leaves, one at a time, and dip in sauce. Discard prickly choke.
Makes 4 servings.

Fresh Asparagus Mimosa

2-1/2 to 3 lb asparagus
1/2 teaspoon salt
1 hard-cooked egg
1/4 cup butter or margarine, melted
2 tablespoons lemon juice

1. Cut off tough ends of asparagus. Wash stalks well. With vegetable parer, scrape skin and scales from stalks.
2. In large skillet, add salt to 1-1/2 inches water; bring to boiling. Add asparagus spears; boil vigorously, covered, 8 to 10 minutes.
3. Meanwhile, separate white and yolk of the hard-cooked egg. Chop white and yolk separately.
4. Drain asparagus well. Arrange on platter. Drizzle with butter. Sprinkle egg white over asparagus, then egg yolk. Just before serving, sprinkle with lemon juice.
Makes 6 servings.

Fresh Asparagus with Hollandaise

2 to 2-1/2 lb asparagus
Boiling water
1-1/2 teaspoons salt
1/4 cup butter or margarine, melted
Hollandaise Sauce, page 22

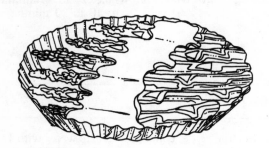

1. Break or cut off tough ends of asparagus. Wash asparagus well under cold running water. (If asparagus is sandy, scrub with brush. With vegetable parer, scrape the skin and scales from stalks.)
2. Bunch stalks together; tie with string, or use a rubber band. Place upright in deep saucepan. Add boiling water (about 2 inches deep) and the salt.
3. Return to boiling; cook, covered, 15 to 20 minutes. Pierce lower part of stalks with fork, to see if they are tender. Be sure not to overcook.
4. Drain asparagus well, reserving liquid to use in sauce and being careful not to break stalks. Arrange in heated vegetable dish; pour butter over all. Serve with Hollandaise Sauce. (Or, if desired omit Hollandaise, and serve with lemon wedges.) Makes 4 to 6 servings.
Note: You may use bottom of double boiler, with the top inverted over asparagus as cover.

Chinese-Style Asparagus

2 to 2-1/2 lb fresh asparagus
1/3 cup butter or margarine
1/2 teaspoon salt
Dash pepper

1. Break or cut off tough ends of asparagus stalks. Wash asparagus tips well with cold water; if necessary, use a soft brush to remove grit. With a vegetable parer, scrape skin and scales from lower part of stalk only.
2. With a knife, cut stalks on the diagonal, making bias slices about 1 inch long and 1/4 inch thick.
3. In large skillet with tight-fitting cover, heat butter with 1/3 cup water to boiling. Add asparagus, salt, and pepper; cook, covered and over high heat, 5 to 8 minutes, adding a little more water if necessary. Asparagus should be tender when pierced with fork, and water should be evaporated.
Makes 6 servings.

Old-Fashioned Baked Beans

3 cups dried navy (Great Northern) beans (1-1/2 lb)
3/4 lb salt pork
1 medium onion
2 teaspoons salt
1/4 cup light-brown sugar, firmly packed
2 teaspoons dry mustard
1 cup light molasses

1. Wash beans, discarding imperfect ones. Cover beans with 2 quarts cold water; refrigerate, covered, overnight.
2. Next day, turn beans and water into 6-quart kettle.
3. Bring to boiling; reduce heat, and simmer, covered, 30 minutes. Drain, reserving liquid.
4. Preheat oven to 300F.

5. Trim rind from salt pork. Cut pork almost through, at half-inch intervals.

6. Place onion in bottom of 4-quart bean pot or casserole. Add beans; bury pork, cut side down, in center of beans.

7. Heat reserved bean liquid to boiling.

8. Mix remaining ingredients. Stir in 1 cup boiling bean liquid. Pour over beans. Add boiling liquid just to cover beans—about 1-1/2 cups.

9. Bake, covered, 6 hours. Stir once every hour, so beans cook evenly. If they seem dry after stirring, add a little boiling water.

10. To brown top of beans, remove cover for last half hour of baking time.

Makes 8 servings.

Quick Boston Baked Beans

4 cans (1-lb size) pork and beans with tomato
   sauce or with molasses
5 slices bacon
1 cup coarsely chopped onion
1/2 cup light molasses
1/2 cup catsup
1 teaspoon dry mustard

1. Preheat oven to 400F. Turn beans into a 3-quart casserole or bean pot.

2. In skillet, sauté bacon and onion until onion is golden—5 minutes.

3. Remove from heat. Add molasses, catsup, and mustard; mix well. Gently stir into beans.

4. Bake, uncovered, 45 minutes, or until beans are hot and bubbly.

Makes 8 to 10 servings.

Barbecued Lima Beans

1 lb large dried lima beans
1 teaspoon salt

Sauce:
6 slices bacon, cut in 1-inch pieces
1 cup chopped onion
1/2 cup chopped green pepper
1 cup bottled barbecue sauce
1 can (8 oz) tomato sauce

1. Cover beans with 5 cups cold water. Refrigerate, covered, overnight.

2. Next day, turn beans and liquid (do not drain) into a 4-quart kettle or Dutch oven; add salt. Bring to boiling; reduce heat, and simmer gently, covered and stirring occasionally, 1 hour, or until beans are tender and liquid is almost absorbed.

3. Meanwhile, make Sauce: In large saucepan, sauté bacon until crisp. Remove bacon; drain on paper towels.

4. In hot bacon drippings, sauté onion and pepper until tender—about 10 minutes. Add barbecue sauce and tomato sauce. Stir into beans.

5. Preheat oven to 325F.

6. Turn bean mixture into a 3-quart casserole; bake, uncovered, 30 minutes. Garnish with bacon just before serving.

Makes 8 servings.

Festival Beets

1-1/2 lb beets
1/2 cup sugar
1 tablespoon cornstarch
1/4 teaspoon salt
1/2 cup cider vinegar
2 tablespoons orange or ginger marmalade
2 tablespoons butter or margarine

1. Gently wash beets, leaving skins intact. Remove leaves.
2. Place beets in large saucepan. Cover with cold water; bring to boiling. Reduce heat; simmer, covered, 45 minutes, or until beets are tender.
3. Drain beets. Cover with cold water; slip off skins. Cut beets into 1/2-inch cubes; set aside.
4. In medium saucepan, combine sugar, cornstarch, and salt; mix well. Stir in vinegar.
5. Over medium heat, bring to boiling, stirring constantly. Mixture will be thickened and translucent.
6. Add marmalade and butter; heat, stirring, until butter melts.
7. Add beets; cook, over low heat, stirring occasionally, until beets are heated through—about 10 minutes.
Makes 6 servings.

Orange Beets

1 can (1 lb) sliced beets, drained
2 tablespoons orange marmalade
1 tablespoon cider vinegar
2 tablespoons butter or margarine
1/2 teaspoon salt

1. Combine all ingredients in medium saucepan.
2. Cook, over low heat, stirring occasionally, until beets are heated through.
3. Turn into serving bowl. Serve hot.
Makes 4 servings.

Broccoli with Lemon Sauce

2-1/2 to 3 lb broccoli
Boiling water
Salt
2 eggs, separated
2 tablespoons heavy cream
2 tablespoons lemon juice
4 tablespoons butter or margarine

1. Trim broccoli; wash thoroughly. Split each stalk lengthwise into halves or quarters, depending on size.
2. Place broccoli in large saucepan. Add boiling water to almost cover; add 1 teaspoon salt. Cook, covered, 10 minutes, or until tender. Drain. Keep warm.
3. Meanwhile, in top of double boiler, beat egg yolks with cream and 1/4 teaspoon salt until thickened and light colored. Gradually beat in juice.
4. Place over hot, not boiling, water; cook, beating constantly with wire whisk, until mixture thickens slightly. Remove double boiler from heat, but leave top over hot water.
5. Add butter, 1/2 tablespoon at a time, beating after each addition until butter is melted. Remove top from hot water.
6. In small bowl, beat egg whites until soft peaks form when beater is slowly raised. Fold into yolk mixture.

7. Arrange broccoli on heated serving platter. Top with sauce, and, if desired, garnish with lemon slices.
Makes 6 to 8 servings.

Broccoli Amandine

1 bunch fresh broccoli (about 1-1/2 lb)
Boiling water
1/2 teaspoon salt
1/2 cup slivered almonds
1/4 cup butter or margarine
2 tablespoons lemon juice

1. Wash and trim leaves from broccoli. If stalks are very large, split lengthwise through flower and all. Arrange in single layer in bottom of large skillet.
2. Pour 1/2 cup boiling water over broccoli; sprinkle with salt. Cook, covered, over medium heat 8 to 10 minutes, or until stalks are just tender and water is evaporated.
3. Meanwhile, sauté almonds in 1 tablespoon butter until golden. Add remaining butter and lemon juice. Heat until butter melts. Pour over broccoli.
Makes 4 to 6 servings.

Broccoli Polonaise

2 pkg (10-oz size) frozen broccoli spears*
4 tablespoons butter or margarine
1/3 cup soft white-bread crumbs
4 teaspoons lemon juice
* Or use 2 packages frozen broccoli spears in butter sauce, omitting butter in step 3.

1. Cook broccoli as package label directs.
2. Meanwhile, slowly heat 1 tablespoon butter in a small skillet. Add bread crumbs, and sauté until golden-brown. Remove crumbs, and set aside.
3. In same skillet, melt remaining butter with lemon juice.
4. Drain broccoli. Add lemon butter; toss gently until evenly coated. Turn into serving dish; sprinkle with browned crumbs.
Makes 6 servings.

Brussel Sprouts in Cheese Sauce

2 pkg (10-oz size) frozen brussels sprouts

Cheese Sauce:
2 tablespoons butter or margarine
2 tablespoons flour
1/2 teaspoon dry mustard
3/4 teaspoon salt
Dash pepper
Dash cayenne
1 cup milk or light cream
1 cup grated natural sharp Cheddar cheese (1/4 lb)

1. Using a large saucepan, cook brussels sprouts as package label directs. (Cook about 8 minutes or until tender.)
2. Make Cheese Sauce: In small saucepan, slowly melt butter (do not brown); remove from heat; stir in flour, mustard, salt, pepper, cayenne and milk until smooth.
3. Bring to boiling, stirring until thickened. Reduce heat; add cheese; cook, stirring, until cheese is melted and mixture is smooth.
4. Drain brussels sprouts; turn them back into saucepan. Heat slightly to dry out. Pour cheese sauce over top.
Makes 6 servings.

Buttered Cabbage Wedges

1 head cabbage (about 2-1/2 lb)
1 teaspoon salt
1/2 cup butter or margarine
Freshly ground black pepper

1. Discard outer leaves from cabbage; wash head; cut cabbage into 8 wedges.
2. Pour 1/2 cup water into large skillet; bring to boiling. Add salt, then cabbage. Cook, covered, over medium heat 8 minutes.
3. Add butter; stir until melted and cabbage is coated. Sprinkle with pepper before serving.
Makes 8 servings.

Spicy Red Cabbage with Apples

1 quart shredded red cabbage (1 lb)
2 tart cooking apples, pared and sliced
1/4 cup red-wine vinegar
1-1/4 teaspoons salt
1/3 cup sugar
4 whole cloves
3 tablespoons butter or margarine

1. In medium saucepan, combine all ingredients with 1/2 cup water.
2. Cook, covered, over medium heat until cabbage is tender—about 25 minutes; stir occasionally.
Makes 4 to 6 servings.

Buttery Grated Carrots

2 lb carrots
1 tablespoon salad oil
1/4 teaspoon finely chopped garlic
1/2 teaspoon salt
1/8 teaspoon pepper
1/4 cup butter

1. Pare carrots; grate on medium grater into large skillet with tight-fitting cover.
2. Toss with oil, garlic, salt, pepper, and 2 tablespoons water. Cook, covered, over medium heat, stirring occasionally, 10 to 12 minutes, or until tender.
3. Remove from heat. Toss lightly with butter until carrots are coated.
Makes 4 to 6 servings.

Buttery Grated Turnips

1. Use 3 lb white turnips instead of carrots. Proceed as above, but cook turnips 15 minutes, or until tender.
2. Then, to evaporate liquid, cook, uncovered, over very low heat, 5 minutes.
3. Remove from heat. Toss with butter, 2 tablespoons lemon juice, and 1/4 cup chopped parsley until turnips are coated.
Makes 4 to 6 servings.

Buttery Grated Beets

1. Use 2 lb beets instead of carrots. Proceed as above, but cook beets 20 minutes, or until tender.
2. Remove from heat. Toss lightly with butter and 2 tablespoons lemon juice until beets are coated. Makes 4 to 6 servings.

Braised Carrots

1 tablespoon butter or margarine
1 tablespoon salad oil
2 cups thinly sliced (on diagonal), pared carrots (about 9)
1/2 teaspoon salt

1. In hot butter and oil in medium skillet, cook carrots, stirring, 1 minute.
2. Add 2 tablespoons water and the salt; cook tightly covered, over low heat until carrots are fork-tender—7 to 8 minutes. Stir once to prevent sticking.
Makes 4 to 6 servings.

Lemon-Glazed Carrots

1 lb carrots
Salt
Boiling water
3 tablespoons butter or margarine
2 tablespoons sugar
4 thin slices lemon

1. Wash carrots; pare; cut diagonally into 1-inch pieces.
2. Place in medium saucepan with enough salted boiling water to cover; simmer, covered, 15 minutes, or until tender. Drain.
3. Melt butter in heavy medium skillet. Stir in sugar; add lemon slices and carrots; cook over medium heat, stirring occasionally, until carrots are glazed.
Makes 4 servings.

Carrots with Fresh Mint

24 small carrots (2 lb)
Boiling water
1 teaspoon salt
2 tablespoons butter or margarine
2 tablespoons sugar
2 tablespoons chopped fresh mint leaves

1. Wash carrots, but do not pare. Place in large skillet. Add boiling water, to partly cover, and the salt; simmer, covered, 10 minutes, or until carrots are tender.
2. Drain carrots. Hold the carrots under cold running water, and peel off their tender skin.
3. Melt butter in large skillet. Add sugar, mint, and carrots. Cook over low heat, turning carrots frequently, until they are nicely glazed.
4. Turn into serving dish. Garnish with mint sprigs, if desired.
Makes 8 servings.

Brown-Sugar Glazed Carrots and Onions

1 lb carrots, pared
Boiling water
1 teaspoon salt
1 lb small white onions, peeled

Glaze:
1 cup light-brown sugar, firmly packed
1 tablespoon cornstarch
1/4 cup butter or margarine
1/8 teaspoon nutmeg
3 tablespoons lemon juice

1. Slice carrots, on the diagonal, 1-1/2 inches thick.
2. In 3-quart saucepan, in 1 inch boiling water, with the salt, bring carrots and onions to boiling.
3. Reduce heat; simmer, covered, 20 to 25 minutes, or just until vegetables are tender. Drain well.
4. Meanwhile, make Glaze: In large skillet, combine sugar and cornstarch. Gradually stir in 2 tablespoons water to make a smooth mixture. Add butter, nutmeg, and lemon juice.
5. Bring to boiling, stirring constantly; boil 5 minutes, stirring occasionally. Mixture will be thickened and translucent.
6. Add vegetables to glaze. Cook, uncovered, 5 minutes, turning gently so they become glazed on all sides.
Makes 4 servings.

Orange-Glazed Carrots

1-1/2 lb medium carrots
Boiling water
1 teaspoon salt
1/4 cup orange juice
1 tablespoon sugar
2 tablespoons butter or margarine
1 medium orange, thinly sliced

1. Wash carrots in cold water, scrubbing well. Cut off stem end; do not pare.
2. Place carrots in 10-inch skillet with tight-fitting cover. Add boiling water to measure 1 inch and the salt. Bring back to boiling; reduce heat, and simmer, covered, 10 minutes, or until just tender but not mushy.
3. Drain; cool 10 minutes; then peel skin with knife.
4. In medium skillet, combine orange juice, sugar, butter, and orange slices. Add carrots; simmer gently, spooning glaze over carrots, 5 to 10 minutes, or until tender.
Makes 6 servings.

Cauliflower Polonaise

1 large cauliflower (about 2-1/2 lb)
Boiling water
1-1/2 teaspoons salt
3 slices lemon
1 hard-cooked egg, coarsely chopped
1 tablespoon chopped parsley
1/2 cup butter or margarine, melted
3 tablespoons lemon juice
1/2 cup pkg prepared croutons

1. Trim leaves and stem from cauliflower. Place, stem side down, in large kettle. Cover with boiling water. Add salt and lemon slices. Bring to boiling; reduce heat; simmer, covered, 20 to 25 minutes, or until tender. Drain.
2. To serve: Place whole cauliflower in warm serving dish. Sprinkle with hard-cooked egg and parsley. Combine butter with lemon juice and croutons. Pour over cauliflower.
Makes 6 to 8 servings.

Cauliflower Garni

1 head cauliflower (about 2 lb)
2 tablespoons lemon juice
Boiling water
1-1/2 teaspoons salt
1/4 cup butter or margarine
2 tablespoons chopped onion
1 tablespoon chopped parsley
1 tablespoon chopped pimiento
Parsley sprigs

1. Wash cauliflower. Remove leaves, leaving bottom row intact. Make two 1/2-inch-deep gashes across stem.
2. Brush top of cauliflower with 1 tablespoon lemon juice.
3. Place cauliflower, stem end down, in colander. Place colander in large kettle. Add boiling water to kettle to cover the stem of cauliflower only, not the flowerets. Add salt to boiling water.
4. Bring water back to boiling. Cover kettle tightly; reduce heat; simmer, covered, 45 to 55 minutes, or just until stem of cauliflower is tender when tested with fork.
5. Meanwhile, in hot butter in small skillet, sauté onion until tender. Remove from heat.
6. To serve: Remove cauliflower to serving platter; brush top with rest of lemon juice.
7. Spoon sautéed onion with melted butter over top of cauliflower; then sprinkle with chopped parsley and pimiento. Garnish with parsley sprigs. Pass more melted butter, if desired.
Makes 4 to 6 servings.

Cauliflower Surprise

1 large head cauliflower (2 lb)
Salt
Boiling water
2 egg yolks
2 tablespoons heavy cream
1/2 teaspoon sugar
1/2 teaspoon monosodium glutamate
Paprika
2-1/2 tablespoons lemon juice
1/4 cup butter
2 egg whites

1. Wash cauliflower thoroughly. Cut into flowerets. Cook, covered, in 1 inch lightly salted boiling water until tender—about 10 minutes. Drain well; keep warm.
2. Meanwhile, in top of double boiler, beat egg yolks with cream until thickened and light colored. Beat in 1/2 teaspoon salt, the sugar, monosodium glutamate, and 1/4 teaspoon paprika.
3. Place over hot, not boiling, water. With wire whisk, gradually beat in lemon juice; cook, beating constantly, until mixture is consistency of heavy cream. Remove from heat, but leave over hot water.
4. Add butter, 1/2 teaspoon at a time, beating after each addition until butter is melted. Remove from hot water.
5. Beat egg whites just until soft peaks form when beater is slowly raised. Fold into lemon mixture.
6. Mound cauliflowerets in heated serving dish. Top with sauce, and sprinkle with paprika.
Makes 6 servings.

Cauliflower with Shrimp Sauce

2 heads cauliflower (2 lb each)
2 tablespoons lemon juice
2 teaspoons salt
1 can (10-1/2 oz) condensed cream-of-shrimp
    soup, undiluted
1/3 cup light cream
1/3 cup tomato juice

1. Trim leaves and stems from cauliflower; wash thoroughly. Make two 1/2-inch-deep gashes across stems. Brush tops with lemon juice.
2. Place cauliflower, stem ends down, on rack in shallow roasting pan. Add enough water to just cover stems. Add salt to water.
3. Bring to boiling; steam gently, covered, 40 to 45 minutes, or until stems of cauliflower are tender. (Use sheet of foil if pan has no cover.)
4. Turn soup into medium saucepan. Stir in cream and tomato juice; bring to boiling, stirring frequently. Keep warm.
5. Drain cauliflower very well; place in heated serving dish. Spoon sauce over top.
Makes 8 to 10 servings.

Corn on the Cob

8 ears of corn
Butter or margarine, melted
Salt
Pepper

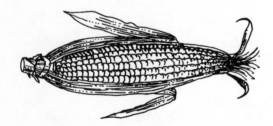

1. Cook corn as soon as possible after purchasing. (Keep refrigerated until cooking.)
2. In 6-quart kettle, start heating 4 quarts water.
3. Remove husks and silk from corn. Break off stem end of corn.
4. With tongs, slip ears of corn one by one into boiling water.
5. Cover kettle; return to boiling; boil gently 5 minutes.
6. With tongs, remove cooked corn from water to heated serving platter. Serve at once, with melted butter, salt, and pepper.
Makes 4 servings.

Corn Griddlecakes

2/3 cup unsifted all-purpose flour
1 teaspoon baking powder
1/2 teaspoon salt
2 teaspoons sugar
1 tablespoon finely chopped onion
1 can (12 oz) whole-kernel corn, drained
2 eggs, well beaten
1/4 cup butter or margarine, melted
1/2 cup milk

1. Sift dry ingredients onto a piece of waxed paper.
2. In medium bowl, combine chopped onion, corn, and beaten eggs. Blend in melted butter, the milk, and sifted dry ingredients.
3. Spoon 1/4 cup batter for each griddlecake onto preheated, lightly greased griddle. Gently pat griddlecakes into uniform shape. When bubbles stop breaking on surface, turn; bake until second side is golden-brown. Serve with butter and maple syrup.
Makes 10 to 12.

Corn off the Cob

4 cups fresh corn kernels, cut from cob
1 cup heavy cream
1 teaspoon sugar
1/2 teaspoon salt
Dash pepper
1/4 cup butter or margarine

1. Combine all ingredients in medium saucepan.
2. Simmer, covered, 10 minutes; or until tender.
Makes 6 servings.

Corn Fritters

1-1/4 cups unsifted all-purpose flour
2-1/4 teaspoons baking powder
3/4 teaspoon salt
1 egg, separated
3/4 cup milk
1-1/2 tablespoons salad oil
1 can (12 oz) whole-kernel corn, drained
Salad oil or shortening for deep-frying
Maple or maple-flavored syrup

1. Sift flour with baking powder and salt. In small bowl, with rotary beater, beat egg white until stiff peaks form when beater is slowly raised.
2. In medium bowl, with same beater, beat egg yolk, milk, and 1-1/2 tablespoons salad oil until smooth.
3. Gradually add flour mixture, beating until smooth. Fold in egg white gently. Add corn; stir until well combined.
4. In electric skillet or heavy saucepan, slowly heat salad oil (at least 2 inches deep) to 375F on deep-frying thermometer.
5. Into hot oil, drop corn mixture by large spoonfuls (about 1/4 cup), a few at a time. Deep-fry, turning once, about 5 minutes, or until golden-brown. Drain well on paper towels. Serve hot, with hot maple syrup.
Makes 4 or 5 servings.

Souffléed Corn

6 ears fresh corn*
1/2 cup butter or margarine
1/2 cup sugar
1 tablespoon flour
1/2 cup evaporated milk, undiluted
2 eggs, well beaten
1-1/2 teaspoons baking powder
1 tablespoon butter or margarine, melted
1/4 cup sugar
1/2 teaspoon cinnamon
* Or use 2 cans (12-oz size) whole-kernel corn.

1. Preheat oven to 350F. With a sharp knife, cut corn from ears (4 cups), and set aside.
2. In medium saucepan, heat 1/2 cup butter with 1/2 cup sugar until butter is melted. Stir in flour until well blended. Remove from heat.
3. Gradually stir in milk. Add eggs and baking powder; mix well. Fold in corn. Turn into buttered 1-quart casserole.
4. Bake 40 minutes, or until knife inserted in center comes out clean. Brush with melted butter. Sprinkle with sugar and cinnamon.
Makes 6 to 8 servings.

Corn Pudding

2 pkg (10-oz size) frozen corn, thawed and drained
3 eggs, well beaten
1/4 cup unsifted all-purpose flour
1 teaspoon salt
1/4 teaspoon white pepper
1 tablespoon sugar
Dash nutmeg
2 tablespoons butter or margarine, melted
2 cups light cream

1. Preheat oven to 325F. Lightly grease a 1-1/2-quart casserole.
2. In a large bowl, combine corn and eggs; mix well.
3. Combine flour, salt, pepper, sugar, and nutmeg. Stir into corn mixture.
4. Add butter and cream; mix well. Pour into prepared casserole. Set casserole in pan; pour hot water to 1-inch depth around casserole.
5. Bake, uncovered, 1 hour and 10 minutes, or until pudding is firm and knife inserted in center comes out clean. Serve hot.
Makes 8 servings.

Perfect Fried Eggplant

2 eggs, beaten
1 teaspoon salt
Dash pepper
1 cup pkg dry bread crumbs
2 tablespoons grated Parmesan cheese
1 medium eggplant (about 1 lb)
Salad oil or shortening for frying
Salt

1. In shallow dish, mix eggs, salt, and pepper.
2. Combine crumbs and cheese on waxed paper.
3. Cut unpeeled eggplant, crosswise, into 1/8-inch-thick slices. Dip in egg, then in crumb mixture, coating completely.
4. Meanwhile, in large, heavy skillet, slowly heat salad oil (at least 1/4 inch).
5. Sauté eggplant until golden-brown—about 3 minutes on each side. Drain on paper towels. Sprinkle lightly with salt.
Makes 4 servings.

Eggplant Fritters

2 medium eggplants (2 lb)
1 tablespoon salt
Salad oil or shortening for deep-fat frying

Batter:
1 cup unsifted all-purpose flour
1 teaspoon baking powder
1/2 teaspoon salt
Dash pepper
2 eggs, well beaten
2/3 cup cold milk
1 tablespoon salad oil

Lemon wedges

1. Wash eggplants; peel. Cut crosswise into slices 1/2 inch thick; then cut into 1/2-inch sticks. In large bowl, toss eggplant with salt. Let stand 20 minutes; drain. Dry eggplant well on paper towels.
2. Meanwhile, in electric skillet or deep-fat fryer, slowly heat oil (at least 1-1/2 inches) to 375F on deep-frying thermometer.
3. Make Batter: Sift flour with baking powder, salt, and pepper into medium bowl.
4. Add eggs, milk, and oil to flour mixture, beating with a portable electric mixer until smooth and well combined.
5. Dip eggplant sticks into batter, coating completely.

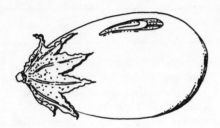

6. Shake off excess batter. Deep-fry 2 minutes on each side, or just until golden-brown. (Fry only enough at one time to fit easily into skillet.)

7. Remove with slotted spoon; drain on paper towels. Keep warm in very low oven while frying rest. Sprinkle with salt, if desired. Serve with lemon wedges.

Makes 6 to 8 servings.

Eggplant-and-Tomato Casserole

2 medium-size eggplants (about 2-1/2 lb)
Boiling water
Salt
1/4 cup salad oil
2 cloves garlic, finely chopped
2 tablespoons flour
2 cans (1-lb size) stewed tomatoes, undrained
2 teaspoons sugar
1 teaspoon paprika
1/8 teaspoon pepper
1/8 teaspoon dried basil leaves
1/2 cup grated Parmesan cheese

1. Preheat oven to 375F. Lightly grease a 2-quart casserole.

2. Wash and pare eggplants; cut into 2-inch cubes. In a 6-quart saucepan, in small amount of boiling, salted water, simmer eggplant 10 minutes. Drain.

3. Meanwhile, in hot oil in large skillet, sauté garlic until golden—about 3 minutes. Remove from heat.

4. Stir in flour, tomatoes, sugar, paprika, pepper, and basil. Cook, stirring, over medium heat, until mixture boils and is thickened.

5. In prepared casserole, layer eggplant cubes alternately with tomato mixture, to fill casserole. Top with grated cheese.

6. Bake 30 minutes, or until lightly browned.

Makes 6 to 8 servings.

Green Beans Hollandaise

2 lb fresh green beans
2 cups boiling water
2 teaspoons salt

Hollandaise Sauce:
5 egg yolks
2/3 cup butter or margarine, melted
2/3 cup boiling water
3 tablespoons lemon juice
1/2 teaspoon salt
Dash cayenne

1. Wash beans; cut off ends. Cut diagonally into 2-inch pieces.

2. Place in large skillet with 2 cups boiling water and 2 teaspoons salt. Boil gently, covered, 12 to 15 minutes, or until tender.

3. Meanwhile, make Hollandaise Sauce: In top of double boiler, with wire whisk or fork, slightly beat egg yolks. Slowly stir in butter. Gradually add boiling water, beating constantly.

4. Cook over hot, not boiling, water (water in double-boiler base should not touch pan above), stirring constantly, just until thickened. Remove from hot water. Gradually beat in lemon juice, salt, and cayenne.

5. Drain beans well; turn into serving dish. Toss with Hollandaise, and serve immediately.

Makes 8 servings.

French-Style Green Beans

1 lb fresh green beans
1 teaspoon salt
Boiling water
3 tablespoons butter or margarine

1. Wash beans under cold running water; drain.
2. With tip of paring knife, trim ends of beans. Then cut each in half lengthwise. (If beans are large and wide, cut in thirds.)
3. Place beans in 2-1/2-quart saucepan. Add salt and boiling water to measure 1 inch.
4. Boil beans gently, covered, 12 to 15 minutes, or just until they are tender-crisp.
5. Drain beans, and toss with butter.
Makes 4 servings.

Steamed Italian Green Beans

1 pkg (10 oz) frozen Italian green beans
2 tablespoons butter or margarine
Dash dried marjoram, basil, and savory leaves
1 teaspoon sugar
1/2 teaspoon salt
Dash pepper

1. Preheat oven to 375F.
2. On sheet of heavy-duty foil (about 18 by 15 inches), place frozen beans, rest of ingredients, and 1 tablespoon water. Close foil tightly to prevent leakage; place on cookie sheet. Steam in oven 40 minutes.
3. Serve beans in their liquid.
Makes 3 or 4 servings.

Mushroom Ratatouille

2 medium green peppers
2 medium zucchini
1 lb small mushrooms
1 medium onion, peeled
1/2 cup salad oil
2 cloves garlic, peeled and split
4 medium tomatoes, peeled
1-1/2 teaspoons salt
1/4 teaspoon pepper
1/2 teaspoon dried thyme leaves

1. Wash peppers; halve, and remove ribs and seeds. Cut crosswise into 1/4-inch-thick slices. Wash zucchini; cut into 1/2-inch-thick slices. Cut mushrooms into halves. Thinly slice onion.
2. In 1/4 cup hot oil in large skillet or Dutch oven, sauté green pepper, onion, and garlic until tender —about 5 minutes. With slotted spoon, remove to a large bowl; discard garlic.
3. Add 2 tablespoons oil to skillet, and heat. Add zucchini, and sauté, turning frequently, just until tender—about 10 minutes. With slotted spoon, remove zucchini to same bowl.
4. Add remaining oil to skillet, and heat. Add mushrooms, and sauté until golden—about 5 minutes.
5. Cut tomatoes into large pieces; add to mushrooms, along with sautéed vegetables, the salt, pepper, and thyme. Stir gently just to combine.
6. Simmer, covered, 5 minutes, or until very hot and bubbly.
Makes 12 servings.

Sautéed Mushrooms

18 large mushrooms (1-1/4 lb)
1/4 cup butter or margarine
1 teaspoon dried marjoram leaves
1/2 teaspoon salt

1. Wash mushrooms; trim ends of stems.
2. Melt butter in large skillet. Add mushrooms; sprinkle with marjoram and salt.
3. Sauté mushrooms, turning frequently, 15 minutes, or until golden and tender.
Makes 6 servings.

Mushrooms in Sour Cream

3 tablespoons butter or margarine
1 cup chopped onion
1-1/4 lb fresh mushrooms, sliced 1/4 inch thick
1 teaspoon salt
1 teaspoon paprika
1/2 teaspoon pepper
1/4 cup chopped parsley
1 cup dairy sour cream

1. In hot butter in medium skillet, sauté onion until golden—about 5 minutes.
2. Add mushrooms and 1/2 cup water; simmer, covered (adding more water, if necessary) until mushrooms are tender—about 15 minutes.
3. Add salt, paprika, pepper, 2 tablespoons parsley, and the sour cream. Heat very slowly, stirring, until thoroughly hot. Before serving, sprinkle with rest of parsley.
Makes 6 servings.

Savory Stuffed Mushrooms

12 to 16 fresh medium mushrooms
1/2 cup butter or margarine
3 tablespoons finely chopped green pepper
3 tablespoons finely chopped onion
1-1/2 cups fresh-bread cubes (1/4 inch)
1/2 teaspoon salt
1/8 teaspoon pepper
Dash cayenne

1. Preheat oven to 350F.
2. Wipe mushrooms with damp cloth. Remove stems, and chop stems fine; set aside.
3. Heat 3 tablespoons butter in large skillet. Sauté mushroom caps only on bottom side 2 to 3 minutes; remove. Arrange, rounded side down, in shallow baking pan.
4. Heat rest of butter in same skillet. Sauté chopped stems, green pepper, and onion until tender—about 5 minutes.
5. Remove from heat. Stir in bread cubes and seasoning. Use to fill mushroom caps, mounding mixture high in center.
6. Bake 15 minutes.
Makes 6 to 8 servings.

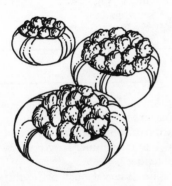

Baked Onions

8 medium yellow onions (3 lb)
4 chicken-bouillon cubes
3 tablespoons butter or margarine, melted
1/2 teaspoon paprika
Dash pepper

Crumb Topping:
1/3 cup packaged dry bread crumbs
2 tablespoons butter or margarine, melted
1/2 teaspoon salt
1/8 teaspoon dried thyme leaves

1. Peel onions. Place in large saucepan, along with bouillon cubes and 2 quarts water; bring to boiling. Reduce heat; simmer, covered, 30 minutes, or until onions are tender. Drain.
2. Preheat oven to 400F. Line a shallow baking pan with foil.
3. Place 3 tablespoons butter, the paprika, and pepper in foil-lined pan. Add onions; toss to coat well with butter. Bake 10 minutes.
4. Meanwhile, make Crumb Topping: In small bowl, combine crumbs, butter, salt, and thyme. Sprinkle over tops of onions. Bake 10 minutes longer.
Makes 8 servings.

Fried Onion Rings

1 large Bermuda onion (3/4 lb)

Batter:
1 cup sifted all-purpose flour
1 teaspoon salt
1-1/2 teaspoons baking powder
1 egg yolk
3/4 cup milk
1 tablespoon salad oil
1 egg white

Shortening or oil for deep-fat frying

1. Peel onion; slice about 1/4 inch thick; separate into rings. Cover with cold water, and let stand 30 minutes. Drain, and spread out on paper towels.
2. Meanwhile, make Batter: Sift flour, salt, and baking powder into medium bowl; set aside.
3. Beat egg yolk slightly in bowl; then stir in milk and salad oil. Add to flour mixture, stirring until smooth.
4. Beat egg white until soft peaks form. Fold into batter.
5. Heat 1 inch of melted shortening in saucepan or skillet to 375F on deep-frying thermometer.
6. Dip onion rings in batter (let excess batter drip into bowl); drop several rings at a time into hot fat, and fry until golden. Drain on paper towels. Keep warm while frying rest.
Makes 4 to 6 servings.

Buttered Parsnips

2 lb parsnips
Boiling water
2 tablespoons butter or margarine
1/2 cup light-brown sugar, firmly packed
1-1/4 teaspoons salt

1. Wash parsnips. Pare; cut lengthwise into quarters; cut quarters into 3-inch pieces.
2. Place in medium saucepan. Add boiling water to measure 1 inch; simmer, covered, 20 minutes, or just until tender.
3. Drain, if necessary (most of liquid will have evaporated). Cool slightly; remove core from parsnips.

4. Melt butter in same saucepan, over medium heat. Stir in sugar and salt.
5. Add parsnips; stir gently, over low heat, until parsnips are well coated. Serve at once.
Makes 6 servings.

Creamed Onions

2 lb small white onions, peeled*
Salt
3 tablespoons butter or margarine
2 tablespoons flour
Dash pepper
Dash nutmeg
1-1/4 cups milk
2 tablespoons packaged dry bread crumbs
* Or you may use 2 cans (15-1/2-oz size) small white onions.

1. In medium saucepan, place onions, 1 teaspoon salt, and enough cold water to cover.
2. Bring to boiling. Reduce heat, and simmer, covered, 20 to 25 minutes, or until tender. Drain onions, reserving 1/2 cup liquid.
3. Melt 2 tablespoons butter in medium saucepan; remove from heat. Stir in flour, 1/2 teaspoon salt, the pepper, and nutmeg until smooth. Gradually stir in milk and reserved onion liquid.
4. Bring to boiling, stirring constantly; boil gently 1 minute. Add onions, and simmer 2 minutes.
5. Melt remaining butter; mix with bread crumbs.
6. Turn onions into serving dish; sprinkle buttered crumbs over top.
Makes 6 to 8 servings.

Buttered Peas, French Style

4 large lettuce leaves
3 lb fresh young peas, shelled*
1 teaspoon sugar
1/2 teaspoon salt
Dash pepper
2 tablespoons butter or margarine
* Or use 1 pkg (10 oz) frozen tiny peas. Cook as directed in Steps 1 to 3, 8 minutes. Spread peas with a fork; cook 8 minutes longer, or just until peas are tender. Makes 3 servings.

1. Line medium-size, heavy skillet with tight-fitting cover with 3 large lettuce leaves.
2. Add peas; sprinkle with sugar, salt, and pepper.
3. Dot with butter; top with another lettuce leaf. Cook, tightly covered, over medium heat 10 to 15 minutes, or until tender.
4. To serve, remove lettuce.
Makes 4 servings.

German-Fried Potatoes

4 medium potatoes (about 1-1/4 lb), pared
1/4 cup butter or margarine
Salt
Pepper

1. Slice potatoes, crosswise, into 1/8-inch-thick slices.
2. In hot butter in large skillet, sauté potato slices, turning occasionally, until golden-brown and tender.
3. Sprinkle with salt and pepper.
Makes 4 servings.

Perfect Baked Potatoes

4 medium to large baking potatoes (about 2-1/2 lb)
Butter or margarine
Salt
Pepper
Paprika
Dairy sour cream (optional)
Crumbled crisp bacon (optional)
Finely chopped green onion (optional)

1. Preheat oven to 425F.
2. Scrub potatoes well under cold running water. Dry thoroughly with paper towels. With fork, prick skins over entire surface. (Brush potatoes with salad oil if you like skins soft after baking.)
3. Place potatoes right on oven rack, and bake 50 to 60 minutes, or until they are easily pierced with fork or feel soft when squeezed.
4. Slash an X in top of each potato. Then, holding potato with pot holders, squeeze ends so steam can escape and potato fluffs up.
5. Add a pat of butter to each; sprinkle with salt, pepper, and paprika. Or top with sour cream and bacon or green onion.
Makes 4 servings.

Lyonnaise Potatoes

1/3 cup butter or margarine
6 medium potatoes (about 2 lb), pared and thinly
   sliced
1-1/2 cups sliced onion
1/2 teaspoon salt
Dash pepper
2 tablespoons chopped parsley

1. In hot butter in large, heavy skillet, sauté potato and onion slices, turning frequently, until golden-brown and tender—15 to 20 minutes.
2. Sprinkle with salt, pepper, and parsley.
Makes 6 servings.

French-Fried Potatoes

Single-Frying Method

1. Pare as many Idaho potatoes as desired. Cut lengthwise into 3/8-inch-thick slices. Then cut slices lengthwise into strips 3/8 inch wide. Rinse in cold water; drain well on paper towels.
2. Meanwhile, heat salad oil or shortening in deep-fat fryer* (filling at least one third full) to 385F on deep-frying thermometer.
3. Cover bottom of fryer basket with a single layer of potatoes; lower basket slowly into fat. Fry 5 or 6 minutes, or until potatoes are golden-brown and tender.
4. Remove potatoes; drain well on paper towels. Sprinkle with salt. Keep warm while frying rest of potatoes.
* Or use an electric skillet, following manufacturer's directions.

French-Fried Potatoes

Double-Frying Method

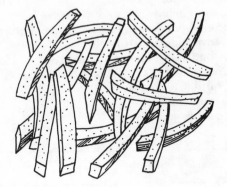

1. Pare as many Idaho potatoes as desired. Cut lengthwise into 3/8-inch-thick slices. Then cut slices into strips 3/8 inch wide. Rinse in cold water; drain thoroughly on paper towels.
2. Meanwhile, heat salad oil or shortening in deep-fat fryer* (filling at least one third full) to 360F on deep-frying thermometer.
3. Cover bottom of fryer basket with a single layer of potatoes; lower basket slowly into fat. Fry 4 minutes, or until potatoes are tender but not browned.
4. Remove potatoes; drain well on paper towels. Keep at room temperature until ready to complete cooking. Reserve oil.
5. Before serving, reheat oil to 375F on deep-frying thermometer.
6. Cover bottom of fryer basket with 2 layers of potatoes; fry 1 minute, or until potatoes are golden.
7. Remove potatoes; drain well on paper towels. Sprinkle with salt. Keep warm while frying rest of potatoes.
* Or use an electric skillet, following manufacturer's directions.

Scalloped Potatoes

3 lb potatoes
4 medium onions, thinly sliced
Boiling water
3 teaspoons salt
3 tablespoons butter or margarine
2 tablespoons flour
1/4 teaspoon pepper
1/8 teaspoon paprika
2-1/4 cups milk
2 tablespoons chopped parsley

1. Preheat oven to 400F. Lightly grease 2-quart casserole.
2. Wash, pare, and thinly slice potatoes; measure 8 cups.
3. Cook potatoes and onions, covered, in small amount of boiling water, with 2 teaspoons salt, about 5 minutes, or until slightly tender. Drain.
4. Melt butter in saucepan. Remove from heat. Stir in flour, pepper, paprika, and remaining salt until smooth. Blend in milk.
5. Cook, stirring, over medium heat, to boiling point, or until thickened and smooth.
6. In prepared casserole, layer one third of potatoes and onions. Sprinkle with 1 tablespoon parsley; top with one third of sauce. Repeat. Then add remaining potatoes and onions, and top with remaining sauce.
7. Bake, uncovered, 35 minutes, or until top is browned and potatoes are tender when pierced with fork.
Makes 6 to 8 servings.

New Potatoes with Lemon Butter

3 lb small new potatoes
Boiling water
Salt
1/2 cup butter or margarine
3 tablespoons lemon juice
2 tablespoons finely snipped chives, parsley
  or mint

1. Scrub potatoes. Pare a strip of skin, about 1/2 inch wide, around center of each potato. Place in medium saucepan; add boiling water to measure 2 inches and 1/2 teaspoon salt.
2. Bring to boiling; boil gently, covered, 20 minutes, or until potatoes are tender. Drain. Return to heat several minutes, to dry out.
3. Melt butter in small saucepan. Stir in lemon juice, chives, and 1/2 teaspoon salt. Pour over potatoes, turning to coat well.
4. Turn into serving dish.
Makes 8 servings.

Potatoes au Gratin

1-1/2 cups light cream
2 lb new potatoes, pared and very thinly sliced
1-1/2 teaspoons salt
1/4 teaspoon pepper
1 cup grated Gruyère cheese (6 oz)

1. Preheat oven to 350F. In small saucepan, heat cream just until bubbles form around edge of pan.
2. Pour 1/4 cup cream into a 1-1/2-quart shallow baking dish. Arrange one third potatoes in dish; sprinkle with one third salt, dash pepper, and one third cheese; add one third of remaining cream. Repeat twice, using rest of ingredients.
3. Set baking dish in shallow pan. Pour hot water to 1-inch level around dish.
4. Bake 30 minutes, covered. Then bake, uncovered, 1 hour longer, or until potatoes are tender.
Makes 8 servings.

Golden Whipped Potatoes

2 lb carrots, pared
1-1/2 lb potatoes, pared
1/4 cup warm milk
2 tablespoons soft butter or margarine
1/4 teaspoon nutmeg
3/4 teaspoon salt
Dash pepper

1. Cut carrots into 1-inch chunks. Quarter potatoes. Combine carrots, potatoes, and 2 cups water in 3-1/2-quart saucepan; bring to boil, covered.
2. Reduce heat; simmer 40 minutes, or until vegetables are very tender. Drain well.
3. Return vegetables to saucepan; beat, with portable electric mixer (or mash with potato masher), until smooth. Then heat slowly, stirring, over low heat, to dry out—about 5 minutes.
4. Add milk, 1 tablespoon butter, nutmeg, salt, and pepper; beat until fluffy. Pile lightly into serving dish. Top with rest of butter.
Makes 6 to 8 servings.

Fluffy Mashed Potatoes

8 medium potatoes (about 2-1/2 lb)
Boiling water
1 tablespoon salt
1 cup milk
1/4 cup butter or margarine

1. Pare potatoes; cut in quarters. Cook in 1 inch boiling water with salt, covered, until tender—20 minutes. Drain well; return to saucepan.
2. Beat, with portable electric mixer (or mash with potato masher), until smooth. Heat, slowly, stirring, over low heat, to dry out—about 5 minutes.
3. In saucepan, heat milk and butter until butter melts—don't let milk boil.
4. Gradually beat in hot milk mixture until potatoes are smooth, light, and fluffy.
Makes 6 to 8 servings.

Savory Roast Potatoes

1/2 cup butter or margarine
8 large baking potatoes (about 4 lb)
1 tablespoon seasoned salt
1/2 cup chicken broth

1. Preheat oven to 350F. Melt butter in a 13-by-9-by-1-3/4-inch baking pan.
2. Pare potatoes; roll in melted butter, to coat well. Sprinkle with seasoned salt.
3. Bake, uncovered, 1 hour. Remove pan from oven; turn potatoes. Add chicken broth.
4. Bake 1 hour longer, turning several times.
Makes 8 servings.

Sweet-and-White-Potato Casserole

6 medium white potatoes (about 2 lb)
Boiling water
1 can (1 lb, 1 oz) vacuum-pack sweet potatoes
3/4 cup milk
3/4 cup butter or margarine
2 teaspoons salt
Dash pepper

1. Pare white potatoes; cut in quarters. In large saucepan, in boiling water to cover, cook, covered, until tender—about 20 minutes. Drain well; leave in saucepan.
2. Meanwhile, in small saucepan, heat sweet potatoes over low heat. Add to white potatoes.
3. In same saucepan, heat milk and 1/2 cup butter until butter melts.
4. With electric mixer at low speed, mash potatoes until smooth. Gradually beat in hot milk mixture, salt, and pepper; beat at medium speed until potatoes are light and fluffy.
5. Turn into heated 1-1/2-quart, heatproof serving dish. Melt remaining butter; brush over potatoes. Run under broiler a few minutes, to brown top. Taste, and add more salt, if necessary.
Makes 6 to 8 servings.

Whipped Potatoes and Rutabaga

1-1/2-lb rutabaga
3-1/4 teaspoons salt
2 lb potatoes
1/8 teaspoon pepper
1/2 cup butter or margarine, melted
1/4 cup light cream
Chopped parsley

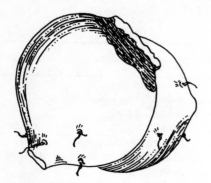

1. Wash rutabaga; pare. Cut into 1-inch cubes—you should have 4 cups cubes.
2. In 1 inch boiling water with 1 teaspoon salt in medium saucepan, simmer rutabaga, covered, about 30 minutes, or until it is very tender. Drain.
3. Meanwhile, pare potatoes. Cut into 1-inch cubes—you should have 4 cups cubes.
4. In 1 inch boiling water with 1-1/4 teaspoons salt in large saucepan, simmer potato, covered, 20 minutes, or until tender. Drain.
5. In the large saucepan, combine rutabaga with potato. Place over low heat several minutes, shaking pan occasionally to dry vegetables. Remove from heat.
6. Add remaining teaspoon salt, the pepper, and melted butter to vegetables. Mash with potato masher, or beat with portable electric mixer, until mixture is smooth and well combined.
7. Place over low heat. Gradually add cream, beating constantly with mixer or wire whisk. Continue to beat until mixture is very fluffy and heated through.
8. Pile into serving dish; sprinkle with chopped parsley.
Makes 6 to 8 servings.

Rutabaga in Cream

1 rutabaga (about 3 lb)
2 teaspoons salt
Boiling water
1 cup heavy cream
1 tablespoon flour
1 teaspoon sugar
Dash pepper
1 tablespoon chopped parsley

1. Cut rutabaga into quarters; pare. Cut into 1-inch cubes.
2. In 3-quart saucepan, add rutabaga and 1 teaspoon salt to 1 inch boiling water; bring back to boiling. Reduce heat; simmer, covered, 25 minutes, or just until rutabaga is tender.
3. Drain rutabaga well. Return to saucepan.
4. Combine cream, flour, sugar, pepper, and rest of salt. Pour over rutabaga; mix gently to combine.
5. Cook, uncovered, over low heat, about 15 minutes, or until rutabaga mixture is heated through; stir occasionally.
6. Turn mixture into a shallow, heat-proof serving dish. Run under broiler, 6 inches from heat, until cream becomes golden and puffs up slightly. Sprinkle chopped parsley over top of rutabaga.
Makes 4 to 6 servings.

Orange-Glazed Sweet Potatoes

4 large sweet potatoes or yams (about 3 lb)
Boiling water
2 teaspoons salt
1/8 teaspoon pepper
4 tablespoons light-brown sugar
2 teaspoons grated orange peel
1 cup orange juice
1/4 cup butter or margarine

1. Wash yams. Place in large saucepan. Cover with boiling water; add 1 teaspoon salt.
2. Bring to boiling; reduce heat, and simmer, covered, 35 to 40 minutes, or until tender.
3. Drain potatoes; let cool. Peel; slice crosswise into 1/4-inch-thick slices.
4. Meanwhile, preheat over to 350F. Grease a 12-by-8-by-2-inch baking dish.
5. Arrange half of potatoes, in a single layer, overlapping slightly, in prepared dish. Sprinkle with 1/2 teaspoon salt, dash pepper, 2 tablespoons brown sugar, and 1 teaspoon orange peel.
6. Repeat layering with rest of potatoes, salt, pepper, brown sugar, and orange peel. Pour over orange juice.
7. Cover dish with foil; bake 30 minutes, or until potatoes are bubbly; baste occasionally.
8. Remove cover. Dot potatoes with butter; bake, uncovered and basting occasionally, 30 minutes longer.
Makes 4 to 6 servings.

Sweet Potatoes Hawaiian

6 sweet potatoes (3 lb)*
Boiling water
1 can (8-1/2 oz) crushed pineapple
1/2 cup butter or margarine, melted
1/3 cup granulated sugar
1 teaspoon cinnamon
1/2 cup chopped pecans
1/3 cup light-brown sugar, firmly packed
1/4 cup butter or margarine, melted
* Or use 2 cans (1 lb, 2 oz size) sweet potatoes. Proceed as in Step 3, above, adding 1/4 cup reserved pineapple syrup. Bake potato mixture in 2-quart casserole at 375F for 20 minutes.

1. Scrub potatoes well; cut each in half. Cook in boiling water to cover 20 minutes, or just until tender; drain. When cool enough to handle, scoop potato out of shells, being careful to keep shells intact.
2. Preheat oven to 375F. Drain pineapple, reserving syrup.
3. In large bowl, combine sweet potato, pineapple, 1/2 cup butter, granulated sugar, and cinnamon. Beat until well blended and creamy. Fold in pecans.
4. Dip potato shells in reserved pineapple syrup. Arrange in shallow baking dish. Fill with potato mixture. Sprinkle with brown sugar, and drizzle with melted butter.
5. Bake 15 minutes, or until bubbling hot.
Makes 6 servings.

Flambéed Sweet Potatoes

6 medium sweet potatoes (about 2-1/2 lb)*
Boiling water
1/3 cup butter
1 cup brown sugar, firmly packed
1/2 cup orange juice
1/2 teaspoon salt
1/2 cup slivered toasted almonds
1/3 cup brandy
* Or use 2 cans (1-lb, 2-oz size) sweet potatoes;
continue with Step 3.

1. Scrub potatoes. Place in large saucepan, cover with boiling water; bring back to boiling. Reduce heat, and simmer, covered, 30 minutes, or until tender.
2. Drain; let cool. Peel, and halve lengthwise.
3. Melt butter in large skillet. Add brown sugar, orange juice, and salt; bring to boiling, stirring until sugar is dissolved. Boil syrup gently 5 minutes.
4. Add potatoes, turning carefully to coat with syrup; heat 5 minutes. Sprinkle with almonds.
5. Heat brandy gently in small pan. Light with match; pour, flaming, over potatoes.
Makes 6 servings.

Sweet-Potato or Yam Soufflé

6 egg whites
1/2 teaspoon salt
1/4 cup sugar
1 can (1 lb, 8 oz) sweet potatoes or yams,
   drained*
1/4 cup sugar
1/4 teaspoon cinnamon
1/4 teaspoon mace
1 tablespoon grated orange peel
1 cup light cream
* Or use 2 cups mashed, cooked fresh sweet potatoes or yams.

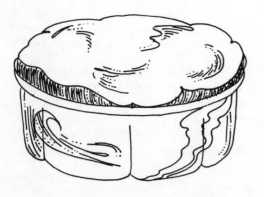

1. In large bowl, let egg whites warm to room temperature—about 1 hour. Also, preheat oven to 375F.
2. With electric mixer at high speed, beat egg whites with salt just until soft peaks form when beater is slowly raised. Gradually add 1/4 cup sugar, beating until stiff peaks form when beater is slowly raised.
3. In another large bowl, using same beater, combine sweet potatoes, 1/4 cup sugar, the cinnamon, mace, and orange peel. Beat at high speed until mixture is smooth—2 minutes.
4. Meanwhile, in small saucepan, heat cream to boiling. Slowly add to sweet-potato mixture, beating until combined.
5. With wire whisk or rubber scraper, using an under-and-over motion, fold sweet-potato mixture into egg whites just until combined.
6. Gently turn into a 1-1/2-quart, straight-sided soufflé dish. Bake 45 minutes, or until puffy and golden-brown. Serve at once, with butter, if desired.
Makes 8 servings.

Candied Sweet Potatoes

3/4 cup light-brown sugar, firmly packed
1/2 cup light corn syrup
1/4 cup butter or margarine
1/4 teaspoon salt
6 pared, cooked, large sweet potatoes, halved
   lengthwise; or 1 can (1 lb, 1 oz) vacuum-pack
   sweet potatoes

1. In large, heavy saucepan or Dutch oven, combine sugar with corn syrup, butter, and salt.
2. Bring to boiling over low heat, stirring until butter melts and sugar is dissolved.
3. Reduce heat; add sweet potatoes, arranging in a single layer. Baste well with syrup; cook, covered, over very low heat, turning once, 15 minutes.
4. Remove cover; cook, basting occasionally, 15 minutes longer, or until potatoes are well glazed.
Makes 6 servings.

Sweet-Potato-and-Pineapple Casserole

2 cans (1-lb, 1-oz size) vacuum-pack sweet
   potatoes, undrained
1 can (8-3/4 oz) crushed pineapple, undrained
1/8 teaspoon nutmeg
1 teaspoon salt
2 tablespoons light-brown sugar
1/4 cup butter or margarine, melted

Crunchy Topping:
1/3 cup light-brown sugar, firmly packed
1/2 cup butter or margarine, melted
2 cups cornflakes

1. Preheat oven to 325F.
2. Turn potatoes into a large bowl; mash smoothly. Add pineapple, nutmeg, salt, 2 tablespoons sugar, and 1/4 cup butter; mix with fork until well combined.
3. Turn into a 1-1/2-quart shallow baking dish, spreading evenly.
4. Make Crunchy Topping: In a medium bowl, mix sugar with butter. Add cornflakes; toss until cereal is well coated. Sprinkle evenly over sweet potato mixture.
5. Bake, uncovered, 40 minutes, or until topping is brown and crisp.
Makes 8 to 10 servings.
Note: Flavor is even better if made day before and reheated for serving.

Fresh Spinach Mimosa

4 lb fresh spinach*
1-1/2 teaspoons salt
1 clove garlic, split
3 tablespoons butter or margarine, melted
2 tablespoons lemon juice
1 hard-cooked egg yolk, sieved
* Or use 3 packages (10-oz size) frozen leaf
spinach. Cook as package label directs, adding
garlic to salted water. Drain; continue as above.

1. Wash spinach thoroughly, and remove stems. Place in Dutch oven with only the water clinging to the leaves. Add salt and garlic.
2. Cook over medium heat, covered and stirring occasionally, 4 to 6 minutes, or just until leaves are wilted.
3. Drain spinach well; remove and discard garlic. Return spinach to Dutch oven. Add butter and lemon juice; toss until well blended. Turn into serving dish; sprinkle with egg yolk.
Makes 8 servings.

Salsify Provençal

2 jars (14-oz size) salsify strips
1/4 cup butter or margarine
1 clove garlic, finely chopped
1/3 cup finely chopped parsley
1 teaspoon salt
1/8 teaspoon white pepper

1. Drain salsify. Melt butter in skillet.
2. Add drained salsify, garlic, parsley, salt, and pepper; toss lightly.
3. Cook, covered, over medium heat until heated through—8 to 10 minutes.
Makes 6 servings.

Spinach with Sour Cream

2 lb fresh spinach, or 2 pkg (10-oz size)
  frozen chopped spinach
1 teaspoon salt
3/4 to 1 cup dairy sour cream

1. Wash spinach; remove and discard large stems. Place in large saucepan with just the water clinging to leaves. Cook, covered, tossing with a fork once or twice, 5 minutes, or until just tender. Drain very well. Chop coarsely. If using frozen spinach, cook as label directs; drain very well.
2. Return spinach to saucepan. Add salt and sour cream; toss to mix well. (If using frozen spinach, omit 1 teaspoon salt, but add salt to taste.) Heat, over low heat, until heated through.
Makes 4 to 6 servings.

Creamed-Spinach Ring

2 lb fresh spinach, or 2 pkg (10-oz size)
  frozen chopped spinach
Grated Parmesan cheese
4 tablespoons butter or margarine
1/2 cup chopped onion
1 cup light cream
1 teaspoon salt
1/2 teaspoon sugar
Dash pepper
Dash nutmeg
4 eggs
1/2 cup fresh bread crumbs (2 slices)
1/3 cup grated Swiss or Gruyère cheese

1. Wash spinach; remove and discard large stems. Place in large kettle with just the water clinging to leaves. Cook, covered, tossing with a fork once or twice, 5 minutes, or until spinach is just tender. Drain very well. Chop coarsely. If using frozen spinach, cook as package label directs; drain very well.
2. Preheat oven to 350F. Grease a 4-1/2-cup ring mold well, and dust with grated Parmesan cheese.
3. In hot butter in large saucepan, sauté onion until tender—about 5 minutes. Add spinach, cream, salt, sugar, pepper, and nutmeg; heat just to boiling. Remove from heat.
4. In large bowl, beat eggs slightly. Add bread crumbs and Swiss cheese; gradually stir in spinach mixture.
5. Turn into prepared mold. Set mold in baking pan on oven rack; pour boiling water into pan to depth of 1-1/2 inches. Place a piece of waxed paper over top of mold.
6. Bake 30 to 35 minutes, or until knife inserted in center of spinach mixture comes out clean.
7. Loosen mold around edge with a small spatula.

Invert onto heated serving plate. Fill center of ring with Lemon-Glazed Carrots, page 533, if desired. Makes 6 to 8 servings.

Summer Squash Creole

2 lb small summer squash
4 bacon slices, diced
1/2 cup chopped green onion
1 teaspoon salt
Dash pepper
2 medium tomatoes, peeled and cubed

1. Wash squash. Cut, on the diagonal, into slices 1/2 inch thick.
2. In large skillet, sauté bacon until crisp; remove bacon, and reserve.
3. In bacon drippings, sauté green onion until tender—about 3 minutes.
4. Add squash, salt, and pepper; toss lightly. Cook, covered, over low heat, about 15 minutes, or just until squash is tender.
5. Add tomatoes; toss to combine. Cook, covered, 1 minute longer.
6. Turn into serving dish; sprinkle with bacon. Makes 6 servings.

Summer Squash with Dilled Sour Cream

2-1/2 lb small summer squash
1/4 cup butter or margarine
1/2 cup sliced onion
1-1/4 teaspoons salt
1/8 teaspoon pepper
1 tablespoon snipped fresh dill
1 cup dairy sour cream, at room temperature
Sprigs of fresh dill
Paprika

1. Wash squash. Cut squash, on the diagonal, into slices 1/2 inch thick.
2. In hot butter in large skillet, sauté onion until tender—about 5 minutes.
3. Add squash, salt, pepper, and snipped dill to skillet; toss lightly to combine.
4. Cook, covered, over low heat, 12 to 15 minutes, or just until squash is tender. Stir occasionally.
5. Drain squash, if necessary. Turn into serving dish. Spoon sour cream over squash. Top with dill sprigs; sprinkle with paprika.
Makes 6 servings.

Honey-Spice Acorn Squash

3 medium acorn squash
1/4 cup butter or margarine, melted
1/4 teaspoon cinnamon
1/2 teaspoon salt
1/4 teaspoon ginger
1/3 cup honey

1. Preheat oven to 375F.
2. Scrub squash. Cut in half lengthwise; remove seeds and stringy fibers.
3. Arrange, cut side down, in shallow baking pan. Surround with 1/2 inch hot water.
4. Bake 30 minutes.
5. Combine remaining ingredients. Pour off excess liquid from baking pan; turn squash cut side up.
6. Pour sauce into cavities; bake 15 minutes, basting now and then with sauce.
Makes 6 servings.

Baked Acorn Squash

4 (1-lb size) acorn squash
4 tablespoons butter or margarine
2 tablespoons coarsely grated orange peel
2 tablespoons coarsely grated lemon peel
2 tablespoons orange juice
2 tablespoons lemon juice
2 tablespoons sherry
Salt

1. Preheat oven to 350F. Cut squash in half; with a spoon, remove seeds and strings. Place, skin side up, on buttered 15-by-10-by-1-inch baking pan.
2. Bake until tender—40 minutes; remove from oven. Turn each squash half over, and prick flesh with fork. Dot each with 1/2 tablespoon butter. Sprinkle each with 3/4 teaspoon mixed orange and lemon peel.
3. In small bowl, combine orange juice, lemon juice, and sherry. Spoon mixture over squash and into holes in center. Sprinkle each with a little salt.
4. Return to oven, and bake 15 to 20 minutes longer, basting once or twice with liquid in center.
Makes 8 servings.

Winter Squash with Orange

2 pkg (12-oz size) frozen winter squash
1/4 teaspoon grated orange peel
2 tablespoons orange juice
1/4 cup butter or margarine
2 tablespoons light-brown sugar
1/2 teaspoon salt
Dash nutmeg

1. Cook squash as package label directs.
2. Add remaining ingredients, mixing well. Cook, over low heat, 5 minutes, stirring occasionally.
Makes 4 servings.

Stewed Tomatoes and Okra

2 tablespoons butter or margarine
1 medium onion, thinly sliced
1 pkg (10 oz) frozen okra
1 can (1 lb) stewed tomatoes
3/4 teaspoon salt
1/4 teaspoon pepper

1. In hot butter in large skillet, sauté onion just until tender—about 5 minutes.
2. Add remaining ingredients; cook gently, covered, 15 to 20 minutes, or until okra is tender.
Makes 6 to 8 servings.

Pan-Broiled Tomato Halves

3 large tomatoes (1-1/2 lb)
1-1/2 teaspoons seasoned salt
1/4 teaspoon pepper
1 tablespoon sugar
1/4 cup butter or margarine
2 tablespoons packaged dry bread crumbs
2 tablespoons chopped green onion

1. Cut out stem end of tomatoes; cut tomatoes in half crosswise.
2. Combine seasoned salt, pepper, and sugar; mix well. Sprinkle evenly over cut sides of tomatoes.
3. In hot butter in large skillet, sauté tomato halves, cut sides down, about 2 minutes, or until soft but not mushy.

4. Turn tomatoes. Baste with pan juices, and sprinkle with bread crumbs. Cook 1 minute longer.
5. With slotted utensil, remove tomatoes to serving platter; sprinkle green onion over top.
Makes 6 servings.

Baked Tomato Halves

2 large tomatoes (about 1 lb)
4 tablespoons butter or margarine
1/4 cup finely chopped onion
1 teaspoon prepared mustard
1/2 teaspoon Worcestershire sauce
2 slices white bread, torn into coarse crumbs
2 teaspoons chopped parsley

1. Preheat oven to 350F. Wash tomatoes and remove stems. Cut in half crosswise. Place, cut side up, in small shallow baking pan.
2. In 2 tablespoons hot butter in small skillet, sauté onion until tender. Stir in mustard and Worcestershire. Spread on tomato halves.
3. Melt remaining butter in same skillet. Stir in bread crumbs and parsley. Sprinkle over tomatoes.
4. Bake, uncovered, 20 minutes, or until tomatoes are heated through and crumbs are golden-brown.
Makes 4 servings.

Sautéed Squash and Tomatoes

1 lb yellow summer squash or zucchini
1/4 cup butter or margarine
1 cup thinly sliced onion
1 teaspoon salt
1/8 teaspoon pepper
3/4 teaspoon dried basil leaves
1 can (8 oz) stewed tomatoes

1. Wash squash well, scrubbing with a brush. Slice into 1/2-inch-thick diagonal slices.
2. In butter in medium skillet with tight-fitting cover, sauté onion, stirring, until golden—about 3 minutes.
3. Add squash and remaining ingredients; toss lightly to combine.
4. Cook, covered, over medium heat 10 to 15 minutes, or until squash is tender.
Makes 6 servings.

Turnips Florentine

1 lb white turnips (about 4 medium)
Boiling water
1/2 teaspoon salt
1 teaspoon instant minced onion
1 tablespoon lemon juice
2 tablespoons butter or margarine
1/2 cup finely chopped raw spinach

1. Wash turnips; pare. Cut each into quarters.
2. In 1 inch boiling water, in small saucepan, combine turnips with salt and onion.
3. Cook, covered, 25 to 30 minutes, or until turnip is tender.
4. Drain turnips well. Mash till smooth.
5. Return mashed turnips to heat. Cook, over low heat, 1 to 2 minutes to dry out.
6. Add lemon juice, butter, and spinach, mixing well. Serve at once.
Makes 4 servings.

Zucchini with Fresh Herbs

8 small zucchini (2 lb)
1 teaspoon salt
Dash pepper
1/4 cup butter or margarine, melted
2 tablespoons chopped parsley
1 tablespoon snipped chives or dill
1 tablespoon lemon juice

1. Wash zucchini; cut on diagonal into 1/4-inch-thick slices.
2. In medium skillet with tight-fitting cover, bring 1/3 cup water with the salt and pepper to boiling.
3. Add zucchini; cook, covered, over medium heat 10 minutes, or until just tender, not mushy; water should be evaporated.
4. Add butter, parsley, chives, and lemon juice; toss gently to combine. Turn into heated serving dish.
Makes 6 servings.

Sautéed Zucchini and Green Peppers

3 slices bacon, cut in 1-inch pieces
1/2 cup sliced onion
2 red peppers, cut into strips
1 green pepper, cut into strips
1 medium zucchini, cut into 1/2-inch-thick
  slices (1/2 lb)
1/2 teaspoon salt
1/4 teaspoon dried thyme leaves
Dash pepper

1. In large skillet, sauté bacon until crisp. Remove bacon bits, and set aside. In hot drippings, sauté onion until tender—about 5 minutes.
2. Add pepper strips and zucchini; sprinkle with salt, thyme, and pepper. Cook, covered, over medium heat 15 minutes, or just until vegetables are tender.
3. Turn into serving dish. Sprinkle with bacon.
Makes 4 to 6 servings.

Zucchini, Corn, and Tomatoes

2 lb zucchini
1/4 cup butter or margarine
1/2 cup thinly sliced onion
1-3/4 teaspoons salt
Dash pepper
1/2 teaspoon dried oregano leaves
3 medium tomatoes, peeled and cut into eighths
1 can (12 oz) whole-kernel corn, drained

1. Scrub zucchini very well with stiff vegetable brush; do not pare. Cut zucchini, on the diagonal, into slices 1/2 inch thick.
2. In hot butter in large skillet, sauté onion until tender—about 5 minutes.
3. Add zucchini, salt, pepper and oregano; mix well. Bring to boiling; reduce heat; simmer, covered and stirring occasionally, 15 minutes, or until zucchini is tender.
4. Add tomatoes; cook, uncovered, 5 minutes longer.
5. Add corn; cook a few minutes longer, or until the corn is heated through.
Makes 6 to 8 servings.

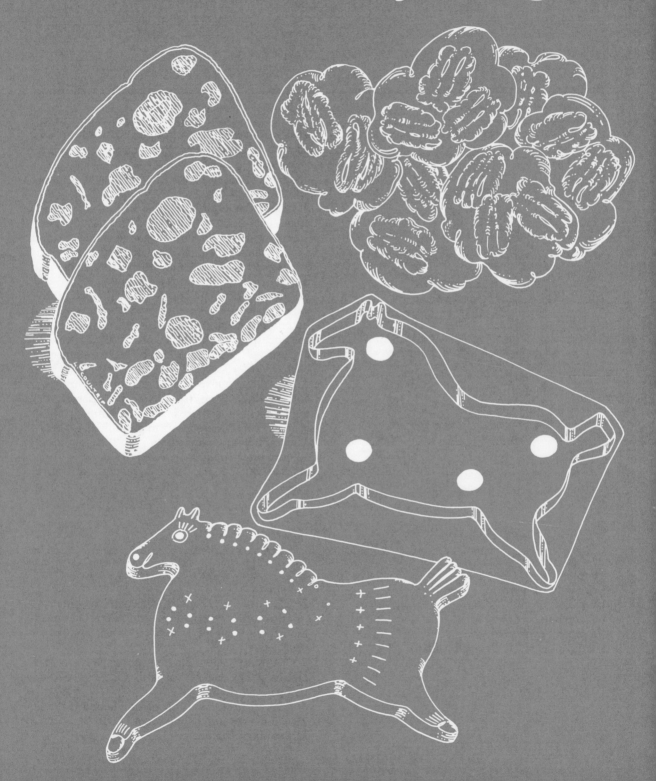

Nothing is more welcome than a gift you have made yourself. Here is a collection of Christmas goodies—candies, cookies, cakes and puddings—that will make the friendliest of all Christmas gifts to friends and family.

Candied Grapefruit and Orange Peel

2 large grapefruit (about 2-3/4 lb) or 4 large navel
    oranges (about 2-1/2 lb)
3 cups sugar
1/4 cup light corn syrup

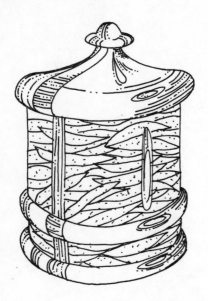

1. With sharp knife, remove peel from grapefruit or oranges in quarters.
2. In heavy, 6-quart saucepan, place peel and 2 quarts water. Bring to boiling; reduce heat, and simmer, covered, 30 to 40 minutes, or until peel is tender.
3. Drain; cool slightly. Carefully scrape excess pulp from peel.
4. In same saucepan, combine 1 cup water, 2 cups sugar, and the corn syrup. Cook over medium heat, stirring constantly, until sugar is dissolved and syrup comes to boiling. Continue cooking, without stirring, to 235F on candy thermometer, or until a little in cold water forms a soft ball.
5. Add grapefruit or orange peel; simmer gently, stirring frequently, 30 to 40 minutes, or until peel becomes translucent. (To prevent scorching during cooking, lift peel off bottom of pan several times.)
6. Turn peel and syrup into bowl. Let stand in a cool, dry place, covered, overnight.
7. Next day, remove peel from syrup to wire rack, and let drain 3 hours. Then, with scissors, cut into 1/4-inch-wide strips. Roll in remaining sugar, coating well. Place on rack to partially dry—about 3 hours. Roll in sugar again.
8. Store peel in a tightly covered container.
Makes about 1 pound candied grapefruit or orange peel.

Walnutty Caramels

2 cups sugar
1 cup light corn syrup
1 cup light cream
1/4 cup butter or margarine
1 teaspoon vanilla extract
1-1/2 cups coarsely chopped walnuts

1. Line an 8-by-8-by-2-inch pan with foil; lightly butter foil.
2. In a heavy, 3-1/2-quart saucepan, combine sugar, corn syrup, cream, and butter. Cook over medium heat, stirring with wooden spoon, until sugar is dissolved.
3. Continue cooking, stirring occasionally, to 245F on candy thermometer, or until a little in cold water forms a firm ball.
4. Remove from heat. Stir in vanilla and walnuts. Turn into prepared pan; let cool 1 hour.
Makes about 2 pounds.

Burnt-Almond Candy

1-1/3 cups almonds, with skins on
1 cup sugar

1. In heavy, medium skillet, combine almonds, sugar, and 1 cup water. Bring to boiling, stirring until sugar melts. Reduce heat; simmer until almonds make a popping sound—15 to 20 minutes.
2. Remove from heat. Stir until sugar crystallizes (mixture will become dry).
3. Return to heat; cook over low to medium heat until sugar starts to melt and clings to almonds, forming a glaze—15 minutes.
4. Turn out onto a greased cookie sheet to cool. Separate almonds with a fork. Cool completely. Store in container with tight-fitting lid, in a cool, dry place.
Makes about 2 cups.

Sugar Nuts

1 cup brown sugar, firmly packed
1/2 cup granulated sugar
1/2 cup dairy sour cream
1 teaspoon vanilla extract
2 cups walnut halves

1. Combine both kinds of sugar and the sour cream in medium saucepan. Cook over medium heat, stirring, until sugar is dissolved.
2. Continue cooking, without stirring, to 238F on candy thermometer, or until a little in cold water forms a soft ball. Remove from heat.
3. Add vanilla and walnuts. Stir gently until all nuts are coated.
4. Turn onto waxed paper; with a fork, separate the nuts. Let dry.
Makes about 1 pound.

Hazelnut Truffles

3/4 cup hazelnuts
6 squares (1-oz size) semisweet chocolate
1/3 cup heavy cream
1-1/3 cups confectioners' sugar
1 egg white
1 tablespoon Grand Marnier, Cointreau, or rum

1. Grind hazelnuts in a blender or in a Mouli grater. Line bottom of a 9-by-5-by-3-inch loaf pan with waxed paper.
2. In small, heavy saucepan, combine chocolate and cream. Heat over low heat just until chocolate is melted. Remove from heat.
3. In medium bowl, combine nuts, sugar, and egg white. With wooden spoon, stir until combined. Stir in chocolate mixture and liqueur, to combine well.
4. Turn into prepared pan, or use to fill fluted paper bonbon cups. Refrigerate until firm. Cut into 3/4-inch squares. Store, covered, in refrigerator.
Makes about 60 pieces.

Tyrolean Honey Cookies

1/4 cup candied orange peel
1/4 cup candied lemon peel
1-1/2 cups whole unblanched almonds
3/4 cup honey
1-1/4 cups granulated sugar
1 tablespoon grated fresh lemon peel
1/4 cup lemon juice
1-1/2 tablespoons kirsch or brandy
4 cups sifted* all-purpose flour
Dash salt
1 teaspoon baking soda
1 teaspoon cinnamon
Dash cloves
Dash nutmeg
1 cup confectioners' sugar
Candied red cherries
* Sift before measuring.

1. Put candied orange and lemon peel and almonds through fine blade of food grinder. Or grind in blender until very fine.
2. In medium saucepan, bring honey and granulated sugar just to boiling, stirring (do not boil). Add fresh lemon peel and lemon juice. Set aside to cool—10 minutes. Then add ground peel and almonds and the kirsch.
3. Into a large bowl, sift flour with salt, baking soda, cinnamon, cloves, and nutmeg. Make well in center of flour mixture; pour in fruit-and-honey mixture. Work together, with a kneading motion, until well combined. Dough will be quite stiff.
4. Preheat oven to 350F.
5. Divide dough into 4 parts. Refrigerate 3 parts until ready to use. Between 2 sheets of waxed paper, on slightly dampened surface, roll out one part to form a rectangle 6 by 8 inches, 1/4 inch thick. Cut into 16 rectangles. Place, about 1 inch apart, on ungreased cookie sheets.
6. Bake about 10 minutes, or just until golden.
7. Repeat with rest of dough.
8. In small bowl, combine confectioners' sugar with 3 tablespoons water; stir to mix well. Brush over cookies while they are still warm. Decorate with bits of candied cherries.
9. Store in a tightly covered jar or plastic container, in a cool, dry place, several weeks.
Makes 64.

Cinnamon Stars

1/3 cup egg whites (about 2 egg whites)
1-1/4 cups granulated sugar
1-1/2 cups unblanched almonds, ground
1-1/2 tablespoons cinnamon
1 cup sifted confectioners' sugar

1. In small bowl of electric mixer, let egg whites warm to room temperature—about 1 hour.
2. With electric mixer at medium speed, beat egg whites until soft peaks form when beater is raised.
3. Add 1-1/4 cups granulated sugar to egg whites, 2 tablespoons at a time, beating after each addition. Continue to beat until mixture is thick and glossy—about 10 minutes.
4. In medium bowl, combine the almonds with cinnamon. Stir in egg-white mixture; mix to combine well.
5. Refrigerate dough, covered, overnight.
6. Lightly sprinkle wooden board or pastry cloth with flour and granulated sugar. Roll out dough, one half at a time, 1/4 inch thick.

7. Using 3-inch star cookie cutter, cut out cookies. Place, 1 inch apart, on lightly greased cookie sheets.

8. Let cookies stand, uncovered, at room temperature 2 hours.

9. Preheat oven to 300F. In small bowl, combine confectioners' sugar with 2 tablespoons water; mix until smooth.

10. Bake cookies 20 minutes. Brush tops with glaze; bake 5 minutes longer.

11. Remove cookie sheets to wire racks; let cookies cool several minutes. With spatula, carefully remove the cookies to wire racks to cool completely. Makes about 2-1/2 dozen.

Pfeffernuesse

Cookie Dough:
2-1/2 cups unsifted all-purpose flour
1/2 teaspoon ground cloves
1/2 teaspoon nutmeg
1/2 teaspoon cinnamon
1/4 teaspoon ground ginger
1/4 teaspoon black pepper
1/4 teaspoon ground cardamom
1/4 teaspoon baking soda
2 eggs
1 cup dark-brown sugar, packed
1/3 cup finely chopped walnuts

Glaze:
3 cups granulated sugar
Dash cream of tartar
2 egg whites

1. Make Cookie Dough: Sift flour with cloves, nutmeg, cinnamon, ginger, pepper, cardamom, and baking soda. Set aside.

2. In large bowl, with electric beater at high speed, beat 2 eggs and the brown sugar until light—about 5 minutes.

3. At low speed, beat in flour mixture and nuts until well combined. Dough will be sticky.

4. Preheat oven to 375F. Lightly grease cookie sheets.

5. With wet hands, pinch off dough by tablespoonfuls. Roll into 1-inch balls.

6. Place on prepared cookie sheets. Bake 12 to 15 minutes. Remove to wire rack to cool.

7. Meanwhile, make Glaze: In large saucepan, combine sugar, cream of tartar, and 1 cup water. Bring to boiling over medium heat, stirring until sugar is dissolved. Boil, without stirring, 5 minutes, or until mixture forms a 2-inch thread when dropped from a spoon, or to 235F on candy thermometer.

8. Meanwhile, in medium bowl, with electric mixer at medium speed, beat egg whites until stiff peaks form when beater is raised. Pour syrup in continuous stream into egg whites, beating constantly. Beat until mixture thickens slightly.

9. Drop cookies, a few at a time, into glaze; with fork, turn to coat completely. Lift out, and place on wire rack to dry.

10. Store in tightly covered container about 1 week, to mellow.

Makes about 3-1/2 dozen.

Pecan Pralines

1 cup granulated sugar
1 cup light-brown sugar, packed
1/2 cup light cream
1-1/2 cups pecan halves
2 tablespoons butter or regular margarine

1. In 2-quart, heavy saucepan, combine sugars and cream. Over medium heat, bring to boiling, stirring occasionally with wooden spoon. Continue cooking, stirring occasionally, to 228F on candy thermometer, or until syrup spins a 2-inch thread when dropped from spoon.
2. Add pecans and butter. Cook over medium heat, stirring frequently, to 236F on candy thermometer, or until a little in cold water forms a soft ball.
3. Remove pan to wire rack. Let cool 10 minutes—to 200F. Stir about 1 minute, or until slightly thick but still glossy.
4. Drop by rounded tablespoonfuls, 3 inches apart, onto sheet of foil or double thickness of waxed paper. Pralines will spread into large patties. If mixture becomes too stiff, stir in a drop or two of cold water.
5. To store: Arrange in layers in plastic refrigerator container or tin with tight-fitting lid, with waxed paper between layers. Store in a cool, dry place. Makes 1 dozen.

Pecan Crescents

2 cups unsifted all-purpose flour
1 cup butter or regular margarine, softened
1 cup ground pecans or hazelnuts
1/2 cup unsifted confectioners' sugar
1/8 teaspoon salt
1 teaspoon vanilla extract
1/4 teaspoon almond extract

Vanilla Sugar:
3-inch strip vanilla bean, cut up
2 cups sifted confectioners' sugar

1. In large bowl, combine flour, butter, nuts, 1/2 cup sugar, the salt, and extracts. Mix, with hands, until thoroughly combined. Refrigerate, covered, 1 hour.
2. Make Vanilla Sugar: In electric blender, combine cut-up vanilla bean and 1/4 cup confectioners' sugar; cover; blend at high speed about 8 seconds. Combine with remaining confectioners' sugar on a large sheet of foil.
3. Preheat oven to 375F.
4. Shape cookies: Form dough into balls, using 1 tablespoon dough for each. Then, with palms of hands, form each ball into a roll 3 inches long.
5. Place, 2 inches apart, on ungreased cookie sheets. Curve each to make a crescent. Bake 12 to 15 minutes, or until set but not brown.
6. Let stand 1 minute before removing. With spatula, place hot cookies in vanilla sugar; turn gently to coat both sides. Cool completely.
7. Store in a tightly covered crock or cookie tin in a cool, dry place.
8. Just before serving, coat with additional vanilla sugar, if desired.
Makes about 3-1/2 dozen.

Chocolate Fudge Deluxe

3 cups sugar
1 env unflavored gelatine
1 cup milk
1/2 cup light corn syrup
3 squares (3 oz) unsweetened chocolate
1-1/4 cups butter or margarine
2 teaspoons vanilla extract
1 cup coarsely chopped walnuts

1. Butter an 8-by-8-by-2-inch pan.
2. In a 3-1/2-quart saucepan, mix sugar with dry gelatine. Add milk, corn syrup, chocolate, and butter.
3. Cook over medium heat, stirring frequently, to 238F on candy thermometer, or until a little in cold water forms a soft ball that flattens when removed from water.
4. Remove from heat; pour into a large mixing bowl. Stir in vanilla. Cool 25 minutes.
5. Beat with wooden spoon until candy thickens. Stir in walnuts. Spread in prepared pan. Let cool; then cut into squares.
Makes about 2-1/2 pounds.

Spritz Wreaths

2 cups sifted* all-purpose flour
1/4 teaspoon salt
3/4 cup butter or regular margarine, softened
1/2 cup sugar
1 egg yolk
1 teaspoon vanilla extract, or 1/2 teaspoon almond extract
Cinnamon candies, angelica, miniature multicolor nonpareils
* Sift before measuring.

1. Refrigerate ungreased cookie sheets until ready to use.
2. Preheat oven to 375F. Sift flour with salt. Set aside.
3. In large bowl, with electric mixer at medium speed, beat butter, sugar, egg yolk, and vanilla until smooth and fluffy.
4. At low speed, beat in flour mixture until smooth and well combined. Fill cookie press with dough. Make one or all of the following shapes.
5. Wreaths: Use star disk. Force dough onto cold cookie sheet in a 12-inch strip; cut strip into 3 parts. Form each part into a circle. Decorate wreaths with cinnamon candies and bits of angelica.
6. Christmas trees: Use Christmas-tree disk. For each, stand press upright on cold cookie sheet; force out dough, to form a tree. Reverse handle of press slightly, to cut off dough. Sprinkle the trees with nonpareils. Cookies should be 1-1/2 inches apart.
7. Rosettes: Use a rosette disk. For each, stand press upright on cold cookie sheet; force out dough to form a rosette. Reverse handle of press slightly, to cut off dough. Cookies should be 1-1/2 inches apart.
8. Bake cookies 8 to 10 minutes, or until light golden. Remove to rack; cool. Store in airtight container.
Makes 3 dozen.

Hot Mincemeat Pie

2 jars (1-lb, 2-oz size) prepared mincemeat
2 tablespoons brandy
1/4 cup sherry
1 pkg (11 oz) piecrust mix
1 egg yolk
1 tablespoon light cream

Hard Sauce:
2/3 cup soft butter or margarine
1 or 2 tablespoons brandy
2 cups unsifted confectioners' sugar

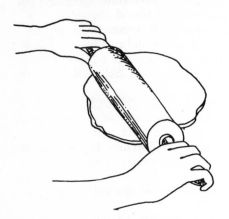

1. In medium bowl, combine mincemeat, brandy, and sherry; mix well.
2. Prepare piecrust mix as the label directs. Form into a ball.
3. On lightly floured surface, roll out half of pastry to form a 12-inch circle. Fit into a 9-inch pie plate. Preheat oven to 425F.
4. Turn mincemeat filling into pie shell; trim pastry to the edge of the pie plate.
5. Roll out remaining pastry to form a 12-inch circle. Make several slits near center for steam vents; adjust pastry over filling. Trim pastry evenly, leaving a 1/2-inch overhang all around.
6. Fold edge of top crust under bottom crust; press together to seal. Crimp edge decoratively. Lightly brush top, but not edge, with egg yolk beaten with light cream.
7. Bake 30 to 35 minutes, or until crust is golden-brown.
8. Meanwhile, make Hard Sauce: In small bowl, with electric mixer, combine all ingredients; beat at medium speed until smooth and fluffy—2 minutes. Store in refrigerator, covered.
9. Cool pie partially on wire rack. Serve warm with hard sauce.
Makes 8 or 9 servings.

Easy Christmas Cherry Cake

1 cup butter, softened
2 cups sugar
1 teaspoon almond extract
8 eggs
4 cups unsifted all-purpose flour
1 pkg (15 oz) light raisins
1 jar (8 oz) candied cherries
1 jar (8 oz) chopped candied citron

1. Preheat oven to 300F. Grease a 10-inch tube pan. Line bottom and side with brown paper; grease paper.
2. In large bowl, with electric mixer at medium speed, beat butter with sugar and almond extract until light and fluffy.
3. Add eggs, one at a time, beating well after each addition.
4. At low speed, gradually beat in flour.
5. Add raisins, cherries, and citron; with spoon, mix until well combined. Turn into prepared pan.
6. Bake about 2 hours and 25 minutes, or until cake tester inserted near center comes out clean.
7. Let cool in pan on wire rack 30 minutes. Turn out of pan; let cool completely on rack.
Makes 5-pound cake.

Best of All Fruitcakes

1 lb golden raisins
1/2 lb seeded raisins
1/4 lb currants
1/2 cup dark rum or brandy
1 lb candied pineapple
1/2 lb candied red cherries
1/4 lb candied citron
1/8 lb candied lemon peel
1/8 lb candied orange peel
2 cups unsifted all-purpose flour
1/2 teaspoon mace
1/2 teaspoon cinnamon
1/2 teaspoon baking soda
1/4 lb almonds, shelled, blanched, and coarsely
    chopped
1/4 lb walnuts or pecans, shelled and coarsely
    chopped
1/2 cup butter or regular margarine, softened
1 cup granulated sugar
1 cup brown sugar, packed
5 eggs, slightly beaten
1 tablespoon milk
1 teaspoon almond extract
Rum or brandy
1 can (8 oz) almond paste
Frosting Glaze, page 567
Angelica
Candied red cherries

1. In large bowl, combine raisins and currants. Add 1/2 cup rum; toss to combine. Let stand, covered, overnight.

2. Next day, line a 10-inch tube pan: On heavy brown paper, draw an 18-inch circle, and cut out. Set pan in center of circle; draw around base of pan and tube. With pencil lines outside, fold paper into eighths; snip off tip. Unfold circle; cut along folds to second circle. Grease both the tube pan and unpenciled side of paper well. Fit paper, greased side up, into pan.

3. Prepare fruits: With sharp knife, cut pineapple in thin wedges; cut 1/2 pound cherries in half; cut citron and lemon and orange peels into very thin strips. Add to raisins and currants; mix well.

4. On sheet of waxed paper, sift 1-1/2 cups flour with spices and baking soda. Set aside. Preheat oven to 275F.

5. Combine remaining 1/2 cup flour with nuts and fruits; toss lightly.

6. In large bowl of electric mixer, at medium speed, beat butter until light. Gradually beat in granulated sugar, then brown sugar, beating until very light and fluffy.

7. Beat in eggs, milk, and almond extract until thoroughly combined.

8. At low speed, beat in flour mixture, mixing just until combined. Turn batter into fruit and nuts. Mix well with hands.

9. Turn into prepared pan, pressing batter down in pan evenly all around.

10. Bake 3 hours and 15 minutes, or until a cake tester inserted near center comes out dry.

11. Let cake stand in pan on wire rack 30 minutes to cool slightly. Turn out of pan; gently remove paper. Let cool completely.

12. To store: Wrap cake in cheesecloth soaked in rum or brandy. Place in a cake tin with a tight-fitting cover. Add a few pieces of raw, unpeeled apple. (As cheesecloth dries out, resoak in rum or brandy.) Store in a cool place several weeks.

13. To decorate cake for serving: Roll almond paste between 2 sheets of waxed paper into an 8-inch circle. Remove top sheet of paper. Invert paste onto cake; remove paper. With sharp knife, trim edge of paste; then press paste to cake. Spread paste with Frosting Glaze, letting it run down side of cake. Cut angelica into thin slices. Cut cherries in half. Decorate cake.

Makes a 5-pound fruitcake.

Dutch Tile Cookies

1-3/4 cups unsifted all-purpose flour
1-1/2 teaspoons baking powder
1/8 teaspoon salt
3/4 cup butter or regular margarine, softened
3/4 cup sugar
1 teaspoon vanilla extract
1/4 teaspoon almond extract
Blanched whole almonds, halved
Red and green candied cherries, cut in bits

1. Preheat oven to 375F. On sheet of waxed paper, sift flour with baking powder and salt; set aside.
2. In large bowl, with wooden spoon, beat butter with sugar and vanilla and almond extracts until smooth. Gradually add flour mixture, stirring until well combined. Dough will be stiff. Divide in half.
3. On slightly dampened surface, between 2 sheets of waxed paper, roll out half of dough into a 7-1/2-inch square. Cut into 25 (1-1/2-inch) squares. Decorate each with a nut half and bits of cherries. Place, 2 inches apart, on ungreased cookie sheets.
4. Bake 10 to 12 minutes, or just until lightly browned. Remove to wire rack; cool completely. Repeat with remaining dough.
5. To store cookies: When completely cool, place in tightly covered jar or tin container. Store in a cool, dry place.
Makes 50.

White Fruitcake

Fruit Mixture:
4 cans (4-1/2-oz size) blanched almonds, coarsely chopped
2 pkg (10-oz size) light raisins
1 jar (8 oz) diced candied citron
1 jar (8 oz) candied red cherries, halved
1 jar (4 oz) candied pineapple slices, cut into strips
1/4 cup brandy

Cake Batter:
1-1/2 cups butter or regular margarine, softened
2 cups sugar
1 teaspoon almond extract
6 eggs
4 cups unsifted all-purpose flour
3/4 cup milk

Brandy
1 can (8 oz) almond paste
Frosting Glaze, below
Angelica
Candied citron
Candied cherries

1. Prepare Fruit Mixture: In large kettle, combine almonds, raisins, diced citron, 1 jar cherries, the pineapple, and 1/4 cup brandy; mix well. Let stand at room temperature, covered, overnight.
2. Next day, line a 10-inch tube pan: On heavy brown paper, draw a 16-1/2-inch circle, and cut out. Set pan in center of circle; draw around base of pan and tube. With pencil lines outside, fold paper into eighths; snip off tip. Unfold circle; cut along folds to circle drawn around base of pan. Grease both tube pan and paper well; fit paper, greased side up, into pan.
3. Preheat oven to 275F.
4. Make Cake Batter: In large bowl, with electric mixer at high speed, beat butter, sugar, and almond extract until smooth and fluffy. Add eggs, one at a time, beating after each addition until light and fluffy.
5. At low speed, beat in flour (in fourths) alternately with milk (in thirds), beginning and ending with flour.
6. Add batter to fruit mixture; mix until well combined. Turn the batter into the prepared pan, packing lightly.
7. Bake 3-1/4 hours, or until cake tester inserted in cake comes out clean. Let cool completely in pan on wire rack. Turn out of pan; peel off paper.

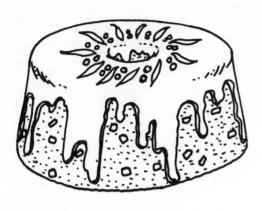

8. Wrap cooled cake in cheesecloth that has been soaked in 1/3 cup brandy. Then wrap very tightly in plastic film or foil. Store in refrigerator. Resoak cheesecloth with brandy as it dries out—about once a week. Store cake 5 to 6 weeks, to develop flavor.

9. To decorate before serving: Roll almond paste between 2 sheets of waxed paper into an 8-inch circle. Remove top sheet of paper. Invert paste onto top of cake; remove paper. With sharp knife, trim edge of paste; then press paste to cake. Spread paste with Frosting Glaze, letting it run down side of cake. Cut angelica to make stems for flowers. Cut candied citron and cherries for the leaves and petals. Decorate cake.

Makes a 7-pound tube cake.

Frosting Glaze

1-1/2 cups confectioners' sugar
2 tablespoons light cream
1/4 teaspoon almond extract

In small bowl, combine sugar, cream, and extract; beat until mixture is smooth.

Steamed Plum Pudding

1 jar (8 oz) diced mixed candied peel
1/4 lb suet, finely chopped
1/3 cup finely chopped walnuts or pecans
1-1/2 cups raisins
1 cup currants
1 tablespoon cinnamon
1-1/2 teaspoons ground ginger
1/4 teaspoon nutmeg
1/2 teaspoon allspice
1/4 teaspoon salt
1 cup sugar
1/2 cup strawberry or cherry preserves
2 cups packaged dry bread crumbs
4 eggs
2 tablespoons milk
1/3 cup rum or brandy
1/3 cup sherry
Pudding Sauce, below

1. Chop candied peel very fine.

2. In large bowl, combine peel, suet, nuts, raisins, currants, spices, salt, sugar, preserves, bread crumbs.

3. In medium bowl, beat eggs until very thick. Beat in milk.

4. To fruit-spice mixture, add beaten egg mixture with rum and sherry. Stir with large spoon to mix well.

5. Turn batter into a well-greased 1-1/2-quart pudding mold with tight-fitting cover. Cover mold, and place on trivet in large kettle. Pour in enough boiling water to come halfway up side of mold. Cover kettle.

6. Steam pudding 5 hours. (Water in kettle should boil gently; add more water as needed.)

7. Remove mold to wire rack; uncover; let cool completely in mold. Invert on wire rack; lift off mold.

8. To store: Wrap pudding in plastic film, then in foil. Store in refrigerator several weeks.

9. To serve: Return pudding to mold; cover, and steam, as directed above, 50 minutes, or until thoroughly hot. Serve at once with Pudding Sauce. Makes 10 to 12 servings.

Pudding Sauce

1 pkg (3 oz) cream cheese, softened
1 egg
1 cup confectioners' sugar
2 tablespoons butter or margarine, softened
1 teaspoon lemon juice
Pinch salt
1 cup heavy cream, whipped
About 2 tablespoons golden rum, or 1/2 to
  1 tablespoon rum extract

1. In medium bowl, with spoon, beat cheese until light. Add egg, sugar, butter, lemon juice, and salt; beat well.
2. Fold in whipped cream and rum just until combined.
3. Refrigerate, covered.
Makes 3 cups.

Swiss Biberli

Dough:
1 cup honey
2/3 cup sugar
1-1/2 teaspoons grated lemon peel
2 tablespoons brandy, rum, or kirsch
4 cups unsifted all-purpose flour
2 teaspoons baking soda
1 teaspoon ground anise
1/4 teaspoon cinnamon
1/4 teaspoon ground ginger
1/4 teaspoon ground cloves
1/4 teaspoon ground coriander

Filling:
3 cups blanched almonds
1 cup sugar
1/2 cup apricot jam
1/3 cup honey
1 tablespoon grated lemon peel
3 tablespoons lemon juice
1-1/2 teaspoons almond extract

Glaze:
1-1/2 cups sugar

1. Make Dough: In small saucepan, combine 1 cup honey, 2/3 cup sugar, and 2 tablespoons water. Heat, stirring, just until sugar dissolves—do not boil.
2. Let cool until lukewarm—about 20 minutes. Stir in 1-1/2 teaspoons lemon peel and the brandy.
3. Into large bowl, sift flour with baking soda, anise, cinnamon, ginger, cloves, and coriander. Add honey mixture; mix with wooden spoon to a stiff dough; then knead until smooth. Shape into a ball.
4. Refrigerate, covered, 2 days.
5. Make Filling: Grind almonds, using fine blade of grinder, or use electric blender. In medium bowl, combine almonds, 1 cup sugar, the jam, honey, lemon peel, juice, extract; mix until blended. Set aside.
6. Preheat oven to 350F. Lightly grease cookie sheets.
7. Divide dough in half; return half to refrigerator. On lightly floured surface, roll out dough, 1/4 inch thick, into a 10-inch square. Cut crosswise, to make 4 strips.
8. Place 5 to 6 tablespoons filling in a 1/2-inch-wide mound down center of each strip of dough. Bring edges of dough over filling, to overlap; press gently, to seal. Place rolls seam side down. Repeat with remaining dough and filling.
9. Cut filled rolls into 1-inch pieces, using sharp floured or moistened knife. Place seam side down on prepared cookie sheets.
10. Bake 20 minutes, or until light brown.
11. Meanwhile, make Glaze: In small saucepan, combine sugar with 1/2 cup water. Bring to boiling, stirring until sugar is dissolved. Boil 5 to 7

minutes, until it forms 2-inch thread when dropped from spoon, or to 230F on candy thermometer.

12. Remove hot cookies to wire rack, and brush with glaze. Cool completely. Pack in airtight containers, to mellow for several weeks.

Makes about 80.

Springerle

4 cups sifted* all-purpose flour
1 teaspoon baking powder
1/2 teaspoon salt
4 eggs
2 cups granulated sugar
2 teaspoons grated lemon peel
2 tablespoons anise seed
Confectioners' sugar
* Sift before measuring.

1. Sift flour with baking powder and salt twice; set aside.
2. In large bowl of electric mixer at high speed, beat eggs until thick and lemon-colored—about 5 minutes.
3. At medium speed, gradually beat in granulated sugar, 2 tablespoons at a time, beating after each addition. Continue to beat until mixture is thick and smooth—about 10 minutes—occasionally cleaning side of bowl with rubber scraper.
4. Add flour mixture and lemon peel to egg mixture; with a wooden spoon, mix well until mixture is smooth.
5. Refrigerate dough, covered, overnight. Also, refrigerate springerle rolling pin.
6. Lightly grease 2 large cookie sheets; sprinkle each with 1 tablespoon anise seed.
7. Divide dough into 3 parts. Refrigerate until ready to roll out.
8. Sprinkle pastry cloth or wooden board lightly with confectioners' sugar.
9. Roll one part of dough on pastry cloth, to coat with sugar; then roll out to an 8-by-5-1/2-inch rectangle. Repeat with remaining dough.
10. Remove springerle pin from refrigerator. Coat surface lightly with confectioners' sugar. Starting from long side, slowly roll pin once, firmly and evenly, over dough, to make designs. (If dough sticks to springerle pin, peel off with a spatula.)
11. With floured sharp knife, carefully cut along straight lines in dough, to make individual cookies.
12. With wide spatula, transfer cookies to prepared cookie sheets, placing them 1/2 inch apart. Let stand, uncovered, at room temperature overnight.
13. Next day, preheat oven to 325F. Bake cookies 15 minutes, or just until light golden. Remove to wire rack; cool completely.
14. Store springerle in tightly covered container in a cool, dry place 2 to 3 weeks before serving.

Makes about 4-1/2 dozen.

Dundee Cake

2 cups sifted* all-purpose flour
1 teaspoon baking powder
1/2 teaspoon salt
1/8 teaspoon nutmeg
1 cup dried currants
3/4 cup diced mixed candied fruits and peels
3/4 cup seeded dark raisins
1/2 cup light raisins
1/4 cup candied cherries, halved
3/4 cup butter or regular margarine, softened
2/3 cup sugar
3 eggs
3 tablespoons sliced blanched almonds
* Sift before measuring.

1. Preheat oven to 325F. Grease well a 9-inch tube pan.
2. Reserve 2 tablespoons flour. Sift remaining flour with baking powder, salt, and nutmeg. Set aside.
3. In medium bowl, combine currants, candied fruits and peels, raisins, cherries, and reserved flour; mix well. Set aside.
4. In large bowl, with electric mixer at medium speed, beat butter with sugar until light and fluffy. Add eggs, one at a time, beating well after each addition.
5. At low speed, gradually add flour mixture, beating until well combined.
6. Stir fruit mixture into batter until combined. Turn into prepared pan; smooth top with spatula. Sprinkle with almonds; gently press into top.
7. Bake 60 to 65 minutes, or until cake tester inserted in center comes out clean. Let cool in pan on wire rack 15 minutes. Remove from pan; let cool completely.
Makes a 9-inch tube cake.

Fruitcake Cookies

2-1/2 cups sifted* all-purpose flour
1 teaspoon baking soda
1 teaspoon salt
1 teaspoon cinnamon
1 cup butter or regular margarine, softened
1-1/2 cups sugar
2 eggs
4 pkg (8-oz size) pitted dates, coarsely chopped
2 jars (4-oz size) cubed candied pineapple, finely chopped
1 cup candied cherries, quartered
1 can (3-1/2 oz) sliced almonds, coarsely chopped
1 cup walnuts, coarsely chopped
* Sift before measuring.

1. Preheat oven to 400F. Sift flour with baking soda, salt, and cinnamon; set aside.
2. In large bowl, with wooden spoon, or portable electric mixer at medium speed, beat butter, sugar, and eggs until light and fluffy.
3. Stir in flour mixture until well combined. Add fruits and nuts, mixing well.
4. Drop by level tablespoonfuls, 2 inches apart, onto ungreased cookie sheets.
5. Bake 8 to 10 minutes, or until golden-brown. Let stand 1 minute. Remove to wire rack; cool.
Makes about 8 dozen.

Menus for Entertaining

Festive Friday Dinner

Planned for Six

Gazpacho*
Fillets of Sole Florentine*
Crisp Potato Sticks
Bibb Lettuce
with
Oil and Vinegar Dressing
Toasted Herb Rolls
Warm Apricot Soufflé*
with
Whipped Cream
or
Old-Fashioned Strawberry Shortcake*
Chilled White Wine
Coffee

Formal Dinner

Planned for Six

Cocktails
Salted Nuts
Royal Consommé Madrilène*
Toasted Crackers
Rack of Lamb Provençal*
Browned New Potatoes
Stuffed Mushrooms*
Red Bordeaux or Burgundy
Green Salad Bowl
Rolls   Butter
Chocolate-Nut Torte*
or
Crème de Menthe Sherbet*
Demitasse
Liqueurs

An Italian Dinner

Planned for Six

Melon with Port
Veal Scallopini*
Noodles with Pesto Sauce*
Sautéed Zucchini and Green Peppers*
Bread Sticks   Butter
Biscuit Tortoni*
or
Spumoni*
Chilled White Wine
Coffee

First Taste of Spring

Planned for Six

Fresh Asparagus Vinaigrette*
Roast Capon with Herbs*
Buttered Rice and Mushrooms
Lemon-Glazed Carrots*
Crisp Toasted English Muffins
Strawberry Snow with
Custard Sauce*
Coconut Macaroons
Coffee

A Sunday in May

Planned for Six to Eight

Eggs Mayonnaise*
Roast Leg of Lamb*
Grilled Tomato Halves
Buttered Fresh Asparagus
Salad of Mixed Spring Greens
Crisp French Bread
Fresh Pineapple in Shell* with Lemon Sherbet
Fudge Brownies*
Tea/Coffee

Special Spring Dinner

Planned for Six to Eight

Cold Ratatouille*
Roast Leg of Lamb en Croûte
with Mushroom Stuffing*
Buttered Whole Green Beans
White Turnips   Salad of Mixed Greens
Warm Buttered French Bread
Apricot-Glazed Poached Pears*
Red Bordeaux
Coffee

Dinner at Eight

Planned for Six to Eight

Cocktails
Mousse of Chicken Livers*
Cream-of-Winter-Squash Soup*
Duckling à l'Orange*
Wild and White Rice
Savory Stuffed Mushrooms*
Green Salad with Endive
Hot Rolls   Sweet Butter
Chocolate Pots de Crème*
Almond Lace Wafers*
Red Burgundy
Coffee

A Little French Dinner

Planned for Four

Snails in Garlic Butter*
or
Moules Marinière*
Coq au Vin*
with
New Potatoes
Petits Pois
French Bread   Sweet Butter
Crème Brûlée* with Strawberries
or
Chocolate Mousse*
Red Burgundy
Demitasse

A Warm Weather Menu

Planned for Four

Cold Cucumber Soup*
Poached Salmon Steaks in White Wine*
Parsleyed New Potatoes
Fresh Asparagus Mimosa*
Toasted English Muffins
Lime Sherbet with Strawberries*
or
Lemon Chiffon Pie*
Chilled White Wine
Iced Coffee

A Man's Favorite Dinner

Planned for Four

Guacamole with Crisp Vegetables*
London Broil with Sautéed Onions*
Maitre d'Hôtel Butter Sauce*
Perfect Baked Potatoes*
Baked Tomato Halves*
Hot Garlic Bread*
Apple Dumplings,* Cinnamon Ice Cream Sauce*
Red Wine
Coffee

Patio Spring Dinner

Planned for Six to Eight

Chilled Tomato Consommé
Roast Leg of Veal in White Wine*
Casserole of Potatoes au Gratin*
Fresh Spinach Mimosa*
Sautéed Mushrooms
Basket of Hot Rolls   Butter
Honolulu Coconut Pie*
Chilled White Wine
Coffee

Buffet in Springtime

Planned for Six to Eight

Chilled Avocado Halves au Naturel
(Avocado Halves filled with
Oil and Vinegar Dressing)
Roast Stuffed Veal en Gelée*
Buttered New Potatoes with Fresh Mint
Green Beans Hollandaise*
Hot Cheese Rolls
Strawberries in May Wine*
Chilled White Wine
Coffee

Christmas Holiday Dinner

Planned for Eight to Ten

Hot Cheese Bacon Puffs*
Jellied Consommé with Red Caviar*
Roast Beef*
Yorkshire Pudding* or Savory Roast Potatoes*
Buttered Peas with Mushrooms
Cauliflower Surprise*
Hearts of Celery or Fennel, Cherry Tomatoes,
Radishes and Scallions on Ice
Hot Rolls   Butter
Steamed Plum Pudding
with
Pudding Sauce
or
Glazed Lemon-Cream-Cheese Cake*
Red Burgundy
Coffee

Traditional Thanksgiving

Planned for Eight to Ten

Hors d'Oeuvre
Chilled Caviar   White Toast Rounds
Lobster Bisque with Sherry*
Golden Roast Turkey*
Old-Fashioned Dressing*
Giblet Gravy
Cranberry-Apple Relish*
Butternut Squash or Glazed Sweet Potatoes*
Broccoli with Lemon Sauce*
Grapefruit-and-Avocado Salad Platter*
Assorted Hot Rolls   Butter
Old-Fashioned Pumpkin Pie*
Ice Cream Turkeys
White or Rosé Wine   Cider
Coffee
Liqueurs

New England Thanksgiving

Planned for Six to Eight

Corn-and-Clam Chowder*
Roast Stuffed Pheasant or Turkey*
Giblet Gravy*
Baked Acorn-Squash Halves*
Broccoli Polonaise*
Crisp Relishes   Cranberry Jelly
Buttered Hot Biscuits or Cornbread Squares
Warm Maple-Squash Pie*
or
Baked Indian Pudding*
with Vanilla Ice Cream
Hot Mulled Cider*
Coffee

A Creole Thanksgiving

Planned for Six to Eight

Liver Pâté en Gelée*
Roast Turkey Flambé
with Oyster-and-Pecan Dressing*
Giblet Gravy
Compote of Fresh Oranges and Cranberries
Sweet Potato and Pineapple Casserole*
Cauliflower Polonaise*
Tossed Green Salad Bowl
Hot Buttered Rolls
Hot Mincemeat Pie* with Hard Sauce
Champagne
Coffee

Holiday Weekend Brunch

Planned for Six to Eight

Grilled Grapefruit with Kirsch*
Eggs Benedict*
Baked Tomato Halves*
Coffeecake,* Hot Cornbread*
Strawberry Preserves
Champagne
Coffee

A Ladies' Luncheon

Planned for Six

Hot Madrilène
Warm Asparagus-and-Swiss-Cheese Tart*
Tossed Green Salad Bowl
Hot Rolls
Spanish Melon or Honeydew with Strawberries
Poundcake Squares*
Coffee/Tea

Modern Thanksgiving

Planned for Six to Eight

Hot Clam Broth with Tarragon*
Turkey au Vin* with Mushrooms,
Onions, and New Potatoes
Tossed Green Salad
Crusty French Bread   Cranberry Relish
Grape-Sherbet Ring
Warm Spongecake
Beaujolais
Coffee

An Easter Buffet

Planned for Eight

Spring Lettuce Soup*
Baked Ham with Curried Fruit*
Orange-Glazed Sweet Potatoes*
Cold Asparagus Vinaigrette*
Assorted Hot Rolls   Butter
Frozen Maple Mousse*
Rosé Wine
Coffee
Liqueurs

Hearty Sunday Breakfast

Planned for Eight

Fresh-Orange Spritzer*
or Honeydew with Lime Slices and Mint Sprigs
Buttermilk Pancakes with
Strawberries and Sour Cream*
Maple Syrup
Baked Ham, Sausage, and Bacon*
Warm Danish Pastry
Coffee

A Very Informal Buffet

Planned for Eight to Ten

Cantaloupe and Honeydew Melon with Prosciutto
Moussaka* or Manicotti*
Garden Salad Bowl*
Salt Sticks   Butter
Floating Heart Ritz*
Red or White Wine
Coffee

The Cocktail Party

Planned for Twenty

Daiquiri Punch* Bowl and other drinks
Cheese Pâté Pineapple*
Assorted Crackers
Guacamole Dip with Crisp Vegetables*
Cocktail Shrimp*
Chafing Dish of Swedish Meatballs*
Savory Steak Slices*
Basket of Party Rye Bread
Salted Nuts
Coffee

A Cocktail Party Buffet

Planned for Twenty

Caviar-Cream-Cheese Ball*
Pumpernickel Party Rounds
Rumaki or Swedish Meatballs*
Quiche Lorraine*
Ginger-Glazed Baked Ham*
Buttered French Bread Slices
Cocktail Olives*   Assorted Nuts
Cocktails
Coffee

Summer Sunday Brunch

Planned for Six

Bloody Marys
or Chilled Cantaloupe Soup*
Lobster Newburg*
Oatmeal Toast   Bar-le-Duc
Coffee

For Weekend Guests

Planned for Six to Eight

Piñas Coladas* or Orange-Lemon Mist
Ham and Eggs in a Cloud*
Baked Cherry Tomatoes
Warm Coffeecake Squares*
Strawberry-Jam Crescents*
Coffee

A Winter Buffet

Planned for Eight to Ten

Tureen of Pumpkin Soup*
Paella* or Chicken Tetrazzini*
or Breast of Chicken in Madeira Sauce*
Tossed Green Salad Bowl
Poppyseed and Sesame Seed Crescent Rolls*
Meringue Torte*
or
Pineapple in Crème de Menthe*
Brownies*
Chilled White Wine
Coffee

Italian-Style Buffet

Planned for Eight

Antipasto Platter
of
Roasted Peppers,* Eggplant Appetizer*
Pickled Garden Relish*
Our Favorite Lasagna*
Salad of Lettuce, Watercress, and Fennel
Italian Whole Wheat Bread   Butter
Peaches in Marsala*
with Amaretti (Macaroons)
Red Chianti
Caffè Espresso

Tea for the Committee

Planned for Ten to Twelve

Pineapple-Apricot-Nut Loaf*
or
Lemon Tea Bread*
with Sweet Butter
Toasted English Muffins
Strawberry Jam
Almond Tile Cookies*
Petits Fours*
Hot Tea*

Lunch on the Terrace

Planned for Six to Eight

Hot Tomato Consommé* Cheese Straws*
Curried-Chicken Salad in Avocado Halves*
Curry Accompaniments (Chutney, Salted
Peanuts, Chopped Cucumber, Chopped Tomato,
Kumquats, Coconut Chips)
Hot Popovers*
Fresh Orange Sherbet*
Coffee/Iced Tea

A Late Supper

Planned for Six to Eight

Jellied Madrilène
Curried Crabmeat Crêpes*
Leek and Endive Vinaigrette*
Assorted Hot Rolls   Butter
Raspberry Sherbet*
with
White and Gold Angel Cake*
Rosé Wine or Champagne
Coffee

A Curry Supper

Planned for Six

Shrimp Curry or Breast of Chicken Curry
Fluffy White or Saffron Rice*
Braised Fresh Spinach
Curry Accompaniments
(Chutney, Chopped Green Pepper, Salted
Peanuts, Cucumber Slices, Diced Tomato, Sliced
Banana, Pineapple Chunks)
Toasted Buttered English Muffins
Honolulu Coconut Pie*
or
Lemon- or Lime-Curd Tarts*
White Wine
Coffee

Nutrition & Meal Planning, Low-Calorie Cooking

With nutrition facts seeming to change so frequently, many homemakers wonder whether it is possible for them to feed their families adequately. Yet it is really quite easy for menus to add up to good nutrition. We need nutrients for three purposes: To provide materials for growth and replacement of muscle tissue, to provide a source of energy (measured as calories), and to provide materials for regulating body processes. Some nutrients help in only one of these functions; others, in more than one.

To help you plan menus that include adequate amounts of protein, fat, carbohydrate, vitamins and minerals that we need in our diets every day, the United States Department of Agriculture has developed an easy-to-follow menu plan.

All you have to know to plan nutritionally balanced meals is the four basic food groups and how much of each belongs in the daily menu. (See chart— Eating for Health and Beauty, page 579.) The milk group consists of milk, cheese, ice cream and other made-with-milk desserts. Adults need a minimum of two servings a day, children three servings a day, and teen-agers four servings a day. The meat group, which includes poultry, fish, eggs, dried peas and beans, usually serves as the main course for at least two meals a day. Fruits and vegetables should add up to four daily servings; one should be a green or yellow vegetable, and at least one should be citrus fruit or tomato. And finally, four helpings of bread or cereal in any of their many forms complete the daily diet. With these simple rules firmly fixed in mind, you can begin the intriguing business of improvising, putting the basics together in a variety of attractive combinations.

To get you started, we present seven days' worth of menus for breakfast, lunch and dinner based on these principles of meal planning. Each of the four food groups is represented in the proper amounts each day. Foods have been selected to complement one another in color, flavor and texture, for the greatest appetite appeal. And the day's eating is distributed, as it should be, among a real breakfast, a planned lunch, and a balanced dinner. If you want to ring your own variations on our menus, follow this general pattern:

Breakfast should consist of fruit or juice (this is a good place to make sure of vitamin C); cereal with milk, or eggs, or meat; an energy food (toast, roll or coffeecake); beverage.

Lunch should include two to three ounces of cheese, meat, poultry, or fish, or two eggs; bread, roll, potato, or spaghetti; one vegetable and one fruit (either may be raw or cooked); and a beverage. Dinner should be made up of three to four ounces of meat, fish, or poultry; a helping of potato, rice, macaroni, noodles, or bread; one or two servings of vegetables (raw or cooked); a dessert; and a beverage.

Our menus presuppose a family with growing children. If there are teen-agers (especially teen-age boys) or a man whose job is a physically strenuous one, portions may have to be increased and perhaps augmented with extra sweets and fats.

On the other hand, weight-watchers would do well to observe these rules:

From the milk group, choose skim milk, dry cottage cheese, or skim-milk cheese as often as possible. Avoid cream, ice cream, and butter.

In the meat group, emphasize fish and lean meat. Cut all fat from meat. Pass up gravies and sauces. Serve fruit unsweetened or with a noncaloric sweetener, vegetables plain or with very small amounts of lower-calorie margarine, and salads with low-calorie dressing.

Use skim milk on cereals; keep bread to minimum requirements; and avoid extras, such as crackers, cookies, cakes, pies, and rolls.

Eating for Health and Beauty

Plan menus to include the recommended number of servings from each of these four basic food groups. The following menus are for one week and give you an idea of the possibilities.

Note: All the other minerals and vitamins you need you will get in these same foods—milk, meat, fruits, vegetables, cereals and breads. That's the reason for eating a balanced diet.

Food You Need Every Day	You Need It For	Why You Need It
Milk 1 pint for adults 1 quart for teen-agers 1-1/2 pints for subteens	Protein Other good sources: cheese, eggs, meats, poultry, fish, dried beans	1. For muscles for good posture and good figure 2. For smooth, healthy skin 3. For silky hair and strong fingernails 4. For good red blood; to make antibodies to fight disease 5. To make children grow
	Calcium Other good sources: cheese, cottage cheese, yoghurt, ice cream	1. To make strong, straight bones 2. To keep bones strong 3. For beautiful teeth
	Vitamin A Other good sources: liver, egg yolks, butter, cheese, fortified margarine, yellow vegetables, green leafy vegetables	1. So your eyes will adapt quickly to changes in light 2. To keep your skin smooth and unblemished 3. For high resistance to infection 4. For vim and vigor
	Vitamin D From vitamin-D milk. Other good sources: sunshine, cod-liver oil	1. To make and keep bones and teeth strong
Meat 2 servings (4 to 5 ounces in all) meat, fish, poultry, eggs, or dried beans or peas (You should have 3 to 4 eggs and liver in some form each week)	Protein	See Milk
	Iron Other good sources: molasses, rolled oats, raisins, whole wheat, dried apricots	1. To make red blood cells—the oxygen-carrying cells 2. For strong, normal fingernails
	B Vitamins Other good sources: milk, cheese, egg yolks, whole-grain or enriched bread or cereals, green leafy vegetables (spinach, broccoli), peanuts, bananas	1. To give you bounce-back from fatigue 2. To keep your eyes clear 3. To keep your heart and nerves working right 4. For good digestion and appetite 5. To prevent dry skin
Fruits and Vegetables 1/2 to 3/4 cup citrus fruit (oranges, grapefruit, lemons, limes, tangerines) or other fruits or vegetables high in vitamin C	Vitamin C Other good sources: strawberries, broccoli, red and green peppers, Brussels sprouts, tomatoes, cauliflower, cabbage, cantaloupe	1. To keep all body cells healthy and strong—bones, muscle, skin, nerves, blood vessels, etc. 2. To keep gums and teeth tip-top 3. To keep resistance to infection high 4. To speed recovery from injury 5. To keep you from bruising easily
4 servings (1/2 to 3/4 cup each) other fruits or vegetables, one of which is green or yellow	Vitamin A Best sources: carrots, sweet potatoes, yams, spinach, tomatoes, yellow squash, dried apricots, green leafy vegetables	See Milk
Whole-Grain or Enriched Cereals and Breads 4 to 6 servings (bread, cereals, macaroni, noodles, rice, cornmeal, grits)	Iron B Vitamins Carbohydrates	See Meat See Meat For energy

Breakfast	Lunch	Dinner
Chilled Orange-Grapefruit Juice Crisp Rice Cereal Milk Buttered Whole-Wheat Toast Strawberry Jam Hot Cocoa with Whipped Cream Coffee	Egg Salad and Lettuce in Buns* Carrot and Celery Sticks, Pickles, Olives Oatmeal Icebox Cookies, page 154 Cinnamon Applesauce Milk/ Tea	Pineapple-Glazed Baked Ham Loaf* Baked Sweet-Potato Casserole Buttered Italian Green Beans Cucumber Coleslaw Buttered Cornbread Squares Chilled Canned Pear Halves with Chocolate-Ice-Cream Sauce Milk/Coffee

Egg Salad and Lettuce in Buns

1/3 cup mayonnaise or cooked salad dressing
2 tablespoons finely chopped sweet gherkins
2 tablespoons finely chopped onion
2 tablespoons finely chopped parsley
1-1/2 tablespoons juice from sweet gherkins
1/2 teaspoon salt
1/2 teaspoon prepared mustard
1/8 teaspoon pepper
6 hard-cooked eggs, chopped (about 2-1/4 cups)
Crisp lettuce
4 large buns, split and buttered

1. In medium bowl, combine mayonnaise, gherkins, onion, parsley, gherkin juice, salt, mustard, and pepper; mix well. Add eggs, mixing until well blended.
2. Use, with lettuce, to fill buns.
Makes 4 servings.

Pineapple-Glazed Baked Ham Loaf

1 cup milk
1 egg
2 tablespoons catsup
2 tablespoons prepared mustard
1 teaspoon salt
1/8 teaspoon pepper
2 cups soft white-bread crumbs
1-1/2 lb ground cooked ham (6 cups)
1/2 lb ground pork
1/2 lb ground veal
2 tablespoons finely chopped onion
2 tablespoons chopped parsley

Glaze:
1 can (8-1/2 oz) sliced pineapple
1/4 cup light-brown sugar, firmly packed
2 tablespoons cider vinegar
1/2 teaspoon ground ginger
8 maraschino cherries

1. Preheat oven to 350F.
2. In large bowl, combine milk, egg, catsup, mustard, salt, and pepper; beat until well blended. Stir in bread crumbs; let stand several minutes.
3. Add ham, pork, veal, onion, and parsley; mix well. In shallow baking pan, shape meat mixture into loaf about 11 inches long and 5 inches wide.
4. Bake, uncovered, 30 minutes.
5. Meanwhile, make Glaze: Drain juice from pineapple into small saucepan. Add sugar, vinegar, and ginger; bring to boiling, stirring. Cut pineapple slices in half; add with cherries to boiling mixture. Reduce heat and simmer 5 minutes. Remove from heat.
6. Remove ham loaf from oven. Pour half of glaze, without fruit, over top. Bake 30 minutes. Arrange some of fruit on ham loaf; cover with remaining glaze. Bake 20 minutes longer.
7. With wide spatulas, remove ham loaf to warm platter. Spoon glaze from pan over top. Serve with remaining fruit and, if desired, catsup.
Makes 8 to 10 servings.

Breakfast	Lunch	Dinner
Chilled Prunes and Orange Sections Buttered Toaster Corn Cakes Strawberry and Apricot Jams Milk/Coffee	Beef-and-Vegetable Soup Quick Pizzas* Chocolate Pudding Milk/Tea	Braised Swiss Steak, Family Style* Poppy-Seed Noodles Casserole of Green Beans and Mushrooms Tossed Green Salad Whole-Wheat Bread Butter Cheese and Crackers Fresh Fruit Bowl Milk/Coffee

Quick Pizzas

4 English muffins
Butter or margarine
1 can (8 oz) tomato sauce with mushrooms
1 cup grated mozzarella cheese (4 oz)
4 slices bacon, cooked but not crisp; or 1 can (2 oz) anchovy fillets
Dried oregano leaves
Grated Parmesan cheese

1. Split muffins; spread lightly with butter. Place, cut side up, on cookie sheet or rack of broiler pan. Broil until muffins just start to get golden-brown. Remove from oven.
2. Spread each half with tomato sauce, and sprinkle with mozzarella—about 2 tablespoons of cheese on each. Quarter bacon slices, and add to muffins, dividing evenly. Or add anchovy fillets. Sprinkle each with about 1/8 teaspoon oregano and some Parmesan.
3. Broil until cheese bubbles and browns slightly. Serve at once, with more Parmesan.
Makes 4 servings.

Braised Swiss Steak, Family Style

2-lb round steak, 1-1/2 inches thick
2 tablespoons flour
1 teaspoon salt
1/4 teaspoon pepper
2 tablespoons salad oil
2 medium onions, cut into eighths
1 can (1 lb) stewed tomatoes
1 bay leaf

1. Wipe steak with damp paper towels.
2. Combine flour, salt, and pepper. Sprinkle half over one side of steak; pound into meat, using wooden mallet or rim of saucer. Repeat on other side.
3. In hot oil in Dutch oven or large skillet, brown steak well on both sides—15 to 20 minutes in all. Brown onion along with steak last 5 minutes.
4. Stir in stewed tomatoes and bay leaf; bring to boiling. Reduce heat, and simmer, covered, 2 hours, or until meat is tender.
5. To serve: Remove steak to heated serving platter. Remove bay leaf. Pour some sauce over steak, and pass the rest.
Makes 4 to 6 servings.

Breakfast	Lunch	Dinner
Chilled Orange Juice Soft-Cooked Egg on Buttered Whole-Wheat Toast Spiced Sugar Doughnuts Cocoa/Coffee	Cup of Tomato Soup Cottage-Cheese Summer Salad* Boston Brown Bread Butter Glazed Ginger Cookies, page 148 Milk/Iced Tea	Crown Roast of Spareribs* with Corn-Bread Stuffing Buttered Peas Yellow Squash Sliced Tomatoes with Herb Salad Dressing Chunky Applesauce and Apricots with Spiced Cream Milk/Coffee

Cottage-Cheese Summer Salad

1 lb cream-style cottage cheese
1/3 cup grated pared carrot
1/3 cup diced pared cucumber
1/3 cup finely chopped green onion
Crisp lettuce leaves

1. In medium bowl, mix cottage cheese with carrot, cucumber, and green onion until well blended.
2. Place mixture in lettuce leaves on serving platter.
Makes 4 servings.

Crown Roast of Spareribs with Corn-Bread Stuffing

2 racks of spareribs (about 4 lb)
1/4 teaspoon salt
1/2 cup butter or margarine
1/2 cup chopped onion
1/2 cup chopped green pepper
1 can (8 oz) cream-style corn
1/2 cup milk
1/2 teaspoon dried marjoram leaves
1 pkg (8 oz) corn-bread-stuffing mix
3/4 cup bottled barbecue sauce

1. Preheat oven to 350F. Wipe spareribs with damp paper towels. Trim by cutting a strip from bottom of ribs, so each rack will be 7 inches high all the way across; save trimmings. Shape the two racks into a standing crown, with meaty side of ribs facing out; fasten with skewers or wooden picks. Sprinkle with salt.
2. Line a small roasting pan with heavy-duty foil. Place meat crown in pan; tuck reserved trimmings inside crown, against ribs. Add 2 cups water to pan.
3. Roast, covered, 1-1/4 hours.
4. Meanwhile, in hot butter in large skillet, sauté onion and green pepper until tender—about 5 minutes. Stir in corn, milk, and marjoram; bring to boiling. Remove from heat. Add corn-bread-stuffing mix; stir until moistened. Set aside.
5. Remove crown from oven. Pour off pan drippings, reserving 1/2 cup. Stir reserved drippings into corn-bread stuffing.
6. Brush entire crown with some of barbecue sauce; spoon stuffing into center. Cover center and ends of ribs with foil.
7. Roast, basting occasionally with remaining barbecue sauce, 35 to 45 minutes longer, or until ribs are glazed and slightly browned.

8. So stuffing will not fall out, lift foil lining with crown to serving platter; then remove top foil, and carefully tear off foil that shows around base of crown.
Makes 6 servings.

Breakfast	Lunch	Dinner
Fruit-Juice Drink (with Vitamin C) Very-Special Oatmeal* Maple Sugar Milk Hot Buttered Toast Marmalade Milk/Coffee	Hawaiian "Ham"-and-Baked-Bean Casserole* Carrot and Celery Sticks Peanut Butter Cookies, page 159 Chocolate Milk/Tea	Tomato Juice on the Rocks with a Twist of Lemon Braised Liver with Onions Scalloped-Potato Casserole Green-Cabbage Wedges Lemon-Buttered Beets Dark-Brown Bread Butter Baked Apples with Vanilla Pudding Sauce, page 182 Milk/Tea

Very-Special Oatmeal

1-1/4 teaspoons salt
2 cups old-fashioned rolled oats
1/2 cup seedless raisins
1/3 cup coarsely chopped unblanched almonds
1 cup hot chunky applesauce
6 to 8 maple-sugar candies or use brown sugar

1. In medium saucepan, bring 4-1/2 cups water and the salt to boiling. Stir in oats and raisins; boil gently, stirring occasionally, 7 to 10 minutes. Remove from heat.
2. Stir in almonds; cover, and let stand a few minutes.
3. To serve: Layer oatmeal and applesauce in 6 to 8 individual bowls. Top each with a maple-sugar candy. Serve with cream or milk.
Makes 6 to 8 servings.

Hawaiian "Ham"-and-Baked-Bean Casserole

2 cans (1-lb size) pork and beans in tomato sauce
1 can (13-1/2 oz) pineapple chunks, drained
2 tablespoons minced onion
1 teaspoon dry mustard
1 can (12 oz) luncheon meat
Whole cloves
2 tablespoons light-brown sugar

1. Preheat oven to 350F.
2. Turn beans into 1-1/2-quart baking dish. Gently stir in pineapple, onion, and mustard.
3. Cut luncheon meat into quarters lengthwise; then cut each piece in half crosswise, to make 3-1/2-by-3/4-by-3/4-inch pieces. Score each, and arrange on beans to make stripes. Stud each piece of meat with 2 or 3 cloves, and sprinkle with brown sugar.
4. Bake, uncovered, 30 minutes, or until beans are bubbling.
Makes 6 servings.

Breakfast	Lunch	Dinner
Fresh Grapefruit Halves Hot Orange Biscuits* Butter or Margarine Strawberry Jam Crisp Bacon Milk/Coffee	Favorite Tuna Salad* Crackers and Cheese Fresh Fruit Easy Sugar Cookies, page 149 Strawberry Milk Shakes Tea	Baked Lamb-Chop-and-Potato Hot Pot* Buttery Green Beans Mixed-Green Salad Bowl Buttered Hot Rolls Applesauce-Date Cake, page 119 Milk/Coffee

Orange Biscuits

1 tablespoon granulated sugar
1 tablespoon brown sugar
2 tablespoons grated orange peel
2 cups packaged biscuit mix
2/3 cup milk

1. Preheat oven to 450F.
2. Mix sugars and 1 tablespoon peel. Set aside.
3. Prepare biscuit mix as the label directs for drop biscuits, using 2/3 cup milk and adding rest of peel.
4. Drop dough by tablespoons onto greased cookie sheet. Top each with orange sugar.
5. Bake 10 to 12 minutes, or until golden on top. Makes 10 to 12 biscuits.

Baked Lamb-Chop-and-Potato Hot Pot

6 shoulder lamb chops (about 3-1/2 lb)
1/4 cup flour
2 teaspoons salt
1/2 teaspoon pepper
1 can (10-3/4 oz) condensed chicken broth, undiluted
2 teaspoons bottled steak sauce
1 lb onions, peeled and sliced
6 carrots, pared and sliced (1/2 lb)
6 potatoes, pared and sliced (1-1/2 lb)

1. Preheat oven to 350F. Trim excess fat from lamb chops. Heat trimmed fat in large, heavy skillet.
2. On waxed paper, combine flour, salt, and pepper. Dip chops in flour mixture, coating lightly. Reserve remaining flour mixture.
3. In hot fat, brown chops on both sides. Remove from heat. Remove chops from skillet.
4. Stir reserved flour mixture into 2 tablespoons drippings in skillet until smooth. Gradually stir in chicken broth and steak sauce; bring to boiling, stirring constantly. Reduce heat; simmer 1 minute. Remove from heat.
5. In 3-1/2-quart casserole, layer half of onion and carrot; cover with browned chops. Add half of potato and the remaining onion. Overlap remaining potato and carrot slices over top. Pour broth mixture over all.
6. Bake, covered, 2 hours, or until meat and potatoes are tender.
Makes 6 servings.

Favorite Tuna Salad

3/4 cup mayonnaise or cooked salad dressing
1 tablespoon grated onion
1/2 teaspoon salt
1/8 teaspoon pepper
2 cans (7-oz size) solid-pack tuna, drained
1/2 cup sliced celery
1/4 cup chopped green pepper
1/2 cup diced sweet gherkins
Crisp salad greens
1 tomato, sliced
2 hard-cooked eggs, cut into wedges
Chopped parsley

1. In medium bowl, combine mayonnaise, onion, salt, and pepper; mix well.
2. Add tuna, celery, green pepper, gherkins; toss until well blended. Refrigerate, covered, about 2 hours, to blend flavors and chill.
3. At serving time, line serving platter with salad greens; mound tuna salad in center. Garnish with tomato slices, egg wedges, parsley.
Makes 6 servings.

Breakfast	Lunch	Company Dinner
Fresh Grapefruit Halves with Orange Sections*	Grilled Deviled-Cheese Sandwiches*	London Broil, page 354
Pecan Pancakes with Butter and Warm Maple Syrup	Carrot and Cucumber Sticks	Sautéed Sliced Mushrooms
Crisp Bacon	Chilled Canned Peaches and Pears	Lemon-Buttered New Potatoes
Milk/Coffee	Butterscotch Ice Box Cookies, page 155	Broiled Tomato Halves
	Milk/Tea	Tossed Salad of Mixed Greens with Roquefort Dressing
		Warm Garlic-Buttered French Bread
		Floating Island, page 174
		Milk/Coffee

Grilled Deviled-Cheese Sandwiches

8 slices white bread
1 pkg (8 oz) sharp-process-American-cheese slices
8 teaspoons pickle relish
1/3 cup soft butter or margarine
1 tablespoon prepared mustard
Midget sweet gherkins
Cherry tomatoes
Pitted ripe olives

1. Preheat sandwich grill or electric skillet as manufacturer directs.
2. Top 4 bread slices with a slice of cheese. Spread each with 2 teaspoons pickle relish. Then add remaining cheese slices and bread.
3. In small bowl, beat butter with mustard until well blended. Spread half of mixture over tops of sandwiches.
4. Place, buttered side down, on grill. Spread with remaining butter mixture. Grill until golden-brown on both sides.
5. Make kebabs, placing a gherkin, tomato, and olive on wooden pick. Use to garnish sandwiches.
Makes 4 servings.

Fresh Grapefruit Halves with Orange Sections

2 grapefruit, chilled
4 teaspoons honey
2 oranges, sectioned, chilled, and drained
Mint leaves

1. Halve grapefruit. Cut out centers, and remove any seeds. With grapefruit knife, cut around each section, to loosen.
2. Drizzle each half with 1 teaspoon honey. Lift alternate sections of grapefruit, and place an orange section behind each.
3. Place remaining orange sections in center of halves. Garnish with mint.
Makes 4 servings.

Breakfast	Lunch	Dinner
Chilled Grapefruit Juice	Bowl of Creamy Corn Chowder*	Broiled Hamburgers, page 372
Double-Boiler Scrambled Eggs*	Lettuce-and-Cucumber	Sautéed Mushrooms
Toasted English Muffins	Salad in Rolls	Baked Macaroni and Tomatoes
Butter or Margarine	Apples, Bananas, Grapes	au Gratin*
Plum Jam	Milk/Tea	Buttered Green Peas
Milk/Coffee		Radishes, Celery, Carrot Sticks
		Buttered and Herbed
		Toasted English Muffins
		Honey-Baked Pears
		Nutmeg Ice Cream
		Milk/Coffee

Baked Macaroni and Tomatoes au Gratin

4 tablespoons butter or margarine
2 tablespoons packaged dry bread crumbs
1/4 cup chopped onion
1/4 cup dairy sour cream
1/2 teaspoon salt
Dash cayenne
2 cans (15-oz size) macaroni with cheese sauce
3 hard-cooked eggs
1 large tomato, sliced
Parsley sprigs

1. Preheat oven to 350F.
2. Melt butter in small skillet. Remove 2 tablespoons, and toss with bread crumbs. Set aside.
3. In remaining hot butter in skillet, sauté onion until golden—about 3 minutes. Remove from heat. Add sour cream, salt, cayenne; mix well.
4. Turn 1 can macaroni with cheese sauce into 1-1/2-quart casserole. Quarter 2 eggs; arrange on macaroni. Add sour-cream mixture, then remaining can of macaroni with cheese sauce, spreading evenly. Arrange tomato slices around edge; sprinkle with buttered crumbs.
5. Bake, uncovered, 30 to 35 minutes, or until hot and bubbly around edge. Slice remaining egg, and use with parsley to garnish casserole.
Makes 6 servings.

Double-Boiler Scrambled Eggs

8 eggs
1/2 cup milk
1/2 teaspoon salt
1/8 teaspoon pepper

1. In top of double boiler, combine eggs, milk, salt, and pepper. With rotary beater, beat until well blended.
2. Cook over gently boiling water, stirring occasionally, 10 to 15 minutes, or until eggs are of desired doneness.
Makes 4 servings.

Creamy Corn Chowder

2 slices bacon, diced
1 small onion, thinly sliced
2 medium potatoes, pared and diced (2 cups)
1 can (1 lb, 1 oz) cream-style corn
1-1/2 cups milk
2 tablespoons butter or margarine
1-1/4 teaspoons salt
1/2 teaspoon sugar
1/8 teaspoon pepper
Chopped parsley

1. In medium saucepan, sauté bacon and onion until onion is golden.
2. Add potatoes and 3/4 cup water; bring to boiling. Boil gently, covered, about 10 minutes, or until potatoes are tender but not mushy.
3. Add corn, milk, butter, salt, sugar, and pepper; simmer, covered, 10 minutes, or until hot.
4. Serve in soup bowls. Garnish with parsley.
Makes 6 to 8 servings.

Dieting and Low-Calorie Cooking

Our basic pattern for sensible dieting is geared to approximately 1,500 calories per day. You may need to alter this according to individual needs. If you're a serious dieter or must diet periodically, our low-calorie recipes will make your dieting easier. We've reduced the caloric count normally found in the individual recipes with the help of lower-calorie foods and prepared products.

Basic Diet Pattern

Here is an outline for three meals a day which includes the foods you should eat to keep fit, in amounts that add up to about 1,500 calories.

Breakfast
1 serving fruit high in vitamin C, as orange, grapefruit, strawberries, or cantaloupe
1 egg
1 slice whole-wheat toast
1 pat butter or margarine
1 glass skim milk

Lunch
2 eggs, or 1/2 cup cottage cheese, or 2 slices (1 oz each) cheese, or about 3 ounces cooked meat, poultry, or fish
1 serving Free vegetable
1 serving 35-Calorie vegetable
1 slice bread
1 pat butter or margarine
1 serving 60-Calorie fruit
1 glass skim milk

Dinner
About 3 ounces cooked meat, poultry, or fish
1 small potato, or 1 medium ear of corn
1 serving Free vegetable
1 serving 35-Calorie vegetable
1/2 pat butter or margarine, or 1/2 tablespoon mayonnaise or cooked salad dressing
1 serving 60-Calorie fruit

1 glass skim milk

Free Vegetables

The following vegetables are relatively so low in calories that you may eat up to a cupful of them without counting the calories.

Asparagus
Bean sprouts
Broccoli
Brussels sprouts
Cabbage
Cauliflower
Celery
Cucumber
Eggplant
Endive
Green beans
Green peppers
Lettuce
Mushrooms
Radishes
Sauerkraut
Spinach
Summer squash (crookneck, pattypan, zucchini)
Tomatoes
Watercress

35-Calorie Vegetables

No need to bother with elaborate calorie counting: These vegetables average about 35 calories for each half cupful. Eat a variety, and count each at the one simple figure.

Artichokes
Beets
Carrots
Peas
Winter squash, as acorn or Hubbard
Yellow turnips

Vegetables needn't be dull because you have to give up slathering them with butter and rich sauces. Try seasoning them with seasoned salt and seasoned pepper; a teaspoon or two of chopped fresh herbs, as parsley, basil, mint, and thyme; a grating of lemon rind; or a squeeze of lemon. Dress them, even hot ones, with low-calorie salad dressing.

60-Calorie Fruits

Here is a list of fresh fruits in amounts that average about 60 calories if you don't eat the same fruit every day, but eat a variety. When fresh fruits are not available, choose from the large selection of diet-pack canned ones. You will find the calorie count marked on the label.

1 medium apple
3/4 cup unsweetened applesauce
3 medium apricots
1 small banana
3/4 cup blackberries
3/4 cup blueberries
1/2 medium cantaloupe
15 cherries
2 figs, dried or fresh
1/2 large grapefruit
3/4 cup grapefruit juice
1 cup grapes
1 wedge (1/8) honeydew melon
1 medium orange
1/2 cup orange juice
1 large peach
1 medium pear
1 cup diced pineapple
2 large plums
1 cup strawberries
1-1/2 cups watermelon balls

Some Low-Calorie Foods To Look For

Look for the many low-calorie foods—all aids to the dieter—in the diet section of your supermarket: liquid diet meals in many flavors; noncaloric sweeteners; low-calorie beverages and sodas; low-calorie salad dressings; fruits and fruit juices canned without sugar; low-calorie jams and jellies; dietetic cookies and crackers; low-calorie puddings and gelatin desserts; low-calorie dessert topping; frozen ice milk; low-calorie complete meals (soup, main dish, and dessert); and the low-calorie cheeses and dairy products.

Frisky Sour

2 cans (10-1/2-oz size) condensed beef broth
8 ice cubes
1/4 cup lemon juice

1. Put broth, ice cubes, lemon juice, and 2/3 cup cold water in large shaker or jar with tight-fitting lid.
2. Cover, and shake well.
3. Serve in chilled glasses.
Makes 6 servings; 22 calories each.

Low-Calorie Onion-Soup Dip

1 cup yoghurt
1 cup diet cottage cheese
3 tablespoons dry onion-soup mix
1/4 teaspoon chili powder

1. In medium bowl, combine yoghurt and cottage cheese until well blended. Stir in the dry onion-soup mix and chili powder.
2. Refrigerate the dip, covered, 3 hours, to chill well and to let flavor develop.
3. Arrange on tray with an assortment of crisp vegetables and chilled shrimp.
Makes 2 cups dip; 13 calories in a tablespoon.

Tomato Bouillon

2 teaspoons butter or margarine
3/4 cup chopped onion
1/2 cup chopped celery, with leaves
1 can (46 oz) tomato juice
1 bay leaf
1/2 teaspoon dried oregano leaves
1/4 teaspoon seasoned salt
1/8 teaspoon pepper

1. In hot butter in medium saucepan, sauté onion until golden—about 3 minutes.
2. Add celery, tomato juice, bay leaf, oregano, seasoned salt, and pepper; bring to boiling. Reduce heat, and simmer, stirring occasionally, 15 minutes.
3. Strain. Serve hot or cold.
Makes 8 servings, 3/4 cup each; 41 calories each.

Boiled Brisket of Beef

1 onion, stuck with 2 whole cloves
4-lb brisket of beef, trimmed of fat
1 cup cut-up celery, with tops
1 cup cut-up carrots
1/4 cup coarsely chopped parsley
1 bay leaf
3 whole black peppercorns
1 tablespoon salt
Few sprigs parsley
Horseradish Sauce, page 590

1. Bring 2 quarts water to boiling in large kettle. Add all ingredients, except parsley sprigs; bring to boiling.
2. Reduce heat; simmer, covered, 3 hours, or until meat is tender.
3. Garnish with parsley sprigs; serve with Horseradish Sauce.
Makes 6 servings; 4 pieces (each 1-1/2-by-1-by-1 inch), 280 calories, per serving.

Crab Salad

2 cans (7-1/2-oz size) king-crab meat, drained
1/2 cup low-calorie mayonnaise
2 tablespoons chopped parsley
2 tablespoons snipped chives
1 teaspoon Worcestershire sauce
1/2 teaspoon lemon juice
1 cup diced pared cucumber
Crisp lettuce cups
4 hard-cooked eggs, sliced

1. If necessary, remove cartilage from crabmeat.
2. In medium bowl, combine mayonnaise, parsley, chives, Worcestershire, and lemon juice; mix well. Add crabmeat and cucumber; toss.
3. Refrigerate, covered, until well chilled—about 1 hour.
4. To serve: Arrange lettuce cups on 4 serving plates. Fill with salad. Garnish with sliced egg.
Makes 4 servings; 232 calories each.

Low-Calorie Beef Stew

2 lb boneless beef chuck, cut into 1-1/2-inch cubes
1/2 cup chopped onion
16 small white onions, peeled (1 lb)
16 small fresh mushrooms (1/2 lb)
3 tablespoons flour
1/8 teaspoon pepper
2 teaspoons meat-extract paste
2 tablespoons tomato paste
1-1/2 cups Burgundy
1 can (10-1/2 oz) condensed beef broth, undiluted
1 bay leaf

1. Heat Dutch oven. Add beef cubes, a few at a time, and quickly brown on all sides. Remove, and set aside.
2. Add 1 cup water and the chopped onion to Dutch oven; bring to boiling. Reduce heat; simmer just until water evaporates—about 10 minutes.
3. Add whole onions; cook until slightly brown. Add mushrooms; cook, stirring frequently, until golden-brown—about 3 minutes.
4. Remove from heat. Stir in flour, pepper, meat-extract paste, and tomato paste until well blended. Gradually stir in the Burgundy and beef broth.
5. Preheat oven to 350F.
6. Bring wine mixture to boiling, stirring constantly. Remove from heat. Add beef and bay leaf; mix well.
7. Bake, covered, 1-1/2 hours, or until beef is tender.
Makes 8 servings; 238 calories each.

Broiled Calves' Liver

6 slices (1-1/2 lb) calves' liver
1/4 cup low-calorie French dressing
1 can (3 oz) sliced mushrooms, drained

1. Brush both sides of liver with dressing.
2. Place on broiler rack; broil, 4 inches from heat, 4 minutes.
3. Turn; then broil 2 minutes on other side.
4. Cover with mushrooms; broil 2 minutes.
Makes 6 servings; 1 slice, 176 calories, each.

Cottage-Cheese Topping for Baked Potatoes

1/2 cup dry cottage cheese
1/4 cup dairy sour cream
1 tablespoon snipped chives
1/4 teaspoon salt
Dash pepper

1. Combine all ingredients in blender container. Cover; blend at high speed 1 minute, or until mixture is creamy.
2. Serve on baked potatoes.
Makes 3/4 cup; 17 calories in 1 tablespoon.

Horseradish Sauce

1 cup (8 oz) yoghurt
1/2 teaspoon salt
1/8 teaspoon pepper
1 teaspoon prepared horseradish

1. Combine all ingredients in small bowl.
2. Refrigerate, covered, until well chilled—about 1 hour. Serve cold.
Makes 1 cup; 2 tablespoons, 14 calories, per serving.

Herb-Broiled Lamb Chops

12 rib lamb chops, 1 inch thick
2 teaspoons dried basil leaves
2 teaspoons dried marjoram leaves
2 teaspoons dried thyme leaves
2 teaspoons salt

1. Wipe chops with damp cloth.
2. Mix other ingredients; rub into both sides of chops. Chill, covered, 1 hour.
3. Place on broiler rack, 4 inches from heat; for medium rare, broil 6 minutes on one side, 4 minutes on other.

Makes 6 servings; 2 chops, 256 calories, per serving.

Cottage-Cheese Salad in Tomato Halves

3 medium tomatoes
1 carton (12 oz) diet creamed cottage cheese
1/3 cup grated pared carrot
1/3 cup diced pared cucumber
1/3 cup finely chopped green onion
4 radishes, coarsely grated
1/2 teaspoon salt
1 tablespoon low-calorie Italian-style dressing
Crisp lettuce
Parsley or dill sprigs

1. Cut tomatoes in half crosswise. With spoon, scoop out pulp and seeds. Drain.
2. In medium bowl, combine cottage cheese, carrot, cucumber, onion, radishes, drained tomato pulp, salt, and dressing; mix lightly. Spoon into tomatoes.
3. Arrange on lettuce on salad plates. Garnish with fresh parsley or dill sprigs.

Makes 6 servings; 67 calories each.

Deviled Lobster

1 bay leaf
1 lemon, sliced
1 teaspoon sugar
1 teaspoon salt
3 (8-oz size) frozen rock-lobster tails
1 can (3 oz) button mushrooms
1 tablespoon flour
1/2 cup skim milk
1/2 teaspoon seasoned salt
1/2 teaspoon soy sauce
1 egg yolk
1 tablespoon dry sherry
1 tablespoon grated Parmesan cheese

1. In large saucepan, combine 4 cups water, the bay leaf, lemon slices, sugar, and salt; bring to boiling. Add lobster tails; boil gently 10 minutes. Drain.
2. Meanwhile, drain liquid from mushrooms into a 1-cup measure; add water to make 1/2 cup. Gradually stir into flour in small saucepan. Add milk, seasoned salt, and soy sauce.
3. Bring to boiling, stirring constantly. Reduce heat, and simmer 3 minutes.
4. In small bowl, beat egg yolk; gradually stir in hot mixture. Return to saucepan, and cook, stirring, just to boiling. Remove from heat; stir in wine.
5. Remove lobster meat from shells, being careful to keep shells intact. Cut meat into bite-size pieces. Add, with mushrooms, to sauce; cook over medium heat just until heated through.
6. Spoon into lobster shells. Sprinkle each with 1 teaspoon Parmesan.
7. Broil, 2 inches from heat, just until cheese is golden-brown—2 to 3 minutes.

Makes 3 servings; 213 calories each.

Lamb Kebabs

4-1/2- to 5-lb shank-end leg of lamb
1/2 cup bottled low-calorie Italian-style dressing
1/4 cup lemon juice
1/2 teaspoon garlic salt
1/8 teaspoon cracked black pepper
10 mushrooms
10 cherry tomatoes
2 zucchini (about 1/2 lb)
1 green pepper

1. Cut lamb from bone; trim fat from meat. Cut lamb into 40 cubes, each about 1-1/2 inches. Place in a shallow baking dish.
2. In 1-cup measure, combine dressing, lemon juice, garlic salt, and pepper; mix well. Pour over lamb; turn meat to coat all pieces well.
3. Refrigerate, covered, 4 hours.
4. Trim mushrooms. Wash tomatoes and zucchini. Cut zucchini into 1-inch pieces. Cut green pepper into 1-inch squares.
5. On each of 10 skewers, arrange a cherry tomato, lamb cube, mushroom, lamb cube, green-pepper square, lamb cube, zucchini chunk, lamb cube, square of green pepper.
6. Broil, about 4 inches from heat, turning once, until of desired doneness and browned—about 20 minutes for medium.
Makes 10 servings; 241 calories each.

Pineapple-Mint Frappé

1 can (1 lb, 4 oz) pineapple chunks in pure juice
2 tablespoons coarsely chopped mint leaves

1. Set aside 5 pineapple chunks for garnish. Turn remaining pineapple and the liquid into a 9-inch square pan. Place in freezer until almost completely frozen—will take about 1-1/4 hours.
2. Turn into electric blender, along with chopped mint; cover; blend at low speed just until smooth, but not melted.
3. Spoon into 5 sherbet glasses. Top each frappé with a reserved pineapple chunk and a mint sprig, if desired.
Makes 5 servings; 90 calories each.

Lime-Pineapple Parfait

2 cups boiling water
1 pkg (5/8 oz) low-calorie lime-flavored gelatine (2 env)
1 can (12 oz) unsweetened pineapple juice
1 can (8 oz) pineapple tidbits in pineapple juice
6 tablespoons refrigerated whipped topping

1. Pour boiling water over gelatine in large bowl, stirring until gelatine is dissolved.
2. Stir pineapple juice and undrained pineapple tidbits into gelatine.
3. Refrigerate, stirring occasionally, until consistency of unbeaten egg white—about 1 hour.
4. Pour into 6 parfait glasses. Refrigerate until firm.
5. To serve, top each parfait with 1 tablespoon whipped topping.
Makes 6 servings; 83 calories each.

Index

A

Acorn squash
  baked, 554
  honey spice, 553
  how to buy and cook, 526
Alcoholic drinks, 76-82
  champagne punch, 78
  Christmas punch, 76
  cranberry-bourbon punch, 77
  daiquiri punch, 77
  Ella Brennan's milk punch, 78
  Irish coffee, 68, 302
  Margaritas, 321
  old English eggnog, 79
  peach brandy eggnog, 80
  pink champagne punch bowl, 77
  planter's punch bowl, 79
  rosé wine spritzer, 82
  rum swizzles, 80
  sangría, 81
  syllabub, 81
  wassail bowl, 81
  whiskey sour punch, 80
Ale, wassail bowl, 81
Alfredo sauce, 464
Almond(s)
  candy, burnt, 559
  cherry flip, 187
  cinnamon stars, 560
  cookies, 271
  junket, 271
  lace wafers, 158
  tart, 420
  tile cookies, 288
  Turkish cookies, 152
Amaretti (macaroons), 311
Ambrosia bowl, 180
Anadama batter bread, 115
Anchovy antipasto salad, 62
Angel food cakes, 129-33
  how to cut, 118
  McCall's Best, 129
  White-and-Gold, 136
Anise toast, 313
Antipasto salad, anchovy, 62
Appetizers, 43-66
  anchovy antipasto salad, 62
  artichokes with lemon sauce, 527
  asparagus and Swiss cheese tart, 66
  avocado halves, California style, 61
  beef-tartare canapés, 55
  blini, 62
  blue-cheese spread, 48
  caviar, 60
  caviar cream cheese ball, 48
  Cheddar-beer spread, 48
  Cheddar in sherry, 50
  cheese-bacon puffs, 50
  cheese-pâté pineapple, 49
  chili con queso with raw vegetables, 52

  clams oregano, 60
  cocktail macadamias, 47
  cocktail olives, 47
  cold ratatouille, 64
  coquilles Saint Jacques, 66
  deviled eggs, 223
  eggplant, 45
  eggs en gelée, 61
  eggs mayonnaise, 63
  first courses, 60-66
  Greek cheese pie, 52
  grilled grapefruit with kirsch, 63
  guacamole dip with crisp vegetables, 45
  herring in dill sauce, 58
  herring in sour cream, 59
  holiday cheese ball, 48
  hot cheese pastries, 51
  liver pâté en gelée, 58
  lobster cocktail, 64
  marinated artichokes, 44
  melon with prosciutto, 63
  moules marinière, 276
  mousse of chicken livers, 46
  onion soup dip, low calorie, 589
  parmesan cheese leaves, 53
  pâté tart, 65
  pickled mushrooms, 45
  pineapple-cheese ball, 46
  pissaladière, 54
  quiche Lorraine, 52
  rumaki, 56
  savory Edam cheese, 47
  savory steak slices, 56
  scallops Provençale, 65
  shrimp with apricot sauce, 268
  shrimp cocktail, 62
  shrimp toast, 265
  smoked salmon canapés, 57
  snails in garlic butter, 276
  spring dip, 46
  steak tartare, 56
  stuffed grape leaves, 44
  Swedish cold salmon with mustard sauce, 59
  Swedish meatballs, 55
  Swiss cheese fondue, 50
  Swiss cheese fritters, 49
  Swiss cheese and tomato fondue, 51
  tea eggs, 264
  Williamsburg cheese straws, 54
Apple cider
  pie, deep-dish, 428
  sauce for ham, 498
Apple(s)
  baked, with vanilla pudding sauce, 182
  and baked pork chops, 378
  chicken Waldorf salad, 473
  cobbler, 205
  custard, baked, 176
  -cranberry relish, 342
  crème-de-menthe and crème-de-cassis jelly, 330

  dumplings, 426
  filling for blintzes, 210
  flan, fresh, 413
  glazed, 447
  kuchen, 294
  La Velle's plum chutney, 331
  pie, perfect, 24-25
  pie, French, 290
  pie, upside-down, 414
  slices, warm, with custard sauce, 301
  and sour cream slaw, 483
  with spicy red cabbage, 532
  stuffing for roast pork, 376
  tarte tatin, 290
Applesauce
  country, 183
  -date cake, 119
Apricot(s)
  flambé, brandied, 191
  fritters, 172
  glaze, 143, 431
  -glazed poached pears, 180
  -pineapple-nut loaf, 86
  pinwheels, 111
  sauce, 215, 268
  -sherry jelly, 328
  soufflé, 204
  upside-down cake, 123
  -yoghurt-orange soup, 519
Arroz con pollo, 323
Artichoke(s), French or Italian
  halves, 296
  how to buy and cook, 524
  with lemon sauce, 309
  marinated, 44
  soup, cream of, 516
  with tarragon butter, 527
Artichoke(s), Jerusalem
  how to buy and cook, 524
  relish, 338
Asparagus
  Chinese style, 528
  fresh, with Hollandaise, 528
  how to buy and cook, 524
  mimosa, fresh, 527
  quiche, 284
  soup, chilled cream of, 516
  and Swiss cheese tart, 66
  vinaigrette, fresh, 476
Aspic see also GELATINE SALADS
  crisp cucumber, 486
  tomato, 484
Aunt Cal's garden relish, 340
Avocado(s)
  dressing, 492
  frappé, 516
  guacamole dip with crisp vegetables, 45
  guacamole salad mold, 485
  guacamole-and-tomato salad, 482
  halves, California style, 61
  and pink grapefruit salad platter,

B

B & B custard pudding, 177
Baba au rhum, 288
Babka, 108
Bacon
  and baked trout, 272
  cheese puffs, 50
  how to cook, 386
  quiche Lorraine, 52
  rumaki, 56
  scrambled eggs, 224
Baked
  acorn squash, 554
  apple custard, 176
  apples with vanilla pudding sauce, 182
  bean and "ham" casserole
    Hawaiian, 583
Baked (continued)
  beans, old-fashioned, 528
  beans, quick Boston, 529
  custard, 173
  eggs Gruyère, 229
  fillets thermidor, 243
  fruit flambé, 181
  haddock, New England style, 242
  ham in cider, 381
  ham in crust with Cumberland
    sauce, 380
  ham, fruit-glazed, 383
  ham, ginger-glazed, 384
  ham loaf, pineapple-glazed, 580
  ham, maple-glazed, 382
  ham and scalloped potatoes, 382
  ham steak with hot mustard fruit, 385
  Indian pudding, 179
  lamb chop and potato hot pot, 584
  macaroni and cheese, 465
  macaroni and tomatoes au gratin, 586
  manicotti with cheese filling, 20-21
  meringue shell, 211
  noodles Romanoff, 463
  onions, 542
  pear bread pudding, 177
  pie shell, 412
  pork chops and apples, 378
  potatoes, cottage cheese topping
    for, 590
  potatoes, perfect, 544
  rice custard, 173
  spiced rhubarb, 185
  striped bass, 241
  stuffed breast of veal, 401
  stuffed fish, 241
  stuffed pork chops, 379
  tomato halves, 555
  trout and bacon, 272
  veal loaf, 401
  Virginia ham, 384
  ziti casserole, 232
Bakery breads, ways to serve, 95-96

Baking powder biscuits, 90
Baklava, 298
Bamboo shoots, 264
Banana(s)
  bread, holiday, 85
  coconut pie, 425
  fritters, 171
  ice cream milk shake, 75
  split, 192
Bar cookies, 160-62
  chocolate fudge brownies, 160
  dream bars, 161
  filled oatmeal-date bars, 162
  scotch oatmeal shortbread, 160
  toffee crisps, 161
Barbecue sauce, 391
  California style, 503
  Don's, 503
Barbecued
  lamb riblets, 391
  lima beans, 529
  spareribs, maple-, 380
Barley pilaf, 461
Basic
  cooking techniques, 33
  cooking terminology, 34-36
  cooking utensils, 37-38
  diet pattern, 587
  four food groups, 578
    chart, 579
  French or oil and vinegar salad
    dressing, 492
  puffy omelet, 228
  sweet batter, for dessert
    fritters, 171
  vanilla ice cream, 196
  white sauce, 496
Bass, baked striped, 241
Basting sauces
  for broiled fish, 239
  for Cornish hens, 446
Batter breads, 114-15
  anadama, 115
  honey whole wheat casserole, 114
  Virginia Sally Lunn, 115
Batter for tempura, 315
Bavarian cream, strawberry, 188
Bay scallops, 258
Bean(s)
  Aunt Cal's garden relish, 340
  baked, old-fashioned, 528
  baked, quick Boston, 529
  black, soup with rum, 520
  brown, Swedish-style, 325
  cassoulet, 280
  curd, 264
  garbanzo salad, 477
  green, French style, 540
  green, hollandaise, 539
  green, how to buy and cook, 524
  Italian green, 540
  kidney bean salad, 477
  lima, barbecued, 529
  lima, how to buy and cook, 525

  pasta e fagioli, 304
  refried, 319
  salad bowl, three-bean, 477
  wax, how to buy and cook, 524
  white, with leg of lamb, 278
Bear claws, 110
Béarnaise sauce, 22-23
  blender, 496
Beef, 347-372
  à la mode, 357
  balls Bourguignon, 368
  balls stroganoff, 367
  borsch with sour cream, 511
  Bourguignon, 277
  braising, 356-63
  brisket
    boiled, 365, 589
    pot roast, 358
  broiling and pan-broiling, 352-56
  broth, frisky sour, 588
  chuck steak
    Florentine, 355
    with vegetables, braised, 360
  corned beef
    hash, 366
    New England boiled dinner, 366
  filet of, in brioche, 350
  filet of, Burgundy, 350
  five-flavor, 265
  flank steak
    London broil, 354
    stroganoff, 363
  ground beef, 366-72
  beef balls Bourguignon, 368
    beef balls stroganoff, 367
    bobotie, 367
    chili con carne and
      enchiladas, 320
    Greek meatballs with lemon
      sauce, 297
    hamburger roulade, 369
    hamburgers, 372
    Italian spaghetti and
      meatballs, 370
    lasagna, our favorite, 464
    Madras curried meatballs, 368
    meatball and mozzarella
      filling for pizza, 310
    meatballs and sauerkraut
      soup, 515
    moussaka, 16-17
    roast meat loaf, 369
    steak tartare, 56
    stuffed cabbage rolls, 371
    stuffed eggplant creole, 372
    Swedish meatballs, 55
    tacos with green-chile salsa, 318
    tamale casserole, 370
    upside-down chili pie, 371
  how to buy beef, 346
  London broil, 354
  and peppers, 269
  pot roasts
    beef à la mode, 357

five-flavor beef, 265
with noodles, country, 359
sauerbraten, 292
sauerbraten with gingersnap
sauce, 361
Swedish, 357
with vegetables, 360
with vegetables, herbed, 358
roasts, 347-52
eye-round Provençale, 352
prime ribs, 348
rib roast, how to carve, 42
savory, with Yorkshire
pudding, 349
timetable, 348
short ribs, savory braised, 359
simmering and stewing beef, 363
steak(s)
broiling timetable, 353
and kidney pie, 272
with marrow sauce, 356
with mustard and herbs, 355
and peppers, 269
au poivre, 277
sirloin with red wine, 354
slices, savory, 56
Swiss, braised family style, 362
stew(s)
Hungarian goulash, 365
low calorie, 590
with parsley dumplings, 14-15
ragout, 364
and vegetable, 364
stroganoff, 362
sukiyaki, 316
tartare canapés, 55
tongue, boiled, 405
and vegetable soup, hearty, 510
Wellington, 350
Beer-cheddar spread, 48
Beet(s)
beef borsch with sour cream, 511
buttery grated, 533
festival, 530
how to buy and cook, 525
orange, 530
pickled, 343
soup with dill, 521
Beignets and French crullers, 172
Belgian endive, 468
and cold leeks vinaigrette, 479
Benne-seed cookies, 147
Berry pie, fresh, 414
Best of all fruitcakes, 565
Best of all pizzas, 309
Best cherry pie, 417
Best French dressing, 493
Beverages, 67-82
alcoholic drinks, 76-82
banana shake, 75
caffè espresso, 68, 70
cappuccino, 68
champagne punch, 78
chocolate-mint soda, 76

Christmas punch, 76
coffee for a crowd, 69
coffee, percolator, 68
coffee, vacuum-type, 68
cranberry-bourbon punch, 77
cup of cheer, 71
daiquiri punch, 77
double strawberry soda, 76
drip coffee, 69
Ella Brennan's milk punch, 78
fresh lemonade, 72
fresh orange spritzer, 72
frisky sour, 588
frosted punch bowl, 78
frosted strawberry float, 74
fruit drinks and punches, 71-73
glögg, 325
golden refresher, 72
hot mulled cider, 72
ice block, 78
ice cream milk shakes, 75
iced tea, 71
Irish coffee, 68, 302
maple milk shake, 75
Margaritas, 321
Mexican hot chocolate, 319
mint chocolate, 73
mocha chocolate, 73
mocha frosted, 75
old English eggnog, 79
old-fashioned hot chocolate, 73
orange chocolate, 73
orange eggnog, 74
orange-sherbet freeze, 76
peach brandy eggnog, 80
peanut butter shake, 75
piñas coladas, 81
pineapple lemon soda, 76
pineapple-orange blush, 73
pineapple shake, 75
pink champagne punch bowl, 77
planter's punch bowl, 79
raspberry shake, 75
rosé wine spritzer, 82
rum swizzles, 80
sangría, 81
sodas, 76
spiced chocolate drink, 73
spiced cocoa, 74
spicy eggnog, 74
strawberry milk shake, 75
syllabub, 81
tea, 70
tea for 25, hot, 70
Turkish coffee, 68
Viennese coffee, 68
wassail bowl, 81
whiskey sour punch, 80
Bibb lettuce, 468
Biberli, Swiss, 568
Bing cherry salad, 488
Biscuit
mix shortcake, 207
tortoni, 312

Biscuits, 90-91
baking powder, 90
cheese, 91
drop, 91
orange, 584
Bisque
cold shrimp, 519
lobster, 509
Black bean soup with rum, 520
Blackberry pie, fresh, 414
Blanc mange
chocolate, 174
coconut, 174
mocha, 174
vanilla, 174
Blender béarnaise sauce, 496
Blender hollandaise sauce, 499
Blini, 62
Blintzes, 209
apple filling, 210
blueberry filling, 210
cheese filling, 210
cherry filling, 209
Blueberry(ies)
buttermilk pancakes, 97
cake muffins, 88
cheese pie supreme, 420
filling, for blintzes, 210
glaze, 168
-and-peach pie, 415
pie, fresh, 414
sally lunn, 92
surprises, 109
Blue cheese
holiday cheese ball, 48
salad dressing, 492
salad dressing, creamy, 489
spread, 48
Bluefish, baked stuffed, 241
Blum's coffee-toffee pie, 419
Boiled
beef brisket, 365
brisket of beef, 589
corned beef brisket, New England
Dinner, 366
crabs, 251
dressing, 489
live lobsters, 254
rock lobster tails, 255
shrimp, 259
tongue, 405
Bordelaise sauce, 497
Borsch, beef, with sour cream, 511
Boston baked beans, quick, 529
Boston lettuce, 468
Bouillabaisse, 275
Bouillon, tomato, 589
Bourbon
-cranberry punch, 77
Ella Brennan's milk punch, 78
Bow ties, 112
Braised
carrots, 533
chuck steak with vegetables, 360

partridges, 406
pot roast of lamb, 388
short ribs, savory, 359
Swiss steak, family style, 362
veal chops, 398
Braising
beef, 356-63
meat, general directions, 347
Bran buttermilk muffins, 88
Brandied
apricots flambé, 191
caramel flan, 320
partridges, 406
Brandy
-peach eggnog, 80
sauce, 216
Bread(s)
anadama batter, 115
apple kuchen, 294
babka, 108
baking powder biscuits, 90
batter breads, 114-15
bear claws, 110
biscuits, 90-91
blueberry buttermilk pancakes, 97
blueberry cake muffins, 88
blueberry sally lunn, 92
blueberry surprises, 109
bow ties, 112
brioche, 116
brioche dough, 351
brown-sugar muffins, 89
-and-butter pickles, 334
buttermilk bran muffins, 88
buttermilk pancakes, 96
caraway rye, 103
cheese biscuits, 91
cheese muffins, 89
coffeecakes, 91-92
cornbread, 93
corn muffins, 93
corn sticks, 94
crescents, 109
crisp herb bread, hot, 95
crispy herb rolls, 96
daily needs, 578
date-nut, 84
date-nut muffins, 90
double cornbread, 93
drop biscuits, 91
French toast, 97
garlic, 95
griddlecakes, 97
holiday banana, 85
honey whole wheat casserole, 114
horns, 110
H. R. M.'s favorite waffles, 98
jelly doughnuts, 113
lemon tea, 85
Maureen's soda, 300
McCall's basic white, 102
McCall's best nut, 84
muffins, 87-90
orange biscuits, 584

Bread(s) (continued)
pancakes and waffles, 96-97
pineapple-apricot-nut loaf, 86
pinwheels, 111
pizzas, best of all, 309
popovers, 94
potato, old-fashioned, 103
prune, 86
pudding
B & B custard, 177
baked pear, 177
pumpkin loaves, 87
quick breads, 83-98
sweet, 84-87
raisin-caraway soda, 300
refrigerator potato rolls, 12-13
salt crescent rolls, 96
savory cheese, 86
sour cream crumbcake, 92
Southern spoon bread, 94
spiral cinnamon raisin, 107
stollen, 112
strawberry jam crescents, 95
streusel-layered coffeecake, 91
stuffing, 455
Swedish limpa, 105
sweet roll dough, 108
Swiss braided loaves, 105
tortillas, 317
Virginia sally lunn, 115
waffles, 326
whole-wheat, 104
whole-wheat soda, 301
yeast breads, 99-116
overall directions, 100-1
sweet, 107-13
Breaded cod fillets, 247
Breakfast(s)
hearty Sunday, menu, 575
nutritional guidelines, 578;
menus, 580-87
Breast of chicken curry, 441
**Breast of chicken in Madeira
sauce, 444**
Brioche, 116
Brioche dough, 351
Brisket of beef, boiled, 365, 589
Brisket pot roast, 358
Broccoli
amandine, 531
how to buy and cook, 525
Italian style, 308
with lemon sauce, 530
polonaise, 531
Broiled
calves' liver, 590
chicken with parsley butter, 437
coconut topping, 143
fish, 239
lamb chop grill, 392
lamb chops, savory mushroom
stuffing, 391
leg of lamb slices with sauce
maître d'hôtel, 390

live lobsters, 256
liver, 403
rock lobster tails, 256
salmon steaks, crispy, 240
salmon or swordfish steaks,
parsley-lemon butter, 240
Broiling
beef, 352-56
meat, general directions, 346
pan-broiling, 347
timetable for steaks, 353
Broth see also SOUP
cottage, 299
Brown beans, Swedish style, 325
Brown gravy, 503
Brown rice, 458
Brown sugar
glazed carrots and onions, 534
how to measure, 33
muffins, 89
shortbread cookies, 149
Brownies, chocolate fudge, 160
Brunch menus, 574-75
hearty Sunday breakfast, 575
holiday weekend, 574
summer Sunday, 575
for weekend guests, 575
Brussels sprouts
in cheese sauce, 531
with chestnut sauce, 274
dilly vegetables, 339
how to buy and cook, 525
Buffet menus, 573-76
Easter, 574
Italian-style, 576
in spring, 573
very informal, 575
winter, 576
Burgundy gravy, 504
Burnt-almond candy, 559
Butter
cakes, 123-29
crisps, 157
frosting, coffee, 138
herb, for chicken Kiev, 10
lemon, 242, 256
orange, 215
parsley, 500
parsley-lemon, 240
sauce, maître d'hôtel, 500
spiced pear, 331
tarragon, with artichokes, 527
tarragon-chive, 242
whipped, 98
Buttered
cabbage wedges, 532
linguine parmesan, 463
parsnips, 542
peas, French style, 543
Buttermilk
bran muffins, 88
-lemon soup, 520
pancakes, 96

Butternut squash, cream-of-winter-squash soup, 509
Butterscotch
icebox cookies, 155
sauce, 216
Buttery
grated beets, 533
grated carrots, 532
grated turnips, 532
B vitamins, sources of, chart, 579

C

Cabbage
apple and sour cream slaw, 483
beef borsch with sour cream, 511
buttered, 377
colcannon, 299
creamy coleslaw, 479
Harvey House slaw, 478
how to buy and cook, 525
red, 293
rolls, stuffed, 371
Scandinavian, 325
soup, green, 507
sour cream coleslaw, 478
spicy red, with apples, 532
wedges, buttered, 532
Cacciatore, chicken, with polenta, 305
Caesar salad, 469
Caffè espresso, 68, 70
Cakes, 117-37
applesauce-date, 119
apricot upside-down, 123
baba au rhum, 288
baking notes, 118
butter or "conventional," 123-29
chocolate, Colette's, 286
chocolate fudge, 127
chocolate-mousse dessert, 136
chocolate, perfect, 26-27
chocolate poundcake, 135
clove, with caramel frosting, 124
coconut chiffon, 130
cutting notes, 118
diplomat, 208
Dundee, 570
easy upside-down, with mix, 123
fillings, 143-44
favorite one-egg, 120
freezing notes, 118
fresh lemon, 132
fresh orange spongecake, 132
general directions, 118
gold petits-fours, 122
hot milk spongecake, 132
how to frost a layer cake, 138
ingredients for, 118
Irish tea, 302
jelly roll, 133
lemon pudding, 179
madeleines, 289
McCall's best angel food, 129

McCall's best chocolate loaf, 124
McCall's best daffodil, 131
McCall's best devil's food, 123
McCall's best gold, 119
McCall's best spicecake, 125
macaroon, 126
marble loaf, 125
with mixes, 136-37
mocha chiffon, 130
Neapolitan, 137
notes on cakes, 118
oatmeal praline, 128
one-bowl or "quick," 119-23
pineapple upside-down, 122
pink-and-white petits fours, 134
poundcake, 28-29
removing cakes from pans, 118
Scotch chocolate squares, 121
silvery white, 120
sour cream fudge, 121
storing notes, 118
tests for doneness, 118
tomato soup-spice, 128
walnut poundcake loaf, 134
walnut-raisin, 126
white-and-gold angel, 136
Calcium, sources of, chart, 579
Calcutta mulligatawny soup, 511
California cheese and rice casserole, 234
California style
avocado halves, 61
barbecue sauce, 503
Calorie counting, 578
basic diet pattern, 587-88
fruits, 588
vegetables, 588
Calves' liver
broiled, 403, 590
pan-fried, 403
venetian style, 404
Canapés, 44-60, see also
HORS D'OEUVRES and SPREADS
beef tartare, 55
cheese-bacon puffs, 50
smoked salmon, 57
Candied
grapefruit and orange peel, 558
sweet potatoes, 551
Candy(ies) see also CONFECTIONS
burnt-almond, 559
chocolate fudge deluxe, 563
hazelnut truffles, 559
pecan pralines, 562
walnutty caramels, 558
Canned meat, storage of, 346
Canning jelly, 328
Cannoli, 313
shells, 314
Cantaloupe soup, chilled, 517
Cantonese lobster, 269
Capon, roast, with herbs, 449
Cappuccino, 68

Caramel(s)
custard, 176
custard flan, 324
custard mold, 175
flan, brandied, 320
frosting, easy, 140
sauce, 216
soufflé, cold, 204
walnutty, 558
Caraway
noodles, 291, 463
-raisin soda bread, 300
rye bread, 103
Carbohydrates, sources of, chart, 579
Cardinal sauce, 216
Carrots
braised, 533
buttered, 377
buttery grated, 532
dilled whole, 338
with fresh mint, 533
golden whipped potatoes, 546
how to buy and cook, 525
lemon-glazed, 533
and onions, brown sugar-glazed, 534
orange-glazed, 534
sticks, dilled, 338
Carving
crown roast of lamb, 389
ham, 41
leg of lamb, 40
standing rib roast, 42
turkey, 39
Casseroles see also POT ROASTS and STEWS
arroz con pollo, 323
baked eggs Gruyère, 229
baked lamb chop and potato hot pot, 584
baked macaroni and tomatoes au gratin, 586
baked manicotti with cheese filling, 20-21
baked ziti, 232
barbecued lima beans, 529
bobotie, 367
breast of chicken in Madeira sauce, 444
cheese lasagna, 233
cheese-and-rice, California, 234
chicken cacciatore, 438
chicken Tetrazzini, 439
coq au vin with new potatoes, 442
corn pudding, 538
eggplant parmigiana, 307
eggplant and tomato, 539
John Wayne's cheese, 231
Hawaiian "ham" and baked bean, 583
Hungarian veal for a crowd, 400
moussaka, 16-17
old-fashioned baked beans, 528

orange-glazed sweet potatoes, 549
paella, 322
pasta e fagioli, 304
potatoes au gratin, 546
quick Boston baked beans, 529
scalloped crab, 253
scalloped potatoes, 545
souffléed corn, 537
sweet potato and pineapple, 551
sweet-and-white potato, 547
tamale, 370
turkey ragout, 451
Cassoulet, 280
Cauliflower
garni, 535
how to buy and cook, 525
polonaise, 534
with shrimp sauce, 536
surprise, 535
Caviar, 60
blini, 62
-cream cheese ball, 48
red, jellied consommé with, 515
Cecilia's omelet, Spanish-style, 228
Cereals and grains, 460-62
daily needs, 578
date-nut rolls, 160
fried cornmeal mush, 462
gnocchi, 461
hot buttered grits, 462
oatmeal, very special, 583
polenta, 460
Champagne
Christmas punch, 76
punch, 78
punch bowl, pink, 77
sherbet, pink, 201
Chantilly cream, 217
Charts
eating for health and beauty,
578-79
guide to serving cheese with fruit,
235-36
timetables
for baking ham, 380
for broiling steaks, 353
for roasting beef, 348
for roasting chicken, 437
for roasting lamb, 386
for roasting pork, 374
for roasting turkey, 451
for roasting veal, 395
vegetables, 524-27
weights and measures, 34
Cheddar cheese
-bacon puffs, 50
-beer spread, 48
holiday cheese ball, 48
muffins, 89
-pâté pineapple, 49
in sherry, 50
soup, 508
straws, Williamsburg, 54

Cheese, 231-36 *see also* COTTAGE
CHEESE *and* CREAM CHEESE
bacon puffs, 50
baked eggs Gruyère, 229
baked ziti casserole, 232
ball, holiday, 48
biscuits, 91
bread, savory, 86
caviar-cream cheese ball, 48
Cheddar in sherry, 50
cherry cheese pie supreme, 420
chile con queso with raw
vegetables, 52
Edam, savory, 47
fondue, Swiss, 50
filling for blintzes, 209
filling for baked manicotti, 20-21
fritters, Swiss, 49
with fruit, 234
guide to serving, 235-36
golden buck, 231
how to serve, 234-36
John Wayne's casserole, 231
kinds of, described, 235-36
lasagna, 233
lasagna, our favorite, 464
leaves, parmesan, 53
macaroni and, baked, 465
muffins, 89
omelet, 227
pastries, hot, 51
pâté pineapple, 49
pie, blueberry supreme, 420
pie, favorite, 419
pie, Greek, 52
pineapple ball, 46
potatoes au gratin, 546
quiche Lorraine, 52
and rice casserole, California, 234
ricotta, cannoli, 313
salad dressing
Roquefort or blue, 492
Roquefort or blue, creamy, 489
sandwiches, grilled deviled, 585
sauce, 497
sauce for Brussels sprouts, 531
-scrambled eggs, 224
soufflé, fabulous, 232
soup, Cheddar, 508
spread, blue, 48
spread, Cheddar-beer, 48
straws, Williamsburg, 54
Swiss, and asparagus tart, 66
and tomato filling for pizza, 310
and tomato fondue, Swiss, 51
Cheesecakes, 164-68
glazed lemon cream, 166
glazes for, 167-68
Lindy's famous, 164
Ratner's marble, 166
strawberry and cream, 165
Chef's salad, 471
Cherry(ies)

-almond flip, 187
cheese pie supreme, 420
easy Christmas cake, 564
filling for blintzes, 209
glaze, red, 167
jubilee, 191
pie, best, 417
pinwheels, 111
salad, bing-, 488
Chestnuts
roasted, 274
sauce, for Brussels sprouts, 274
Chicken, 435-45
arroz con pollo, 323
basquaise, 281
breast of, in Madeira sauce, 444
breasts, pâté-stuffed, 444
broiled, with parsley butter, 437
broiler, described, 436
cacciatore, 438
cacciatore with polenta, 305
Calcutta mulligatawny soup, 511
cobb salad with Russian dressing,
471
coq au vin with new potatoes, 442
curry, 441
drumsticks, crispy, 443
golden-fried, 440
gravy, 504
Kiev, 10-11
livers
mousse of, 46
mushroom dressing, 455
party pâté, 57
rumaki, 56
sautéed, 403
paprikash, 440
picnic, 443
poached, with vegetables, 438
roast capon with herbs, 449
roast stuffed, 436
roaster, described, 436
roasting timetable, 437
salad, 472
curried, 474
pineapple, 472
Waldorf, 473
soup, cream of, 322
for stewing, described, 436
sweet-and-sour, 442
Tetrazzini, 439
with toasted almonds, 268
wrap-ups, crusty, 443
Chicory, 468
Chiffon cakes
coconut loaf, 130
how to cut, 118
mocha, 130
Chiffon pies
freezing, 410
lemon, 424
Chilled
cantaloupe soup, 517

cream of asparagus soup, 516
Chile con queso with raw vegetables, 52
Chile salsa, green, 319
Chiles rellenos, 318
Chili
and enchiladas, 320
pie, upside-down, 371
sauce, old-fashioned, 336
Chinese cooking, 264-71
almond cookies, 271
almond junket, 271
apricot sauce, 268
asparagus, 528
beef and peppers, 269
chicken with toasted almonds, 268
egg drop soup, 266
five-flavor beef, 265
fried rice, 266
fruit bowl, 270
ingredients described, 264
lobster Cantonese, 269
shrimp with apricot sauce, 268
shrimp toast, 265
steamed rice, 267
subgum fried rice, 266
sweet-and-sour fish, 270
sweet-and-sour pork, 267
tea eggs, 264
Chinese mushrooms, 264
Chinese parsley, 264
Chive-lemon sauce, 497
Chive-tarragon butter, 242
Chocolate
blanc mange, 174
butter cream frosting, 141
cake
Colette's, 286
fudge, 127
marble loaf, 125
McCall's best devil's food, 123
McCall's best loaf, 124
mousse dessert, 136
perfect, 26-27
poundcake, 135
sour cream fudge, 121
squares, Scotch, 121
cheesecake, Ratner's marble, 166
-cinnamon ice cream, 198
cream pie, 422
crème, 287
curls, 287
-custard filling, 144
drink, spiced, 73
frosting
butter cream, 141
cocoa cream, 139
quick fudge, 140
for Scotch cake squares, 121
for tartlets, 433
sour cream, 139
whipped cream, 139
fudge brownies, 160
fudge deluxe, 563

fudge sauce, 218
glaze, 143
for éclairs, 170
for petit four cookies, 151
hazelnut truffles, 559
kiss-peanut butter cookies, 156
Mexican hot, 319
mint drink, 73
mint soda, 76
mocha drink, 73
mocha frosted, 75
mousse, 212
mousse pie, 422
nut torte, 213
old-fashioned hot, 73
orange drink, 73
peanut butter pinwheels, 153
pots de crème, 287
sauce, deluxe, 217
quick, 217
soufflé, 30-31
spiced cocoa, 74
toffee crisps, 161
Toll House crunch cookies, 159
whip, Mrs. Simmons', 187
Chowder
corn, 513
corn-and-clam, 512
creamy corn, 587
Manhattan clam, 513
New England clam, 513
New England fish, 514
quick Cape Cod clam, 521
Christmas
cherry cake, easy, 564
cooking *see* HOLIDAY DELIGHTS
holiday dinner menu, 574
punch, 76
Chuck steak Florentine, 355
Chuck steak with vegetables, 360
Churros (Spanish doughnuts), 323
Chutney, La Velle's plum, 331
Cider
cup of cheer, 71
hot mulled, 72
rum swizzles, 80
Cinnamon
-chocolate ice cream, 198
cookies, Mexican, 321
ice cream sauce, 218
raisin bread, spiral, 107
stars, 560
Cioppino, 250
Clam(s)
broth with tarragon, 507
chowder, corn-and-, 512
chowder, Manhattan, 513
chowder, New England, 513
chowder, quick Cape Cod, 521
fried, 251
hard-shell, 250
how to buy and prepare, 250
oregano, 60
paella, 322

sauce, white, for spaghetti, 466
soft-shell, 250
Cloud ears, 264
Clove cake with caramel frosting, 124
Club steaks, broiling timetable, 353
Cobb salad with Russian dressing, 471
Cobbler, apple, 205
Cocktail(s)
lobster, 64
macadamias, 47
Margaritas, 321
olives, 47
party menus, 575
shrimp, 62
Cocoa cream frosting, 139
Cocoa, spiced, 74
Coconut
blanc mange, 174
chocolate icing, 121
chiffon loaf cake, 130
-custard pie, slipped, 424
date-nut rolls, 160
dream bars, 161
macaroon cake, 126
pie, banana, 425
pie, Honolulu, 425
piñas coladas, 81
seven-minute frosting, 142
tarts, miniature, 434
topping, broiled, 143
Codfish
baked stuffed, 241
cakes, 248
fillets, breaded, 247
Coffee
butter frosting, 138
cappuccino, 68
for a crowd, 69
drip type, 69
espresso, 68, 70
how to make, 68
jelly with custard sauce, 190
Irish, 68, 302
kinds described, 68
percolator, 68
spice seven minute frosting, 142
-toffee pie, Blum's, 419
Turkish, 68
vacuum-type, 68
Viennese, 68
Coffeecakes, 91-92
apple kuchen, 294
blueberry sally lunn, 92
sour cream crumbcake, 92
streusel-layered, 91
Colcannon, 299
Cold
caramel soufflé, 204
cucumber soup, 518
leeks and endives vinaigrette, 479
plum soup, 520
ratatouille, 64
roast veal loaf, 402
shrimp bisque, 519

soups, 515-20
Coleslaw
  creamy, 479
  Harvey House, 478
  sour cream, 478
  -stuffed peppers, 336
Colette's chocolate cake, 286
Collards, 526
Compote, rumtopf, 332
Confectioners' sugar, how to measure, 33
Confections *see also* CANDIES
  candied grapefruit and orange peel, 558
  sugar nuts, 559
Conserve, cranberry, 332
Consommé
  hot tomato, 506
  jellied, with red caviar, 515
  Madrilène, royal, 506
Converted rice, described, 458
Cookies, 145-62
  almond, 271
  almond lace wafers, 158
  almond tile, 288
  amaretti (macaroons), 311
  anise toast, 313
  baking directions, 146
  bar cookies, 160-62
  benne-seed, 147
  brown sugar shortbread, 149
  butter crisps, 157
  butterscotch icebox, 155
  chocolate fudge brownies, 160
  chocolate kiss-peanut butter, 156
  cinnamon stars, 560
  date-nut rolls, 160
  date-and-walnut pinwheel, 154
  dream bars, 161
  drop cookies, 147-49
  Dutch tile, 566
  easy no-roll sugar, 149
  filled oatmeal-date bars, 162
  Finnish logs, 156
  freezing directions, 146
  fruitcake, 570
  ginger crinkles, 158
  glazed ginger, 148
  jewel, 158
  mailing cookies, 146
  Mexican cinnamon, 321
  molasses-raisin drop, 147
  molded cookies, 156-60
  oatmeal icebox, 154
  oatmeal-raisin, 157
  old-fashioned filled, 150
  old-fashioned sugar, 152
  orange-oatmeal, 148
  peanut butter, 159
  peanut butter pinwheels, 153
  pecan balls, 157
  pecan crescents, 562
  petit-four, 150
  petticoat tails, 155

pfeffernuesse, 561
  refrigerator cookies, 153-55
  sand tarts, 151
  sandwich, 151
  Scotch oatmeal shortbread, 160
  shell sundaes, strawberry, 193
  springerle, 569
  spritz wreaths, 563
  storing cookies, 146
  Swiss biberli, 568
  toffee crisps, 161
  Toll House crunch, 159
  Turkish, 152
  Tyrolean honey, 560
Cooking, introduction to, 9-42
  basic techniques, 33
  basic utensils (list), 37-38
  carving, 38-42
    ham, 41
    leg of lamb, 40
    standing rib roast, 42
    turkey, 39
  cutting terminology, 37
  food weights and measures, 34
  how to measure, 33
  oven temperatures, 34
  recipes, how to tackle, 33
  top-of-the-range terminology, 34-35
Cooking School (illustrated lessons) 10-31
  baked manicotti with cheese filling, 20-21
  béarnaise sauce, 22-23
  beef stew with parsley dumplings, 14-15
  chicken Kiev, 10-11
  chocolate soufflé, 30-31
  hollandaise sauce, 22-23
  moussaka, 16-17
  perfect apple pie, 24-25
  perfect chocolate cake, 26-27
  poundcake, 28-29
  refrigerator potato rolls, 12-13
  summer baked ham, 18-19
Coq au vin with new potatoes, 442
Coquilles Saint Jacques, 66
Cottage broth, 299
Cottage cheese
  and chive omelet, 227
  salad in tomato halves, 591
  spring dip, 46
  summer salad, 582
  topping for baked potatoes, 590
  Welsh curd tarts, 273
Country applesauce, 183
Country pot roast with noodles, 359
Corn
  chowder, 513
  chowder, creamy, 587
  -and-clam chowder, 512
  how to buy and cook, 525
  off the cob, 537
  on the cob, 536
  on the cob, pickled, 335
  fritters, 537

griddlecakes, 536
  muffins, 93
  pudding, 538
  relish, Iowa, 337
  relish, quick, 343
  relish, sweet, 337
  souffléed, 537
  sticks, 94
  tomatoes and zucchini, 556
Cornbread, 92-94
  cornbread, 93
  corn sticks, 94
  double cornbread, 93
  -dressing balls, 454
  oyster dressing, 455
Corned beef
  brisket, New England boiled dinner, 366
  hash, perfect, 366
Cornish hens, roast, with walnut stuffing and wine sauce, 445
Cornmeal
  baked Indian pudding, 179
  mush, fried, 462
  polenta, 460
Cornstarch pudding, blanc mange, 174
Crab(s), crabmeat, 251-54
  boiled, 251
  curried, crêpes with, 252
  how to buy and prepare, 250
  salad, 589
  sautéed soft-shell, 254
  scalloped, 253
  sherried, 252
Cranberry
  -apple relish, 342
  -bourbon punch, 77
  conserve, 332
  jellied mold, 341
  -orange dressing, 454
  salad mold, 485
  sherbet, 200
  -tangerine or -orange relish, 342
  walnut relish, 341
Cream Chantilly, 217
Cream cheese
  caviar ball, 48
  frosting, 141
  holiday cheese ball, 48
  hot cheese pastries, 51
  -pâté pineapple, 49
  pie, glazed, 419
  pineapple-cheese ball, 46
  pudding sauce, 568
Cream cheesecake
  glazed lemon, 166
  Lindy's famous, 164
  Ratner's marble, 166
  strawberry, 165
Cream pies, 422-26
  chocolate, 422
  banana coconut, 425
  Honolulu coconut, 425
  lemon chiffon, 424

lemon meringue, 423
maple squash, 426
old-fashioned pumpkin, 423
pastry cream for tartlets, 432
rum cream for fruit tarts, 430
slipped coconut custard, 424
Cream puffs, 168-73
cream puff dough, 168
custard filling for, 171
éclairs, 170
French crullers and beignets, 172
madelons, 169
miniature, 169
profiteroles, 192
strawberry profiteroles, 170
Cream soups, 507-10
artichoke, 516
asparagus, chilled, 516
chicken, 322
peanut, 508
pumpkin, 508
spring lettuce, 510
winter squash, 509
Cream toppings for pies, 422, 424
Creamed
onions, 543
spinach ring, 552
Creamy
corn chowder, 587
rice pudding, 178
Creamy salad dressings, 488-91
avocado, 492
blue cheese or Roquefort, 489
boiled, 489
creamy, 471
cucumber yoghurt, 491
curry, 489
ginger, 491
golden gate, 489
green mayonnaise, 491
honey lime, 491
lemon mayonnaise, 488
mayonnaise, 488
poppy seed, 491
Russian, 490
sour cream, 490
thousand island, 490
Creamy scrambled eggs, 225
Crème brûlée, 291
Crème-de-menthe and crème-de-cassis jelly, 330
Crème de menthe sherbet ring with strawberries, 200
Creole
sauce, 498
shrimp with white rice, 260
stuffed eggplant, 372
summer squash, 553
Crêpes
with curried crabmeat, 252
Suzette, 215
Crescents, 109
poppy-seed, 96
salt, 96

sesame-seed, 96
strawberry jam, 95
Crisp cucumber aspic, 486
Crispy broiled salmon steaks, 240
Crispy chicken drumsticks, 443
Crispy herb rolls, 96
Crown roast of lamb, filled with sautéed mushrooms, 389
Crown roast of spareribs with cornbread stuffing, 582
Crullers, French, and beignets, 172
Crumb topping for baked onions, 542
Crusty chicken wrap-ups, 443
Cucumber(s)
aspic, crisp, 486
pickled, 478
and salmon salad, fresh, 475
soup, cold, 518
in sour cream, sliced, 478
-yoghurt dressing, 491
Curly endive, 468
Cumberland sauce, 499
Cup of cheer, 71
Currant-jelly glaze, 431
Curried
basting sauce for fish, 239
chicken salad, 474
crabmeat, crêpes with, 252
fruit for summer baked ham, 18-19
Madras meatballs, 368
Curry
accompaniments, 262, 441
Calcutta mulligatawny soup, 511
chicken, 441
dressing, 489
sauce, 441
Senegalese soup, 517
shrimp, 262
supper menu, 576
Custards, 173-79
B & B pudding, 177
baked, 173
baked apple, 176
baked pear bread pudding, 177
baked rice, 173
brandied caramel flan, 320
caramel, 176
caramel flan, 324
caramel mold, 175
chocolate crème, 287
crème brûlée, 291
English trifle, 178
filling for cream puffs, 171
floating island, 174
French, with raspberry sauce, 177
pears vefour, 212
pie, 424
pie, slipped coconut, 424
pots de crème, 287
royal (garnish for consommé), 506
sauce, English, 218
sauce, pour, 217
sauce, with warm apple slices, 301
strawberry rum sundaes, 191

zabaione, 312
Cutting terminology, 37

D

Daffodil cake, McCall's best, 131
Daiquiri punch, 77
Dandelions, 526
Date(s)
-applesauce cake, 119
-nut bread, 84
-nut muffins, 90
-nut rolls, 160
-oatmeal bars, filled, 162
old-fashioned filled cookies, 150
-and-walnut pinwheel cookies, 154
Deep-dish pies, 427-28
apple-cider pie, 428
peach pie, 428
pear pie, 427
Deep-frying meat, 347
Delmonico steaks, broiling timetable, 353
Deluxe chocolate sauce, 217
Dessert sauces, 215-20
apricot, 215
brandy, 216
butterscotch, 216
caramel, 216
cardinal, 216
chocolate, deluxe, 217
chocolate, quick, 217
cinnamon-ice cream, 218
cream Chantilly, 217
custard, for warm apple slices, 301
English custard, 218
fudge, 218
hard, 218
Irish whiskey, 303
marshmallow, 219
nutmeg hard, 219
orange, 215
pineapple, 219
pour custard, 217
pudding, 568
raspberry, 184, 220
sabayon, 286
strawberry, 98, 219
vanilla pudding, 182
Desserts, 164-215 *see also* CAKES, COOKIES *and* PIES
almond junket, 271
ambrosia bowl, 180
apple kuchen, 294
apple cobbler, 205
apple dumplings, 426
apricot fritters, 172
apricot-glazed poached pears, 180
apricot soufflé, 204
B & B custard pudding, 177
baba au rhum, 288
baked custard, 176
baked apples with vanilla pudding sauce, 182

baked custard, 173
baked fruit flambé, 181
baked Indian pudding, 179
baked pear bread pudding, 177
baked rice custard, 173
baked spiced rhubarb, 185
baklava, 298
banana fritters, 171
banana split, 192
basic vanilla ice cream, 196
biscuit tortoni, 312
blanc mange, 174
blintzes, 209-10
brandied apricots flambé, 191
brandied caramel flan, 320
cannoli, 313
caramel custard, 176
caramel custard flan, 324
caramel custard mold, 175
cherries jubilee, 191
cherry-almond flip, 187
Chinese fruit bowl, 270
chocolate cinnamon ice cream, 198
chocolate crème, 287
chocolate mousse, 212
chocolate nut torte, 213
chocolate pots de crème, 287
chocolate soufflé, 30-31
coffee jelly with custard sauce, 190
cold caramel soufflé, 204
country applesauce, 183
cranberry sherbet, 200
cream puffs, 168
creamy rice pudding, 178
crème brûlée, 291
crème de menthe sherbet ring
    with strawberries, 200
crêpes Suzette, 215
custard filling for cream puffs, 171
custards and puddings, 173-79
diplomat cake, 208
éclairs, 170
English trifle, 178
fig sorbet, 201
floating heart ritz, 199
floating island, 174
French crullers and beignets, 172
French custard with raspberry
    sauce, 177
fresh fruit dessert salad, 483
fresh orange sherbet, 202
fresh peach kuchen, 206
fresh pineapple luau, 185
fresh pineapple in shell, 186
fresh strawberry à la Colony, 195
fresh strawberries with mint, 184
fresh strawberries in port, 184
fritters, basic sweet batter, 171
frozen lemon cream, 197
frozen maple mousse, 198
fruit, 179-86
gelatine desserts, 187-190
glazed lemon cream cheesecake,
    166

heavenly lemon meringue, 210
homemade strawberry ice cream,
    196
ice cream, 190-99
individual strawberry shortcakes,
    208
lemon pudding cake, 179
lime pineapple parfait, 592
lime sherbet with strawberries,
    202
Lindy's famous cheesecake, 164
macaroon-stuffed peaches, 182
madelons, 169
meringue torte, 214
miniature cream puffs, 169
Mrs. Simmons' chocolate whip,
    187
Nesselrode ice cream cake, 194
oranges Orientale, 181
orange soufflé surprise, 203
old-fashioned strawberry short-
    cake, 206
peach shortcake, 207
peaches in marsala, 313
pear tatin, 211
pears in port, 180
pears sabayon, 183
pears véfour, 212
peppermint ice cream, 196
peppermint ice cream sundae pie,
    193
pink champagne sherbet, 201
pineapple in crème de menthe, 185
pineapple mint frappé, 592
pineapple shells filled with lemon
    ice, 194
pots de crème, 287
profiteroles, 192
prune whip with custard sauce,
    182
pudding sauce, 568
raspberries sabayon, 286
raspberry sherbet, 201
Ratner's marble cheesecake, 166
Saint Peter's pudding, 188
snow pudding, 190
soufflés, 202-5
spumoni, 311
steamed plum pudding, 567
strawberries à la Blue Fox, 214
strawberries in May wine, 189
strawberries and pineapple with
    sour cream, 183
strawberries with raspberry
    sauce, 184
strawberries Romanoff, 184
strawberry Bavarian cream, 188
strawberry cookie shell sundaes, 193
strawberry and cream cheesecake,
    165
strawberry parfait, 195
strawberry profiteroles, 170
strawberry-rum custard sundaes,
    191

strawberry snow with custard
    sauce, 189
waffles, 326
warm apple slices with custard
    sauce, 301
watermelon basket, 186
zabaione, 312
Deviled
    cheese sandwiches, grilled, 585
    eggs, 223
    lobster, 591
Devil's food cake, McCall's best, 123
Dieting
    basic pattern, 587-88
    low calorie recipes, 588-92
    nutrition and meal planning,
        577-92
    rules to observe, 578
Dill, beet soup with, 521
Dill sauce, herring in, 58
Dilled carrot sticks, 338
Dilled whole carrots, 338
Dilly vegetables, 339
Dinner menus for entertaining, 572-75
    at eight, 573
    buffet in spring, 573
    Christmas holiday, 574
    Creole Thanksgiving, 574
    Easter buffet, 575
    festive Friday, 572
    first taste of spring, 572
    formal, 572
    Italian, 572
    little French, 573
    man's favorite, 573
    modern Thanksgiving, 575
    New England Thanksgiving, 574
    patio spring, 573
    special spring, 572
    Sunday in May, 572
    traditional Thanksgiving, 574
    warm weather, 573
Dinner menus for good nutrition, 580-87
    nutritional guidelines, 578
Diplomat cake, 208
Dips see also SPREADS
    chile con queso with raw vege-
        tables, 52
    eggplant appetizer, 45
    guacamole with crisp vegetables,
        45
    onion soup, low calorie, 589
    spring, 46
    Swiss cheese fondue, 50
    Swiss cheese and tomato fondue,
        51
Don's barbecue sauce, 503
Double boiler scrambled eggs, 587
Double cornbread, 93
Double strawberry soda, 76
Doughnuts
    French crullers and beignets, 172
    jelly, 113

Spanish churros, 323
Dow see, 264
Dream bars, 161
Dressings, salad, 488-94
avocado, 492
basic French or oil and vinegar, 492
best French, 493
boiled, 489
creamy, 471
creamy blue cheese or Roquefort, 489
cucumber yoghurt, 491
curry, 489
French, 492
fresh mint, 494
ginger, 491
golden gate, 489
green goddess, 473
green mayonnaise, 491
honey lime, 491
lime, 494
mayonnaise, 488
poppy seed, 491
Roquefort or blue cheese, 492
Russian, 490
sour cream, 490
sour cream for fruit, 490
special French, 493
thousand island, 490
vinaigrette, 493
white wine French, 494
zesty French, 494
Dressings (stuffings), 454-56
bread, 455
chicken-liver-mushroom, 455
cornbread balls, 454
cornbread oyster, 455
cranberry-orange, 454
old-fashioned, 456
sausage, 446
sausage-oyster-and-pecan, 456
Drip coffee, 69
Drop biscuits, 91
Drop cookies, 147-49
benne-seed, 147
almond tile, 288
amaretti, 311
easy no-roll sugar, 149
fruitcake, 570
glazed ginger, 148
molasses raisin, 147
orange-oatmeal, 148
Dry beans
cassoulet, 280
old-fashioned baked, 528
pasta e fagioli, 304
refried, 319
Swedish style brown, 325
white, leg of lamb with, 278
Duck, roast wild, 406
Duckling à l'orange, 448
Duckling with turnips, 280

Dumplings
apple, 426
parsley, 14-15
Dundee cake, 570
Dutch tile cookies, 566

E

Easter buffet, menu, 575
Easy
caramel frosting, 140
Christmas cherry cake, 564
no-roll sugar cookies, 149
Éclairs, 170
custard filling for, 171
Edam cheese, savory, 47
Egg(s), 221-30
all about, 222
baked, Gruyère, 229
Benedict, 230
deviled, 223
-drop soup, 266
fried, 223
en gelée, 61
golden buck, 231
grades of, 222
and ham in a cloud, 230
hard-cooked, 222, 265
how to cook, 222
-and-lemon sauce, 295
mayonnaise, 63
omelet, basic, 226
omelet, basic puffy, 228
omelet, Cecilia's Spanish style, 228
omelet, cheese, 227
omelet, cottage cheese and chive, 227
omelet fines herbes, 226
omelette Mère Poulard, 283
omelet, puffy Spanish, 229
poached, 223
with ham, 223
ranchero, 317
salad and lettuce in buns, 580
scrambled, 223-25
à la Suisse, 225
bacon, 224
cheese, 224
creamy, 225
double boiler, 587
Mexican style, 224
mushroom, 225
skillet, 224
soft-cooked, 222
spinach frittata, 308
stuffed, 325
tea, 264
Eggnog
old English, 79
orange, 74
peach brandy, 80
spicy, 74
Eggplant, 526

appetizer, 45
cold ratatouille, 64
Creole, stuffed, 372
fritters, 538
moussaka, 16-17
parmigiana, 307
perfect fried, 538
and tomato casserole, 539
Ella Brennan's milk punch, 78
Enchiladas and chili, 320
Endive, 468
Endive, Belgian, and cold leeks vinaigrette, 479
English cooking, 272-74
baked trout and bacon, 272
Brussels sprouts with chestnut sauce, 274
custard sauce, 218
savory roast beef with Yorkshire pudding, 349
steak-and-kidney pie, 272
Welsh curd tarts, 273
English trifle, 178
Entertaining, menus for, 571-76
Equivalents, weights and measures, chart, 34
Escarole, 468
Espresso, caffè, 68, 70

F

Fabulous cheese soufflé, 232
Farina, gnocchi, 461
Fats, how to measure, 33
Favorite
cheese pie, 419
lasagna, 464
one-egg cake, 120
tuna salad, 585
Festival beets, 530
Feta cheese
Greek cheese pie, 52
hot cheese pastries, 51
spinach pie, 296
1500 calorie diet pattern, 587-88
Fig sorbet, 201
Filet of beef Burgundy, 350
Filet of beef Stroganoff, 362
Filet steaks, broiling timetable, 353
Filled cookies, old-fashioned, 150
Filled oatmeal-date bars, 162
Fillets of sole
bonne femme, 243
Duglère, 246
Florentine, 245
Marguery, 244
Queen Victoria, 244
with tarragon-chive butter, 242
Filling(s)
apple, for blintzes, 210
blueberry, for blintzes, 210
cheese, for blintzes, 210
cherry, for blintzes, 209
chocolate custard, 144

chocolate whipped cream, 139
crabmeat, curried, for crêpes, 252
custard, for cream puffs, 171
date, for old-fashioned cookies, 150
fresh-orange, 144
lemon, 143
lemon, for heavenly meringue, 210
lemon, for tartlets, 431
mocha whipped cream, 139
for pizza
    meatball and mozzarella, 310
    salami and sweet peppers, 310
    tomato and cheese, 310
rum cream, for fruit tarts, 430
sherry cream, for strawberries, 214
vanilla cream, 144
Finnish logs, 156
First courses, 60-66, *see also* SOUP
anchovy antipasto salad, 62
artichokes with lemon sauce, 527
asparagus and Swiss cheese tart, 66
avocado halves, California-style, 61
blini, 62
caviar, 60
cold ratatouille, 64
coquilles Saint Jacques, 66
eggs en gelée, 61
eggs mayonnaise, 63
grilled grapefruit with kirsch, 63
lobster cocktail, 64
melon with prosciutto, 63
moules marinière, 276
pâté tart, 65
scallops provençale, 65
shrimp with apricot sauce, 268
shrimp cocktail, 62
snails in garlic butter, 276
Fish, 237-48, *see also* SHELLFISH *and names of fish*
baked, 240
baked fillets thermidor, 243
baked haddock, New England style, 242
baked stuffed, 241
baked trout and bacon, 272
baked striped bass, 241
balls, Norwegian, 326
basting sauces for broiling, 239
bouillabaisse, 275
breaded cod fillets, 247
broiled salmon or swordfish steaks, parsley lemon butter, 240
broiling timetable, 239
chowder, New England, 514
cioppino, 250
codfish cakes, 248
crispy broiled salmon steaks, 240
fillets of sole bonne femme, 243
fillets of sole Duglère, 246
fillets of sole Florentine, 245
fillets of sole Marguery, 244
fillets of sole Queen Victoria, 244

fillets of sole with tarragon-chive butter, 242
grilled (sautéed), 247
herring in dill sauce, 58
herring in sour cream, 59
how to buy, 238
how to store, 238
en papillote, 240
poaching, 243
salmon steaks poached in white wine, 246
Swedish cold salmon with mustard sauce, 59
sweet-and-sour, 270
trout amandine, 248
tuna salad, favorite, 585
Five-flavor beef, 265
Flaky pastry, 411-12
Flambéed sweet potatoes, 550
Flan
caramel custard, 324
fresh apple, 413
strawberry, 285
Flank steak
broiling timetable, 353
London broil, 354
savory slices, 56
stroganoff, 363
Flat bread
Arab, souvlakia, 297
tortillas, 317
Florentine chuck steak, 355
Floating heart ritz, 199
Floating island, 174
Flounder *see* FILLETS OF SOLE
Flour, in bread baking, 100
how to measure, 33
Fluffy mashed potatoes, 547
Fluffy white rice, 458
Fluted tart shells, 429
Food groups, basic four, 578
chart, 579
Food weights and measures, 34
Fondant frosting, 141
Fondue, Swiss cheese, 50
Swiss cheese and tomato, 51
Four-minute frosting, 142
Frankfurters, 372-73
goulash, 373
how to heat, 373
lentil soup with, 521
and sauerkraut in beer, 373
Freezing
cakes, 118
cookies, 146
pies, pie shells, 410
French bread from bakery
garlic bread, 95
hot crispy herb bread, 95
French cooking, 274-91
almond tile cookies, 288
apple pie, 290
asparagus quiche, 284
baba au rhum, 288

beef à la mode, 357
beef Bourguignon, 277
bouillabaisse, 275
brioche, 116
cassoulet, 280
chicken basquaise, 281
chocolate crème, 287
cold ratatouille, 64
Colette's chocolate cake, 286
coquilles Saint Jacques, 65
crème brûlée, 291
French crullers and beignets, 172
French custard with raspberry sauce, 177
French dinner, menu, 573
duckling à l'orange, 448
duckling with turnips, 280
glazed vegetables, 285
gnocchi Parisienne, 279
leg of lamb, French style, 390
leg of lamb with salsify, 278
leg of lamb with white beans, 278
lobster soufflé, Plaza Athenée, 282
madeleines, 289
moules marinière, 276
mushroom ratatouille, 540
omelette Mère Poulard, 283
onion soup, 506
pissaladière, 54
potage printanier, 275
potatoes Anna, 283
potatoes Niçoise, 284
pots de crème, 287
quiche Lorraine, 52
raspberries sabayon, 286
scallops Provençale, 65
snails in garlic butter, 276
soupe au pistou, 274
steak au poivre, 277
strawberry flan, 285
tarte tatin, 290
French dressing, 492
best, 493
special, 493
white wine, 494
zesty, 494
French-fried potatoes, 544-45
French green salad, 470
French potato salad, 481
French-style buttered peas, 543
French-style green beans, 540
French toast, 97
Fresh
apple flan, 413
asparagus with hollandaise, 528
asparagus mimosa, 527
asparagus vinaigrette, 476
-berry pie, 414
grapefruit halves with orange sections, 586
ham, roasting timetable, 374
ham hocks, country style, 378
lemonade, 72

mint dressing, 494
orange filling, 144
orange sherbet, 202
orange spritzer, 72
peach and green grape pie, 421
peach kuchen, 206
pears in port, 180
pineapple luau, 185
salmon and cucumber salad, 475
spinach mimosa, 551
spinach salad, 470
strawberries à la Colony, 195
strawberries with mint, 184
strawberries in port, 184
strawberry glacé pie, 421

Fried
chicken, golden, 440
clams, 251
cornmeal mush, 462
eggs, 223
onion rings, 542
oysters, 257
rice, 266
scallops, 258
scallops, shrimp, and sole, 259

Frisky sour, 588
Fritters
apricot, 172
banana, 171
basic sweet batter, 171
corn, 537
eggplant, 538
Swiss cheese, 49

Frosted
punch bowl, 78
strawberry float, 74
tartlets triumphant, 432

Frosting(s), 138-42, *see also* GLAZES
and TOPPINGS
Frosting(s) (continued)
chocolate butter cream, 141
chocolate sour cream, 139
chocolate, for tartlets, 433
chocolate whipped cream, 139
cocoa cream, 139
coconut seven-minute, 142
coffee butter, 138
coffee spice seven-minute, 142
cream cheese, 141
easy caramel, 140
fondant, 141
four-minute, 142
glaze, 567
half 'n' half seven-minute, 142
how to frost a layer cake, 138
mocha whipped cream, 139
orange, 142
peanut butter, 140
pink peppermint seven-minute,
142
quick fudge, 140
seafoam, 142
seven-minute, 142
vanilla, for tartlets, 433

Frosty daiquiri punch, 77
Frozen desserts *see also* ICE CREAM
and SHERBET
biscuit tortoni, 312
floating heart ritz, 199
lemon cream, 197
maple mousse, 198
Frozen meat, storage of, 346
Frozen tomato frappé, 517
Fruit *see also* names of fruits
bowl, Chinese, 270
cheese with, 234-36
compote, rumtopf, 332
curried, for summer baked ham,
18-19
daily needs, 578
Fruit desserts, 179-86
ambrosia bowl, 180
apricot-glazed poached pears, 180
baked apples with vanilla pudding
sauce, 182
baked fruit flambé, 181
baked spiced rhubarb, 185
Chinese fruit bowl, 270
country applesauce, 183
fresh pears in port, 180
fresh pineapple luau, 185
fresh pineapple in shell, 186
fresh strawberries with mint, 184
fresh strawberries in port, 184
macaroon-stuffed peaches, 182
oranges Orientale, 181
peaches in marsala, 313
pear tatin, 212
pears sabayon, 183
pears véfour, 212
pineapple in crème de menthe, 185
prune whip with custard sauce,
182
Saint Peter's pudding, 188
strawberries à la Blue Fox, 214
strawberries in May wine, 189
strawberries and pineapple with
sour cream, 183
strawberries with raspberry
sauce, 184
strawberries Romanoff, 184
watermelon basket, 186
Fruit drinks, 71-73, *see also* PUNCHES
cup of cheer, 71
fresh lemonade, 72
fresh orange spritzer, 72
golden refresher, 72
hot mulled cider, 72
pineapple-orange blush, 73
swizzles, 80
Fruit-glazed baked ham, 383
Fruit mustard, hot, 385
Fruit pies, 413-18
banana coconut, 425
best cherry, 417
blueberry cheese, supreme, 420
cherry cheese, supreme, 420
deep-dish apple cider, 428

deep-dish peach, 428
deep-dish pear, 427
French apple tart, 290
fresh apple flan, 413
fresh berry, 414
fresh strawberry glacé, 421
lemon chiffon, 424
lemon meringue, 423
open-face plum, 415
peach-and-blueberry, 415
peach and green grape, 421
peach streusel, 416
pear tatin, 211
perfect apple, 24-25
rhubarb lattice, 416
spiced plum, 418
strawberry Devonshire glacé, 421
strawberry flan, 285
tarte tatin, 290
upside-down apple, 414
Fruit salads, 483-84, *see also* GELA-
TINE SALADS
apple and sour cream slaw, 483
fresh-fruit dessert, 483
ginger-and-fresh fruit mold, 487
green-and-white, 484
orange and onion, 484
pink grapefruit and avocado platter, 483
Fruit tarts, 430
tartlets, triumphant, 432
Fruitcake(s)
best of all, 565
cookies, 570
Dundee cake, 570
white, 566
Fudge
brownies, chocolate, 160
cake, chocolate, 127
cake, sour cream, 121
deluxe, chocolate, 563
frosting, quick, 140
sauce, 218

G

Game, 405-8
brandied partridges, 406
braised partridges, 406
roast wild duck, 406
roast venison with wine, 407
smothered quail, 407
squab in sour cream, 407
venison pot roast, 408
Garbanzo bean salad, 477
Garlic bread, 95
Garlic butter, shrimp in, 260
Gazpacho, 518
salad bowl, 481
salad, molded, 486
Gelatine, eggs en gelée, 61
Gelatine desserts, 187-90
cherry-almond flip, 187
coffee jelly with custard sauce, 190

Mrs. Simmons' chocolate whip, 187
Saint Peter's pudding, 188
snow pudding, 190
strawberry Bavarian cream, 188
strawberries in May wine, 189
strawberry snow with custard
sauce, 189
Gelatine salads, 484-88
bing cherry, 488
cranberry mold, 485
crisp cucumber aspic, 486
ginger and fresh fruit, 487
guacamole salad mold, 485
jellied cranberry, 341
molded gazpacho, 486
perfection, 487
tomato aspic, 484
German cooking, 291-94
apple kuchen, 294
caraway noodles, 291
fried potatoes, 543
pfeffernuesse, 561
potato pancakes, 294
potato salad, 480
red cabbage, 293
sauerbraten, 292
with gingersnap sauce, 361
sauerkraut and pork, 292
smoked loin of pork, 293
springerle, 569
stollen, 112
Giblet gravy, 504
Ginger
cookies, glazed, 148
crinkles, 158
dressing for salads, 491
-and-fresh fruit salad mold, 487
-glazed baked ham, 384
root, 264
Gingersnap sauce, 498
Glaze(s) see also FROSTINGS and
TOPPINGS
apricot, 143, 431
blueberry, 168
brown sugar, 534
chocolate, 143, 151, 170
currant jelly, 431
frosting, 567
lemon, 143
orange, 142
pineapple, 168
red cherry, 167
strawberry, 167
Glazed
apples, 447
cream cheese pie, 419
ginger cookies, 148
ham loaf, 383
lemon-cream-cheesecake, 166
smoked pork with buttered carrots and cabbage, 377
smoked shoulder butt, 376
tartlets triumphant, 432
vegetables, 285

Glögg, 325
Gnocchi, 461
Parisienne, 279
Gold cake, McCall's best, 119
Gold petits-fours cake, 122
Golden
buck, 231
-fried chicken, 440
-gate dressing, 489
needles, 264
refresher, 72
roast turkey, 452
whipped potatoes, 546
Goose, roast stuffed, 446
Goulash
frankfurter, 373
Hungarian, 365
pork-and-sauerkraut, 377
Graham cracker pie shell, unbaked, 411
Grains and cereals, 460-62
fried cornmeal mush, 462
gnocchi, 461
hot buttered grits, 462
polenta, 460
Grape leaves, stuffed, 44
Grapes, green, and peach pie, 421
Grapefruit
grilled, with kirsch, 63
juice, cup of cheer, 71
juice, rum swizzles, 80
halves with orange sections, 586
and orange peel, candied, 558
pink, and avocado salad platter,
483
Gravy, 503-4, see also SAUCES
brown, 503
Burgundy, 504
chicken, 504
giblet, 504
Greek cooking, 295-98
artichoke halves, 296
baklava, 298
cheese pie, 52
egg and lemon sauce, 295
hot cheese pastries, 51
meatballs with lemon sauce, 297
roast leg of lamb Olympia, 295
souvlakia, 297
spinach pie, 296
stuffed grape leaves, 44
Green beans
French style, 540
hollandaise, 539
how to buy and cook, 524
Italian, 540
salade Niçoise, 473
Green
cabbage soup, 507
chile salsa, 319
goddess salad, 473
grape and peach pie, 421
mayonnaise, 491
peppers and zucchini, sautéed, 556
Green salads, 468-71

Caesar, 469
French, 470
fresh spinach, 470
garden salad bowl, 471
old-fashioned lettuce bowl, 470
Green tomato pickles, sour, 333
Green-and-white fruit salad, 484
Greens (collards, dandelions, kale, and
spinach), how to buy and cook,
526
Griddlecakes, 97
corn, 536
Grill, mixed, 392
Grilled
deviled cheese sandwiches, 585
grapefruit with kirsch, 63
Grilling meat, 346
Grits, hot buttered, 462
Ground beef, 366-72
beef balls Bourguignon, 368
beef balls stroganoff, 367
beef tartare canapés, 55
bobotie, 367
broiling timetable, 353
hamburger roulade, 369
hamburgers, 372
Italian spaghetti and meatballs,
370
Madras curried meatballs, 368
meatballs and sauerkraut soup,
515
moussaka, 16-17
roast meat loaf, 369
steak tartare, 56
stuffed cabbage rolls, 371
stuffed eggplant Creole, 372
Swedish meatballs, 55
tamale casserole, 370
upside down chili pie, 371
Guacamole
dip with crisp vegetables, 45
salad mold, 485
-and-tomato salad, 482
Gumbo, shrimp, 261

H

Haddock
baked, New England style, 242
baked, stuffed, 241
fillets of sole bonne femme, 243
Norwegian fish balls, 326
Halibut, New England fish chowder,
514
Ham, 380-85
baked in cider, 381
baked in crust with Cumberland
sauce, 380
baked, fruit-glazed, 383
baked, ginger-glazed, 384
baked, maple-glazed, 382
baked, and scalloped potatoes, 382
baking timetable, 380
and eggs in a cloud, 230

fresh, roast, 374
fresh, roasting timetable, 374
hocks, fresh, country style, 378
how to carve, 41
lentil soup with, 514
loaf, glazed, 383
loaf, pineapple-glazed baked, 580
loaf, upside-down, family favorite, 385
poached eggs with, 223
prosciutto, melon with, 63
steak, baked, with hot mustard fruit, 385
summer baked, 18-19
Virginia baked, 384
Hamburger *see also* GROUND BEEF
hamburgers, 372
roulade, 367
Hard-cooked eggs, 222, 265
Hard sauce, 218
nutmeg, 219
Harvey House slaw, 478
Hash, perfect corned beef, 366
Hawaiian
"ham" and baked bean casserole, 583
sweet potatoes, 547
Hazelnut truffles, 559
Head lettuce, 468
Hearty soups, 510-15
beef borsch with sour cream, 511
beef and vegetable, 510
Calcutta mulligatawny, 511
corn chowder, 513
corn and clam chowder, 512
lentil with ham, 514
Manhattan clam chowder, 513
meatballs and sauerkraut, 515
New England clam chowder, 513
New England fish chowder, 514
old-fashioned split pea, 512
oyster stew, 512
Heavenly lemon meringue, 210
Herb
bread, hot crisp, 95
-broiled lamb chops, 591
butter, for chicken Kiev, 10
rolls, crispy, 96
Herbed
basting sauce, 239
pot roast with vegetables, 358
Herring in dill sauce, 58
in sour cream, 59
Hoisin sauce, 264
Holiday banana bread, 85
Holiday cheese ball, 48
Holiday delights, 557-70
best of all fruitcakes, 565
burnt almond candy, 559
candied grapefruit and orange peel, 558
chocolate fudge deluxe, 563
cinnamon stars, 560
Dundee cake, 570

Dutch tile cookies, 566
easy Christmas cherry cake, 564
frosting glaze, 567
fruitcake cookies, 570
hazelnut truffles, 559
hot mincemeat pie, 564
pecan crescents, 562
pecan pralines, 562
pfeffernuesse, 561
pudding sauce, 568
Saint Peter's pudding, 188
springerle, 569
spritz wreaths, 563
steamed plum pudding, 567
stollen, 112
sugar nuts, 559
Swiss biberli, 568
Holiday delights (continued)
Tyrolean honey cookies, 560
walnutty caramels, 558
white fruitcake, 566
Hollandaise sauce, 22-23
blender, 499
for green beans, 539
Homemade ice creams and frozen desserts, 195-99
basic vanilla ice cream, 196
chocolate cinnamon ice cream, 198
floating heart ritz, 199
frozen lemon cream, 197
frozen maple mousse, 198
peppermint ice cream, 196
strawberry ice cream, 196
strawberry parfait, 195
Homemade noodles, 464
Homemade sherbets, 199-202
cranberry, 200
crème de menthe ring, 200
fresh orange, 202
fig, 201
lime, 202
pink champagne, 201
raspberry, 201
Hominy grits, hot buttered, 462
Honey
baklava, 298
cookies, Tyrolean, 560
how to measure, 33
-lime dressing, 491
-spice acorn squash, 553
whole wheat casserole bread, 114
Honeydew melon with prosciutto, 63
Honolulu coconut pie, 425
Horns, 110
Hors d'oeuvres, 44-60, *see also* CANAPÉS *and* FIRST COURSES
beef tartare canapés, 55
blue cheese spread, 48
caviar, 60
caviar-cream cheese ball, 48
Cheddar in sherry, 50
Cheddar-beer spread, 48

cheese-bacon puffs, 50
cheese-pâté pineapple, 49
chile con queso with raw vegetables, 52
clams oregano, 60
cocktail macadamias, 47
cocktail olives, 47
deviled eggs, 223
eggplant appetizer, 45
Greek cheese pie, 52
guacamole dip with crisp vegetables, 45
hot cheese pastries, 51
herring in dill sauce, 58
herring in sour cream, 59
holiday cheese ball, 48
liver pâté en gelée, 58
marinated artichokes, 44
mousse of chicken livers, 46
onion soup dip, low calorie, 589
parmesan cheese leaves, 53
pickled mushrooms, 45
pineapple-cheese ball, 46
pissaladière, 54
quiche Lorraine, 52
rumaki, 56
savory Edam cheese, 47
savory steak slices, 56
shrimp toast, 265
spring dip, 46
steak tartare, 56
stuffed grape leaves, 44
Swedish cold salmon with mustard sauce, 59
Swedish meatballs, 55
Swiss cheese fondue, 50
Swiss cheese fritters, 49
Swiss cheese and tomato fondue, 51
tea eggs, 264
Williamsburg cheese straws, 54
Horseradish sauce, 496
low calorie, 590
sour cream, 498
Hot
buttered grits, 462
cheese pastries, 51
chili oil, 264
chocolate, Mexican, 319
chocolate, old-fashioned, 73
crisp herb bread, 95
dogs, *see* FRANKFURTERS
-milk spongecake, 132
mincemeat pie, 564
mulled cider, 72
mustard fruit, 385
tomato consommé, 506
tea for 25, 70
H. R. M.'s favorite waffles, 98
Hungarian
chicken paprikash, 440
goulash, 365
veal casserole for a crowd, 400

I

Ice block, 78
Ice cream, 190-99
    basic vanilla (crank freezer type), 196
    chocolate cinnamon, 198
    peppermint, 196
    strawberry, 196
    strawberry parfait, 195
Ice cream desserts
    Blum's banana split, 192
    brandied apricots flambé, 191
    cherries jubilee, 191
    fresh strawberries à la Colony, 195
    ice cream cinnamon sauce, 218
    nesselrode ice cream cake, 194
    peppermint ice cream sundae pie, 193
    pineapple shells filled with lemon ice, 194
    strawberry cookie shell sundaes, 193
    profiteroles, 192
    spumoni, 311
    strawberry-rum custard sundaes, 191
Ice cream drinks, 74-76
    banana shake, 75
    chocolate mint soda, 76
    double strawberry soda, 76
    frosted strawberry float, 74
    maple milk shake, 75
    mocha frosted, 75
    peanut butter shake, 75
    pineapple shake, 75
    raspberry shake, 75
    root beer float, 76
    strawberry shake, 75
Ice cubes for punch bowls, 71
Ice ring with fruit, 79
    strawberry, 77
Iceberg lettuce, 468
Icebox cookies, 153-55
    butterscotch, 155
    date and walnut pinwheel, 154
    peanut butter pinwheels, 153
    petticoat tails, 155
    oatmeal, 154
Iced tea, 71
Icicle pickles, old-fashioned, 335
Icing see also FROSTINGS
    Chocolate, for Scotch cake squares, 121
Indian pudding, baked, 179
Individual strawberry shortcakes, 208
International cheeses described, 235-36
International cooking, 263-326
    Chinese, 264-71, see CHINESE
    Dutch tile cookies, 566
    English, 272-74, see ENGLISH
    French, 274-91, see FRENCH
    German, 291-94, see GERMAN
    Greek, 295-98, see GREEK
    Irish, 298-303, see IRISH
    Italian, 304-14, see ITALIAN
    Japanese, 314-16, see JAPANESE
    Mexican, 317-21, see MEXICAN
    Polish babka, 108
    Scandinavian, 324-26, see SCAN-DINAVIAN
    Spanish, 322-24, see SPANISH
    Swiss biberli, 568
    Swiss braided loaves, 105
    Tyrolean honey cookies, 560
Introduction to cooking, 9-42
    carving, 38-42
      ham, 41
      leg of lamb, 40
      standing rib roast, 42
      turkey, 39
    cooking school, illustrated, 10-31, see COOKING SCHOOL
    cutting terminology, 37
    food weights and measures, 34
    how to measure ingredients, 33
    oven temperatures, 34
    recipes, how to tackle, 33
    top-of-the-range terminology, 34-35
    utensils (list), 37-38
Iowa corn relish, 337
Irish cooking, 298-303
    caraway-raisin soda bread, 300
    colcannon, 299
    cottage broth, 299
    Dundee cake, 570
    Irish coffee, 68, 302
    lamb stew, 300
    Maureen's soda bread, 300
    steamed raisin pudding with Irish whisky sauce, 303
    tea cake, 302
    warm apple slices with custard sauce, 301
    whole-wheat soda bread, 301
Iron, sources of, chart, 579
Italian cooking, 304-14
    amaretti (macaroons), 311
    anise toast, 313
    artichokes with lemon sauce, 309
    best of all pizzas, 309
    biscuit tortoni, 312
    broccoli, Italian style, 308
    cannoli, 313
      shells, 314
    chicken cacciatore, 438
      with polenta, 305
    chicken tetrazzini, 439
    eggplant parmigiana, 307
    Italian dinner menu, 572
    Italian spaghetti and meatballs, 370
    Italian-style buffet menu, 576
    meatball and mozzarella filling for pizza, 310
    minestrone, 304
    pasta e fagioli, 304
    peaches in marsala, 313
    pizza sauce, 310
    Roman veal scallopini, 305
    salami and sweet peppers filling for pizza, 310
    spaghetti and meatballs Napoli, 306
    spinach frittata, 308
    spumoni, 311
    stewed sweet peppers, 308
    traditional tomato and cheese filling for pizza, 310
    veal parmigiana, 306-7
    zabaione, 312
Italian green beans, 540
Italian ham (prosciutto), melon with, 63

J

Jams, jellies and preserves, 327-44 see JELLIES and PRESERVES
    Tropical jam, 329
Japanese cooking, 314-16
    batter for tempura, 315
    rice with mushrooms, 314
    sauce for tempura, 316
    sukiyaki, 316
    tempura, 315
Jellied
    consommé with red caviar, 515
    cranberry mold, 341
Jelly(ies), 328-30
    apricot-sherry, 328
    crème de menthe and crème de cassis, 330
    directions for, 328
    doughnuts, 113
    port wine festival, 328
    rhubarb, 330
    -roll cake, 133
    tarragon-wine, 329
Jerusalem artichoke relish, 338
Jewel cookies, 158
John Wayne's cheese casserole, 231
Junket, almond, 271

K

Kabobs, lamb, 592
Kale, 526
Kidney(s)
    lamb, braised, 405
    -and-steak pie, 272
    veal Provençale, 404
Kidney bean(s)
    salad, 477
    soupe au pistou, 274
    three-bean salad bowl, 477
Kneading bread, 100
Kuchen
    apple, 294
    fresh peach, 206
    pie shell, 416

L

Lace wafers, almond, 158
Lamb, 386-94
  cottage broth, 299
  braised pot roast, 388
  chop(s)
    broiled, savory mushroom
      stuffing, 391
    grill, broiled, 392
    herb broiled, 591
    mixed grill, 392
    -and-potato hot pot, baked, 584
  crown roast filled with sautéed
    mushrooms, 389
  how to buy, 346
  kabobs, 592
  kidneys, braised, 405
  leg of
    broiled slices with sauce maître
      d'hôtel, 390
    French style, 390
    how to carve, 40
    roast, 386
    roast en croûte with mushroom
      stuffing, 387
    roast Olympia, 295
    roast, Swedish style, 388
    with salsify, 278
    with white beans, 278
  moussaka, 16-17
  pie with dill, 394
  rack of, 393
    Provençale, 394
  riblets, barbecued, 391
  roasting timetable, 386
  souvlakia, 297
  stew, 300
    with dill, spring, 393
Lasagna, cheese, 233
Lasagna, our favorite, 464
Lattice pie, rhubarb, 416
La Velle's plum chutney, 331
Leaf lettuce, 468
**Leeks and endives vinaigrette, cold,
479**
Leg of lamb
  broiled slices with sauce maître
    d'hôtel, 390
  French style, 390
  how to carve, 40
  roast, 386
  roast en croûte with mushroom
    stuffing, 387
  roast Olympia, 295
  roast, Swedish style, 388
  with salsify, 278
  with white beans, 278
Lemon
  butter, 242, 256
  -buttermilk soup, 520
  chiffon pie, 424
  chive sauce, 497
  cream, frozen, 197

  cream cheesecake, glazed, 166
  -curd tarts, 434
  -and-egg sauce, 295
  filling, 143
  glaze, 143
  -glazed carrots, 533
  golden refresher, 72
  mayonnaise, 488
  meringue, heavenly, 210
  meringue pie, 423
  parsley butter, 240
  pineapple soda, 76
  pudding cake, 179
  sandbakels, 431
  sauce, artichokes with, 309
    broccoli with, 530
    with Greek meatballs, 297
  spongecake, fresh, 132
  tea bread, 85
Lemonade, fresh, 72
Lemony basting sauce, for fish, 239
Lentil soup with frankfurters, 521
  with ham, 514
Lettuce, 468
  salad bowl, old-fashioned, 470
  soup, spring, 510
Lima beans, barbecued, 529
  how to buy and cook, 525
Lime
  -curd tarts, 434
  honey salad dressing, 491
  salad dressing, 494
  sherbet with strawberries, 202
  pineapple parfait, 592
Limestone lettuce, 468
Lindy's famouse cheesecake, 164
Linguine parmesan, buttered, 463
Liquids, how to measure, 33
Liver
  broiled, 403
  broiled, calves', 590
  calves', Venetian-style, 404
  pan-fried, 403
  pâté en gelée, 58
  pâté tart, 65
Livers, chicken, sautéed, 403
Loaf of bread, how to shape, 101
Lobster(s)
  bisque, 509
  boiled live, 254
  broil rock lobster tails, 255
  broiled live, 256
  broiled rock lobster tails, 256
  Cantonese, 269
  cocktail, 64
  deviled, 591
  how to buy and prepare, 250
  Newburg, 255
  soufflé, Plaza Athenée, 282
  sauce, 500
  and shrimp in white wine, 261
  tempura, 315
  thermidor, 255

Lobster(s) (continued)
  varieties of, 254
London broil, 354
Long grain white rice (described), 458
Low calorie foods, 578
Low calorie recipes, 588-92
  beef stew, 590
  broiled brisket of beef, 589
  broiled calves' liver, 590
  cottage cheese salad in tomato
    halves, 591
  cottage cheese topping for baked
    potatoes, 590
  crab salad, 589
  deviled lobster, 591
  frisky sour, 588
  herb broiled lamb chops, 591
  horseradish sauce, 590
  lamb kabobs, 592
  lime pineapple parfait, 592
  onion soup dip, 589
  pineapple mint frappé, 592
  tomato bouillon, 589
Luau, fresh pineapple, 185
**Luncheon meat, "ham" and baked bean
casserole Hawaiian, 583**
Luncheon menus for entertaining
  on the terrace, 576
  ladies', 574
**Luncheon menus for good nutrition,
580-87**
  nutritional guidelines, 578
Lyonnaise potatoes, 544

M

Macadamias, cocktail, 47
Macaroni
  baked, and tomatoes au gratin, 586
  baked ziti casserole, 232
  basic directions for cooking, 462-63
  and cheese, baked, 465
  pasta e fagioli, 304
  salad, 482
  -tuna supper salad, 476
Macaroon(s)
  amaretti, 311
  cake, 126
  -stuffed peaches, 182
Madeleines, 289
Madelons, 169
Madras curried meatballs, 368
McCall's best
  angel food cake, 129
  basic white bread, 102
  daffodil cake, 131
  devil's food cake, 123
  chocolate loaf cake, 124
  gold cake, 119
  nut bread, 84
  spicecake, 125
  zucchini bread-and-butter pickles,
    334

Mâitre d'hôtel butter sauce, 500
Mailing cookies, 146
Main dish salads, 471-76
    chef's, 471
    chicken, 472
    chicken pineapple, 472
    chicken Waldorf, 473
    cobb, with Russian dressing, 471
    curried chicken, 474
    fresh salmon and cucumber, 475
    green goddess, 473
    Pacific coast summer, 475
    salade Niçoise, 473
    shrimp and roasted peppers, 474
    tuna-macaroni supper, 476
Manhattan clam chowder, 513
Manicotti, baked, with cheese filling, 20-21
Maple
    -barbecued spareribs, 380
    -glazed baked ham, 382
    milk shake, 75
    mousse, frozen, 198
    squash pie, 426
Marble loaf cake, 125
Margaritas, 321
Marinade for sweet-and-sour fish, 270
Marinara sauce for spaghetti, 465
Marinated
    artichokes, 44
    mushroom salad, 476
    rice salad, 480
Marmalade, tomato, 332
Marsala
    peaches in, 313
    zabaione, 312
Marshmallow sauce, 219
Maureen's soda bread, 300
Mayonnaise, 488
    green, 491
    lemon, 488
Meal planning *see also* MENUS FOR ENTERTAINING
    breakfast, 578
        sample menus, 580-87
    dinner, 578
        sample menus, 580-87
    eating for health and beauty, chart, 578-79
    low calorie, basic diet pattern, 587
    lunch, 578
        sample menus, 580-87
    menus for good nutrition, seven days' worth, 580-87
    nutrition and dieting, 577-92
Measures and weights, chart, 34
Measuring ingredients, 33
Measuring tools, list, 37-38
Meat, 345-408, *see also* BEEF, GAME, LAMB, PORK, VEAL, VARIETY MEATS
    basic cookery, 346-47
        braising, 347

        broiling and grilling, 346
        deep-frying, 347
        pan-frying, 347
        roasting, 346
        simmering in water and stewing, 347
    daily needs, 578
    how to buy, 346
    how to store, 346
Meatball(s)
    beef balls Bourguignon, 368
    beef balls stroganoff, 367
    Greek, with lemon sauce, 297
    Italian spaghetti and, 370
    Madras curried, 368
    and mozzarella filling for pizza, 310
    -and-sauerkraut soup, 515
    and spaghetti, Napoli, 306
    Swedish, 55
Meat loaves
    baked veal loaf, 401
    cold roast veal loaf, 402
    glazed ham, 383
    pineapple-glazed baked ham, 580
    roast, 369
    upside-down ham, family favorite, 385
Meat pie, lamb, with dill, 394
Medium grain white rice, described, 458
Melon
    cantaloupe soup, chilled, 517
    with prosciutto, 63
    salad mold, ginger-and-fresh fruit, 487
    watermelon basket, 186
    watermelon pickle, Mrs. Lamb's, 334
Menus for entertaining, 571-76
    brunch for weekend guests, 575
    buffet in spring, 573
    Christmas holiday dinner, 574
    cocktail party, 575
    cocktail party buffet, 575
    Creole Thanksgiving, 574
    curry supper, 576
    dinner at eight, 573
    Easter buffet, 575
    festive Friday dinner, 572
    first taste of spring, 572
    formal dinner, 572
    hearty Sunday breakfast, 575
    holiday weekend brunch, 574
    Italian dinner, 572
    Italian-style buffet, 576
    ladies' luncheon, 574
    late supper, 576
    little French dinner, 573
    lunch on the terrace, 576
    man's favorite dinner, 573
    modern Thanksgiving, 575
    New England Thanksgiving, 574
    patio spring dinner, 573

    special spring dinner, 572
    summer Sunday brunch, 575
    Sunday in May, 572
    tea for the committee, 576
    traditional Thanksgiving, 574
    very informal buffet, 575
    warm weather menu, 573
    winter buffet, 576
Menus
    low calorie diet pattern, 587
    seven days' worth for health and beauty, 578-87
Meringue
    lemon, heavenly, 210
    pie, lemon, 423
    shell, baked, 211
    torte, 214
Mexican cooking, 317-21
    beef tacos with green chile salsa, 318
    brandied caramel flan, 320
    chile con queso with raw vegetables, 52
    chiles rellenos, 318
    chili and enchiladas, 320
    cinnamon cookies, 321
    eggs ranchero, 317
    green chile salsa, 319
    guacamole dip with crisp vegetables, 45
    hot chocolate, 319
    Margaritas, 321
    refried beans, 319
    tortillas, 317
Mexican-style scrambled eggs, 224
Milk, daily needs, 578
Milk drinks, 73-75
    banana shakes, 75
    Ella Brennan's punch, 78
    frosted strawberry float, 74
    maple shake, 75
    Mexican hot chocolate, 319
    mint chocolate, 73
    mocha chocolate, 73
    mocha frosted, 75
    old-fashioned hot chocolate, 73
    orange chocolate, 73
    orange eggnog, 74
    peach brandy eggnog, 80
    peanut butter shake, 75
    pineapple shakes, 75
    raspberry shakes, 75
    spiced chocolate, 73
    spiced cocoa, 74
    spicy eggnog, 74
    strawberry shake, 75
Mincemeat pie, hot, 564
Minestrone, 304
Miniature cream puffs, 169
Mint
    chocolate drink, 73
    chocolate soda, 76
    dressing, fresh, 494
    -jelly sauce, 499

Mix(es)
    biscuit mix shortcake, 207
    cake mix cakes, 136-37
Mixed grill, 392
Mocha
    blanc mange, 174
    chiffon cake, 130
    chocolate drink, 73
    frosted, 75
    whipped cream filling and
        frosting, 139
Molasses, how to measure, 33
    -raisin drop cookies, 147
Molded cookies, 156-60
    almond, 271
    almond lace wafers, 158
    butter crisps, 157
    chocolate kiss peanut butter, 156
    date-nut rolls, 160
    Finnish logs, 156
    ginger crinkles, 158
    jewel, 158
    Mexican cinnamon, 321
    oatmeal raisin, 157
    peanut butter, 159
    pecan balls, 157
    pecan crescents, 561
    pfeffernuesse, 561
    spritz wreaths, 563
    toll house crunch, 159
Molded salads *see* GELATINE
SALADS
Monosodium glutamate, 264
Moules marinière, 276
Moussaka, 16-17
Mousse
    of chicken livers, 46
    chocolate, 212
    frozen maple, 198
**Mozzarella and meatball filling for
pizza, 310**
Mrs. Lamb's watermelon pickle, 334
Mrs. Simmons' chocolate whip, 187
Muffins, 87-90
    blueberry cake, 88
    brown sugar, 89
    buttermilk bran, 88
    cheese, 89
    corn, 93
    date-nut, 90
Mulled cider, hot, 72
Mulligatawny soup, Calcutta, 511
Mush, fried cornmeal, 462
Mushroom(s)
    chicken liver dressing, 455
    pickled, 45
    ratatouille, 540
    relish, 343
    rice pilaf, 460
    rice with, 314
    salad, marinated, 476
    sauce, 244, 497
    sautéed, 389, 541
    savory stuffed, 541
    scrambled eggs, 225
    in sour cream, 541
    stuffing for roast leg of lamb, 387
    stuffing, savory, for lamb chops, 391
    veal chops with, 399
Mussel(s)
    how to buy and prepare, 250
    moules marinière, 276
Mustard
    fruit, hot, 385
    sauce, 59, 378, 499
        quick, 500

N

Navy beans *see* DRY BEANS
Neapolitan cake, 137
Nesselrode ice cream cake, 194
New England
    boiled dinner, 366
    clam chowder, 513
    fish chowder, 514
    -style baked haddock, 242
New potatoes with lemon butter, 546
Newburg
    lobster, 255
    sauce, 501
Niçoise, salade, 473
Noodles
    Alfredo, 464
    basic directions for cooking, 462-63
    buttered linguine parmesan, 463
    caraway, 291, 463
    cottage pot roast with, 359
    homemade, 464
    parmesan, 463
    Romanoff, baked, 463
    with pesto sauce, 466
    poppy seed, 463
Norwegian fish balls, 326
Nut(s)
    bread, McCall's best, 84
    chocolate torte, 213
    cocktail macadamias, 47
    -date bread, 84
    -date muffins, 90
    -date rolls, 160
    hazelnut truffles, 559
    pecan crescents, 562
    pecan pralines, 562
    praline paste for tartlets, 432
    -pineapple-apricot loaf, 86
    sugar, 559
Nutmeg hard sauce, 219
Nutrition, 577-92
    basic four food groups, 578
        chart, 579
    dieting and meal planning, 577-92
    eating for health and beauty, 578
        chart, 579
        menus, seven days' worth, 580-87
    low calorie recipes, 588-92
        basic diet pattern, 587-88

O

Oak leaf lettuce, 468
Oatmeal
    -date bars, filled, 162
    icebox cookies, 154
    -orange cookies, 148
    praline cake, 128
    -raisin cookies, 157
    shortbread, Scotch, 160
    toffee crisps, 161
    very special oatmeal, 583
Oil and vinegar salad dressing, 492
Okra and stewed tomatoes, 554
Old English eggnog, 79
Old-fashioned
    baked beans, 528
    chili sauce, 336
    dressing (stuffing), 456
    hot chocolate, 73
    filled cookies, 150
    icicle pickles, 335
    lettuce salad bowl, 470
    potato bread, 103
    pumpkin pie, 423
    sliced tomatoes, 481
    split pea soup, 512
    strawberry shortcake, 206
    sugar cookies, 152
Olives, cocktail, 47
Omelets, 226-29
    basic puffy, 228
    Cecilia's, Spanish-style, 228
    cheese, 227
    cottage cheese and chive, 227
    fines herbes, 226
    omelette Mère Poulard, 283
    puffy Spanish, 229
Onion(s)
    baked, 542
    and carrots, brown sugar-glazed,
        534
    creamed, 543
    glazed vegetables, 285
    and orange salad, 484
    rings, fried, 542
    small white, how to buy and
        cook, 526
    soup dip, low calorie, 589
    soup, French, 506
    white rice with, 459
Open-face plum pie, 415
Orange(s)
    -apricot-yoghurt soup, 519
    beets, 530
    biscuits, 584
    -braised pork chops, 378
    butter, 215
    chocolate drink, 73
    -cranberry dressing, 454
    -cranberry relish, 342
    crêpes Suzette, 215
    eggnog, 74
    filling, fresh, 144

frosting, 142
and grapefruit peel, candied, 558
glaze, 142
-glazed carrots, 534
-glazed sweet potatoes, 549
golden refresher, 72
-oatmeal cookies, 148
and onion salad, 484
Orientale, 181
-pineapple blush, 73
sauce, 215, 448
sherbet, fresh, 202
soufflé surprise, 203
spongecake, fresh, 132
spritzer, fresh, 72
winter squash with, 554

Oriental cooking see CHINESE COOK-
ING and JAPANESE COOKING
Our favorite lasagna, 464
Oven-steamed rice, 459
Oven temperatures, 34
Oyster(s)
availability of, 257
cornbread dressing, 455
fried, 257
how to buy and prepare, 250
pecan and sausage dressing, 456
Rockefeller, 257
stew, 512

P

Pacific coast summer salad, 475
**Paella (rice with clams and shrimp),
322**
Pan(s)
-broiled tomato halves, 554
-broiling beef, 353
-broiling meat, 347
oven pans, list, 37
top-of-the-range pans, list, 37
-fried liver, 403
-frying meat, 347
Pancakes, 96-97
blini, 62
blintzes, 209-10
blueberry buttermilk, 97
buttermilk, 96
corn griddlecakes, 536
crêpes with curried crabmeat, 252
crêpes Suzette, 215
griddlecakes, 97
potato, 294
Parfait(s)
lime-pineapple, 592
strawberry, 195
Parmesan cheese
buttered linguine, 463
eggplant parmigiana, 307
leaves, 53
noodles, 463
veal parmigiana, 306-7
Parsley
butter, 500

dumplings, 14-15
lemon butter, 240
sauce, 496
Parsnips, buttered, 542
how to buy and cook, 526
Partridges
braised, 406
brandied, 406
Party
crown roast of pork with apple
stuffing, 376
menus, see MENUS FOR
ENTERTAINING
pâté, 57
**Pasta (macaroni, spaghetti and
noodles), 462-66**
baked macaroni and cheese, 465
baked macaroni and tomatoes
au gratin, 586
baked noodles Romanoff, 463
baked ziti casserole, 232
basic directions for cooking, 462
buttered linguine parmesan, 463
caraway noodles, 291, 463
chicken Tetrazzini, 439
e fagioli, 304
homemade noodles, 464
Italian spaghetti and meatballs, 370
lasagna, cheese, for a crowd, 233
lasagna, our favorite, 464
macaroni salad, 482
macaroni-tuna supper salad, 476
noodles Alfredo, 464
parmesan noodles, 463
poppy seed noodles, 463
spaghetti with marinara sauce, 465
spaghetti and meatballs Napoli,
306
spaghetti with pesto sauce, 466
spaghetti with white clam sauce,
466
Pastry see also PIES
for almond tart, 420
baklava, 298
for Blum's coffee-toffee pie, 419
cream, for tartlets, 432
flaky, for 1-crust pie, 411
flaky, for 2-crust pie, 412
hot cheese hors d'oeuvres, 51
parmesan cheese leaves, 53
pie shell, baked, 412
pie shell, kuchen, 416
spinach pie, 296
tart shells, fluted, 429
tartlet shells, 433
for upside-down apple pie, 414
Williamsburg cheese straws, 54
Pâté
liver, en gelée, 58
party, 57
-stuffed chicken breasts, 444
tart, 65
Pea(s)
buttered, French-style, 543

how to buy and cook, 526
split, soup with ham, quick, 522
split, soup, old-fashioned, 512
yellow, soup with pork, 324
Peach(es)
-and-blueberry pie, 415
brandy eggnog, 80
and green grape pie, fresh, 421
kuchen, fresh, 206
macaroon-stuffed, 182
in marsala, 313
pie, deep-dish, 428
shortcake, 207
spiced, 340
streusel pie, 416
Peanut butter
chocolate kiss cookies, 156
cookies, 159
frosting, 140
ice cream milk shake, 75
pinwheels, 153
Peanut soup, cream of, 508
Pear(s)
bread pudding, baked, 177
butter, spiced, 331
-marmalade tarts, 429
pickled, 344
pie, deep-dish, 427
poached, apricot-glazed, 180
in port, fresh, 180
sabayon, 183
tatin, 211
véfour, 212
Pearl barley pilaf, 461
Pecan(s)
balls, 157
crescents, 562
pie, Southern, 418
pralines, 562
-sausage-and-oyster dressing, 456
Pepper(s)
and beef, 269
coleslaw-stuffed, 336
green, and zucchini, sautéed, 556
relish, 342
roasted, 344
and shrimp, 474
sautéed sweet, 376
stewed sweet, 308
sweet, and salami filling for pizza,
310
Peppermint
ice cream, homemade, 196
ice cream sundae pie, 193
seven minute frosting, pink,
142
Percolator coffee, 68
Perfect
apple pie, 24-25
baked potatoes, 544
chocolate cake, 26-27
corned beef hash, 366
fried eggplant, 538
Perfection salad, 487

Pesto sauce for spaghetti, 466
Petits fours
    cookies, 150
    gold cake, 122
    pink and white, 134
Petticoat tails, 155
Pfeffernuesse, 561
Phyllo pastry leaves
    baklava, 298
    hot cheese pastries, 51
    spinach pie, 296
Pickled
    beets, 343
    corn on the cob, 335
    cucumbers, 478
    garden relish, 341
    mushrooms, 45
    pears, 344
    vegetables, 344
Pickles and relishes, 333-44
    dilled carrot sticks, 338
    dilled whole carrots, 338
    directions for pickles, 333
    old-fashioned icicle, 335
    Mrs. Lamb's watermelon, 334
    sour green tomato, 333
    spiced peaches, 340
    zucchini bread-and-butter, 334
Picnic chicken, 443
Pies and small pastries, 409-34, *see also*
  PASTRY
    almond tart, 420
    asparagus quiche, 284
    asparagus and Swiss cheese tart,
      66
    banana coconut, 425
    best cherry, 417
    blueberry cheese, supreme, 420
    Blum's coffee-toffee, 419
    cherry cheese, supreme, 420
    chocolate cream, 422
    chocolate mousse, 422
    custard, 424
    deep-dish, 426-28
      apple-cider, 428
      peach, 428
      pear, 427
    favorite cheese, 419
    freezing pies, 410
    French apple, 290
    fresh apple flan, 413
    fresh berry, 414
    fresh peach and green grape, 421
    fresh strawberry glacé, 421
    frosted tartlets triumphant, 432
    fruit tarts, 430
    general directions for pies, 410
    glazed cream cheese, 419
    glazed tartlets triumphant, 432
    Greek cheese, 52
    Honolulu coconut, 425
    lamb with dill, 394
    lemon chiffon, 424
    lemon meringue, 423

    lemon sandbakels tartlets, 431
    lemon tarts, 434
    lime tarts, 434
    maple squash, 426
    miniature coconut tarts, 434
    mincemeat, hot, 564
    old-fashioned pumpkin, 423
    open-face plum, 415
    peach-and-blueberry, 415
    peach streusel, 416
    pear-marmalade tarts, 429
    pear tatin, 211
    peppermint ice cream sundae, 193
    perfect apple, 24-25
    pissaladière, 54
    quiche Lorraine, 52
    rhubarb lattice, 416
    rum cream, for fruit tarts, 430
    slipped coconut-custard, 424
    Southern pecan, 418
    spiced plum, 418
    spinach, 296
    steak-and-kidney, 272
    strawberry Devonshire glacé, 421
    strawberry flan, 285
    tarte tatin, 290
    tips for pie bakers, 410
    upside-down apple, 414
    upside-down chili, 371
    very special pies, 418-22
Pie crusts *see* PASTRY
Pie shells
    baked, 412
    graham cracker, unbaked, 411
    kuchen, 416
    meringue, baked, 211
    unbaked, 411
Pilaf, barley, 461
Pilaf, rice, 460
Piñas coladas, 81
Pineapple
    -apricot-nut loaf, 86
    cheese ball, 46
    cheese pâté, 49
    chicken salad, 472
    in crème de menthe, 185
    fresh, luau, 185
    fresh, in shell, 186
    glaze, 168
    -glazed baked ham loaf, 580
    ice cream milk shake, 75
    lemon soda, 76
    lime parfait, 592
    -mint frappé, 592
    -orange blush, 73
    sauce, 219
    shells filled with lemon ice, 194
    and strawberries with sour cream,183
    and sweet potato casserole, 551
    sweet potatoes Hawaiian, 549
    tropical jam, 329
    upside-down cake, 122
Pink
    champagne punch bowl, 77

    champagne sherbet, 201
    grapefruit and avocado salad
      platter, 483
    peppermint seven minute frosting,
      142
    and white petits fours, 134
Pinwheels, 111
    date-and-walnut, 154
    peanut butter, 153
Pissaladière, 54
Pizza(s)
    best of all, 309
    fillings for, 310
    quick, 581
    sauce, 310
Planter's punch bowl, 79
Plum(s)
    chutney, La Velle's, 331
    pie, open-face, 415
    pie, spiced, 418
    pudding, steamed, 567
    soup, cold, 520
Poached
    chicken with vegetables, 438
    eggs, 223
    eggs with ham, 223
    fish, 243
    salmon steaks in white wine, 246
Polenta, 460
    chicken cacciatore with, 305
Popovers, 94
Poppy seed
    crescents, 96
    dressing, 491
    noodles, 463
Pork, 373-86, *see also* BACON, HAM,
  and SAUSAGE
    cassoulet, 280
    chops
      and apples, baked, 378
      baked stuffed, 379
      orange-braised, 378
      Swiss, with mustard sauce, 378
    crown roast with apple stuffing,
      376
    fresh ham hocks, country style, 378
    how to buy, 346
    maple-barbecued spareribs, 380
    roast fresh ham, 374
    roast with herb gravy, 374
    roast with sautéed peppers, 375
    roasting timetable, 374
    and sauerkraut, 292
    and sauerkraut goulash, 377
    smoked loin of, 293
    smoked shoulder butt, glazed, 376
      with buttered carrots and
      cabbage, 377
    spareribs, crown roast of, with
      cornbread stuffing, 582
    sweet and sour, 267
    yellow pea soup with, 324
Porterhouse steaks, broiling timetable,
353

Port wine festival jelly, 328
Pot roast
    beef à la mode, 357
    braised chuck steak with
      vegetables, 360
    braised lamb with browned
      potatoes and mint gravy, 388
    brisket, 358
    herbed beef with vegetables, 358
    with noodles, country (beef), 359
    sauerbraten, 292
    sauerbraten with gingersnap
      sauce, 361
    Swedish (beef), 357
    veal, 398
    veal with mushroom sauce, 398
    venison, 408
Potage printanier, 275
Potato(es) *see also* **SWEET**
    POTATOES
    Anna, 283
    au gratin, 546
    baked, cottage cheese topping for,
      590
    baked, perfect, 544
    bread, old-fashioned, 103
    casserole, sweet-and-white, 547
    colcannon, 299
    fluffy mashed, 547
    French-fried, 544-45
    German-fried, 543
    golden whipped, 546
    how to buy and cook, 526
    and lamb chop hot pot, baked, 584
    lyonnaise, 544
    new, with lemon butter, 546
    Niçoise, 284
    Pacific coast summer salad, 475
    pancakes, 294
    quick vichyssoise, 522
    rolls, refrigerator, 12-13
    salad, delicatessen deluxe, 480
    salad, French, 481
    salad, German, 480
    salade Niçoise, 473
    savory roast, 547
    scalloped, 545
    scalloped, and baked ham, 382
    whipped, and rutabaga, 548
Pots de crème, 287
Poultry, 435-56
    buying and storage, 436
    capon, roast, with herbs, 436
    chicken, 436-44, *see* CHICKEN
    Cornish hens, 445
    duckling à l'orange, 448
    duckling with turnips, 280
    goose, roast stuffed, 446
    squab in sour cream, 407
    stuffings for, 454-56, *see*
      STUFFINGS
    terminology, 436
    turkey, 450-53
      au vin, 450

    breast marsala, 452
    golden roast, 452
    how to carve, 39
    ragout, 451
    roast flambé, with oyster and
      pecan dressing, 453
    roasting timetable, 451
Poundcake, 28-29, 134-35
    chocolate, 135
    cooking lesson, 28-29
    pink and white petits fours, 134
    walnut loaf, 134
Pour custard sauce, 217
Praline(s)
    cake, oatmeal, 128
    paste for tartlets, 432
    pecan, 562
Preserves, 327-44
    apricot-sherry jelly, 328
    Aunt Cal's garden relish, 340
    coleslaw-stuffed peppers, 336
    cranberry-apple relish, 342
    cranberry conserve, 332
    cranberry-tangerine or -orange
      relish, 342
    crème-de-menthe and crème-de-
      cassis jelly, 330
    dilled carrot sticks, 338
    dilled whole carrots, 338
    dilly vegetables, 339
    Iowa corn relish, 337
    jellied cranberry mold, 341
    Jerusalem artichoke relish, 338
    La Velle's plum chutney, 331
    Mrs. Lamb's watermelon pickle,
      334
    mushroom relish, 343
    old-fashioned chili sauce, 336
    old-fashioned icicle pickles, 335
    pickled beets, 343
    pickled corn on the cob, 335
    pickled garden relish, 341
    pickled pears, 344
    pickled vegetables, 344
    pepper relish, 342
    port wine festival jelly, 328
    quick corn relish, 343
    rhubarb jelly, 330
    roasted peppers, 344
    rumtopf, 332
    salsa fria, 342
    sour green tomato pickles, 333
    spiced peaches, 340
    spiced pear butter, 331
    sweet corn relish, 337
    tarragon wine jelly, 329
    tomato marmalade, 332
    tropical jam, 329
    walnut cranberry relish, 341
    zucchini bread-and-butter pickles,
      our best, 334
Profiteroles, 192
    strawberry, 170
Prosciutto, honeydew melon with, 63

Protein, sources of, chart, 579
Prune
    bread, 86
    butter pinwheels, 111
    whip with custard sauce, 182
Pudding(s)
    B & B custard, 177
    baked Indian, 179
    baked pear bread, 177
    cake, lemon, 179
    chocolate blanc mange, 174
    coconut blanc mange, 174
    corn, 538
    creamy rice, 178
    mocha blanc mange, 174
    Saint Peter's, 188
    sauce, 568
    snow, 190
    steamed plum, 567
    steamed raisin with Irish whisky
      sauce, 303
    vanilla blanc mange, 174
    Yorkshire, 349
Puffy Spanish omelet, 229
Pumpkin
    loaves, 87
    pie, old-fashioned, 423
    soup, cream of, 508
Punch(es), *see also* **EGGNOGS**
    champagne, 78
    Christmas, 76
    cranberry-bourbon, 77
    cup of cheer, 71
    daiquiri, 77
    Ella Brennan's milk, 78
    frosted bowl, 78
    how to serve, 71
    ice block for, 78
    ice ring for, with fruit, 79
    pink champagne, 77
    planter's, 79
    rum swizzles, 80
    sangría, 81
    syllabub, 81
    wassail bowl, 81
    whiskey sour, 80

Q

Quail, smothered, 407
Quiche
    asparagus, 284
    Lorraine, 52
Quick Boston baked beans, 529
Quick breads, 83-98
    apple kuchen, 294
    with bakery breads, 95-96
    baking powder biscuits, 90
    biscuits, 90-91
    blueberry buttermilk pancakes,
      97
    blueberry cake muffins, 88
    blueberry sally lunn, 92
    brown sugar muffins, 89

buttermilk bran muffins, 88
buttermilk pancakes, 96
caraway-raisin soda bread, 300
cheese biscuits, 91
cheese muffins, 89
crispy herb rolls, 96
coffee cakes, 91-92
cornbreads, 92-94
    muffins, 93
    sticks, 94
date-nut bread, 84
date-nut muffins, 90
double cornbread, 93
drop biscuits, 91
French toast, 97
garlic bread, 95
griddlecakes, 97
H. R. M.'s favorite waffles, 98
holiday banana bread, 85
hot crisp herb bread, 95
lemon tea bread, 85
Maureen's soda bread, 300
McCall's best nut bread, 84
muffins, 87-90
orange biscuits, 584
pancakes and waffles, 96-97
pineapple-apricot-nut loaf, 86
popovers, 94
poppy-seed crescents, 96
prune bread, 86
pumpkin loaves, 87
salt crescent rolls, 96
savory cheese bread, 86
sesame-seed crescents, 96
sour cream crumbcake, 92
Southern spoon bread, 94
strawberry jam crescents, 95
streusel-layered coffee cake, 91
sweet breads, 84-87
whole-wheat soda bread, 301

Quick
Cape Cod clam chowder, 521
chocolate sauce, 217
corn relish, 343
fudge frosting, 140
mustard sauce, 500
pizzas, 581
split pea soup with ham, 522
vichyssoise, 522

Quick and easy relishes, 341–44
corn, 343
cranberry-apple, 342
cranberry-tangerine or -orange, 342
jellied cranberry mold, 341
mushroom, 343
pepper, 342
pickled beets, 343
pickled garden, 341
pickled pears, 344
pickled vegetables, 344
roasted peppers, 344
salsa fria, 342
walnut cranberry, 341

R

Rack of lamb, 393
Provençale, 394
Raisin
bread, spiral cinnamon, 107
-caraway soda bread, 300
-molasses drop cookies, 147
-oatmeal cookies, 157
pudding, steamed, with Irish
    whisky sauce, 303
-walnut cake, 126
Raspberry(ies)
cardinal sauce, 216
ice cream milk shake, 75
pie, fresh, 414
sabayon, 286
sauce, 220
sauce, strawberries with, 184
sherbet, 201
Ratatouille
cold, 64
mushroom, 540
Ratner's marble cheesecake, 166
Recipes, how to tackle, 33
Red cabbage, 293
spicy, with apples, 532
Red-cherry glaze, 167
Red snapper
baked stuffed, 241
sweet-and-sour fish, 270
Red wine steak sauce, 501
Refried beans, 319
Refrigerator cookies, 153-55
butterscotch icebox, 155
cinnamon stars, 153
date and walnut pinwheel, 154
oatmeal icebox, 154
peanut butter pinwheels, 153
petticoat tails, 155
Refrigerator potato rolls, 12-13
Relishes, 333-44
Aunt Cal's garden, 340
cranberry-apple, 342
cranberry-tangerine or -orange,
    342
dilled carrot sticks, 338
dilled whole carrots, 338
dilly vegetables, 339
directions for, 333
Iowa corn, 337
jellied cranberry mold, 341
Jerusalem artichoke, 338
mushroom, 343
pepper, 342
pickled beets, 343
pickled garden, 341
pickled pears, 344
pickled vegetables, 344
quick corn, 343
quick and easy, 341–44
roasted peppers, 344
salsa fria, 342
spiced peaches, 340

sweet corn, 337
walnut cranberry, 341
Rémoulade sauce for seafood, 502
Rhubarb
baked spiced, 185
jelly, 330
lattice pie, 416
strawberry soup, 519
Rib roast of beef, how to carve, 42
Rib steaks, broiling timetable, 353
Rice, 457-60
arroz con pollo, 323
and cheese casserole, California,
    234
converted (described), 458
custard, baked, 173
fried, 266
fluffy white, 458
kinds of, 458
with mushrooms, 314
old-fashioned fluffy white, 458
oven-steamed, 459
packaged precooked white
    (described), 458
paella, 322
pilaf, 460
pilaf, mushroom, 460
pudding, creamy, 178
saffron, 459
salad, marinated, 480
and spinach ring mold, 459
steamed, 267
stuffed grape leaves, 44
subgum fried, 266
white (described), 458
white, with onions, 459
wild, 458
wild and white, 459
Rich meat gravy, 503
Ricotta cheese, cannoli, 313
Ring mold, rice and spinach, 459
Roast beef, 347-52
eye round Provençale, 352
filet of, Burgundy, 350
filet of, in brioche, 350
savory, with Yorkshire pudding,
    349
prime ribs, 348
standing rib, how to carve, 42
timetable, 348
Wellington, 350
Roast capon with herbs, 449
**Roast Cornish hens with walnut
    stuffing and wine sauce, 445**
Roast chicken
stuffed, 436
timetable, 437
Roast goose, stuffed, 446
Roast wild duck, 406
Roast lamb
crown, filled with sautéed
    mushrooms, 389
leg of, 386

en croûte with mushroom
stuffing, 387
French style, 390
how to carve, 40
Swedish style, 388
timetable, 386
Roast meat loaf, 369
Roast pork
fresh ham, 374
with herb gravy, 374
glazed smoked shoulder butt, 376
with buttered carrots and
cabbage, 377
party crown, with apple stuffing,
376
and sauerkraut goulash, 377
with sautéed peppers, 375
timetable, 374
Roast stuffed veal en gelée, 396
Roast turkey
flambé with oyster and pecan
dressing, 453
golden, 452
how to carve, 39
timetable, 451
Roast veal
Florentine, 395
leg of, in white wine, 397
loaf, cold, 402
stuffed, en gelée, 396
timetable, 395
Roast venison with wine, 407
Roast wild duck, 406
Roasted peppers, 344
Roasting meat, 346
Rock Cornish hens, 445
Rock lobster tails, boiled, 255
broiled, 256
tempura, 315
Rolled cookies, 149-52
cinnamon stars, 560
brown sugar shortbread, 149
cutting and decorating, 151
Dutch tile, 566
old-fashioned filled, 150
old-fashioned sugar, 152
petit-four, 150
springerle, 569
Swiss biberli, 568
Turkish, 152
Tyrolean honey, 560
Rolls
bear claws, 110
blueberry surprises, 109
bow ties, 112
brioche, 116
crispy herb, 96
horns, 110
pinwheels, 111
poppy-seed crescents, 96
refrigerator potato, 12-13
salt crescent, 96
sesame-seed crescents, 96
strawberry jam crescents, 95

sweet, 108-12
sweet roll dough, 108
Romaine lettuce, 468
Roman veal scallopini, 305
Romanoff noodles, baked, 463
Root beer float, 76
Roquefort salad dressing, 489, 492
Rosé wine spritzer, 82
Round steak
braised Swiss, family style, 362
broiling timetable, 353
with marrow sauce, 356
Royal consommé madrilene, 506
Rum
cream, for fruit tarts, 430
daiquiri punch, 77
old English eggnog, 79
piñas coladas, 81
planter's punch bowl, 79
-strawberry custard sundaes, 191
swizzles, 80
wassail bowl, 81
Rumaki, 56
Rumtopf, 332
Russian blini, 62
Russian dressing, 490
Rutabagas
in cream, 548
how to buy and cook, 527
whipped potatoes and, 548
Rye bread
caraway, 103
Swedish limpa, 105

S

Sabayon sauce, 286
Saffron rice, 459
Saint Peter's pudding, 188
Salad dressing(s), 488-94
avocado, 492
basic French or oil and vinegar,
492
best French, 493
boiled, 489
creamy, 471
creamy blue cheese or Roquefort,
489
cucumber yoghurt, 491
curry, 489
French, 492
fresh mint, 494
ginger, 491
golden gate, 489
green goddess, 473
green mayonnaise, 491
honey lime, 491
lime, 494
mayonnaise, 488
poppy seed, 491
Roquefort or blue cheese, 492
Russian, 490
sour cream, 490
sour cream for fruit, 490

special French, 493
thousand island, 490
vinaigrette, 493
white wine French, 494
zesty French, 494
Salad(s), 467-88
apple and sour cream slaw, 483
bing cherry, 488
Caesar, 469
chef's, 471
chicken, 472
chicken pineapple, 472
chicken Waldorf, 473
cobb, with Russian dressing, 471
cold leeks and endives vinaigrette,
479
cottage cheese summer, 582
cottage cheese in tomato halves,
591
crab, 589
cranberry mold, 485
creamy coleslaw, 479
crisp cucumber aspic, 486
curried chicken, 474
delicatessen deluxe potato, 480
egg, for sandwiches, 580
French green, 470
French potato, 481
fresh asparagus vinaigrette, 476
fresh fruit dessert, 483
fresh spinach, 470
fresh salmon and cucumber, 475
fruit, 483-84, *see* FRUIT SALADS,
GELATINE SALADS
garbanzo bean, 477
gazpacho bowl, 481
gelatine, 484-88, *see* GELATINE
SALADS
ginger and fresh fruit mold, 487
green goddess, 473
green and white fruit, 484
greens, care of, 469
kinds of, 468
guacamole salad mold, 485
guacamole and tomato, 482
Harvey House slaw, 478
jellied cranberry mold, 341
kidney bean, 477
macaroni, 482
main dish, 471-76, *see* MAIN
DISH SALADS
marinated mushroom, 476
marinated rice, 480
marinated sliced tomatoes, 482
molded gazpacho, 486
old-fashioned lettuce bowl, 470
old-fashioned sliced tomatoes, 481
orange and onion, 484
Pacific coast summer, 475
perfection, 487
pickled cucumbers, 478
pink grapefruit and avocado
platter, 483
salade Niçoise, 473

shrimp and roasted peppers, 474
sliced cucumbers in sour cream, 478
sour cream coleslaw, 478
three-bean salad bowl, 477
tomato aspic, 484
tuna, favorite, 585
tuna-macaroni supper, 476
Salami and sweet peppers filling for pizza, 310
Sally lunn
blueberry, 92
Virginia, 115
Salmon
and cucumber salad, fresh, 475
Pacific coast summer salad, 475
smoked, canapés, 57
steaks, broiled, parsley-lemon butter, 240
steaks, crispy broiled, 240
steaks poached in white wine, 246
stuffed eggs, 325
Swedish cold, with mustard sauce, 59
Salsa fria, 342
Salsify, leg of lamb with, 278
Salsify provençal, 552
Salt crescent rolls, 96
Sand tarts, 151
Sandbakels, lemon, 431
Sandwich cookies, 151
Sandwich(es)
egg salad and lettuce in buns, 580
grilled deviled cheese, 585
souvlakia, 297
Sangría, 81
Sauces, dessert, 215-20
apricot, 215
brandy, 216
butterscotch, 216
caramel, 216
cardinal, 216
chocolate, deluxe, 217
chocolate, quick, 217
cinnamon-ice cream, 218
cream Chantilly, 217
custard, for warm apple slices, 301
English custard, 218
fudge, 218
hard, 218
Irish whisky, 303
marshmallow, 219
nutmeg hard, 219
orange, 215
pineapple, 219
pour custard, 217
pudding, 568
raspberry, 184, 220
sabayon, 286
strawberry, 219
vanilla pudding, 182
Sauces and gravies, 495-504
apple cider, for ham, 498
apricot, for shrimp, 268

barbecue, 391
California style, 503
Don's, 503
basic white, 496
basting, for broiled fish, 239
basting, for Cornish hens, 446
béarnaise, 22-23
blender, 496
bordelaise, 497
brown gravy, 503
Burgundy gravy, 504
cheese, 497, 531
chestnut, 274
chicken gravy, 504
Creole, 498
Cumberland, 499
curried basting, for fish, 239
curry, 441
dill, herring in, 58
egg and lemon, 295
giblet gravy, 504
gingersnap, 498
green chile salsa, 319
herbed basting, for fish, 239
hollandaise, 22-23
blender, 499
for green beans, 539
horseradish, 496
low calorie, 590
sour cream, 498
lemon
artichokes with, 309
with broccoli, 530
-chive, 497
with Greek meatballs, 297
lemony basting, for fish, 239
lobster, 500
lobster cocktail, 64
maître d'hôtel butter, 500
marinara, for spaghetti, 465
mint jelly, 499
mushroom, 244, 497
mustard, 59, 378, 499
quick, 500
Newburg, 501
old-fashioned chili, 336
orange, for duckling, 448
parsley, 496
parsley butter, 500
pesto, for spaghetti, 466
pizza, 310
red wine steak, 501
rémoulade, 502
seafood cocktail, 501
shrimp, 536
shrimp cocktail, 62
sour cream horseradish, 498
spaghetti, 465–66
Spanish, 501
sweet-and-sour, for fish, 270
tarragon sour cream, 502
tartar, 502
tartar sour cream, 502
tempura, 316

tomato
for chiles rellenos, 318
for spaghetti and meatballs Napoli, 306
for veal parmigiana, 307
truffle, 350
white clam, for spaghetti, 466
white wine, 447
wine, for Cornish hens, 446
wine, for fillets of sole, 245
Sauerbraten, 292
with gingersnap sauce, 361
Sauerkraut
and franks in beer, 373
and meatballs soup, 515
and pork, 292
and pork goulash, 377
smoked loin of pork, 293
Sausage-oyster-and-pecan dressing, 456
Sausage stuffing, 446
Sautéed
chicken livers, 403
mushrooms, 389, 541
scallops, 258
soft-shell crabs, 254
squash and tomatoes, 555
sweet peppers, 376
zucchini and green peppers, 556
Savory
braised short ribs, 359
cheese bread, 86
Edam cheese, 47
mushroom stuffing, 391
roast beef with Yorkshire pudding, 349
roast potatoes, 547
steak slices, 56
stuffed mushrooms, 541
stuffing for baked pork chops, 379
Scalloped
crab, 253
potatoes, 545
potatoes and baked ham, 382
Scallops
Brittany style, 258
coquilles Saint Jacques, 66
fried, 258
how to buy and prepare, 250
Provençale, 65
sautéed, 258
shrimp and sole, fried, 259
tempura, 315
varieties of, 258
Scampi, 260
Scandinavian cooking, 324-26
cabbage, 325
glögg, 325
herring in sour cream, 59
Norwegian fish balls, 326
spritz wreaths, 563
stuffed eggs, 325
Swedish cold salmon with mustard sauce, 59
Swedish limpa bread, 105

Swedish meatballs, 55
Swedish pot roast, 357
Swedish-style brown beans, 325
waffles, 326
yellow pea soup with pork, 324
Scotch
chocolate cake squares, 121
oatmeal shortbread, 160
Scrambled eggs, 223-25
à la Suisse, 225
bacon, 224
cheese, 224
creamy, 225
double boiler, 587
Mexican style, 224
mushroom, 225
skillet, 224
Sea bass, sweet-and-sour fish, 270
Sea scallops, 258
Seafood *see* FISH *and* SHELLFISH
cocktail sauce, 501
rémoulade sauce for, 502
Senegalese soup, 517
Sesame oil, 264
Sesame seed, benne-seed cookies, 147
Sesame-seed crescents, 96
Seven-minute frosting, 142
coconut, 142
coffee spice, 142
pink peppermint, 142
seafoam, 142
Shaping bread loaves, 101
Shellfish, 249-62
boiled crabs, 251
boiled live lobsters, 254
boiled rock lobster tails, 255
boiled shrimp, 259
bouillabaisse, 275
broiled live lobsters, 256
broiled rock lobster tails, 256
cioppino, 250
clam broth with tarragon, 507
clams oregano, 60
clams, varieties of, 250
coquilles Saint Jacques, 66
corn and clam chowder, 512
crab salad, 589
crêpes with curried crabmeat, 252
deviled lobster, 591
fried clams, 251
fried oysters, 257
fried scallops, 258
fried scallops, shrimp, and sole, 259
hard-shell clams, 250
how to buy and prepare shellfish, 250
lobster Cantonese, 269
lobster cocktail, 64
lobster Newburg, 255
lobster sauce, 500
lobster soufflé, Plaza Athenée, 282
lobster thermidor, 255
Manhattan clam chowder, 513

Shellfish (continued)
moules marinière, 276
New England clam chowder, 513
oysters Rockefeller, 257
paella (rice with clams and shrimp), 322
quick Cape Cod clam chowder, 521
rémoulade sauce for seafood, 502
sautéed scallops, 258
sautéed soft-shell crabs, 254
scalloped crab, 253
scallops Brittany style, 258
scallops Provençale, 65
scampi, 260
seafood cocktail sauce, 501
sherried crabmeat, 252
shrimp with apricot sauce, 268
shrimp cocktail, 62
shrimp Creole with white rice, 260
shrimp curry, 262
shrimp in garlic butter, 260
shrimp gumbo, 261
shrimp and lobster in white wine, 261
shrimp sauce, for cauliflower, 536
shrimp toast, 265
snails in garlic butter, 276
soft-shell clams, 250
tempura, 315
white clam sauce, spaghetti with, 466
Sherbet
cranberry, 200
crème de menthe ring with strawberries, 200
fig sorbet, 201
fresh orange, 202
homemade, 199-202
lime, with strawberries, 202
orange sherbet freeze (drink), 76
pineapple shells filled with lemon ice, 194
pineapple lemon soda, 76
pink champagne, 201
raspberry, 201
Sherried crabmeat, 252
Sherry
-apricot jelly, 328
cream, 214
syllabub, 81
Shrimp
with apricot sauce, 268
bisque, cold, 519
boiled, 259
Creole, with white rice, 260
cocktail, 62
curry, 262
in garlic butter (scampi), 260
gumbo, 261
how to buy and prepare, 250
and lobster in white wine, 261
paella, 322
and roasted peppers, 474

sauce, for cauliflower, 536
scallops and sole, fried, 259
supplies of, 259
tempura, 315
toast, 265
Shortbread
brown sugar cookies, 149
Scotch oatmeal, 160
Shortcake(s), 205-8
apple cobbler, 205
biscuit mix, 207
peach, 207
strawberry, individual, 208
strawberry, old-fashioned, 206
Short grain white rice (described), 458
Short ribs of beef, savory braised, 359
Silvery white cake, 120
Simmering beef, general directions, 363
Simpson lettuce, 468
Sirloin steak(s)
beef stroganoff, 362
broiling timetable, 353
with mustard and herbs, 355
with red wine, 354
sukiyaki, 316
Skillet scrambled eggs, 224
Sliced
cucumbers in sour cream, 478
tomatoes, old-fashioned, 481
Smoked
loin of pork, 293
salmon canapés, 57
Smothered quail, 407
Snails in garlic butter, 276
Snow pudding, 190
Soda bread
caraway-raisin, 300
Maureen's, 300
whole-wheat, 301
Soda(s)
double strawberry, 76
mint chocolate, 76
orange sherbet freeze, 76
pineapple lemon, 76
Soft-cooked eggs, 222
Soft-shell crabs, sautéed, 254
Sole, fillets of
baked, thermidor, 243
bonne femme, 243
Duglère, 246
Florentine, 245
Marguery, 244
Queen Victoria, 244
scallops, and shrimp, fried, 259
with tarragon-chive butter, 242
Soufflé(s)
apricot, 204
caramel, cold, 204
cheese, fabulous, 232
chocolate, 30-31
dessert, 202-5
lobster, Plaza Athenée, 282
orange surprise, 203
sweet potato or yam, 550

Souffléed corn, 537
Soup(s), 505-22
    avocado frappé, 516
    beef borsch with sour cream, 511
    beet with dill, 521
    black bean with rum, 520
    bouillabaise, 275
    with canned soups, 520-22
    Cheddar cheese, 508
    chilled cantaloupe, 517
    chilled cream of asparagus, 516
    clam broth with tarragon, 507
    cold, 515-20
    cold cucumber, 518
    cold plum, 520
    cold shrimp bisque, 519
    corn chowder, 513
    corn and clam chowder, 512
    cottage broth, 299
    cream, 507-10
    cream of artichoke, 516
    cream of chicken, 322
    cream of peanut, 508
    cream of pumpkin, 508
    cream of winter squash, 509
    egg drop, 266
    French onion, 506
    frozen tomato frappé, 517
    gazpacho, 518
    green cabbage, 507
    hearty, 510-15
    hearty beef and vegetable, 510
    hot tomato consommé, 506
    jellied consommé with red caviar, 515
    lemon buttermilk, 520
    lentil with frankfurters, 521
    lentil with ham, 514
    lobster bisque, 509
    Manhattan clam chowder, 513
    meatballs and sauerkraut, 515
    minestrone, 304
    New England clam chowder, 513
    New England fish chowder, 514
    old-fashioned split pea, 512
    orange-apricot-yoghurt, 519
    oyster stew, 512
    potage printanier, 275
    quick Cape Cod clam chowder, 521
    quick vichyssoise, 522
    royal consommé madrilène, 506
    Senegalese, 517
    soupe au pistou, 274
    spring lettuce, 510
    strawberry-rhubarb, 519
    tomato bouillon, 589
    yellow pea, with pork, 324
Sour cream
    coleslaw, 478
    crumbcake, 92
    dilled, with summer squash, 553
    dressing, 490
    dressing for fruit, 490

frosting, chocolate, 139
fudge cake, 121
herring in, 59
horseradish sauce, 498
spinach with, 552
tartar sauce, 502
tarragon sauce, 502
Sour green tomato pickles, 333
Southern pecan pie, 418
Southern spoon bread, 94
Souvlakia, 297
Soy sauce, 264
Spareribs
    crown roast of, with cornbread stuffing, 582
    maple-barbecued, 380
Spaghetti
    basic directions for cooking, 462-63
    chicken Tetrazzini, 439
    Italian, and meatballs, 370
    with marinara sauce, 465
    and meatballs Napoli, 306
    with pesto sauce, 466
    sauces, 465–66
    with white clam sauce, 466
Spanish cooking, 322-24
    arroz con pollo, 323
    caramel custard flan, 324
    churros (doughnuts), 323
    cream of chicken soup, 322
    paella (rice with clams and shrimp), 322
    sangría, 81
Spanish omelet, puffy, 229
Spanish sauce, 501
Spanish-style omelet, Cecilia's, 228
Special French dressing, 493
Spice cake
    McCall's best, 125
    tomato soup, 128
Spiced
    chocolate drink, 73
    cocoa, 74
    peaches, 340
    pear butter, 331
    plum pie, 418
Spicy
    eggnog, 74
    red cabbage with apples, 532
Spinach
    frittata, 308
    in green salads, 468
    how to buy and cook, 526
    mimosa, fresh, 551
    pie, 296
    and rice ring mold, 459
    ring, creamed, 552
    salad, fresh, 470
    with sour cream, 552
Spiral cinnamon raisin bread, 107
Sponge cakes, 129-33
    fresh lemon, 132
    fresh orange, 132

how to cut, 118
hot milk, 132
jelly roll, 133
Spoon bread, Southern, 94
Split pea soup with ham, quick, 522
    old-fashioned, 512
Spread(s) see also DIPS
    blue-cheese, 48
    caviar cream cheese ball, 48
    Cheddar-beer, 48
    Cheddar in sherry, 50
    cheese pâté pineapple, 49
    eggplant appetizer, 45
    holiday cheese ball, 48
    liver pâté en gelée, 58
    mousse of chicken livers, 46
    party pâté, 57
    pineapple-cheese ball, 46
    savory Edam cheese, 47
    steak tartare, 56
Spring
    dip, 46
    lamb stew with dill, 393
    lettuce soup, 510
Springerle, 569
Spritz wreaths, 563
Spumoni, 311
Squab in sour cream, 407
Squash
    acorn, baked, 554
    acorn, honey-spice, 553
    acorn, how to buy and cook, 526
    pie, maple, 426
    soup, cream-of-winter, 509
    summer, Creole, 553
    summer, with dilled sour cream, 553
    summer, how to buy and cook, 526
    and tomatoes, sautéed, 555
    winter, how to buy and cook, 526
    winter, with orange, 554
    zucchini and green peppers, sautéed, 556
    zucchini with fresh herbs, 556
    zucchini, corn, and tomatoes, 556
Standing rib roast, 348-49
    how to carve, 42
Steak(s)
    braised Swiss, family style, 362
    broiling timetable, 353
    chuck, Florentine, 355
    flank, stroganoff, 363
    -and-kidney pies, 272
    London broil, 354
    with marrow sauce, 356
    with mustard and herbs, 355
    au poivre, 277
    sauce, red wine, 501
    slices, savory, 56
    sirloin, with red wine, 354
    tartare, 56
Steamed
    plum pudding, 567
    raisin pudding with Irish whiskey sauce, 303

rice, 267
Stew(s)
    beef Bourguignon, 277
    beef, low calorie, 590
    beef, with parsley dumplings, 14-15
    beef ragout, 364
    beef and vegetable, 364
    fish, bouillabaise, 275
    fish, cioppino, 250
    how to simmer meat, 347, 363
    Hungarian goulash, 365
    lamb, with dill, spring, 393
    lamb (Irish), 300
    oyster, 512
    pork and sauerkraut goulash, 377
    turkey ragout, 451
Stewed
    sweet peppers, 308
    tomatoes and okra, 554
Stollen, 112
Strawberry(ies)
    à la Blue Fox, 214
    Bavarian cream, 188
    cardinal sauce, 216
    cookie shell sundaes, 193
    and cream cheesecake, 165
    and crème-de-menthe sherbet ring, 200
    Devonshire glacé pie, 421
    flan, 285
    float, frosted, 74
    fresh, à la Colony, 195
    fresh, with mint, 184
    glacé pie, fresh, 421
    glaze, 167
    ice cream, homemade, 196
    ice cream milk shake, 75
    ice ring, 77
    jam crescents, 95
    lime sherbet with, 202
    in May wine, 189
    parfait, 195
    and pineapple with sour cream, 183
    in port, fresh, 184
    profiteroles, 170
    with raspberry sauce, 184
    -rhubarb soup, 519
    Romanoff, 184
    -rum custard sundaes, 191
    sauce, 219
    shortcake, individual, 208
    shortcake, old-fashioned, 206
    snow with custard sauce, 189
    soda, double, 76
    syrup, 98
    tropical jam, 329
Streusel
    -layered coffeecake, 91
    pie, peach, 416
Striped bass, baked, 241
    sweet-and-sour fish, 270

Stroganoff
    beef, 362
    beef balls, 367
    flank steak, 363
Strudel pastry leaves
    baklava, 298
    hot cheese pastries, 51
    spinach pie, 296
Stuffed
    cabbage rolls, 371
    eggplant Creole, 372
    eggs, 325
    grape leaves, 44
    mushrooms, savory, 541
    pork chops, baked, 379
Stuffing(s)
    apple, with party crown roast of pork, 376
    bread, 455
    chicken-liver-mushroom, 455
    cornbread dressing balls, 454
    cornbread oyster dressing, 455
    cranberry-orange dressing, 454
    old-fashioned dressing, 456
    mushroom, for roast leg of lamb, 387
    for poultry, 454-56
    savory, for baked pork chops, 379
    savory mushroom, for lamb chops, 391
    sausage, 446
    sausage-oyster-and-pecan, 456
    walnut, for Cornish hens, 445
    for whole fish, 241
Subgum fried rice, 266
Sugar
    cookies, easy no-roll, 149
    cookies, old-fashioned, 152
    nuts, 559
Sukiyaki (cooked at table), 316
Summer baked ham, 18-19
Summer squash
    Creole, 553
    with dilled sour cream, 553
    how to buy and cook, 526
    sautéed zucchini and green peppers, 556
    zucchini, corn, and tomatoes, 556
    zucchini with fresh herbs, 556
Sundae(s)
    pie, peppermint ice cream, 193
    strawberry cookie shell, 193
    strawberry-rum custard, 191
Supper menus for entertaining
    curry, 576
    late, 576
Swedish
    cold salmon with mustard sauce, 59
    limpa bread, 105
    meatballs, 55
    pot roast, 357
    -style brown beans, 325

    -style roast leg of lamb, 388
Sweet
    corn relish, 337
    peppers and salami filling for pizza, 310
    peppers, sautéed, 376
    peppers, stewed, 308
Sweet potato(es)
    candied, 551
    casserole, and white, 547
    flambéed, 550
    Hawaiian, 549
    how to buy and cook, 526
    orange-glazed, 549
    and pineapple casserole, 551
    soufflé, 550
Sweet quick breads, 84-87
    date-nut, 84
    holiday banana, 85
    lemon tea, 85
    McCall's best nut, 84
    pineapple-apricot-nut loaf, 86
    prune, 86
    pumpkin loaves, 87
Sweet rolls, 108-12
    bear claws, 110
    blueberry surprises, 109
    bow ties, 112
    crescents, 109
    dough, 108
    horns, 110
    pinwheels, 111
Sweet-and-sour
    chicken, 442
    fish, 270
    pork, 267
Sweet and white potato casserole, 547
Sweet yeast breads, 107-8
    babka, 108
    spiral cinnamon raisin, 107
    stollen, 112
Swiss biberli, 568
Swiss braided loaves, 105
Swiss cheese
    and asparagus tart, 66
    fondue, 50
    fritters, 49
    quiche Lorraine, 52
    and tomato fondue, 51
Swiss pork chops with mustard sauce, 378
Swiss steak, braised, family style, 362
Swordfish steaks, broiled, parsley-lemon butter, 240
Syllabub, 81
Syrup, how to measure, 33
    strawberry, 98

T

Tacos, beef, with green chile salsa, 318

Tamale casserole, 370
Tangerine-cranberry relish, 342
Tarragon
    butter, with artichokes, 527
    chive butter, 242
    clam broth, 507
    sour cream sauce, 502
    -wine jelly, 329
Tart(s), 426, 429-34, see also
    TARTLETS
    almond, 420
    asparagus and Swiss cheese, 66
    coconut, miniature, 434
    fruit, 430
    lemon-curd, 434
    lime-curd, 434
    pâté, 65
    pear-marmalade, 429
    shells, fluted, 429
    tarte tatin (upside-down
        apple), 290
    Welsh curd, 273
Tartar Sauce, 502
    sour cream, 502
Tartlet(s)
    chocolate frosting for, 433
    lemon sandbakels, 431
    shells, 433
    triumphant, frosted, 432
    triumphant, glazed, 432
    vanilla frosting for, 433
T-bone steaks, broiling
    timetable, 353
Tea
    eggs, 264
    how to brew, 70
    iced, 71
    kinds of, 70
    menu, for the committee, 576
Temperature(s)
    for baked ham, 380
    oven, 34
    for roast beef, 348
    for roast lamb, 386
    for roast pork, 374
    for roast veal, 395
    for roast turkey, 451
Tempura, 315
    batter for, 315
    sauce for, 316
Terms used in cooking, 34-36
    cutting, 37
Thanksgiving menus, 574-75
    Creole, 574
    modern, 575
    New England, 574
    traditional, 574
Thawing
    cakes, 118
    pies, pie shells, 410
Thermidor
    baked fillets, 243
    lobster, 255
Thousand island dressing, 490
Three-bean salad bowl, 477

Timetable(s)
    for baking ham, 380
    for broiling steaks, 353
    for roasting beef, 348
    for roasting lamb, 386
    for roasting pork, 374
    for roasting veal, 395
    for roasting turkey, 451
Toast
    anise, 313
    French, 97
Toffee
    -coffee pie, Blum's, 419
    crisps, 161
Toll House crunch cookies, 159
Tomato(es)
    aspic, 484
    and baked macaroni
        au gratin, 586
    bouillon, 589
    and cheese filling, traditional,
        for pizza, 310
    cold ratatouille, 64
    consommé, hot, 506
    corn, and zucchini, 556
    and eggplant casserole, 539
    frappé, frozen, 517
    gazpacho, 518
    and guacamole salad, 482
    halves, baked, 555
    halves, cottage cheese salad in, 591
    halves, pan-broiled, 554
    marmalade, 332
    old-fashioned chili sauce, 336
    old-fashioned sliced, 481
    marinated sliced, 482
    pickles, green, sour, 333
    pissaladière, 54
    pizza sauce, 310
    salsa fria, 342
    sauce for chiles rellenos, 318
    sauce marinara, 465
    sauce for spaghetti and
        meatballs Napoli, 306
    sauce for veal parmigiana, 307
    -soup spice cake, 128
    and squash, sautéed, 555
    stewed, and okra, 554
    and Swiss cheese fondue, 51
Tongue, boiled, 405
Topping(s) see also FROSTINGS,
    GLAZES
    apricot glaze, 431
    broiled coconut, 143
    cottage cheese for baked
        potatoes, 590
    crumb, for baked onions, 542
    currant jelly glaze, 431
    rumtopf, 332
    whipped butter, 98
    whipped cream lattice, 424
Torte(s)
    chocolate nut, 213
    meringue, 214
Tortillas, 317

beef tacos with green chile salsa, 318
chili and enchiladas, 320
eggs ranchero, 317
Tossed salads, 468-71
    Caesar, 469
    French, 470
    fresh spinach, 470
    garden salad bowl, 471
    old-fashioned lettuce bowl, 470
Tropical jam, 329
Trout
    amandine, 248
    baked, and bacon, 272
Truffle sauce, 350
Truffles, hazelnut, 559
Tuna
    -macaroni supper salad, 476
    Pacific coast summer salad, 475
    salad, favorite, 585
    salade Niçoise, 473
Turkey, 450-53
    au vin, 450
    breast, marsala, 452
    golden roast, 452
    how to carve, 39
    ragout, 451
    roast, flambé, with oyster and
        pecan dressing, 453
    roasting timetable, 451
Turkish coffee, 68
Turkish cookies, 152
Turnips
    buttery grated, 532
    with duckling, 280
    Florentine, 555
    glazed vegetables, 285
    how to buy and cook, 527
    yellow, see RUTABAGAS
Tyrolean honey cookies, 560

U

Unbaked pie shell, 411
    graham cracker, 411
Upside-down
    apple pie, 414
    apple tart (tarte tatin), 290
    apricot cake, easy, with cake
        mix, 123
    chili pie, 371
    ham loaf, family favorite, 385
    pineapple cake, 122
Utensils, how to buy, 37
    list, 37-38

V

Vacuum-type coffee, 68
Vanilla
    blanc mange, 174
    -cream filling, 144
    frosting, for tartlets, 433
    ice cream, basic, 196
    pudding sauce for baked
        apples, 182

Variety meats, 403-5
boiled tongue, 405
braised lamb kidneys, 405
broiled calves' liver, 590
broiled liver, 403
calves' liver, Venetian-style, 404
veal kidneys Provençale, 404
pan-fried liver, 403
sautéed chicken livers, 403
Veal, 395-402
birds with bread stuffing, 402
breast of, baked stuffed, 401
casserole for a crowd,
Hungarian, 400
chops, braised, 398
chops with mushrooms, 399
how to buy, 346
kidneys Provençale, 404
loaf
baked, 401
cold roast, 402
parmigiana, 306-7
pot roast, 398
pot roast with mushroom
sauce, 398
roast, Florentine, 395
roast leg of, in white wine, 397
roast stuffed en gelée, 396
rolls, marsala, 399
roulades, 400
scallopini, Roman, 305
Vegetable salads, 476-82, *see also*
GELATINE SALADS
cold leeks and endives
vinaigrette, 479
creamy coleslaw, 479
delicatessen deluxe potato, 480
French potato, 481
fresh asparagus vinaigrette, 476
garbanzo bean, 477
gazpacho bowl, 481
German potato, 480
guacamole and tomato, 482
Harvey House slaw, 478
kidney bean, 477
macaroni, 482
marinated mushroom, 476
marinated rice, 480
marinated sliced tomatoes, 482
old-fashioned sliced tomatoes, 481
perfection, 487
sliced cucumbers in sour
cream, 478
sour cream coleslaw, 478
three-bean salad bowl, 477
Vegetable(s), 523-56, *see also*
names of vegetables
Aunt Cal's garden relish, 340
basic cookery chart, 524-27
and beef soup, hearty, 510
and beef stew, 364
braised chuck steak with, 360
buying chart (in season), 524-27
daily needs, 578

dilly, 339
gazpacho (soup), 518
glazed, 285
guacamole dip with, 45
herbed pot roast with, 358
minestrone, 304
mushroom ratatouille, 540
pasta e fagioli, 304
pickled, 344
pickled garden relish, 341
poached chicken with, 438
pot roast with, 360
potage printanier, 275
raw, chile con queso with, 52
soupe au pistou, 274
sukiyaki, 316
Venison
pot roast, 408
roast with wine, 407
Very special oatmeal, 583
Vichyssoise, quick, 522
Viennese coffee, 68
Vinaigrette dressing, 493
Virginia
ham, baked, 384
sally lunn, 115
Vitamins, sources of, chart, 579

W

Wafers, almond lace, 158
Waffles
H. R. M.'s favorite, 98
Scandinavian, 326
Walnut
cranberry relish, 341
-and-date pinwheel cookies, 154
poundcake loaf, 134
-raisin cake, 126
stuffing, for Cornish hens, 445
Walnutty caramels, 558
**Warm apple slices with custard
sauce, 301**
Wassail bowl, 81
Water chestnuts, 264
Watercress, 468
Watermelon
basket, 186
pickle, Mrs. Lamb's, 334
Wax beans, how to buy and cook, 524
Weights and measures (chart), 34
Weight-watching, 587-88
low calorie recipes, 588-92
Wieners *see* FRANKFURTERS
Welsh curd tarts, 273
Whipped
butter, 98
cream frosting, chocolate, 139
cream frosting, mocha, 139
cream lattice, 424
potatoes and rutabagas, 548
Whiskey sour punch, 80
White
bread, McCall's basic, 102

cake, silvery, 120
fruitcake, 566
-and-gold angel cake, 136
rice, fluffy, 458
rice with onions, 459
sauce, basic, 496
wine French dressing, 494
wine sauce, for roast stuffed
goose, 447
Whitefish, baked stuffed, 241
Whole-wheat
bread, 104
honey casserole bread, 114
soda bread, 301
Wild rice, 458
and white rice, 459
Williamsburg cheese straws, 54
Wine
festival jelly, port, 328
how to serve, 82
jelly, tarragon, 329
sangría, 81
sauce, for Cornish hens, 446
sauce, for fillets of sole
Florentine, 245
spritzer, rosé, 82
steak sauce, red, 501
Winter squash
acorn, baked, 554
acorn, honey-spice, 553
how to buy and cook, 526
with orange, 554
soup, cream of, 509

Y

Yam(s), *see* SWEET POTATOES
how to buy and cook, 526
soufflé, 550
Yeast breads, 99-116
all about yeast, 100
anadama batter, 115
babka, 108
batter breads, 114-15
bear claws, 110
best of all pizzas, 309
blueberry surprises, 109
bow ties, 112
brioche, 116
brioche dough, 351
caraway rye, 103
crescents, 109
honey whole-wheat casserole, 114
horns, 110
how to knead, 100
how to shape loaves, 101
jelly doughnuts, 113
McCall's basic white, 102
old-fashioned potato, 103
pinwheels, 111
refrigerator potato rolls, 12-13
spiral cinnamon raisin bread, 107
stollen, 112
Swedish limpa, 105

sweet yeast breads, 107-13
sweet yeast rolls, 108-12
Swiss braided loaves, 105
tips for bread bakers, 100
Virginia sally lunn, 115
whole-wheat, 104
Yeast cake, baba au rhum, 288
Yellow pea soup with pork, 324
Yellow turnips *see* RUTABAGAS
Yoghurt

cucumber dressing, 491
soup, orange-apricot, 519
Yorkshire pudding, 349

Z

Zabaione, 312
Zesty French dressing, 494
Ziti (macaroni) casserole, baked, 232
Zucchini *see also* SUMMER SQUASH

bread and butter pickles, our
best, 334
chicken basquaise, 281
cold ratatouille, 64
corn, and tomatoes, 556
with fresh herbs, 556
and green peppers, sautéed, 556
how to buy and cook, 526
mushroom ratatouille, 540
sautéed squash and tomatoes, 555